JOURNAL OF
ASIAN AND AFRICAN STUDIES

JOURNAL OF
ASIAN AND AFRICAN STUDIES

EDITOR: K. ISHWARAN

DEPARTMENT OF SOCIOLOGY AND ANTHROPOLOGY, YORK UNIVERSITY
TORONTO 12, CANADA

VOLUME VIII

LEIDEN
E. J. BRILL
1973

CONTENTS

Journal of Asian and African Studies

EDITOR: K. ISHWARAN

DEPARTMENT OF SOCIOLOGY AND ANTHROPOLOGY
YORK UNIVERSITY
TORONTO 12, CANADA

Volume VIII — Numbers 1-2
January and April 1973

E. J. BRILL — PUBLISHERS — LEIDEN

Journal of Asian and African Studies

| Volume VIII | JANUARY and APRIL 1973 | Numbers 1-2 |

CONTENTS

JOURNAL OF ASIAN AND AFRICAN STUDIES

The *Journal of Asian and African Studies*, published by E. J. Brill, Leiden, Holland, is a quarterly publication issued in January, April, July, and October. Each number is of about eighty pages in length.

The Journal, edited by a board of scholars from all over the world who are specialists in Asian and African studies, presents a scholarly account of studies of man and society in the developing nations of Asia and Africa. It endeavours to fulfill a need in the field in that it unites contributions from anthropology, sociology, history, and related social sciences into a concerted emphasis upon building up systematic knowledge and using the knowledge derived from pure research for the reconstruction of societies entering a phase of advanced technology.

ALL EDITORIAL CORRESPONDENCE, including papers, notes and news covering research projects, associations and institutions, conferences and seminars, foundations and publications, and other activities relevant to Asia and Africa, should be addressed to: K. Ishwaran, Editor, J.A.A.S., Department of Sociology, York University, Downsview, Ontario M3J 1P3, Canada.

BOOKS FOR REVIEW (AFRICA) should be sent to: John M. Janzen, Department of Anthropology, University of Kansas, Lawrence, Kansas, 66044, U.S.A., and (ASIA) to Edward R. Beauchamp, College of Education, University of Hawaii, Wist Annex 2-222, 1776 University Avenue, Honolulu, Hawaii 96822, U.S.A.

BUSINESS CORRESPONDENCE, including subscriptions, change of address, additional off-prints, etc., should be addressed to:

E. J. BRILL — LEIDEN, THE NETHERLANDS

Subscription price of Volume VIII (1973): Gld. 56.— *plus postage and packing.*

Please do not send money with your order. The publisher will invoice you and will then be pleased to receive your remittance.

MANUSCRIPT STYLE GUIDE

Manuscripts of articles should be not more than 7000 words. Unsolicited papers will not be returned unless postage paid. Submit two copies of the article and retain a copy for your own files. Prepare copy as follows:

1. Type double-spaced on white 8-1/2″ × 11″ standard paper, with a 2″ margin at the left hand side and a 3″ space above the titles of both articles and reviews.
2.* Tables should be typed on separate pages, numbered consecutively and given headings. Footnotes for tables appear at the bottom of the tables. Insert a location note at the appropriate place in text, e.g., "Table 1 about here".
3.* Figures, maps and other line drawings are to be submitted in black Indian ink about twice the intended final size on good quality tracing paper. Insert a location note at the appropriate place in text.
4. Articles and reviews are to be submitted in their *final form* so that they require no further alterations. It is the obligation of authors to carefully proof read their material before submission to the journal. Owing to increasing costs, the publisher is compelled to charge authors for corrections other than printer's errors.

   *Tables, graphs, figures, etc., should be used sparingly.

● Bibliographical references should be cited in the text by the author's last name, date of publication and page, e.g., (Anderson 1972: 105) or, if the author's name is mentioned in the text, by the date and page reference only, e.g., (1972: 105). ● Footnotes are to appear as notes at the end of articles and are to be used only for substantive observations and not for purpose of citation. ● With dual authorship, give both last names; for more than two use "et al" (see 3 below). ● If there is more than one reference to the same author and year, distinguish them by using letters (a, b) attached to year of publication in the text and reference appendix (see 2 below). ● For institutional authorship supply minimum identification, e.g., (U.N.E.S.C.O. 1971: 67).

Entries in the references should be in alphabetical order of authors and should include: name and initials of author(s), date, title, name of periodical, volume number (arabic numerals to be used throughout), pagination (for periodicals), place of publication and publisher. e.g.,

1. Frolic, B. Michael
      1971   "Soviet urban sociology". International Journal of Comparative Sociology XII (December): 234–251.
2. Greenberg, Joseph H.
      1965a   "Linguistics" pp. 416–41 in Robert A. Lystad (ed.), The African World: a survey of social research. New York: Frederick A. Praeger.
      1965b   "Urbanism, migration and language" pp. 50-59, 189 in K. Huyper (ed.), Urbanization and Migration in West Africa. Berkeley and Los Angeles: University of California Press. (Reprinted in Man in Adaptation, the Bio-social Background, ed. by Y. A. Cohen, 259–67. Chicago: Aldine Publishing Co., 1968.)
3. Kaser, D., et al
      1969   Library Development in Eight Asian Countries. New Jersey: Scarcecrow Press.
4. Southall, Aidan W.
      1970   "The illusion of tribe" pp. 28–50 in P. C. W. Gutkind (ed.), The Passing of Tribal Man in Africa. Leiden: E. J. Brill.

Book reviews should not exceed 800 words and should not contain footnotes; references to other works should be incorporated in the text; page references should be given when quotations from the book are included.

Galley proofs of articles will be sent to authors (from the publisher), who should use the standard method of proof correction. Corrected proofs should be returned to publisher as soon as possible; where proofs are not returned in time, the Editor reserves the right to send the printers his own corrected proof of contributors article which will be the basis of the final article. Proofs are intended for checking, NOT RE-WRITING and authors are most strongly reminded that material should be submitted ready for the printer.

Authors receive 25 free offprints of their article (8 free offprints for book reviews). Additional offprints of articles can be supplied at cost price and must be ordered and paid for when the corrected proofs are returned to the printer.

PUBLISHER: E. J. Brill, Leiden, The Netherlands

Journal of Asian and African Studies, VIII, 1–2

In Search of a Communist Development Model: The Soviets' Political Economy of India

STEPHEN CLARKSON

University of Toronto, Toronto, Ontario, Canada

In Pursuit of a Communist Model

W HEN THE COLD war was turning Western scholars' attention toward the political future of Africa, Asia and Latin America, one could scarcely read an article on the position of the developing countries in international affairs without encountering some reference to the communist model that threatened, like some international pied piper, to attract the elites of the Afro-Asian nations into the socialist bloc. Just what constituted this model, however, was not quite so clear as one first thought. Was it the historical experience of development in the Soviet bloc? If so, there would be not one but a multiplicity of models, one for each sacred father – Lenin's or Novotny's, Tito's or Mao's. Worse, in the case of the more long-lived, such as Stalin, there would be a model for each stage of communist construction over which he had presided: that of forced industrialization and collectivization, of the patriotic war, of post-war reconstruction. Each aspect of each model was presumably in some way appropriate to the national conditions obtaining in each particular communist regime, but which part of which model was relevant to a given developing country? And who was to decide what was relevant and what was not? If the leadership in each country was to choose, our communist model would vary in addition with the needs and ambitions of each national leader: for Nehru it was above all the magic of five-year planning, for Nkrumah it was the single party system; for others the lesson might be the nationalization of foreign companies.

A more obvious, though less familiar, sense in which there has always been an identifiable communist model specifically relevant for each developing country is the analysis of its problems by the scholars from a particular communist country. By dissecting their writings one should be able to extract their "model" for development, at least on those problems they are most concerned about.

The Soviet analysis of India offers one of the best cases for applying this approach, for among marxist-leninists the Soviets have devoted the most re-

sources to studying the developing countries and their writings on India over
the past two decades are abundant enough to permit satisfactory generalizations concerning their analysis.[1] Even when considering the Soviet marxist-
leninist publications on a major third-world country like India, it is not obvious
a priori whether there is a *model* defined as a coherent diagnosis of India's
problems and a prescription for their solution. There is certainly no single
development strategy which has been deduced from the economic and historical
experience of the USSR. There is much analysis varying not just in quality from
author to author but varying also dramatically over time. As official Soviet
ideology has gone through several distinct phases since the October revolution
influenced by changes in the internal economic or political situation as by the
external international position of the Soviet Union, so have Soviet analysts
seen India as a highly developed capitalist economy on the brink of a socialist
revolution (1921-28), a colonial economy in the hands of a reactionary bourgeoisie (1928-41), an important economic and industrial base for the British,
their war-time allies (1941-45), a continuing colony in the British-American
Empire (1947-53) and a truly independent and progressive third-world power
(1955-present). Despite the wild fluctuations in these phases of Soviet Indology,
these variations are best seen as politically inspired interpretations within a
generally stable analytical paradigm, the marxist-leninist political economy.
In any case since Krushchev's de-stalinization of Soviet marxism and his positive reorientation of Soviet foreign policy towards independent third world
countries invalidated the major theses of the stalinist analysis, Moscow's orientalists were forced to recast their interpretation to allow for the possibility of
progressive social and economic development within non-communist, ex-
colonial countries. The resulting post-stalinist school of thought presented a
development model centred round the concept of state capitalism. This was
more than an economic model. It was a political economy paradigm based on
three major postulates: the historical position maintained that the emergence
of a powerful socialist bloc enabled third world countries to pass from a feudal
to a socialist stage through an accelerated state capitalist stage; the economic
proposition asserted that a gradual transition to socialism was possible through
the expansion of the state sector under long-term planning; the class analysis
held that the national bourgeoisie could direct this transition with internal
support from progressive proletarian and peasant forces. Whatever industry or
sector of the economy was under discussion, a common analytical framework
was applied. What was the size of the private sector and which class interests
were served by it: the foreign monopolies, the local monopoly bourgeoisie, the
national bourgeoisie, the petty bourgeoisie, the proletariat or the peasantry?
What was the relative size of the public sector and the means used to stimulate
its growth (nationalization, joint ventures or new investment)? What instruments does the state have for controlling this industry or sector?

1   See the classified bibliography of selected Soviet writings on the developing countries in
    general and India in particular in my *L'analyse soviétique des problèmes indiens du sous-
    développement (1955–1964)* Mouton, Paris and the Hague, 1971, pp. 163–252.

This paradigm was flexible: it could distinguish countries by their degree of progressiveness from feudal states where the landlord class was dominant through to non-capitalist regimes where radical leaderships were in power. Within the same country it could respond to new developments – a regressive shift from state capitalism controlled by the national bourgeoisie to monopoly state capitalism controlled by the monopoly capitalists in conjunction with foreign monopolies or vice versa. The prescriptions were as clear as the diagnosis: industrialize through progressive takeover by the public sector while modernizing agriculture by large scale production and profiting from favourable aid from the socialist bloc whose friendship would permit increasing independence from imperialist commercial and corporate control.

While the Soviet development model as articulated in the mid 1950s was clear in its rough outline, it was not certain whether it could maintain its theoretical consistency and conceptual clarity as Soviet scholars applied its hypotheses to empirical analysis of individual developing countries. In actual practice the experience of the past fifteen years has demonstrated two general laws:

(1) The increase in quantity and quality of Soviet analysis led to increasing debate within the Soviet developmental school leading to a more interesting analysis whose original model, however, tended to fragment under the strain.

(2) The quality of the analysis varied inversely with the political or ideological sensitivity of the problem under research.

By examining briefly four key areas of the Soviet analysis of India from the worst (Indian politics) to the best (Indian agriculture) one can see how the Soviet model of Indian development has been undermined as the quality of writing has improved.

The Worst: Political Analysis

In marxism-leninism there is no autonomous political science as an independent discipline. Political analysis is observed in larger discussions of the economy and class struggle. This does not prevent the Soviets from providing careful analysis of the parties and politics in some political systems. However, the serious study of politics remains the main gap in Soviet Indology. In the analysis of parties there is a virtual void. While half the propaganda brochure, *Contemporary India: The Distribution of Class and Political Forces*, is devoted to Indian communism this is no way reduces the need for a serious study of India's political parties, including the communist parties (Kutsobin 1963). Two aspects of politics in India – the nationality question (Dyakov 1966, Kazakov 1967) and the social and intellectual content of political ideologies[1] – have been the

---

1 See *Obshchestvenno-politicheskaya i filosofskaya mysl' Indii* (India's philosophical and socio-political thought), Moscow, IVL, 1962, 263 p.; I. R. Gordon-Polonskaya, *Musul'manskie techeniya v obshchestvennoi mysl' Indii i Pakistana* (Kritika "musul'manskogo natsionalizma") (Moslem currents in India's and Pakistan's social thought: a critique of "Moslem nation-

object of some attention. Otherwise one must glean the Soviet view of political life in India from their sociological analysis of class contradictions and from discussions of the linkages between the corporate sector and the national bourgeois leadership. The model is clear at least by inference: the proletariat should take over. However the analysis is so inadequate that the prescription has to be taken as an act of faith. While it is asserted that the national bourgeoisie is acting in the interests of the people as a whole, there is no explanation of what political mechanics make this possible especially when it appears in their writings that the communist party is the instrument for expressing the public's true interests.

Second Worst: Foreign Investment, Aid and Trade

While the Soviet analysis of Indian politics seems to be paralysed by the fear of hurting the Indian communist party the Soviet analysis of India's external economic relations is similarly deformed by political considerations. In reading Soviet works on foreign investment, aid and trade one detects two distinct lines. The ideologically most coloured line demonstrates an acute manicheism which sees imperialist aid as exploiting, shackling and unwanted, while economic relations with the socialist bloc are liberating, developing and sought after. The they-are-bad, we-are-good line is qualified by another theme which seems designed less for fellow communists than for the leaderships of the developing countries. Here they accept that the developing countries require external sources of capital accumulation, admit that the socialist countries cannot alone provide all the third world's needs, reject a quota as high as one percent of GNP as a legitimate quantity for socialist aid and maintain that the imperialist countries should give more aid as repayment for previous colonial exploitation. Now while defending the virtues of socialist aid they recognize its "tied character" – tied in rubles and tied to specific projects. Although they denounce the western exploitation of developing countries through "non-equivalent exchange" (the charging of high prices for western exports but paying low prices for third world exports), they concede that Soviet trade is equally based on world prices. When criticizing private foreign investment, they recognize its positive economic consequences without feeling the need to impugn its bad motivations (Alexsandrov, Mel'man 1967b: 105–7). This increased balance strengthens the thrust of the basic Soviet case: on the one hand national independence is endangered by direct investment and too much aid and, on the other, India has concrete advantages to gain from the increase of commercial exchange with the socialist countries.

---

alism"), Moscow, IVL, 1963, 326 p.; *Ideologicheskie techeniya sovremennoi Indii* (Modern India's ideological currents), Moscow, Nauka, 1965, 196 p.; A. D. Litman, *Filosofoskaya mysl' nezavisimoi Indii (akademicheskie sistemy i religioznofilosofskie ucheniya)* (Independant India's philosophical thought: academic systems and religious-philosophical teaching), Moscow, Nauka, 1966, 268 p.

When the reader makes a synthesis of the Soviet discussion of aid and trade, comparing the critique of western investment and aid with the qualities of socialist aid and trade he perceives a diagnosis and a prescription not very different from the left liberal position of scholars such as Gunnar Myrdal. What is disappointing is the lack of rigor in their attack on western investment.

Soviet analysis of Indian external economic relations with capitalist countries remain surprisingly shallow (Clarkson 1967). As for India's relations with the socialist bloc, Soviet publications continue to rely for their information on foreign documentation. It is still disappointing that the Soviets do not provide a really detailed analysis of their own aid and trade with India all the more as an evaluation of its characteristics is still very positive. Yershov's book (Yershov, 1965) about the particularly happy and successful cooperation of the socialist countries in constructing in India a state oil industry against the concerted opposition of the Western oil cartel has not led to further studies of this kind. With the ideological line broken down by the qualifications scattered through the texts, the Soviet model is more implicit than intact in its external dimension.

Better: The Economy and the State

Although the rhetoric of a revolutionary solution has never been entirely dropped from the Soviet analysis, the call for "fundamental socio-economic transformations" has become increasingly divorced from the concrete analysis produced by Moscow specialists. When analyzing the internal economy Soviet scholars come closest to their Western colleagues' discussion of a mixed economy and become even more optimistic about the developmental role of the state sector than their Western counterparts. Offsetting their institutional optimism, however, is their concern about the direction taken by the class struggle.

In fact the current Soviet assessment of the Indian situation considers the ruling national bourgeoisie to be increasingly linked with the big landowners and foreign monopolies. While in the 1950's the Soviets felt that state capitalism would lead India towards a transition to the socialist path, in the 1960's they observed a capitalist economy characterized by a highly developed heavy industry (Aleksandrovskaya 1968: 260) and a high concentration of capital (Savel'ev 1967: 209–210). It is both as cause and effect of this strengthening of capitalism that the character of India's state capitalism and the nature of its class relations have evolved.

Overall they identify a struggle going on between the two possible types of capitalist development, the conservative path taken by the big bourgeoisie in cooperation with the foreign monopolies and the radical path leading to real democratic transformation (Levkovsky, 1966: 629–636). This struggle is focused around the role played by the state in regulating and participating in economic development. While state capitalism still remains at the centre of the Soviet economic analysis, this concept has lost the theoretical status it enjoyed ten years ago before the declaration of "non-capitalism" as a new law of development for radical regimes in the third world.

A sober assessment of the regulatory activity of the state is printed in the important volume published by the Institute of the Peoples of Asia, *Problems of Socio-economic Development in Independent India*, which discusses the various means of control allowing the government "to use the anarchic processes of capitalist accumulation to develop the national economy." (Batalov et al, 1967: 9–16) The Soviet analysis becomes a type of score-keeping with the achievements of state capitalism being measured against its failures. State capitalism's success is seen in its having directed private capital into heavy industry. But the regulation policy has had serious failures: the failure to exercise control over the smallest enterprises has led to an excessive increase in small-scale production; the attempted regulation of prices and internal trade has nevertheless not succeeded in suppressing speculation in food and imported goods.

As for the nationalized industrial sector, there again state capitalism reveals weaknesses. Public enterprises have used very large amounts of capital but make very small profits (Solonitskii, Ul'rikh 1968: 107). As a result, the government is now investing in light and food industries where the return is more rapid but the development contribution less progressive. It is also creating new governmental organisations able to act directly on such problems as grain distribution. The diminished effectiveness of state control entails a greater degree of freedom for the forces of the capitalist market. This is why the Soviets regret that state capitalism is adapting to the mixed economy and not vice versa (Batalov et al 1967: 27).

The Soviet economists find the proof that state capitalism can no longer dominate the anarchic laws of the capitalist market in the disappointing results of planning. The failures experienced in the execution of the third five-year plan demonstrate the weakness of governmental action on the private sector (Batalov et al 1967: 24). The different analysts have their own dialectical evaluation of the problem: for some, the increased capital investment encouraged by the planning system helped break the old economic structure but at the same time accelerated the rise of the private capitalist sector (Batalov et al 1967). In Lozovaya's analysis even if planning is aimed at the abolition of old economic disparities, the planning experience has brought new ones to light: unutilized capacity in industry, unbalanced development of complementary branches, increased dependence on imports, insufficient expansion of the energy sector[1] (Lozovaya 1966: 158–159). In theory, the strong point of planning is its ability to mobilize capital. But in his study on the financing of the five-year plans Egorov underlines the inadequate revenue coming from the public sector firms. Observing that the plans' financing depend more and more on private sources of capital, he has serious reservations about the planning system's capacity to direct national economic development. Worse still, the concessions made to free enterprise could even become the "starting point for the country's slide into the state

---

[1] See also the general review of Indian planning in the preface by A. I. Levkovskii in the Russian translation of D. Gadgil, *Planirovanie i ekonomicheskaya politika v Indii* (Planning and economic policy in India), Moscow, IIL, 1963, pp. 5–17.

monopoly capitalist path." (Egorov 1967: 214) Thus the danger that India's state capitalism will be transformed into its reactionary form becomes greater as the progressive aspects of the state's regulatory activity are overshadowed by the action of private enterprise. Because of the failure to execute fundamental socio-economic transformations, state capitalism is unable to realize its two main aims mobilizing the productive forces and increasing the rate of accumulation (Bragina 1965: 226).

The corollary of state capitalism's reduced effectiveness is reinforcement of private enterprise at the summit where the concentration of capital is highest. "Monopoly capital" is studied first of all as an economic sector whose high level of organization and technology is due, according to Loshakov to its close links with the imperialist monopolies (Loshakov 1967a: 64, 1967b). What makes these links with the western corporate giants so serious for the Soviet analysts is their ideological implications for the overall trend of India's economic development. In his progress report on the rise of big business in India, Maev emphasizes the threat that the reactionary strategy of the monopolies presents in economic policy: they are striving to transform India's economy on to the Western model (Maev 1964a: 161, 1964b: 21–36). Although he considered in 1964 that monopoly capitalism – the subordination of the state to the monopolies – had not yet triumphed in India, his later assessments show a growing pessimism in this regard (1966: 120–127, 1967: 118–123). To make the political point very clearly, Savel'ev warned in *International Affairs*, in April 1967, that the growing activity of the Indian monopolist bourgeoisie was seriously threatening to deflect India from "its established path of neutrality in foreign policy" (1967: 35).

The exact significance of this extension of monopoly capital in India is the subject of an important debate centred around the analysis of the Indian social classes. According to Shirokov and Reisner the big monopoly bourgeoisie is not monolithic and has not succeeded in dominating the lower groups of the bourgeoisie, especially because of Nehru's policy of maintaining a balance among the classes (1966: 207). Aleksandrov and Melman assert on the contrary that the big bourgeoisie dominates the petty bourgeoisie just as much through its economic power as by its political organization (1967a: 158). They also note that the middle bourgeoisie still plays an important role despite the small expansion of its size.

Savel'ev thinks it is better to consider together the small and middle capitalists since these two strata face the same economic difficulties. As they demonstrate practical agreement on the main political and social questions, they can lead a common front against the domination of big capital (1967: 205–206). But Shirokov and Reisner feel that the significance of these differences inside the bourgeoisie should not be exaggerated. These conflicts cannot trancend the main social contradiction, namely, the antagonism dividing the workers on one hand from all the groups of the exploiting class on the other (1966: 204). This debate continues as the Soviets pursue their research on the industrial classes which form the core of their analysis of developing India's capitalism (Gordon

1967: 193–219, 245–256; Reisner & Shirokov 1967: 240–244). When Madam Gandhi nationalizes the banks, the Soviets cheer; when a new concession is made to a foreign investor they grumble.

The extent to which state capitalism has passed from a development model in itself to a framework for analysis can be seen in the introduction by some Soviet scholars of serious discussion of small-scale, labour-intensive enterprise. The careful statistical analysis by Kuz'min showing how in certain industries artisanal production is more efficient in terms of capital investment than large-scale industry has in one blow taken Soviet analysis out of a fixation on size but shattered the coherence of the Soviet message (1969).

Best: Agrarian Capitalism and the Class Struggle

The Soviet analysis is most vigorous and scholarly, most firmly based on marxist-leninist theory and on empirical research in that area which is furthest removed from the concerns of party politics and cold-war diplomacy, agriculture. It is in rural sociology that the Soviet academic tradition finds its roots in pre-revolutionary soil.

From the early 1950's the analysis of India's agrarian problems has been the strongest part of the Soviet analysis whether measured by the quality of its research or by the sophistication of its methodology. The intervening years have allowed the agrarian analysts to consolidate their advance by concentrating their efforts on a few selected issues.

The basic problems for the Soviet agrarian analysts is defining what historical stage agrarian development has reached. For India they have to their satisfaction resolved the 1950's debate on the relative importance of feudalism versus capitalism, in favour of the latter. As a result of the agrarian reforms introduced by the Indian National Congress in the 1950's the feudal agrarian system is in a state of transition to capitalist agricultural relations. Capitalism has now won out as the dominant trend in the Indian countryside.[1] In saying that Indian agriculture is directed toward capitalism the Soviets do not mean that capitalist farms are the major producers at the present moment. While pointing out how far capitalism has progressed, the Indologists have put greater emphasis on the pre-capitalist aspects of the village. In actual fact, with only 40 to 45 per cent of national income coming from capitalist-type enterprises, the major part of the national revenue is still produced by the pre-capitalist sector. Since the growth of capitalism in agriculture is slower than the breakdown of small-commodity production (Gurvich 1967: 139), the Soviets are paying increasing attention to these transitional structures. Rastyannikov notes that the expanding share by commercial farms in the agricultural produce being sold on the market is only gradual. Although in some regions the degree of

---

1 "Izmeneniya v sotsial'no-klassovoi strukture Indii" (Changes in India's social and class structure) in *Problemy ekonomicheskogo i sotsial'nogo razvitiya nezavisimoi Indii*. Moscow, Nauka, 1967, pp. 105–107.

commercialization is high, the agrarian bourgeoisie is not yet the main supplier of commercialized grain (1967: 192). The pre-capitalist commodity production sector is still placing obstacles in the way of the bourgeoisie's development toward capitalism. The system of state taxes and the longevity of transitional property forms are preventing the agrarian bourgeoisie as a class from separating from the small peasantry even though the latter remain ready for the transition to capitalism. Why does this not happen?

Rastyannikov and Maksimov have devoted a large part of a recent book to answering this question. The nature of primitive accumulation does not encourage capitalist development and even restrains its progress (1965). The agrarian capitalists that have appeared, are forced to choose between the two conflicting paths of capitalist development: the radical (peasant) direction and the conservative (landlord) path. The conservative tendency is dominant thanks to the close ties linking big urban capital with the large landowners (Rastyannikov 1967: 178). The government's conservative agricultural policy is thus responsible for the failure of rural capitalism to develop. By maintaining in place the large landlords and abandoning radical agrarian reforms, pre-capitalist vestiges have been allowed to survive.

But this is not a unanimous point of view in Moscow. Rudin considers that capitalist development is prevented less by such subjective factors as the government's policy than by the objective problem of relative overpopulation. In his view no radical reform will produce a de facto transformation in the village economy as long as the colossal reserve supply of labour ready to work at any price keeps growing (Rudin 1967: 178).

The struggle for land reforms of the 1950's is no longer the focus of attention for the Soviets who are much more interested in the state's regulatory action in the agricultural marketplace than in the land struggle. State capitalism is much less effective here than it is in industry: the efforts to control agrarian prices have only had a partial effect; the government has not created a sector of state agricultural enterprises so that planning in agriculture has not been effective either (Lozovaya 1966: 147). Congress' agrarian policy consists of large capital investment in programmes of communal development, cooperatives and agro-technical improvements from which only the large landowners and well-off peasants benefit (Orleanskaya 1962: 49–59, 1964: 50–59).

The technical aspects of agriculture still interest the Soviets especially as they identify the backward state of agricultural technology as a determinant of agriculture's low productivity which, in its turn, slows down its rate of growth. As for the food crisis which remains as far from a solution in their view as it did in 1951, the Soviet authors no longer speak as they once did of the enormous potential of India's resources. Mironova, in her brochure on *India's Food Problem*, provides a detailed study of the grain market, its degree of commercialization, the role of speculation and usury capital in the fluctuation of prices, and the insufficient measures taken by the government to improve this situation (1967). She supports recommendations that are directed at creating a complete state network for selling cereal grains. An article by Rastyannikov recom-

mending protectionism for agricultural prices demonstrates the same empirical approach to governmental policy on important middle-range problems
(1968).

The greater prominence given recently by Soviet Indologists to specific
policy recommendations makes their analyses more meaningful to the non-
marxist reader. Such advice given in terms of the existing situation does not
prevent their reaffirming their more grandiose solutions consistent with Soviet
doctrine. But the exact nature of the "radical transformation" without which,
in their view, a solution of the agrarian problem is not possible still remains
imprecise and insufficiently argued in the Soviet writings. Between the concrete
recommendations and dazzling panaceas, the Soviets also recommend programmes of action such as the democratization and expansion of cooperatives
for the small peasants that will, in their view, promote agricultural development in the middle term (Batalov et al 1967: 35). Although these recommendations in agrarian policy lack sufficient argumentation to support them, they
reflect the priority given to socio-economic analysis over political considerations in the Soviet analysis of India's agriculture.

The priority of analysis over slogans is especially clear in the Soviets' discussion of the agrarian classes. The agrarian proletariat is of special interest.
But their analysis of it is less and less dominated by old marxist-leninist for-
mulae. It is true that Kotovsky concludes his study of the agrarian labourers by
stating in dramatic tones that the entry of tens of millions of proletarians and
semi-proletarians "in the path of active class struggle will inevitably provoke a
decisive change in the distribution of political forces in the country" (1967:
164). Nevertheless his article's interest lies much less in such rhetoric than in
his descriptions of the socio-economic situation of the agricultural workers.
Although proletarians in the economic sense, they remain peasants in their
socio-psychology since a very large percentage still cultivate a little land. Given
the low concentration of rural workers (very few farms outside the plantations
employ more than one or two), the problem of caste and of religion (30% of
agrarian workers are untouchables or belong to a classified tribe), the prospects
of agrarian worker unity seem much less bright than Kotovsky's conclusion
would suggest. As Semenova shows, the organization of agrarian workers by
caste produces contradictory results: caste organization helps politicize the
poorest strata of the countryside but slogans of class peace weaken their revolutionary force (1967: 142).

The consideration given the traditional element in the countryside is probably the most remarkable change in the Soviet analysis during these past years.
In his introduction to *Castes in India*, Kotovsky breaks with the old Soviet view
that caste is only disguised class. He underlines especially the historic stability
of the caste system and its increased importance in current social and political
conflict (1965: 37, 40). Levin provides a penetrating discussion of the role of
caste in the formation of bourgeois groups (1965: 233–261). Though the caste
problem is given prominence in this collection of articles, this new awareness of
the continuing importance of the traditional elements has not yet been absorb-

ed by all Russian Indologists many of whom continue to dismiss the traditional as anachronistic.

Thus we can see that, as Soviet analysts of Indian development problems become more empirical and more open to Western scholarly inputs, differences of opinion amoung them become more visible and the coherent inter-relation of all parts of their model breaks down.

General Assessment

Taking the best of recent Soviet writings on India one can see an increase in their originality and independence. As a school of underdevelopment marxist-leninist Indology has honed both its conceptual system and extended its applied research.

Although the style of the Soviet authors retains its displeasing characteristics – unresolved contradictions, quotations of doctrinal documents of the Party as infallible authority, hyperbolic generalizations – it would be wrong to be led astray by these weaker aspects of contemporary Indology in the Soviet Union. For in applying their methodology to the Indian reality, they have made continued progress, to use their words, in both depth and breadth. They are looking more closely at aspects of rural problems of which they had only begun the study in the fifties and they are advancing on new fronts (caste and overpopulation) that till now had remained either ignored or taboo.

In any analysis there is a tension between theoretical proposition and empirical description. The Soviets are most often criticized for letting the former dominate the latter. But in their agrarian and economic analysis, empirical study increasingly takes precedence over doctrinal generalizations. The statement that capitalism is winning out in Indian agriculture does not prevent their doing research on the problem of the pre-capitalist, small-production sector. Their interest in India's transition to a non-capitalist path does not prevent them from making a detailed analysis of private and even monopoly industry. The areas where the application of the marxist-leninist methodology is no longer an obstacle to good analysis have increased. Their conclusions are less determined by a priori political judgments. One can now complain that their analysis does not lead to clear ideological conclusions. Does, for instance, the lack of progress in the formation of new capitalist classes in the country increase the prospects of class conflict as Rastyannikov maintains or the contrary as Kotovsky's analysis of the caste system seems to suggest? The price of academic difference is diversity in their conclusions.

Another sign of the growing freedom of Soviet Indology can be seen in the good relationship between Moscow and Delhi that has been maintained despite the numerous warnings by Soviet research writers on the growth of reaction in India and the monopolization of its economy. Soviet Indologists can now complain that their diplomats do not read their writings enough before making their foreign policy.

The maintenance of a friendly diplomatic atmosphere has, however, helped professionalize Indology in the USSR. Despite the spectacular change toward a Pakistan-Soviet rapprochement, political and economic relations between the Soviet Union and India continued stable all the more since the Tashkent agreement and the Indo-Soviet Treaty when Moscow asserted its role as the grand priest of good relations between the Asian neighbors of China. As a result, contacts of Soviet Indologists with India have grown through scientific exchanges, research trips made in India, and the translation of foreign works on India.

Marxist-leninist Indology thus is getting away from its original monolithic state while remaining a school with a quite distinct approach. But to say that there is now a definite Soviet analysis of underdevelopment applied to the Indian case does not mean that it prescribes coherent solutions to the problems analyzed. As noted above, Soviet authors sometimes give recommendations for governmental action to resolve concrete problems. This advice is supported by political and economic arguments.

One must simply accept as an article of faith that India's entry upon the non-capitalist path will mark the true beginning of solving India's problems from agricultural production to the caste system (Potemkin, Sandakov 1968: 66–67). Even the "minimum programmes" are scarcely supported by an adequate amount of argument. Potemkin and Sandakov support without comment the electoral program of the Indian Communist Party, recommending general democratic transformations to divert the big bourgeoisie's sources of accumulation into the state's coffers (Shatalon 1967: 74).

The same absence of reasoning is true of class strategy recommandations. Thus when Rastyannikov and Maksimov draw class conclusions from their study on India's agrarian capitalism, they speak facilely of a strategy of "antifeudal unity" of the working class and the peasantry, "the most massive force of the people." These old slogans of class strategy are repeated without any very evident relationship with the preceeding analysis which, on the contrary, emphasizes the absence of class consciousness, the difficulties in organizing the country and the lack of ideological rapport between industrial proletariat and the poor people in the country.

While in its vocabulary and its style, this is clearly an "ideological" analysis, retaining the use of traditional marxist-leninist concepts and formulas, it is ultimately very moderate. Awarding state capitalism a progressive character has some clear implications. It removes any blame for the miserable state of the people from the economic system, casting responsibility back to the previous historical period, that of colonial domination. Furthermore the enshrining of state capitalism as a progressive historical stage of development gives it a kind of moral right to direct the course of the country's current economic development. The concept of historical stage implies, of course, some end to the period, but an extreme precision in periodization is not the forte of marxist-leninists: imperialism has represented the "highest stage of capitalism" in the West for almost half a century. For the state capitalist period, the Soviet analysis does not furnish us with indices precise enough to indicate what signs, apart from a reactionary shift in foreign policy, would announce the end of this progressive stage in India's development. As long as the bourgeois national government is considered by the Kremlin to be friendly towards Soviet policies, nothing indicates what would constitute an end to the state capitalist stage. For this reason the post-Stalinist analysis appears to have opened an ideological door to the acceptance of capitalism in the Afro-Asian world as can be seen when Yershov holds out India's state capitalist policy of fighting the oil monopolies as holding "the promise of freedom from the oil monopolies for many countries" (Yershov 1965: 180).

Despite the language which sounds the conventional bells of the marxist world view, this Soviet analysis of Indian development hardly brandishes the red flag. Gradualist and revisionist in its acceptance of evolutionary progress under bourgeois reforms, this analysis is quite clearly non-revolutionary, as the Chinese are not slow to point out. It is not, however, for the unbeliever to cry heresy. We can speculate that the *raison d'être* of this moderate line lies in the requirements of Soviet diplomacy: if the Soviet Union deems India's friendship worth several hundred millions of rubles in economic aid, it is important that this good neighbor policy be justified by and consistent with the ideological analysis. Whatever the geopolitical reasons, we can see that the Soviet model of development, as found in the post-Stalinist writings of India, is closely patterned on the economic system as it is actually operating. While preferring as much socialization as possible, it is still tolerant of private capitalism; while denouncing the reactionary attempts of big capital to subvert the independence of the public sector, it admits that Tata can work hand in glove with the state's policy of heavy industrial development; while pointing out that Indian planning is not of the "scientific socialist" type, the Soviet analysis accepts the principle of its efficacy in a mixed economy. In a word, the Soviet model is neither a revolutionary call to arms nor an oversimplified formula for a quick industrialization. Though maintaining a distinctive tone and style of both impatience and optimism, it recognizes that there is still a long row to hoe. Agreeing in major areas with the analysis of Western experts, it can hardly be credited with playing some occult role as diplomatic aphrodasiac in the Seduction of the Uncommitted Nations.

"Politics," it has been said, "is the delicate use of blunt instruments." The real reason why the Soviet analysis of India's as of other countries' problems should be taken seriously is to be found both in the sensitivity with which their concepts are manipulated and in the simplicity of the conceptual model itself. At a time when the over-developed theoretical structures of Western social scientists are being challenged for irrelevance by intellectuals in the developing countries, the significance of a much more stable, less exciting and even simplistic marxist-leninist paradigm may be gaining much wider acceptance, especially as the failures of welfare economics to cope with the magnitude of India's problems becomes increasingly evident.

REFERENCES

ALEKSANDROV, M. A. and MEL'MAN, S. M.
   1967a Book review of L. I. Reisner and G. K. Shirokov, "Sovremennaya indiiskaya burzhuaziya". *Narody Azii i Afriki*, I.
   _____
   1976b "Privlechenie resursov iz-za rubezha" (Attracting resources from abroad) in *Problemy ekonomicheskogo i sotsial'nogo razvitiya nezavisimoi Indii* (Problems of independant India's social and economic development). Moscow: Nauka.

ALEKSANDROVSKAYA
   1968 "Industrializatsiya razvivayushchikhsya stran i otnoshenie k nei razlichnykh klassov i sotsial'nykh sil" (The industrialization of the developing countries and its relationship with different social and class forces) in *Klassy i klassovaya bor'ba v razvivayushchikhsya stranakh* (Classes and the class struggle in the developing countries). Moscow: Mysl'.

BATALOV, A. L. GURVICH, R. P., KOTOVSKII, G. G., REISNER, L. I. and SHIROKOV, G. K.
   1967 "Itogi razvitiya narodnogo khozyaistva" (A balance sheet of the national economy's development) in *Problemy ekonomicheskogo i sotsial'nogo razvitiya nezavisimoi Indii.* Moscow: Nauka.

BRAGINA, E. A.
   1965 Book review of Charles Bettleheim, L'Inde indépendante. *Narody Azii i Afriki* III.

CLARKSON, Stephen
   1971 *L'analyse soviétique des problèmes indiens du sous-developpement (1955–1964)*. Paris and The Hague: Mouton.

CLARKSON, Stephen
   1967 "Manicheism Corrupted: The Soviet View of Aid to India". *International Journal* XXII (Spring): pp. 253–264.

DYAKOV, A. M.
   1966 *The National Problem in India Today*. Moscow: Nauka.

EGOROV, I. I.
   1967 *Finansirovanie planov ekonomicheskogo razvitiya Indii* (The financing of India's economic development plans). Moscow: Nauka.

GORDON, L. A.
   1967 "Gorodskoi nesel'skokhozyaistvennyi proletariat" (The urban non-agrarian proletariat) in *Problemy ekonomicheskogo i sotsial'nogo razvitiya nezavisimoi Indii*. Moscow: Nauka, pp. 193–219.
   1967 "Intelligentsiya i sluzhashchie" (The intelligentsia and civil servants) in *Ibid.* pp. 245–256.

GORDON-POLONSKAYA, I. R.
   1963 *Musul'manskie techeniya v obshchestvennoi mysl' Indii i Pakistana (Kritika "musul'manskogo natsionalizma")* (Moslem currents in India's and Pakistan's social thought: a critique of "Moslem nationalism"). Moscow IVL.

GURVICH, R. P.
   1967 "Krest'yanstvo" (The peasantry) in *Problemy ekonomicheskogo i sotsial'nogo razvitiya nezavisimoi Indii*. Moscow: Nauka.

(No author)
   1965 *Ideologicheskie techeniya sovremennoi Indii* (Modern India's ideological currents). Moscow: Nauka.

(No author)
   1967 "Izmeneniya v sotsial'no-klassovoi strukture Indii" (Changes in India's social and class structure) in *Problemy ekonomichiskogo i sotsial'nogo razvitiya nezavisimoi Indii*. Moscow: Nauka.

KAZAKOV, V. I.
   1967 *Bor'ba za sozdanie natsional'nykh shtatov v nezavisimoi Indii* (The Struggle to found national states in independant India). Moscow: Nauka.

KOTOVSKII, G. G.
  1965   Introductory article in *Kasty v Indii* (Castes in India). Moscow: Nauka.
KOTOVSKII, G. G.
  1967   "Sel'skokhozyaistvennyi proletariat i poluproletariat" (The agrarian proletariat
          and semi-proletariat) in *Problemy ekonomichiskogo i sotsial'nogo razvitiya nezavisimoi
          Indii*. Moscow: Nauka.
KUTSOBIN, P. V.
  1963   *Sovremennaya Indiya. Rasstanovka Klassovykh i politicheskikh sil* (Modern India:
          Redistribution of class and political forces). Moscow: Izd. Pol., Lit.
KUZ MIN, S. A.
  1969   *The Developing Countries, Employment and Capital Investment.* New York: International
          Arts and Sciences Press.
LEVIN, S. F.
  1965   "Ob evolyutsii musul'manskikh torgovykh kast v svyazi s razvitiem kapitalizma"
          (On the evolution of Moslem trading casts and their links with the development of
          capitalism) in *Kasty v Indii* (Casts in India). Moscow: Nauka.
LEVKOVSKY, A. I.
  1966   *Capitalism in India.* Bombay: People's Publishing House.
LEVKOVSKII, A. I.
  1963   Preface in the Russian translation of D. Gadgil, *Planirovanie i ekonomicheskaya politika
          v Indii* (Planning and economic policy in India). Moscow IIL.
LITMAN, A. D.
  1966   *Filosofoskaya mysl' nezavisimoi Indii (akademicheskie sistemy i religioznofilosofskie ucheniya)*
          (Independent India's philosophical thought: academic systems and religious-
          philosophical teaching). Moscow: Nauka.
LOSHAKOV, Yu. I.
  1967a   "Indiiskii monopolistischeskii kapital" (Indian monopoly capital). *Vestnik Mos-
          kovskogo Universiteta* Seriya VII 3.
  1967b   "Kontsentratisiya priozvodstva i monopolii sovremennoi Indii" (Concentration of
          Production and monopolies in modern India). Moscow: Thesis abstract.
LOZOVAYA
  1966   "Indiya" (India) in *Plany-programmy ekonomicheskogo razvitiya stran Azii* (The eco-
          nomic development plans of Asian countries). Moscow.
MAEV, O. V.
  1964a   "Ekonomicheskaya programma indiiskikh monopolistov" (The economic program
          of Indian monopolists). *Narody Azii i Afriki* 5.
  1964b   "Indiiskii monopolisticheskii kapital" (Indian monopoly capital). *Narody Azii i
          Afriki* 1.
MAEV, O. V.
  1966   "Indiiskii monopolisticheskii kapital: zapadnoindiiskie gruppy" (Indian mono-
          poly capital: Western groups). *Mirovaya Ekonomika i Mezhdunarodnye Otnosheniya*,
          No. 8.
  1967   "Indiiskii monopolistischeskii kapital: vostochnoindiiskie gruppy" (Indian mono-
          poly capital: Eastern groups). *Mirovaya Ekonomika i Mezhdunarodnye Otnosheniya*, No. 3.
MIRONOVA, E. I.
  1967   *Prodovol'stvennaya problema v Indii* (The food problem in India). Moscow: Nauka.
(No author)
  1962   *Obshchestvenno-politicheskaya i filosofskaya mysl' Indii* (India's philosophical and socio-
          political thought). Moscow IVL.
ORLEANSKAYA, L. K.
  1962   "K voprosu o razvitii proizvodstvennykh zemledel'cheskikh kooperativov v Indii"
          (Concerning the development of agrarian production cooperatives in India). *Krat.
          Soob, INA*, No. 51.
  1964   "Sel'skokhozyaistvennye sbytovye kooperativy v Indii" (The agricultural marketing
          cooperatives in India). *Krat. Soob, INA*, No. 75.

POTEMKIN, Yu. V. and SANDAKOV, V. A.
  1968   "Problema nakopleniya v razvivayushchikhsya stranakh" (The problem of accumulation in the developing countries) in *Klassy i klassovaya bor'ba v razvivayushchikhsya stranakh*. Vol. II. Moscow: Mysl'.
RASTYANNIKOV, V.G.
  1967   "Ekspluatatorskaya verkhushka derevni i formirovanie sel'skoi burzhuazii" (The exploiting summit in the villages and the formation of the agrarian bourgeoisie) in *Problemy ekonomicheskogo i sotsial'nogo razvitiya nezavisimoi Indii*. Moscow: Nauka.
RASTYANNIKOV, V. G.
  1968   "Price Policy and Food Production". *Amrita Bazar Patrika*, March 8.
RASTYANNIKOV, V. G. and MAKSIMOV, M. A.
  1965   *Razvitie kapitalizma v sel'skom khozyaistve sovremennoi Indii* (The development of capitalism in modern India's agriculture). Moscow: Nauka.
REISNER, L. I. and SHIROKOV, G. K.
  1967   "Gorodskaya promyshlennaya i torgovaya burzhuaziya" (The urban industrial and trading burgeoisie) in *Problemy ekonomichiskogo i sotsial'nogo razvitiya nezavisimoi Indii*. Moscow: Nauka.
REISNER, L. I. and SHIROKOV, G. K.
  1966   *Sovremennaya indiiskaya burzhuaziya* (The modern Indian bourgeoisie). Moscow: Nauka.
RUDIN, L.
  1967   Book review of V. G. Rastyannikov and M. A. Maksimov, Razvitie kapitalizma v sel'skom khozyaistve sovremennoi Indii. *Narody Azii i Afriki*, No. 2.
SAVELYEV, N.
  1967   "Monopoly Drive in India". *International Affairs* (April).
SAVEL'EV, N. A.
  1967   "Natsional'naya burzhuaziya" (The National bourgeoisie) in *Klassy i klassovaya bor'ba v razvivayushchikhsya stranakh*. Volume I. Moscow: Mysl'.
SEMENOVA, N. I.
  1967   "Bor'ba sel'skokhozyaistvennykh rabochikh Indii" (India's agrarian workers' struggle) in *Krest'yaenskoe dvizhenie v stranakh Vostoka* (The peasant movement in Eastern countries). Moscow: Nauka.
SHATALOV, I. M.
  1967   "The Third World and the Scientific and Technical Revolution". *International Affairs* (May).
SOLONITSKII, A. S. and UL'RIKH, O. D.
  1968   "Puti stanovleniya i razvitiya gosudarstvennogo sektora v osvobodivshikhsya stranakh" (Ways of creating and developing the State sector in liberated countries) in *Klassy i klassovaya bor'ba v razvivayushchikhsya stranakh*. Volume II. Moscow: Mysl'.
YERSHOV, Y.
  1965   *India: Independence and Oil*. Moscow: Progress.

Mechanization and the Division of Labor: A Study of Farm Families in the Beka'a Plain of Lebanon

AGOP K. KAYAYAN AND DAVID G. FRANCIS

Ohio State University, Columbus, Ohio, U.S.A.

Introduction

THE RECENT rises in income among the populations in developing countries and the governments' encouragement to purchase productive items have stimulated investment in various types of machinery. In the agricultural sector the trend toward farm mechanization is progressing at a rapid pace. As an example, in 1964, Lebanon imported tractors for the total value of more than 7,000,000 Lebanese Pounds (U.S. $2,300,000) (Republique Libanaise: 766–772). The social effects of such rapid farm mechanization have been only briefly investigated.

One possible effect of the increasing use of farm machinery is the release of agricultural labor and the resulting movement to urban centers. Conflicting findings have been reported in this area. Tanyol indicates that mechanization increased the rate of rural-urban migration in Turkish villages (1959: 198–218). Both Johl (1971) in India, and Saab (1960) in Lebanon, however, indicate that in the long term mechanization increases the need for manpower in the rural areas through more intensive use of agricultural land and the creation of new occupational categories.

These findings may actually complement each other if a temporal distinction is made. In the short run a movement of population seems to occur away from the rural areas to the urban centers. But in the long run there may be a reverse movement of population due to increases in the intensity and diversity of the agricultural production process.

Morsink (1965) reported an increasing rate of rural-urban migration in Lebanon. He has further indicated the unpreparedness of the urban areas to provide employment, housing, and services to rural migrants. The potentially serious problem of the adequacy of adjustment of rural migrants to urban areas remains to be investigated.

The implications of technological change on the division of labor were studied early in the development of sociological theory. Durkheim postulated that the adoption of technological innovations by members of a social group changes its patterns of division of labor. He further indicated that such rapid changes lead to a situation of anomie among group members (1966: 353–372). More recently, Simone de Beauvoir, in her analysis of the division of labor between the sexes, argued that while initially the division of labor was based on physical and physiological differences, it crystallized into traditional beliefs (1949: 12–42). Firth (1957: 82–83) and Mead (1962: 16) supported Beauvoir in attributing the establishment of a division of labor between the sexes to physical and physiological differences. Gross (1958: 327–328) added the influence of age as an intervening variable. Dube (1965: 168–174) provided a comprehensive set of variables including age, sex, caste, and social status as being related to the division of labor in Indian communities.

The purpose of this article is to assess the effects of farm mechanization on certain aspects of the division of labor among farm families on the Central Beka's Plain of Lebanon.

Methodology

In order to study the association between farm mechanization and the division of labor, it was initially intended that two categories of farmers be studied: mechanized and non-mechanized. This attempt was unsuccessful since totally nonmechanized farmers, similar to mechanized farmers in their farming patterns, were difficult to find. Decision was thus made to study farmers at different levels of mechanization.

It was hypothesized that the higher the level of mechanization on the farm:

(1) The less would be the amount and tiresomeness of work performed by the farmer, his wife and his children;

(2) The more leisure time would be available to all members of the family;

(3) The more technical and mechanical skills would be acquired by farmers and/or their sons;

(4) The fewer would be the number of relatives living in the nuclear family or being supported by its income;

(5) The higher would be the children's attendance at school.

Measurement of Variables

The central variable considered by the study is the level of mechanization of the farmer. In order to measure this variable each farmer was asked about the crops he raised and the number of *dunums*[1] of each. It was found that wheat, barley, onions, potatoes, and tomatoes were the major crops of the area. Wheat and potatoes showed considerable variation in mechanization level and were universally raised. They were thus selected for further examination. The farmers

---

1   One Lebanese *dunum* equals 1,000 square meters or 0.1 hectare.

were then asked to specify the operations performed by tractor for each of these two crops. Based on these responses a formula was developed to measure the farmers' levels of mechanization as follows:

$$M = \frac{N}{T} \times 100 \times C$$

M stands for the degree or level of mechanization of each farmer, N for the number of mechanized operations in the growing of wheat and potatoes, T for the total number of operations that could be mechanized, and C for a correction factor related to the number of years the tractor had been in use.[1] Thus "level of mechanization" indexed the proportion of operations mechanized in relation to the total for which machinery could possibly have been employed, taking into consideration the length of time of tractor use. In the villages studied, there were ten operations each for wheat and potato crops that could be mechanized. The following example illustrates the formula: Farmer A mechanized four operations for wheat and three for potatoes, and he had been using the tractor for seven years. Since the correction for this period is 1.3, the farmer's level of mechanization would be:

$$\frac{(4 + 3)}{(10 + 10)} \times 100 \times 1.3 = 45.5$$

The correction was used on the assumption that the longer the period of tractor use, the higher would be the level of mechanization. The decreasing rate of increase of the correction was judged necessary on the assumption that in the early years of machinery use the farmer's level of mechanization and its resulting mental and psychological changes increase, but tend to increase at a lower rate with time. This correction hopefully brings the formula closer to reality. It would probably have to be modified for use in studying different cases of mechanization in different areas. The values could, of course, alter the distribution of level of mechanization to some extent.

    Among the other variables examined, accuracy of measurement of amounts and tiresomeness of work[2] were dependent upon farmers' recall. This was also true for amounts of leisure time. These variables were recorded for the periods before and after mechanization. The farmer responded to all questions including those pertaining to his wife and children.

    Amount of work performed was subsequently calculated per *dunum* of land cultivated on the basis of the information provided by the farmers.

    Technical and mechanical skills were measured from farmers' responses to

---

1 The correction factor was given an arbitrary value of 1.0 for 1–5 years of tractor use, 1.3 for 6–10 years, and 1.4 for more than 10 years use.

2 Amounts of work and leisure were calculated from average numbers of hours reported per day for every season of the year for all family members. Tiresomeness of work was indexed by response to the question: "Is your work at present (much more, more, same, less, much less) tiresome than before you mechanized?"

questions concerning their and their sons' abilities to drive and repair a tractor.

Number of relatives living in the nuclear family or being supported by it was calculated directly from the farmer responses.

School attendance was determined using the official school records of the village schools attended by the children of the respondents.

Choice of Villages and Farmers in the Sample

Three villages (Bednayel, Housh el Rafaka and Timnin Tahta) in the Beka'a Plain were chosen for the study. These villages are geographically within ten kilometers of each other. They are about 25 kilometers from each of two larger towns which are capitals of *mohafazats* (largest administrative divisions). All three villages are situated along the main highway running between Beirut and the city of Baalbeck. The American University of Beirut maintains a local Agricultural Research and Education Center which provides extension services to these villages.

Farming patterns and crops are similar in all three villages. These villages are exclusively Shi'ite, one of the major Islamic sects in the Middle East. Control was thus established for one of the most important intervening variables since religion by itself could account for many differences in patterns of the division of labor within the family. Sociological and economic studies have been conducted in these villages by Stevens (1959) and Fetter (1961). Farmers had therefore been introduced to the idea of being interviewed for academic purposes.

Since the respondents in the sample could not be selected beforehand on the basis of their levels of mechanization, it was decided to interview all land owning farmers in the three villages. A complete list of farmers in each village was provided by its *mukhtar* (elected village head). This list was cross-checked by asking farmers in each village to give the names of other farmers in their village. Very few names resulted for addition to the original list. The total number of farmers included in the three villages was 113. Or these, 31 were not interviewed because, in most cases, they were not found at home when a third visit was made. Thus, the total number of interviewees was 82 of which 31 were from Bednayel, 35 from Housh el Rafaka and 16 from Timnin Tahta. The number of farmers who were not interviewed may have reduced the representativeness of the sample. There was, however, no reason to believe that they represented any particular category of response.

For purposes of statistical analysis farmers were divided into low, medium, and high levels of mechanization based on formula scores as previously discussed. The chi-square test and its correlate for determining homogeniety in the sample populations were used to determine significance of variation. The probability level of 0.05 was considered sufficient to test the significance of relationships between variables.

Discussion of Findings

Characteristics of the Respondents

Of the 82 farmers interviewed, the average age was 49.9 years, whereas the average age of their wives was 42.1. All the farmers except one were married and the average length of married life for the sample was 25.2 years. It was interesting to note that these facts support the common belief that early marriages in Middle Eastern villages are commonly practiced and highly valued. Only two farmers, of the 82 interviewed had two wives each.

Farmers' average level of education was relatively low since 22 farmers (27 percent) did not attend school at all. Twenty-three others (28 percent) had only one to three years of education. In most cases the type of school attended by the latter group was a Coranic village school. Twenty-five farmers attended school for four to six years, but the number of farmers who continued to complete the ninth grade dropped sharply to eight (10 percent of the sample). Only two interviewees had finished their high school education; one studied at a technical school and the other was enrolled at the Lebanese University.

Compared to farmers, wives had an extremely low average level of education. Seventy-five percent of them had not attended school. Another 18 percent had one to three years of education. Only two women completed the sixth grade and three completed the ninth grade.

The respondents' average family size was 8.1 members. When the relatives living with or being supported by the family were considered, this number increased to 9.2.

Tractors were introduced in the three villages about 20 years ago but apparently came into more common usage only during the last 10 years. The length of time which tractors had been in use by the respondents ranged from two to twenty years. Eleven farmers in the sample used their own tractors, whereas 71 farmers (87 percent) rented tractors from the owners. There were twelve tractors in use in the three villages. The implements used with tractors were mainly two and five-bottom moldboard plows, discs, combines, trailers, and a new type of threshing implement.

Findings In Relation to Hypotheses

As seen in Table 1 the level of mechanization was not significantly associated with the amount of work performed by farmers, their wives, or their children. It is interesting to note in the case of male children that the relationship not only was not significant but was actually in the opposite direction from the one expected. The higher the level of mechanization the larger was the number of farmers who had sons helping in one or more operations. This might be attributed to the help of sons of more highly mechanized farmers in the performance of agricultural operations requiring new mechanical skills.

Level of mechanization and farmers' tiresomeness of work were significantly related. The chi-squares test for homogeneity indicated that the difference in sample proportions between "low" and "high" levels of mechanization was significant for both those who perceived "little or no change" in the tiresomeness of their work and those who felt their work was "much less tiresome". The data indicated that the higher the level of mechanization the higher was the number of farmers who felt their work had become much less tiresome. This finding was congruent with the unexpected relationship found between level of mechanization and amount of work performed by male children.

Similarly, Table 1 shows a significant association between level of mechanization of farmers and their wives' tiresomeness of work. The work of wives of more highly mechanized farmers was less tiresome than that of less mechanized farmers. The chi-square test for homogeneity indicated that the difference was significant between proportions of wives of farmers at "high" and "low" levels of mechanization.

Farmers' levels of mechanization and amounts of leisure were positively and significantly associated. The chi-square test of homogeneity indicated that there were significant differences in proportions of farmers having specified amounts of

Table 1

Summary of Hypotheses, Statistical Tests Applied and Support Levels

	Null Hypotheses	Tests Applied	x^2 Value	Signifi- cance	Support/ Reject
1.	There is no significant difference in amounts of work performed (hours/ year/dunum) by farmers, wives and children at different levels of mechanization.				
	A. There is no significant difference in amount of work performed by *farmers* at different levels of mechanization.	x^2, x^2 for homogeneity	6.57	< .05	Support
	B. There is no significant difference in amount of work performed by *wives* at different levels of mechanization.	x^2, x^2 for homogeniety	3.25	< .05	Support
	C. There is no significant difference in amount of work performed by *female children* at different levels of mechanization.	x^2	5.20	< .05	Support
	D. There is no significant difference in amount of work performed by *male children* at different levels of mechanization.	x^2	1.77	< .05	Support
	E. There is no significant difference in the tiresomeness of work (in the farmers' opinions) of *farmers* at different levels of mechanization.	x^2, x^2 for homogeneity	17.12	> .05	Reject

Null Hypotheses	Tests Applied	x^2 Value	Signifi- cance	Support/ Reject
F. Wives.	x^2, x^2 for homogeneity	12.06	> .05	Reject
G. Female children.	x^2	1.81	< .05	Support
H. Male children.	x^2	.40	< .05	Support
2. There is no significant difference (in the farmers' opinions) in amounts of leisure available to farmers, wives and children at different levels of mechanization.				
A. There is no significant difference in amounts of leisure available to *farmers* at different levels of mechanization.	x^2, x^2 for homogeneity	10.77	> .05	Reject
B. Wives.	x^2	9.43	< .05	Support
C. Children.	x^2	2.15	< .05	Support
3. There is no significant difference in the abilities of farmers and/or their sons to perform minor repairs at different levels.	x^2	.75	< .05	Support
A. There is no significant difference in the tractor driving ability of farmers and/or their sons at different levels of mechanization.	x^2	4.98	< .05	Support
4. There is no significant difference in the number of relatives living with and/or being supported by families on farms at different levels of mechanization.	x^2, x^2 for homogeneity	10.36	> .05	Reject
5. There is no significant difference in the rates of children's absence from school among children from farms at different levels of mechanization.	x^2	2.15	< .05	Support

leisure time at "low" and "high" levels of mechanization. The data thus demonstrated that more highly mechanized farmers had a higher average numbers of hours of leisure per day than less mechanized farmers. This relationship again, was in agreement with the earlier finding concerning male children's help. More mechanized farmers viewed their present work as less tiresome, had more leisure time available, and a larger number of them had sons helping in one or more agricultural operations.

Level of mechanization and amount of leisure were not significantly associated for other members of the respondents' families.

Concerning the third hypothesis, level of mechanization and farmers' and/or their sons' ability to drive and perform minor tractor repairs were not found to be significantly related. Tractor repairs had to be performed outside the villages, in a district center about 25 kilometers from the study area. Thus mechanization, at the time of the study, had not seemed to create new occupational categories in the villages.

The significant and positive relationship stated in the fourth hypothesis between levels of mechanization and number of relatives living with and/or being supported by the farm families was not found. Rather the finding, significant at the .05 level, was in the *opposite* direction from the one hypothesized. It was expected that at higher levels of mechanization there would be less need for help from relatives therefore reducing the occurrences of the extended family. Table 2 presents findings which are contradictory to this conventional explanation of the extended family phenomenon in the Middle East. As can be observed in this table farmers mechanized at a "medium" level least frequently (17 percent) had relatives living with or being supported by the family. Almost three times as many highly mechanized farmers (51 percent) had one or more relatives living with or being supported by them. The chi-square homogeneity test indicated that the differences in proportions between farmers of "medium" and "high" levels of mechanization were significant both for those who had no relatives and those who had one or more relatives living with or being supported by them.

Since the highly mechanized farms were also the larger farm owners, it could be inferred that the Islamic prescription of *Zakat* (almsgiving) is operative in these villages.

Table 2

The effect of farm level of mechanization on the number of relatives living with and/or being supported by the respondent families

Level of Mechanization	No relatives		One or more relatives		Total	
	No.	%	No.	%	No.	%
"Low" (Scores 20–34)	19	41	11	32	30	37
"Medium" (Scores 35–49)	19	41	6	17	25	30
"High" (Scores 50 or more)	9	18	18	51	27	33
Total	47	100	35	100	82	100

$$x^2 = 10.3589 \ p > 0.05$$

Concerning the last hypothesis, children's school attendance was not found to be significantly related to their fathers' levels of mechanization. This finding must be cautiously interpreted, however, since only 22 of the children's records of school attendance could be located.

Conclusions

Since the present investigation surveyed only 82 farmers it must actually be considered a pilot study. The findings were not meant to be conclusive but rather to indicate a topical direction for future research. In that the hypotheses – based upon the "conventional wisdom" concerning effects of mechanization upon farm life – were only marginally supported, the need for further research of the nature indicated becomes even more apparent.

In contrast to previous findings of Saab (1960) in Lebanon as well as Johl (1971) in India, no evidence was found of mechanization leading to an increase in occupational categories in the study area. Rather, the farm machinery was being taken to the nearest urban area for repair! With only 12 tractors in the three villages studied; however, the area must be recognized as being in the beginning stages of mechanization. Higher levels of mechanization will increase the need for local repair services.

The significant increase in amounts of leisure time available to farmers and their wives as well as the reduction in tiresomeness of their farm work have interesting policy implications. These would prove useful in planning for the future social and economic development of the area. According to community needs, which would have to be determined, it might be effective to establish some small-scale industrial activity. Secondary processing of agricultural products could possibly be handled more efficiently in the rural areas. Adult educational programs may be of interest to those in the area. Regardless of the focus, however, the findings indicate the critical necessity of community development planning in order to balance the progress that is presently being achieved.

REFERENCES

DUBE, S. C.
  1965 *Indian Village*, London: Routledge and Kegan Paul.
DURKHEIM, Emile
  1966 *The Division of Labor in Society*, New York: The Free Press.
FETTER, G. C.
  1961 *Attitudes Toward Selected Aspects of Rural Life Among Central Beka'a Farmers*, Publication No. 13, Beirut: American University of Beirut.
FIRTH, R.
  1957 *Human Types*, London: Thomas Nelson and Sons.
GROSS, E.
  1958 *Work and Society*, New York: The Thomas Y. Crowell Company.
JOHL, S. S.
  1971 "Mechanization, Labor-Use and Productivity in Indian Agriculture," Occasional Paper No. 23, Columbus: The Ohio State University.
MARASCULIO, L. A.
  1971 *Statistical Methods for Behavioral Science Research*, New York: McGraw Hill Book Company.
MEAD, Margaret
  1962 *Male and Female*, New York: The New American Library.
MORSINK, H. J. A.
  1965 "Rapid Urbanization in the Arab Countries and Its Social, Economic, Physical, and Administrative Problems," *Al-Abhath: Quarterly Journal of the American University of Beirut*, 18.
République Libanaise
  1965 *Commerce Exterieur, Année 1964*, Beyrouth.

SAAB, G.
1960   *Motorisation de l'Agriculture et Developpment Agricole au Proche-Orient*, Paris: SEDES.

STEVENS, R. D.
1959   "Capital Formation and Agriculture in Some Lebanese Villages," Ph. D. Dissertation, Ithaca: Cornell University.

TANYOL, C.
1959   "Tractor Giren 50 Koyde Nufus Hareketlerin ve Ictimai Degismelerinin Kontrolu," *Sosyologi Dezgisi*, 13–14.

Occupational Preferences of College Students in North India*

YOGENDRA K. MALIK AND JESSE F. MARQUETTE

The University of Akron, Akron, Ohio, U.S.A.

LITERATURE on occupational choices suggests that in modern industrial societies based upon capitalism, individuals have freedom to select their occupations. (Ginzberg 1951: 3). It is conceded, however, that the young adult's occupational aspirations and his selection of a job are influenced by such factors as socialization by his family, his peer group and his school (Musgrave 1967: 33).

In the case of traditional societies, however, it is assumed that occupational choices are both limited and largely determined by such factors as caste, family status, religion, and other ascriptive norms (Ginzberg 1951: 3). India is described as a traditional society, presently undergoing the process of modernization. Since 1947, a democratic political system has existed in India. There has been a politicization of the masses, and a constant, though slow process of industrialization is taking place. What impact has this change in the external environment had on the interrelationship between a youth's social origin and his selection of a particular occupation? The answer to this question will not only give us some idea of the interrelationship between the traditionally accepted ascriptive norms and occupational preference, but will also be indicative of changing patterns of social norms and values in a transitional society. It should be pointed out here that some recent studies on occupational distributions in India appear to demonstrate that despite urbanization, industrialization, and some change in traditional occupational patterns, caste and religion still remain the dominant determinant of one's occupation. For example, in his study of occupational differentiation in South India, Noel P. Gist concludes that "the caste system as a determinant in occupational choice is still a dynamic

* The senior author wishes to express his gratitude to Professors S. M. Sud of Doaba College, Jullundur; Ram Pal Vidyalankar of Government College, Malerkotla; and R. C. Chaudhary of Ludhiana for their valuable assistance in conducting the surveys in their colleges. He also wishes to acknowledge his debt to Dr. Paul Weidner, Chairman of the Political Science Department, University of Akron, the administrative officials of the various colleges in India for their cooperation in assisting the completion of this project. The authors also wish to acknowledge the assistance of Penny Marquette in the preparation of this manuscript.

force" (Gist 1954b: 131). He further adds that "High status castes are oriented towards high status occupations and vice-versa" (Gist 1954a: 130). With reference to North India, S. P. Jain's study of a small town community also arrived at the conclusion that "occupational differentials" were still based upon "religion and hierarchy of castes" (Jain 1967: 309, Rutha 1970: 248). These conclusions, however, are based upon studies of the populations of either small towns or large cities. None of these studies focus solely on the occupational choices of those born and educated in a free India.

Occupational choice is viewed as a developmental process. Ginzberg, et al, stress that it is at the age of eighteen and above that a young adult is first in a position to make a "realistic" choice of his occupation (Ginzberg 1951: 95). It therefore becomes important to investigate the occupational preferences of college youth. It is the objective of this paper to investigate the inter-relationship between college students' occupational preferences and their social origins.

Universe of the Study

The student population for this study was selected from Ludhiana and Jullundur, two large cities, and Malerkotla, a medium-sized town, all situated in the Punjab state of North India. Ludhiana and Jullundur, each with a population of 400,000 or above, have diversified economies built around medium and small-scale industries (Pathak 1970: 1091). Both cities are the headquarters of their district governments and both house numerous technical and educational institutions. According to the 1961 census, Jullundur district's population was 54 percent Hindu, and 44 percent Sikh. In Ludhiana district on the other hand, the Hindus are a minority (33.7%) and the Sikh (63%) a majority (Census of India 1961: 31). Both of the cities, however, are predominantly Hindu, Jullundur having the larger Hindu population (60% as compared to 55% in Ludhiana) (Wallace 1967: 71).

Malerkotla has a population of approximately 50,000, including the largest concentration of Muslims in the state. It is a market town, heavily dependent on agriculture. The town was formerly the headquarters of a princely state.

Sample and Methodology

In Punjab, institutions providing college level are of three types: (1) Denominational colleges (here called private colleges) run by Hindu, Sikh or other sectarian organizations; (2) Government colleges run by the state government; and (3) Exclusively women's colleges, managed and run either by the state government or by sectarian organizations.

To achieve a fair representation of these different segments of the student population, two private colleges (one Hindu and one Sikh), two state colleges (one urban and one rural), and two women's colleges (one state and one Hindu) were selected for the study.

The data were collected by the senior author on the basis of a structured questionnaire administered to the students during a class hour. The selected classes were the first year (freshman) and the third year (graduating) classes in Liberal Arts and Sciences. In the three private colleges, all students of the first and third year classes, present on that day, were asked to fill out the standardized questionnaire. At the request of the officials, the questionnaire was administered only to randomly selected sections of the freshman and graduating classes at the government colleges. The completed questionnaires were collected at the end of the hour. The total number of respondents came to 2,275, ninety percent being the response rate.

Hypotheses

To continue distribution of occupational opportunities according to traditional criteria, the stratification system must enjoy generalized normative support. The unequal ascription of occupational status must be seen as just and appropriate. In a changing and modernizing society, however, whether or not traditional ascription is seen as just, it is not likely to be seen as appropriate. Thus, our major hypothesis, simply put, is that the children of free India are likely to order their occupational preferences according to criteria other than ascribed status. The corresponding null hypotheses are: (1) There exists a significant relationship between the respondent's caste and his occupational preference, (2) There exists a significant relationship between the respondent's religious background and his occupational preference.

If, as Ginzberg suggests, the young adult is unable to make a realistic occupational choice until late adolescence, we would expect the college to play a major role in determining occupational aspirations (Ginzberg 1951: 96). Therefore, our third null hypothesis is: (3) There is no significant relationship between the college attended and the respondent's occupational choice.

We would, however, expect the father's occupation to be a significant background factor in the respondent's socialization, and as such, to affect both the choice of school and the choice of occupation. Our fourth and fifth null hypotheses are thus: (4) No significant relationship exists between the respondent's choice of school and his father's occupational status, and (5) No significant relationship exists between the respondent's occupational aspirations and his father's occupational status.

Finally, we wished to examine the relationship between the desire for job security and the respondent's background. Following the results of work by LaPalombara and Waters with Italian youth, we postulated a relationship between the desire for occupational security and the respondent's residential background (LaPalombara 1961: 39). LaPalombara found that respondents from rural areas were far more concerned with job security than respondents from urbanized and industrialized areas. LaPalombara argues that respondents from the more deprived rural areas show a marked aversion to risk-taking in their occupational goals. Rural youth are thus more prone to desiring occupations within the civil service which provide greater job security, but lower possibilities for advancement. We tested the null hypothesis that (6) There exists no significant relationship between place of residence and employment preference.

Analysis and Summary of Findings

We are dealing with a sample of college students, and as such, their occupational expectations are limited to a few higher status occupations. All respondents will have aspirations in the direction of upper status white collar positions. In terms of actual occupational choices, we find that the most desirable occupation for the young adult is teaching (26.1%), followed by civil service (22.1%), military service (17.1%), business (11.1%), law (9.1), medicine (8.1%), and scientific research (5.1%). Engineering, a highly prestigious occupation, draws only 2.1% of the youths, and such occupations as journalism, stewardess, artist and social service are preferred by an insignificant minority of the students.

It is when we compare the young adults' occupational preferences with their parents' actual occupations that we discover a very high degree of expected occupational mobility on the part of the college students. The young adults' occupational preferences stand in sharp contrast to their parents' reported occupations. Only 33% of the parents hold such white collar jobs as civil service, teaching, and professional positions such as law or medicine. Fully a third of the respondents reported parent occupations in either agriculture or laboring occupations, and another third reported parent occupations in business. In contrast, only 11% of the respondents indicated business-oriented work aspirations, while 70% indicated white collar occupations. It is this presumption of occupational mobility which lies at the heart of our research. Is this apparent occupational and social mobility significantly different from what could have been expected under the traditional social system; or has the process of social change resulted in major alterations in the manner by which life chances are distributed in Indian society?

In order to test our first hypothesis concerning the relationship between caste and occupational expectation, we tested the relationship between caste and parents' actual occupation. This test establishes a meaningful basis of comparison for our examination of inter-generational change. As expected, there is an extremely high level of relationship between parents' occupation and caste, the contingency coefficient being 0.5363 (Table I).

When we examine the relationship of the young respondents' occupational choice and caste we find, contrary to our original hypotheses, that the relationship is still significant (Table II). However, the contingency coefficient for Table II (0.1636) indicates that there is a lower level of correlation between the respondents' occupational preferences and caste than was found with their parents. Obviously, the ability of the stratification system to effect occupational choice has greatly declined among the young Indians.

Table 1

Father's Work Rank by Caste [a]

| | Work Rank | | | |
	High	Moderately High	Moderately Low	Low
Caste	High	Moderately High	Moderately Low	Low
Upper	18.6%	11.4%	11.1%	7.5%
Lower Upper	34.8%	52.3%	9.3%	15.7%
Middle	24.3%	7.6%	63.2%	10.2%
Lower Middle	12.8%	18.4%	7.8%	22.0%
Lower	9.5%	10.3%	8.7%	44.5%
N =	580	673	497	254

$x^2 = 809.28$ @ 12 d.f.
P < .001 CC = .5363

For this study, castes reported by the respondents were ranked as follows: Brahman-Upper; Khshatriya-Lower Upper; Jat (land owning agriculturists) – Middle; Vaish, Aggrawal, Jain and non-Jat – Lower Middle; and Ramdasi, Chamar and Sudra – Low. For the parent occupations, Government Service, Medicine and Law – High; Business – Moderately High; Teaching and Agriculture – Moderately Low; Laboring occupations – Low.

Table 2

Respondents' Caste by Respondents' Expected Job

| | Work Rank [a] | | | |
	High	Moderately High	Moderately Low	Low
Caste	High	Moderately High	Moderately Low	Low
Upper	14.2%	11.5%	13.5%	12.5%
Lower Upper	25.8%	45.6%	30.2%	33.8%
Middle	30.2%	19.7%	25.1%	23.7%
Lower Middle	14.4%	11.3%	18.6%	15.8%
Lower	15.3%	11.8%	12.5%	14.2%
N =	810	390	811	562

$x^2 = 57.01$ @ 12 d.f.
P < .0001 CC = .1636

For this study, castes reported by the respondents were ranked as follows: Brahman-Upper; Khshatriya-Lower Upper; Jat (land owning agriculturists) – Middle; Vaish, Aggrawal, Jain and non-Jat – Lower Middle; and Ramdasi, Chamar and sudra – Low. Occupational preferences of the respondents were ranked Civil and Military Service – High; Medicine and Business – Moderately High; Law, Science, Engineering – Moderately Low; Teaching and Other – Low.

Since our primary concern is whether or not the processes of social change have led to a decline in the relationship between ascription and occupational choice, we tested the subsidiary hypothesis that individuals from urbanized environments would be less amenable to choice by ascription. Table III presents the correlation of caste level and occupational preference controlling for the effect of rural versus urban background. Table III provides a dimension not available through comparison of Tables I and II, namely the significance of social environment. The results shown in Table III indicate that respondents

Table 3

Respondent's Caste Position by Occupational Preferences Controlling for Social Background[a]

Caste Rank	Rural Respondent's Preference				Urban Respondent's Preference			
	High	Mod. High	Mod. Low	Low	High	Mod. High	Mod. Low	Low
Upper	9.2%	8.1%	15.0%	8.8%	20.1%	13.3%	12.1%	14.7%
Lower Upper	11.0%	29.4%	11.3%	17.5%	42.4%	56.6%	45.7%	45.1%
Middle	45.8%	39.7%	43.6%	42.5%	12.9%	8.8%	9.8%	11.0%
Lower Middle	14.1%	11.0%	15.8%	14.9%	15.9%	11.6%	20.8%	16.0%
Lower	20.0%	11.8%	14.3%	16.2%	9.7%	11.6%	11.6%	13.2%
N =	426	136	133	228	373	249	173	319

$$x^2 = 36.66 @ 12 \text{ d.f.}$$
$$P < .001 \quad CC = .1955$$

$$x^2 = 22.18 @ 12 \text{ d.f.}$$
$$P = \text{N.S.} \quad CC = .1397$$

For this study, castes reported by the respondents were ranked as follows: Brahman-Upper; Khshatriya-Lower Upper; Jat (land owning agriculturists) – Middle; Vaish, Aggrawal, Jain and non-Jat – Lower Middle; and Ramdasi, Chamar and Sudra – Low. Occupational preferences of the respondents were ranked Civil and Military Service – Moderately High; Law, Science, Engineering – Moderately Low; Teaching and Other – Low.

from more rural, and hence more traditionally oriented regions, still retain some willingness to abide by the occupational prescriptions of the stratification system. Urban respondents, on the other hand, demonstrate no significant relationship between their occupational intentions. There is an obvious and major impact of exposure to modern life styles on the individuals' desire to order his working future in accord with more modern behavior patterns. Two parallel trends are apparent from these data. First, it is clear that members of the younger generation as a whole are far less predisposed to accept their place in the traditional status order than their parents; and second, the more urbanized the area of the individual's childhood, the less willing he is to accept ascriptive determination of his occupation.

Corollary to the differential assignment of social perquisites by the stratification system is the normative justification of this inequality by the religious order. If the average young Indian is less willing to accept ascription of occupation than his parents were, we would expect to find a similar breakdown in the relationship between religious affiliation and occupation. Table IV confirms our suspicions, with a decline in the contingency coefficient from 0.37 for the parents' occupations to 0.08 for the respondents. Clearly, this closely parallels the result of the analysis of caste position and occupation. Social change is affecting both the traditional distribution of available life chances and the acceptance of the religious justification for that distribution.

Table 4

Religious Affiliation and Occupational Status[a]

	Parent Occupational Status				Respondent Status			
Religion	*High*	*Mod. High*	*Mod. Low*	*Low*	*High*	*Mod. High*	*Mod. Low*	*Low*
Hindu	29.4%	46.4%	10.5%	13.7%	36.3%	20.5%	14.9%	28.3%
Sikh	26.5%	19.8%	42.4%	12.4%	42.4%	17.6%	15.5%	24.6%
Other	26.4%	32.2%	17.2%	24.1%	24.9%	11.6%	18.6%	34.9%
N =	603	727	530	292	859	418	338	596

$x^2 = 338.78$ @ 6 d.f. $x^2 = 15.77$ @ 6 d.f.
P < .001 CC = .3688   P = N.S. CC = .0841

Occupational preferences of the respondents were ranked Civil and Military Service – High; Medicine and Business – Moderately High: Law, Science, Engineering – Moderately Low; Teaching and Other – Low.
For the parent occupations, Government Service, Medicine and Law – High; Business – Moderately High; Teaching and Agriculture – Moderately Low; Laboring occupations – Low.

If ascriptively determined, occupational choice would undoubtedly be affected at an early age. If, however, ascriptive norms are not the primary factor in determining occupational choice, we may proceed to test the proposition derived from the argument by Ginzberg that in the measure the individual has rejected traditional influences, we would expect later socialization processes to have greater impact. Our particular concern is in determining the level of relationship between the respondent's college choice and his occupational choice. Table Va presents the tabulation of college choice by occupational preference for the respondents, and Table Vb presents the same tabulation for the parents.

Both tabulations indicate significant relationships between choice of college and occupational choice, or parent's occupation. To determine the independent effect of socialization experiences in college, we must be able to differentiate between two equally reasonable sequences of influence. First, it is possible that the current occupational status of the parent determines the child's choice of college, which in turn affects the child's choice of occupation. Second, it is possible that the current occupational status of the father has an independent

Table 5

Occupational Status by College Attendance Respondent's Preference and Parent's Occupation[a]

College	Va-Respondent				Vb-Parent			
	High	Mod. High	Mod. Low	Low	High	Mod. High	Mod. Low	Low
Government	34.6%	9.4%	16.4%	39.5%	26.7%	43.5%	20.0%	9.7%
D.C.[b]	46.1%	27.1%	12.3%	14.4%	24.6%	35.0%	20.9%	19.5%
K.M.V.[c]	24.9%	17.3%	16.3%	41.4%	32.6%	41.1%	21.5%	4.9%
L.K.C.[d]	47.8%	21.3%	16.0%	14.9%	28.8%	16.0%	36.4%	18.8%
N =	866	420	338	598	605	727	537	294

$x^2 = 237.65$ @ 9 d.f.
$P < .001$ CC = .3108

$x^2 = 182.43$ @ 9 d.f.
$P < .001$ CC = .2789

a   Occupational preferences of the respondents were ranked Civil and Military Service – High: Medicine and Business – Moderately High; Law, Science, Engineering – Moderately Low; Teaching and Other – Low.
   For the parent occupations, Government Service, Medicine and Law – High: Business – Moderately High; Teaching and Agriculture – Moderately Low; Laboring occupations – Low.
b   Hindu Denominational College.
c   Women's Hindu Denominational.
d   Sikh Denominational.

Table 6

Parent's Occupational Status by Child's Occupational Preference

Status-Parents' Occupation[a]	Child's Preference[a]			
	High	Moderately High	Moderately Low	Low
High	31.7%	29.1%	24.6%	24.2%
Moderately High	24.6%	46.0%	38.6%	34.8%
Moderately Low	28.1%	15.9%	23.7%	26.5%
Low	15.6%	9.0%	13.1%	14.5%
N =	826	402	321	566

$x^2 = 76.12$ @ 9 d.f.
$P < .001$ CC = .1864

Occupational preferences of the respondents were ranked Civil and Military Service – High; Medicine and Business – Moderately High; Law, Science, Engineering – Moderately Low; Teaching and Other – Low.
For the parent occupations, Government Service, Medicine and Law – High; Business – Moderately High; Teaching and Agriculture – Moderately Low; Laboring Occupations – Low.

Table 7

Parents' Occupation by Childs' Occupational Preference Controlling for College Choice[a]

Parents' Occupation	Government School Students' Preference				D.C.[b] Students' Preference				K.M.V.[c] Students' Preference				L.K.C.[a] Students' Preference			
	H	MH	ML	L	H	MH	ML	L	H	MH	ML	L	H	MH	ML	L
High (H)	32.1[e]	17.0	20.9	26.4	28.1	26.7	21.1	13.8	42.5	38.6	28.4	26.6	30.3	31.0	28.2	23.1
Moderately High (MH)	35.8	62.3	50.5	42.3	25.7	55.3	45.1	17.5	32.7	43.4	41.9	43.6	12.0	28.4	17.6	10.3
Moderately Low (ML)	22.3	7.5	19.8	21.8	23.3	10.7	21.1	32.5	22.1	16.9	20.3	23.4	39.3	25.9	32.9	41.0
Low (L)	9.8	13.2	8.8	9.5	22.9	7.3	12.7	36.3	2.7	1.2	9.5	6.4	18.4	14.7	21.2	25.6
N =	193	53	91	220	253	150	71	80	113	83	74	188	267	116	85	78

$x^2 = 18.91$ @ 9 d.f. $x^2 = 78.37$ @ 9 d.f. $x^2 = 17.49$ @ 9 d.f. $x^2 = 24.99$ @ 9 d.f.

P = N.S. CC = .1812   P < .001 CC = .3520   P = N.S. CC = .1918   P = N.S. CC = .2092

Occupational preferences of the respondents were ranked Civil and Military Service – High; Medicine and Business – Moderately High; Law, Science, Engineering – Moderately Low; Teaching and Other – Low. For the parent occupations, Government Service, Medicine and Law – High; Business – Moderately High: Teaching and Agriculture – Moderately Low; Laboring occupations – Low.

and significant impact on both the child's choice of college, as well as his choice of occupation. To successfully distinguish between these two possibilities it is first necessary to establish whether there exists some apparent relation between the father's current occupational status and the respondent's occupational preference. The data in Table VI indicate that there is, in fact, a significant relationship between parent's occupation and the child's preference. We may determine whether or not this relationship is artifactual by controlling for the effect of college choice.

Controlling for the effect of college choice, Table VII presents the relationship between parent's occupation and respondent's preference. In three of the four colleges, the previously apparent relationship is now insignificant. We may, therefore, contend that the appropriate comprehension of the significance of the father's occupational status lies in its being a partial determinant of the choice of college. Beyond that indirect influence, our respondents seem to possess a relatively high degree of freedom of choice in their occupational aspirations.

Our final concern is with the relationship between the respondent's residential background and his desire for occupational security. To test this hypothesis in the Indian case, we dichotomized the occupational preferences of our respondents into public and private. We placed preferences aimed at Civil and Military service into the public category, and all other responses into the private category. Table VIII presents the cross-tabulation of this dichotomous variable with rural versus urban residence. There is a statistically significant relation-

Table 8

Rural/Urban Residence by Public/Private Employment Preference

	Employment Preference	
Residence	*Public*	*Private*
Rural	53.9%	40.3%
Urban	46.1%	59.7%
N =	852	1327

$$x^2 = 37.89 \text{ @ } 1 \text{ d.f.}$$
$$P < .001 \text{ CC} = .1307 \text{ Q} = .2671$$

ship between residence and security orientation, but the degree of relationship is not nearly as strong as that reported by LaPalombara. Obviously, the less mobilized and more deprived the area from which the respondent comes, the more likely he is to desire regulated and secure employment. As the level of relationship is relatively low, $CC = 0.13$, it is very difficult to infer any substantively significant result of this tendency in terms of its impact upon the quality of government service. To the degree that this tendency indicates a desire for security, rather than opportunity, we might expect a higher proportion of these respondents to develop a time-serving, rather than innovative, approach to their work tasks. This possibility is belied by the fact that when we relate employment preference to scales of desired social change and achievement orientation, approximately equal numbers of respondents from both employment categories score high on desire for change and achievement orientation. The results of this portion of the analysis are, therefore, inconclusive.

Conclusions

This study was undertaken to determine the relationship between a young adult's occupational aspirations and his social origin in a transitional society. As the study focuses on college-going adults between the ages of 19 and 25, our findings are relevant only to this segment of Indian society. Our study does reveal some important changes taking place in this traditional society which can be summarized as follows:

(1) In contrast to the findings of Jain in Uttar Pradesh and Gist in South India, our study demonstrates that both caste and religion are becoming increasingly insignificant in determining a young adult's occupational choice. This may be the result of a change in environment as well as a result of exposure to higher education.

(2) We also find that respondents belonging to lower castes, and thus of lower social origins, have the same occupational aspirations as respondents from upper castes. This shows a positive orientation towards upward social mobility. With the spread of higher education, young adults are increasingly likely to reject their traditional lower status in the society and become more achievement oriented.

(3) Furthermore, our study demonstrates that the respondent's area of residence, and to a lesser extent his fathers occupation, have more influence on his occupational choice than his caste or his religion. The youth coming from rural areas are far more willing to accept their traditional occupations than the urban youth.

(4) Traditionally, the state colleges occupy a highly prestigious position in the educational structure of India. They are known to have better faculties and they attract highly motivated students. But our study demonstrates that the students educated in such colleges do not necessarily have the highest occupational aspirations. Actually, it is significant that a majority of our respondents, regardless of the college they attend, have high occupational aspirations. This indicates that college attendance seems to be exercising a threshold effect. If an individual overcomes the obstacles to college attendance, his occupational aspirations are then primarily a result of influences other than ascriptive norms.

(5) If this trend toward a declining relationship between occupation and such ascriptive norms as caste and religion continues, the Indian society is likely to develop a system of stratification based upon occupation rather than ascription.

REFERENCES

GINZBERG, Eli, et al.
    1951　*Occupational Choice: An Approach to a General Theory.* New York: Columbia University Press.
GIST, Noel P.
    1954a　"Caste Differentiation in a North Indian Community". *American Sociological Review* XVIIII (April): 130.
    1954b　"Occupational Differentiation in South India". *Social Forces* 33:6 (December): 131.
Government of India, Census Commissioner, Census of India 1961, paper No. 1 of 1963; and *Religion* (New Delhi: Manager of Publications, 1963), 31–34.
JAIN, S. P.
    1967　"Occupational Differentiation in a North Indian Community". *Man in India* 43:4 (October–December): 309.
LAPALOMBARA, J. and WATERS, J. B.
    1961　"Values, Expectations and Political Predispositions of Italian Youth". *Midwest Journal of Political Science* V (February): 39–58.
MUSGRAVE, P. W.
    1967　"Towards a Sociological Theory of Occupational Choice". *Sociological Review* XV (March): 33–46.
PATHAK, H. P.
    1970　"Small-Scale Industries in Ludhiana". *Economic and Political Weekly* V (July): 1,091–1,097.
RUTHA, S. N.
    1970　"Religion and Occupational Differentiation". *Man in India* 50:3 (July–September): 248–256.

The Tutsi and the Ha: A Study in Integration

JAMES L. BRAIN

State University of New York, New Paltz, New York, U.S.A.

THE PAST decade has been the witness of bloody conflict between the
former ruling elite of the Tutsi and the agricultural Hutu in the countries of
Rwanda and Burundi. While it is true that Rwanda probably represented the
stratified caste structure in its most extreme form, a very similar form of social
structure did exist in the neighboring area of Buha in what is now Tanzania,
and to date no comparable conflict and bloodshed has occurred. It is the purpose of this essay to examine why this was so. Although the colonial powers in
their wisdom excised Rwanda and Burundi from formerly German Tanganyika after the First World War, and gave them to Belgium, this did not, of
course, alter the ethnic and cultural makeup of the area. Thus Buha, which
under German administration had been separated from the Belgian Congo by
Ruanda-Urundi, now found that it formed the frontier of British Tanganyika,
and joined Belgian territory. In reality this did little to hinder local trade and
movement between the areas, in spite of the police and customs posts set up on
the main roads. Census figures (see Appendix) show that almost half the population of Kibondo District in Buha was composed of people classified as Rundi,
and in the late 1950s efforts of local agricultural extension officers to improve
the quality of tobacco offered for sale to B.A.T. Ltd (British American Tobacco
Company Ltd) were nullified by the discovery that it was far more lucrative to
sell *any* tobacco of any type across the border in Burundi than to grade and
select leaf for sale through legitimate channels. Culturally and linguistally
there is nothing to choose between Rundi and Ha (I studied the Ha language
through the medium of a Rundi grammar), why then the great difference in
historical events over the past few years? It is my intention to show that this
difference stemmed partially at least from a historical accident brought about
by the policies of the European colonial powers.

The area known as Buha spreads over three administrative districts of
western Tanzania–Kigoma, Kasulu, and Kibondo. The whole area is bounded
to the east by Unyamwezi, to the south by Ufipa, to the north by Buzinza, and
to the west by Lake Tanganyika and Burundi. Although the Ha are numerically one of the largest peoples of Tanzania, 289,789 in the 1957 Census, and think
of themselves as one people having a common language and culture, there is not

now nor has there been in the past, a kingdom of Buha as a whole, and if we group the Interlacustrine Bantu peoples into sub-groups, the Ha fall into the pattern exemplified by the Soga, Haya, Zinza, and Sukuma, rather than the larger kindoms such as Bunyoro or Ankole. Audrey Richards described the former as "multiple kingdom tribes, composed that is, of a series of small principalities, each with its own hereditary ruler." (Richards 1959: 2). Polycephalous would be an appropriate term to classify Buha. The entire Interlacustrine area is characterized to a greater or lesser extent by the presence of a caste of aristocrats claiming a different ethnic origin from that of the farmers over whom they ruled[1], providing a good example of the conquest state situation, though Maquet's remark that it was probably "an infiltration rather than a conquest" is considered correct (Maquet 1961: 12)[2]. In Buha this ruling caste is known by the name found in Rwanda and Burundi, the Tutsi (*Umututsi* pl. *Abatutsi*), sometimes rendered as Tusi or Tussi. The Hima or Huma, who are probably the same people, are in Buha reckoned as one of the Tutsi clans. One of the confusing points for the newcomer to the area is that whereas the whole area is known as Buha, that is to say in common Bantu usage, the land of the Ha people, all of the people are not called the Ha, who are the middle of the three castes – the Tutsi, the Ha, and the Kiko, the same three found in Burundi and Rwanda under the names of Tutsi, Hutu, and Twa. In practice this difficulty is not a reality since the total population is referred to by the name of the kingdom, e.g. Muhambwe has the *Abahambwe* people, Buyungu has the *Abayungu* in the same sort of way as Burundi has the *Barundi*, Bunyoro the *Banyoro* etc., though in the case of Buha "kingdom" is rather a grandiose title for such small areas.

Scherer, a Dutch scholar, carried out research in this area from 1951–3 and reported that there were only two castes, the Tutsi and the Ha (Scherer 1959: 845), and this has been repeated by La Fontaine utilizing his material (La Fontaine 1959: 214). My own research showed that three castes are known, and, it was said, still existed at that time (1959–60). I did not personally make contact with any of the Kiko, but was assured by several informants that they existed in the district.[3] A myth of origin recorded by an early British administrator was checked with informants and found to be known, though it is evident that Scherer did not consult all available sources since he notes that "the origin of the name Ha is obscure" (Scherer 1959: 842). Since it provides one of the clearest "charters for social action" that one could imagine for what Maquet terms "the premise of inequality" (Maquet 1961) it is given in full here.

---

1 With the exception of Buganda, which will be considered later.
2 I am not taking seriously Murdock's assertions about the origins of the Nima/Tutsi (1959: 350).
3 It seems almost incredible that Scherer did not consult either the District Book or Kibondo or *Tanganyika Notes and Records*. There are a number of interesting mentions of the Kiko, e.g. they are said to be called Kiko as a pejorative term and their real name is *Banyahoza* who have their own language (Moffett 1943: 54–75; Macquarie 1940: 61–7) and later we are told that they have a number of different names all equated with the Twa, e.g. *Banyungwe, Bakimbili*, and again *Banyahoza* (Procter 1960: 48–50).

Long ago there came from Urundi a man of the Bahumbi (i.e. the ruling clan) named Ruhaga Ruantobo accompanied by his wife and two brothers in search of a pleasent country in which to live. After much wandering they came to a river and sat down to rest. Ruhaga's youngest brother saw that this river was full of fish and hippopotamus. He said to his two elder brothers "I will stay here and make my home and feed on the flesh of fish and hippopotamus." They left him there and a little further on came to an anthill near which was seen ripe millet and maize and all kinds of food crops. Ruhaga's second brother said "I will stay here and till the ground and make a nice farm." Ruhaga and his wife went on alone and a day later came to a beautiful savanah full of strange animals which were engaged in suckling their young. Now the strange thing about these animals was that they did not flee into the bush at the sight of the two human beings, Nay, further they allowed these humans to milk them. Ruhaga was delighted with the behaviour of the animals and with the milk which they gave and he said to his wife "We will make a house here for ourselves and a house for these animals and we will herd them and live on their milk." And this they did. Later on they learnt to make butter and ghee from the milk that was left over, and this they smeared on their bodies. When they had been settled for some time Ruhaga bethought himself of his two brothers and of persuading them to come and live with him. So he packed a parcel of food including this new butter, and set off.

He came first to the house of the farmer and said to him "Oh brother, I have discovered a beautiful country abounding with strange animals on whose milk and butter I live. Come and set up house with me. Behold I have brought you some of this butter that you might see it for yourself."

But his brother replied "I do not want your butter. I am quite happy where I am living on my millet and beans. Leave me alone and go on your way." "Very good" said Ruhaga, "from henceforth I shall impose on you the duty of supplying me with food, honey, and beer. From the sweat of your brow shall I live." And so from that day on it has been the custom of the Baha to supply their Muhumbi chief with presents of food. As he was going away Ruhaga said to his brother, "From now on you are no longer Muhumbi but Muha, for you shall give me whatever I require." (Note, the verb *kuha* means "to give", hence *Muha* is "a giver").

From thence Ruhaga went on to his youngest brother and told him the same story and showed him the butter, but his brother too made the same reply as the first, saying "I am quite happy with my diet of fish. Leave me in peace."

To him Ruhaga said, "Henceforth you shall be an outcast among men. You shall be denied access to the house of your chief. You shall dwell by the banks of this river and shall never leave it. Your work will be to fish and to make pots. The pots you make you shall send to me whenever I ask for them." And so from that day the Bakiko dwell by the river and fish, and supply cooking pots to their Muhumbi chief.

(Lumley 1928)

The myth makes clear why the Tutsi reject the appellation of Ha, in that a *Muha* is a giver, and we shall return to this point. The Kiko caste does seem to exist still, but as with the Twa in Rwanda their numbers were probably always insignificant, where they were assessed as making up only 0.67% of the population (Maquet 1961: 10), and we shall not concern ourselves further with them except to say that I accept the general proposition that they were probably the aboriginal inhabitants of the area before the arrival of the Bantu-speaking Ha agriculturalists. The Kiko, like the Tutsi, have adopted the Ha language.

The Tutsi may not precisely have conquered the country so much as infiltrated it, in Maquet's phrase (1961: 12 and c.f. the Alur, Southall, 1953), though the effect may not have been very different. The important point was probably that they were able to impose their cultural values on the whole country by their military superiority. The particular value which is here relevant was that of the overwhelming superiority of cattle over any other form of wealth, so that gradually the Ha accepted clientage to Tutsi herders by the acceptance of loans of cattle in the patron-client relationship known as *ubugabire* (see Tawney 1944). Scherer notes that both the Ha and the Tutsi owned cattle, but it is my view that cattle were brought to the area by the Tutsi since the only breed to be seen is that of the very characteristic "Ankole" type, with quite extraordinarily long and beautiful horns, emphasis on which appears in dances in Tutsi culture. Thus, if cattle were owned by Ha it would have been as a result of clientage, when some of the offspring of the original cattle loaned to the Ha client were allowed to be kept by him, so that over time he built up a herd which was partly the property of his Tutsi patron, and partly his own. Some of the early British administrators commented on the arrogance of Tutsi patrons, who referred to a client as *Muha wanje* – my Ha man, as though he were a slave. This was to misunderstand the relationship, which although it may be characterized as exploitative, nevertheless involved duties and obligations on the part of the patron to his client, as well as the other way round, so that *Muha wanje* should be translated as "my giver", i.e. one who supplies grain and beer in return for sharing the cattle and for protection. A client was *umugabire* to his *sebuja* or *databuja* – father of service, but the word *umugabire* comes from the verb *kugabura*, which means not only "to give out" but also "to share in" (and can also mean "to take part in a sacrifice"), so that an *umugabire* could be viewed as "one who shares".

A further possible reason for the acceptance of Tutsi domination could be that they probably introduced the cult of the Cwezi spirits to the area. There is considerable confusion in the traditions of all the interlacustrine peoples about this mysterious people, who apparently came from somewhere in the north and later as mysteriously disappeared. In some accounts they seem to be the same people as the Hima, in others they are the same as the Lwo-speaking Bito, whoo ruled Bunyoro. Oberg records of the Cwezi from Ankole tradition that "they were like the Bahima, but more brilliant ... they wore bark cloth and went about in cow-hide sandals. Their women covered their faces in public and were guarded by eunuchs ... they were great hunters and magicians." (Oberg 1940: 123). It is explicit in the Ankole tradition that the founder of the royal dynasty was Ruhinda, a member of the Cwezi who was persuaded to remain behind and brought with him the drum which became the symbol or royalty and symbolic of the sovereignty of the entire people (there are similar drums among the Ha). The *Bahinda* clan which he thus founded is to be found all over the area and provides the ruling dynasty of the Buzinza and Buhaya areas. It is also conceivable that the Humbi (*Abahumbi*), the ruling dynasty of the Kibondo area of Buha, may originally have been of this clan since it is known that the Hinda clan exists in the area as one of the Tutsi clans, and Burton, who was an acute observer, recorded that the ruling clans of Buha were "of *Wahinda* or princely origin" (Burton 1860: 70). Whatever or whoever the Cwezi may have been, their memory remains in the widespread spirit cult of the same name. In Ankole this is known as *Emandwa*, in Rwanda as *Imandwa*, in Bunyoro people become possessed by Cwezi spirits, in Busumbwa and Buha males and females join the secret society known as the *Abacwezi* (also mentioned as *Baswezi, Baswesi, Waswezi, Bachwezi*). It is possible too that membership in this society may have been one of the factors responsible for the lessening of hostility between Ha and Tutsi, since it is possible for both castes to join, as well as both sexes. An account of the initiation rites for the society is given by the late Hans Cory (1955), and it is clear from this that a systematic attempt is made to break down customary behavior, presumably in the hope that by so doing, the reversal of normal standards of behavior will acquire mystical power for the initiates, particularly is this true of the ritual act of symbolic incest. Functionally, however, it seems also probable that these rites have the effect of lessening resentment of Tutsi domination on the part of the Ha, and similarly, one might postulate, reduce female resentment of male domination. It would be interesting to find out the extent to which the society still wields political power in the independence period, since it was evident that its power under the traditional system during the period of colonial rule was very considerable. It was alleged by some that the Cwezi society had a hierarchical organization paralleling that of the Mwami and sub-chiefs, and certain observed facts seemed to substantiate this.

It is difficult to make an accurate assessment of the proportion of Tutsi to Ha, since it is suspected that census figures do not differentiate the two. It is true that Tutsi appear on the 1957 census, but only seem to be about 1% of the total population, and it is thought that these are a group of pastoral Tutsi living in a very inaccessible part of the extreme south-east of Kibondo district, whom it proved impossible to visit. It is estimated by Oberg that the Hima numbered only 10% of the total Ankole people (Oberg 1940: 126), and by Maquet that the Tutsi in Rwanda were never more than 10–15% of the total Rwanda people (Maquet 1961: 144). Probably the same sort of ratio was found among the Ha, though Scherer makes no comment on the census figures, which show 2% for the whole of Buha, though his data on the homesteads he examined show that approximately 10% of 168 homesteads were of Tutsi affiliation (Scherer 1959: 865). Oberg's comment on the proportions is significant. He notes that:

> In this connextion we must always remember that the Bairu had to supply a population only one-tenth its own size. Had the numbers been reversed, exploitation would not, perhaps, have been successful.
>
> (1940: 126)

The presence of large numbers of Rundi has already been mentioned, but a further comment on them is necessary. Culturally and linguistically they are almost indistinguishable from Ha, and tend to be reckoned as and to count themselves today as Ha (thus reinforcing the suggestion that the Ha and the Hutu are in fact the same). The proportion varies from area to area, but in some parts it amounts to a large-scale immigration from Burundi. The reasons for this movement are probably threefold. Firstly, many Rundi were glad to escape the severity of Belgian rule, which local accounts claimed to be much harsher than British. Secondly, there exists an acute land shortage in much of Burundi, whereas Kibondo district has a huge surplus. In 1959–60 I estimated that only about one third of the available agricultural land of Kibondo was occupied. Thirdly, and perhaps most importantly, was the fact that during the British colonial era it was customary to base a chief's or headman's salary on the number of taxpayers in his area, and thus it became a regular practice for headman on the border to encourage an immigration of Rundi, who in many cases were their kinsmen or affines. There was at that time a constant flow of movement backwards and forwards over the international frontier which totally disregarded the customs and police posts on the official roads, and at markets held near the border it was customary for all the petty traders to have a pile of both Francs and Shillings available for change, and for all of them, even though illiterate, to know the fluctuating rate of exchange.

While the Tutsi made up only a small proportion of the population, their political influence was disproportionately great. Each small kingdom was organized hierarchically with a *Mwami* (pl. *Abami*) at its head, and in theory at least he/she (since there have been several female *Mwamis*, two at the time I was there) controlled all the land resources. The organization was feudal in type, the *Mwami* making over sections of the kingdom to sub-chiefs called *abatwale* (sing. *umutwale*), who in turn allocated small areas to headmen, who were also called *abatwale*. The use of the same term for the two tiers of authority seems to illustrate well the feudal nature of the system. To distinguish these two categories the adjective indicating "large" or "small" is used, thus a sub-chief was described in full as *umutwale munini* – a great *umutwale*, and a headman as *umutwale muto* – a small one. The derivation of the word is probably from the verb *kutwala* – to take and/or hold, and this certainly fits the circumstances. Scherer states that the lowest authorities were known as *bateko*, sing. *muteko* (op cit: 214), and equates these with the pre-Tutsi localized patrilineage heads.[1] In early reports in the district book this word was mentioned in Kibondo but was not known to informants in my time. The earlier use of it in this area, however, was confined to a ritual figure. Whether the term *umutwale* was later applied to the *umuteko* to fit in with the idealized feudal political system is hard to say, but seems probable. The sub-chiefs in 1959–60 were all Tutsi with one exception, a Ha married to a Tutsi woman, and this was clearly so unusual that whenever he was mentioned everyone would immediately say of him, "But he's married to a Tutsi ..." The headmen were, on the other hand, exclusively Ha. Ideally, as has been mentioned, the headman held land by favor of the sub-chief in direct line from the *Mwami*, but the reality was that the headmen were the heads of patrilineages dominant in any particular area because of their early arrival as

---

1 This does fit in with a report in 1936 to the effect that before the arrival of the Tutsi, the Ha were ruled by "Teko who at the present day are the priests of the tribe." (Griffiths 1936: 73), but by the time of my stay in 1959 none of my informants knew the word.

the first settlers. How this took place I was able to observe. The Ha are great colonizers, and it is common for men to move to totally new locations every few years, frequently miles from the old homesteads, When some settlers have begun to open up a new area, others rapidly immigrate there too, so that there is a gradual build-up of population of which finally the *Mwami* becomes cognizant. He then notifies the local sub-chief to choose a headman, who will be ratified. In fact the whole process is the other way round, that is to say, the senior man of the incoming group, providing that he is competent and acceptable to the others in the area, becomes the headman *de facto*, and this situation is accepted by the sub-chief and then ratified by the *Mwami*. A very interesting point here is that the ancestral cult among the Ha does not prevent this movement to new areas as it does elsewhere, when abandonment of the ancestral graves is difficult. The reason is simple. The Ha believe that the spirits reside in the wild fig trees which are planted to encircle a homestead, so that when people move they take with them cuttings from the old trees to plant in the new area, providing, as it were, "instant ancestors". One might also suggest that this movement inhibited the growth of large-scale corporate lineages, prevented too much authority being vested in local leaders, and may well have had a part in reducing tension between Ha and Tutsi, in that surplus land would always make it possible to escape from too tyrannical a rule, whereas in Burundi and Rwanda land is notoriously in short supply, greatly reducing mobility.

It is suggested that the major reason for the absence of physical conflict between Tutsi and Ha arose in the period between the end of the First World War and the assumption of administrative control of the area by Great Britain under a League of Nations Mandate. In a report contained in the district book dated 1921, the then District Officer, C. J. Bagenal, described some of the events of this period, when for a time the area was temporarily under Belgian administration. At first there were several changes made in control, but finally, he says:

> ...the balance of Kibondo district was divided, a portion being handed back to Ujiji, and a portion (which comprised the present chiefdoms of Muhambwe and Buyungu) was retained by Urundi. These districts were placed under an Urundi chief named Kirarangania, who made very little attempt to administer them, using them merely as an area in which to loot food and cattle. The Boma at Kibondo was left unoccupied and on two occasions during the last eighteen months a Belgian officer who visited Kibondo accompanied by a crowd of Warundi, was attacked and forced to retire, the Warundi losing twelve men killed by arrows. The country of Kasulu and Kibondo which was said to have contained 100,000 head of cattle and one million small stock, had been absolutely stripped. I doubt if there are 10,000 head of cattle in the whole district, while small stock can scarcely be found at all. All the way along the border the natives on my approach simply fled headlong into the bush; such a state of affairs can hardly be imagined under European administration. It will take years for the country to recover and for the government to regain the confidence of the natives.

We have seen how the clientage system was based upon loan of cattle. In these circumstances it is evident that the Tutsi were totally unable to continue to operate such a system, except on a very small scale by a minority of wealthy patrons. Not only was the whole clientage structure undermined, but if they were to survive at all the Tutsi had no alternative to starvation other than to undertake the demeaning (in their traditional view) practice of agriculture, about which they no doubt had to seek advice from the Ha. This situation was doubtless exacerbated by the spread of tsetse fly throughout this whole area. Not only was this disastrous for the remaining cattle, and probably reduced their numbers still more, but in the 1930s the Trypanosomiasis underwent the change which transformed it into human Sleeping Sickness, to an extent that the colonial government found it necessary to move part of the population forcibly to prevent their being wiped out. This forced move was not understood at the time and still rankled in 1959–60, since among other things it had entailed the abandonment of the royal settlement and the royal graves (the kings were mummified and interred in a cave). If both cattle and human populations become reduced then bush tends to increase, and if bush increases (Brachystegia and Combretum known as *Miyombo*) then tsetse is provided with ideal conditions for its propagation. At the time when I was in the area it had become customary to have an annual turnout of all adult men for bush clearing to combat the spread of tsetse, a communal effort which was deeply resented, and finally a tax was added to the annual poll tax to finance permanent clearing gangs.

The total result of all the foregoing was to make it virtually impossible to tell Ha from Tutsi by occupation, and although some Tutsi were readily identifiable by their features and height, this was quite unreliable as an indicator of status.

One further point should be considered in this total situation. During the period of British administration Buha became one of the recruiting areas for work on sisal estates, and SILABU (Sisal Labour Bureau, an association of employers sanctioned by the government), operated recruiting posts and camps in the area. Since little other chance existed of making money, many young men went away for two or three year periods, while others went for shorter periods to work for African coffee farmers in Buganda. While it is not claimed that this was in any sense an ideal situation, it must be realized that it did have important effects on the social organization. Traditionally a young man had to depend on his father and his father's siblings to provide him with bridewealth, but by undertaking wage labor it became possible for a young man to obtain sufficient money for his own bridewealth, thus effectively diminishing the authority of fathers, and indeed the authority of his father's generation (c.f. Beattie 1960: 52), and similarly this had the effect of downgrading the importance of clientage as a means of gaining status. This downgrading would also, of course, diminish the importance of the Tutsi as a group.

Considering this whole picture leads to reflection on the situation found in some of the other interlacustrine kingdoms. Perhaps the most sophisticated of all was Buganda, but in this case, as Richards notes, there were "practically no traces of the caste-like system which has been considered to be characteristic of these peoples" (Richards 1959: 51). So much was this so that Mair does not even mention the ethnic background of the peoples in her major work on the Ganda (1934). Why the breakdown of the caste system should have taken place in Buganda and not in Ankole, Rwanda, or Burundi, is open to speculation, but to speculate is to suggest hypotheses which might later be tested. Two reasons come to mind. The first is that the geographical situation of Buganda makes it more suitable than the other kingdoms for the production of bananas, the major food crop, and because of the all-year round supply the problem of having a food surplus was solved without storage difficulties, so that social and political differentiation was made feasible to a greater extent than in many areas of Africa. The second reason, and one which depends on the first to some extent, is that of the tsetse fly. As we have seen in the case of Buha, the removal of the Tutsi cattle meant the end of domination through cattle clientage, but whereas in that case the reason was raids from Burundi, in the case of Buganda it could have been just a natural encroachment of the tsetse. Mair notes that:

> Nowadays, the number of cattle has decreased very much through sleeping sickness and other epidemics, while the Baganda can no longer replenish their herds from those of their neighbours, and one sees very few except in Kyagwe.
>
> Mair, op cit, 106–7

Beattie too, writing of Bunyoro, where the caste system still did exist, comments that "the distinction between Hima and Iru is of decreasing importance" (1960: 12), and makes several mentions of the losses of cattle in Bunyoro, for instance he notes that:

> Long ago Nyoro had great herds of cattle. But these have been practically wiped out by war and disease, and there are now only a few thousand head, mostly in a favored corner of the country which is free from tsetse fly, carrier of the fatal cattle disease trypanosomiasis.
>
> op cit, 1–2, and c.f. pp. 22–3

To summarize then, the interlacustrine area was characterized by conquest-state type kingdoms of varying size, but all, with the exception of Buganda, had until recently two, three, or sometimes four castes of different ethnic origin, the ruling caste valuing cattle above all as wealth, and maintaining their privileged position by clientage, this clientage depending largely on cattle for its operation. Whereas in Rwanda and Burundi the rift between the ruling Tutsi/Hima caste and the farming Hutu became so acute that disastrous armed conflict has occurred between Tutsi and Hutu since independence, this was not the case elsewhere. It is suggested that the major reason for this lay in the reduction of cattle populations. It is further suggested that in the case of Buganda the disappearance of the caste system before the arrival of the European colonial powers may have been partly due to this cause, aided by the ideal conditions for banana culture.

APPENDIX

Census Figures for Kibondo District of Buha

1928

Buyungu (one of two kingdoms)	Ha	18,449
	Rundi	10,207
	Subi	4,798
	Zinza	2,622
	Tutsi	47
	Total	36,123
Muhambwe	Ha	12,315
	Rundi	13,539
	Tutsi	271
	Total	26,125
Total for whole District		62,248

1931

	Ha	37,233
	Rundi	35,356
	Subi	5,257
	Zinza	3,320
	Tutsi	296
	Total	81,462

1957

	Ha	62,496
	Rundi	49,680
	Subi	3,897
	Zinza	1,841
	Tutsi	650
	Others	1,558
	Total	120,104

The small number of Tutsi is explained by the fact that they only account for the pastoral Tutsi residing in the south-east.

REFERENCES

BAGENAL, C. J.
    1921   Report in Kibondo District Book.
BEATTIE, John
    1960   *Bunyoro: an African Kingdom*. New York: Holt, Rinehart and Winston.
BURTON, Sir R.
    1860   *The Lake Regions of Central Africa*. London.
GRIFFITHS, J. E. S.
    1936   "The Aba-Ha of the Tanganyika Territory", *Tanganyika Notes and Records*, No. 2, 72–6.

LaFontaine, J.
  1959 "The Ha", in *East African Chiefs*. Edited by Audrey Richards; London: Faber and Faber, 212–28.
Lumley, E. K.
  1928 Report in Kibondo District Book.
Macquarie, C.
  1940 "Water Gipsies of the Malagarasi", *Tanganyika Notes and Records*, No. 9, 61–7.
Mair, Lucy P.
  1934 *An African People in the Twentieth Century*. London: Routledge and Kegan Paul, 65.
Maquet, J. J.
  1961 *The Premise of Inequality*. London: Oxford University Press.
Moffett, J. P.
  1943 "A Raft on the Malagarasi", *Tanganyika Notes and Records*, No. 16, 54–75.
Murdock, G. P.
  1959 *Africa: Its Peoples and their Culture History*, New York: McGraw-Hill.
Oberg, K.
  1940 "The Kingdom of Ankole in Uganda" in *African Political Systems*. Edited M. Fortes and E. E. Evans–Pritchard, London, New York: Oxford University Press, 121–62.
Procter, J.
  1960 "Did You See Me From Afar?" *Tanganyika Notes and Records*, No. 54, 48–50.
Richards, A. I.
  1959 *East African Chiefs*. Editor, Introduction and "The Ganda", London: Faber and Faber.
Scherer, J. H.
  1959 "The Ha of Tanganyika", *Anthropos*, 54, 841–904.
Southall, Aidan
  1956 *Alur Society*. Cambridge: Cambridge University Press.
Tawney, J. J.
  1944 "Ugabire: a Feudal Custom among the Waha", *Tanganyika Notes and Records*, No. 17, 6–9.

Value Orientation among Migrants in Ankara, Turkey: A Case Study[1]

Hacettepe University, Ankara, Turkey

SINCE 1950, there has been a dramatic increase in net immigration into the urban areas in Turkey (Robinson 1958: 397–405). This migration is partly the consequence of new opportunities created in the cities as a result of economic developments since the establishment of the Republic in 1923. But at the same time, large numbers of migrants are also motivated by increased unemployment and underemployment in the villages, resulting from population pressure on the land and changes in land tenure (Kıray 1968: 87–102; Kıray and Hinderink 1968: 497–528). The impact of this migration on future development in Turkey will be substantial both from the pressures that will be exerted on future economic planning and from the social problems involved in large numbers of persons having to adapt to the cities.[2]

This paper reports the results of a study of workers in Ankara (Turkey's capital city) who have migrated there from the rural areas. This particular group of migrants was studied in order to examine from a social psychological perspective their acculturation into the city: their jobs, standard of living, participation in urban patterns of behavior and their attitudes and values Examining migration from the viewpoint of individual migrants may give insights into the development of migrant ideologies as they are exposed to the process of urban stratification.

Modernism versus Traditionalism as Value Systems

There are a number of ways in which the adaptation of migrants in a developing country can be examined from a social psychological perspective. One approach has been to see adaptation as a shift in cognitive values from a

---

1 The study was financed by a grant given by the Ford Foundation. The author wishes to thank Professor Mübeccel Kıray, Professor Şerif Mardin, Professor Fred Shorter, and Doc. Dr. Oğuz Arı for their help while undertaking the study.
2 Many of these rural-urban migrants are absorbed by temporary working in western Europe for two or three years at a time. At least a million Turkish workers are employed in Europe, especially in West Germany.

more or less traditional value system to a more or less modern value system (Schnaiberg 1970: 71–85) The assumption is that as an individual is exposed to modernizing influences, he will shift his values to more modern ones (Lerner 1958; Smith and Inkeles 1966: 353–377; Feldman and Hurn 1966: 378–395; Inkeles 1970: 208–225).

This approach has come recently under increasing criticism (Fanon 1959: esp. 21–101; Gusfield 1967: 351–362; Rudolph and Rudolph 1967; Frank 1969: 21–94; Frank 1971). Substantial evidence has accumulated to demonstrate that there need not be a conflict between traditional and modern values; that traditional practices can co-exist with modern practices in the urban areas of developing countries (Duocastella 1955: 319–337; Abu-Lughod 1961: 22–32; Bruner 1961: 507–521; Suzuki 1964: 208–216; Gutkind 1965: 48–60; Zachariah 1966: 378–392; Buechler 1970: 62–71; Petersen 1971: 560–573). There has, therefore, been a shift towards describing some of the determinants of individual adaptation and treating change as a multi-dimensional phenomena, rather than as a uni-dimensional phenomena in which a person is either traditional or modern (Chance 1965: 372–393; Graves 1967: 306–321).

This latter approach will be taken in this study. Historically, Turkey has been exposed to significant ideological influences emanating from Europe, especially since 1923 (Mardin 1962; Lewis 1968; Keddie 1972; 39–57; Mardin 1973: 169–190). The religious state was secularized, bureaucratic feudalism was re-oriented towards urban industrial capitalism, the legal system was changed from a religious law to a western European law, the alphabet was Latinized, and a number of laws were passed and political pressures enacted which attacked feudal and Islamic customs. The army was also strongly secularized and universal conscription for men was established. The pushing of a modern, western political philosophy, of course, met much resistance which are still acting themselves out, but as a consistent value orientation for the society, it has had a dramatic and widespread effect. It could be assumed that all migrants have been exposed to these influences prior to coming to the urban areas through the education system, the mass media, marketing systems, and the army, and that all migrants will be oriented to some extent towards accepting beliefs, attitudes and values of the urban sector. However, it is an empirical question whether the value positions of migrants in the urban areas actually do correspond to these historical conflicts in values, and whether their value positions reflect solely ideological influences or life style differences.

Theoretical Model

The hypothesis here is that there are two general determinants of the modernization value position of migrants. The first is the extent to which a migrant has been exposed to western, urban influences prior to coming to the cities. The second is the extent to which the individual's experiences in the city confirm his commitment to accepting these western urban values. In particular, the extent to which the individual achieves a satisfactory job and standard of living will affect to a large extent whether his belief in the city was justified or not. Further, it could be assumed that his exposure to earlier influences was itself related to his experiences in the village and his previous economic conditions so that his acceptance of these influences is not a passive acceptance of "propaganda" from the city but an interpretation of his life style given information that he has received. It is felt that the data in this study are consistent with this view and while they do not unequivocably validate the model, values and attitudes of migrants cannot be understood without reference to the economic conditions of their life style.

METHOD

The Sample: University Workers in Ankara

The group of migrants studied were male workers at the Middle East Technical University, who were interviewed by Turkish social science students during the summer of 1969. The criteria for selection were that they had to be male, born in a provincial town or village, and to have migrated to Ankara from the provinces (rather than from another large city). The Turkish census's definition of a rural village is 2000 persons or fewer and an urban area as 10,000 persons or more, but these were felt to be necessarily restrictive; there are large towns which depend substantially on the agricultural sector, rather than on industry and services. Therefore, arbitrarily 64,000 persons or fewer for a town or village was taken as a criterion for including a worker as a migrant to the urban areas. In all, there were 449 workers in the university (excluding administrative and academic staff) and out of these, 392 met the criteria for selection and were interviewed. Nonetheless, the majority of these workers came from small towns and villages; 90% came from towns of 16,000 persons or fewer, and 60% came from villages of 1000 persons or fewer. Further, virtually all of those interviewed came from their place of birth.

There are several characteristics which make the sample interesting to study but perhaps less typical of all migrant groups. First, compared to other jobs in Ankara, working at the university is a good job. The workers are unionized and though they do not have automatic tenure, they are eligible for a union pension at age 65. They receive automatic annual increments as well as pay raises accompanying promotion. Thus, the job provides relative security and would be expected to maximize individual adaptation. Second, the workers encompass different occupational skill levels. While approximately half are unskilled workers and are similar to other employed migrant groups in Ankara, a significant number are more skilled. Some of these workers, therefore, would be expected to be more adapted to the city than others. Third, the university is an institution which symbolizes change for Turkey and has been seen as one of the key elements in the change process since the beginning of the Republic

(Frey 1964: 205–235). Therefore, these workers are continually exposed to strong western, urban influences through their work setting.

The Interview Schedule

The workers were interviewed using a precoded questionaire with 159 items. Each of the questions asked the person the extent to which something was true for him with the emphasis always on subjective meaning. While there were undoubtedly distortions in their perceptions, especially for questions concerning events that may have happened years before, it was felt that what is important for an individual is how he perceives events, rather than whether those perceptions are correct or not.

Six general areas were emphasized in the questionaire: 1) the individual's job in the university, his income and standard of living; 2) the extent to which he participated in urban behaviors; 3) his evaluation of his experiences in the city; 4) attitudes and beliefs related to traditional-modern value conflicts in Turkey; 5) a description of his family background and the village from which he came; and 6) motives that affected his coming to Ankara.

The questions were both asked and coded by the interviewers. Inter-rater reliability was very high. This was tested by pairing off interviewers for twenty-four interviews. One interviewer would ask the questions but both would code the answers separately. The scores of the two questionaires were then correlated with each other in order to see general similarity in coding. For the twenty-four paired interviews, the mean correlation was 0.93 with a range from 0.84 to 0.98. All the interviewees were encouraged to answer all the questions, but in the few cases where an answer was not given, the mean response for the whole sample was coded.

Method of Analysis

The analysis is in terms of concept-scales (or indices) and the correlations (Pearson "r") among these scales. The logic of the method is to define clusters of "like" items which are combined into a single index in order to improve predictability by compounding variances. Essentially, the method involves, first, defining clusters of items which are assumed to measure the same social property. This was done in constructing the questionaire. Second, in order to see if the items in a concept actually do fall together, the items are subjected to internal consistency tests by inter-correlating all the items in a concept cluster. If an item does not correlate positively with others in the concept (preferably significantly), it is dropped. Third, the items in a concept are then correlated with the items from other concepts to determine whether or not they all showed the same pattern of correlations. Finally, the items were grouped to form a single index (or concept-scale) which could then be correlated with other indices. The method, thus, balances theoretical meaning with empirical consistency. Since each subject answered all questions (or were coded for all questions), then for each question and for each correlation between questions, the sample size is 392.

For the analysis of the attitudes and beliefs, however, a factor analysis was used. In this case, each of the 33 attitude and belief items were condensed into the simplest possible descriptive structure in order to approximate general value orientations. The method of principle component analysis was used (Harman 1960), with the number of factors being extracted determined by the number of latent roots greater than 1.00 (Guttman 1954: 149–161). A rotated orthogonal factor solution was produced using the simple loadings method (Jennrich and Sampson 1966: 313–323). In this method, the primary factor loadings are rotated, rather than the primary reference structure, using the quartimin criterion (Carroll 1953: 23–28).

FINDINGS

Job, Income, and Standard of Living

The workers occupied four different skill levels.

Unskilled Workers	49%
Semi-Skilled Workers	23%
Skilled Workers	21%
Highly-Skilled Workers	7%
	100%

Compared to the occupational skill level of their fathers', 51% advanced beyond their fathers' skill level, whereas only 1% showed a decrease. Similarly, in terms of education level, 85% showed an intergenerational increase and 13% showed a decrease. Eighty-five percent of the workers had completed primary school and 15% had gone beyond primary school. As would be expected, there is a high correlation between education level and job level ($r = 0.43$) and between job level and salary ($r = 0.57$). About 10% also had outside jobs and 9% reported that other family members worked.

The salary level of these workers is quite good relative to other migrant jobs in Ankara, but in examining their standard of living, the relative advantage of their salary did not translate itself into a high standard of living.[1] Only 15% lived in an apartment and only 9% had central heating (the two most desired attributes of standard of living). Only 16% had a radio, 22% had electricity, 52% had a bathroom, and 54% had a toilet in the house. In terms of

---

1 In 1969, the average take-home salary of these workers was 698 Turkish Lira per month. In 1962, the average monthly income of a sample living in the squatter housing areas of Ankara (*Gecekondu*) was 435 Turkish Lira per month (M.E.T.U. Urban Sociology Research Seminar 1962). Many university graduates also received only 600–800 T.L. per month, especially when they worked for the government.

living space, the average for the group is similar to the national average for main city districts: 2.46 rooms per household compared to 2.53 nationally (Turkish Census 1965: 690).

There are probably two reasons that their standard of living is not particularly high. First, for many individuals a certain proportion of their income is sent to someone in the village and, second, in spite of the higher salaries of these workers compared to other migrant groups, inflation in Ankara and other cities is high and eats away at "surplus" income. After sending money home and paying for necessities, there is not much money left over for renting a large apartment, for buying consumer durables, or for accumulating capital in order to invest. When the way these workers evaluate their income and standard of living was examined, their perceptions corresponded to their actual economic condition, though mediated by reference points. Eighty-one percent evaluated their job as good or very good in relation to other jobs in the village, 70% evaluated their job as good or very good in relation to other jobs in the university, 64% evaluated their job as good or very good in relation to other jobs in the city, but only 26% evaluated their standard of living as good or very good. Most of the migrants feel successful in having their job, but few feel they have a high standard of living.

Participation in Ankara

A majority of these migrants have been in Ankara for a fairly long time (mean = 9.7 years), so that the period of immediate adjustment for most is over. It would be expected, therefore, that most of the workers would have adopted urban-oriented behavior and would have decreased their contacts with their home village or town. This was measured by two concept-scales: New Culture Contacts and Old Culture Contacts. New Culture Contacts measured the extent to which the individual was being exposed to urban contacts, either through personal contacts or through the mass media, while Old Culture Contacts measured the extent of contacts that the person still maintained with his home. In the initial stages of migration, most migrants maintain contacts with their village or town, an effect which facilitates urban participation (Levine 1973: 355–368). But after five years or so, the amount of contact with the village does decrease. In this study, the correlation of Old Culture Contacts with time in Ankara decreases (Table 1). As a worker stays in the city, he loses contact slowly, though the amount of contacts with the villages and towns is still quite high. Twenty-one percent of these workers visit their home frequently or very frequently and 25% send money home frequently or very frequently. But 47% receive letters from home frequently or very frequently and 58% receive visitors from home frequently or very frequently. There is undoubtedly a lessening of visiting the village after a number of years, compared to writing, partly because some relatives and friends die off and others come to the city, and partly because of increased involvement in city life.

Table 1

Relationships between Education, Urban Exposure, Standard of Living, and Urban Participation
Pearson "r" Correlations (N = 392)

	Time in Ankara	Old Culture Contacts	Educa- tion Level	Index of Standard of Living	Skill Level of Job	New Culture Contacts
Time in Ankara	–	–.21	0.10	0.21	0.32	0.14
(no. of years)		**	*	**	**	*
Old Culture Contacts		–	0.01	–.08	–.06	0.04
Education Level Obtained			–	0.49	0.43	0.36
				**	**	**
Index of Standard of Living[1]				–	0.46	0.23
					**	**
Skill Level of Job					–	0.19
						**
New Culture Contacts						–
Significance Levels: (two-tailed test)	N = 392					

* = r > .099	or	< –.099: P < .05
** = r > .14	or	< –.14: P < .005

1   The standard of living index was composed of the worker's income divided by the number of people being supported, the type of housing, and the list of commodities mentioned earlier.

Similarly, there is a slow increase in city contacts over time, but as can be seen from Table 1, mere time in the city is not itself sufficient to increase New Culture Contacts substantially; available income and the person's educational background apparently are more important determinants. This can be seen by taking the individual items. Only 30% go the cinema frequently or very frequently and only 10% participate in formal social activities in Ankara frequently or very frequently. On the other hand, 69% read a newspaper frequently or very frequently, 73% listen to the news on the radio everyday, and 56% talk to the students frequently or very frequently. The high frequency of these latter "inexpensive" activities would suggest that there is no lack of intention on the part of these workers to be exposed to urban behavior, but the lack of available income is an inhibiting factor.

Educational experience is, however, even more important in aiding New Culture Contacts and the effect of education on urban participation is greater than its mediating effect in providing a better job and a higher income.[1] On the other hand, there is no simple relationship between education level and Old

1   The partial correlation of the Index of Standard of Living with New Culture Contacts becomes 0.06 when Education is partialled out.

Culture Contacts indicating that participation in urban behaviors does not necessarily imply a decrease in contact with the village, a result borne out in Table 1. It would appear, though, that education is more important in increasing New Culture Contacts than the income level of the person, a result which appears to somewhat contradict the initial model.

Attitudes, Beliefs, and Value Orientations

The relatively high income of these workers combined with the length of their stay in the city might lead us to expect that they would also become more urban in their attitudes and beliefs. Thirty-three attitude and belief items which contrasted "Traditional" and "Modern" values were chosen. The items reflected four areas of historical contrast: 8 items measuring religious values, subdivided into religious practices, social religiosity, and the acceptance of religion in politics; 11 items measuring the contrasts between the rural areas and the urban areas (rural vs. urban identity, evaluation of villagers and city people, acceptance of a centralized agricultural vs. decentralized industrial economy); 7 items looked at the worker's aspirations for himself and his son. There were also 7 items that should measure differences in behavior patterns between city people and rural people: the person's tendency towards isolation vs. sociability, his bedtime, his estimate of the ideal marriage age and his estimate of the ideal family size. These 33 items were condensed into 13 variables – 9 concept scales and 4 single items – using the method of concept-scales, and then checking it with a factor analysis.

The relationship between the 13 attitude and belief variables suggests a picture of three or more value orientations for these workers. The 13 variables were factor analyzed using the method described earlier. The orthogonal factor solution yielded five factors, which accounted for 55% of the matrix. Table 2 presents the rotated, orthogonal solution.

Taking a factor loading of $\pm$ .40 as the cut-off point and a factor loading of $\pm$ .35 to $\pm$ .39 as indicating a weak association, the factors can be described. The first factor has only one variable loading on it – the worker's estimate of the ideal size family. The second factor has three variables loading on it: having high socio-economic aspirations for his son, having high salary expectations for himself in five years time, and believing that the ideal marriage age should be relatively late in life. These all go together and suggest that *Future Economic Prospects* would be a reasonable label for this factor; some workers have good future economic prospects and some have less good prospects.

The third factor has two variables loading on it, negatively, and one variable is weakly loaded on it, positively. Being less sociable (i.e. more isolated) is associated with having lower aspirations for owning personal possessions (radio, refrigerator, automobile) and these are associated slightly with believing that religion should not be separated from politics. Because Religion-in-Politics also loads on factor V, the emphasis in this factor is on the first two variables so that *Socially Visible Possessions* (or lack of them) seems an appropriate label for this

Table 2

Factor Analysis of 13 Attitude and Belief Indices
Rotated Factor Structure (N = 392)

(cs): indicates concept-scale

	I	II	III	IV	V
Ideal Family Size	0.99	0.00	0.04	0.03	0.06
Ideal Marriage Age	0.09	0.52	0.05	0.02	−.19
Salary Expectations in Five Years	−.03	0.65	0.10	0.01	−.29
Socio-Economic Aspirations for Son (cs)	−.14	0.67	−.11	−.01	0.32
Centralized, Agricultural Economy (cs)	−.12	−.33	0.28	0.07	0.33
Sociability (cs)	−.07	−.17	−.75	−.03	0.14
Aspirations for Personal Possessions (cs)	−.03	0.05	−.69	0.26	0.01
Identification with Villagers (cs)	−.01	0.27	−.02	−.62	0.06
Evaluation of Villagers (cs)	0.02	0.21	0.13	−.70	0.14
Evaluation of City People (cs)	0.14	−.09	−.06	0.54	0.44
Religious Practice (cs)	0.03	−.00	0.03	−.05	0.68
Social Religiosity (cs)	0.13	−.20	−.22	−.12	0·66
Religion in Politics	−.03	−.19	0.37	0.12	0.37

factor; some workers are more isolated and don't desire personal possessions while others are more sociable and aspire to owning these commodities. Factor IV has three variables loading on it. A high evaluation of city people is associated with a correspondingly low evaluation of villagers and a low identification with the village and with villagers. This factor has been named *Urban Identity* (or *Rural Identity*, taking the opposite). Factor V has three variables loading on it and one variable loading weakly on it. Participating frequently in religious practices is associated with applying religious criteria to social behavior (emphasizing going to Mecca, that his son should go to Koran school, that friends and politicians should be good Muslims) as well as being weakly associated with believing that religion should not be separated from politics. These variables, however, are also associated with having a high evaluation of city people. The three religious variables indicate a general religious orientation, but the fourth variable would suggest that this religiosity is urban rather than rural or traditional. Withholding interpretation for the present, therefore, this factor can be sub-divided into two parts: a *General Religiosity* and an *Evaluation of City People*. The Centralized, Agricultural Economy scale fails to load strongly on any one factor, but has minor loadings on three factors.

Seven value scales were made up by combining the variables loading beyond the cut-off point on each factor in a simple additive manner. *Centralized Agricultural Economy* was treated as a separate scale, as was *Evaluation of City People*. Thus, factor IV becomes *Rural Identity*, emphasizing the rural orientation. Religion-in-Politics was included in *General Religiosity*, rather than in *Socially Visible Possessions* because it correlated more highly with the individual variables making up the former than with the variables making up the latter.

The factor analysis, of course, produces an orthogonal solution, which does not permit any association to exist between the various factors (or very minimal association after rotation). However, when the seven scales are inter-correlated it is apparent that there are relationships between these variables (Table 3).

Table 3

Value Orientations: Correlations Among Seven Value Scales
Pearson "r" Correlations (N = 392)

	Future Econ. Pros.	Ideal Family Size	Socially Visible Poss.	Eval. of City People	General Relig.	Central. Agricul. Economy	Rural Identity
Future Economic Prospects	–	0.07	–.20 **	–.18 **	–.31 **	–.10 *	0.08
Ideal Family Size		–	–.12 *	–.11 *	0.09	0.04	0.02
Socially, Visible Possessions			–	0.21 **	0.14 **	0.03	–.06
Evaluation of City People				–	0.28 **	0.07	–.21 **
General Religiosity					–	0.13 *	0.05
Centralized, Agricultural Economy						–	0.06
Rural Identity							–

Significance Levels: (two-tailed test)	N = 392

* = r > .099	or	< –.099: P < .05
** = r > .14	or	< –.14: P < .005

Having high future economic prospects is negatively related to being religious and to believing in a centralized, agricultural economy, a result which would appear consistent with a modern-traditional split. Having good economic prospects, however, is also negatively related to aspiring to owning consumer commodities and to evaluating city people highly, variables that would intuitively seem modern. At the same time, these latter variables all relate positively to each other; evaluating city people highly and aspiring to ownership of consumer goods are related to being religious. There is no simple modern-traditional split among these attitudes. In addition, general religiosity does not appear to be indicative of a traditional value orientation. There is only a weak relationship with believing in a centralized, agricultural economy and there is no simple relationship with identifying with the rural areas. There is, however, a negative relationship between rural identity and evaluating city people highly.

Nonetheless, the relationships between these variables, though significant, are not very strong. They represent tendencies, rather than clear-cut patterns. However, these data could indicate that there may be two or three value systems operating among these workers. The first type – *Urban Modern* – is associated with having good economic prospects and with not being religious, not being feudal oriented, not being unrealistically aspiring, and not being over-accepting of city people and would appear to correspond with the historical urban-rural dichotomy. The second type – *Urban Identity* – appears to represent a synthesis of the conflicting values. Workers who identify strongly with city people are highly sociable, aspiring to ownership of consumer goods, but at the same time they are also very religious. The third type seems to reflect a strong *Rural Orientation* where the individual rejects city people, identifies with villagers and with the village, but he may or may not be religious.

Urban Conditions and Value Systems

These three value types are, of course, "Ideal" abstractions from the data, but the interpretation suggests that though all of these workers are migrants, several value orientations can emerge. The process of migration is not uniform in its effects and the differences may reflect differences in experience as well as differences in background. In order to explore this further, these seven value scales were related to the acculturation indices measuring the economic conditions of the workers, the amount of urban participation, and the worker's evaluation of his acculturation (Table 4).

An *Urban Modern* orientation is more related to a high social mobility pattern than are the other two value types. The better the person's job, the higher his standard of living, the more his own socio-economic status exceeds that of his father, and the more urban participation he shows, then the higher are his future economic prospects.[1] Conversely, the *Urban Identity* type appears more related to a low social mobility pattern. The less skilled the worker's job, the lower his standard of living, the less his own socio-economic status exceeds that of his father, and the less urban participation he shows, then the more likely he is to evaluate city people highly, aspire to own consumer commodities that are socially visible, and to show a general religiosity. The *Rural Oriented* type appears more related to the low mobility pattern, though few of the correlations for Rural Identity and Centralized, Agricultural Economy are significant. Ideal Family Size does not show a meaningful relationship to any of the acculturation indices.

Looking at the worker's evaluation of his life in Ankara, the *Urban Identity* type is happier with his life style than the other two types. The more highly the

1 An index of the Socio-Economic Status of the Father was constructed by taking the father's occupational skill level and adding it to the father's educational level and the mother's educational level. Differences between the worker and his father could be compared by taking their respective job skill levels and educational levels.

Table 4

Urban Acculturation and Value Orientation: the Effects of Urban Exposure, Standard of Living, and
Urban Participation on Values
Pearson "r" Correlations (N = 392)

Acculturation Indices:	Future Econ. Pros.	Ideal Family Size	Socially Visible Poss.	Eval. of City People	General Relig.	Central. Agricul. Economy	Rural Identity
			Value Scales				
Time in Ankara	0.17 **	−.01	−.05	−.10	−.07	−.03	−.08
New Culture Contacts	0.27 **	−.01	−.02	−.06	−.13 *	−.07	−.09
Skill Level of Job	0.31 **	0.02	−.10 *	−.10 *	−.27 **	−.08	−.08
Index of Standard of Living	0.26 **	0.05	−.20 **	−.08	−.37 **	−.09	−.07
Index of Father–Son Mobility	0.41 **	0.06	0.03	−.24 **	−.51 **	−.10 *	0.03
Index of General Evaluation of Ankara[1]	−.25 **	0.07	0.12 *	0.46 **	0.36 **	0.11 *	−.22 **

Significance Levels: N = 392
(two-tailed test)

* = r > .099   or   < −.099: P < .05
** = r > .14   or   < −.14: P < .005

1 The Index of General Evaluation of Ankara was composed of the worker's perceived sense of adjustment, his perceived job success, his perceived standard of living, his evaluation of Ankara if he had to recommend it to a friend, his commitment to staying in the city, and his perceptions of whether he would migrate to Ankara if he could choose again.

worker evaluates city people, the more he is religious, the more he aspires to own personal possessions, and the more he believes in a centralized, agricultural economy, then the more highly he evaluates his experiences in living in the city. There seems to be no antithesis between being religious and accepting city life. The *Urban Modern* type and the *Rural Oriented* type are less happy with their urban experiences. The relative unhappiness of the *Urban Modern* may reflect a different frame of reference from the other two; workers who are more educated evaluate their urban experiences lower than workers who are less educated.

With the exception of higher future economic prospects, the time spent in Ankara for a worker does not bear any relationship to the value scales. The effects of urban conditions are far more important on value orientation than merely residing in the city.

Background Experience and Value Systems

These value systems are also related to the individual's background, though to a much lesser extent. An index of the Level of Economic Development of the Village was constructed by combining a number of questions about the village.[1] These indices, as well as the worker's perception of his parents' educational and occupational aspirations towards him, were related to the seven value scales (Table 5).

Table 5

Background and Value Orientation: the Effects of Village Economy, Family Status, and Educational
Achievement on Values
Pearson "r" Correlations (N = 392)

Background Indices:	Value Scales						
	Future Econ. Pros.	Ideal Family Size	Socially Visible Poss.	Eval. of City People	General Relig.	Central. Agricul. Economy	Rural Identity
Level of Development of Village	0.12 *	0.11 *	−.01	−.03	−.00	0.02	0.03
Socio-Economic Status of Father	0.13 *	−.02	−.06	−.10 *	−.16 **	0.07	−.01
Occupational Aspirations Expressed by Parents	0.16 **	0.01	−.13 *	−.06	−.02	0.01	0.05
Educational Aspirations Expressed by Parents	0.09	−.03	−.04	−.07	−.09	0.05	0.03
Education Level Obtained	0.30 **	0.00	−.16 **	−.19 **	−.36 **	−.06	0.05
Significance Levels: (two-tailed test)	N = 392						

$* = r > .099$ or $< -.099: P < .05$
$** = r > .14$ or $< -.14: P < .005$

---

1   The Level of Economic Development of the Village was composed of items measuring the size of the village, whether the village was a plateau or mountain village (plateau villages are more developed generally), the type of crops grown in the village (commercial crops require a greater investment than grain crops), how many tractors were in the village, how much land area was cultivated by tractors, how much of the land used commercial fertilizers, to what extent there was cooperative irrigation in the village, the proportion of villagers who worked in non-agricultural occupations, how many families lived on small crafts in the village, and the extent of money lending in the village.

The most consistent relationship to the seven value scales is the individual's educational level. The more educated the worker, then the higher are his future economic prospects and the less likely he is to be religious, the less likely he is to evaluate city people highly, and the less likely he is to be socially aspiring of consumer commodities. The *Urban Modern* type, therefore, has a more educated background while the *Urban Identity* type is less educated. Further, the strength of association to the value scales by educational level is of the same order as the economic conditions in Table 4. As urban orientation is related to both the amount of education the individual has received and his present economic position. Table 5 shows that a few of the other relationships are statistically significant, but the pattern is one of low or statistically insignificant correlations.

Motives for Migration and Value Systems

Three types of motivations characterized the sample group. For most, economic reasons underlie the decision to migrate, both in terms of "push" factors in the village or town and "pull" factors in Ankara. For example, when asked how much land the worker had in the village, 59% indicated that they had little or no land. On the other hand, 89% stated that most if not all of the other male villagers owned land. It appears that many were encouraged to move partly because of lack of land, whereas those who stayed are perceived as having some land, though we cannot check whether this perception is accurate. Seventy-five percent felt strongly that they migrated because of the situation in the village and 78% perceived that other villagers who migrated to Ankara had very low incomes. The primary pull factor drawing workers to Ankara is also economic. Eighty-five percent felt strongly attracted to Ankara because of work possibilities and 81% felt strongly attracted by standard of living possibilities. These six items were combined into a concept-scale: *Economic Motives.*

A second type of motivation lay in the attraction of the city because of living possibilities, and was also widespread: educational opportunities (80% strongly attracted), desire to live in a more free way (73% strongly attracted), desire to become a city person (62% strongly attracted) and entertainment possibilities (31% strongly attracted). These items have also been combined into a concept-scale: *Pull of the City.* For a few persons, being strongly attracted because of family contacts (23%) and friend contacts (15%) was a third motivation. The low emphasis on family and friends in the city has to be seen in relation to the first two "opportunity" motivations; friends and family are useful and desirable, but as a prime reason are less important than necessities and opportunities (see similar results in Berardo 1967: 541–554).

When these three motivations (and the age at which the worker arrived in Ankara) were related to the seven value scales, a pattern of motivations appeared that distinguished the three general value systems (Table 6).

Workers who arrived at younger ages had better future economic prospects, whereas those who arrived at older ages are more religious, more aspiring to

Table 6
Motives for Migration and Value Orientation
Pearson "r" Correlations (N = 392)

Migration Motives:	Value Scales						
	Future Econ. Pros.	Ideal Family Size	Socially Visible Poss.	Eval. of City People	General Relig.	Central. Agricul. Economy	Rural Identity
Economic Motives	−.03	−.02	0.11 *	0.04	0.19 **	0.14 **	0.13 *
Pull of the City	0.04	0.06	0.02	0.29 **	0.15 **	0.03	−.11 *
Family, Friends	0.03	0.11 *	0.03	0.02	0.02	0.04	0.02
Age of Arrival	−.12 *	0.19 **	0.16 **	0.08	0.24 **	0.14 **	0.01

Significance Levels: (two-tailed test)	N = 392

* = r > .099	or	< −.099: P < .05
** = r > .14	or	< −.14: P < .005

consumer commodities, more feudal in their orientation and believe in a larger ideal family size. This might suggest that the *Urban Modern* type had better economic prospects than the other two types when he arrived, though this must be taken cautiously as these are perceptions of events which happened years before. Workers who indicated a greater intensity of economic motives are more likely to be religious, believing in a centralized, agricultural economy, aspiring to personal possessions, and identified with the rural areas. This is characteristic of the values representing both the *Urban Identity* and the *Rural Oriented* type. The difference between these latter two, in fact, may be represented by the strength of their attraction for Ankara. Those workers who were more "pulled" to the city are more likely to evaluate city people highly, more likely to be religious, but are less likely to identify with the rural areas. It appears, therefore, that workers who moved less out of economic necessity (younger, more educated, and from a slightly higher status family) are more likely to be *Urban Modern* in their value orientation, whereas workers who came more out of economic necessity are more likely to be either an *Urban Identity* type or *Rural Oriented*.[1]

Discussion

The evidence in this study tends to support the hypothesis that cognitive

---

1   The correlation of Education Level and Age of Arrival is −.27 while the correlation of Father's *S–E* Status and Age of Arrival is −.12.

value positions of these workers are products of both their exposure to modernizing influences through education and the economic conditions of their life style in the city, although the levels of correlations are generally not very great. Further, the exposure of workers to educational influences is itself related to economic conditions in their village or town and the extent to which economic necessity dictated their coming to the city (data not presented). In a more developed area, there is likely to be a school and individuals are more likely to be exposed to modernizing institutions, such as a marketing system or a state cooperative. If they come from a wealthier family, then they are more free to develop their educational potential and will be encouraged to succeed, if merely to maintain their family status. There are undoubtedly other indirect influences that would affect a developed village or town and, certainly, a person who came from a higher status family in the area. This is not to play down the importance of educational achievement itself. Nonetheless, exposure to education has to be seen in the light of other conditions that exist in a village or small town, and not merely be treated as an institutional "given".

The three value systems inferred from the data indicate three possible responses to the historical conflicts of values that have affected Turkey. Speculating a little, the evidence possibly shows that these three value systems reflect three ideological positions held by migrants that are consequences of their economic experiences in the city. One type of migrant accepts the urban, middle-class beliefs (the *Urban Modern*). His economic condition is relatively well-off and he finds that he is able to increase his urban participation. He, consequently, accepts the aspiration levels of the middle-classes and compared to these levels, he feels less adjusted and happy about his life. His ideology is that of entry into the middle-classes: *Embourgeoisment*.

A second type of migrant (the *Urban Identity*) comes from a poorer background and has a more limited education. When he obtains a stable job, although his standard of living is not at all high, he feels very successful. He rejects his background and over-compensates in his acceptance of the city and city people. He is more "urban" than the *Urban Modern* and desires strongly to have material acquisitions, though he still maintains religious behavior. His economic prospects are restricted. His ideology is that of *Emulation* as he adopts the success symbols of the middle-classes and identifies with their success. The third type of migrant also comes from a poorer background and also has had only an elementary education. His job and standard of living are similar to that of the "emulator" and his economic prospects are as limited. But rather than identify with the symbols of the middle-classes, he rejects the city and re-identifies with rural areas and with traditional practices. His ideology is that of *Traditionalism*.[1]

Whether future studies will support this interpretation remains to be seen.

---

1 This would suggest that traditionalism as a coherent ideology develops in the urban areas and is associated with people being blocked economically, rather than merely being an appendage of rural social structure. See for analogies Barber (1941: 177–183) and Worsley (1957).

Since these workers represent a relatively advantaged migrant group, these patterns may not held for other groups and should be treated with caution. But what is certain is that, for the time being, economic prospects for migrants in the cities are becoming limited. If the urbanization of Ankara and other cities continues without proper industrial development, the possibilities for the participation and integration that these workers show will decrease for future migrants and for less privileged groups. The problem of migrant adaptation, then, will become the problem of underdevelopment.

REFERENCES

ABU-LUGHOD, Janet
     1961   "Migrant adjustment to city life: the Egyptian case". American Journal of Sociology 67: 22–32.

BARBER, Bernard
     1941   "Acculturation and messianic movements". American Sociological Review 6: 663–668. (Reprinted in Comparative Perspectives on Social Change, ed. by S. N. Eisenstadt, 177–183. Boston: Little, Brown, and Co., 1968.)

BERARDO, Felix
     1967   "Kinship interaction and communications among space age migrants". Journal of Marriage and the Family 29: 541–554.

BRUNER, Edward M.
     1961   "Urbanization and ethnic identity in North Sumatra". American Anthropologist 63: 508–521.

BUECHLER, Hans C.
     1970   "The ritual dimension of rural-urban networks: the fiesta system in the northern highlands of Bolivia" pp. 62–71 in William Mangin (ed.), Peasants in Cities. Boston: Houghton Mifflin.

CARROLL, J. B.
     1953   "An analytical solution for approximating simple structure in factor analysis". Psychometrika 18: 23–28.

CHANCE, N. A.
     1965   "Acculturation, self-identification, and personality adjustment". American Anthropologist 67: 372–393.

DUOCASTELLA, R.
     1955   "Problems of adjustment in the case of internal migration: an example in Spain". Reprinted in Readings in the Sociology of Migration, ed. by Clifford J. Jansen, 319–337. Oxford: Pergamon Press, 1970.

FANON, Frantz
     1959   A Dying Colonialism. Harmondsworth: Pelican (English edition 1970).

FELDMAN, Arnold S. and HURN, Christopher
     1966   "The experience of modernization". Sociometry 29: 378–395.

FRANK, Andre G.
     1969   "Sociology of development and underdevelopment of sociology" pp. 21–94 in Andre G. Frank, Latin America: Underdevelopment or Revolution. New York: Modern Reader.

FRANK, Andre G.
     1971   Capitalism and Underdevelopment in Latin America. Harmondsworth: Pelican.

FREY, Frederick W.
     1964   "Education – Turkey" pp. 205–235 in Robert E. Ward and Dankwart A. Rustow (eds.), Political Modernization in Japan and Turkey. Princeton: Princeton University Press.

GRAVES, Theodore D.
    1967 "Acculturation, access, and alcohol in a tri-ethnic community". American Anthropologist 69: 306–321.
GUSFIELD, Joseph R.
    1967 "Traditional and modernity: misplaced polarities in the study of social change". American Journal of Sociology 72: 351–362.
GUTKIND, Peter C. W.
    1965 "African urbanism, mobility and the social network". International Journal of Comparative Sociology 6: 48–60.
GUTTMAN, L.
    1954 "Some necessary conditions for common-factor analyses". Psychometrika 19: 149–161.
HARMAN, H. H.
    1960 Modern Factor Analysis. Chicago: University of Chicago Press.
INKELES, Alex
    1970 "Making men modern: on the causes and consequences of individual change in six developing countries". American Journal of Sociology 75: 208–225.
JENNRICH, R. I. and SAMPSON, P. F.
    1966 "Rotation for simple loadings". Psychometrika 31: 313–323.
KEDDIE, Nikki R.
    1972 "Intellectuals in the modern Middle East: a brief historical consideration". Daedalus 101 (Summer): 39–57.
KIRAY, Mübeccel B.
    1968 "Values, social stratification and development". Journal of Social Issues 24: 87–102.
KIRAY, Mübeccel B. and HINDERINK, Jan
    1968 "Interdependencies between agroeconomic development and social change: a comparative study conducted in the Çukurova region of southern Turkey". Journal of Development Studies 4: 497–528.
LERNER, Daniel
    1958 The Passing of Traditional Society. Glencoe: Free Press.
LEVINE, Ned
    1973 "Old culture – new culture: a study of migrants in Ankara, Turkey". Social Forces 51: 355–368.
LEWIS, Bernard
    1968 The Emergence of Modern Turkey. Oxford: Oxford University Press, 2nd. edition.
MARDIN, Şerif
    1962 The Genesis of Young Ottoman Thought. Princeton: Princeton University Press.
MARDIN, Şerif
    1973 "Center-periphery relations: a key to Turkish politics?". Daedalus 102 (Winter): 169–190.
M.E.T.U. Urban Sociology Research Seminar
    1962 Quoted in Mübeccel B. Kıray, "Squatter housing: fast de-peasantization and slow workerization in underdeveloped countries". Paper presented to 7th World Congress of Sociology, Urban Sociology Research Group. Ankara: Middle East Technical University, p. 4.
PETERSEN, Karan K.
    1971 "Villagers in Cairo: hypotheses versus data". American Journal of Sociology 77: 560–573.
ROBINSON, R. D.
    1958 "Turkey's agrarian revolution and the problem of urbanization". Public Opinion Quarterly 22: 397–405.
RUDOLPH, Lloyd I. and RUDOLPH, Suzanne H.
    1967 The Modernity of Tradition. Chicago: University of Chicago Press.

SCHNAIBERG, Allan
    1970   "Rural-urban residence and modernism: a study of Ankara Province, Turkey".
            Demography 7: 71–85.
SMITH, David and INKELES, Alex
    1966   "The OM scale: a comparative socio-psychological measure of individual modern-
            ity". Sociometry 29: 353–377.
SUZUKI, Peter
    1964   "Encounters with Istanbul: urban peasants and village peasants". International
            Journal of Comparative Sociology 5: 208–216.
Turkish Census
    1965   Genel Nüfus Sayımı. Ankara: Devlet İstatistik Enstitüsü, 1969. Table 56b, p. 690.
WORSLEY, Peter
    1957   The Trumpet Shall Sound. London: MacGibbon and Kee.
ZACHARIAH, K. D.
    1966   "Bombay migration study: a pilot analysis of migration to an Asian metropolis".
            Demography 3: 378–392.

RESEARCH COMMUNICATIONS

Note: The *Journal of Asian and African Studies* invites communications in the form of short articles and reports about ongoing research, not exceeding 5,000 words, both in the empirical and theoretical fields.

EDITOR

1. The *Sande* and some of the Forces that inspired its Creation or Adoption with some References to the *Poro*

J. V. O. RICHARDS

University of Lagos, Akoka, Yaba, Nigeria

In the Mende[1] community, religious activities such as initiation rites, ancestor worship and social counselling require group interaction and involvement. These activities are capable of stimulating the growth of group organisations, fraternities, cultural institutions and as in this study, secret societies. These societies are characterised by an elaborate ritual, a social life and religious beliefs which are capable of binding members together and of reinforcing traditional social ties between individuals. In such societies, the link between the supernatural world and the members is sometimes strengthened by the art forms they generate. These art forms are used to maintain social and political equilibrium and to guarantee security for every member in the face of the hazards of life as well as to impart form and content to the social activities of these societies.

Among the Mende, almost the full range of motivations for the arts is controlled by the *Bundu* Society (*Sande*). This is a female initiation secret society in which the women wear a wooden helmet mask called *sowei*. This secret society is found in many areas of West Africa with slight organisational differences occasioned by the cultural awareness and religious attachments of its members who in many cases look up to the masked figure (sometimes called *Sowei*), as representative of their divine and mystical protector.

In the *Sande*, art with its corresponding stabilising, integrating and educational functions plays a vital role in sustaining group loyalty. When such a society supports art, change in the forms generated is acceptable only within narrow limits. Any art tradition devoted to the expression of spiritual values, for example the Byzantine or the Buddhist, sets a space limit on excessive self-expression and promotes instead what may be thought of as group expression. This is not a prohibitive or inhibitive limitation, but one that disavows egocentrism in the artist, and encourages a slow but steady refinement of the existing models.

---

1 The Mende with a high density of population and numerous secret societies for men and women occupy an area of roughly 12,000 square miles in the eastern and south-western parts of Sierra Leone Province, and a much smaller area in the adjoining corner of Liberia.

Before examining what factors motivate the creation or adoption of a secret society such as the *Sande* or the *Poro* which is the men's society, it is necessary to discuss some of the propositions that have become current in recent years. The exploratory study by M. Watkins in 1943 had very little to say about the social and religious factors involved in the creation or evolution of the *Sande* beyond a few general remarks on its role in Mendeland. In addition, the recent theoretical studies on the *Sande* by Augustus Caine (1959), Kenneth Little (1967), and Harry Sawyerr (1968) are confined to listing, describing and explaining the various roles of the *Sande*. Their studies as does that of Watkins, emphasize the importance of the *Sande* in coordinating the diverse and conflicting elements of Mende culture and transmitting them from one generation to another. This initiation Society they posit, provides a galaxy of counsellors to plan the type of education that guarantees a steady stream of technical competence in various crafts and skills vital to the Mende industrial complex. In so doing, the *Sande* provides rational guidance, inspiration and challenge as well as patterns for understanding the complexities and philosophical theories of Mende culture.

While one is impressed by the contributions of Watkins, Caine, Little and Sawyerr to the understanding of the diverse roles of the *Sande*, Little goes still further to list myths and oral traditions associated with the origin of the *Poro* Society. In his analysis he employs the often-cited account on the creation of the Poro Society among the Mende by Colonel H. G. Warren. Warren believes

> ...that it was brought about by the death of the first Mende chief. This chief had the reputation of being very powerful and, on his death, his principal attendants, fearing that when his death was made known to his people there would be trouble in the country and a general split-up of the Mende tribe, it was decided that they would keep his death secret. It so happened that the chief had an impediment which made him talk through his nose, so a suitable person had to be found to impersonate him. When the person was found, he was sworn on the chief's corpse and other medicines that he would not reveal the secret. So effective was this, that others were gradually told the secret and likewise sworn to have "one word". (Warren 1919: 8–9.)

What is important in the light of the general argument of this study is the fact that the *Poro* was established by the Mende to ensure ethnic cohesion as Warren's account seems to indicate.

The Colonel was an Englishman employed as a District Officer in Sierra Leone. He was initiated into the *Poro* Society, but did not advance beyond the first grade. In the search for evidence on the beginnings of the *Poro* Society, his account has been consistently employed by other writers such as F. Migeod. From Migeod (1927: 232–233), we know that the Colonel was handicapped by an inadequate knowledge of the Mende language, and this obviously limited his participation in all the activities of the Society. Furthermore, whatever secrets he learnt while in the *Poro* died with him.

Today, the *Poro* Society is one of the most powerful secret societies of the Mende, whose nocturnal activities are designed to bring about forced seclusion of non-members. At present, women, children and non-members are strictly forbidden to approach its sacred groves. In fact, the operation of the Society is such that although some of the powerful members in the religious hierarchy are women[1], *Poro* laws operate to keep them at a respectful distance from most of its deliberations. Formerly, any woman caught trespassing on *Poro* grounds was put to death. In recent times, this practice has been considerably modified and any woman who mistakenly trespasses is forced to undergo initiation or she is redeemed by paying a very high fee.

Perhaps this is why Mende women wanted to have a powerful secret society that would balance the role of the *Poro*. As my informant explained, what the women needed was some kind of social and religious association that would promote an egalitarian position for women and ensure for them a more favourable status and an active participation in the socio-religious life of the Mende. In addition, the women wanted considerable freedom for their sex, and the creation or adoption of a powerful secret society with a wide range of powers was an effective way to guarantee this right. As *Poro* laws ensure that women and non-members stay indoors when its *Gbeni* makes its seasonal rounds of the town, so too do *Sande* rules operate to keep men in awe of thier masked dancer (*Sowei*).

To enforce its strict laws and rights, the creative leaders of the *Sande* had to utilize masks that personalised the protective deity of the Society, and the mystic force which inheres in it. These masks are very sacred in the Society and every member of the Mende community consciously or unconsciously acquires some reverence or awe for them. It is not unusual to see other masked dancers unmask in public, but any non-member who attempts to watch a *Sowei* remove the mask (*sowei*) for some airing would be guilty of a serious offence. The fine for such an offence is not very high; but exculpation from the guilt may require the performance of certain cleansing acts which may awe a superficial observer who has not been admitted into the mysteries of the *Sande*. However, the spirit inhabiting the mask (sowei) and the unmatchable authority with which it endows its wearer are admitted by all Mende peoples.

Absence of Data on the Origin of the Sande

In Sierra Leone, data on the creation and development of the *Sande* and *Poro* are scarce. In addition, systematic studies on the roles of the *Sande* and its art forms are of uneven quality and far from abundant. Apparently throughout the Mende region, many of the initiated members of the *Sande* are reluctant to offer even the minimal information on when or how their Society began, and it is reasonable to suppose that this aspect of *Sande's* secret is not available to non-members. Furthermore, the body of laws and medicines of *Sande*, my informant reaffirmed, are all designed to bring destruction on those who betray the oath of secrecy which every initiated member is required to take.

However, despite the absence of decisive evidence on the beginnings of the *Sande* and *Poro*, it is possible from available data and from field research to formulate some hypothetical assumptions on why these Societies were created and the interconnection of their art with their socio-religious activities. These

---

1   The *Mbole* who takes care of the *Poro* spirit's pipe and razor used during the initiation of new members is a woman. T. J. Alldridge (1901) states that she is considered to be both man and woman: a quality described as "*Deh-boi*" in *Poro* language.

assumptions will necessarily involve the problem of causation, the analysis of which will vary considerably in the *Poro* and the *Sande* where the hypotheses can be tested with consistent results. In fact, almost all the results can be verified by observation, and the hypotheses themselves are capable of both objective and subjective analytical assessment.

Hypotheses on the Origin of the Sande

In attempting to examine some of the factors associated with the creation and development of the *Sande*, one becomes involved in the question of why such a society was formed. The analysed data at our disposal permit one to say that the *Poro* and the *Sande* arose partially out of the needs for cohesion, inner security and education. These needs are interrelated; and among the Mende, they operate collectively to make the creation of a secret society necessary. Throughout this study, the term *survival needs* will be applied to avoid the cumbersome repetition of these three needs. This term is appropriate since the forces of cohesion, inner security and education are necessary for the survival of the Mende peoples.

Although this study does not intend to prove *in toto* the importance of these *survival needs* for the creation and development of the *Sande*, it does prove the dependence of *survival needs* on art. Since this study also examines some of the factors limiting change in the art forms of the *Sande*, the dependence of *survival needs* on art is important for three reasons. First, change in the art forms will affect the response of members to *survival needs* Second, these art forms constitute an external expression of the founding ancestors of the *Sande*. Change therefore (in the art forms), would necessarily precipitate changes in the unifying ancestor myths that supply an answer to *survival needs*. Third, changes in art will definitely lead to changes in the various aspects of *survival needs*.

A sample survey of secret societies in Mendeland showed that without individual and communal demands for *survival needs* the leader of an space ethnic group do not set out to form a secret society such as the *Sande* or the *Poro*. The above needs and their relevance to the survival of the Mende community determines the type of secret society to be created. The act of creation is the responsibility of the creative leader who formulates policies codes and conducts that govern the activities of the secret society created. He also draws up laws that would subordinate the interest of the individual to the welfare of the whole community. In the *Sande*, the present leaders are women gifted in the traditions of the group as well as great religious and moral leaders who employ myths and mysteries in explaining phenomena.

To discuss the problems associated with puberty rites, childbirth and motherhood, Mende women have to organise themselves into a secret society such as the *Sande*. This explains why this organisation is characterised by elaborate educational and religious activities designed to meet the *survival needs* of the Mende. Membership is open to every female member of the community participation in the activities of this Society is essential in the development of the Mende "tribal personality" and the establishment of behaviour patterns. Among the Mende, the earlier years of girlhood are the time to inculcate the formative principles of womanhood, which by their very nature ensure the initiates a place in the community. The age for admission into *Sande* is between the ages of 12 and 16; but older girls may also be admitted.

Testing the Hypotheses

In testing the hypotheses, the variables which constitute *survival needs* will be examined in the light of what is known about the Mende peoples. This test will be necessary in order to prove whether all the variables yield adequate results when used in determining the factors responsible for the creation of the *Sande* or *Poro*.

Need for Cohesion

The Mende community as we know it today once existed as a looseknit confederation of ethnic groups, local families, and clans whose internal cohesion was in most cases too weak to withstand the hostile contacts the Mende have been experiencing with their neighbours. What the Mende community needed was some cohesive force that would bind peoples with differing idiosyncrasies but similar cultural and historical traditions into a powerful ethnic group with considerable "one word" strong enough to resist external agression. Such cohesion was ensured by the establishment of secret society with absolute powers to control the domestic and administrative activities of everyday life. The benefits of such cohesion becomes obvious in times of uncertainty and acute social stress.

A familiar historical case was that which existed in Mendeland in 1898 when the Mende confronted the British over the issue of hut (house) tax. Earlier, the introduction of "civilised laws" by the British to replace ethnic laws and the enactment of the *Poro* Ordinance that removed the *Poro's* embargo on the harvesting of palm fruits, made foreign intrusion unbearable to the Mende. The masses who feared that their way of life was threatened turned to the *Poro* for ethnic solidarity. Formerly the rapping on a tortoise shell summoned *Poro* members, but during the 1898 Mende rising, it was a burnt leaf that was passed round to summon members to war. This was a clever device contrived to deceive the British and to ensure cohesive response from members of the Society.

For ethnic cohesion to be effective, these secret societies must propagate some unifying myth or philosophy essential for controlling the moral and spiritual conduct of their members. In the *Sande*, art is one of the vehicles by which this unifying myth or philosophy is given external expression and conveyed to members during initiation. During the initiation ceremonies, the art forms ensure that every member of the Society has a claim of descent from a common ancestor and so members consider themselves to be culturally one family.

Today there are more members in the *Poro* and the *Sande* than in any other similar association. The cohesion that these Societies foster has in the past constituted a threat to Christianity in its bid to convert indigenes of Sierra Leone and Liberia. The result was that missionaries in 1958 vandalised *Sande* camps in Liberia, and tried to expose their activities to non-members. The repercussion was swift and drastic. The Government of Liberia stepped in and fined the missionaries $600 each and sentenced them to one year imprisonment.[1] In such times of natural hazards or molestation ,the *Sande* in all large towns have their *Sowei* ready to take up their cudgel against intruders.

The Need for Inner Security

In Mendeland, inner security had top priority in the schedule of necessities. The evil forces of witchcraft, magic, juju and evil spirits had to be counteracted; and so too were the less hostile forces such as drought, thunder and other forces of nature. Since ancestors and natural phenomena could influence the lives of the Mende for good or evil, these forces had to be controlled by pacification rites, which in the *Sande* call for the use of art. Furthermore, the ability of the creative leaders to control forces hostile to the survival of their community satisfied the demands of the Mende for inner security in an incomprehensible world. Eventually, the prerogative to harness these forces for peaceful or harmful use was invested in the *Poro* and the *Sande*.

In Mendeland, where the possession and use of supernatural powers are highly valued because they are restricted and controlled, membership of the *Poro* or *Sande* guarantees the right to invoke these powers for use in times of insecurity. In addition, the Mende believe that there is no activity in life that cannot be aided by certain conjurations from the Koran, or their sacred myths. In order to be effective, these citations must be meticulously word-perfect; their arrangement is taught to older members of the *Sande* and *Poro*. Also the need for a concrete apparatus to guarantee inner security has induced the *Poro* and *Sande* to employ the services of *mori* men to prepare protective charms which most often are worn around the neck or waist of the initiate. Further evidence collected in many areas of Mendeland seems to support the efficacy of these charms; but it is not necessary for the purpose of this study to describe the supernatural outlook of the Mende beyond what has been collated in earlier studies.

Another concrete device for satisfying the demands of members of the *Sande* for inner security and protection are the art forms. The Society and its members needed some form of external expression of the spirit or protector who continually watches over them. This protector usually takes abode in a sculpture charged with the infinite powers of a supreme being (*Ngewo*) and transmitted through his divine hierarchy of spirits, Again, while giving spiritual dignity to the ritual objects and charms used in the ceremonies of the Society, these art forms act as intermediaries between the world of ancestors and the secret societies. Whenever these art forms are in the midst of *Sande* members, they give them a feeling of security in the future and also help to perpetuate the optimism so obvious in the art forms themselves.

The art is ritualistic, communal and effective as a sacred device for maintaining inner security and social order among members. The presence of the

---

1 This was a calculated attempt to pacify the natives who obviously disapproved of foreign intervation in their socio-religious affairs. See *Liberian Age*, 16/5/58, Monrovia, Liberia.

art is an external manifestation of the spirit associated with the secret society. In the *Sande*, art counteracts the centrifugal forces of fear, and provides an integrating glue that binds members together. The integrating force is achieved by invoking the supernatural powers of the ancestral spirits which the art personifies. These spirits are the founding ancestors of the community, on whose good-will the group depends for its spiritual and material prosperity. The power to control these spirits rests with the members who form the religious hierarchy of the Society.

The officials in the hierarchy of the Society can be stratified according to their importance in the Society. For the purpose of this analysis, three grades will be described with the highest grade – the *Majo* – as the seat of power. The *Majo* is comparable to the president of a large professional institution in status and is regarded with considerable awe and respect by men and women. In the same grade are the *Sowei* or *Sowa;* these are the people who are responsible for teaching the initiates the Mende traditional ways of life, as well as preparing them for future "careers" as mothers and housewives.

Next in grade are the *Ligba* (sometimes referred to as *Ligba-wa* and *Ligba-wo*, that is the high *Ligba* and the low *Ligba*. They are charged with the sacred duty of initiating the girls. The professional dancers are called *Ndoli mo* and are women who have acquired professional competence in dancing. The masked dancer who entertains the public is called *Sowei Ndoli mo;* less important is the clown dancer called *Gonde*.

In the third grade are the *Klawa* who act as counsellors for the initiates. The *Klawa* are very responsible persons who act as a liaison between the *Majo* and the initiates, as well as between the *Sande* and the parents of the initiates. In the western sense of the word, they are "public relations women."

In *Sande*, the *Sowei*, and *Ligba* are charged with the responsibility of providing protection and social security for other members of the Society. For instance, men who molest *Sande* girls or infringe *Sande* rules are arrested by the *Sowei* and tried before a local chief. In such situations, the *Sowei* wears a mask, and attended by a few *Ligbanga* (plural of *Ligba*), escorts the accused to the chief where the judgement is given.

When the *Sowei* wears the mask of the *Sande*, she personalises the spirit or protector of the Society, and no man has been known to ignore her command or wishes. Even heavy fines levelled on accused persons have always been promptly paid. By subjecting men to its rules, the *Sande* guarantees the maintainance of some sort of respect for the rites and activities of the Society.

The Need for Education

Another distinctive feature of *Sande* was the planning of the educational curriculum for the members within the community it serves. The fact that Mende children had to transmit to future generations the philosophies and myths of the group, the creation of secret societies became a community obligation. In *Sande*, women can work together to perpetuate and revitalise knowledge, skills and values essential for the welfare of the community.

The *Sande* disseminates information on spinning, weaving, fishing, net making, house and mother craft. The education programme covers all aspects

of their culture which will in future help the initiate to mature into adulthood
equipped with skills and social sentiments which membership of the Mende
community entails. Today this training, as M. A. S. Margai (1948) suggested,
has been expanded to include simple anatomy, nursing, physiology, sanitation
and first-aid as well as a wide variety of domestic science subjects. Also in the
Sande the girls are taught the medicinal use of herbs in addition to dancing and
learning to sing Mende songs.

In the *Sande*, drama, songs and dances combine to create the most melodra-
matic manifestation of Mende culture. In these festive rites, philosophical doctrines can be expounded to the initiates. They learn from songs and dances what
cannot be transcribed in literature. Their meaning may appear obscure to an
outsider, but for them each movement in the dance or stanza in the song
conveys certain ideas readily understood by the initiates. Before the acquisition
of the art of writing, these plays, dances and songs were the only effective method
of recording and transmitting facts about sacred history of the Mende community. Even today, this educational function of the *Sande* forms an integral
part of the Society's curriculum and all initiates are taught the secrets of ex-
tracting significance and meaning from such rites.

In non-literate societies, it is only natural that art should have an educational function, the traces of which are still discernible among certain African
ethnic groups. In Africa, demands for education through secret societies and
art are culturally variable, and the variability has three poles. First, art provides an easy means of non-verbal communication, as with the Woyo proverb
pot lids in Cabinda. Second, art records vital historical information, as in the
Benin plaques or the rock paintings and engravings at Tassili and Ahaggar.
Third, it develops the entrancing mysteries of the invisible world, as *Sande*
masks manifest, or enshrines the folk lore and folk ways of the group, as in the
Ashanti gold weights.

A good example of the use of art as a means of communication is the
sculpted Woyo pot lids in Cabinda. They are invested with a variety of de-
cipherable messages calculated to convey a wife's grievances to her husband
and thus minimize the risks of unhealthy arguments. In such communities, men
are the recipients of the awe and respect traditional African marriages guarantee. For instance, when there is a disagreement in the family, the wife is not
supposed to talk back. Such an attitude by no means implies inequality between the sexes, rather it limits the possibilities of arguments. In Cabinda,
when a woman's rights are infringed by her husband, she buys the appropriate
pot lid, and covers her husband's food with it when he is entertaining his
friends who will eventually intercede on her behalf and *call the palaver*. These
pot lids convey a pictorial message and so act as a communication device.
Against this mode of representation, are the ancient bronze plaques of Benin
in which art was used to record important historical events.

A striking demonstration of art as a language of spiritual expression is
found in *Sande* masks. These masks are representations of spiritual and mythological symbols translated into wood and designed to express a spiritual message so complete that future generations can do no more than learn from its
mysteries. In fact, *Sande* art forms represent sacred traditions drawn from many
levels of time and human consciousness. More than that, these art forms transmit to future generations the myths and mysteries of the sacred world, and are

calculated to awaken feelings of respect for traditional order. In this connection, it is therefore necessary to impose some limitations on their composition and execution, for change in the art forms will involve change in the myths and spiritual symbolism that inspired their creation.

REFERENCES

ALLDRIDGE, Thomas J.
    1901   *The Sherbro and its Hinterland*, MacMillan, London.
CAINE, Augustus
    1959   *A Study and Comparison of the West African "Bush" School and the Southern Lesotho Circumcision School.* An unpublished N.U. Thesis.
LITTLE, Kenneth L.
    1967   *The Mende of Sierra Leone: A West African People in Transition.* Rev. ed. London, Rouledge and K. Paul, New York, Humanities Press.
MARGAI, M. A. S.
    1948   "Welfare work in a Secret Society", *Journal of African Affairs*, vol. 47, no. 189.
MIGEOD, F. W. H.
    1908   *A View of Sierra Leone*, Brentano's, New York.
SAWYERR, Harry and HARRIS, W. T.
    1968   *The Springs of Mende Belief and Conduct*, Freetown, Sierra Leone Univeristy Press.
WARREN, Harold G.
    1919   "Secret Societies", *Sierra Leone Studies*, no. 3 in microfilm, Northwestern University Library.
WATKINS, M. H.
    1943   "The West African Bush School", *American Journal of Sociology*, vol. XIVIII, no. 6.

2. The Problem of Chinese Education in Malaysia* and Singapore

KEITH WATSON

Reading, United Kingdom

One of the most explosive issues in post independent Malaysia and Singapore has been that of Chinese education. Both countries now seem to have come to terms with the problem, on the surface at least. However it is possible that the delicate position could be completely undermined by subversive forces at any given time and I wish in this article to trace how the problem arose and how it has been dealt with in different ways by the two countries.

(a) *Early settlements: 16-19 Centuries*

According to Purcell (1966: 238 ff, 1956: 1) although Chinese traders went to Malacca from China during the Fifteenth Century, and although the King, Parameswara, paid homage to the Emperor of China in 1405 there were no real settlers, apart from a few temporary traders, until the arrival of the Por-

---

*   This refers to peninsula Malaya, now West Malaysia.

tuguese during the Sixteenth Century. In fact it was only through the help of a number of Chinese merchant junks that the Portuguese won so easily. By 1678 there was a small community of Chinese numbering 852 outside and 40 inside the fort of Malacca. By 1760 this settlement had increased to 3,989. Exactly one hundred years later, in 1860, the number had reached 10,039. It was, however, only after the hoisting of the British flag first in Penang and then in Singapore, that Chinese immigration to the Malay peninsula began in earnest. This has been outlined elsewhere (Purcell, Gungwu 1959) and I do not intend to repeat the story here. A word, however, should be mentioned about the early settlers.

Apart from merchants, artisans and traders and a number of soldiers who hoped to improve their lot overseas some of China's worst characters settled in Nanyang. Fighting between rival secret society gangs become an all too common picture. Singapore was in a state of lawlessness during the riots of 1831. Five hundred were killed in one week in fighting in 1851 and four hundred were killed in similar riots in 1854 (Purcell 1966: 249 ff). Taiping in Perak was founded and developed by Chinese rebels from the T'aiping Rebellion in China (1849–60) (Cheng 1949: 16). It was because of the lawlessness of the rival Chinese gangs that finally led to British intervention in the Malay states. Yet in establishing law and order the British authorities showed scant interest in the social framework or educational development of this large minority group. Admittedly a Chinese "protectorate" was established in 1877 but no officer with a knowledge of Chinese was appointed to the Education Department until 1917. As a result trouble was stored up for the future.

(b) *The Development of Chinese Education during the Nineteenth Century*

Because of the differences in religious outlook and in attitudes towards eating pork and because so many of the Chinese communities were all-male there was little intermarriage and assimilation as in Siam. The Chinese community kept itself apart from the Malays. There would have been little mixing of the children. The majority of children would have had no schooling, but a number would have had a traditional Chinese education (Purcell 1936) and would have attended what Skinner called "Chinese writing schools" (Skinner 1957: 135). Still others would have attended classes provided by missionaries in the mission and Free Schools. However, influenced by what they had seen of English medium education and in view of the indifference of the British authorities

> "who could see no reason why the Government of these States should educate children to make them suitable citizens for China and Southern India, apart from what services they may be able to render here as Chinese or Tamil interpreters" (Ann. 1898: 5–6)

certain prominent Chinese businessmen decided to establish their own private schools.

In 1885 the Anglo-Chinese Free School in Singapore was opened by Mr Gan Eng Song (Chelliah 1947: 96) to provide a free English education for children of poor Chinese parents: in 1886 the American Methodist Mission opened another Anglo-Chinese school; and in the same year Mr Lee Cheng Yan founded the Hung Choo Free School (Siang 1923: 292), a Chinese medium school run on English lines. In 1891 the Singapore Chinese Educational Institute was opened. For over ten years it offered evening classes at the Raffles Institute in English history and literature, Chinese history and literature, mathematics and shorthand (Siang 1923: 256–8). Mr Gan Eng Song opened yet another school in 1893. It was to be bi-lingual and when opening it Sir Cecil Clementi Smith, the Governor, commented that

> "...The school might be devoted to the study of English, but I am glad to know that a knowledge of Chinese will also be gained here, which to me appears an essential part of the education of a Chinese boy..." (Doraisamy 1969: 83–4)

Unfortunately the school failed and became a purely English medium school.

These few schools were merely the beginning of a renewed interest in education amongst the Chinese. The real impetus for the development and modernization of Chinese education gathered momentum during the late 1890s and after the turn of the century as a result of the reform movement and changes taking place within China proper (Purcell 1936). Between 1900 and 1919 at least twenty important Chinese schools were opened by pioneers like Dr Lim Boon Keng or Mr Seng Ong Siang (1923: 126–130) and by members of different language and clan associations. The most famous of them were Ch'ung-cheng (1905), Yang-cheng (1905), Yin-hsiu (1906), Ch'i-fa (1906), Ai-t'ung (1912), Kwang-fu (1916), Hsiu-ya (1918), Kwang-yang (1918) and Kung Shang (1920). The first girls' school opened in 1911. By 1918 there were 39 Chinese primary schools and their numbers steadily increased to 205 by 1928 and 329 by 1938.

This growing interest in education amongst the Chinese coincided with increasing nationalism, especially in the years preceding and following the 1911 revolution. In the years before the revolution rival schools were established by groups loyal to the Chinese Royalists and by groups loyal to the Chinese Nationalists; in the years following the revolution schools became increasingly nationalist and during the 1930s, communist. The schools were modelled along Japanese and Western lines.

> "A blend of traditional cultural chauvinism and modern nationalism directed their entire teaching process towards creating a highly charged atmosphere of youthful militancy." (van der Kroef 1964: 97)

Their curriculum was identical with that in the mainland schools. There was a strong emphasis on creating a military spirit, with drilling, uniform and the singing of patriotic songs. Schools were guided by the Three Principles of Sun-Yat Sen, nationalism, democracy, livelihood – which, when translated into educational terms, meant industrial training, military training and "training for democracy". Industrial training was reflected in the introduction of arts and craftwork and commercial studies into the curriculum, military training by the drilling previously mentioned and "training for democracy" was little more than the inculcation of propaganda and political thought. The latter was better taught in the night schools that began to spring up at this time.

The government chose to ignore these developments, at least in their early stages, and it is therefore all the more to the credit of the local Chinese that they provided and staffed these schools entirely from their own funds and private resources. Cheeseman, writing in 1931, had this to say of them:

> "The interest of the Chinese in education is proverbial. Their record in Malaya does them the greatest credit... In almost every village, even in the remotest districts, there is a Chinese school to be found, usually entirely financed by locally collected funds, to which it is not uncommon for every member of the community to be a willing and regular contributor." (Cheeseman 1931: 40)

Enthusiasm, however, did not necessarily imply quality, and the Director of Education, Singapore, wrote in the Annual Report of 1917 that Chinese schools were poorly staffed and equipped, that they seemed to take a greater interest in military exercises than in learning and that they were generally controlled by the Chinese government with scant regard for any local authority.

But the period of laissez-faire on the part of the British authorities was rapidly ending. Two developments finally brought about government intervention and both of them had their roots in intense Chinese nationalism. The first was the beginning of the National Language Movement in 1917 and the decision to adopt Kuo Yu (Mandarin) as the medium of instruction in all Chinese schools. It became apparent all too soon, that with the development of Kuo Yu as the medium of instruction, Chinese schools

> "were becoming instruments of propaganda for political parties outside Malaya whose objectives were often entirely opposed to the policy of the Malayan governments or their Education Departments. Quite apart from the use of education for out and out subversiveness, it was clear that the governments could not leave uncontrolled the system of education turning out boys and girls who were to all intents and purposes members of a foreign state, owing no duty to the country they lived in; the teachers were nearly all China born, recent arrivals in Malaya and often of extremist views." (Purcell 1966: 229)

With the rapid increase in the number of Chinese schools such a situation could not be ignored.

The second development was the serious rioting of 1919 following the Treaty of Versailles. The Chinese felt bitter that the Japanese had been granted rights over the former German possessions in Shantung province and instead of celebrating the Allied victory they turned to expressing their views in rioting and civil disturbance: the government, decidedly alarmed, decided to intervene.

(c) *The Period of Conflict – 1920–41*

Government intervention was in the form of the School Regulation Ordinance (1920), which was justified on political, educational and welfare grounds, though there seems little doubt that the main motive was political, for in the preamble to the ordinance it was said that

> "the teaching (in the schools) shall be not of such kind that is against the interests of the government of the colony."

The Ordinance aimed at controlling the schools through registration both of the schools and their managers and of the teachers; through the enforcement of regulations regarding the conduct of the schools; and through powers to close the schools if they were found to be teaching revolutionary matter.

As in Siam there were loud protests and petitions were drawn up to prevent the ordinance from becoming law. Nevertheless by 1921 91 schools and 254 teachers had agreed to register. Several more schools decided to register after 1923 when, in return for the right of inspection, the government agreed to pay grants-in-aid to Chinese schools at the rate of $10 per head. But that the government expected a greater response is clear from the Annual Report for Education, 1926 for the Director of Education complained that

> "no applications for grants were refused, but Chinese schools in the Straits Settlements have not, generally speaking, shown any desire to seek government assistance or submit to the slight measure of control involved by the acceptance of a grant." (Ann. 1926)

Chinese suspicion was understandable. In Old China schooling was largely a private matter and all government interference was suspect. In Malaya the Chinese had hitherto been left to provide their own schooling and to suddenly be told that the government was going to take an interest came as a shock. Inevitably therefore they sought ways and means of evading the law, though as soon as loopholes were found the law was amended to righten the restrictions. Thus amendments were made in 1925, 1926, 1929, 1932, 1937 and 1938.

In addition to the old traditional type of school, of which there were 120 (with 2539 pupils) in 1931 and 158 (with 4646 pupils) in 1938 (Purcell 1966: 278), three main types of Chinese school developed in Malaya: schools run by committees of district or surname associations or groups of Chinese families; pseudo-public schools organized by one or more teachers who selected their own "committee members" – (eg shopkeepers); and private schools run purely as a commercial proposition. According to Purcell the traditional and private schools had to be seen to be believed.

> "Most of them were dirty, ill-ventilated, and ill-lighted basements, outhouses, or attics: sanitation was non-existent; skin diseases were common among the pupils: the hubbub of pupils 'backing' their lessons was deafening to any European who came within range." (1966: 278)

In spite of the restrictions imposed by registration Chinese education both progressed and apparently improved.

> "Imposing school buildings, many with well-equipped laboratories and libraries, sprang up everywhere; teachers were trained, and textbooks were modernized. This progress must be accounted for partly by the strength of the system itself, partly by the lead which the 'mother country' (China) provided during these crucial years." (Doraisamy 1969: 87)

The Chinese government established a Bureau of Education (Ta-Hsueh Yuan) in June 1927. An Overseas Education Commission with special responsibility for the education of overseas Chinese, was made a part of it. In January 1928 this commission demanded the registration of all overseas Chinese schools. When in February 1928 the Commission was absorbed into the Overseas Affairs Bureau of the Chinese Ministry of Foreign Affairs, it meant that Chinese schools were placed in a considerable dilemma. On the one hand they were expected to obey the Chinese government and teach according to the Chinese syllabus based on Sun-Yat Sen's Three Principles, on the other they were expected to register with the local government in Malaya, and obey its regulations.

Nevertheless in spite of these difficulties the number of Chinese schools rose dramatically during the 1920s and 1930s and by 1938 there were 49,271 enrolled in Chinese schools in the Straits Settlements and the Federated Malay States. Of these 28,411 were enrolled in Chinese schools in the Straits Settlements, especially in Singapore, as opposed to 10,591 Chinese enrolled in English medium schools (see Table 1). In the Federated Malay States on the other hand more Chinese were enrolled in English schools (26,974) than in Chinese schools (20,860).

Table 1*

Year	Enrolments in Chinese Medium Schools		
	No of Chinese Schools	No of Pupils	No of Chinese at Govt & Aided Schools
1918	39	c 1950	6288
1928	205	14321	8194
1938	329	28411	10591

*   Ann. Education Reports (Straits Settlements).

The British authorities were not in principle opposed to either the KMT or to Chinese nationalism but having ignored the development of Chinese education for so long they suddenly found themselves confronted, during the 1920s and 1930s, with a variety of problems which were as threatening to their rule as they were unexpected.

The realization that Chinese schools were generally inferior to English ones in construction, instruction and sanitation was probably not unexpected. It was this however that led to offers of grants-in-aid, which although not readily accepted at first, came to be more readily sought after the 1930–32 economic depression. By 1938 $341,369 was being paid in grants to Chinese schools.

But the realization that the schools, and the Hailam night schools in particular were little more than centres for communist and nationalist propaganda[1] that the textbooks were decidedly anti-British in tone; and that with the controlling influence of the Nationalist Chinese Government over Chinese education in Malaya, many Chinese would grow up imbued with a spirit of Chinese nationalism, viewing China and not Malaya as their home, led the British authorities to take drastic action.

Textbooks for use in Chinese schools in Malaya were generally either printed at the Commercial Press or the Chung Hua Press, both in Shanghai. From 1925 a great deal of anti-foreign, and especially anti-British, material was introduced trying to portray the British as brutal imperialist oppressors. The government therefore took the only action feasible. It banned the importation of textbooks and appointed two firms in Singapore to produce a series free from sedi-

---

1   According to Purcell ("The Chinese in South East Asia" op. cit. p. 337) "Some schools were not educational institutions at all, merely centres of Communist propaganda, especially the Hailam night schools for adults where Marx, Lenin, Engels and other Communist authors were studied by pupils who had not enough general education to understand anything except the message of opposition to the local government."

tious material. Unfortunately the new books still took China, and not Malaya, as their model for references.

The fact that the Chinese government regarded the overseas Chinese as its citizens, sent inspectors to look at the schools and even offered grants-in-aid, was also viewed with serious misgivings, especially at a time when thoughts were being turned towards creating a sense of national unity. It was felt that if such a situation persisted the chances of racial harmony would be greatly weakened.

Accordingly in 1929 the new Governor, Sir Cecil Clementi, banned the KMT in Malaya. This decision struck at the very roots of Chinese propaganda since it affected all those schools that had registered with the Chinese government. Instead of being controlled by the Chinese government and following a syllabus based on the Three Principles, these schools now had to follow a syllabus laid down by the British Education authorities and had to accept inspection. The Chinese government protested strongly, but to no avail.

The policy of control was not entirely successful since when the Sino-Japanese war broke out in 1937, the Chinese in Malaya responded magnificently in raising money for a relief fund for the mother country. Nevertheless more and more schools sought financial aid from the government and became aided schools, subject to the same control as the English aided schools.

During the Japanese occupation the Chinese suffered terribly for their anti-Japanese stance. Some of their schools were forced to stay open and were expected to teach Japanese. At first only 4 hours and later only 2 hours of Chinese were allowed to be taught each weak. The majority of Chinese opted not to go to school.

(d) *Post War Developments (1946–70)*

With a return to more peaceful conditions, following the war and a re-examination of education policy in both Malaya and Singapore, Chinese schools began to spring up rapidly, though recognition of their equality with other language medium schools in the system meant that the majority became aided schools rather than private ones. In Malaya 139,191 were enrolled in Chinese primary schools by 1947. By the time of independence in 1956 this figure had reached 250,692. Chinese secondary schools likewise made rapid progress. There had only been a few before the war and enrolments were just over 3000 (3215) in 1938. Because of the war by 1947 enrolments were only 2692. But then followed a decade of expansion and by 1957 30,052 were enrolled in Chinese Middle Schools. Only a comparatively small number, 5426, were enrolled in private secondary schools. The British authorities sought to encourage Chinese schools, particularly in the New Villages, as it was felt that Chinese children would thus be prevented from cooperating with the Communists. Yet because funds still came from predominantly private sources many schools did become centres of Chinese Communist propaganda (Franke 1965: 182).

Although the government paid lip-service to recognising the different language medium schools it became apparent from a fairly early stage that they hoped to absorb Chinese education increasingly into the state system. The Barnes Committee (Report of the Committee on Malay Education 1951) that was set up to look into Malayan education in 1950 was both by its tone and its constitution strongly biassed against the Chinese. By proposing the creation of a bilingual primary school and the gradual abolition of non-Malay schools the Chinese rightly felt that there was an attack on their own hard won educational achievements. In their reply to the Barnes proposals (the Fenn-Wu report) the Chinese rightly attacked British indifference to their plight and determined that Chinese schools

> "cannot be eliminated until the Chinese themselves decide that they are not needed, which will happen only if and when there is an adequate and satisfactory alternative." (1951: 10)

The thinking behind the Barnes Report – the ultimate suppression of Chinese education because of its threat to Malayan unity – has influenced future thinking in Malaya. Although in post-independent Malaya, as a result of the Razak Report's recommendations, Chinese primary schools have been given equal ranking status with other schools, at secondary they level have been forced to become either National-type schools with Malay or English as the medium of instruction and Chinese reduced to a subject only, or to become independent. Many of them have opted for the latter. As Franke says:

> "Due to the drastic restriction of Chinese as a teaching medium quite a number of private Chinese secondary schools – among them some of the best and largest in Malaya – have declined government assistance and so far retained their independent status." (1965: 185)

However this independence poses still other problems, for the public examinations are held only in English and Malay, and those Chinese who have doggedly pursued a Chinese education find themselves at a disadvantage in face of those who have opted for English or Malay secondary education: they frequently fail their examinations. Moreover Chinese diplomas are not recognised, so that if a Chinese student wishes to continue his education at tertiary level he must either become proficient in Malay (or English) or go elsewhere – to Taiwan or Singapore. Until 1969 degrees from Singapore (Nanyang University) were not recognised: from Taiwan they are still not recognised.

Such discrimination ruthlessly pursued in the name of Malayan nationalism causes resentment, bitterness and frustration. When linked with job discrimination, especially in government posts, in favour of Malays, frustration runs even deeper. Many Chinese still feel rootless and though they have a strong economic hold on the country, should their economic position be also threatened they might become more rebellious. The government can point to the fact that their policy is seemingly working. Enrolments in private Chinese secondary schools have begun to decline. Enrolments in private Chinese primary schools have declined dramatically since 1961, when Chinese medium secondary schools ceased to exist. Enrolments in assisted Chinese medium schools have also begun to fall as a percentage – from 31.8% in 1956 to 27.0% in 1967 – of total enrolments. Yet beneath the surface there is still simmering resentment. This occasionally flares up in racial rioting. It is potentially an explosive situation. Unfortunately

> "the identification of Chinese education with political extremism ... leads to a certain reluctance on the side of responsible educators to make in public suggestions in favour of Chinese education." (Franke 1965: 190)

The situation in Singapore has been both different and potentially more dangerous, yet the solutions worked out have apparently been extremely successful.

In the years following the war Chinese schools sprang up rapidly. By 1946 there were already 66 open and by 1953 81,000 of the 163,000 enrolments were in Chinese schools. The government deliberately fostered English education as a means of discouraging Chinese education which they feared was becoming increasingly subversive, but they were quite prepared to integrate Chinese schools into the state system on an aided basis provided that one third of the primary school curriculum, one half of the junior middle school curriculum and two-thirds of the senior middle school curriculum was in English. Many teachers feared they would lose their jobs and the communists succeeded in fomenting student unrest and strikes during 1953/54 and at periodic intervals thereafter. The chief organisers seemed to be the Chinese Middle Schools Students' Union.

The situation was sufficiently bad by 1955 that the government appointed an All-Party Legislative Committee on Chinese Education

> "to investigate the situation in Chinese schools in Singapore and to make recommendations for the improvement and strengthening of Chinese education in the interests of Chinese culture and orderly progress towards selfgovernment and ultimate independence." (Report 1956: 1)

Described as "by far the most important document on Chinese education in Singapore" (Doraisamy 1969: 93) the report traced the causes of Chinese discontent and felt that Chinese schools should not only be given equal treatment with all other schools but that they should be integrated, as aided schools, into the state system. Only by breaking down "the mutual exclusiveness between the two streams of education – English and vernacular", and only by creating amicable conditions for intermingling through bilingual or trilingual schools could a multi-racial society be created and "progress towards self-government and ultimate independence (be) achieved."

The report was accepted and when the White Paper and then the Education Ordinance of 1957 were published Chinese schools were for the first time given parity of treatment. Thenceforth the policy in Singapore has been to allow students to pursue their studies in Chinese from primary to tertiary level, provided they also learn English and Malay. By 1964 the majority of Chinese schools had become government aided and had accepted a more Malaysian approach in the textbooks. In that year there were only two private Chinese secondary schools and nine private Chinese primary schools left.

However it was not simply parity that helped ease the crisis in the schools. It was also the banning of the Chinese Middle Schools Students' Union as a political and disruptive force. The Report looking into the Union's activities summed up the situation as follows:

> "The integral place of the Chinese middle schools in the education system of Singapore is fully accepted. But the activities of this union are undermining the essential characteristics of Chinese education and are preventing the full contribution of the Chinese middle school to the development of a Singapore and Malayan loyalty. It has taken part in political activities and industrial disputes in a way which proves it has been used as a Communist front organization ... it has persistently ... combined with other Com-

munist front organizations to take part in demonstrations the purpose of which was political... The members of the union intimidated 'striking' children to flout the authority of their teachers, have organized 'protest' meetings on school premises, and have intimidated teachers and students who have refused to accept their nomination... The union has developed the Communist modelled system of study known as 'Hsueh-Hsih' and has transferred not only the method but also its content to the Singapore Chinese middle school." (1956: 19)

Only when the particularly vicious activities of this union had been brought under control was the hope of more peaceful development within the schools made possible.

One other running sore in Chinese education in both Malaya and Singapore has been that of tertiary education. Until 1953 the only provision at higher education level was in the medium of English, so that if Chinese students wished to continue their studies in Chinese they had to go overseas, either to China, Hong Kong or Taiwan. With the closing of Communist China to overseas students, pressures built up within Malaya – or rather Singapore – demanding higher education facilities in Chinese. Resentment that higher education was only available to those who had passed through English medium schools was exploited by the Communists.

"The whole question of the use of English and Chinese in school or out came to be inextricably interwoven with the emotionally charged demands of national pride and cultural identity in a British colonial setting." (van der Kroef 1964: 100)

In 1953 a group of enterprising Chinese businessmen decided to found a Chinese university, Nanyang, on a beautiful site at Jurong in Singapore (Buttwell 1953). It opened there in 1956. Unfortunately although the idea was good and the original founders acted from the highest motives all was not well. The first Chancellor, Am Lin Yutang was forced by the Communists to resign before the university officially opened. Students influenced by the Middle Schools Students' Union began to proceed to the university and in a very short time began to foment strikes, unrest and protest marches. The anxiety amongst the authorities was all too apparent and in an effort to get to the root cause of the trouble and reform the university various committees were established (Buttwell 1953). Gradually common sense and understanding prevailed, by 1969 the university and its degrees were recognised by the government, and higher education facilities were made readily, though not freely, available to those students who had pursued a Chinese medium education from primary level.

The differences in approach between Malaysia and Singapore towards Chinese education are interesting. Whereas the Malay government allows Chinese primary schools, it hopes that they will eventually disappear. To speed up this process it has banned all but private Chinese secondary schools since 1961. There is no tertiary outlet for specifically Chinese speaking students. Textbooks have a strong Malaysian bias and Chinese is merely a subject on the curriculum. It is hoped thereby to achieve not only assimilation of the Chinese into Malaysian society but also, through multi-racial secondary schools, to create a Malaysian society. The Singapore Government on the other hand has not only encouraged Chinese education at both primary and secondary level, it has also made grants to Nanyang University and provides Chinese medium education in other institutions of higher education, most notably Singapore Polytechnic. Although textbooks have a strong Malaysian bias and the Chinese are expected to learn English and Malay an atmosphere of toleration rather than suppression prevails. That in the past the Communists have exploited Chinese schools is true, but the chances of achieving a harmonious and multi-racial society in Singapore seem fraught with less dangers than in Malaysia.

REFERENCES

1898   Annual Education Reports.
1926   Annual Report of Education Straits Settlements.
BUTWELL, R. A.
    1953   "A Chinese University for Malaya". Pacific Affairs 26, 3.
CHEESEMAN, H. R.
    1931   Compulsory Education in Malaya. Overseas Education.
CHELLIAH, D. D.
    1947   A Short History of the Educational Policy of the Straits Settlements. 1800–1925 circa. Singapore: Government Press.
CHENG, T. D.
    1949   "The Education of Overseas Chinese: A Comparative Study of Hong Kong, Singapore and the East Indies". unpublished MA Thesis, University of London.
DORAISAMY, T. R. (ed.)
    1969   150 Years of Education in Singapore. Singapore: TTC Publications.
FRANKE, W.
    1965   "Problems of Chinese Education in Singapore and Malaya". Malaysian Journal of Education II (December).
PURCELL, V.
    1966   "The Chinese in Malaya and Singapore" in The Chinese in South East Asia. Oxford: Oxford University Press.
    1956   The Chinese in Modern Malaya. Singapore: Donald Moore.
PURCELL, V. and WANG GUNGWU
    1959   A Short History of the Nanyang Chinese. Singapore: Eastern Universities Press Ltd.
PURCELL, V.
    1936   Problems of Chinese Education. London: Kegan Paul, Trench, Trubner.
    1951   Report of a Mission invited by the Federation Government to study the problem of the Education of Chinese in Malaya (Fenn-Wu Report). Kuala Lumpar.
    1951   Report of the Committee of Malay Education. Kuala Lumpar.
SONG ONG SIANG
    1923   One Hundred Years of History of the Chinese in Singapore. London: John Murray.
Government of Singapore
    1956   Singapore Chinese Middle Schools Students's Union. Singapore.
SKINNER, G. W.
    1957   Chinese Society in Thailand: An Analytical History. Ithaca: Cornell University Press.
VAN DER KROEF, J. M.
    1964   "Nanyang University and the Dilemmas of Overseas Chinese Education". China Quarterly 20 (October–December).

BOOK REVIEWS

A. Fukiau, *N'Kongo ye nza yakun'zungidila* (Le Mukongo et le monde qui l'entourait: Cosmogonie-Kongo). In KiKongo with French translation by C. Zamenga and an introduction by J. M. Janzen. Kinshasa, Office Nationale de la Recherche et du Développement, Recherches et Synthèses No. 1, 1969, 179pp., fig. 56, 175K, $ 3.50.

André Fukiau is an unusual young man. Most of his contemporaries with similar education have eagerly taken up bureaucratic jobs in town but Fukiau has returned to his home village to found a secondary school devoted to Kongo culture, agricultural techniques, and African studies, with an emphasis on African languages. As he himself has repeatedly written, to make progress the Congolese must first take stock of their ancestral heritage, which is systematically neglected in the nation's educational system in favor of European values and ideologies. A Congolese intellectual who wants to write analytically about his ancestral culture is burdened by the double handicap of the heritage of colonial condescension, which constrains him to write primarily to justify rather than to analyse, and the difficulty of translating metaphysical concepts into foreign languages. Conscious of these burdens, Fukiau has chosen to address himself to his fellow countrymen in KiKongo. In the second half of the book Fukiau's text is translated into French by C. Zamenga, who comes, like the author, from the Manianga region of the Lower Congo. Much of the ethnographic detail presented is peculiar to Manianga, but the significance of the work as a whole transcends the local perspective.

Fukiau takes as his starting point Kongo cosmogony, a subject the ethnographers have not seriously investigated. In the beginning the androgynous creature Mahungu circled the palm tree of God and found himself divided into two, male and female; unable to reconstitute the original unity, the two reconciled themselves by inventing marriage. This story enables Fukiau to establish the dominant theme of Kongo religion, wholeness achieved by the union of opposites. The descendants of Mahungu, according to legend, were decimated, divided, and scattered by a flood, a famine and the loss of the sword of chiefship, the source of order. The flood remains in the form of the mythical river Nzadi, sometimes identified with the Congo River. The focus of ritual and political endeavor is to restore harmony in the universe and reconcile the two worlds now separated by Nzadi.

In ritual the principal symbols of the divided universe are crosses, water, and the colors white, black and red, of which white is the color of the other world (*ku mpemba*) and red the color of mediators between the worlds (*min'kambakani*). Fukiau explores the function of mediation in the Manianga cult of Lemba, of which he gives by far the most detailed account yet published, based on extensive research. Lemba died out under the impact of the colonial government and the Kimbanguist prophetic movement (*kingunza*) to which Fukiau devotes the next chapter. Shorter chapters on rites of reconciliation (*bindokila*) and the limitations of human action constitute the real conclusion of the work, although there is another short (and unsatisfactory) chapter on totems and a final poem on the nationalist theme, "Africa my country, awake, turn again to our ancestors."

The rich detail in Fukiau's accounts of rituals undoubtedly make this the most valuable contribution to our knowledge of Kongo religion since Van Wing's *Etudes Bakongo: Religion et Magie* (1938). In addition, the book provides a key to a general understanding of the religion such as ethnographers have never been able to find, their resolute empiricism having concealed from them the formal system of abstractions that Fukiau reveals. This is nevertheless a difficult book to use. The author is not at all scrupulous about confounding personal interpretations with traditional wisdom; at the beginning of the book, in particular, the reader is asked to accept a mixture of fanciful etymology and dubious history ambiguously derived from published and unpublished versions of tradition. Fukiau has read much of the existing ethnography in French, and occasionally reveals his debt to the anthropologist John M. Janzen, who writes the introduction. His study, therefore, is no naive report of folk beliefs, nor is it a scholar's detached appraisal. It is in some ways the highly personal document of a young Congolese who feels called to rediscover and reaffirm the pattern of thought that his ancestors followed and which continues to govern the thinking of most BaKongo.

The translator has done well by an extremely difficult text. Fukiau makes a point of stretching the vocabulary and structure of KiKongo to show that it is itself a fit vehicle for a treatise in social science, thus reversing the prevailing tendency among educated BaKongo to make French the language of intellectual discourse. The translation is not literal and is no substitute for the original. Janzen's introduction ably summarises the argument of the work and its significance for the study of Kongo culture. Fukiau's study is nominally the first of a series which will be a valuable one if its successors maintain this standard.

Haverford College
Haverford, U.S.A.

Wyatt MacGaffey

N. Mansergh, *The Commonwealth Experience.* New York, Frederick A. Praeger, 1969, 471 pp., $ 12.50.

In this important study, Professor Mansergh directs attention to a familiar story: "the historical process which had affected the lives of millions and which had culminated in the national freedom and association in partnership... of the majority of peoples whose destinies were formerly determined by the greatest of European empires" (p. 413). It was a complex process producing, as the author's careful phrases suggest, a limited achievement, and it is analysed here with skill and precision.

The first section of the book, "the Foundation Members and the Nature of Their Association," with emphasis upon Canada reviews the origins of the Commonwealth in the colonies of settlement. In the second, covering the period, 1914–1947, emphasis is placed on the impact of war which both excited national aspirations and defined the limits of cooperation and association. His analysis of the pivotal place of the Dominion settlement in Ireland in the wider context of Imperial history is a special strength of this section. The latter part of the book which considers the devolution of power in the dependent empire and more especially in India after 1945 is in some respects the least satisfactory. To suggest, for example, that London yielded possessions in Africa because of the persuasiveness of Asian anti-colonialism (an assertion which Professor Mansergh seems to deny and then to affirm, p. 349) requires more discussion than is given to it. African independence movements, while certainly owing a great deal to outside sources, had their own unique roots, reaching back to the earliest days of colonial rule and before. Consideration of the post-independence relationship with the former rulers was similarly a matter which had exercised political leaders in British Africa well before the 1950's.

At every stage, the author stresses the fragility of the Commonwealth. "Liberal" histories (a reference to an earlier generation of textbooks), he argues, have misinterpreted its development by suggesting that self-government grew easily and even inevitably within a framework of association. "...The question is rarely, if ever, asked whether it was not more important that Joseph Chamberlain should have 'killed' Home Rule than that Gladstone should have proposed it" (p. 7). Professor Mansergh is himself far from repudiating the progressive view of Commonwealth history, but he is very properly concerned as well with those who had "other designs and other visions." Neither the particular visions of Cecil Rhodes nor Eamon de Valera have received the attention they deserve in the textbooks. At the least such men stand out as the "catalysts of change", as individuals who forced statesmen to a reassessment of the direction of policy.

Of those who, by their vision or their policies, contributed more directly to the achievement of "national freedom and association in partnership", the author singles out three for special consideration: Mackenzie King, ever vigilant to the machination of Empire; Smuts, who saw acutely that dominion aspirations, generated in war, would have to be recognised and who had, by 1921, suggested a formula; and Nehru, the statesman most attuned to the crises which overtook the twentieth century empire. Of the three it is Nehru who emerges as *the* "Man of the Commonwealth". As the "architect of its Asian membership", he was "the very archetypal figure of those later days" (pp. 18–19). These are not choices, evidently, which will satisfy all of his readers. His selection does, however, complement the main theme of the book, and underline his contention that, in the development of the Commonwealth, the decisive initiatives came more often from the periphery than from the centre.

Professor Mansergh has produced a valuable study, cognisant of recent scholarship, illuminated, particularly in constitutional matters, by a comparative approach and suggestive in its interpretations. There is a useful bibliographical essay, although the lists of national and regional histories appended to the essay are highly selective and less useful. A large number of well-chosen illustrations are included. It is to be hoped that this volume will stimulate analogous studies of other aspects of Commonwealth History (race relations, for example), the want of which constitutes a serious gap in its historiography.

Queen's University   A. H. JEEVES
Kingston, Canada

Sandra Wallman, *Take Out Hunger: Two Case Studies of Rural Development in Basutoland.* London, The Athlone Press, University of London, 1969, ix + 178 pp. No price given.

Economics, politics and communication are fundamentally related to the success or failure of planned change. This is no more or less true in Basutoland than elsewhere. The disturbing aspect of the two case studies presented in this book – a land reclamation scheme and a tractor-hire service – is that in spite of reasonably good preparation and planning, serious problems arose as the projects moved from the drawing board to the field.

In Chapter 2 the author provides a good description of the political structure of Basutoland as it existed in 1964 – a trinity comprised of the chieftainship, the British and the elected politicians, in which "...no one is finally responsible for anything; ...each sector can blame the other if something goes wrong; ...more time is spent in trying to decide who should do something than in actually doing it; and... politics... are characterized by an atmosphere of perpetual, if sometimes veiled, mistrust."

Chapter 3 discusses the village economy of Basutoland in substantial detail, including household surveys, and adds to the swelling body of evidence that African farmers are rational, economic men. Migration of village males to South Africa for wage employment has adversely affected traditional village life and raises fundamental questions as to the effect of large-scale labor migration on social welfare when externalities are introduced for consideration.

Chapters 4 and 5 discuss the land reclamation scheme in Taung Ward (1958–1961) and the tractor-hire scheme in Mafeteng district (1961–1964) respectively. Both are essentially analyses of failures. The subsequent apparent success of the tractor-hire scheme is more or less attributed to the ability of the project manager to transcend those elements of failure which the author infers were inherent in the political framework at that time.

While considering a myriad of political, social and economic factors the book fails to convey a sense of the relative importance of the respective variables involved in the failure of the two schemes. For example, inadequate attention was given to alternative income opportunities facing farmers displaced by the Taung reclamation scheme or to the risk of livestock thefts embodied in pasturing them further from home. A quantitative analysis of the factors involved might have indicated that economic factors were mainly responsible for the failure of the scheme. From the statements of farmers quoted by the author, I suspect this was, in fact, the case.

Similar questions arise with respect to the tractor-hire scheme. A reasonable hypothesis would be that the previous failure of a similar scheme had in fact resulted in a negative reaction by the farmers, only to be overcome by demonstrated success. Whether this was in fact the case or whether other political and communication factors were more important must remain unanswered.

Explaining rural change or the lack of it in terms of dominant influences is not inconsistent with an integrated interdisciplinary approach to the subject. Indeed, whether one interprets a demonstration effect as a communication process or an economic process via risk reduction may as often as not be a question of semantics. Yet I cannot help but feel that cumbersome administrative machinery out of touch with rural life is any more relevant in Basutoland than elsewhere in Africa. It is unfortunate indeed that data for the study were not more systematically gathered so as to admit of statistical analysis. For while the author is to be commended for her perceptive insights and her comprehensive approach, she can be faulted for failing to give the reader a grasp of the relative importance of the many factors considered in her study.

Michigan State University   THOMAS ZALLA
East Lansing, U.S.A.

D. Parkin, *Neighbours and National in an African City Ward*. Berkeley and Los Angeles, University of California Press, 1969, 228 pp., tables, maps, figures and plates.

Some will say this book about Kenyans in Kampala, Uganda, is a great book, outstanding history; some will say it is only a good book, fair anthropology. Depending on the reader's interest, either view is justifiable.

From its beginnings around the old capital of the Bugunda kingdom, the whole Kampala-Mengo agglomeration has developed into a commercial, administrative, and communications center for the modern country of Uganda, much larger than the old kingdom alone. Mengo has been inhabited largely by Ganda, the "Host" people; Kampala largely by Europeans, Asians, and other non-Ganda "Migrants". Kampala-East, the city ward which is the locus for this book, has a heavy concentration of Africans migrant from Kenya. These Luo and Luhya are the "neighbors and nationals" to which the title refers.

Although most of this book is a report on the lives of Luo, Parkin presents his data in terms of a general super-tribal cultural dichotomy between "Hosts" (Ganda and those people from politically centralized societies who are affiliated with them in Mengo, the Soga, Nyoro, Toro, Ankole, and Rwanda) and "Migrants" (foreigners from politically uncentralized lineage-based societies, the Luo, Luhya, Acholi, Lango, Lugbara, Kiga, Iru, Samia, Padole and Jonam). He argues that these broad cultural differences – expressed in town by "Migrants" in terms of tighter kinship control, stronger ideology of brother-hood, and less emancipation of women – coincide with modern political and economic cleavages. Thus, even if Kenya Migrants, who were dominant in Kampala East just prior to the independence of Uganda (1962), were all forced to return "home" to Kenya, their place in the general social scheme would be taken by other "Migrants" culturally like the Kenyans but from Uganda and therefore not disfranchised as were all Kenyans in 1963. "Very loosely, then, Kampala East is something of a microcosm of the city in the presumably future joint participation in its affairs by local and migrant tribes" (p. 11).

This potential relevance, the opportunity to deal with an important future-oriented problem, is lost as the book proceeds through detailed, well-docu-mented, cases of political, kinship, and association events that focus on Kenya "Migrants" in the process of retracting, instead of on Uganda "Migrants" who might be coming on. The book becomes more a history of the episode of Luo experience in Kampala than a scientific treatise examining general principles of urbanism and ethnicity.

It would be very exciting to investigate intensively that part of the Kenya

Migrants' (Luo, Luhya) experience that is relevant to the carrying on of the Migrant tradition (by Ugandans). Instead, Parkin puts much emphasis on that which seems unique to the Kenyans and their times and their circumstances. He is intrigued with how the Kenya Migrants adjust to disfranchisement, with how they maintain as much of their economic and social status as they could without displeasing those in power, and with how they keep prepared for eventual repatriation if necessary. There is nothing uninteresting in all this – in fact there is nothing uninteresting in the entire book – but the future-oriented question perplexes and is never resolved.

The city council housing estates in which Parkin made his observations, and participated to the extent that a European and non-resident could, are Nakawa and Naguru, fairly high in the residential status hierarchy of Kampala localities for non-Ganda. Differentiating between "locality" (the wider concept) and "neighborhood" (the narrower) he finds that both have status implications but that for the men, those attached to locality are most important while for the women, their wives, the implications of neighborhood are more important. "It is men who join associations, become leaders, send deputations to make claims to the housing authorities and take decisions about moving..." (p. 60). "Women tend to be much more restricted physically. Many of them spend on average only half of the year in town, returning home twice a year for periods of three months for digging and planting, and for harvesting. Only wives of the very high status have jobs, while most women have domestic and child-rearing chores around the house and so are limited physically to the immediate neighborhood..." (p. 60). "The policy of allocating houses according to economic status has the result that in any one neighborhood of from ten to twenty houses, there will be a general parity of economic status among householders" (p. 62). Successful men, "leaders", move up from neighborhood to neighborhood and from locality to locality.

Migrant men marry Migrant (not Host) women but not always women of their own tribe. These migrant marriages are generally sanctioned by the kinsmen of both parties. In fact, Parkin emphasizes the degree to which "Migrants share a highly complicated system of negative sanctions deriving from the tribal system" (p. 103). The ideology of brotherhood, that derives from rural kinship, is useful for political and economic and moral reasons in maintaining a wide and effective network of associates, "brothers" in an extended sense, around any one person in the city. All this is more true for Migrants, especially Luo, than it is for Hosts, especially Ganda.

So the Kenya Migrants, using a flexible ideology of brotherhood that helped maintain ties in Kampala, in other towns, and even in Kenya, developed a series of "tribal" associations (clan associations, location or subtribal associations, tribal unions) manifestly aiming at mutual aid, recreations, or political support, but latently helping to maintain a wide network of communication that served many purposes for Migrants both as neighbors and as nationals. This wide network made possible communication with the ultimate source of authority (in Kenya) which was an important factor enabling the Kenyans to be in a position to undertake a phase-out from Kampala without too much personal and social dislocation, if this became necessary" (p. 148).

In a concluding chapter, Parkin attempts several separable things. First he reviews the historical process he has been describing: the interaction of status grouping, ethnic distinction, and national affiliation in the special context of Uganda at the time of achieving independence.

"In summary, the whole process described is of tribal ties, ideology, and ceremony being used to express an acceptance of national political change while enabling the status system and certain common economic interests to continue relatively unaltered" (p. 182).

Secondly, he considers whether there is some generalization to be made concerning ethnic cultural differences and urbanization. After brief references to such considerations by others (Gluckman, Mitchell, Epstein, Banton, Fraenkel, and Little) he states what he calls a rough and obviously tautological distinction: "Other things being equal, societies among whom even nowadays much of rural social life is mediated through extended families or local descent groups, especially agnatic ones, tend to provide the best conditions for the existence of effective kin networks in town. Societies which generally lack these rural features and mediate many of their social relations through patron-client relationships, often of a non-kinship nature, allow for the existence of extensive urban kin networks which are not, however, so consistently effective for an ego and which are rarely mobilized over issues to do with family life at home" (pp. 185–186).

This reviewer is not so much concerned about the tautological quality of the statement as he is about the roughness of these distinctions couched in terms that imply precision. Here, Parkin contrasts "effective" with "extended" as if there is a distinction that is unidimensional and clear. The context in which Epstein (1961), Mayer (1966), and Boissevain (1968), use these terms, referring to different parts of the same egocentric network, made their meaning obvious. "Effective" has to do with accomplishment; "extended" has to do with scale. The two are not mutually exclusive, as Parkin elsewhere notes when he speaks of the advantages of the Migrants' wide system of relationships based on the flexible idea of brotherhood: "the network has to be both extended and effective for this system to work" (p. 146). If he believes these components are important Parkin should define them unambiguously.

The third consideration in the concluding chapter is the problem of urbanism: How can the urban whole be characterized? Parkin sees two orders in the urban system, each with its "structural" and "cultural" aspects:

"There are thus two 'structures': a first-order one of the widest level concerning the distribution of power, authority, and economic opportunity...; and a second-order one of the urban domestic life of individual ethnic groups...

"There are two 'cultural' systems: an ideology of kinship and traditional custom which emanates from urban domestic life but which becomes a diacritical and syncretic characteristic of individual ethnic groups and tribespeople in political and economic contexts; and a collection of notions centering on a common pursuit of prestige and status symbols, and reinforced by values set on 'non-tribalism' at neighborhood and national level" (p. 192).

In this attempt to characterize the urban system as a whole Parkin is close to a universally important conception relevant to all societies but most especially to those with multi-ethnic communities. But his own presentation of the complex is weakened, in this book, because he did not really study the second-order structure, the domestic domain, except as it is expressed in the extrinsic aspects of marriage. I hope he will give us, in another book, a more complete analysis in accord with this seminal interpretation of urbanism as a process at several levels.

University of Wisconsin   ALVIN W. WOLFE
Milwaukee, U.S.A.

W. H. Wriggins, *The Rulers Imperative: Strategies for Political Survival in Asia and Africa.* New York, Columbia University Press, 1969, 275 pp., $ 10.00.

Professor Wriggins proposes that "The challenge facing leaders in Asia and Africa is how to combine sufficient power to sustain continuity for a period permitting governmental effectiveness, while seeking means to permit those necessary elements of representation, openness to innovation and access to rising groups, without which sound and humane government in an era of rapid change cannot be established or sustained" (p. 263). His proposition would certainly be accepted by almost all the leaders of Africa and Asia; and perhaps by many in Europe and America! He sets out to examine the major tactics employed by a number of Asian and African leaders in composing their strategy. He divides these tactics into the uses of personality, organization, ideology, rewards, intimidation, economic development, political participation and foreign policy; and he points out that most policies are composed of several of these ingredients. As the main examples he studies are Sukarno, Nasser, Bouguiba, Nkrumah, Bandaranaike, Nehru and Ayub, it will be realized that several kinds of amalgam are revealed in these policies.

I have no doubt that this book is a valuable addition to the study of the problems which face leaders in developing nations. It will be particularly useful to political scientists, if only because it reveals that political policies – even those aimed simply at survival – cannot be understood by looking at politics alone. I find the chapter in which the advantages and disadvantages of economic development are set side by side especially persuasive. It is good to note that recognition is now beginning to be shown of the agonising dilemma facing all leaders in choosing between short-term gains which are politically advantageous, and the longer-term measures which are essential for serious development but may lead to unpopularity; and between rural and urban growth.

Nevertheless, I have to strike a cautionary note, even in a short review. There is a constant danger in much current writing on Africa and Asia, even more prevalent in North America than in Europe, of analysis being Euro-American oriented. It is not just that there are localised mistakes here – Nkrumah "barricaded" himself in Flagstaff House, not Christianborg Castle – but certain judgements seem to me to be irrelevant when viewed from within the society concerned. Nkrumah certainly isolated himself from realistic criticism and advice; but it was not his authoritarianism which caused his downfall. If he had been successful – successful in combining economic growth with social justice he would not have been removed. One has only to recall the incident of Azikiwe, who, though proved to have misused public funds, still retained popular support because of his contribution to their progress, to see the point. Similarly, and even more importantly, with Wriggins' treatment of Nyerere, where he relies too much on Bienen's work, the data for which is now outdated. Nyerere is trying to combine ideology, economic development and political participation. The core of what has happened since Bienen left Tanzania is a devolution from centralised government. Whether it succeeds or not will largely depend on new economic initiatives which are certainly no longer "vague". Small criticisms in a book worth serious reading.

London, England   JOHN HATCH

Colin Leys (ed.), *Politics and Change in Developing Countries: Studies in the Theory and Practice of Development.* Cambridge, Cambridge University Press, 1969, 288 pp., $ 7.50.

In his introduction to this symposium, Professor Leys does not try to relate the individual papers too closely to a single theme: the authors differ widely in their academic interests, and their contributions are correspondingly diverse. However, the essays do share a common perspective, and it is this which provides the volume with its underlying coherence. During the past decade the study of developmental processes has experienced a profound change of mood. The infectious self-confidence of the pioneers, and their enthusiastic commitment to behaviouralism, have passed out of fashion, while the overwhelming predominance of American initiative has also become slightly less marked. Growing numbers of students from Europe and the Third World are entering the field at a time when fundamental assumptions are undergoing critical rethinking, and they bring to the task of reappraisal the distinctive preoccupations of their varied intellectual backgrounds. Here nine social scientists from the British sphere of influence are engaged in a search for new bearings; each, within the limits of his subject, reviewing the ground covered by his predecessors, analysing their methodological shortcomings, and attempting to identify promising lines for future enquiry.

In some cases the results of empirical research are used to support their critique. Professor Morris-Jones, for example, introduces data on aspirant legislators in India into his discussion of political recruitment. Similarly, in examining the single-party state as a developmental model, Martin Staniland tests conventional wisdom on the question against the complex reality of the Ivory Coast. David Feldman looks at social change in rural Tanzania, bringing generalisations about the relationship between ideology and action down to earth with an investigation of decision-making among peasant farmers. And Robert Dowse offers a workmanlike survey of the existing literature on the role of the military in development, laced with a few observations of his own on the situation in Ghana.

Other chapters are pitched at a slightly higher level of abstraction, but none loses sight of the need to operationalise the concepts which it employs. In the broadest terms, a contribution by the late Peter Nettl, to whom the book is dedicated, deals with the whole issue of theory-building. Why is it, Nettl asks, that we seem unable to shake ourselves free of so many traditional categories of analysis? Why do we cling to the conservative vocabulary of structuralism, when our new awareness of process so often casts doubt upon the validity of institutional identities? And why do we not address ourselves more seriously to the great problems of development which we so glibly acknowledge, but so little understand – problems like those involved in population pressure and racial conflict? Equally stimulating are the excellent account by Bernard Schaffer of the intricacies of development administration, and a piece by Colin Leys himself on the study of planning; both are replete with policy and research implications, and both should become required reading for anyone with even the most tangential interest in the organisation of government for economic and social change.

Complaints about omissions may seem inappropriate, because the volume makes no claim to be comprehensive. However, the editor lists a number of areas in which the established strengths of British scholarship could enrich the study of development, and it is a pity that only two chapters are explicitly concerned with exploring – as opposed to utilising – these resources. Admittedly Alec Nove's essay on Russia is disappointing in its failure to examine fully the relevance of Soviet studies to general theory, but Joan Vincent's discussion of recent departures in anthropology shows how useful such an approach can be. This is an era of inter-disciplinary exchange, but no specialist can keep abreast of all the latest thinking in related fields; he needs the kind of intelligent updating which Dr. Vincent provides. Although her paper suffers from an attempt to include too much within a limited compass, it makes one wish, not only for a more leisurely treatment, but also for similar efforts in other sectors which Leys mentions – economics, for instance, and history.

Naturally the contributions do not all possess an equal originality of thought, and no reader will find them all equally rewarding. But they do maintain a consistently high standard in their grasp of material and clarity of expression and, in an area where such virtues are all too rare, this in itself must be regarded as a recommendation. Moreover, at their best, they reveal an impressive depth of learning and analytical insight; the person who does not find food for thought among them must be either remarkably erudite, or remarkably dull.

Makerere University College   JOHN D. CHICK
Kampala

P. Robson and D. A. Lury (eds.), *The Economies of Africa.* Evanston, North-western University Press, 1969, 528 pp. No price given.

This collection of 10 essays by 15 authors possessing considerable back-grounds in African economic studies is a commendable collaborative effort. The result is a good summation of the general economic problems in Africa and a detailed account of 13 particular economies which affords valuable material for comparative analysis of national economies. The special problems of integration and regionalism are examined in essays on the East African countries and the economy of Central Africa.

The rapid pace of political change in Africa in the 1960's has tended to reveal and underscore inadequacies of data for policy formulation. There are new needs emphasizing careful planning in order to achieve sound economic and social development in the near future. The African economies, like most of the developing world, operate as open systems in which difficulties of export expansion and domestic and foreign capital mobilization temper aspirations for national growth. These topics have been consistently emphasized in the essays.

In their introduction, the editors stress the problems of gaining insights through comparative studies of similar and dissimilar economic conditions. The selection of African countries and the patterns of analysis reflect this concern. The African continent presents a formidable array of divergencies of considerable challenge to the comparative approach. The editors also outline the difficulties of finding and using common tools and measurement of data for the purpose of description and comparison.

Each of the country surveys follows a similar format which facilitates comparisons particularly in the concluding statement for each survey. (The index of the book, incidentally, might have been more full for aiding comparisons.) Limitations of space in the chapters preclude full examinations of many of the interesting policy problems which have arisen in recent years. The short excellent examination of planning in Nigeria, for example, breaks off at a point where the more important tasks are about to be examined. However, a short list of selected readings is appended to each chapter as a guide to these interests.

Not all types of economies in Africa are dealt with in this book. Those countries selected represent only about one third of the land mass and roughly the same proportion of the population of the continent. What is selected, however, is representative of the spectrum of the major forces of change in the country as a whole. A more complete coverage would have led to confusion. There is some overlap in the countries selected with those included in the 1968 volumes of the International Monetary Fund, which apparently were not available at the time of writing.

The authors of the materials in this book have kept the needs of the student in mind. In addition, the experience of the researcher and policy adviser have been judiciously incorporated. The student of contemporary African economic development, therefore, is well served by this comprehensive yet selective survey.

University of New Hampshire   KENNETH J. ROTHWELL
Durham, U.S.A.

D. Buxton, *Travels in Ethiopia*. New York, Praeger, 1967, 138 plates, 2 maps, 176 pp., $ 7.50.

Travelers, like missionaries, are never completely trustworthy. In Ethiopia this incredulity is intensified. So many purposeful ill-informed adventurers and missionaries – be they religious or political – have skimmed the surface of Ethiopia that a bizarre image of that country and the people who live in it is readily available. All one has to do is go to a good library, choose almost any of the books, shelves of them, and convince oneself that this is indeed a medieval kingdom, tyrannical at the top and enslaved at the bottom, unwashed, stagnant, rich in potential, but certainly improvable.

David Buxton's recently reprinted *Travels in Ethiopia* is a genteel exception: he has only one bias. He prefers thatched roofs to corrugated metal ones.

Buxton's travels were motivated by two sources. One was to survey possible breeding areas of the desert locust. His other was to explore and understand, in the time he had, the intricate monastic and clerical life of highland Ethiopia. The first motive took him into areas where self-announced brave men feared to tred, were killed, or endured historic sufferings. His description of the Dankali is the sanest in print, and his photographs are magnificent. The second motive, investigating the rock-hewn cliffside monasteries provides a lesson in patience. Most of the sites Buxton mentions have not since been investigated by inquisitive outsiders who are now pouring into Ethiopia, nor will they be unless they have Buxton's tact.

Speaking of the Dankali, who call themselves 'Afar, Buxton says, "Of all the nomad tribes of the Ethiopian deserts the Danakil have earned for themselves the most sinister reputation for ferocious savagery." Of this there is no doubt. He continues, "...My own reception among the Danakil, during two trips to different parts of their deserts, had been friendly enough. And I have wandered far among their villages, unarmed and unescorted." Insiders may compare this with Nesbitt's horrifying description of crossing the Danakil desert as reported in *Desert and Forest* and elsewhere.

Speaking of his rope ascent to one of the creviced monasteries, Buxton says, "...some monks had appeared at the top and were peering down at us, protesting at our audacity." When he reached his goal, "The Abbot with a retinue of monks was awaiting us, and gave us a most friendly welcome." Again, one must see the photograph to appreciate the situation.

Travelers and missionaries must always be doubted. They and their followers are usually sponsored by sources wishing to intensify contact to their own advantage. Buxton's Desert Locust Control, probably responsible for saving hundreds of thousands of lives from starvation, nevertheless collects information regarding things other than 'hoppers these days. Currently Americans are the dominant travelers and missionaries, the vectors of change. Buxton might be unsettled if he knew his remote monastery was fewer than two hundred miles from several thousand U.S. troops stationed in Asmara.

Still, the gentility of Buxton is comforting. He says, (*Geographical Journal*, 1949: 172) "...I valued very highly the experience of sharing the life of a community whose customs, founded on the most ancient traditions, belong essentially to an earlier and to me a congenial age. This was one of the compensations for living in a country where life is necessarily a strain, since the inquisitive foreigner is not really welcome."

State University of New York   SIDNEY R. WALDRON
Binghampton, U.S.A.

R. Chambers, *Settlement Schemes in Tropical Africa; A Study of Organization and Development.* London, Routledge & Kegan Paul, 1969, xvi + 234 pp., £ 2.15.

It was Dwight Waldo who, reviewing a collection of books on management, characterised them by referring to the old tale of the blind man describing an elephant. Chambers is far from blind, and the animal he is describing is unmistakeable!

Settlement Schemes in Tropical Africa is an attempt to locate such schemes within the genus *organisations*. Robert Chambers has had extensive field experience with one particular scheme – the Mwea Irrigation Scheme in Kenya – and has had the opportunity to study a number of other schemes in tropical Africa. His approach has been to identify the emerging organization and those environmental elements which were critical for its creation, or which became critical for its survival. After an opening part in which Chambers places tropical African development schemes in their socio-economic-political-administrative setting, he describes the Mwea Scheme from its inception in 1952/53 until the time of writing – 1967. The third part of the book is an analysis of settlement schemes as organizations; the final part presents a typology of settlement schemes together with some tentative conclusions.

The book is fascinating and frustrating. Its fascination comes from the impression of intimacy with the Mwea Scheme and from the clarity with which Chambers handles his data. The frustration – for this reviewer – comes from his failure to make explicit use of the valuable tools available for the gathering, analysis, and interpretation of data about organizations.

The detailed description of the emergence and adaptation of the Mwea Scheme is one of the most insightful accounts of organizational life in the literature. It provides, at an institutional level, what Dalton (*Men Who Manage*) gave us at the managerial and technical levels in the Milo study. Perhaps the richest aspect of Chamber's account is the attention given to the dynamics of the relationships between the Mwea Scheme and the principal elements in the task environment. The data give a vivid description of the coalitions that formed and re-formed and the search for survival goals and for criteria of assessment which would satisfy the dominant elements on whose approval the continuance of the Scheme depended.

The descriptive sections of the book are excellent. Chambers' analysis is perceptive and comes closer to a sense of dynamism than almost any other writing in this field. Every statement made, every conclusion offered, is consistent with general systems theory, and with the propositions which can be derived from that fruitful source of integrative ideas. Anyone familiar with James Thompson's propositions (*Organizations in Action*) will find himself continually applying these ideas to the material contained in Chambers' book and will be gratified at the closeness of the fit. The fact that the Mwea Scheme reacted to its particular environmental constraints in the way described is all the more convincing because Chambers gives no sign of having heard of Thompson's ideas.

In the final part of the book, Chambers essays a typology of developmental schemes. He approaches the task with humility, and is able to derive a logical scheme of classification based primarily on the degree of control over the technical core of the undertaking. The three main classes, two of which are sub-divided, are then used to classify the schemes referred to in the book. The resulting arrangement seems valuable in distinguishing real from superficial differences in the various schemes as organizations. Here again, it is surprising that Chambers did not take the one further step and link development schemes with an existing typology of formal organizations.

The bibliography, to which extensive reference is made throughout the book, contains mainly works from the literature of development schemes. There are only two or three references to the literature on organizations, although much of the writings suggests that Chambers is familiar with the British writing in this field.

The book will be rewarding reading for all of those who work in, and think about, organizations. Although seeming to have specific relevance only for development schemes, the book has achieved its author's goal of being a contribution to the wider understanding of organizations as such; and to the recognition that for all their apparent differences, development schemes are part of the genus *organization*. Robert Chambers has demonstrated his ability as a perceptive observer and a skilful writer – it is to be hoped that we hear more from him.

Western Australian Institute of Technology   C. E. CARR
Perth, Western Australia

Kwame Nkrumah, *A Handbook of Revolutionary Warfare.* New York, International Publishers, 1969, 122 pp., $ 1.50.

The problem of rapid transformation of undeveloped countries into modern industrialised societies has received considerable attention of scholars and statesmen. However, this problem is often seen in terms of obstacles to economic development posed by the traditional character of such societies. Many scholars and statesmen conceive the problem also in terms of encouraging the development of liberal democracy and capitalism. Excepting "studies on the left" the equally difficult and important problem of transforming a clientele state with its clientele economic and political structures into a "genuinely" independent state is seldom admitted or frankly discussed. But evasion of this issue, however convenient it may be for those who wish to preserve the existing international economic *status quo* does not eliminate the problems which the clientele states of the undeveloped countries must eventually confront. It is partly this problem of transforming clientele states into genuine autonomy which Kwame Nkrumah attempts to deal with in *A Handbook of Revolutionary Warfare.*

Probably Nkrumah has always been a revolutionist. But while in power in Ghana, he was certainly a reluctant revolutionist. His actions and policies were ambivalent in so far as his revolutionary objectives were concerned, his brand of "socialism" indistinguishable from those of some of Ghana's neighbouring states. He has since been ousted from power, and from Ghana. Thus *A Handbook of Revolutionary Warfare* is written by a committed revolutionary socialist and pan-African nationalist.

The book is addressed to revolutionaries or potential revolutionaries in the undeveloped countries, especially Africa. The author explains to the initiates or revolutionary activists the nature and world strategy of imperialism and neo-colonialism, the problem of puppet governments and the need for a continental organization for combating these forces which exploit the masses of the African people. He is convinced that genuine economic and political liberation of all Africa can only be achieved by revolutionary armed struggle against the remnants of colonialism and racism in Southern Africa and the Portuguese colonies, and against imperialism, neo-colonialism and the puppet governments which perpetuate the regime of clientele economies in the independent African States. The positive objectives of the armed struggle include the attainment of African unity – i.e., a continental Union Government of Africa – and socialism.

Nkrumah acknowledges the contribution made by nationalism based on the territorial configurations established by the colonial powers to the formal transfer of political power to Africans. This represents only the first phase of the anti-imperialist struggle. Although this sort of nationalism may be relevant for the territories still under colonial and racists' rule, the need to transform "sham independence" of the clientele states to genuine autonomy now makes it an anachronism. Therefore, the next phase of the African liberation movement must embrace the whole continent and it must include a commitment to revolutionary socialism, which alone can transform the clientele status of African states with their clientele economic and political structures into genuine independence.

The author describes in some detail the form which the politico-military organisation of the revolutionary movement should take. He advocates the establishment of an All-African People's Revolutionary Party, the All-African Committee for Political Co-ordination, and the All-African People's Revolutionary Army. The All-African People's Revolutionary Party should draw its membership from peasants, workers, members of co-operative movements and student organisations whose revolutionary awareness is high. Membership could be drawn also from the revolutionary petty bourgeoisie, the patriotic bourgeoisie, nationalist bureaucratic bourgeoisie, and revolutionary outsiders. In this regard Nkrumah attacks as a myth the denial by some African socialists of the existence of a working class in Africa and debunks the notion of "African socialism". The basic principles and techniques of guerilla warfare, its strategy and tactics are explained. Several charts are employed for purposes of illustration.

Both revolutionary activists, especially the initiates are bound to learn something from this manual of instruction. But others who are not interested in making a revolution will find the book interesting as a testament of a contemporary African revolutionist. They would be impressed by the grandiosity of Nkrumah's vision, and horrified by the means which the author believes should be employed for translating the dream of a United Socialist State of Africa into reality. Many will find his scheme wholly unrealistic in the present African circumstances.

University of Ibadan   E. U. Essien-Udom
Ibadan, Nigeria

Emmanuel John Hevi, *The Dragon's Embrace: The Chinese Communists and Africa.* New York, Frederick A. Praeger, 1966, 152 pp., $ 5.95.

Emmanuel John Hevi's *The Dragon's Embrace* is a curious book. The thesis is clear and simple. Africa needs peace to develop. And she needs to be left alone (except for economic and technical assistance without strings) in order to develop rapidly and solidly. Thus she must reject decisively China's call to revolution and the violent overthrow of established regimes. Since China has so clearly marked herself as an "enemy of peace", Africans must be wary of her conspiracies as well as her example.

On the surface this book is a polemic. Although China is not responsible for all the world's evils, virtually everything that the Chinese People's Republic does is regarded by Hevi as dangerous. The only exceptions are a number of statements by China's officials, which Hevi likes to quote, if for no other reason than to demonstrate where actual policy in his estimation diverges from political pronouncement.

Regarding China in Africa, Hevi's position practically coincides with the position of the United States Department of State. Moreover, a number of other facts lead one to the serious suspicion that Hevi's work is not only approved by some U.S. governmental agency, but may well be sponsored by some such group. Granted, hard evidence is absent to prove conclusively my supposition. But circumstantial evidence is temptingly convincing. Here are just two examples that lead me to this idea. In English-speaking Africa, and elsewhere in the world a "student edition" of Hevi's first book. *An African Student in China* (1962), is sold for considerably less than the cost of most other cheap paperbacks. The price is equivalent to about 25 U.S. cents. It is published by Fawcett Publications, although the original hardbound American edition was released by Frederick A. Praeger, the publisher of *The Dragon's Embrace*. In order to gain greater readership in the developing world, it seems clear that some U.S. government body was willing to underwrite the costs of printing and circulation of this student edition.

Frederick A. Praeger himself has admitted to a close association and susceptibility to governmental pressures. In 1967 he stated that his house had published "15 or 16 books" at the suggestion of the CIA. Most of these books dealt with Communist countries or nations in peril of the Communist takeovers. He refused to comment when asked if the CIA had ever financed a book in whole or in part and when asked if his link with the CIA continued to exist. Moreover he stated that his concern had published considerably more books following the suggestions of "somebody connected with the Pentagon" or as a result of funding by USIA than the "15 or 16" stemming from CIA influence (*New York Times*, February 24, 1967). I am not positive that *The Dragon's Embrace* is a product of governmental "suggestion" but the possibility is not slim.

Secondly, in the beginning of Chapter Three, Hevi borrows heavily from an account of Chou En-lai's speech in Somali that included the famous statement that "revolutionary prospects are excellent throughout the African continent." What is strange is that the account he employs by Peter Kumpa appeared in the *Baltimore Sun* of February 9, 1964. To be sure, an author may draw his material from wherever he can. Elsewhere he also refers to an article in Italian in the Italian periodical, *Vita*, dated 1966. Given the fact that this book is not especially well researched or copiously documented, (there are only 33 footnotes in all) and the fact that after his return from China in 1962 until 1966, this native Ghanaian lived in exile in Nigeria, it seems highly unlikely that the author would have had the opportunity to read or even to secure on a regular basis copies of the *Sun* and *Vita*. More likely he researched the book or it was researched and documented for him by someone who had access to a rather complete library or file system. Someone in or around Washington, D.C. would not be a bad guess. Either Hevi or his research assistants knew where to go in order to find quickly the kinds of information he was after.

The result is a book that expresses views strikingly like those of the U.S. Government. He regards the Vietnamese War, as does the Pentagon, as a "confrontation between the United States and China." He continually praises the Nationalist Chinese on Taiwan. He insists that the "second scramble" for Africa is not among the former colonialists and the United States but rather between the Soviet Union and the Chinese People's Republic. He also talks of the "Sino-Nkrumah conspiracy" and attacks Mao Tse-tung's view of nuclear war. Superficially then, the polemics of this volume are as glaring as Communist Chinese propaganda posters. They are compounded by tone and flippant prose. One example – describing Russian Ambassador to Guinea Daniel Solod's expulsion from that country, Hevi writes that "Toure's boot [was] applied squarely to his [Solod's] back side."

But although the primary message and purpose of this book is to point out the genuine dangers of China's policies in Africa and in general the dangers of any kind of close involvement with Communist states, there are parts that seem to take a different position. He has some constructive criticisms of Africa's leaders. On occasion he takes issue with America's use of force around the world, expressing ideas akin to Senator Fulbright's "Arrogance of Power" thesis. He defends the CPR military aid to Tanzania since it is overt and checked by military aid from counter-poles. Of course the underlying purpose of the book is to point up the perils of a too close involvement with any Great Power that is in a position to weaken you by conspiring against you or by withdrawing unilaterally its assistance to you. Thus it would be unwise to regard this as purely a propaganda effort. Hevi is essentially a concerned African nationalist who wants his people to be free to make decisions unencumbered by undue outside interference or influence and he wants Africa to develop as rapidly as she can. His experiences in China doubtless embittered him to that regime and under-standably he cannot help but pour forth his bile in these volumes. At one point he writes, "Today, however, I sit here, receive and am influenced by ideas set down in books and newspapers or broadcast by radio from all over the world." It is not difficult to see why the influences on Mr. Hevi should be so onesided. But coming from an African nationalist they are surprisingly opinionated, bitter, and curiously pro-Western.

Case Western Reserve University   KENNETH W. GRUNDY
Cleveland, U.S.A.

John Wright, *Libya*. New York, Fredrick A. Praeger, c. 1969 (Nations of the Modern World Series), 304 pp., $ 7.50.

It would perhaps be fair to say that the series of which this book is a part (Nations of the Modern World, Praeger) has not been particularly noteworthy from a number of points of view, and the present book seems to be no exception. This book is not really a solid history of Libya. Nor is it a social history attempting to bring together significant cultural concepts of the Libyan past into a relevant framework by which the present may be better understood. It does not offer us theories by which Libyan events can be apprehended and which may be relevant elsewhere in comparative analyses. And lastly, while Mr. Wright refers to Arab nationalism in his discussion, he does not really provide a sufficient context by which past and present Libyan politics and political goals can be understood. In order to have even that latter kind of discussion make sense, he would have had to discuss colonialism and imperialism somewhat more, and to have spelled out in greater detail, the actual impact the Arab-Israeli dilemma has made on Libyan social and political life.

It would be quite proper to say, however, that Mr. Wright should not be criticized for not writing a book which the reviewer would have preferred. He should be assessed in terms of the intent of the book written and its actualities. Mr. Wright set out to write a general history of Libya, and indeed he has. But one must ask two questions before the value of the book can be determined: a) to which audience is the book addressed?; and b) what does it have to offer that audience?

Since so little is available in English on Libya as such, one could assume that the book was directed to a general audience, but also thought of as a book for university level courses on the Middle East. It seems somehow unsatisfactory for both audiences.

For the general audience, he offers a chronological account of the various invasions that crossed the Libyan shore filled with dates and enormous amounts of trivia. One almost gets the feeling that he was enchanted by the details of the vast primary sources which he asserts to have examined, and thus a series of unconnected facts appear in the book. A typical sentence is:

> The Byzantine provincial governor withdrew with his army into the port of Teuchira, which was still walled and provided private baths for the governor and his staff and public ones for the troops. (p. 77)

Secondly, the first eight chapters of the book, with few exceptions, do not offer either anything much new factually from what Charles Andre Julien offers in his more famous, *Histoire De L'Afrique Du Nord* (Payot, Paris, 1956) nor does one get a sense of the general socio-cultural environment. Only if one is already aware of Islamic history, the pre-Islamic culture of the area, and the specifies of Maghrebian history, does Wright's book make some sense. But presumably, if one is familiar with these, Wright's book would not be read by that person. It is always distressing to have an oversimplified book which only a specialist can understand.

In short, for the general reader, Wright has not known how to bring into his general history the relevant cultural themes and socio-historical influences, as they came to play in the Libyan context. While from Chapter 9 on he is more informative, especially during the Italian period, the weaknesses of his earlier chapters do not permit the full potential of his later chapters to emerge.

These same comments are true for the student audience, especially those just beginning their studies of North Africa and the Middle East. Additionally, however, the student aims to identify those ideas or idea systems which help not only to explain the past and present, but to anticipate the future of a people, their social system, etc. Wright does not really direct the student to the possible sources of those sets of ideas which purport to explain Libyan events, and over which students may debate according to their own criteria. Thus, for example, in Chapter 17, "The Years of Debate" (pp. 191–2–7), which allegedly explains the debate involved in developing the form and direction of an Independent Libya, Wright does not really make explicit the ideological bases and their full implications for Western power and influence in the area as well as for Arab nationalism. Further, by eliminating any significant discussion of Israel vis-a-vis the Arab world, the student would additionally be pressed to understand the larger significance of the recent coup in Libya as well as its reaction to the lack of Lebanese support for the Palestinian Commandos.

Again, in short, by not including some coherent discussion of these forces as they relate to Libya, Wright, by default, permits the ideas of popular propaganda to dominate explanation not only of Libya, but Libya as part of the Arab World, and indeed the Arab World itself.

The Arabs consider themselves ultimately to belong to one Arab nation. They are presently split up into eighteen different nations, which they consider to be artificial, and which were created as a result of the colonial period. Arab nationalism means simply the reconstruction of the Arab nation. However, there are a number of Arab governments which are conservative (the monarchies, and the Western-type nations such as Tunisia and Lebanon), and are primarily influenced by the former colonial powers, and the West in general. These influences keep the Arab nation from being reconstituted, or so Arabs believe. The establishment of the State of Israel by conquest of Palestine, in the midst of the Arab world, and the attachment of that State to the Western political, economic, and technological systems, tends to impede the development of a modern Arab nation. Thus with each success Israel has, the greater are the internal pressures in the Arab world to shake off conservative governments, to unite the Arab people, and to check Israeli advances.

Governments such as that of the Arab Republic of Egypt articulate Arab nationalism. Egypt has attempted to encourage the complete independence of Arab nations from the West and the East and to seek the ideological and institutional bases by which Arab nations may become one. The emergence of the Palestinian Commando after the 1967 war has encouraged this further as they seek support in the Arab world in dealing with Israel.

Within this larger context, the ideological debate over the orientation and form of Arab nationalism can be understood, and specific events within each of the countries can also be better understood, Thus, the Libyan coup could be anticipated, and its actions understood. The various attempts within Saudia Arabia directed against the monarchy can also be understood. And Arab hostility toward the Lebanese Government for controlling the operations of the Palestinian Commandos from its soil can also be understood.

While we must give credit to Mr. Wright for his attempt to fill in a rather large gap on informative works on Libya, we must conclude, however, that his general history is too general in some ways and too specific in ways that are not meaningful. It joins the shelf of books in this series which represent a good idea that did not work out.

Simmons College   ELAINE C. HAGOPIAN
Boston, U.S.A.

R. M. Prothero, *Migrants and Malaria in Africa.* Pittsburg, University of Pittsburg Press, 1965, 148 pp., $ 1.50.

Among the more attractive features of Social Science research in Africa are
the high frequency of inter-disciplinary studies, and the fact that applied work
can also be of fundamental importance. One of the better examples of this type
of research is the book under review. Prothero has presented a study which is
highly competent, which welds together the work of many disciplines, and
which is clearly in an applied field, for the intention of the research was to
demonstrate the effects of mobility on malaria transmission. At the same time
it is one of the most comprehensive sources of data on migrations in Africa.
    For social scientists, the interest of the book will lie in this area, for we are
gradually finding that African societies are highly mobile. Indeed, among the
leading causes/results of social change are certain types of movements, notably
labour migrations and urbanization. Yet, at the same time, our lack of knowledge about migrations – regretfully, we have even less knowledge about the
basic facts (volume, timing, pattern) than we have about the characteristics
(who moves and why) – is monumental, as Prothero has noted (p. 45). In this
book he has bound together the available information on many of the migrations,
and has thus added to the demographic inventory of Tropical Africa. However,
I was disappointed that he was not able to overcome some of the difficulties
inherent in research on migration in West Africa. The West African chapter
mainly concerned itself with problems inherent in certain pilot eradication
projects, rather than attempting to give an overview. Perhaps, he might have
increased Chapter 3, on the various patterns of migration, so as to provide, in
tabular form if necessary, a summary of what is known about the direction,
estimated volume and general characteristics of significant movements in each
region of Africa. Some of these data have been published elsewhere, some of it
is contained in other chapters, but such a summary would have been extremely
valuable.
    This criticism and a few minor quibbles aside – the map on p. 48 of my copy
was very poorly produced – one must say that his major argument comes through
very forcefully. In this way Prothero has served the social sciences very faithfully, for he has demonstrated that for all aspects of African development a
knowledge of the societies concerned is essential; more specifically, before
malaria eradication can be achieved with any degree of success African governments must have more data on migratory movements, and, this in turn will
involve intergovernmental co-operation.

Cornell University   IAN POOL
Ithaca, U.S.A.

A. J. Bruwer, *Zimbabwe Rhodesia's Ancient Greatness.* Johannesburg, Keartland
(distributed by Tri-Ocean, San Francisco), 1965, 74 illustrations, 152 pp.,
$ 9.00.

There has long been a need for a new study of Zimbabwe setting it in its
context of African history. Most unfortunately this is not such a study though

its title may tempt the unwary into believing that this is a work of historical scholarship. Mr. Bruwer, a South African economist, who visited Rhodesia on three occasions in 1963, scathingly rejects the work of three generations of archaeologists including Gladys Caton-Thompson and Roger Summers as "politico-archaeology" because they assigned the stone buildings to the second millennium AD. and to Bantu societies. He seeks to show that Zimbabwe, the 2,000 or more gold mines and the Inyanga terraces were the work of Phoenicians who first of all came to exploit the metal ores from 332–64 BC., later colonized the area from 64 BC.–633 AD. and were finally cut off from their Eastern Mediterranean bases by the expansion of Islam in the seventh century AD. From 1150 till the arrival of the Pioneer Column in 1890 he contends that the area went "back to Bush". He marshalls no convincing evidence to support this hypothesis. He constantly compares Zimbabwe to Aztec structures in Mexico and interprets all spiral or concentric circle designs as being symbolic of the sun-god Baal or the moon-goddess Astarte, as are also the towers at Zimbabwe. He dismisses contrary evidence based on painstaking analysis of pottery and beads as being "rudimentary and unsatisfactory". The annular occupation units around stone paved pits at Inyanga he sees as Phoenician grain silos and the stonework is compared to the neolithic and early bronze age stone ruins on Malta. He claims that archaeologists have ignored cult objects like the figurines and soapstone birds which he thinks are representations of the phoenix which are for him characteristic of Phoenicia and the origin of the name Phoenicia.

Bruwer relies on his emotions in most of his arguments against the weight of archaeological evidence and decries the winds of change which were "whipped up by ruthless propaganda into a destructive hurricane" which he considers responsible for much of the acceptance of "politico-archaeology". In a book dedicated to Mr. Ian Smith, he uses such arguments as it is "out of character" for Bantu to put up stone structures, or that the mines are unrelated to the Bantu as the Bantu have no name for gold or that the Bantu never constructed agricultural terraces, nor did they have highly developed religions. It is unfortunate that Mr. Bruwer presents no real evidence for his Phoenicians, he illustrates no Phoenician pottery from Rhodesia whilst he claims that no burials have been found since Phoenician burials are too deep for the archaeologist to find. Every bead is diagnosed as Phoenician but he presents no comparative analysis of Phoenician and Rhodesian beads.

The evidence, however, for a second millennium dating of Zimbabwe is inescapable. Pottery, the most abundant of finds, is closely dated not only by radiocarbon dates but also by association with Chinese porcelain of the fourteenth and fifteenth centuries AD. The mines have sealed within them Rhodesian iron age pottery dating from the eighth century AD. but without a single associated object of Eastern Mediterranean manufacture. Negroes elsewhere in Africa, in Mauretania, Senegal, Guinea and Ghana were exploiting gold before 1400 AD. so why not their Bantu speaking relations in Rhodesia? Many of the finest art objects of Africa from Ife, Benin, the Congo bespeak of the organization and religion of the contemporaries of the occupants of Zimbabwe. Careful excavation has demonstrated the building sequence at Zimbabwe and shown that the most impressive walls date from a period after 1300 AD. Not even archaeologists in the service of the Smith regime contend that Zimbabwe is either contemporary with the Phoenicians or owes its structure to outside influence. Terraces are certainly found in East Africa and if every stone structure had to have a Phoenician origin the Phoenicians must have had a busy time throughout Africa! Had analogies been wanted for the Inyanga stone ruins Bruwer need only have looked at the University of Witwatersrand's impressive programme of mapping stone enclosures in the Transvaal, where Dr. Revil Mason's team has located more than 2,000 ruins and securely dated them to a post 1500 AD. context.

The only merit of this rather pathetic *apologia* of pre-1910 explorers and diggers, like Theodore Bent and R. N. Hall, is some excellent photographs of Zimbabwe illustrated by permission of the Rhodesian Department of Tourism. This is perhaps one of the worst examples of selective comparative history to appear in recent years and by comparing random objects out of context an equally implausible case could be made for Zimbabwe as an Indonesian or South American colony. However hard the romantics may try, Zimbabwe remains a monument to the technical skill of the ancestors of Rhodesia's African majority.

University of Ghana   MERRICK POSNANSKY
Accra, Ghana.

M. Lawrence, *Long Drums and Cannons: Nigerian Dramatists and Novelists.* New York, Praeger, 1969, 209 pp., $ 5.95.

Recently there have been several critical studies of contemporary African literature most especially those comprehensive works by Jahnheinz Jahn and Wilfred Cartey. Against these extensive studies Margaret Lawrence's new book may appear to have obvious limitations, but her restrictions allow her to undertake effectively concentrated rather than diffuse discussion of the area she has selected for her analysis. She deals only with Nigerian literature – though admittedly this is a substantial part of contemporary African writing. She also concerns herself only with the novel and the drama; avoiding the extensive area of published poetry. The structure of this book is the simplest possible. Each of the major authors get a chapter: Wole Soyinka, J. P. Clark, Chinua Achebe, Amos Tutuola and Cyprian Ekwensi. In a rather hurried terminal chapter labelled "Other Voices" Miss Lawrence deals with the novelists, Aluko, Amadi, Nwankwo, Nwapa, Nzekwu and Okara. The structure within each chapter is equally simple. Each major work is recorded in chronological order, its plot is described and comments, sometimes skimpy but regularly very shrewd, are added. It is the manner of a good lecture survey.

The fact that Miss Lawrence is herself a writer rather than an academic lends a particular preception to her remarks. She does not feel impelled to develop any overall explanations and theories concerning the birth of this new literature. Rather she takes the published novels and plays as her texts and makes comments which elucidate their complexities and explain their backgrounds.

Her longest chapter is the first one discussing the work of Wole Soyinka and it makes nearly a third of the book. This is probably about a fair estimate of the relative merit of this most distinguished writer. Soyinka still remains the one unquestionable genius amongst African writers to date. The very length of this chapter allows a closer inspection of the works of Soyinka than has yet been attempted. It also demands a very intensive analysis for the chapter is too long to be sustained by mere generalizations and plot summaries. Happily Miss Lawrence is at her best here. She skilfully unravels the complex threads of Soyinka's fascinating but difficult first novel, *The Interpreters*. She does not shrink from analysing the complicated structure of *A Dance of the Forest*, a play commonly neglected by critics in favor of easier analysis of the simpler humor of *Lion and the Jewel*. Although too rarely discussed it is acknowledged that *A Dance* raises themes which are central to Soyinka's entire philosophy. It explores motifs which permeate his poetry and forshadow the later development of his last play *The Road*. Miss Lawrence's discussion of the last confusing (and perhaps confused) scene of *A Dance*, with its mixture of symbols, part personal, part Yoruba tribal, is masterly. She reviews the effect of the alternative endings and with persuasive critical logic, manages to create a single coherent sequence that will coordinate the diffuse elements of myth and drama, ritual and theater with which Soyinka concludes his major play. This chapter with its original and authoritative interpretation is a valuable addition to published study in this field.

Against this chapter the other briefer ones appear inevitably more sparse and generalized but they are also invariably intelligent and competent. This review may appear to have stressed the restrictions of this work, its limitation of geography and genre. That would be unfair. It is restricted but deliberately so. Within its selected area it is as useful and informative as any study yet published in the field of African literature. If I had to advise a reader or student of one book that would be the most useful introduction to this new writing I think it would be Margaret Lawrence's volume. I would recommend it for the precise and commonsense explanations it gives concerning writings which have too often been treated by critics not as works of literature but as anthropological, linguistic or political evidence of contemporary African conditions. Margaret Lawrence brings us back to the recognition that these are authors as well as racial and national spokesmen and it is a valuable and healthy reminder.

University of California   John F. Povey
Los Angeles, U.S.A.

P. Rigby, *Cattle and Kinship among the Gogo: A Semi Pastoral Society of Central Tanzania*. Ithaca, Cornell University Press, 1969, xvi + 355 pp., 11 plates, 3 maps, 19 figures, 14 tables, $ 13.50.

In this analysis of kinship among the Gogo of Central Tanzania Rigby has tried to apply tools developed in the study of segmentary systems to a highly amorphous (or should one say diffusely structured) society. The attempt has been only partially successful.

The Gogo are enough to dismay the most persistent ethnographer. Not only do they have no corporate unilineal descent groups on which one could hang the analytical hat. Their boundaries with other tribes are fuzzy, there are important dialectical variations from one end of the society to the other and cultural features which might characterize them are generally indistinct. Rigby's most prominent conclusion about these people is that the "politico jural domain cannot be described formally as a set of patrilineal descent groups which provide the basis for corporate political action and local organization," and the pattern of residence cannot be seen outside of a consideration of the cycle of development of domestic groups, the property relations which provide its mainspring (principally control of cattle), and the early fission of agnatic groups and the role of affinal relationships.

Certain parts of his analysis have special interest. For one thing, Rigby is not swayed by conventional views of cattle in Africa. Gogo men have as a primary aim the accumulation and control of a large number of livestock, and cattle serve as the basic "value units" in Gogo society for the evaluation of anything from wives and children to the seriousness of an offense. Further, livestock can be converted into agricultural products in times of famine. In general Rigby is more economically sophisticated than the tradition from which he derives (Radcliffe-Brown, Fortes et al). His analysis of the MB/ZS relationship of the Gogo points up in the way these roles are played the importance of the economics of marriage transactions.

Yet Rigby is plainly in the structural-functional tradition, whose deficiencies are continually exposed when placed in a comparative framework. Theoretical assertions while plausible are ad hoc and particularistic. For example, Rigby is impressed by the stress on affinal relations in Gogo society feeling that this derives from the lack of patrilineal corporate groups to go along with their patrilineal ideology. In my work with the Turu, neighbors to the northwest of the Gogo and culturally very similar to them, I was also impressed by the stress on affinity, yet the Turu are seemingly the direct opposites of the Gogo in that they rigidly demarcate corporate patrilineal segmentary lineages. Whatever the cause of the prominence of affinity, this suggests that the degree of corporacy is not it. Typical of structural-functional analysis, its highly trained practitioners reward us with the depth and intensity of their investigations, but disappoint us with the low level reached by their theory.

For those who are concerned about the style in which an ethnography is written, Rigby's book is aggressively analytical making few concessions to the reader. He is particularly prone to extensive footnotes, cross-references to his other publications on the Gogo, and extensive use of the Gogo language, in the use of which he apparently became exceptionally skilled.

In sum, this book is the first extensive account of one of the group of cattle oriented people of central Tanzania and is therefore a valuable addition to the anthropological ethnographic collection.

Indiana Univeristy   HAROLD K. SCHNEIDER
Bloomington, U.S.A.

D. F. McCall, N. R. Bennett and J. Butler (eds.), *Eastern African History.* Boston University Papers on Africa, vol. 3, New York, Praeger, 1969, 245 pp., $ 17.50.

Here are eight papers delivered at Boston University in 1965 or 1966.

Harold C. Fleming opens with an essay on the classification of West Cushitic. He concludes that it must be considered as an independent branch of Afro-Asiatic. Even though he uses Swadesh's one hundred wordlist with caution and really as a general vocabulary, the reviewer remains a bit sceptical about the division into basic and cultural vocabulary that is so often made. McCall follows up with an essay on loanwords in Swahili and makes a plea for trying to establish the relative chronology of these. Part I of his essay tells us all about loanwords in general, and does so very well. Bruce Trigger discusses the relation between culture history and geography in the Sudan. His major points stand, but most of the data adduced have been replaced by recent works of authors such as Michaelovsky, Shinnie, Yusuf Fadl Hasan and Trigger himself.

The first essay in more conventional history is Robert L. Hess' tale about Falasha history. It is a fascinating story expertly done and very well written. Maybe some of the fascination stems from the fact that so much about the Falasha still remains unknown. Ralph A. Austen takes R. Oliver to task about *ntemiship* in Western Tanzania for having suggested that the political organization of the Nyamwezi represented an earlier "stage" in the evolution of the interlacustrine states. Austen argues for differences stemming from differences in environment and goes on to argue that it was the age grouping organizations in Nyamwezi which made the organization of caravans first possible.

How France signed a treaty with Zanzibar in 1846 is Bennett's story. He adds to G. B. Freeman Grenville's *The French at Kilwa Island*, Oxford 1965, which one must be read now against the background provided by J. B. Kelly, *Britain and the Persian Gulf*, 1785–1880, Oxford 1968, and can be further extended by J. A. Kieran's article on the subsequent treaty of 1862 in *The Canadian Journal of African Studies*, II, 2, 1968, p. 147–166.

The last two papers deal with Rwanda and adjoining districts of Uganda. Alison des Forges probably regrets now that she ever wrote a paper on the White Fathers in Rwanda when she was still a graduate student and had not done any original research yet. She did not even use all the available sources in print and her anthropology is too much based on a single source. The content is weak throughout, but the comparative section is ludicrous. Elizabeth Hopkins focuses on Kigezi in her discussion of the International Boundary and Colonial Control. It all remains very theoretical, with data adduced mainly as illustrations. Again she uses very few sources and misses some very important developments. Her anthropology of Kigezi is quite poor, and a fog of jargon smothers it all.

The cruel passage of time has scarred almost every single paper. Why did they have to wait until 1969 when they were written in 1965/6? As for the format the book reads like the issue of a Journal and the Editors should abandon the series and considering the proceedings rather for *African Historical Studies* where the articles would be more accessible and presumably could be published faster.

The greatest criticism here goes to the publisher. His printing is drab, the footnoting suggests padding and the maps are carelessly drawn. All this for $ 17.50. What do they imagine their public is? Pigeons? This more than any any factor will effectively restrict the audience of the authors to readers in University libraries within the United States only.

University of Wisconsin   J. VANSINA
Milwaukee, U.S.A.

M. O. Beshir, *The Southern Sudan: Background to Conflict.* New York, Praeger, 1968, 192 pp., appendices, table and maps, $ 7.50.

For millions of Sudanese, independence fostered great expectations, an acute awareness of the immense obstacles that prevent their fulfillment, and a growing impatience with the incumbent rulers who have a limited understanding of what needs to be done. Many come to believe that the "new class" and the "bureaucratic bourgeoisie" are fundamentally corrupt. This is so because the Sudanese ruling elite, like their counterparts in most African states, have no ideological key beyond a common-place nationalism. This ideological bankruptcy has committed their people to the old life of wretchedness. Decolonisation was expected to realize not merely the establishment of a new state of the achievement of sovereignty, but also a fundamental commitment to change which would in part transform the oppressed spectators into privileged actors. Instead, the former order built by the British over half a century is perpetuated by Sudanese politicians (themselves creatures of the old order), who led the national movement and who govern the country today. Such politicians are viewed by their people as nothing but directors-general of a corporation of profiteers.

In the span of five years, 1953–58, the gap between the ruler and the ruled grew wider to be rapidly filled by the military which left the country at the mercy of the colonial counter-offensive as is seen today in the rebellion in the Southern Sudan.

The problem of the Southern Sudan which is the subject-matter of this brief, remarkable work of Mr. Beshir is not typical of Africa alone. The author has successfully described and placed the problem in its historical context. In eight well-documented chapters, he gives us a clear picture of the history of the Southern provinces from before 1898 to 1964. In three outstanding chapters, the so-called "Southern Policy" is traced from its genesis in 1920 through 1953. Here, although the author avoids value judgments, we are appalled by the insidious, systematic British and missionary attempts to implement a two-nation policy. While the British ruled, this policy was doomed to failure because of its contradictions and disastrous effects on the development of the South. It survives, however, today, to be echoed by certain southern politicians. That such is the case is made clear in chapters VIII–IX, and is upheld by the account of events leading to and during the "Round Table Conference" which is the subject of Chapter X. Mr. Beshir places the blame squarely where it belongs: on the Northern and Southern politicians. The people of the Sudan in both North and South are victims of these hopelessly inept men who are ill-prepared to meet the challenge of building a united modern Sudan for the sake of an African continent not interested in balkanization. The author's diagnosis of the problem is penetrating and illuminating, but his proposals for a solution are uncertain, for they emphasize legal forms rather than social content. This is not a shortcoming in terms of the book's stated purpose to "describe and expose certain issues about the Southern Sudan problem." The issues are complex. But, the author cogently argues, if the politicians in the Sudan learn these "certain issues", ignorant and blind attempts at resolution will be replaced by knowledgeable and informed ones. Mr. Beshir deserves our appreciation if not our gratitude for making available this long overdue work. The book is essential in being successful in what it professes to achieve and its valuable appendices enhance further its importance. Indeed, rarely has so much been said in so few pages.

McGill University   A. ABU ZAYD
Montreal, Canada

Christopher Clapham, *Haile-Selassie's Government.* New York, Praeger, 1969, xiv + 218 pp., $ 7.50.

With so many of her sister states on the Continent in search for a "tradition étatique", the government of Ethiopia derives directly from an indigenous political system held together over two thousand years by a common faith and, most important, by the unifying position of the Emperor. This straight line of continuity, unencumbered by the traumas of colonialism, is not only a source of romantic memory and myth but it has also preserved traditional political forms which are still relevant. Peculiar too are the problems such a polity faces when trying to modernize its machinery. It is these problems and efforts to which this long overdue and adsorbing study by Christopher Clapham addresses itself.

The essence of this form of "Palace government" is the pivotal and multi-functional role of the Emperor who controls every aspect of administration mainly as a catalyst and legitimizer and whose authority and approval are required literally for every descision. He presides over a class of courtiers who are recruited from the main social and regional sectors of the country into a readily accepted relationship of subservience and sycophancy. What political process there is, works through a system of elusive personal connections. Government takes a domestic atmosphere and because of their small size, their inter-related membership, and the almost Kafkaesque omnipresence of the Palace the various factions hang together as a fairly homogeneous political elite. The Emperor stands at the apex, not only of an administrative hierarchy, but also of a hierarchy of informers, and is the sole arbiter between the vying factions. Although he has absolute powers, enshrined in the Constitutions of 1931 and 1955, these must be made good by effective leadership in balancing these forces and maintaining a consensus. The present Emperor has proven a master tactician and his assiduous ascension and self-preservation over a period of fifty years (well documented in the book) have been due to his success in embodying the characteristic Amhara penchant for secrecy, ambiguity, caution, subsurface activity, adaptability, and capacity for manipulating others. Undoubtedly the most fascinating parts of the book are those depicting the intrigue-ridden feuds and factional in-fighting which comprise the political dynamic in such a system. Small wonder that much of the data has been gathered through years of patient detective work from a number of undisclosed sources, and that the book has apparently already been banned in the country. The style is free from the deadening tedium of contemporary jargon about "political development" though the price to be paid for this refreshing change, it seems, has been an almost total refraining from making comparative or conceptualized generalizations. As well, the book, cast in the contrast between traditionalism and institutionalization, is deliberately restricted to an analysis of the central government, with little attempt to relate the political forms to Ethiopia's economic and social system, or the central institutions to political structures at the local level.

One weakness of the personalized Palace government, operating without parties and formalized interest groups, is poor communication, and inadequate information about general grievances (witness the December 1960 revolt or the potentially perilous growth of ethnic separatism in Eritrea and among the Galla). Another is its built-in resistance to delegation so necessary for the impetus to introduce change. Thus the administrative modernization which has taken place since 1941 has been simply the result of the rise of a new generation using new methods of systematized and decreasingly personal administration. In institutional terms, it has reflected the decline of such traditional bodies as the Imperial Secretariat, and the development of such modern ones as the Council of Ministers, the Prime Ministry, the bicameral Parliament, and new budgetary techniques, to which Mr. Clapham devotes an illuminating chapter each. But these institutional innovations do not seem to have affected the foundations of the system. The upshot is a dual structure of government, with traditional modes continuing behind a facade of modern institutions. Most important, though the Emperor has steadily withdrawn from the field of day-to-day administration, his basic role as legitimizer and integrator has remained intact. Yet it is on developing some alternative source of legitimate authority that the post-Haile-Selassie course of Ethiopia hinges.

McGill University   F. A. KUNZ
Montreal, Canada

E. C. Rowlands, *Teach Yourself Yoruba.* The English Universities Press Ltd., 1969, 276 pp., $ 2.65.

"Teach Yourself Books" have appeared for close to forty languages. All of them share one quality of highly dubious value – it is not likely that anyone except a rare specialist can really teach himself any second language with only a book to guide him. Even Rowlands' statement, "To acquire a good pronunciation it is advisable to hear the sounds from the lips of a Yoruba" (p. 5), is pathetically feeble. Such listening, along with imitation and constant correction, is rather in the category of absolutely essential. Considerable experience in classroom teaching of Yoruba (and several other African languages) has fully demonstrated that virtually every learner needs regular supervision and explanations that even the best teaching materials do not provide. Fortunately, some speakers of Yoruba (many more than of most African languages) are not only satisfactory models, but rather competent teacher-guides as well. If one's purpose is only to learn to read a language, a book alone may possibly suffice, though using only a book is most inefficient; however, Rowlands' continued emphasis on pronunciation (especially tone), and the relative unimportance of Yoruba as a written language (there just is not much written), make the "teach yourself" concept reprehensibly deceptive for the average would-be learner.

With this serious reservation, it should quickly be added that Rowlands has done a generally admirable job of presenting the phonology and the grammar of Yoruba accurately and in a pedagogically useful way. This book may be genuinely recommended for students (especially of linguistics) who have had a good background in one or more other African tone languages.

Constant and careful attention to tone and to certain occurrences of vowel length is crucial to learning Yoruba, and the author places entirely appropriate emphasis on these aspects of Yoruba structure. He wisely adds two tone marks in phrases and sentences to those required for words in isolation, to account for the effect of a "latent low tone" belonging to an elided vowel (pp. 29–31). He also happily indicates the usually unwritten high tone that marks a noun as the subject of a verb in many combinations (pp. 34–35). He also describes the "associative" tone in noun phrases and before possessive pronouns (pp. 44–47); he could have incorporated this also into his writing system, to the learner's advantage. The widespread pronunciation of four of the subject pronouns with low rather than mid tone is noted in the case of a habitual construction marked by *maa n-*, but unaccountably the same variation before *n-* alone is not mentioned (pp. 60–61).

The absence of a primary singular-plural distinction in Yoruba is noted (pp. 40–42), but a more systematic statement of the contrasting uses of personal and other nouns is possible and desirable. The use of *àwọn* has to do basically with individuation; pluralization is merely an inevitable implication. Similarly, the distinction between verbs generally referring to description and those referring to action could usefully be refined; descriptive verbs in the "simple" construction may refer to the past only if a reference to past time is added (pp. 9–10), while action verbs (pp. 18–19) in the same construction cannot under any circumstances refer to the present.

The label "dependent verb forms" for clauses introduced by *kí* (pp. 71–74) obscures – and the author does not mention – the fact that such clauses are frequently used by themselves: *k'á lọ* "let's go", *k'ó lọ* "he should go, have him go".

On page 67, third person pronouns are erroneously given first person equivalents in English. Fortunately, such slips, as well as printer's errors, are rare in the book. The weaknesses of the work – which by no means predominate – seem generally to be efforts to simplify, which always run the risk of confusing rather than clarifying.

University of California   Wm. E. Welmers
Los Angeles, U.S.A.

A. L. Adu, *The Civil Service in Commonwealth Africa.* New York, Humanities Press (George Allen and Unwin), 1969, 253 pp., $ 6.00.

Mr. Adu's *The Civil Service in Commonwealth Africa* is essentially a revised version and second edition of *The Civil Service in New African States* and represents the author's adjustment to the many changes that have occurred in Commonwealth Africa during the half decade or so that has elapsed since the first edition appeared. His magisterial views, expressed in a suitably lapidarian flow of bureaucratic prose, the breadth of his experience, his intellectual grasp of the problem in hand and his ability to marshall the appropriate arguments to support a particular standpoint are all qualities richly displayed in this book. Adu views the Civil Service as the still centre around which political storms may rage in vain and whose structure if carefully set up can withstand all shocks. The Civil Service can be a blue-print for survival and the present volume provides us with detailed instructions on how to adapt any existing African Commonwealth Civil Service to this end.

Although the author seems almost bemused by the overwhelmingly important role of the bureaucracy in developing countries, it would appear that messages have reached him about disturbing developments in the outside world: African Socialism in the Tanzanian style: complaints about salary differentials: and a general distemper called "accelerated constitutional developments." "Get the structure right" Mr. Adu seems to be urging us and then like Noah you can sit out the flood. As the former head of the Ghana Civil Service, he writes with authority and comments sadly in an introductory page of acknowledgements that Dr. Nkrumah after 1961 "did much to undermine the integrity of the Ghana Civil Service." The author continues in a style that summarizes much of his subsequent argument: "Nevertheless I still feel that the policies which were established during the pre-1961 period not only gave the Ghana Civil Service a firm foundation, but also sustained it through the period of transition so that, helped by structural reforms now being made, it is emerging as a viable instrument for political economic and social change."

Mr. Adu prefers to advance his argument by definition: key terms are defined and as in Aristotelian essentialism a number of critical deductions are subsequently made embodying rules of the game. What should be the relationship of the senior civil servant to his Minister under a one-party regime – given that the basic rule is that "the civil servant should not identify himself with any political party?" (p. 28). Adu's answer seems to be business as usual with an emphasis on special restraint and sensitivity towards political matters (p. 28). This reads remarkably like play it cool and do not embarrass the Minister. What structure is appropriate to new circumstances? The structure of the Service is defined as "the arrangement of the component parts to form an organic whole" (p. 32), which would seem to leave many questions unanswered. What makes the civil servant contented, or rather what structure can provide the possibility of such happiness? Answer: the creation of multiple ladders up which even the humblest aspirant may climb to better things. Mobility is all. Mr. Adu believes firmly that qualities emerge that enable a man to be picked out for promotion. It is interesting to note that among these qualities ambition is not mentioned and this is because the *essence* of a particular grade (Administrative and so on) is contained in its functional definition which does not include the human qualities of those who are to fill the posts. Frankly, the section on remuneration ducks all the issues: the ex-colonialists are blamed for paying inflated salaries but one has scarcely advanced on colonial principles by stating that the levels of present-day salaries are dependent on "general levels in a particular country and they may also change in time" (p. 57).

The basic weakness of Adu's approach to bureaucracy in the new Africa is his failure to think out afresh the bases of a fruitful relationship between administration and politics. And there are few men better equipped than the author to undertake such a study. As it is, British practice is strained beyond credulity to ensure that new wine is put into old bottles. A book to read for those who wish to know the African establishment view on Public Administration.

Lakehead University   GEOFFREY F. ENGHOLM
Thunder Bay, Canada

Tayeb Salih, *Season of Migration to the North.* London, Heinemann, 1969, 169 pp. (Translated from the Arabic by Denys Johnson-Davies), 25/.S.

After having written *The Wedding of Zein* in which, with humour and insight, are depicted scenes from Sudanese village life, Tayeb Salih has made a moderately successful attempt in *Season of Migration to the North* to translate in novel form the problems of acculturation. His method is that of the extended metaphor. The hero, Mustapha Sa'eed represents the first generation of Sudanese to have been faced with the challenge of the West and the narrator, the second.

The action takes place in a Sudanese village where Sa'eed and the narrator meet. Both have had similar training in British schools and have spent a number of years in England. The unsettling effect, observable in other former colonial areas, results in a love-hate relationship with the colonizing power. This feeling is illustrated by Sa'eed's murdering of Jean Morris, his English wife. A similar image is suggested at the end of the book when the narrator attempts to swim across an unnamed river in an effort to reach the northern bank – hence the title of the novel. The issue is left in doubt since the swimmer cries out for help in mid-stream.

On this transparent framework of reference the author has grafted a number of sub-plots which complete the picture. Sa'eed is a womanizer who preys on the numerous females who are irresistibly attracted to his dark features and the promise of erotic adventures which they seem to guarantee. When one of his victims, thrilled at the thought that Sa'eed was born on the banks of the Nile, cries out enthusiastically, "The Nile!", Sa'eed replies with a delightful touch: "Yes. Our house is on the bank of the Nile. So that when I'm lying in my bed at night I put my hand out of the window and idly play with the Nile waters till sleep overtakes me" (p. 39).

If the woman in question is destined to become the prey of Sa'eed's cynicism, he in turn will have to pay the price of his prolonged contact with Western civilization. His desperate attempt to reconcile his past and present leave him no alternative but to commit suicide. The fact that the narrator attempts to reach a "northern" shore strongly suggests that the author sees a final solution. If the second generation cannot quite bridge the gap, then perhaps the third will.

One of the most difficult assignments for the ambitious novelist is to create a work of art which develops on two levels, that of metaphor and reality. Salih's didactic intentions tend to shine through the plot, with the result that the "events" of the story cannot be taken too seriously. The publishers suggest in the introductory notes to be found on the jacket that *Season of Migration to the North* can be compared with E. M. Forster's *Passage to India*. There is little to justify such a claim. Rather, Tayeb Salih has written a worthwhile novel which affords considerable insight into the psychological problems which educated men and women are facing in the developing nations of Africa. *Season of Migration to the North* is hardly the last word, artistically or sociologically speaking, but it does make for pleasant reading.

University of British Columbia   GÉRARD TOUGAS
Vancouver, Canada

N. Long, *Social Change and the Individual: A Study of the Social and Religious Responses to Innovation in a Zambian Rural Community*. New York, Humanities Press (Manchester University Press for the Institute of Social Research, University of Zambia), 1969, 257 pp., $ 8.50.

Long's book is a highly analytical study of social responses to economic change in one parish in the Central Province of Zambia. Based on field research carried out in 1963–64, it is a work in the evolving tradition of social anthropology at the University of Manchester. The book draws a good deal on the recent writings of J. Van Velsen, V. W. Turner, and others. In a compact manner Long tackles the problem of how to analyze rural social change in a meaningful way without becoming entangled in older problems of structuralism, in equilibrium concepts, the need or urge to describe the total social structure, and in functional theories.

The parish in question is small (somewhat more than 1,000 persons), many of its inhabitants have had urban contacts or lived in urban areas at one time or another, and it is going through a process of commercialization of agriculture, using plough techniques. The changes involve the growing of traditional crops as surplus beyond subsistence needs, as well as the recent introduction of tobacco as a commercial product. In addition, there has been the development of a number of small stores, and a considerable increase in modern craft skills, such as carpentry and bricklaying. Many of the innovators belong to Jehovah's Witnesses. Associated with the economic changes there has been a breakdown in the older village settlement pattern of the matrilineally-oriented Central African type into smaller individual settlements of traditional subsistence agriculturalists and of commercial farmers and storekeeper families. In addition, the ranking of social statuses has undergone changes, with new categories introduced and older ones altered in position.

Long operates in terms of three social fields: economic, residential, and social status. He believes that this social field approach frees him from the more formal boundaries of an overall structural study. In the discussion of each social field he uses the description and analysis of specific cases or events, the technique of situational analysis. From the cases he draws conclusions about that field which he then tests with quantitative field data. Here the study breaks new ground, for the problem of selectivity in the use of exemplifying cases is checked through quantitative methods. The approach is valuable, also, in providing insights into the factors that motivate individuals to act in new, as well as more traditional, ways; persons are seen as strategists operating in competitive situations.

In the economic field Long spends a good deal of time discussing problems of labor and work in the traditional and modern farms. He is particularly concerned with relating labor needs to residential patterns, and to the question of kin *vs.* contract labor as a basis of work. The strategy of farming, given the economic situation in the parish and the nature of kin ties and other social relations, becomes a central issue. He then moves to a careful analysis of the village residential pattern and the changes in settlement occurring in the parish, taking two villages as his cases. Here he uses both genealogical analysis and statistics. The third social field, social status, is attacked through the analysis of various linguistic terms for status and authority and then depends heavily on a prestige-rating questionnaire and scale. Here he reverses his usual procedure for he first develops his general ideas of status and then, with a single lengthy case, shows how his categories can be usefully employed in social analysis.

At the end of the book the author raises Max Weber's thesis on the Protestant ethic in terms of the considerable role that members of Jehovah's Witnesses play as innovators in the parish. He discusses those aspects of their religious ethic which he considers especially important to social change and explores the paradox of a people denying the validity of human authority and of status distinctions and yet being highly motivated in these directions as innovators. In his conclusions he cautions that great care is needed in the comparative analysis of religious ethics and social change; different social groups may use various aspects of the same religious ethic in change, and the particular social and economic milieu of each group in question is important.

This is a notable book. Combining concepts of social field, situational analysis, and quantitative techniques, and bringing in data only when directly related to his study, it should serve as a valuable model to both students and professionals. One might quarrel with it at points here and there – the prestige-rating scale needs other supporting quantitative evidence, and Weber's argument is more complex than Long's presentation of it – but the overall sense is of a very neat analysis, a major step forward in the study or rural social change.

University of Washington   Simon Ottenberg
Seattle, U.S.A.

Audrey I. Richards, *The Multicultural States of East Africa.* London, McGill-Queen's University Press, 1969, ix + 123 pp., $ 4.50.

This book consists of a collection of related essays which were given in memory of Professor Keith B. Callard in October, 1966. She discusses the diverse ethnic groups of East Africa, their cultural classifications, the persistence of tribal societies, the new ethnic rivalries – taking Uganda as a case study – and the problems of rural development.

The book suffers from the following disadvantages: First, it contains a number of factual errors. For example (p. 11) The Kabaka was deported in 1953 and not in 1954 (p. 48). He returned in November, 1955 and not in 1954. (p. 51).

She refers to Ganda, Nyoro, Soga etc. whereas the right nomenclature should be Baganda, Banyoro and Basoga. I hope that anthropologists and other writers will in future be rigorous enough to reject the traditional wrong nomenclatures. There are other mistakes which have not been mentioned because of the shortage of space.

Second, she makes a number of important statements which have recently been proved to be either half-true or entirely dubious. For example, on p. 41, she says, "the Karamojong rejected the civilisation of Europe." Recent research has shown that the colonial government tended to preserve Karamoja District as a kind of "human Zoo", in Uganda. In fact, many of the people in Karamoja were not exposed to the so called "civilisation of Europe" (Incidentally she misspelt "Karamojong"). More evidence on the subject will be shown in our forthcoming publication on Uganda. On page 10 she says, "In Uganda, however, Swahili is disliked by the dominant Ganda whose language, Luganda, was taught in schools all over the area..." This is a serious statement because it raises serious questions of linguistic communication in East Africa, inter-tribal, cultural penetration and political integration. And thus it must be backed by serious empirical data. And yet as I have argued elsewhere the question of either rejecting or accepting Swahili or any other language depended largely on its functional utility. Thus Muteesa I, the King of Buganda, learnt Swahili because he used it to procure guns, etc. It has as yet to be established empirically whether the Baganda as a group rejected Swahili especially where it served functional purposes.

On page 86 she says, "All three territories, with Zanzibar now united to Tanzania, have become one-party states and this of course can make a sense of unity." To begin with, the banning of opposition parties in Kenya and Uganda is very recent. Indeed in Uganda it took place in late December, 1969. It is, of course, too early to appraise the likely consequences of banning opposition parties. Suffice it to say that even in Tanzania where a one-party situation was in many ways a spontaneous growth, the phenomenon has not always been an integrating factor.

Third, she relies heavily on Secondary Sources. The book has, of course, positive dimensions. Her analysis of the reasons why tribal societies persist is sound especially when she points out on page 14 that "new economic inequalities created new forms of ethnic rivalry after the granting of independent rule." Her identification of the problems of political integration in Uganda may be controversial but it is candid and has a lot to offer. In fact this little book contains a lot of important economic and political facets dealing with integration which are rewarding.

Makerere University College   APOLO NSIBAMBI
Kampala, Uganda

Alan Milner (ed.), *African Penal Systems*. London, Routledge and Kegan Paul, 1969, xiii + 501 pp., no price given.

Though it may be a rather negative form of praise to put it this way, the first thing to be said about this book is that it is far better than it might have been. It could indeed have been dreadful. A round-up of the penal systems of Africa, state by state, could have been the occasion for a series of "national" contributions in the worst sense, formal, uncritical, and larded with uninformative official statistics. As it is, it has other limitations; but albeit in varying degrees, all the contributors have made some attempt at an independent analysis and assessment, and some contributions are very independent indeed. There is, in short, not much whitewash.

Secondly, several of the contributors make a valiant effort to face three related questions. Are there, or were there, distinctive approaches to the nature of crime and the treatment of offenders characteristic of traditional African cultures? Have such approaches anything to contribute to the solution of modern problems? And how have they affected the present-day treatment of offenders in African states since Independence? The contributors, that is, have seriously tried to bring to their task an anthropological as well as a legal and penological approach to their problems.

Thirdly, though there is much of interest in the first part of the book, which consists of straightforward accounts of the present-day system in several African states, there is greater illumination in depth in the more specialized, albeit less comprehensive, essays in the second part. Among these, Milner and Asuni's impressively scholarly paper on psychiatry and the criminal offender and Welsh's review of the use of the death penalty in South Africa are outstanding contributions to knowledge; while the interesting and otherwise somewhat neglected topic of the penal law in relation to economic development is well analysed by Costa, and the one attempt to assess the experience of imprisonment from the prisoner's point of view is to be found in Tanner's essay in an East African setting.

As Milner points out in his preface, "criminology has not yet begun to flourish in Africa", and the chief limitation of any book on this subject is bound to be lack of material. The main reason for this is simply that, like the penal system itself, research in criminology is grossly under-provided with the necessary resources, though it has to be added that some African governments are secretive about their prisons, as has been shown in recent prosecutions in South Africa. This book is especially valuable accordingly in providing some illuminating insights.

It is not easy to imagine how a work on penology could be exactly cheerful reading; in evaluating the content of such a book, the sort of questions which the humane and (in a broad sense) liberal reader will have in mind will presumably be: Are things worse than they must inevitably be? Granted that the first aim must be the prevention of crime and the protection of the law-abiding public, are offenders treated as humanely as the circumstances permit? Are conditions such as to allow both prisoners and their captors to retain and even develop their human dignity? And in addition, those with a special interest in the recent history of Africa will ask: Were penal conditions unduly harsh under colonial rule? Have they improved or deteriorated since Independence?

This book enables us to answer these questions, at any rate in broad outline; and the answers are mostly in the negative. Though the picture is not one of unrelieved gloom, yet the overwhelming impression is one of "man's inhumanity to man", and first and foremost among the causes must be put the insufficiency of resources. Seidman in his historical perspective of the Ghana prison system, for instance, makes it abundantly clear that a strong and persistent "strain of humane feeling" in the system has been equally persistently frustrated by overcrowding, and in this Ghana does not seem to be untypical. Equally vividly, Milner and Asuni demonstrate the impossibility of affording psychiatric

help to disturbed prisoners in African countries, some of which, such as Bechu-
analand, Swaziland and the Gambia, had no psychiatrists at all, while others
like Cameroon, Gabon, Congo (Brazzaville) Niger Republic and Sierra Leone
had one each, and Nigeria had the largest number of ten, apart from South
Africa – to practice among the whole population, that is, not only among
prisoners. In these circumstances one African psychiatrist's request to see all
charged murderers was refused "on the grounds that the distances were too
large and security arrangements too tenuous for the authorities to be able to
agree. A judge warned the same psychiatrist that he would kill himself with
work if he tried to carry out any such project" (p. 355, note 36).

Secondly, callousness, cruelty, and crudely punitive attitudes – though by
no means universal in Africa, as the last example shows – also make for a degree
of avoidable inhumanity in African penal systems. To quote Seidman again,
with reference to Ghana, but not untypically, "Thus has 'the great object of
reclaiming the criminal' been shrivelled by insufficient funds, and by courts
which have no understanding of the penological problem."

It will come as no surprise to find these factors particularly strong in the
Republic of South Africa. Whether one adopts with Welsh a purely structural
analysis, based on the salient features of South African society, or essays an
Adorno-style explanation in terms of authoritarian personality and (one would
add) ideology, there is a constellation of attitudes and practices which tend to
be found consistently in association and which include racial and social stereotyping, over-categorisation, prejudice, insecurity, and approval of harshly
absolutist practices in the treatment of offenders, including the death penalty.
Where in other countries at a comparable level of civilization "capital punishment has increasingly come under criticism and has in many instances been
abolished,... the government of South Africa has set its face against abolition
or even diminution in the use of the death penalty. The number of persons
executed has dramatically increased over the last two decades, and the range
of offences for which the death penalty may be imposed has widened" (p. 397).
Not only murder and treason but also rape; robbery and housebreaking with
aggravating circumstances; sabotage; and child-stealing and kidnapping may
now be punishable with death. Judicial hangings have been carried out in
recent years at a rising average rate, now of about a hundred a year, while
– though the government admits no such separate category – it appears that
there have been about fifty political executions during the nineteen-sixties.

What of the former colonial regimes? The penal policies and practices of
the metropolitan countries in the nineteenth century were not exactly gentle.
In Britain, for instance, harsh doctrines of less eligibility and penal labour in
the period 1876–1907 left little that could be done to persons who committed
further offences in prison but flogging; and the British system was faithfully
followed in African colonies such as the former Gold Coast, as Seidman's
account makes clear. It was never, in fact, true, that flogging was essentially
something that white men did, or caused to be done, to black men, as poor Fanon's analysis in "The Wretched of the Earth" would lead us to believe; and
African convicts in the eighteen seventies probably fared no worse than their
counterparts in Britain and the other colonial powers of Europe. Equally,
however, as the harshness of the regime in British prisons was relaxed, and
reformation rather than deterrence became officially the chief aim in the treat-

ment of offenders, so also in the prison systems of the British African colonies – though it is fair to add that neither the early harshness nor the later humaneness were in the least degree directly related to African conditions.

An several of the contributions make clear, flogging, once commonplace in prisons in the British colonies, virtually fell into desuetude everywhere during the 1920's and 30's; while the judicial caning of juveniles survived only in a few places, including for instance, Basutoland, partly in the absence of alternative provisions for young offenders, and partly because of strong support in the local culture (p. 184). While it is a further refutation of Fanon, it is accordingly ironic and sad to find that man's inhumanity to man in these respects has certainly not been generally diminished by the end of colonial rule and the setting up of independent African states. While in the Portuguese colonies corporal punishment has not existed for several centuries and capital punishment was abolished in 1870, the independent states of Africa have generally retained the death penalty – in more than one, indeed, there have been public executions since Independence – and there has been a tendency to re-introduce or resort increasingly to various forms of corporal punishment in response to public clamour. The saddest case, perhaps, is Tanzania. The savage floggings of the German East Africa period, a practice strongly reversed under British rule, are apparently remembered there with awe – and with approval, not with revulsion (p. 109); and despite the evident misgivings of Vice-President Kawawa (p. 163, note 83), and the impressive contrary arguments of the Commissioner of Prisons, Mr. Rugimbana (p. 151), the then Tanganyika parliament passed in 1963 a Minimum Sentence(s) Act which can only be described as disgraceful, providing as it does for the compulsory imposition for offences, mostly against property, and many of them trivial, of a period of imprisonment together with corporal punishment of twenty four strokes, administered in two instalments, respectively at the beginning and the end of the imprisonment (pp. 149–51). As already suggested, when one learns of harsh brutality in South Africa one may be appalled, but not astonished. When Tanzania acts in this way, however, the sense of shock is greater; for even though the brutality involved in judicial caning is somewhat less, the regression to harshly punitive attitudes and practices seems sadly at variance with the high moral tone and the pretensions to enlightenment which had come to be associated with the country which framed the Arusha declaration.

University of Leeds   J. E. GOLDTHORPE
Leeds, England

A. Humbaraci, *Algeria: A Revolution that Failed: A Political History since,* 1954. New York, Praeger, 1966, 2 maps, xvi + 308 pp. No price given.

It is not easy to break ground in the political study of a contemporary new nation. The writer faces a multitude of daily events which must be organized into some comprehensible pattern. This can be an immense job in itself, especially with a country like independent Algeria, where policy decisions and political alliances have been one long stream of surprises and apparent contradictions. A second necessity is to probe in depth the underlying social and world environmental context which is responsible for the "political game" at the surface. To fulfill both of these tasks is perhaps too much to demand of a writer in a single book.

Arslan Humbaraci, a Turkish journalist, has made a valuable contribution toward the first of these tasks. In this second major study of post-independence Algerian politics to be published in English (David Gordon's new book appeared in early 1966), Humbaraci does much to clear the air of myths fostered by some, both on the Right and the Left, since 1962. These had usually asserted that Algeria, especially under Ben Bella, was either "crypto-Communist" or "on the threshhold of socialism." Humbaraci is at his best in this "muckraking" function, repeatedly demonstrating how often both the Ben Bella and Boumedienne regimes failed to live up to the promises of their ideological statements. Relying to a considerable extent on his personal contacts with certain Algerian political leaders (with a subsequent regrettable minimum of footnotes), Humbaraci identifies the various areas in which the "image vs. reality" contrast has been the greatest and how large in fact was the gap.

In this context, about one-half of the book discusses Algerian foreign policy. Especially good descriptions are offered of Algeria's relationships with France (and the French Left), the U.A.R., and black Africa. In domestic politics, he gives considerable attention to the power rivalries and conspiracies among the leadership elite, the failure to construct an economic and administrative infrastructure more adequate for Algerian development and more independent from France, and the almost non-existence of the F.L.N. political party. His coverage of the Summer 1962 crisis and the growing buildup of pressures behind the June 1965 coup are particularly useful. His overall assessment of Ben Bella is one of a man with little intellectual depth, poor administrative ability, and few principles other than power accumulation. Boumedienne emerges somewhat better only because of his obvious administrative talents and his apparent desire to avoid "dialogues with the crowds". It would have helped his description of the power struggle, however, if Humbaraci had elaborated more on the role of the U.G.T.A. (trade union movement), the 1963 mobilization of genuine popular enthusiasm through the workers' self-management movement, and the ideology and membership of the groups within the post-coup A.N.P. (army). It is also unfortunate that the writer included a number of gross exaggerations and errors, among them the assertions that only one trade union leader had the courage to resist Ben Bella (p. 105), that the peasants fought during the war for nothing more than to own some land (p. 112), that the main pre-occupation of the self-management unit workers was petty thievery (p. 120), and that the masses never rose out of apathy after the Summer of 1962 (p. 223).

The greatest weakness of the book, however, stems from Humbaraci's intention to offer more than an organized description of the daily reality of Algerian politics. As his title implies, he is attempting to evaluate the whole Algerian experience. Although occasionally referring to certain roots of Algerian political behavior (the relevance of Islam to national identity, the difficulty of finding alternative aid and trade sources, etc.) he never adequately analyzes the extent to which such factors limited in advance the short- and middle-range bounds of Algerian political development. On the basis of Humbaraci's own account, for example, one could well argue that the inability of the political leadership to work together after independence was an *inevitable* result of the wartime split in its ranks. If this is the case, then in what sense is it fair to say that there was even a *possibility*, let alone success or failure, of a post-war economic and social "revolution"? Unfortunately, Humbaraci never clearly defines what he means by "revolution" in the process of demonstrating its "failure". From an absolute perspective, it is obvious that no revolution is successful. If one defines and analyzes at least some of the apparent limitations on progress which existed in advance, however, a much more balanced assessment can be made. Within such a perspective, the shortcomings of the post-1962 years are still evident, and Humbaraci's book definitely contributes to a knowledge of these. But certain elements of successful "social revolution", such as even the limited gains in the realm of workers' self-management, must also be acknowledged even if they are achieved at a slower, less dramatic pace than the Algerian leaders proclaim.

St. Mary's College   DAVID PORTER
St. Mary's City, U.S.A.

A. Abdel-Malek, *Idologie et renaissance nationale, l'Egypte moderne.* Paris Editions Anthropos, Centre National de la Recherche Scientifique, 1969, 575 pp., Fr. 50.

This book brings together and further develops ideas which the author, Anouar Abdel-Malek, of the Centre National de la Recherche Scientifique, has put forward in a number of previously written articles. The result is an extremely interesting and provocative analysis of nineteenth-century-Egypt. Although the author is reputed to have been one of Egypt's leading Marxist thinkers in the period prior to 1959, the analysis does not bear the marks of a rigidly doctrinaire approach to the subject. The author is obviously imbued with a sense of deep devotion to the land of his birth and an admiration for the intellectual awakening which it experienced during the nineteenth century in the wake of the great social, economic and cultural changes effected under the reign of Muhammad Ali, and wishes primarily to provide a theoretical framework for the understanding of that awakening and of the national ideology which it produced. If the point of view is Marxist and universalistic, it is not on that account less sensitive to national concerns and values. The greatest figure of the Egyptian national renaissance, in the judgment of M. Abdel-Malek, is al-Tahtawi (1801–1873), the great nationalist writer, who is also presented here as, in his later years, a great socialist thinker who comes nearest, of all his contemporaries, to a Marxist point of view.

As a theoretician, M. Abdel-Malek treats nineteenth century Egypt as a case study in the phenomenon of national renaissance and emergent national self-expression. Both "infrastructural" and "superstructural" factors are taken into account, the former embracing the institutional foundations of national cultural activity, such as education and the press, the latter comprising the ideology itself, which provides the rationale for the national movement. The ideology of the Egyptian national movement is seen to be conditioned by a variety of factors: the Egyptian sense of a distinctive history, reaching back to time immemorial; the etatism of Muhammad Ali; the Islamic heritage; European thought. These factors to a large extent determine the *problematique* of the Egyptian national renaissance. One of the great problems for national develop-ment has to do with the relationship between the idea of religious community (*ummah*) and that of the nation as such (*watan*). Another problem is that of the symbiosis achieved under the system of etatisme (la symbiose etatique), a symbiosis of ruler and ruled, characteristic of hydraulic societies generally, which stands in the way of true synthesis necessary to nationhood. Because of the deep cleavage in Egyptian society between those who were influenced by Western values as a result of the new education inaugurated by Muhammad Ali and those whose education was of the traditional Islamic type, the ideological superstructure of the Egyptian national renaissance suffered from a fundamental dichotomy between two main currents: Islamic fundamentalism, as represented by Muhammad Abdu, and the liberal modernism of the followers of Tahtawi and others. Still another problem is posed by the confusion of socialism and etatism among Egyptian social thinkers, due in large part to the influence of the Saint-Simonian movement in Egypt.

M. Abdel-Malek's analysis extends to the period of the British occupation, which brought to an end the nineteenth-century Egyptian renaissance, or, as he frequently calls it, the first stage of the Egyptian renaissance, the second having commenced in the present century. The imperialist rule over Egypt is viewed as the dark night of modern Egypt, when imperialist policy deliberately sought to reinforce Islamic traditionalism, particularly in education, as a counter-force to the national movement.

The author leans heavily on secondary sources, i.e. works by contemporary scholars of nineteenth-century Egypt, of which he exhibits a wide command. This study therefore represents little original research; its purpose is rather to apply a particular method of analysis to the important but difficult task of interpreting nineteenth-century Egypt. Not all who read it will agree with the results in every instance, but all should find this attempt at fresh insight stimu-lating.

American University   B. WEISS
Cairo, Egypt

W. T. Newlyn, *Money in an African Context.* Nairobi, Oxford University Press (Studies in African Economics 1), 1967, 156 pp., $ 2.50.

This book seems to be an effort to provide a textbook on general monetary theory which will be of greater interest to African students than the ordinary textbook prepared with only students of advanced countries in mind. The author states in his preface that "this book results from my being asked to give the course of lectures on money and banking at Makerere University College." Mr. Newlyn's conception of how this task should be accomplished seems to be a combination of fairly orthodox, although very effective presentation of general monetary theory with a description of the monetary and banking institutions of three East African countries (Kenya, Tanzania and Uganda). Those readers who are attracted by the title and pick up the book in an expectation of learning something about the difference in the role of money in African societies or cultures and in others, or indeed in learning something about the role of monetary policy in the economic development of African countries, will accordingly be disappointed. The first two chapters on "Outline of Monetary Development" and "Determinants of Stock Money" are almost completely general. The third through the sixth chapters provide some information about the history and organization of the monetary and banking systems of the three countries. The seventh and eight chapters are again almost completely general; and where attempts are made to distinguish the general theory of monetary equilibrium from the East African context, the discussion is highly misleading, if not plain wrong. The author maintains, for example, that "in economies like those of East Africa" (p. 108) investment is less important than exports in a multiplier process. But a generalized multiplicand always includes exports, as well as private investment and government expenditures, and some advanced countries (such as Australia) also have a ratio of exports to income higher than the ratio of investment to income, at least to some years. He also apparently misunderstands the role of savings in a multiplier process, arguing that savings have a smaller role in East Africa because they are not channeled into investment institutions. This fact is of no importance in the multiplier process; all that counts is what share of income is diverted from current consumption. Newlyn also repeats an all too common mistake of saying that the multiplier does not work when there is no idle capacity. Developing countries who accept this error as gospel will find to their sorrow that the multiplier works all too well when there is no idle capacity, taking the form of inflation. The book closes with a chapter on the three central banks, and a final sermon stressing the need for wisdom in the management of central banks, no matter what form the central bank legislation takes.

Neither students of African affairs nor of economic development will learn much from this book. To those who wish a brief survey of the money and banking systems of the three countries, they will find such descriptions here in concise and convenient form.

University of Montreal   BENJAMIN HIGGINS
Montreal, Canada.

R. Lewis, and **Y. Fey,** *Painting Africa White: The Human Side of British Colonialism.* New York, University Books, 1971, xviii :238 pp., $ 12.50.

Somehow it seemed appropriate that "Painting Africa White" – (the less explicit title of the English edition is "The British in Africa") should arrive on my breakfast table the same morning as did the news of the Rhodesian Agreement – perhaps the last attempt that Africa will see to perpetuate the whitewashing process.

This beautifully produced book seems at first sight to be a Coffee Table book for intellectuals who enjoy a joky backward look at the funnier aspects of the departed Colonial era. The illustrations are numerous and splendidly chosen and cover most of the activities of the Whites in Africa over the last 200 or so years – missionary, exploratory, military, administrative, domestic and sporting. Victorian catalogues from the Army and Navy Stores extol the merits of the "Rhorkee" carrying chair for explorers and missionaries, solar topees and double terais, rifles, spine pads and compendious safari chests. There are delightful pictures of the first white nurses and teachers who braved the dangerous trek into the interior of Africa attired in long flannel skirts and whale-boned collars – and many other good things. It is immensely diverting to delve into the shopping lists of the 19th century pioneers and to read from their letters and diaries about their daily lives and adventures. For the pictures alone the book is worth the money.

But there is much more to the book than this. It begins with the first attempt by the British to administer Tangier, part of Charles II's dowry on his marriage to Catharine of Braganza. This ended in failure and a scuttle organised by the ubiquitous Mr. Samuel Pepys – but not before a duckung stool had been installed as punishment for females guilty of malice or gossip which was not, perhaps unfortunately, extended to later British communities in Africa. From the 17th century to modern times, the book traces the British presence in Africa, ending with two modern historical events – the Independence Celebrations in Tanganyika, presided over by British Royalty, and the declaration of U.D.I. in Rhodesia. At the first occasion the British watched the lowering of the Union Jack and departed "with little left but to wonder how the Blacks would ever do without them", while the theme song of white Rhodesia was "They revert. When excited or drunk, they revert". The theme of supposed white superiority repeats itself throughout the long period covered by this book.

The authors believe, and I think prove, that the British though often courageous and generous in uncomfortable and sometimes very dangerous conditions have nearly always been convinced of the basic superiority of white civilisation over black. Interestingly, they suggest that during the peak period of British penetration into Africa, the influence of Darwin was paramount. Much that they found was horrifying – the skull littered execution groves of the Asantehene, the callous cruelty of the Buganda court, the African participation in the slave trade. This, it is argued, served to reinforce the belief that the Africans were far behind the white races in the evolutionary process and only very recently down from the Darwinian trees. Perhaps it also helped to justify the German massacres in East Africa and other atrocities. By and large, however, the British were more paternalistic than brutal.

Victorians, in any case, had a natural tendency to adopt a paternalistic view of the Blacks as they had with the lower classes at home. Their survival in Africa depended on a copious supply of cheap and docile labour. Africans, for their part, felt outraged by the tacit assumption of superiority, combined with economic exploitation, and accentuated by the arrival of white wives at the turn of the century. Of course there were exceptions among the Whites – people who loved and understood Africans, and were loved by them – but in Southern Africa today such people form the endangered minority.

Whether if white people had come to Africa at an earlier period of their own bloodstained history, or had been less self-righteous and more genuinely interested in the positive aspects of African society, the outcome would have been different it is impossible to guess. But it is sad to trace the repetition of attitudes from those of Charles II's administrators down to those of recently arrived white bricklayers in Rhodesia in the 1970's – which make the prospects for interracial partnership in Africa tragically improbable today.

Two criticisms. The book is diffuse and darts disturbingly backwards and forwards up and down the historical and geographical scale – a fault perhaps inevitable in a comparatively short book about a whole Continent. Also, it stops short at the point when large numbers of British and Commonwealth young people are working in Africa without the prejudices which have befogged the past and in a spirit of comradeship and curiosity which may, hopefully, wipe out something of the paternalistic legacy.

London, England   HELEN HOPE

A. F. Isaacman, *Mozambique: The Africanization of a European Institution, The Zambesi Prazos, 1750–1902.* Madison, University of Wisconsin Press, 1972, xviii, 260, maps, tables, $ 17.50.

This book was written with the purpose of placing the subject of the *Prazos* – Crown estates established in the Zambezi basin early in the 17th Century by Portugal – in its correct African historical perspective. The nature of Portugese control over the *Prazos* has not been very clear until very recently. The Portuguese Crown in law could abrogate the charters establishing these *Prazos* but in practice Portugal's control over the Prazos was minimal if not absolutely non-existent. It was the wrong assumption that Portugal determined the growth and future development of the Prazos, that has led commentators and historians of Euro-African relations to see the *Prazo* as an alien institution which remained virtually untouched by the African environment where it operated. Writers who subscribed to this view have always seen the *Prazos* as alien institutions or even as pure and simple transplanted European feudalism.

What Isaacman has done constitutes a departure from this Euro-Centric bias. His conclusion, which is overdrawn to some extent, is that the *Prazo* as it evolved, became more or less an African institution and that by the beginning of the 19th Century the *Prazero* was no longer, strictly speaking, a Portuguese or Goan but a *Muzungu* (racially mixed Afro-Portuguese) who was less Portuguese and more African not only in his world-view but also in colour. Isaacman suggests that the resistance of some of these *Prazeros* against Portuguese attempt at effective occupation of Mozambique during the era of the scramble must be seen as part of the general African Primary resistance against imposition of European rule. His reason apparently for discountenancing the fact that the Matequenhas, the Bongas, the Gouveia and the Pereiras were strictly speaking not Africans and could not have led African resistance movements, is that the Africans who lived in these *Prazos* joined the resistance movements. One can of course deduce from reading the book that most of the Africans who fought on the side of the *Prazeros* were their Achikunda (warrior slaves on the Prazos) whose profession left them no alternative. As Isaacman himself points out the *Prazero's* authority had no traditional sanction and was therefore considered alien and illegitimate in the eyes of the Africans. In spite of this assertion there is an attempt to dismiss the fact that the power the *Prazeros* enjoyed arose out of their relative military superiority over the indigenous African policies. Dr.

Isaacman explains this by suggesting that the kind of master-subject relationship established by the *Prazeros* was not alien to the Zambesi and that it conforms to the earlier pattern of political subjection of the Tonga, Sena, and Chewa Chiefs to their Karanga and Malawi political overlords. This parallel does not necessarily nullify the point of the extra-African origin of the Prazeros.

The book is strong on several points, in spite of the obvious and generous use of social-science jargons, its treatment of the little impression Portuguese colonialism had on African society after centuries of Portuguese rule is very relevant to the on-going debate of Portuguese colonialism in Africa. The book points out the general weakness and inefficiency of Portuguese rule in Africa. The economy of Mozambique contrary to what one would have expected was not based on plantation agriculture. In fact the *Prazeros* were mostly traders. They traded first in Gold and Ivory and by 1821 the economy of Mozambique was based on the slave trade. About 85% of the total value of exports was realised from the legal sale of slaves. The history of the *Prazos* is in fact the history of the failure of plantation agriculture in Mozambique. The slave trade continued to dominate the economy of Mozambique up till the 1850s and like in some parts of West Africa, it destroyed the very foundations of the states and *Prazos* in this area.

This book also confirms the results of earlier researches about the essential differences of African slavery and plantation slavery. Isaacman points out the social mobility enjoyed by African slaves. They could marry sons and daughters of their masters, they were rarely ever sold except in times of extreme crisis.

Another important contribution of this book is the exposure of the myth of 'colour blindness' or lack of racial discrimination in the Portuguese Empire. Isaacman points out that marriage between a "Portuguese" female and a Goan was considered absolutely scandalous and that this kind of racial feeling was encouraged by a 1755 Legislation which enjoined on the *dona* (female estate holders) to marry only European Portuguese men and not Indians from Goa who must have been considered Portuguese with a difference.

The weakest points of the book are that Isaacman occasionally forgets the Central theme of the book and discussions that are not tangent to the main theme are constantly brought into the book thus throwing the whole work out of focus. The treatment of the politics of the area before the advent of the Portuguese is a bit confused; nevertheless this book in spite of its shortcomings is bound to attract the attention of scholars of Portuguese enterprise in Africa.

University of Ibadan   A. OSUNTOKUN
Ibadan, Nigeria

C. P. Potholm, *Four African Political Systems.* Englewood-Cliffs, Prentice-Hall, 1970, pp. 308, No price given.

It is not simply the 'breakdown' of 'democracy' in independent African States since the mid-1960's that has aroused so much interest in African Politics. Nor is it because Africa is simply unique. Rather, it is partly because of all the continents and sub-continents in the world, it is in Africa – particularly south of the Sahara – where there has been such rapid changes in political systems.

Of the several African governments which inherited the Parliamentary system of government, when the white Governors departed in the early 1960's, few, if any, seem to have any resemblance to their 'mother' Parliaments in London or Paris. Part of the explanation lies in the nature of the African societies both before and after the invasion of Africa by the white colonialists; even the existence of Pax Europeanna was unable to mould African societies into 'nations' that could ensure the continuation of the type of democracy prevailing in Europe. Independent Africa is faced with enormous problems: the leadership in most of black Africa was inept, corrupt and simply inefficient; independence itself opened the old wounds of 'tribal rivalries'; the departure of the colonial power removed the only obvious 'enemy' that fostered unity among the Africans; fragile economies dependent on one major cash crop have led to, or been the consequences of, lack of stability and progress; and the general difficulty of African States to cope with endemic world problems has only accentuated an already hopeless situation.

Nowhere are these developments discussed more basically and sympathetically than in Christian P. Potholm's *Four African Political Systems*. In a couple of chapters only, the reader is given a broad spectrum not only of the four Political Systems discussed here – that is, South African, Tanzanian, Somali and Ivoirien – but of almost *all* the African countries south of the Sahara. After reading Potholm's sober analysis of these four political systems, one realizes the extent to which we will remain indebted to this superb, well documented scholarly work.

The author starts off with a useful conceptual framework for comparative Politics (chap. 1). As a background to the discussion of the four African Political Systems, the author discusses political development and modernization in three "broad stages of societal development", namely: traditional, transitional and modern. Chapters 1 and 2 are examples of a clear academic mind at work; for in these two chapters the bases or "models" for the comparative studies of any Political Systems – whether African, Asian or Latin American – are suggested.

We are perhaps too well informed on the barbaric Political System in South Africa to expect any new ground to be uncovered; but, even though, the analysis is superb and the author succeeds in identifying at what level the decisions are really made and in showing how and why "the present form and style of command decision making... are the basic core values of South Africa, and [why] both are non-negotiable, either domestically or internationally" (p. 127), the crucial factor in South Africa's ability to defy the entire world is her strong economy. Thus wealth becomes a crucial criterion not only in the development but also in the actual survival of any African Political System. That is partly why the Ivoirien Political System – in a country with perhaps the highest income per capita in black Africa – has been able to survive in spite of the existence of serious political shortcomings and of the most obvious alienation of the mass of the people from the process of decision-making. In fact, Ivory Coast's present Political System owes its existence and survival largely to the presence of the French troops in the country as well as to Houphouet-Boigny's ability (because of the enormous wealth at his disposal) to reward handsomely his lieutenants who are in turn so committed to the system.

It is perhaps the discussions of the Tanzanian and the Somali Political

Systems that are most exciting. The Tanzanian System presented here is limited to that appertaining on the mainland, where Julius Nyerere has been able to "evolve" a unique Political System in which the existence of one political party has ensured in fact the real meaningful participation of the entire mass population. Thus the Tanzanian Political System ensures that the apparent "poverty" of the people is compensated by their participation in the decision-making processes. Somalia, a poor country like Tanzania, was also able to develop a good Political System until the military *coup* of 1970 which put an end to – or is it only a postponement? – of political activities in that part of the Horn of Africa. The Somali Political System had reached such a stage of development that, despite the several changes of government that occurred before 1970, there was no collapse of the processes of mass participation or decision-making at all levels. In Somalia the "defeated candidates for major political office [were] not shot, exiled or jailed: they [continued] to participate in politics" (p. 206). One of the reasons, however, for Somali unity – compared with elsewhere in Africa – was the oneness of the people to achieve the creation of the "Greater Somalia". There is no doubt, however, that of the four Political Systems under review, it is Tanzania's, despite the fragile economy and other problems common to all the developing nations, that appears most likely to absorb the stresses and strains that have contributed to the collapse of "democracy" elsewhere in Africa. Potholm's book is highly commendable; it is lucid, well documented and a pleasure to read. It is a pity, however, that the publishers did not tell us its price.

Makerere University   PHARES M. MUTIBWA
Kampala, Uganda

A. S. Mathews, *Law, Order and Liberty in South Africa*. Berkeley, University of California Press, 1972, 318 pp., $ 15.00.

A. S. Mathews, Dean of the Faculty of Law at the University of Durban, South Africa, has produced a detailed analysis of the numerous security laws presently in force in South Africa. The book will be of particular interest to the specialist in the South African field as the survey is precise and comprehensive. Mathews' overview makes it clear that discrimination is not merely an unfortunate byproduct of the existing economic structure in South Africa. Nor can the racism practiced by the government be explained solely in terms of acts of personal racial bias. Discrimination is part and parcel of the formal legal system, a calculated effort to deny the black majority of South Africa essential civil liberties. The book places particular emphasis on the discretionary features of these laws which give trusted white officials and judges immense power in the administration and enforcement of measures which again and again exceed reasonable bounds. Mathews' cool, dispassionate analysis invites confidence in his scholarship in an area where much of the literature is charged with rhetoric and short on analytic detail.

For the non-specialist the book will be less interesting. The volume is written in a fairly dry manner. Furthermore, such legislation can only be completely understood in terms of its effects on individuals in South Africa. But if read in tandem with a more personal account of the functioning of these laws (Carlson's *No Neutral Ground*, Crowell, 1973, for example) the extent to which such a set of laws are vital to a regime committed to the denial of basic human rights becomes apparent.

Although his survey of security legislation is clearly the core of this book, Mathews places his overview within the context of chapters which discuss various formulations of the minimum requirements of the rule of law and relates standards to the traditional attitudes of liberal governments. The author makes a fairly tantalizing beginning in comparing the South African approach to parallel laws in the United States, but both his comparison and the general perspective fall short of grappling with these larger problems in a fresh way. These chapters are shot through with references to classical and modern authors, but Mathews himself seems to have little new to offer to the analysis. Often, Mathews is critical of South African security legislation .Nevertheless, the discussion frequently degenerates into word games which seem unnecessary given the evidence amassed in the security legislation Chapters. In one instance, for example, Mathews attempts to distinguish between authoritarian regimes, totalitarian governments and pragmatic oligarchies, a digression which does little to advance the general notions Mathews is proposing.

Despite these criticisms, the book should stimulate further intensive study of the South African legal structure by specialists in the field. Such examinations are a necessary preliminary to a complete understanding of a system unique in its disregard for normal legal standards and its calculated effort to cloak discrimination with the legitimacy afforded by law.

New York University   ROBERT JANOSIK
New York, U.S.A.

J. C. Willame, *Patrimonialism and Political Change in the Congo.* Stanford, Stanford University Press, 1972, xii, 223. $ 8.50.

This book is a refreshing exception to those published doctoral dissertations which are too bookish and oriented more to discipline than subject. This is no doubt so because the author spent much of his time from 1960–65 in the Congo (Zaire Republic) studying provincial institutions and national events as a researcher in the Institute for Social and Economic Research of Lovanium University in Kinshasa and gained a close knowledge of Congolese politics before preparing a dissertation on these matters.

The book sets as its goal the understanding of politics in independent Africa, and in particular, in the Congo. This is no easy task, since such a study must include both the 1960–65 era of seccession rebellion, and administrative fragmentation, and the 1965–70 era following Mobutu's coup and increasingly centrist rule. Drawing theoretical inspiration from the institutional sociology of Weber and Marx, the author interprets the events of the first era as being the logical consequences of "patrimonialism". By patrimonialism is meant, in Weber's sense, 1) the appropriation of public offices as the prime source of status, prestige, and reward for an elite; 2) political and territorial fragmentation through the development of (centrigufal) relationships based on primordial and personal ties; and 3) the use of private armies, militias, and mercenaries as chief instruments of rule. This perspective permits him to postulate, for the disruptive events of 1960–65, an underlying political model whose logical unfolding is predictable, though the political climate was anything but that oftentimes. It is recalled colloquially as the time when the politicians ran away with the country.

The period since then from 1965–70 is marked by a swing of the political pendulum away from patrimonialism to the kind of political centralism identified as "Caesarist bureaucracy": a composite administration made up of the elements inherited from earlier eras – the patrimony of army, urban youth, intelligentsia, and businessmen – welded together into a bureaucratic structure topped by a single authority figure who in this case is, of course, President Mobutu. The unique historical and sociological forces having gone into the formation of this hierarchic combination, – e.g., the absence of any monied elite in the African population, the longtime hold of foreign cartels on the country's resources, to mention two related ones – make this emerging bureaucracy somewhat unique. The author describes in competent terms how a reduction of the number of provinces, the elimination of lower and middle-range decision-making bodies in the governmental hierarchy, and the frequent rotation of cabinet members, the more noticeable reform tactics of the Mobutu government, have gradually created a working government out of the pieces of earlier diverse patrimonies.

It is too early, suggests the author, to predict the durability of the governmental form that is replacing patrimonialism. The process is, in any event, yet incomplete. In the face of what Willame calls the "ultracontemporaneous" status of these events and phenomena, three alternative outcomes may be suggested: The present authoritarian and bureaucratic regime may continue at its present state – a fairly static eventuality that is not likely in view of the instabilities inherent in the structure and its component parts. Key groups may strengthen their existing links with external forces, especially the foreign trusts, and lead the country away from further centralization. A third and most likely possibility, borne out by intervening events, is that the authoritarian and personalistic tendencies will grow stronger, producing a purely dictatorial Caesarist regime with all the attending characteristics of the leader's isolation and non-tolerance of autonomous bases of authority – increasing the likelihood of coups and political assassinations typical of such regimes.

Begun as a careful study of a profoundly interesting and troubled period in Central African political history – the early years of independence – Willame's conclusions bear all the marks of going to press in the midst of recent events that needed to be explained. The book is surprisingly strengthened by such a tentative ending. An appropriate conceptual foundation is provided in terms of which subsequent events can be understood.

University of Kansas   John M. Janzen
Lawrence, U.S.A.

John S. Galbraith, *Mackinnon and East Africa 1878–1885. A study in the "New Imperialism".* London, Cambridge University Press, 1972, Pp. 246 & viii, $ 17.50.

The Imperial British East Africa Company was the stepchild of the great chartered companies in nineteenth century Africa. Little has been written specifically about the company since P. L. McDermott's book in 1895. Regrettably Marie de Kiewiet's thesis on the company which was completed in 1955 was never published. The founder, Sir William Mackinnon, has lacked a biographer and has remained a rather shadowy figure in the history of late Victorian imperialism. Professor John S. Galbraith of UCLA has attempted to remedy some of these deficiencies in this book.

Professor Galbraith takes us through the abortive attempt to create a concessionary company in 1878, the association of Mackinnon with King Leopold of the Belgians, the rivalry with Germany to the foundation of the company in 1888. The brief history of the company between 1888 and 1895 was a chronicle of disaster. Professor Galbraith makes it clear that Lord Salisbury thought good relations with Germany to be more important than East African empire but that he was content to use the company after the demarcation between Britain and Germany in 1886 as the cheapest means of ensuring that the British zone of influence would not be undermined. But it was this imperial role which would lead to the downfall of the company. No private company could compete with the resources of the German state. Furthermore, unlike Nigeria and Southern Africa, there was no real economic base for the IBEA – no minerals, no palm oil, not much wild rubber. Commercial prudence dictated a limited and cautious commercial base on the Coast with gradual penetration of the interior. Government pressure and dreams of glory persuaded the company to finance extremely expensive military operations in Somalia and in Uganda. The inevitable result was bankruptcy and the consequent threat to withdraw from Uganda. Ultimately Lord Rosebery decided, largely as a consequence of Protestant missionary pressures and strategic considerations relating to the control of the Nile, to declare the British East African Protectorate in 1895. The company was discarded and the unfortunate Sultan of Zanzibar forced to pay most of the compensation.

Professor Galbraith has provided an erudite and readable account of these events based on the large number of manuscript resources now available. This monograph is meant to be the prelude to a more general study of the British chartered companies in the nineteenth century. This perhaps explains the focus on the diplomatic background within which the company operated. But the main characters, particularly Sir William Mackinnon, remain shadowy and somewhat enigmatic. A biography is still very necessary. Professor Galbraith remains puzzled at the seeming irrationality of Mackinnon and the other Scots' businessmen involved in the company. But supposedly hard-headed andrational businessmen are just as prone to romantic folly as anyone else.

Canadian Association
of University Teachers

DONALD C. SAVAGE

Nnamdi Azikwe, *My Odyssey: An Autobiography.* New York, Praeger, 1971, pp. 452., $ 12.50.

Dr. Nnamdi Azikiwe's autobiography, *My Odyssey,* is a book that not only inspires but also leads one to reflect deeply. It is a comprehensive personal history of a man destined to play a major role in the political development of Africa and the Federal Republic of Nigeria in particular.

The book is sincerely dedicated to all those human beings "who continue to do good in spite of man's ingratitude" and man's inhumanity to man. It is a book envisioned in two or more volumes to chronicle Dr. Azikiwe's geneological development, his travels, and wholistic life experiences. The first volume quite comprehensively dealt with the early childhood days, the developmental processes in the British West Africa, and the great adventures in the New World.

Dr. Azikiwe was born in Zungeru, Northern Nigeria. Most of his early childhood days were spent at his native Onitsha in the East Central State and the Lagos State of the present Federal Republic of Nigeria. He attended the Methodist Boys' High School in Lagos, and the Hope Waddell Training Institution at Calabar. It was during his attendance at these schools that Zik (as he is affectionately and popularly referred to) encountered the socio-psychological forces that constituted the dynamic elements in his personality development. His personal encounter with Dr. Kwegyit Aggrey of Africa inspired him to manhood and to dream of a great life dedicated to the service for humanity in general and to the political and economic liberation of Africa in particular. He was introduced to great books written by great sons of Africa such as J. B. Danquah and Marcus Garvey, and to the biography of Abraham Lincoln and James A. Garfield of the United States of America.

After many years of nurtured dreams and psycho-spiritual struggles, Zik made his way to the United States of America. Here, he attended Storer College in West Virginia, Howard University, Washington, D.C., Lincoln University in Pennsylvania, Columbia University, and The University of Pennsylvania. In spite of formidable economic and socio-cultural difficulties, he was able to distinguish himself academically as well as athletically. In the course of his experiences, he developed many philosophical principles that were to guide him in the economic and political activities surrounding the development of Africa's struggles to be free from European colonial domination. He learnt to suffer in silence, to struggle with patience, to function with enthusiasm and humility, and above all to be magnanimous, philanthrophic, and grateful. It was indeed to his American experiences that Zik owes much of his principles of operation and the dynamic processes of human relations. He came to the full realization that man's inhumanity to man constitutes a universal pathology that all of mankind must unitedly work to cure. He was able to learn that the incidious elements of white-European institutional racism greatly diffused the economic, political, and social processes that sustained colonialism and the continued repression of the African peoples of this earth. He was able to realize the paradoxial predicament of the African peoples of the world who have continued to maintain an "inside and outside" simultaneous existence in a white-dominated world. No wonder his ultimate resolve to dedicate his life to the seeming eternal struggle to rid Africa of these negative scourges of man's inhumanity to man.

On completion of his academic studies, Zik returned to West Africa to begin his life – dedicated to the liberation struggle in Africa. He inspired many prominent sons of Africa to go to the United States of America in search of the "Golden Fleece" of knowledge. Among these great sons of Africa inspired by Zik, was Dr. Kwame Nkrumah. Zik's pioneer work in African journalism and political ventures began in Ghana. He launched his project armed with a "philosophy of new Africa" which he characterized by the principles of: (1) *Spiritual balance* connoting basic freedom of conscience, thought and opinion; (2) *Social Regeneration* to imply freedom in religious, social, economic, and political dimensions; (3) *Economic determination* to imply self-sufficiency, economic viability, and equity; (4) *Intellectual or Mental emancipation* to imply freedom of thought and expression towards the renaissance of Africa; (5) the *Political risorgimento*, to imply full political control embodying freedom, liberty, the pursuit of happiness, and the total uplift of African human dignity and the respect for African human personality. In spite of formidable odds and the exigency of imponderable forces, Zik was able to distinguish himself in all he dabbled with, economically, socially, culturally, and politically.

He established many newspapers in Ghana and Nigeria, actively participated and encouraged athletics, inspired many Africans to greater heights of political, economic and social existence, and yet emerged a venerable political figure in Africa in spite of people's ingratitude, deliberate distortion of facts, and their amorphous interpretations of Zik's actual role in the political development of Nigeria.

Howard University   P. CHIKE ONWUACHI
Washington, U.S.A.

L. Thompson, (ed.) *African Societies in Southern Africa: Historical Studies.* New York, Praeger (for African Studies Center, University of California), pp. 336, $ 8.75.

This book is a cooperative study and represents the new methods successfully applied to the writing of African history. Leonard Thompson, the editor of the collective volume, acknowledges the important work done by social anthropologists during the past decades through the careful collection of previously unknown evidence on precolonial southern Africa. He believes that it is now the task of the historian to use the vast amount of source material for the study of the process of change in the specific African societies. He does not attribute the neglect of the precolonial phase of South African history to the dearth of source material but to the fact that those who have recorded it represented their own non-African social environment which influenced their choice of perspectives.

To remedy the limited historical approach of past writers the present book undertakes the difficult task of bringing together archeologists, linguists, social anthropologists and historians. Although the latter represent he majority of contributors, even the historians in this volume have used a great deal of evidence and data relating to the social and anthropological structure of African society in their attempt to piece together the fragments of the economic and political history of tribes and chiefdoms. What has emerged is a study which spotlights the early and later Iron Age, the evolution of social relations before the nineteenth century, the destruction of the Zulu and Ndebele kingdoms and the transformation of their societies. In the concluding section the book concerns itself with the exploration of white politics on African society and African reaction during the process of subordination. The authors avoid cliches and are concerned with adding to our knowledge of the African past. In doing so their writings tend to be highly specialized.

To indicate briefly the nature of the material presented, the following sketches may serve as an illustration. Archeologist D. W. Phillipson of the National Monuments Commission in Zambia describes the archeological evidence in Zambia, Rhodesia, Bostwana and South Africa which makes it possible to draw conclusions regarding life in the Early Iron Age. He investigates social relationships in the above areas and in nearby geographical territories and finds that Zambian and Rhodesian cultures were not isolated phenomena but related to developments in adjacent regions. Anthropologist Brian Fagan of the University of California at Santa Barbara rejects the view that Bantu speaking peoples arrived south of the Limpopo at the time of the landing of Van Riebeeck at the Cape. Recent archeological and anthropological studies show that their existence in the area dates back to before 1400 AD. He suggests that archeologists can substantially contribute to the historical understanding of the southern African Bantu population through the study of the iron and copper trade and through the determination of dates and places of origin of the traceable artifacts and raw materials.

Monica Wilson, social anthropologist at the University of Capetown, shows the relevance of kinship studies to the historian. While the anthropologist concerned with the development of a kingdom in one tribe, tries to discover the cause of a particular development, the historian may use these findings to describe the process of growth of a kingdom. Professor Wilson sees other important sources of information in the study of the influence of marriage and kinship on the power and development of lineages and recommends the study of language change in relation to African history.

The question of whether the Sotho and Nguni peoples established themselves in South Africa as the result of mass immigration or whether they developed structured societies due to local developments prior to the nineteenth century is investigated by Martin Legassick of the University of California, Santa Barbara for the Sotho people while Shula Marks of the School of Oriental and African Studies, London, carries the investigation to the northern Nguni. Gerritt Harinck of the University of California, Los Angeles, has studied the interaction between the Khoi and Xhosa chiefdoms in the pre-colonial period and has come to the conclusion that their relationship was largely determined by the cultural compatibility of their societies.

The problem of the transition from small autonomous Nguni systems to Shaka's Zulu kingdom and the nature of the Difaqane and Mfecane among the Bantu-speaking peoples in the nineteenth century are investigated by three writers. Alan Smith of the University of California, Los Angeles concludes that trade with Delagoa Bay and trade monopolies by some rulers may have led to political consolidation. William Lye of Utah State University explains the tendency to Fission among pre-Difaqane Sotho society which was politically

unwise but helped the people to preserve their freedom and avoid subjection
to stronger chiefs after they had been uprooted. He does not consider the
Difaqane between 1822 and 1836 as a period of social destruction but rather as
a phase of social regrouping. And John Omer-Cooper of the University of
Zambia interprets the history of the Mfecane as a process of political change and
not, as has often been done, as a destructive phase of wandering tribes of the
pre-colonial era. Although society in Shaka's kingdom was subjected to an
absolute military despotism, he sees decentralizing tendencies among the Zulus
before Shaka aswell as during Shaka's regime. He comes to similar conclusions
regarding the Ndebele kingdom of Mzilikazi.

The final chapters by David Hammond-Tooke, social anthropologist of
Rhodes University, Anthony Atmore of the School of Oriental and African
Studies, London, and Colin Webb of Natal University concern themselves with
African reaction to the loss of freedom during the period of transition from in-
dependence to colonial status.

The authors of this volume have used a fresh approach to new and old
problems. Their essays betray originality even though the reader will not always
be fascinated by their presentation. Leonard Thompson's chapter on the forgotten factor in southern African history bridges the centuries and provides a
coherent frame for the diversified approaches to history of this multi-author
study of southern Africa. In his brief critical evaluations of the thriteen essays
he has brilliantly succeeded in giving the book the appearance of an organized
whole.

University of Hartford   ANN BECK
Hartford, U.S.A.

Sir Reginald Coupland, *Kirk on the Zambesi, A chapter of African history.*
Oxford, At the Clarendon Press, 1968, pp. 286, $ 8.00.

Sir Reginald Coupland's *Kirk on the Zambesi* was published in 1928. The
reissue of the book by Oxford University Press in 1968 testifies for the excellence
of Coupland's description of Livingstone's expedition to the Zambesi between
1858 and 1863. Many of the problems which the colonial powers experienced
decades later in Central and East Africa are here forcefully described during
their embryonic stage in a fascinating narrative which is still pertinent to the
historian. The scope of the book is not limited to Kirk's early career in Africa
when he served as lieutenant to Livingstone. One learns as much about Livingstone the explorer, the leader of a dangerous expedition, and the man who was
obsessed by his plan to attack slavery through the opening up of central Africa
to commerce and colonization, as one does about the first stage of Kirk's in-
fatuation with the wonders, mysteries and horros of Africa.

Coupland includes large sections of Livingstone's Journals and Kirk's
Diaries, a fact which in itself is of great value to the modern historian. And he
shows convincingly that Livingstone's plan to abolish the slave trade in the
East African interior through commerce and subsequent colonization had no
chance to succeed in 1858. In his description of Livingstone's scheme to improve the quality of African society by changing its economic basis, Coupland

unwittingly touches upon one of our own crucial problems of today. He quotes from bishop Mackenzie's letter to a friend in November 1861 when the bishop justified his interference in the internal affairs of the strife between the Manganja who were the proteges of his mission and the Ajawa who raided the Manganja for slaves. The mission fought off the Ajawa and established peace but Mackenzie questioned the wisdom of imposing a settlement as an outsider. Should the mission have become involved in an African war? Should Englishmen become entangled in the "savage politics" of the natives? Coupland pointed at the dilemma which white western man had to face when he penetrated Central Africa for humanitarian reasons.

Coupland described the overwhelming lure of Africa in a compelling way. Livingstone and Kirk succumbed to it in spite of exhaustion, fever, hunger and depression which plagued them when they were weakened and which were quickly forgotten as soon as they had regained their strength. Coupland painted fine studies in contrast in his character portrait of Livingstone, his fanaticism, dogmatism and dogged determination to proceed with the expedition against unconquerable odds which often made young Kirk question the sanity of his leader. Equally interesting is the portrait of Kirk whose personality was moulded during those five years in Nyasaland. Coupland stressed the impact of climate, disease and untamed nature on the execution of policy during the exploration of the Zambesi, the Shire highlands and the Rovuma river, a factor which later colonial administrators experienced with equal vehemence in the twentieth century.

Of particular interest is the analysis of the Portuguese failure to abolish the slave trade from the coast to the interior, the description of the degenerate state of the Portuguese residents in East Africa and their inability to develop Mosambique. The expedition sponsored by the British government came to an end in 1863 and was judged a failure because "it had only seen things and not done them. It had revealed the obstacles to its full programme of civilization, commerce and settlement; but it had not by any means removed them." And far from suppressing the slave trade, the report stated, it had helped its extension into the interior by opening up the connections between the coast and Lake Nyassa. The fundamental success of Livingstone and Kirk was not seen by their contemporaries. The capture of the last slave caravan west of Lake Nyassa in 1898, however, must be credited to the expedition.

The relevance of Coupland's book to modern African studies is beyond doubt and the specialist as well as the general reader has reason to be satisfied with its reissue.

University of Hartford   Ann Beck
Hartford, U.A.S.

Satish Saberwal, *The Traditional Political System of the Embu of Central Kenya,*
    Nairobi, East African Publishing House, for Makerere Institute of Social
    Research, 1970, pp. 107, 18.50 sh.

The study of "traditional society" frequently confronts the scholar with the worst of both historical and anthropological worlds: direct observation is not possible because change has destroyed the old system, while at the same time documents of the past are unavailable because the traditional institutions produced none. Yet without some grasp of the indigenous baseline, it is often difficult to make sense of contemporary currents of thought and social processes. Furthermore, traditional society is of interest in its own right as comparative material for theory construction and for the insights it can provide about the range of human institutions. These are good reasons for such studies, but is the methodology equally good and do the results live up to the promise?

Professor Saberwal's short description of traditional Embu society is a reconstruction of pre-colonial life, circa 1900, based upon interviews (through interpreters) with a small number of informants. With such a basis, "approximation to the facts is the only attainable goal" and "I accept my informants statements as true when I cannot show them to be false" (p. xvii). Documentation is from the interviews, and 18 "cases" are presented, these being reports of specific ceremonies, relationships, conflicts, and exchanges as recalled by the informants. The account is a synchronic one, describing the parts of the political system, how the parts fit together, and the resultant workings of the system.

The Bantu-speaking Embu, living on the slopes of Mt. Kenya, raised rainfall crops and large and small animal stock (Ch. 1). Their descent groups were conceptually shallow and weak in practice. Age set organization (Ch. 2) was important for individuals moving to warrior and elder status, and for raiding, but it did not generate strong corporate groups. The "genealogical generation" system (Ch. 3) defined the group of ruling elders, who had more ceremonial than temporal authority. Social control and conflict resolution (Ch. 4) were more a matter of persuasion, social pressure, supernatural sanctions, and self help, with little authoritative judgement or legislation possible. The resulting "loosely structured" society (Ch. 5) incorporated a wide range of beliefs and practices and tolerated a substantial amount of deviation.

The weakness of descent groups is attributed to "frequent population movement" which resulted from erratic rainfall. (This explanation seems preposterous given the many peoples from the Horn, the west, and the north of Africa, not to mention the Middle East, who maintain strong descent groups in a context of erratic rainfall and frequent migration.) Migration is also said to have weakened the age sets and generation system, although the latter also suffered from structural defects.

The tone of this work is that of strain from the struggle to extract a full picture from sketchy data, and the effect is flatness, lacking the life of much ethnographic reporting. To the extent that this is inherent in historical reconstruction, we cannot blame the author, who took upon himself an unenviable task. But the result points up both the virtues and joys of direct field observation.

McGill University   PHILIP C. SALZMAN
Montreal, Canada

William B. Cohen, *Rulers of Empire, the French Colonial Service in Africa.* Stanford, Hoover Institution, Stanford University, 1971, pp. 279, $ 9.50.

Based on an impressive amount of research, much of it original, this book promises to give significant information about the training, professional life and attitudes of the men on the spot who, much more than the government they represented, were the true rulers of the French empire. One can therefore regret that it does not entirely fulfill its promise. For one thing, it reflects too closely its origins, as a Ph. D. dissertation. Particularly in the early chapters, it is repetitious and diffuse in places, overloaded with unnecessary quotations. As a result, early French rule does not entirely come into focus and the administrators do not emerge as clear, living personalities. The author feels genuinely at home with his material only when he describes the later stages of French imperial rule, on the basis of his own interviews and the questionnaire he sent in 1965 to all surviving members of the French Corps of Colonial (later Overseas) Administrators. Even then, Cohen tends to take retrospective opinions expressed in the late 1960's too much at face value. More details as to the questionnaire would also help, especially an indication of how many answers were received.

A certain confusion exists as to the actual subject of the book. Seemingly the study of all French colonial civil servants, it only deals with the elite among them, the *administrateurs*, a tightly knit professional corps which formed the executive branch of French colonial service. Why other colonial administrators were excluded from the inquiry is not adequately explained. That, in fact, they were excluded is never clearly stated.

Cohen's work is not without value, although its most useful elements are too often peripheral to its focus. The chapters on the *Ecole Coloniale*, which provided unified though inadequate training for an increasing proportion of *administrateurs*, gives valuable information, much of it new. Equally interesting though less novel is the demonstration of the contradictions inherent in colonial rule, between the republican attitudes of the middle-class bulk of the Corps, their conviction that French values were universally applicable, and their idealization of "native" African societies; between their well-meant attempts at imparting Western benefits to Africans and the exploitative methods associated with French rule. The book's most interesting and novel aspect, at least for this reviewer, is the material concerning the basic French colonial philosophy. Cohen conclusively shows that the dichotomy usually made between French assimilation and British association theories is unfounded. The French wavered between the two approaches, adopting each in turn and never fully carrying them out, because this would ultimately have forced them to relinquish control. Independence itself, granted in 1958–1960, was a last ditch effort to retain control, through economic and cultural ties.

All in all, French rule emerges as ineffectual, too ambitious for the limited means the mother-country was willing to expend on its colonies, and replete with contradictions. The effect on African societies is well described. New "europeanized" elites isolated from traditional African structures were created, through education and military service, but they were excluded from power by their French masters, who were suspicious of them. Traditional chiefs were preferred as intermediaries, even though the structures on which their power rested were gradually whittled away by westernizing programs, rendering them increasingly ineffectual. French rule, neither able to check the spread of African nationalism nor adequately to prepare Africans for self-rule, ultimately failed.

McGill University
Montreal, Canada

PIERRE H. BOULLE

Journal of Asian and Africaj Studies, VIII, 1–2

A. Lerumo, *Fifty fighting years: The South African Communist Party 1921–1971.*
London, Inkululeko Publications, 1971, pp. 216, $ 5.00.

Before any sort of tactics and strategies are worked out, a revolutionary organization must know not only the nature of that to which tactics and strategies are to be applied but also what kind of change is sought. Lack of knowledge of the reality of that which we want to change, like lack of knowledge of the malaise for which a doctor may prescribe a cure, may result in a fatal mistake. In this book a member of the South African Communist Party attempts not only to spell out what the nature of the South African society is, but he reflects back on the strategies and tactics that the party used to grapple with African appression. The book faces squarely the nature of the White settler state and the attitides that resulted from physical conquest of the African people. This is an extremely timely assessment.

Intellectual and ideological confusion is an enemy of clarity and creates chaos. It produces empirical opportunism that is short sighted and that grasps straws while missing the real issues. The struggle for the emancipation of African people cannot succeed until those parties that are fighting for liberation take stock of their past failures and successes.

In South Africa two groups of Whites have historically been concerned with the oppression and exploitation of the African by the White settler state of which they are members; the Liberals and Communists. The history of both groups and the prescriptions they envisaged for the solution of African oppression were handicapped by their membership in the oppressor group. But of the two groups historical testimony would suggest that at least the South African Communist Party, inspite of its failures has understood the nature of African oppression and exploitation. This is not to say that the South African Communist Party has accomplished more, but it is to say that whatever its mistakes might have been, at least it knew precisely what the nature of the problem was. Only their tactics may have been unsuited to the time and place, hence the ability of the party to grow and change.

In this book Lerumo also examines certain aspects of the South African history and social structure to find out the whys and wherefores of the present conjuncture. That is, what various factors emanating from the historical and concrete conditions of South Africa influenced its dynamic present? Secondly, given these historical and structural conditions, what kind of tactics and strategies must a revolutionary organization adopt, if it is to be successful? Thirdly, what kind of future society would eliminate the injustices of the present society?

The South African Communist Party was founded in 1921 and during its fifty years of existence it has experienced several dilemmas involving ideology, strategy and tactics. Like any human effort its mistakes could not be understood in abstraction, but from the conditions and time in which it was born. Lerumo spells out these conditions. They include among others:

1 The relations between Africans as conquered subjects and White settlers as conquerors. The opposition between White settlers and the indigenous peoples they subjugated is the most abdurate, and any successful theory of revolution must take this aspect of South African reality into account. The Communist Party of South Africa failed to understand this reality and Lerumo tells us why.

2 The relations between White and Black in the economic sphere were shaped and given

their character and content by conquest, and the functioning of all other institutions
became distorted by the fact that White settlers became imbued with a conquering
syndrome. The growth of the mining industry based on foreign capital and cheap African
labour was crucial for the growth of the working class and Lerumo explains how conquest
distorted and deformed the South African working class producing theoretical, strategic
and tactical mistakes in the programmes of the South African Communist Party which
had failed to take this into account. The 1922 Rand Revolt faced the party with its crucial
dilemma.

A reviewer can only heighlight what he considers the salient points in a
book. This book is an appraisal of the Party's achievements as well as a frank
analysis of its failures. When the Nationalist Party came to power in 1948, the
Communist Party was the first to be proscribed. This was inspite of its small
numbers. The South African Nationalist Party, like other fascist regime, knew
the potential of the ideas that were advanced by the Party and given the revolutionary nature of our time the Nationalist Party did not want to take any
chances. The specter of "communism" haunts the South African regime like a
nightmare. Maybe Marx was right when he declared in the Communist Manifesto, "A specter is haunting Europe – the specter of communism. All powers
of old Europe have entered into a holy alliance to exorcise this specter: Pope
and Czar, Metternich and Guizot, French radicals and German police spies."
The revolutionary movement in South Africa is facing the unholy alliance of
old world imperialism; Britain, America, West Germany, Japan, France, etc.
have allied themselves with Portugal and South Africa to oxercise the liberation of the Southern African peoples.

University of Connecticut   BERNARD MAGUBANE
Storrs, U.S.A.

Yousef Bedri and George Scott, *The Memoirs of Babikr Bedri. (Translated from
the Arabic,* with an Introduction of P. M. Holt), London, Oxford University
Press, 1969, pp. 250, $ 7.75.

In the words of C. Wright Mills, "Neither the life of an individual nor the
history of a society can be understood without understanding both." This
premise links the larger historical scene with both the inner life and the external
career of an individual and provides the promise of comprehending the framework of modern society through a grasp of history and biography.

This first volume of *The Memoirs of Babikr Bedri,* written originally in Arabic
and now made available in English by Yousef Bedri and George Scott, furnishes
scholars with a wealth of information which realizes this promise as well as
treating the reader to rare wit.

The author, a legend in his lifetime, is the embodiment of all that is imaginative, daring and aspiring in the Sudanese character. As "the father of modern
Sudanese education" (he piloted the first modern chain of schools for both boys
and girls during the early years of Anglo-Egyptian rule), the modern Sudanese
intelligentsia are partly his creation. His achievement has been fundamental to
the passing of traditional society in the Sudan, for the secularization of education
is a significant pillar in the establishment of a modern, secular state. Babikr

Bedri's own schooling in the traditional Islamic sciences (common to all Muslim societies until the early twentieth century and still existent side by side with modern, Western-inspired education in many places) makes his educational advances all the more impressive, especially in that they have contributed to the production of a militant, secular elite.

Thus, Babikr Bedri ranks with other great nineteenth and twentieth century Muslim educators and reformers such as the Indian Sir Sayyid Ahmed Khan and the Egyptian Muhammad Abduh. He may be said, in fact, to have been more innovative than these two well-known figures, particularly with regard to the education of women.

This volume of his memoirs covers the first thirty-seven years of his life, 1864–1901, which makes it an invaluable document for part of the Turco-Egyptian period, the Mahdist interregnum and the early days of the Condominium, none of which has been satisfactorily recorded. Echoing the North African fifteenth century historian-sociologist, Ibn Khaldun, Bedri states that the most accurate history is freshly recorded history, a dictum which he abides by through the use of his phenomenal memory.

Bedri demonstrates his concern with historical social structures by raising various points about the state, the family, the local prison or a religious creed, all of which he relates through drama in which he himself was an actor. In a brillian description of his boyhood and education, his failings and strengths of character, his perception of relationships between social groups and social phenomena, our authour, who was an apt observor of his milieu, offers us an accurate and vibrant picture of Sudanese society during the period which he describes.

Here, for those concerned with the construction of a third world sociology and, hope.ully, a correct political ideology, is a work of meaningful contribution. It is to be hoped that the translators will put us completely into their debt by rendering the second and third volumes of Mr. Bedri's work into English. None of the few mistakes in transliteration or few incomplete notes detracts from the excellent work of the two translators.

McGill University   A. Abu Zayd
Montreal, Canada

Raph Uwechue, *Reflections on the Nigerian Civil War.* New York, Africana Publishing Corporation, 1971, pp. 199, $ 8.95.

This second edition of the volume that appeared in 1969, now considerably revised by the author, should be a part of any collection of secondary sources on the Nigerian Civil War. Well-written and cogent, it is nevertheless, an uneven book, with glaring weaknesses in it. The opening section, for example, which is apparantly designed to acquaint the unfamiliar reader with the origins of the conflict, is so sketchy as to be almost useless. The opening chapter is banal at best and barely relevant now, so soon after the war is over. Other works–including the Nwankwo and Ifejika book, *Biafra and the Making of a Nation*, (Praeger, 1970), though marred by heavy polemic in its later chapters – do a far better job in analysis of the historical roots of the conflict. Mr. Uwechue resorts too frequently to the writings of others, especially Walter Schwarz, in explaining the details surrounding the first coup, which he calls "The Revolution of January 1966"; and often uses unfortunate terminology, as, for example, when he calls the officers who started the first coup, "boys".

In his description of the second coup Mr. Uwechue finally gets to his task and the full horror of that event comes across. The account on pages 43–46 of the nearly genocidal attack on the Ibos is compelling, yet the author's prose remains unemotional, detached, precise. It is interesting that the author repeats the popular theme – which may indeed prove to be accurate as future historians research the events – that Biafra was in effect "pushed out" by the Federal Government's panicky actions after August 1966. It does seem likely, that if the F.M.G. "had not lost its nerve, secession might have been averted". Here Mr. Uwechwue's argument is convincing and makes sense to any witness of those terrible events (including this reviewer) in 1966, though it may be years before fear and prejudice, retribution and blame have waned enough for most Nigerians to accept that fact.

The section pointing out the weaknesses in the highly centralized twelve-state system, and the subsequent six-state proposal, is logical enough and may be sound. It is also unlikely, for, as the author acknowledges himself, it leaves all of "Iboland" and the other eastern minorities intact in one state.

The book includes an interesting explanation for Tanzania's support of Biafra, and a thorough delineation of Britian's "diplomacy". Here the author's experience shows best. Nor does he neglect France, Russia and Portugal. His direct analysis of the western world's "neglect" except in what he calls "destructive aid" is worth reading. One only wishes for a more complete analysis of the deeper causes, matters often discussed in learned articles but rarely made available to the wider public in books of this sort.

In the section dealing with his own proposals for the future there are a few surprises, particularly the call for compulsory military service, which seems highly theoretical and even idealistic. But, the personal, almost biographical analysis of Ojukwu, does a lot to illuminate the man and his incredible and inflexible will, as well as his enormous flaws. There are several intelligent excerpts on the problems of federation, especially regarding the majority areas dominating Nigeria in the past. Regionalism rather than "tribalism" – a much abused term – is examined as a factor to be reckoned with still. In the realm of political ideas, this is the best part of the book.

Uwechue has written a book full of tentative judgements, often compelling insights, sometimes banal but necessary summaries, and deeply humane ideas about what must be done in the future. Either as political analysis or as history, it is a speculative and incomplete work. Perhaps it is too early yet for anyone as close to the Nigerian Civil War as Uwechue was, to write the definitive work which we all await.

City University of New York U.S.A.   KENNETH C. WYLIE

Robert Chambers (ed.), *The Volta Resettlement Experience*. New York, Praeger, 1970, pp. 286, $ 7.00.

There is a lake in east-central Ghana covering over 3000 square miles, where ten years ago 80,000 people lived in over 700 villages, and countless communities and isolated farmsteads, incompassing about 15,000 dwellings. The people have moved or been moved; the physical remains of the villages and communities and farmsteads – dwellings, fields, tree crops – are under water. The Volta River dam project brought on this extensive destruction of capital assets. What then did Ghanaians gain, both those who had their land inundated and those far from the flood plain who will never see the man-made lake? The book under review makes no attempt to answer this question; the authors, including the editor in his "postscript", take it for granted that the project was desirable, and all criticism (and except for Chambers' final section there is virtually none) is based on this presumption.

In his forward Sir Robert Jackson, late of the Royal Navy and the Australian government, and most recently of UNDP, tells us on the first page that, "no propaganda and no white-washing will be found in this book." To an extent, he is correct, for the next ten chapters, all but one written by Ghanaian government officials or employees of the resettlement program, raise none of the fundamental issues. In a sense, however, this is the most fundamental type of whitewash – complete avoidance of issues. *A priori*, one would think that it would be impossible to write or edit a book about a project as controversial as the Volta River dam and make it dull. Yet, this collection of papers presented at the Volta Resettlement Symposium held in Kumasi in March, 1965, is deathly dull, and he who reads it through to the end has established a reputation for admirable, if undiscriminating, diligence. There is some reward from reading Chambers' low-keyed listing of the specifics of the human misery and financial waste of the project after the narrow, bureaucratic and technocratic articles written by those involved in the project.

The most appalling examples of narrow-minded bureaucracy are the chapters on valuation, acquisition and compensation (Chapter 3) and "the social survey" (Chapter 4). The former is a hopelessly narrow legalistic discussion, which leaves the impression that the compensation program amounted to little more than checking through statute books to resolve minor conflicts and uncertainties in the application of the law. When one considers the incredible proliferation of land tenure rules in the flood basin, the potential redistribution of wealth and power inherent in resettlement, and the disruption of the social environment of 80,000 people, it is amazing to read, "No outstanding lessons have been learnt from the experience of valuation of properties and acquisition of sites. No very exceptional problems have been encountered, beyond what had been envisaged..." (p. 75). It is instructive to compare this assessment to Chambers' postscript. One might be forgiven for expecting from a chapter entitled "The Social Survey" some discussion of the social characteristics of the displaced population and the human impact of resettlement. Yet the chapter is restricted to a description of the methodology of the survey, comments on its usefulness for managing the displaced population, and copies of the forms used.

To the extent that chapters 2–11 provide any analysis, it is a crude faith in modernization. The authors concur not only in the inherent desirability of the project, but also that it provided a unique opportunity to "modernize" the tens of thousands of Ghanaians affected. In short, an opportunity for social management on a vast scale was perceived, an opportunity not to be missed. But as Chambers shows, the groundwork for the minimal job of resettlement with no fall in prosperity was not done, much less the work necessary to radically transform the population economically. This desire to use the dam to make a quantum jump in the level of development was at best a bureaucratic illusion, based on the bureaucrats' inherent lack of faith in the potentialities of the people. The early emphasis on self-help quickly gave way to centralized control, leading to standards in housing and ambitious agricultural schemes beyond the administrative capacity of the government, inconsistent with the skill availabilities of the labour force, and inappropriate to ecological realities and the political structure of the population being planned for. The best example of this was the housing provided in the new communities. Self-help was rejected in favour of government built "modern model villages of which the nation could be proud" (p. 21). The settlers, more interested in making their dwellings liveable than whether or not civil servants and visiting experts would glow with pride when passing through the villages, began adapting the structures to their individual needs; the authorities responded with irrelevant building codes and even demolition of "unauthorized" structures.

Even from Chambers' rather limited critique the pattern is clear: people unrooted from their houses as a result of a project about which they were not consulted, transferred to new areas where agricultural land was inadequate even for subsistence in many cases (fed by the World Food Programme), to be harassed and disappointed by petty officials. Further, little emphaty for the plight of the settlers comes out of the book. Despite the tremendous uncertainty facing the displaced population, reluctance on their part is attributed to superstition (see particularly Chapter 5 and its appendices I–III).

What then are the basic issues? First, some attempt at a cost-benefit analysis is called for. Chambers offers a few figures on cost, but they are exclusively financial outlays, and no attempt is made at costing fore-gone production. Second, who benefited from the dam? It is remarkable that no mention is made of the function the dam plays as a subsidy to the consortium exploiting Ghana's bauxite. There are other issues, of course, but these would provide at least an interesting beginning towards understanding why there is today a lake in Ghana were 80,000 people used to live, and whether it was necessary for Ghana's development to flood them out.

University of Sussex   JOHN WEEKS
England

M. Gelfand, *Diet and Tradition in an African culture.* Edinburgh and London, E. & S. Livingstone, 1971, pp. 248, $ 10.00.

This book is a remarkably detailed description of the food resources and eating habits of the Shona people of Rhodesia. To my taste, much of the detail is meticulous to the point of tedium. There are entire chapters comprising natural-historical lists of (edible?) fauna and flora, cross-referenced in Latin and the vernacular, and dotted with descriptions of the technologies of trapping, culling and cooking. The narrative is disjointed, somewhat repetitive, and with no discernible logic or analytic line. This kind of material would have served a better purpose appended after the argument.

The introductory profile of Shona life is given in the same cook book style. It is, of course, relevent that Michael Gelfand is a "proper" doctor, – i.e. a doctor of medicine, not a social anthropologist, and so not necessarily concerned with the rules of ethnographic and literary games. Nonetheless, there are occasional glimpses of Shona social life which are almost poetic. Having earlier described the socialisation of children into the etiquette of eating (in Chapter 3), Gelfand writes (in Chapter 15, p. 214):

"I cannot emphasis sufficiently the calm attitude and peace of mind prevailing during meals in the rural Shona setting. Eating is not to the clock. Mealtimes are very much social occasions and enjoyed in the company of relatives and friends. No Shona eats alone. A meal is almost a spiritual affair and members of the same age group often eat together from a common plate. Each meal symbolises the sharing of the necessities of life with one's kin..."

This and the subsequent speculative glance at the separation of the sexes at mealtimes allow the inference that social relations have an effect on nutritive-digestive processes – a fact too often ignored by purveyors of antacid in North America, and one which food scientists would do well to examine more systematically.

The book in fact becomes rivetting wherever Gelfand's medical and nutritional expertise is allowed to show. The last four chapters are excellent: he is authoritative in his own field and shows a sociological sensitivity notoriously rare in medical practitioners. His comparison of nutritional levels challenges the popular assumption that poor rural people are better nourished than their urban counterparts. The romantic emanations of the countryside cannot compensate for shortages of even the most natural foods. A regular urban diet which includes over-refined and/or poorly-processed food (white sugar is always the arch criminal) may yet maintian better health than the seasonal irregularities of wholesome subsistence fare.

In the context of southern Africa this possibility contradicts both the white supremicist contention that rural life is intrinsically "better" for the African, and the opposite-but-equal liberal notion that contact with urban white society is *ipso facto* "bad" for him. There is more to life than a satisfied stomach, but it is useful to see food and ideology separated occasionally.

University of Toronto   SANDRA WALLMAN
Toronto, Canada

Kit Elliott, *An African School – A Record of Experience.* Cambridge University Press, 1970, pp. 232, $ 7.50.

Kit Elliot narrated, in a moving and lucid prose, his experience as a young Englishman in a Catholic Mission school in the Benue Plateau State of Nigeria. He started his narration by contrasting his previous experience in Birmingham with his new place of abode – a land with christianized children of the pagan tribe – he had read so much about in the Birmingham Reference Library.

His journey into the land began shortly after arriving at the Kano Airport. A white friend had played host to him on the night of arrival and had offered to take him to Jos where he was picked up by his Irish principal. His experience began with his observation of the contrasting attitude of the principal to the students on one hand and to his cook on the other. In one instance, he saw a sick child turned away for coming late to school without pity. In another, he heard the principal's condescending and caustic remark on the innocent bread seller.

A few days later, he met his students only to discover that his language was too sophistocated for them. This initial, classroom experience underscored the challenging nature of his assignment. He made an effort to understand the strange classroom atmosphere arising from the student's background – socially, culturally and economically – all of which were different from his. In his efforts to communicate effectively with his students, he tried to make his subjects, History and English, as real as possible in spite of his initial problem of finding adequate material. In dealing with the first subject, he led his students to study some artifacts dug up from the tin mines nearby and others at the Federal Government Museum in Jos. The same creditable adaptation was applied to the teaching of English by changing from the artificiality of the old grammar approach to the new techniques which train in sentence patterns.

Aside from his regular teaching of English and History, he helped the students through extra-curricular activities. These included the management of a Literary and Debating Society and the production of "Macbeth". To him, what mattered more than the successful performance of this play was its intrinsic value. This included the process of discovery, fellowship, mutual pride in work shared, to mention a few.

On the whole, the author gives an impression of one who tries to write as objectively as possible, however, with an all-pervading sympathy for the people in his new abode. An example of this objectivity can be seen in this statement: "It is humiliating for a teacher to confess that after so many years the children he taught were still strangers to him... Yet all expatriates in Africa are to some extent prisoners of their own authority, upbringing and privileges." In spite of this admitted limitation, he appears to have known and understood the Africans around him more than the common run of expatriates, whether colonial administrators, traders, teachers or missionaries.

At this transitional stage of our national development, this book could be read with profit by all national and state policy makers, teachers and those who are interested in our educational development. As to the world at large, it could help in an impressive way to bring about greater intesnational understanding.

University of Ibadan   S. A. ADEJUNMOBI
Ibadan, Nigeria

Audry C. Smock, *Ibo Politics: The Role of Ethnic Unions in Eastern Nigeria.* Cambridge, Harvard University Press, 1971, pp. xi, 274, $ 10.00.

There is no sure way yet to judge whether field materials collected in

Eastern Nigeria before the Nigerian civil war have any relationship to current existence there, but the basic structural and functional aspects of rural political process are likely to revivify if anything does. Mrs. Smock's analysis of these features in two prewar communities in central Iboland – only a small bit of "Ibo politics" – is thus a welcome addition to Nigerianist social science, not just a tragic farewell. Further, her sophisticated comparative and theoretical concerns with issues of political "development" and "modernization" mark her contribution by opposition to much of the jargon-saturated and homogenized discussion of the so-called "non-Western political process."

Because ethnic associations ("improvement" unions, or associations d'originaires) are the major indigenously-created formal mechanisms through which many West African communities, and especially the Ibo, deal with the macrosystem to which they belong, Mrs. Smock focusses upon them (and in doing so gives us the first full-length study of this widely-reported form). Unfortunately this unit of analysis leads her away from a holistic examination of rural politics, since many formal and informal influentials and influences stand outside the ethnic unions. But it does steer her to a number of important findings.

In the first two parts of the book Mrs. Smock discusses the community politics (influence and leadership, supports and demands, recruitment and output) of Abiriba (a town of 40,000) and Mbaise (a county council area of 225,000 people). To do so, she finds it necessary to examine their ethnic union activities *both in the home areas and in Port Harcourt*, then the oil boom city of Nigeria and a center of major labor migration. Two conclusions of this strategy are that (a) there is no urban/rural psychological or political "gap" in Eastern Nigeria; and (b) although the organizational *form* of political competition is based upon ethnic identities, the *content* is the same "pork barrel" of jobs, amenities, and advancement that it is in most other places.

The third part of the book considers the relationships of the ethnic unions to other political institutions (the NCNC party and local government councils), and to larger questions of political integration and cultural modernization. Here the conclusion is that ethnic identity arises as part of the process of political change, that it is a modern rather than an atavistic political phenomenon, and that it is neither more incompatible nor less legitimate than any other particularistic attachment to class, locality, occupational group or ideological confreres. The problem is to harness "competitive localism" to wider units, not to eradicate it.

Mrs. Smock argues these points with detail almost to a fault. A welcome burst of micropolitical studies has demonstrated the straightforwardness of local political strategies. But having learned that models of modernism and traditionalism in political systems do not help order at least the West African data very well, we still await the elaboration of concepts which do illuminate the dynamics and the directions of these systems. Now we need to scrutinize middle political levels – the civil service, the careers of politicians like the ones who move tangentially through this book on their own missions, the non-local organizations – to see where the gravest flaws of societal control of its political life lie.

McGill University   DAN R. ARONSON
Montreal, Canada

B. S. Hoyle and D. Hillings (eds.), *Seaports and Development in Tropical Africa.*
New York, Praeger, 1970, pp. xvi, 272, $ 13.00.

"Part of the essential infrastructure of modern economic growth is an
outline system of surface transport facilities, serving the developing area both
internally and externally... Within such a basic transport system seaports
occupy a strategic place, for they exist to integrate land and sea transport networks" (p. 225). B. S. Hoyle thus describes the *raison d'être* of this book in which
he is both contributor and joint editor. One general, and thirteen regional
essays by British, French, German, American and African geographers review
different aspects of port development in a continent where overseas linkages have
at times in the past two decades been severely strained, and where major
capital investments in port infrastructure have had a most important place in
development programs. The book is well illustrated by maps and photographs,
very adequately supplied with informative tables, and contains a wealth of
useful information, much of it not previously presented except in government
documents. It is set in a dual context both of African development and of a
period of major innovation in ocean transport. It contains a mine of information, yet it hardly makes a satisfactory book.

The reasons lie partly in the great unevenness of the essays, partly in the
basic concept of the book. The essays vary enormously. Some are mere technical
accounts of the evolution and development of particular ports; some are comprehensive historical interpretations of the role of ports in the regional development of whole segments of the continent; one (on Madagascar) is a discussion
of the state of development in a country with only marginal reference to ports;
one (on seaport evolution in Nigeria by Babafemi Ogundana) is an interpreta-
tive essay of wide span set in a well-considered explanatory model. The scale
varies from a single port to the whole of West or East Africa; the degree to
which non-local literature, and development theory, are introduced varies
from nil to the order of a major contribution.

To this reviewer, however, the major weakness lies in the basic structure of
the book. The isolation of ports as a field of study is entirely reasonable: given a
development policy dominated by external trade the role of ports as potential
growth poles, the emergence of differentiation between ports, and the value of
port investments in stimulating regional development are all proper subjects
for inquiry, and all are touched on in these essays. But the subject demands an
integrated, or comparative treatment. The present book is segmented, patchy,
and hardly at all comparative. The general introductory essay does not pull the
contributions together, and one is left with a collection of data from which solid
conclusions do not emerge. This common failing of books built up from the
solicited contributions of several authors, who do not have an opportunity to
compare manuscripts with one another, is made worse in this case by the wide
differences in the manner in which authors have approached their task. While
the editors in their introductory essay sometimes bring out points of wider
relevance, which the individual authors themselves fail to emphasise, this first
essay falls far short of the integration that might have made the whole book of
far greater value.

The book will most certainly prove useful as a source of data, and certain
of its essays are also a value transcending the limits of their immediate subject

matter. But this sort of collection is always a hit-and-miss affair, and the hits are in the minority. This is a pity, for the book was a commendable enterprise, involving translation of some essays written originally in French, and a most praiseworthy effort to avoid the pitfalls of restriction to one narrow group of authors. It is well produced, and attractively presented. But the essential guiding thread is only hinted at, and nowhere firmly presented to the reader. The result is something much less than the possibilities of the topic.

McGill University   H. C. BROOKFIELD
Montreal, Canada

I. Scott, *Tumbled House: The Congo at Independence.* London, Oxford University Press, 1969, pp. 142, $ 4.25.

Memoirs written several years after an event, even when they provide no new information, can be useful by revealing the attitudes and preconceptions of the author. This book by Sir Ian Scott, British Consul-General and Ambassador to the Congo during the hectic days of 1960–61, is justified on these grounds.

The basic cause of the Congo's collapse into chaos after independence, in Scott's view, was the complete failure of the Belgians to prepare a responsible Congolese political and administrative elite to take over the reins of government. A responsible elite, he implies, would have recognized the indispensability of the Belgians, who were the only persons "able and willing... to help the Congo on its independent feet" (p. 74). Instead, in the 18 months' rush to independence, the leader who developed a "superstitious" hold over a substantial number of his countrymen was the "unscrupulous" and "paranoiac" Patrice Lumumba, who emerges the leading maker of the Congo tragedy. Also heavily to blame, however, were the "extremists" in the United Nations, notably the Indian Rajeshwar Dayal, who showed a strong distrust of the Belgians and continued to back Lumumba even after President Kasavubu had dismissed him from the Premiership. If the United Nations had allowed the Congolese to settle their internal affairs – "it was his own fellow-countrymen" Scott remarks, "who turned away from (Lumumba) and finally killed him" (p. 109) – much of the subsequent turbulence in the Congo and discrediting of the UN would have been avoided.

Yet Scott does note enough facets of the behaviour of the Belgians to warn the reader that there is another side to the story. Sometimes this is barely hinted at; for example, De Gaulle's speech in Brazzaville in August 1958 proposing self-determination produced an "instantaneous" response in the Congo, and during 1960 there was a "steady and visible crumbling of the administration", but Scott gives no real indication that he was aware of the depth of discontent with Belgian rule – discontent which makes much more comprehensible Lumumba's "bitter, accusatory and xenophobic" attacks on the Belgians. He does refer in several passages to the Belgians' attempts to stop Lumumba from taking office, and even to an "unfortunate" episode when the Belgian Consul-General in Equateur Province participated in a separatist movement by the provincial government a few weeks after independence; but while Belgian machinations to retain *de facto* control o₁ the Congo were merely "unfortunate", Lumumba's reactions to them were clear evidence of his instability and suspicious nature.

The insensitivity to Congolese feelings revealed by a memoir such as this leads one to wonder how many collisions between nations stem from blindness rather than genuine conflicts of interest. It is to be expected that an Ambassador should have personal as well as national sympathies in his relations with various political figures in his host country; but it hardly seems satisfactory for his own country's interest when he does not seem to comprehend why persons or goals he regards as wrong or dangerous are widely supported by his hosts. Looking back over ten years, one can plausibly argue that Scott's fears about the disastrous effect Lumumba might have had as leader of the Congo were justified. But whether he sympathized with Lumumba or not, an effective diplomaat should surely have been able to understand those elements of discontent and change in Congolese society to which Lumumba appealed. On the evidence he offers, Scott did not. In accounting for, say, British acquiescence in Katanga's attempts at secession, or more recently her insensitivity to African feelings over the Rhodesian UDI, one wonders whether perhaps too much weight has been given to calculable economic and other interests, and not enough to the blinkered reporting of the man on the spot.

University of Western Ontario   JOHN CARTWRIGHT
London, Canada

P. L. Shinnie, (ed.), *The African Iron Age.* Oxford, Clarendon Press, 1971, pp. 281, plates, figures, £ 3.00.

This excellent volume presents regional syntheses of the Iron Age of Africa written by nine different scholars. The available data vary considerably from region to region, and one cannot but be impressed by the wide variety of source material gleaned for the reconstruction of this stage of African culture history. The authors rely on everything from inferences drawn from the absence of certain stone tool types in archaeological cultures as indicative of the presence of iron, through rock art depictions of iron weapons, classical and even early Chinese literary sources, and the distribution of types of ceramics, to the specific associations of iron or iron slag with C-14 dates in excavated archaeological sites.

The chapters vary in content relative to the kinds of data available for the various regions. Chittick, for example, writing on the Coast of East Africa relies on historical accounts as the archaeological record is silent regarding Iron Age cultures prior to the advent of Muslim traders, whereas Willett on Nigeria, Fagan on Zambia and Rhodesia, and Shinnie on the Eastern Sudan can point to specific sites and dates for the beginnings of iron using. Sutton writing on the Interior of East Africa, and Nenquin on the Congo, Rwanda, and Burundi rely heavily on the distribution and affinities of dimple-based pottery which is known to be an early Iron Age product. In Ghana the evidence for the earlier Iron Age is more inferential and Ozanne points out the Kintampo culture as belonging to the period of iron introduction. In South Africa Inskeep reviews the meagre field data on the subject over the last 20 years, and pleads for some modern interdisciplinary field research.

A picture of the spread of iron working with concomitant socio-cultural changes after iron became common in Egypt in the 7th Century B.C. emerges from the work of these authors. Shinnie notes that it was being worked as well as used at Meroe in the Sudan by 500 B.C., and Mauny records its introduction into the western Sudan several centuries later. Its later appearance in other regions of western Africa is consistent with these dates. To the south Fagan succintly summarises the rapid spread of iron working into the whole of south central Africa by A.D. 400. In Africa south of the Limpopo the ethnographic association of iron working with Bantu speakers still provides the main basis for broader theorizing. The authors do not agree entirely on the routes and mechanisms of the spread of iron technology and the growth of Iron Age cultures, nor indeed should they in the light of present knowledge. It is clear that in certain regions various "Neolithic" aspects of culture did not appear until the advent of iron. Many recognized gaps exist in the full understanding of these processes of change.

This volume is highly recommended for students and professional Africanists alike as a readable and important contribution to our knowledge of Africa.

Simon Fraser University   ROY L. CARLSON
Burnaby, Canada

Frank Willet, *African Art.* New York, Praeger, 1971, pp. 288, $ 8.50.

This is an exemplary study on "African art" that goes well beyond the common masterpiece anthologies with their technically excellent reproductions but misleading texts of wide generalizations on all African art. This work rather introduces the problems that need to be considered in detecting the wide and varied range of African art achievements in a world framework. Examples are repeatedly cited to contradict popular but erroneous generalizations that have arisen in the field. For example, not everywhere where one finds exponential curves, horns, and shells in African art is the underlying meaning that of increasing life force. Complexity, rather than simple generalization, is the theme of the book.

After a wide-ranging introduction a most valuable chapter (II) reviews the development of the study of African art. Willet seeks once and for all time to debunk the "primitive art" concept of African art by tracing its origin within Western art history. The concept should be replaced by specifying art as to its geographical location, thus avoiding the by now inevitable derrogatory value judgement associated with "the primitive". The interpretation of African art, argues the author of the important study of the history of Ife regional styles, must be based on the assumption of dynamic and changing development within a particular regional concentration. Orthogenic development, inter-regional influence, and the European influence should all be considered in a historical framework. The optic of, for example, Olbrecht's permanent Congo style areas, is misleading and to be avoided.

A further chapter (III) takes up these challenges and applies them "towards a history of African art." Working from what are expectedly uneven sources, Willet attempts a trans-Africa review of early rock paintings and ancient sculpture in bronze, rock, and wood. The evidence of chronological controls and style analysis is apparent in this reconstruction of a dimension of African art that has all too often been simply ignored or done sloppily.

Chapter four examines architecture in the same way. Mud, grass, stone, and wood materials have been developed into a profusely rich body of architecture-sculpture of dwellings, granaries, temples, palaces and the like.

In two further companion chapters (V, VI) Willet writes on "looking at" and "understanding" African sculpture, the medium within African art he selects for special attention. Often, he notes, the supreme values employed by museum collectors and curators of African art have been the rarity or the uniqueness of an object. By this process a serious bias enters our perception of African art that ignores how important our tacit knowledge is in our evaluation of a piece of Western art. In African sculpture the full complement of background ideas must be understood too if one is to make a serious and correct evaluation. Lengthy reviews of careful investigations into indigenous aesthetics follow, including work like Thompson's analysis of Yoruba art values. The distinction of religious and ordinary art; the importance of scale, proportion, and other formal determinants of mood and expression are reviewed in careful detail. Lastly, to debunk the myth of the anonymous artist in African art, Willet is especially insistent that the artist himself brings a force into a stylistic tradition, interpreting it for his generation.

A final chapter (VII) extends these valuable perspectives into contemporary African art. In reading this richly, yet appropriately illustrated work (with 261 closely documented reproductions) this reviewer at least gets the impression that the study of African art has matured alongside serious work in other traditions. A highly-recommended work.

McGill University   JOHN M. JANZEN
Montreal, Canada.

Victor T. LeVine, *The Cameroon Federal Republic.* Ithaca, Cornell University Press, 1971, pp. viii, 205, $ 8.50.

One of the difficulties of discussing a book such as this lies in deciding for whom it is produced. If it is intended to be an introduction to Cameroon for the general reader, it provides the kind of up to date information which is unavailable in print elsewhere in an accessible form which makes it extremely useful. If however it is intended to be more than a guide book to Cameroon its usefulness is more problematic.

If one turns to Professor LeVine's earlier work on Cameroon "From Mandate to Independence", one is impressed by the process by which he provides a causal analysis of crucial aspects of Cameroonian reality by way of an historical explanation; the nature of German and French colonialism, the particular nature of the relationship of the Southern Cameroons to Nigeria and the United Kingdom, and the close relationship between President Ahidjo and the French Government following their suppression of the U.P.C.

This analysis forms the starting point of the present work; the difficulty lies in finding any analysis of the post-independence period. There is valuable information on Trade Union and Co-operative Groups, the recent political changes in West Cameroon, and the execution of Ernest Ouandie and the imprisonment of Archbishop Ndongmo last year. Is this sufficient? No, because the explanation of these events does not emerge out of an historical account of colonialism in Cameroon, it requires, as well, a structural analysis of Cameroonian society today.

If I may take two instances which I think illustrate the point: the replacement of John Ngu Foncha by Solomon Muna as Vice-President is dealt with very briefly by Professor LeVine as though it were a game of political musical chairs. It may have been that as well but in spite of Foncha's dispute with the K.N.D.P. it does have to be explained in the light of his position, even if only in popular rhetoric, as one of the "architects of Reunification", and the fact that the U.C. had supposed that he had at least potentially the ability to attract U.P.C. support, a supposition that was certainly mistaken after 1966. If it is regarded as an isolated example of the exercise of President Ahidjo's power, the removal of Dr. Fonlon, another prominent West Cameroonian, from the Federal Ministry of Health this year, is also another isolated example of the same phenomenon. In order to make sense of these events, so that one does more than engage in political gossip, one does need at least the beginning of an explanation of President Ahidjo's position in terms of his relationship to France and the East Cameroonian elite, not so much in terms of textual analysis of the Federal Constitution.

The other example I would like to deal with, shows even more clearly the necessity for providing an explanation of Cameroon today in terms other than those of a series of isolated events. In Professor LeVine's account of the changes that are taking place in the Cameroonian educational system as a result of Reunification he says in conclusion "Nevertheless Cameroon's educational system is being adapted, however slowly, to the realities of unification and the developmental needs of the country" (p. 77). There is a tendency in writing about Cameroon to substitute judgements of how far Reunification is or is not proceeding as planned for an analysis of the reality which this extract exemplifies. More important is the fact that summed up in a bromide is a situation of great strain, periodic crises and interesting experiments.

Professor LeVine's study shows that, however competent, political analysis of this kind has limits as an explanatory method. Perhaps Cameroonian circumstances illustrate these limitations more clearly than would other situations. In a one party state where any opposition tendencies have neither the desire nor the opportunity to declare themselves in public this kind of analysis becomes even more than usual the frantic collecting of fragments of political gossip. The trouble is that in this kind of political situation the availability of gossip is decreasing. The alternative approach is to wait for a visible crisis, a Minister being dismissed for example, and accumulate these instances until a pattern emerges. But patterns do not emerge from examples like that and there is a tendency, as Professor LeVine's book shows, to concentrate on having a description of the most recent events as though being up to date had a special significance. Of course it is important to be aware of what is happening now but one assumes that the significance of the current event is different for the political scientist than for the journalist. This is because for the scholar these events are related to an analysis which explains them and which they modify. In the case of Cameroon, this does mean relating politics to social analysis which is not done by Professor LeVine. The use of statistics and official policy statements is not enough. The methods used in this book, however conscientiously and competently lead to a dead end, they cannot adequately explain the reality of Cameroonian society. And it is important that this reality should be explained not only in order to understand Cameroon but in order that we should be able to work towards providing an explanation of anglophone and francophone post-colonial realities in other parts of West Africa.

University of Ife   CAROLYNE DENNIS

S. Ottenberg, *Leadership and Authority in an African Society: The Afikpo Village Group.* The American Ethnological Society, Monograph 52. Seattle, University of Washington Press, 1971, pp. xvii, 336, maps, photographs, $ 9.50.

This book is, in effect, the second volume of an ethnographic study of Afikpo villages and village-groups, the first of which was the author's *Double Descent in an African Society.* Together these two volumes provide a detailed examination of this eastern Igbo group, better than anything we have been given hitherto on the Igbo. The Afikpo are not, of course, "typical" of all Igbo, as indeed no single segment of that internally diverse ethnic group could be; nevertheless in giving such rich material Dr. Ottenberg certainly illuminates many of the ethnographic problems and raises fascinating issues of comparison with data on other Igbo groups.

Essentially however we should take this new work as primarily a study of one fairly clearly defined African people, and in its own right. The book itself divides into two distinct parts, but inter-connected and mutually illuminating. First Dr. Ottenberg deals with the village. He examines the different structural forms of Afikpo villages and relates these to the double descent kinship system (the subject of his first volume). This leads on to a most valuable analytical account of the age system which, for this reviewer at least, for the first time really shows how that system works and with a concern for detail comparable to the several East African systems described by anthropologists. Like the age-groups and the associated age-grades, the village secret society cross-cuts the descent and kinship system, seemingly almost establishing an autonomous sphere of social and ritual activities. And yet it is intricately involved in village life and its organization and social control. Dr. Ottenberg elects not to give the details of the complex rituals of the secret society (perhaps a third volume may be devoted to that?), but he concentrates on its role within the internal political system of the village, the principal theme of the book's first part. This description of the village concludes with an account of the ward system comprising the residential segments of the unit and whose organization is age based.

In the second part of the book Dr. Ottenberg concentrates on the political organization of the village-group, the maximal Afikpo unit comprising several villages. In this part he not only shows the nature and operation of intervillage organization and activities, but he demonstrates how the same intravillage groups (descent, age, residence, secret society) and the same village leaders operate at the village-group level. The whole comprises a most complex system for, as Dr. Ottenberg points out, an adult male belongs to two matrilineal and two patrilineal descent groups, to a ward, a secret society, an age-group, a sequence of age-grades, and most probably to a few title societies, as well as to a village and the village-group. Beyond this is the rather vaguer Afikpo group, comprising five village-groups, but which does not have the unifying internal political organization of a village-group.

In general, Dr. Ottenberg is not concerned to raise and discuss theoretical issues, although a number are implicit and are illuminated such as to make the book a valuable source to anthropologists. This is rather a thorough-going ethnography of the best kind and superior to anything previously published on the Igbo. Dr. Ottenberg has successfully mined rich sources of data. The one criticism could be that he has not provided the additional case studies, which he surely has, to amplify his analysis.

York University   P. H. GULLIVER
Toronto, Canada

FURTHER PUBLICATIONS FROM E. J. BRILL

Contributions to Asian Studies

Sponsored by THE CANADIAN ASSOCIATION FOR SOUTH ASIAN STUDIES, TORONTO
Canada.

General Editor: K. ISHWARAN, York University, DOWNSVIEW, ONTARIO, Canada

A series containing scholarly papers. Each volume will cover special areas, of Asian countries,
and may be of value for specialists, but also to students and teachers of sociology, anthropology
and political science.

Volume 1: 1971. viii, 204 pages, 8 tables   Gld. 46.—

Contents: INDIA: FAMILY AND MODERNIZATION. D. A. CHEKKI, Kalyan and Goku:
Kinship and modernization in Northern Mysore; K. ISHAWARAN, The interdependence of
elementary and extended family. – CHINA AND INDIA: MAOISM IN CHINA AND
INDIA. HYOBOM PAK, Chinese Communists in the Eastern Three Provinces, 1918–35; J. M.
VAN DER KROEFF, India's Maoists: Organizational patterns and tactics. – PAKISTAN AND
INDIA: POLITICS AND LANGUAGE. W. M. DOBELL, Ayub Khan, a de Gaulle in Asia?;
L. HARRIS, The frontier route from Peshawar to Chitral: Political and strategic aspects of
the "Forward Policy", 1889–1896; L. ZIRING, Politics and language in Pakistan: Prolegomena
1947–1952. – HONG KONG: VOLUNTARY ASSOCIATION. E. JOHNSON, From rural
committee to spirit medium cult: Voluntary association in the development of a Chinese
town; H. J. LETHBRIDGE, A Chinese association in Hong Kong: The Tung Wah. –
MALAYSIA: LAW. INNOVATION AND CHANGE. M. B. HOOKER, Hindu law and
English law in Malaysia and Singapore: A study in the interaction and integration of two
legal systems; M. C. HODGKIN, Overseas graduates as "Innovators" in two developing countries: Malaysia and Singapore; M. RUDNER, Malayan quandary: rural development policy
under the First and Scond Five Year Plans.

Volume 2: RELIGION AND SOCIETY IN PAKISTAN. Edited by AZIZ AHMAD. 1971.
viii, 105 pages   Gld. 40.—

Contents: F. ABBOTT, The historical background of Islamic India and Pakistan; A. AHMAD,
Islam and democracy in Pakistan; S. M. M. QURESHI, Religion and party politics in Pakistan;
H. MALIK, The spirit of capitalism and Pakistani Islam; S. McDONOUGH, The social import
of Parwez's religious thought; S. AHMAD, Islam and Pakistani peasants.

Volume 3: 1973. viii, 166 pages, some tables and figures   Gld. 64.—

Contents: CEYLON: REINCARNATION AND BUDDHISM. B. L. SMITH, Sinhalese
Buddhism and the Dilemmas of Reinterpretation; I. STEVENSON, Characteristics of Cases of the
Reincarnation Type in Ceylon. – INDIA: ECONOMY, POLITICS AND SOCIAL
CHANGE. J. L. MURRAY, Peasant Motivation, Ecology, and Economy in Panjab; Y. K. MA-
LIK, Conflict over Chandigarh: A Case Study of an Interstate Dispute in India; J. S. UPPAL,
Economic Development of Indian States: A Study in Development Contrast; K. G. SAINI,
Economic Performance and Institutional Change: the Experience of India. – INDIA:
RELIGION. M. MAHAPATRA, The Badu: A Service-caste at the Lingaraj Temple at Bhu-
baneswar; C. R. PANGBORN. – INDIA: INTELLECTUALS AND CHANGE. P. C. DEB and
L. A. WENZEL, A Dimension of Change in India: Prestige of occupations Among University
Students; H. S. SANDHU, The Intellectuals and Social Change in India. – INDIA AND PA-
KISTAN: FAMILY. J. H. KORSON, Some Aspects of Social Change in the Muslim Family in
West Pakistan; I. VERGHESE, Is the Kota Society Polyandrous?

Volume 4: TRADITION AND CHANGE IN THERAVADA BUDDHISM: ESSAYS ON
CEYLON AND THAILAND IN THE 19TH AND 20TH CENTURIES. Edited by BARD-
WELL L. SMITH. 1974. viii, 105 pages.   Gld. 42.—

Contents: B. L. SMITH, Introduction; H. BECHERT, Contradictions in Sinhalese Buddhism;
T. FERNANDO, The Western Educated Elite and Buddhism in British Ceylon: A Neglected
Aspect of the Nationalist Movement; B. G. GOKHALE, Anagarick Dhammapala: Toward
Modernity through Tradition in Ceylon; F. E. REYNOLDS, Sacral Kingship and National
Development: the Case of Thailand; S. PIKER, Buddhism and Modernization in Contem-
porary Thailand; F. B. MORGAN, Vocation of Monk and Layman: Signs of Change in Thai
Buddhist Ethics; D. K. SWEARER, Thai Buddhism: Two Responses to Modernity; F. E.
REYNOLDS, Tradition and Change in Theravada Buddhism: A Bibliographical Essay Fo-
cused on the Modern Period.

Journal of Asian

and

African Studies

| Volume VIII | July and October 1973 | Numbers 3-4 |

SPECIAL NUMBER ON CONTEMPORARY PROBLEMS OF PAKISTAN

Guest Editor: J. Henry Korson

CONTENTS

C. M. Turnbull, The Straits Settlements 1826–67 Indian Presidency to Crown Colony (John L. Hill). Eric A. Walker, W. P. Schreiner, a South African (A. M. Keppel–Jones). P. B. Harris, Studies in African Politics (F. A. Kunz). C. S. Nicholls, The Swahili Coast (Michael Mason). J. F. Ajayi and Michael Crowder, Eds. History of West Africa (Michael Mason). Alan Peshkin, Kanuri School Children: Education and Social Mobilization in Nigeria (A. Richard King). Bruce Grindal, Growing Up in Two Worlds: Education and Transition among the Sisala of Northern Ghana (A. Richard King). M. S. M. Semakula Kiwanuka, A History of Buganda. From the Foundation of the Kingdom to 1900 (Michael Mason). D. A. Low, Buganda in Modern History (M. Mason). D. A. Low, The Mind of Buganda (M. Mason). G. L. Caplan, The Elites of Barotseland 1878–1969; A Political History of Zambia's Western Province (M. Mason). H. E. Guenther, The Life and the Teaching of Naropa (B. C. MacAndrews).

JOURNAL OF ASIAN AND AFRICAN STUDIES

The *Journal of Asian and African Studies*, published by E. J. Brill, Leiden, Holland, is a quarterly publication issued in January, April, July, and October. Each number is about eighty pages in length.

The Journal, edited by a board of scholars from all over the world who are specialists in Asian and African studies, presents a scholarly account of studies of man and society in the developing nations of Asia and Africa. It endeavours to fulfill a need in the field in that it unites contributions from anthropology, sociology, history, and related social sciences into a concerted emphasis upon building up systematic knowledge and using the knowledge derived from pure research for the reconstruction of societies entering a phase of advanced technology.

ALL EDITORIAL CORRESPONDENCE, including papers, notes and news covering research projects, associations and institutions, conferences and seminars, foundations and publications, and other activities relevant to Asia and Africa, should be addressed to: K. Ishwaran, Editor, J.A.A.S., Department of Sociology, York University, Downsview, Ontario M3J 1P3, Canada.

BOOKS FOR REVIEW (AFRICA) should be sent to: John M. Janzen, Department of Anthropology, University of Kansas, Lawrence, Kansas, 66044, U.S.A., and (ASIA) to Edward R. Beauchamp, College of Education, University of Hawaii, Wist Annex 2-222, 1776 University Avenue, Honolulu, Hawaii 96822, U.S.A.

BUSINESS CORRESPONDENCE, including subscriptions, change of address, orders for additional offprints, etc., should be addressed to:

E. J. BRILL — LEIDEN, THE NETHERLANDS

Subscription price of Volume IX (1974): Gld. 56.— *plus postage and packing.*

Please do not send money with your order. The publisher will invoice you and will then be pleased to receive your remittance.

MANUSCRIPT STYLE GUIDE

Manuscripts of articles should be not more than 7000 words. Unsolicited papers will not be returned unless postage paid. Submit two copies of the article and retain a copy for your own files. Prepare copy as follows:

1. Type double-spaced on white 8-1/2" × 11" standard paper, with a 2" margin at the left hand side and a 3" space above the titles of both articles and reviews.
2.* Tables should be typed on separate pages, numbered consecutively and given headings. Footnotes for tables appear at the bottom of the tables. Insert a location note at the appropriate place in text, e.g., "Table 1 about here".
3.* Figures, maps and other line drawings are to be submitted in black Indian ink about twice the intended final size on good quality tracing paper. Insert a location note at the appropriate place in text.
4. Articles and reviews are to be submitted in their *final form* so that they require no further alterations. It is the obligation of authors to carefully proof read their material before submission to the journal. Owing to increasing costs, the publisher is compelled to charge authors for corrections other than printer's errors.

*Tables, graphs, figures, etc., should be used sparingly.

• Bibliographical references should be cited in the text by the author's last name, date of publication and page, e.g., (Anderson 1972: 105) or, if the author's name is mentioned in the text, by the date and page reference only, e.g., (1972: 105). • Footnotes are to appear as notes at the end of articles and are to be used only for substantive observations and not for purpose of citation. • With dual authorship, give both last names; for more than two use "et al" (see 3 below). • If there is more than one reference to the same author and year, distinguish them by using letters (a, b) attached to year of publication in the text and reference appendix (see 2 below). • For institutional authorship supply minimum identification, e.g., (U.N.E.S.C.O. 1971: 67).

Entries in the references should be in alphabetical order of authors and should include: name and initials of author(s), date, title, name of periodical, volume number (arabic numerals to be used throughout), pagination (for periodicals), place of publication and publisher. e.g.,

1. Frolic, B. Michael
    1971   "Soviet urban sociology". International Journal of Comparative Sociology XII (December): 234–251.
2. Greenberg, Joseph H.
    1965a   "Linguistics" pp. 416–41 in Robert A. Lystad (ed.), The African World: a survey of social research. New York: Frederick A. Praeger.
    1965b   "Urbanism, migration and language" pp. 50-59, 189 in K. Huyper (ed.), Urbanization and Migration in West Africa. Berkeley and Los Angeles: University of California Press. (Reprinted in Man in Adaptation, the Bio-social Background, ed. by Y. A. Cohen, 259–67. Chicago: Aldine Publishing Co., 1968.)
3. Kaser, D., et al
    1969   Library Development in Eight Asian Countries. New Jersey: Scarcecrow Press.
4. Southall, Aidan W.
    1970   "The illusion of tribe" pp. 28–50 in P. C. W. Gutkind (ed.), The Passing of Tribal Man in Africa. Leiden: E. J. Brill.

Book reviews should not exceed 800 words and should not contain footnotes; references to other works should be incorporated in the text; page references should be given when quotations from the book are included.

Galley proofs of articles will be sent to authors (from the publisher), who should use the standard method of proof correction. Corrected proofs should be returned to publisher as soon as possible; where proofs are not returned in time, the Editor reserves the right to send the printers his own corrected proof of contributors article which will be the basis of the final article. Proofs are intended for checking, NOT RE-WRITING and authors are most strongly reminded that material should be submitted ready for the printer.

Authors receive 25 free offprints of their article (8 free offprints for book reviews). Additional offprints of articles can be supplied at cost price and must be ordered and paid for when the corrected proofs are returned to the printer.

PUBLISHER: E. J. Brill, Leiden, The Netherlands

Journal of Asian and African Studies VIII, 3–4

Introduction

J. HENRY KORSON

University of Massachusetts, Amherst, U.S.A.

PERHAPS the most important development on the world scene during the last generation has been the achievement of national independence by dozens of former colonial territories. The striving for nationhood is rarely smooth, and frequently is attained only after great political and even military struggle.

Pakistan is only one of the nations in South Asia which achieved independence from Great Britain in the early post-war years, and its trials in achieving and maintaining nationhood have been almost unparalleled. The one factor which distinguishes Pakistan from almost all other newly-established nations is its commitment to the religious ideology of Islam, a commitment which was a foundation stone for the new nation. This commitment a generation after independence is no less today, as can be ascertained by a close reading of the new constitution inaugurated in August, 1973. In fact, the nation has from the start referred to itself as "The Islamic Republic of Pakistan."

The problems which the young nation faced in the early years of independence were, indeed, monumental. Since the nation was founded on the ideology of Islam, various political leaders have, from time to time, raised the slogan of "Islamic Socialism." Yet as an agrarian society the concepts of private property and the ownership of land have been, and continue to be the most cherished values.

As has been the case in many other newly-founded nations, the first leaders of Pakistan had no experience in self government and used the model of the Indian Civil Service to establish their own Civil Service of Pakistan. Both, of course, followed the British pattern which had been long established on the subcontinent. Since many Pakistani leaders had served in the Indian Civil Service at various levels of administration, it was not too difficult to establish the Government Administrative Staff College to train additional members to serve the nation. Political parties began to function, and men who had served as leaders of the Pakistan movement in India became the leaders of the new nation.

The Muslim separatist movement before independence was led by unorthodox men like Mohammad Ali Jinnah who had in mind a secular state, but he did not oppose the pressures of the sectarians provided there was freedom for the religious minorities. And this freedom of worship has been maintained. Leadership in a political movement is not to be equated with experience in national leadership and its responsibilities, so that the earliest leaders didn't even have the opportunity to survive their apprenticeships. For eleven years the nation's leadership wallowed in uncertainty and ineffectiveness – perhaps no worse than the leadership of most other newly-formed nations. As is also frequently the case where one unsuccessful regime is followed by another, the military came to the fore, and in 1958 General Mohammad Ayub Khan assumed the presidency.

Every new administration takes the reins of government with high hopes for the resolution of the major problems of its people, and such was the case eleven years later when Ayub Khan stepped down for still another military leader, General Yahya Khan. When the latter assumed office he made it clear that his personal preference was to continue in his military career and that he considered his political role as president to be that of caretaker until national elections could be held. The election of December, 1970, and the disastrous war in East Pakistan that followed left Zulfikar Ali Bhutto, leader of the People's Party of Pakistan (which had won the majority of West Pakistan's seats in the National Assembly) as the man who not only had to carry the burdens of office under "normal" circumstances, but was challenged to retrieve the nation's dignity. By many observers the economy was considered to be in considerable disrepair, and the election campaign promises of the PPP had to be considered by Bhutto and his party leaders as something far more serious than ordinary campaign rhetoric.

When Bhutto assumed the presidency on December 20, 1971 following the cease-fire in East Pakistan/Bangladesh, he wasted little time in organizing his cabinet and setting about instituting many of the reforms he and his party had promised. This brief statement cannot hope to explore all the problems of the nation in those dark days, nor the solutions promised by Bhutto and his administration, because at its birth and since, Pakistan was a nation with exceedingly limited resources, and this enormous handicap presented almost insuperable barriers to the achievement of rapid economic development.

As in the case of so many ex-colonial nations, foreign aid at the start became a *sine-qua-non* not only for the economic development of the nation, but for its very survival. Aid soon became available from many of the western nations, both in the form of outright grants as well as loans and technical assistance. This economic assistance to Pakistan has continued over the years, which has helped spur the development and growth of the economy. Beginning in 1947 and the years following, some of the immigrants from India were able to bring some of their resources, while others with business experience were able to obtain sufficient credit to undertake various enterprises. The leaders of the new nation opted for private enterprise, although the theme of egalitarianism within the framework of Islam was frequently propounded.

Following the disastrous war in East Pakistan, and with the economy in a shambles, the problems that confronted Bhutto were, indeed, monumental and of long standing. Although the PPP won the majority of West Pakistan's seats in the national assembly in the 1970 election, Bhutto lost no time in instituting reforms—many of which had appeared in the party's platform during the campaign. Unlike the previous Five Year Plans, almost all the reforms were out-lined to be achieved by the end of the decade. For example, within three months of taking office, in December, 1971, the Educational Policy for 1972–1980 was announced under that very title.

In this brief introduction, it is impossible to discuss at length the many and varied problems that face the Bhutto regime during the balance of this decade, but the chapters that follow in this small volume are by scholars who have written widely on various aspects of the nation and people of Pakistan since its inception. It should be kept in mind, however, that the chapters that follow were completed in August/September, 1973, and that although they were "con-temporary" as of that time, it is never possible in a work of this kind to make the efforts of the contributors as timely as the daily newspaper. Nevertheless, it is hoped that the reader will profit from the perspectives and insights offered.

The Punjab has not only been the most heavily populated province, but all too often has been considered the power center of the four provinces that constitute contemporary Pakistan. The landholders have always been the major center of political power, and in his chapter "The People's Party Vs. the Punjab Feudalists," Professor Baxter offers some deep insights into some of the long-standing problems of power politics in what was (and perhaps still is) an essentially feudal society.

We are fortunate to have as the contributor of the second chapter, Professor Fazlur Rahman, assess the new Constitution of Pakistan, which was inaugurated on August 14, 1973. In this chapter Professor Rahman makes comparisons with the Interim Constitution of May, 1972, and points up Bhutto's efforts to compromise with the traditionalists. The new constitution does lay greater stress on the basic philosophy of Islam. Furthermore, although the "Islamic Republic of Pakistan" has been the official name used, not until the new Constitution was written has Islam been recognized as the official state religion. One of the compromises Bhutto and the PPP apparently had to make with the opposition was to grant the Islamic Council veto power over the National Assembly. This point has not been widely publicized, and its effect will be interesting to observe.

All too frequently some of the major political problems of newly established nations are internal ones based on ethnic, tribal, and/or regional differences. Since nationhood is a concept rarely found among a people striving for political independence, self interest is usually found to be the overriding element in the difficulties that confront political leaders as they attempt to resolve the young nation's problems. Regionalism, then, can be readily understood from the point of view of self-interest. But when the greatest concentration of population is combined with the concentration of the most productive land in a primarily agricultural society, the result equates with the concentration of political power. The Punjab, then, in [West] Pakistan has played that role since independence, and will undoubtedly continue to do so in the future. Prof. Malik assesses some of the problems of regionalism that the government has attempted to resolve.

In his chapter on Bhutto's foreign policy in the course of his first eighteen months in office, Professor Ziring reviews the background of Bhutto's experience in the nation's foreign affairs, – which had been the Prime Minister's almost total experience and preoccupation in his nation's government. Bhutto served as Ayub Kahn's minister of foreign affairs before their falling out, and, in the intervening years appears to have been largely concerned with Pakistan's relations with India, – and only secondarily with other nations. How successful his stewardship will be will have to await the time when he has completed his service to the nation.

Operating from an essentially weak position at the end of the war in December, 1971, Bhutto has won the admiration of foreign leaders for his astuteness in handling both the nation's foreign policy as well as reaching a working accommodation with the leaders of the minority parties on the nation's most pressing domestic problems.

The status and character of a nation's economic organization is a fairly accurate indicator of that society's economic and social welfare, and, as one of the numerous newly organized nations of the post World war II period, Pakistan has had its difficulties, but also its share of successes. As with so many underdeveloped nations, foreign aid in a variety of forms has been crucial to the development of its economy, and this aid continues to play a vital role today.

With exceedingly limited natural resources and the desire to encourage rapid economic development, successive administrations offered attractive inducements to the entrepreneurial class which not only resulted in high annual economic growth rates, but also resulted in the concentration of great wealth in the hands of relatively few people – the renowned "22 families." Since the election platform of the People's Party of Pakistan laid considerable stress on "Islamic Socialism" and egalitarianism as goals to be achieved for the nation, Professor Gustafson reviews the government's major accomplishments to date: nationalization of [some] of the basic industries; labor reforms, which are aimed largely at the larger companies; land reforms, the results of which are open to question; and the devaluation of the rupee, which Professor Gustafson considers the most fruitful move to date. The loss of East Pakistan, the major source of foreign exchange earnings, has evidently not had the disastrous effects on the economy of Pakistan that had been predicted. Instead, the resurgence of the economy and annual growth rate has surprised many observers.

Although the economic problems that confront the many underdeveloped nations of the world command the major attention of their leaders, all too often the most serious factor that contributes to the continued economic difficulties of these nations is the unabated population increase. With the relatively rapid adoption of modern public health measures the reduction in mortality rates for many of these nations has been quite dramatic. Unfortunately, the same cannot be claimed for efforts to reduce fertility rates on a comparable basis. The result has almost invariably been a sharp and continued net increase in the population, and Pakistan is no exception. Although the official government position has favored the introduction of family planning, the optimistic results that have been reported in the past have evidently been exaggerated. In their paper devoted to Pakistan's population problems, Bean and Bhatti point up some of the difficulties of the governmentally sponsored fertility control program in a traditional society and discuss the prospects for the future.

In this age of rising expectations, perhaps no other item has greater emotional appeal to the masses in the less-developed nations than universal literacy and free education. It is no accident of history that the ex-colonial nations have, as a rule, the weakest systems of education and the highest rates of illiteracy. It doesn't take much imagination on the part of men who seek high office in such nations to attack illiteracy and promise universal (and frequently free) education. And such has been the case in Pakistan. Previous regimes have proclaimed and promised much, but they can show only an erratic record of accomplishment, and one far below the expectations and hopes of either the people or today's leaders.

That Bhutto was serious about educational reform can be judged by the fact that within three months of taking office the *Education Policy, 1972–1980*, was announced and widely published. Although wide-ranging, its major goals were the nationalization of private schools and colleges without compensation; the universalization of free primary (and, later, secondary) education, and a major attack on the problem of illiteracy. Of these three goals, the first has been largely achieved within the first eighteen months; considerable progress has been made toward the second, while universal literacy will undoubtedly take many years to achieve. In the chapter "Bhutto's Educational Reform," I have tried to assess the new education policy and the progress made in the first eighteen months since it was announced.

Four of the chapters: those by Professors Ziring, Gustafson, Malik and Korson, are revised and expanded versions of papers presented at the annual meeting of the Association of Asian Studies in March, 1972, in Chicago.

The People's Party Vs. the Punjab "Feudalists"

CRAIG BAXTER

U.S. Department of State and the United States Military Academy, West Point, U.S.A.

IN ITS MANIFESTO issued prior to the 1970 elections, the Pakistan People's Party (PPP) led by Zulfiqar Ali Bhutto reiterated one of its "programmatic principles" by declaring "the party stands for elimination of feudalism and will take concrete steps in accordance with the established principles of socialism to protect and advance the interests of the peasantry" (1970:29). The manifesto reviewed the land reforms of the Ayub era and criticized them: "Since it was legally permitted, the feudal landowner divided the excess [i.e., land above the permissible ceiling] among the members of his family...in most parts of West Pakistan the feudal owners live in a social system of castes, caste-clans and surviving traditions of joint families. Thus even with his estate divided in this manner, the feudal lord retains his power" (1970:28). To the PPP the "feudal lords constitute a formidable obstacle to progress. Not only by virtue of their wealth, but on account of their hold over their tenants and the neighbouring peasantry, they wield considerable power and are, even at present, a major political force" (1970:28).

The words "even at present" assume, at least in the eyes of the PPP, the existence of feudal political power in the past. It is the purpose of this article to explore the importance of the major landlords in the Punjab in the political system of the province since the introduction of reforms in 1919 and to look at the impact of the PPP on them in the 1970 election. In the pre-independence period the study will be limited to the Muslim seats in the territory which became part of Pakistan after the partition of 1947. The use of the essentially perjorative terms "feudalism", "landlordism" and similar words and their derivatives by opponents of the traditional leadership of the rural areas will not be challenged here, although the present writer does not subscribe fully to such use. An alternative term might well be "squirearchy", under which the local squires performed political roles in which they both protected and defended their own high estate and legislated, perhaps paternalistically, to improve the conditions of the agrarian population in general, or at least those who owned the land they tilled.

What ever may be the correct term the PPP call for land reform was not original. The party which has been credited with furthering the interests of large landlords, the Unionist Party of pre-partition Punjab, was itself founded to protect the samall as well as the large landowner, primarily against the urban (and largely Hindu) commercial and money lending groups. The Muslim League, following closely the program of the Congress Party, called for the break up of large *zamindari* holdings and a moderate program of land reform in both the 1936 and 1946 elections. More equitable distribution of land was again in the Muslim League manifesto in the 1951 Punjab election. And as we have already noted the 1958 revolution of Ayub Khan included among its basic tenets a revision of the land holding patterns in West Pakistan. The 1951 Muslim League received and the 1958 revolution seized a mandate for reform but neither carried out a program to the extent demanded by the PPP. The party of President Bhutto now has that mandate. Its exercise of the mandate is beyond the scope of this article but it can be noted that, using continuing martial law powers. the new president has announced a land reform program.

Unionist Domination

The Government of India Act, 1919, usually known as the Montagu-Chelmsford reforms, introduced major changes in the administration of the provinces of British India. Now a majority of the members of the provincial Legislative Council would be elected and, while the principle of executive responsibility to the Council was not granted, the Council would have expanded control over the acts of the executive. Additionally, the executive departments were divided into two categories: one group, concerned with fiscal and law and order matters, would remain under the jurisdiction of the Governor and would be administered by officially appointed executive councillors; the second, concerned primarily with "nation-building" subjects, would be transferred to ministers appointed by the Governor from among the elected members of the Council. The new system, "dyarchy", would almost inevitably lead to the formation of parties, informally or formally, either within or outside of the Council. The ambiguous position of the Congress on "council entry" meant that in most provinces parties other than the Congress took the lead and these parties generally were formed first within the Council and later extended their activities outside by organizing in order to present a common electoral front. The franchise was severely restricted with eligibility based primarily on property ownership and income qualifications. Constituencies were divided into general (i.e., territorial) and special, the latter including seats for such groups as landholders, university graduates and industrial and commercial interests. The territorial constituencies were divided in two manners: first, seats were assigned to various communities in a system of separate electorates in accordance with the Lucknow Pact between the Muslim League and the Congress in 1916; and, secondly, within the communal allotments seats were assigned to urban and rural electorates.

In the Punjab a total of 64 members of the Council were to be elected from territorial constituencies and seven more from special constituencies. The 64 general seats were divided into twenty non-Muhammadan (seven urban and

13 rural), 32 Muhammadan (five urban and 27 rural) and twelve Sikh (one urban and eleven rural). The seven special constituencies included four for landholders (one for each community plus a separate seat for the Baluch *tumandars*), one for university graduates and two to represent commercial and industrial groups.

Despite the widening of the franchise under the Montagu-Chelmsford reforms the number of eligible voters in the general constituencies was only 3.4 percent of the population (1921) in the 1926 election (Gr. Brit., 1930: 41–43). In this article we are concerned primarily with the Muhammadan rural constituencies in the territory which was to become part of Pakistan. There were nineteen such seats located in fifteen districts lying east of the Ravi and Sutlej rivers. In 1921 these had a Muslim population of 7,191,140 of which 189,157 were eligible to vote in 1926, a percentage of 2.63, which is significantly lower than that of the province as a whole. It can be assumed that virtually all the electors achieved that designation through the property ownership qualification and from the lower percentage of the Muslim population meeting the standard that the land holdings were perhaps larger than in other districts. There was considerable regional variation in the percentage, ranging from about 5 percent in Rawalpindi, Jhelum and Lyallpur districts down to less than 1 percent in Dera Ghazi Khan and Muzaffargarh (Gt. Brit., 1930: 41–43). Generally the ratio of eligible voters was higher in districts containing canal colonies than in non-colony districts, i.e., those districts in which Darling reports the average land holding to be higher (1947: 127 and *passim*).

Elections were held for the Council in 1920, 1923, 1926 and 1930, with the term of the last Council being extended pending the election of members of the new Assembly created under the 1935 Act. In the nineteen seats together with the Muhammadan landholders and the Baluch tumandars, 21 seats in all, only 51 different persons were elected, an average of 2.43 per seat. Only two seats were won by different persons in each election, Lyallpur South and Gujranwala, but in the latter two of the occupants were from the same family. Four members were elected in each of the four elections, Nawab Chaudhury Fazl Ali of Gujrat, Malik Sir Muhammad Firoz Khan Noon of Shahpur, Makhdum Syed Reza Shah Gilani of Multan and Nawab Sir Muhammad Jamal Khan Leghari of the Baluch tumanders seat. Seven more were elected three times, although like those elected four times not necessarily from the same seat on each occasion. Another 13 were elected twice.

Many of those elected, thirteen, were from among those families listed in the compilation of Punjab chiefs sanctioned by the provincial government (Griffin 1940). Many more are included among such notable categories as provincial and divisional *darbaris*. The names form a listing of the squirearchy of Punjab. Extending the time from 1919 to the end of parliamentary government in 1958 – not all listed had members in the 1921–36 Council – one can note the Arain Mians of Baghbanpura (Sir Muhammad Shafi, Mian Muhammad Shah Nawaz, Begum Jahanara Shah Nawaz, Mian Iftikharuddin, Mian Bashir Ahmad), the Mokul family (Sardar Habibullah), and the Qizilbash clan (Nawab Sir Muzaffar Ali Khan Qizilbash) of Lahore District; the Chathas (Riasat Ali, Salahuddin, Nasiruddin) of Gujranwala; the Janjuas of Darapur (Talib Mehdi Khan, Khair Mehdi Khan, Lahrasab Khan), Pirs of Jalalpur (Nawab Sir Syed Mehr Shah) and Khokars (Raja Ghazanfar Ali Khan) of Jhelum; the Pirs of Makhad, the Kot Ghebas (Sir Muhammad Shah Nawaz Khan), the Hayats of Wah (noted below), and the Shamasabad Awans (Nawab Muhammad Amin Khan) of Attock (now Campbellpur); the Noons and Tiwanas (both noted below), the Qureshis (Nawab Muhammad Hayat, Mian Saeed, Mian Zakir), Pirachas (Sheikh Fazle Haq, Sheikh Fazal Ilahi) and the Pirs of Jahanian Shah (Syed Ghulam Muhammad) of Shahpur (now Sargodha); the Wanbachran (Malik Muzaffar Khan) and Kalabagh (Malik Amir Muhammad Khan) families of Mianwali; the Pirs of Rajoa (Syed Ghulam Abbas) and of Shah Jiwana (Syed Mubarik Ali, Syed Abid Husain) and Sials (Nawazish Ali Khan) of Jhang; the Daultanas (see below), Gilanis (eight have held seats from 1921 through 1958), Dahas (Khan Haibat Khan), Qureshis (Murid Hussain, Ashiq Hussain), Gardezis (Syed Ali Husain Shah) and Khaggas (Pir Budhan Shah) of Multan; Gurmanis (Mushtaq Ahmad, Ghulam Jilani) and Dastis (Abdul Hamid Khan) of Muzaffargarh and Legharis (Sir Jamal Khan), Drishaks (Allan Khan, Bahadur Khan), Mazaris (Balakh Sher, Sher Baz) and Pirs of Taunsa Sharif in Dera Ghazi Khan. The listing is long but incomplete as the unravelling of family connections is a difficult task. However, the families noted above held at least 42 of the 84 seats for which elections were held to the Council and at least 53 of the 116 seats for which elections were held in 1936 and 1946 for the Assembly in the districts under study (i.e., four elections at 21 seats each for the Council and two elections at 58 seats each for the Assembly). If the districts of Sialkot, Gujrat, Sheikhupura, Montgomery, and Lyallpur – largely Jat and small holdings – are eliminated the key families won 70 percent of the Council elections and 68 percent of the pre-independence Assembly elections. With almost no exceptions all those elected to the Council and those elected to the first Assembly were associated with the Unionist Party. The 1945–46 contest between the Unionists and the Muslim League will be discussed below.

The founder and principal mover behind the Unionist Party was Mian Sir Fazli Husain (1877–1936). He has been the subject of an excellent biography by his son (Husain, 1946) and an appreciation by an experienced journalist (Ahmad, 1936). Fazli Husain had been a member of the Legislative Council as it existed prior to the Montagu-Chelmsford reforms and was elected in 1920 to the Muhammadan landholders seat. Under dyarchy he was one of two ministers chosen by the Governor, the other being an urban Hindu, Lala Harkishen Lal (Gauba). He remained a minister until he was oppointed an Executive Councillor in 1926. In 1930 he was appointed a member of the Viceroy's Executive Council in New Delhi where he remained until 1935. He again became a minister in the Punjab in 1936 just prior to his death.

In the first Council Fazli Husain was clearly the most prominent and experienced among the Muslim members and it was to him that they looked for leadership. The informal organization of a rural bloc began in the first Council and drew support not only from Muslims but also from rural Hindus under the leadership of Chaudhury Lal Chand and later Chaudhyry Sir Chhotu Ram, who became the leader of the Unionist Party when Fazli Husain joined the Executive Council. The rural Sikh members, while retaining a separate organization, also gave support to the rural bloc; prior to Fazli Husain's appointment to the Executive Council, one of the two members was the Sikh leader Sardar Sir Sundar Singh Majithia (1872–1941). In 1923 the rural grouping formally constituted itself the Punjab National Unionist Party "intended [as] a mass organization of the Punjab peasant proprietors" (Husain 1964: xi). While the party gained support only from rural members of the Hindu and Sikh communities, and not by any means all of the former, it did gain the adherance of the bulk of the urban Muslim members including such prominent members as Dr. Sir Muhammad Iqbal (1877–1938) (Malik 1971: 82–83), Sir Abdul Qadir and Mir Maqbool Mahmud.

The party adopted a sixteen point program which included the constitutional attainment of dominion status and the "statesmanlike" working of the Montagu-Chelmsford reforms to that end. The latter was a rebuff to the Congress of Gandhi and clearly showed a moderate stance as behooved those with property interests. Underlying the operative points was the urban-rural conflict: the achievement of a balance between urban and rural taxation with the clear implication that the land revenue was a greater burden on the rural population that those taxes laid on city dwellers were on them; the checking of "exploitation of economically backward classes by economically dominant classes," and the continuation of the Punjab Land Alienation Act to protect agriculturist against money lenders (Husain 1946: 154–5). Although there were occasional breaks in the ranks on matters which were specifically communal, it was a program on which the rural elite of the Punjab could agree and carry out cooperatively and inter-communally (Ahmad 1967: 57–64).

Three Families

Sir Fazli Husain's immediate family did not continue in electoral politics. One son, Azim, is a high official in the Indian Foreign Service and another, Nasim, served in the Pakistan Foreign Service as did a nephew and son-in-law, Mian Arshad Husain, who became for a short period a Foreign Minister under Ayub Khan. Another son-in-law, Sheikh Manzur Qadir, son of Sir Abdul Qadir, has been prominent in legal affairs and has served as both Chief Justice and Law Minister of Pakistan, while still another is a member of the Noon family but has not been active in politics. Thus there is no lineal continuation of Fazli Husain's political activity, although Azim Husain's book remains perhaps the best single work on the Unionist Party up to 1936.

There are however three other families who were important in the Unionist period and which have members of the family still active in legislative bodies in Pakistan. These are the Hayats of Wah, the Noon-Tiwana group of Sargodha and the Daultanas of Mailsi in Multan District. These are not the only ones of the key families which survived the People's Party onslaught in 1970. There are others but they do not meet the qualification of being among the highest echelon of the Unionists in the past as well as sitting today. These include the Legharis of Dera Ghazi Khan (Sardar Ata Muhammad Khan, Sardar Mahmud Khan), the Pir of Makhad from Campbellpur, Pirachas (Sheikh Fazal Ilahi, a senator), Kalabagh (Malik Muzaffar Khan), Gilani (Faiz Mustafa Shah), Multan Qureshis (Nawab Sadiq Hussain) and Dastis (Amjad Hamid Khan), the names in parentheses being those who sit today in legislative bodies. Several of these were either elected on the People's Party ticket or were elected as independents and joined the PPP later. Thanks to indirect elections for women's seats the Arain Mians of Baghbanpura (Begum Nasim Jehan) and Pirs of Shah Jiwana (Begum Abida Fakr Imam) have also been seated in legislative bodies.

The *Hayats of Wah* have been represented in legislative bodies continuously since 1921 with the exception of late 1921 to 1923 and of 1955–1958, up to the time of the Ayub revolution, and are again represented in the National Assembly. The principal member of the family was Sardar Sir Sikandar Hayat Khan (1892–1942). Sikandar was elected to the Council in 1921, but was soon unseated in an election petition. In 1923 he was returned again from the Attock seat and in 1926 won the Muhammadan landholders seat previously held by Sir Fazli Husain. Sikandar again followed in Fazli Husain's steps when he became a member of the Executive Council in 1930 at the time Sir Fazli was promoted to the Viceroy's Council in Delhi. In early 1935 Sikandar resigned to become Deputy Governor of the Reserve Bank of India but a year later returned to his position in Punjab. The Hayats, however, were not without a voice in the Council chamber as Sikander was replaced in Lahore by his cousin and brother-in-law, Nawab Muzaffar Khan (1879–1951). Muzaffar Khan, as a government official, had several times been a nominated official member of the Council. After the introduction of further reforms and provicial autonomy under the Government of India Act, 1935, and following the death of Sir Fazli Husain, Sikandar became leader of the Unionist Party and first premier of the Punjab. Muzaffar Khan also became a member of the Legislative Assembly and remained so until 1943. Upon Sikandar's death in 1942 his son, Sardar Shaukat Hayat Khan (b. 1915) was elected to the Assembly and made a member of the new cabinet under Sir Khizr Hayat Khan Tiwana. Shaukat was re-elected on a Muslim League ticket in 1946 and also became a member of the Constituent Assembly where he remained until 1954. In 1970 he was elected to the National Assembly as a candidate of the Council Muslim League of which he is now the leader. A younger brother of Sikandar, Sardar Barkat Hayat Khan, was a member of the Legislative Assembly, 1946–1948. One of Sikandar's daughters, Mahmuda Salim Khan, although not involved in electoral politics, was a minister in the West Pakistan cabinet of the Nawab of Kalabagh from 1962 to 1965. Mumtaz Ali Khan, a nephew of Muzaffar Khan, also was an M.L.A. both in the 1946–1948 assembly and in the 1951–55 assembly.

The elder brother of Sikandar, Nawab Sir Liaquat Hayat Khan (1887–1948), was a member of the Indian Police Service and was detailed to the princely state of Patiala in 1923, where he became prime minister in 1930. He was connected by marriage with the Sadiq family of Amritsar which has contributed several members of legislative bodies: Sheikh Muhammad Sadiq was a member of the Council from 1924 to 1936 and the Assembly, 1938–1939; Sheikh Sadiq Hassan was a member of the Central Legislative Assembly, 1923–1926 and 1930–1934, of the provincial Assembly, 1939–1948, and of the Constituent Assembly, 1951–1954; and Sheikh Masood Sadiq was a member of provincial Assembly, 1951–1958, and later a member of the cabinet of the Nawab of Kalabagh. Liaquat also connects the Hayat family with Mir Maqbool Mahmud (d. 1948), whose wife's uncle Liaquat was. Maqbool Mahmud was a member of the Council, 1923–1930, and of the Assembly, 1937–1945, and served a chief parliamentary secretary to Sikandar during the latter period. When not in the legislature Maqbool Mahmud was active in administrative and judicial positions in princely India, notably in Patiala, and at the time of partition he was director of the secretariat of the Chamber of Princes. He was closely tied to the Hayats by marriage: two of his sisters were married to Sikandar, two of his wife's siblings were married to children of Liaquat, and his daughter is the wife of Shaukat Hayat Khan. Maqbool Mahmud also married a daughter of the Sind political leader, Sir Abdullah Haroon.

The collaterals of the Hayat family are numerous as the family did not frequently follow the cross-cousin marriage pattern adopted by many leading Punjab Muslim families. Without detailing the relationships the family is connected through marriages with the Haroons of Karachi; the Amir of Bahawalpur; S. Osman Ali, several times an ambassador of Pakistan; the Baghbanpura Mians; the Quereshis of Multan; author Herbert Feldman; Shakir Durrani, former director of Pakistan International Airlines; Ahmad Bakhsh Khan (M.L.A., 1937–1938); Syed Fida Hasan, a principal adviser to Ayub Khan; Hakim Ahmad Shuja, for years the secretary of the Council and the Assembly; B. A. Kureshi, former chief secretary of West Pakistan – and even Mian Saeed, the star of Pakistan's cricket efforts in the early days of independence. Today, however, the only legislative representative of the direct line of the family is Shaukat.

The *Noons and Tiwanas* of Sargodha District might more correctly be called a "family group" rather than a single family. They have generally worked in political harmony, expecially prior to independence, and have numerous interconnections through marriage. Griffin (1940: I: 191–235) details four branches of the Tiwanas in addition to the Noons. The Noons alone have been represented in legislative bodies continuously since 1921 with an interruption only when Ayub Khan governed without a legislature from 1958 to 1962. One or more Tiwanas occupied seats in Lahore, New Delhi, London (as a member of the Council of the Secretary of State for India), Karachi or Islamabad almost continuously with only brief gaps in 1934–1937 and 1962–1965 in addition to the Ayub martial law period.

The record for longevity in senior positions for Punjabis belongs to Malik

Sir Muhammad Firoz Khan Noon (1893–1970). He was a member of the Council from its inception in 1921 until just before its close in 1936. During that period he served as Minister of Local Government from 1927 to 1931, succeeding Mian Fazli Husain as Unionist representative in the cabinet, and as Minister of Education from 1931 until 1936, when he resigned to become High Commissioner for India in London, an office created under the 1935 Act. However, Noons were not absent from Lahore. Firoz's father Nawab Malik Sir Muhammad Hayat Khan Noon (1875–1943), who had been a nominated member of the Council of State, 1935–1937, was returned from a landholder's constituency in 1936, and a cousin, Malik Sardar Khan Noon, was elected from another landholder's seat in 1943. In 1941 Firoz returned to India to become a member of the Viceroy's Council, holding first the labor portfolio and in 1942 the defense portfolio, the first Indian to be so designated. He was also a member of the Imperial War Cabinet in 1944. He left the Viceroy's Council in September, 1945, to return to the Punjab to campaign as a Muslim Leaguer for the impending election to the Legislative Assembly. He was elected from the Rawalpindi Division Towns urban seat and was also elected to the Constituent Assembly. In 1950 he was appointed Governor of East Bengal and remained in Dacca until 1953 when he was called back to Lahore to become Chief Minister of the province. He was elected to the second Constituent Assembly in 1955 and left office as Chief Minister the same year, pending the creation of the single province of West Pakistan. In 1956 and 1957 he was Foreign Minister in the cabinet of H. S. Suhrawardy and in January, 1958, became Prime Minister of Pakistan. He was in office when the coup led by General Ayub Khan took place in October, 1958. Firoz Khan Noon was barred from electoral politics by the Elective Bodies Disqualification Order (EBDO) of 1959. In the 1962 indirect elections under the Ayub constitution and again in 1965, his eldest son, Malik Nur Hayat Khan Noon (b. 1927) was elected to the National Assembly. Nur Hayat contested the 1970 election for the National Assembly on the ticket of the Pakistan Muslim League (Qayyum) but was defeated by a relative, Malik Anwar Ali Khan Noon (b. 1924) who contested on the People's Party ticket.

Nawab Malik Sir Umar Hayat Khan Tiwana (1874–1944) of the Mitha Tiwana branch held various offices for almost thirty years. He was named to the pre-reform Legislative Council of Punjab in 1904 and to the Imperial Legislative Council in 1909 where he remained until 1920. He was elected to the Council of State, the upper house of the legislature in Delhi, in 1920, but yielded his elective seat in 1925 to Nawab Sir Mehr Shah. Umar Hayat Khan was then nominated to the Council of State in 1926. In 1929 he was appointed to the Council of the Secretary of State for India in London and completed his term in 1934. His son, Nawab Malik Sir Khizr Hayat Khan Tiwana (b. 1900) was elected to the Assembly in 1937 and became Minister of Public Works in the cabinet headed by Sir Sikandar Hayat Khan. On Sikandar's death, Khizr succeeded him as Prime Minister of the Punjab. Running as the titular head of the Unionist Party and against the tide of the Muslim League, Khizr was re-elected in 1946 and briefly headed a coalition ministry including Unionists,

Akalis and Congressmen. Since the fall of his ministry in 1947, prior to partition, Khizr has not taken an active part in politics.

The Mitha Tiwana branch of the Tiwana clan is not the only one which has been active in politics. The Hamoka branch has four members who have held seats in legislatures. Nawab Malik Sir Khuda Baksh Khan (d. 1930) was a member of the Council, 1925–1926, occupying through a by-election the seat vacated by Fazli Husain when he joined the Executive Council (the next general election saw the seat go to Sikandar Hayat Khan unopposed). Khuda Bakhsh's son, Sir Allah Bakhsh Khan (1887–?), followed a civil service career with an appointment to the Central Legislative Asssembly in 1931 and election to the Punjab Legislative Assembly in 1936 and again in 1946. He was considered to be one of the closest advisers of his nephew, Khizr. Also from the Hamoka branch, Malik Fateh Muhammad Khan (b. 1895), was a member of the Assembly 1951–1958, and his son, Malik Muhammad Anwar Khan (b. 1934) was a member of the second National Assembly under Ayub Khan (1965–1969) and was defeated in the 1970 National Assembly election, finishing third behind nominees of the Council Muslim League and the People's Party. The Mundial Tiwanas of Jahanabad have been represented by Nawab Malik Mumtaz Muhammad Khan, member of the Council, 1923–1926, and his son, Nawabzada Malik Muhammad Habibullah Khan (b. 1907), who was a member of the Assembly, 1937–1945 and 1951–1955. Mumtaz Muhammad Khan opposed Khizr in the 1946 election in an intra-clan contest. A Lyallpur branch of the family has been represented by Malik Nadir Ali Khan, who was a member of the National Assembly, 1968–1969. The strong tendency toward inter-marriage among the Tiwanas and the Noons limits the number of politically important collaterals. A relative of the Hamoka branch, Malik Khuda Bakhsh Bucha, was a career civil servant, including a tour as private secretary to Khizr in the forties, and was elevated to the cabinet as Minister of Agriculture by the Nawab of Kalabagh in 1966. He is now special adviser to President Bhutto for agricultural affairs.

Possibly even more intertwined with other political families than the Hayats are the *Daultanas* of Multan District. Among the family itself and its close collaterals only during the period of Ayub's martial law and the time of the second Ayub National Assembly and the Yahya period are Daultanas missing from the legislatures. For immediate family members (those actually named Daultana) the gaps are 1923–1926 and 1958–1970.

Four Daultanas have sat in legislative bodies. The first was Nawab Mian Ahmad Yar Khan Daultana (d. 1940), along with Mir Maqbool Mahmud one of the closest political associates of Sikandar. He was a parliamentary secretary and chief whip of the Unionist Party in the Assembly. Ahmad Yar was a member of the Council, 1921–1923 and 1926–1936, and of the Assembly from 1937 until his death. His cousin and brother-in-law, Mian Allah Yar Khan, won the seat in a by-election in 1940 and was re-elected in 1946, reamining in the Assembly until his death in 1947. At that time Allah Yar's son, Mian Riaz Ahmad Khan, occupied the seat until the Assembly was dissolved in 1948.

The principal member of the family, however, has been Mian Mumtaz Muhammad Khan Daultana (b. 1916). Returning to Lahore after an academic career in England, Mumtaz was elected to the Assembly in the by-election for the West Punjab Landholders seat following the death of Muhammad Hayat Khan Noon. He was elected as a Muslim Leaguer in 1946 from the seat formerly held by his maternal uncle, Chaudhury Sir Shahabuddin, in Sialkot District, leaving the family's home constituency for Allah Yar. He was also elected a member of the Constituent Assembly and was re-elected in 1955. In 1951 he was elected to the provincial Assembly from Multan District and became Chief Minister of the Punjab, holding that post for two years. He was briefly a member of the first Khan Sahib cabinet in West Pakistan and was Defense Minister in the short lived Chundrigar cabinet in 1957. Like Sir Firoz Khan Noon he was disqualified from electoral politics under EBDO, but within the limitations imposed acted as a principal adviser to the Council Muslim League when that party was reorganized. He became president of the party when the EBDO restrictions were removed in 1967 and held office until after the 1970 election in which he was returned to the National Assembly from his home constituency. Daultana remains a member of the Assembly but has accepted an appointment as Ambassador of Pakistan in the United Kingdom.

Ahmad Yar and Chaudhury Sir Shahabuddin, a Jat from Sialkot District, were married to sisters. Shahabuddin was a member of the Council from 1923 until its termination in 1936 and became president (i.e., speaker) of the Council in 1927. He also was briefly a minister. On 1936 he was elected a member of the Assembly and when the new body convened in 1937 he became speaker. Childless, Shahabuddin in a sense "adopted" Mumtaz, who now lives in the Shahabuddin house in Lahore. On his maternal side, Mumtaz is related to a number of political figures including Yusuf Khattak of the Frontier, the Dahas of Multan, and Chaudhury Salahuddin Chatha of Gujranwala (1912–1970), a member of the Assembly, 1951–1958, and of the National Assembly, 1962–1965. One of Mumtaz's susters is married to Nawabzada Mian Muhammad Saeed Qureshi of Sargodha. Saeed Qureshi was a member of the Assembly, 1951–1958. His father, Nawab Mian Muhammad Hayat Qureshi, was an opponent of the Noon-Tiwana group in Sargodha and a member of the Council, 1926–1936. Having defeated a Tiwana in 1926, he was himself defeated in an Assembly contest by Sir Allah Bakhsh Khan Tiwana in 1936 and by another Unionist candidate in 1946. His son, Saeed, as mentioned, won in 1951, and in 1962 another son, Mian Muhammad Zakir, was elected to the National Assembly, and was defeated in 1965 by Muhammad Anwar Khan Tiwana. In 1970, Zakir was elected to the National Asembly as a candidate of his relative Daultana's Council Muslim League. The rivalry between Daultana and the Noon-Tiwana group has been played locally on the Sargodha electoral scene.

Provincial Autonomy

The Government of India Act of 1935, which went into effect in the provinces in 1937, brought substantial changes. Dyarchy was ended and all subjects were transferred to a responsible ministry subject only to limited reserved powers which could be used by the Governor in emergency circumstances. All members of the provincial legislatures were to be elected by a franchise which was substantially enlarged, although it fell far short of universal suffrage. The membership of nominated officials was ended and those special interests which were represented by nominated non-official members would now elect their spokesmen. The division of seats among the three major communities in the Punjab was governed by the Communal Award made by the British following the inability of Indians to agree on a formula at the Round Table Conferences in the early thrities. The Punjab Legislative Assembly, as the new body was denominated, would have 175 members of which 157 would be elected from territorial communal constituencies. General (i.e., Hindu) constituencies would elect 42 (eight urban and 34 rural); Muslim constituencies 84 (nine urban and 75 rural); and Sikhs 31 (two urban and 19 rural). Four seats were allocated to women, two Muslim and one each Hindu and Sikh. Indian Christians were to have two seats; Europeans and Anglo-Indians, one each. Special interests were alloted one seat for university graduates, one for commerce and industry, three for labor and five for landholders (including one for the Baluch tumandars). Muslims were thus guaranteed 87 seats (84 in territorial constituencies, two women's seats and the tumandar seat as all electors in that seat were Muslim) which was one seat short of a majority. In practice they could also expect two additional landholders seats and one (1936) or two (1946) of the labor seats, for a total of 90 or 91. The first election under the new system was held in the winter of 1936–1937 and resulted in a Unionist sweep of the Muslim seats. Two Muslim Leaguers were elected, one leaving the party the day the result was announced. Including Hindu seats won in Haryana by the Chhotu Ram group the Unionists won 96 seats and could count on the support of twenty Sikh members elected on the Khalsa Nationalist ticket (Coupland 1943: 42).

As noted earlier the families identified as dominant in rural areas in the fifteen districts which became part of Pakistan won 53 of the 58 seats at stake. Six of the 21 sitting members of the last Council chose not to contest and eleven of the fifteen who did contest were elected to the Assembly. One, Chaudhury Asadullah, a brother of Chaudhury Sir Muhammad Zafrullah Khan, may have lost as anti-Ahmadi feeling was more clearly expressed with the wider franchise. Another, Sardar Habibullah of the Mokal family, lost to Mian Muhammad Iftikharuddin, who was elected as a Congress candidate. Another lost to Raja Chazanfar Ah Khan, but the Raja, elected on the Muslim League ticket, defected to the Unionists immediately and became a parliamentary secretary. (His notes form the basis of Ahmad, 1967.)

When Sir Fazli Husain returned to Lahore from New Delhi in 1935 he immediately set about the task of organizing the Unionist Party to wage an electoral battle. He was not unaware of factional alignments in the party and set about to try to end them. Sikandar was off in Bombay as Deputy Governor of the Reserve Bank but his lieutenants, especially Nawab Muzaffar Khan, Mir Maqbool Mahmud and Ahmad Yar Khan Daultana, were active on his behalf.[1] Sikandar felt himself to be, and in many ways, was, the senior person in the party after Sir Fazli Husain and were Fazli to remain out of active politics he pictured himself as the leader and prime minister-presumptive under the new reforms.[2] He was not without a serious rival in Sir Firoz Khan Noon who had since 1927 been a minister. In early 1936 Noon was dispatched to London as High Commissioner, leaving a vacancy in the ministry. To forestall a scramble, Sir Fazli himself filled the vacancy in June, 1936. At the same time urban supporters of the Unionists wished to have the party more closely associated with the Muslim League. Among them were Iqbal, Malik Barkat Ali (who was the only Muslim Leaguer elected in 1936 who stayed with the party), and Mian Abdul Aziz Marwada, a former member of the Council who was to come in to the Assembly as an independent. At a meeting with Jinnah at the home of Abdul Aziz, the League leader was told in effect to stay out of the Punjab and not to interfere with the multi-communal politics of the province. In addition to heading off Jinnah, Fazli made strides in reorganization, in financing and in allocation of tickets for the party. He had, however, returned from New Delhi in poor health and the burden resulted in his death in July, 1936. The Unionists would go to the election without their founder (Husain 1946: 297–346; Ahmad 1967: 158–162; Malik 1971: 94–100).

With Noon in England, and with the support of the factional organization led by his close associates, Sir Sikandar Hayat Khan became without challenge the leader of the Unionist Party and first Prime Minister of the Punjab. In his cabinet he included Malik Sir Khizr Hayat Khan Tiwana of the rival group and urban Unionist Mian Abdul Haye as well as the leader of the Hindu Unionists of Haryana, Chaudhury Sir Chhotu Ram. The Sikh member was Sardar Sir Sundar Singh Majithia and Sir Manohar Lal, an urban non-Congress Hindu who had been a minister in the Council period, completed the ministry. At the junior level, parliamentary secretaries and parliamentary private secretaries, eight Muslims (of a total of 16) were appointed and all but one came from the principal families identified earlier.

Space does not permit the detailing of the political developments in the

---

1   As mentioned earlier both Mir Maqbool Mahmud and Nawab Muzaffar Khan were brothers-in-law of Sikandar. A story is told, which may not be correct in detail, that Sikandar and Ahmad Yar Daultana exchanged turbans in order to symbolize their becoming brothers. Sikandar did occasionally refer to Ahmad Yar as "*bhaijan*" in correspondence. Thus far the story seems credible. It is then said that the two men suggested that one of Sikandar's daughters marry Ahmad Yar's son, Mumtaz, to cement further the relationship between the two families. In any event, either she (the daughter), he (Mumtaz) or they did not go along with the plan, if indeed such a plan existed.

2   Actually the leader of the party was Chaudhury Sir Chhotu Ram, but it was inconceivable that a Hindu would be selected as Prime Minister.

province prior to Sikandar's death in December, 1942. The election had shown the Muslim League to be strong in Muslim minority provinces but weak in Muslim majority provinces. At the 1937 session of the League in Lucknow a pact was signed between Jinnah and Sikandar. Ostensibly on the national level it strengthtened the League, as did similar agreements with A. K. Fazlul Haq of Bengal and Sir Muhammad Saadullah of Assam, by bringing the Muslim members of the Unionist Party into the League and gaining the support of the Unionists on *national* issues of concern to the Muslim community. On the other hand it was agreed that the Punjab Muslim League would be reconstituted in accordance with the new membership. And this would give Sikandar and his associates control over the provincial League. Iqbal and others who were in the League prior to the pact were opposed but Jinnah, to gain national support, was willing to yield local control (Iqbal 1942: *passim*; Batalvi 1967: *passim*). Nawab Sir Shah Nawaz Khan of Mamdot (1883–1946) became the president of the provincial league and the Unionists controlled the party rather closely.

At the 1940 session of the Muslim League in Lahore the "Pakistan" Resolution was passed. Among those who seconded the resolution was Sikandar. But it is evident that the "Pakistan" envisioned by Sikandar was a vastly different thing than that which emerged in 1947. Sikandar had published in 1939 his own proposal for a united India in which the highest possible level of provincial autonomy would be part of the scheme and the central government would have limited powers in defense and foreign affairs (Jafri 1967: II: 247–253). The Nawab of Mamdot either wrote or caused to be written another pamphlet, by "A Punjabee", which opposed Pakistan and proposed sub-federations between the provinces and the central government, with the separation of eastern Punjab from the rest of the province (Jafri 1967: II: 263–265). If there were any doubts that old line Unionists were still Unionists and not proponents of Pakistan, the speech by Sikandar in the Assembly on March 11, 1941, would remove them: "...we in the Punjab stand united and will not brook any interference from whatever quarter it may be attempted... [we will tell] meddling busybodies from the ouside, 'Hands off the Punjab'." (Coupland 1943: 252). The "busybody" in question was Jinnah.

The tide, however, was turning against those who supported an economically based, multi-communal party in the Punjab. Reports of Congress interference in Muslim customs in Uttar Pradesh (the Pirpur report) and Bihar (the Sharif report), the failure of the Congress to work with the League especially in Uttar Pradesh and the growing antagonism between the two major communities – these had their effect even in the Punjab. The death of Sikandar removed the strong hand of the Prime Minister. He was replaced by the junior rural Muslim in the cabinet, Sir Khizr Hayat Khan Tiwana, only 42 years old when he took office. It is a matter of conjecture why the Unionists did not turn to its then seniormost member, Nawab Muzaffar Khan, who by his relationship to Sikandar and his political skill in the party might have been able to command a measure of respect, both provincially and nationally, approaching that of Sikandar. Such a move would have precluded a second step taken, the bringing into the cabinet of Sikandar's son, Sardar Shaukat Hayat Khan. (Chhotu Ram, Abdul Haye, and Manohar Lal continued in the cabinet and Sardar Baldev Singh became the Sikh member, replacing Sardar Dasaundha Singh, who in turn had replaced Majithia on the latter's death in 1941.)

Tiwana and Partition

Shaukat, who had been released from the Army to join the cabinet, lost little time before he quarreled with Khizr. While much of the debate was personal, it served as the first major open split in Unionist ranks and, therefore, among the Muslim rural elite. Shaukat soon found allies, especially in Nawab Iftikhar Husain Khan of Mamdot (1906–1969) who was to succeed his father as provincial League president in 1946 and who was not to be a stand-in for Unionist control, and in Mumtaz Daultana, returned from England and soon to become an M.L.A. and general secretary of the provincial League. Khizr attempted to maintain the Sikandar-Jinnah pact and separate national Muslim matters from provincial concerns (Tiwana 1944). Khizr then, and still, does not accept the two nation theory and felt that, in essence, a Muslim majority government in the Punjab would be an important guarantee of the rights of Muslims in a minority province, the reverse being similarly true. Shaukat, the younger Mamdot, Mumtaz Daultana and others felt that the unity of India was not capable of preservation and that the Muslims of the Punjab should stand firmly with their co-religionists throughout the country in the demand for Pakistan. Unionist control eroded, although the party maintained its majority in the Assembly with little difficulty. It is to be noted, however, that neither the Unionists nor the new Leaguers wished to destroy the rural elite control of the province. It was an internecine battle, not one which would have transferred control to the Muslim masses.

By the end of the war and the signal for new provincial elections it appeared that Jinnah's firmness would lead to the realization of his goal of Pakistan, possibly not fully independent but certainly a rearrangement in which the north-east and north-west would be separated from the main central stem of Hindu majority provinces. With this there was an increasing rush of Muslims in the Punjab to join the band-wagon, that is to join the League and desert the cause of Unionism. Of the 79 Muslim Unionists elected in 1936 from the territorial, women's and landholders constituencies (their successors in the case of by-elections) 34 chose not to run in 1946. Of the remaining 45, seventeen took the Muslim League ticket and all won. Those contesting again as Unionists were 26, and only eight of them won. The remaining two contested as independents and one won. In the districts which were very soon to become part of Pakistan 58 rural seats were contested. The Unionists had won all but two in 1936. Of the 56 incumbents, 23 chose not to contest, leaving 33 in the electoral picture. Ten took the ticket of the Muslim League and all won. The Unionist Party nominated 21, of whom eight won. As had been noted earlier the leading families won 27 of the 58 seats in the Pakistan districts. Of these nine were returned as Unionists, seventeen as Muslim Leaguers and one as an independent. It would seem that this split, even with the strong popular tide among Muslims in favor of the Pakistan concept, shows that the traditional leaders even when retaining their Unionist designation were not routed completely, and were able to maintain considerable support. District results for the Unionists in terms of popular vote in 1946 are shown in Table I and serve to reinforce the conclusion that Unionism was not entirely dead.

There has been much controversy over the events following the election of 1946. The official return (GOI 1948: 153–172) gives the following party breakdown. The Muslim League was the largest with 73 seats. The Congress won 51, of whom 42 were Hindus and nine Sikhs. The Unionist Party won 21, all Muslims except for one Indian Christian. The Panthic Party (Akalis) won twenty. Independents won ten seats (one Hindu, two Muslims, two Sikhs, one European, one Anglo-Indian, one Indian Christian and two labor seats, the occupants of which were one Hindu and one Muslim). There was some post-election shifting, the extent of which is a matter of controversy. Nonetheless the Muslim League, now under the leadership of Nawab Iftikhar Husain Khan of Mamdot, did not have a majority nor was it likely to be able to coalesce with any other party in order to attain a majority. At the same time the other three parties were willing to work together to form a majority government. The coalition may have received official blessing. It did fit the Congress strategy of denying the Muslim League a provincial government at the time of important negotiations with the British on the future of India (Azad 1959: 128–129; Sayeed 1968: 217–218).

The Khizr ministry included Nawab Sir Muzaffar Ali Khan Qizilbash and Mian Muhammad Ibrahim Barq of the Unionists, Lala Bhim Sen Sachar and Chaudhury Lehri Singh of the Congress and Sardar Baldev Singh of the Akali Dal. Before its short career was ended Sardar Swaran Singh replaced Baldev Singh, who became Defense Member in New Delhi. Almost immediately the Unionist ministry was beset with a civil disobedience movement launched by the Muslim League. Disturbances grew to such proportions that the government was unable to contain them. In March, 1947, Khizr submitted the resignation of the ministry and the province was placed under the direct rule of the Governor. Rioting, however, continued as the disturbances surrounding the partition of India and of the Punjab began almost as the anti-Khizr movement ended. The partition tragedy has been described elsewhere (see especially Moon 1961: 71 ff).

Mamdot and Factionalism

Following partition the Muslim League assumed the government of that part of the Punjab which went to Pakistan. Iftikhar Hussain Khan of Mamdot was appointed Chief Minister and included in his cabinet Mumtaz Daultana,

Shaukat Hayat Khan, Mian Muhammad Iftikharuddin, and Sheikh Karamat Ali. Three of the five were from leading rural families and Mamdot himself was included in Griffin (1940: I: 229–233) but not included in this study as his home district, Ferozepur, went to India.

Quarrels hit the cabinet almost immediately. Iftikharuddin left the ministry over a disagreement on refugee policy, a part of his portfolio. Neither Daultana nor Shaukat was prepared to accept cabinet discipline and both looked toward the Muslim League organization. Daultana succeeded in capturing the party from its titular leader, the Chief Minister. Shaukat eventually left the League for a time to join with Iftikharuddin in forming the Azad Pakistan Party, a forerunner of the present National Awami Party. The factionalism grew to such an extent that Mamdot was unable to carry on and he resigned in 1948. As no one was then able to form a new ministry, the Governor once again assumed the powers of the ministry and the Assembly.

During the period preceding the 1951 election Daultana acquired virtually complete control of the League. Noon was in East Bengal as Governor although he had hoped for leadership in his home province. Khizr had retired from politics and had spent much of the post-independence period abroad. Shaukat was out of the League. Daultana now isolated Mamdot and caused him also to leave the League and form a separate party, the Jinnah Muslim League (fragments of which joined later with H. S. Suhrawardy's Awami League). The advisors appointed by the Governor to assist him in his work were increasingly nominees of Daultana. The stage was set for the 1951 election.

From Daultana to Ayub

In 1951 Mumtaz Daultana reached one goal he had set for himself: he became Chief Minister of the Punjab. In the election the Muslim League had won 143 of the 197 seats, to 35 for the Mamdot led Jinnah Awami League (actually an alliance of the Jinnah Muslim League and the Awami League) and one each for the Azad Pakistan Party and the orthodox Jama'at-i-Islami; seventeen others were independents. The organization built by Daultana produced the victory in what was the only unified effort by the League after the formation of Pakistan. Among the key families the proportion elected decreased, both as a result of the increased number of seats and of the granting of universal franchise, which perhaps diluted the power of the traditional leadership. It is, of course, not clear how many of those elected were propelled to victory through the support of local leaders from among the elite. Of the 197 seats, 191 were clearly designated for Muslims (including five set aside for women). The others were four for Christians, one "general" (i.e., Hindu) and one for university graduates, which was won by a Muslim. However, of the 191 Muslim seats, 44 were reserved for refugees in double member constituencies. Thus only 147 seats were available to pre-partition residents of West Punjab. Of these at least 31 (21.1 percent) were won by members of elite

families. The Muslim League won 28 of these including a representative each of
the Tiwana and Hayat families, the Jinnah Awami League won one (a Tiwana)
and one, Nawab Qizilbash, was returned as an independent.

In forming his cabinet, Daultana included four from the principal families
(Sardar Abdul Hamid Khan Dasti, Sardar Muhammad Khan Leghari,
Sheikh Fazal Ilahi Piracha and Syed Ali Husain Shah Gardezi) in addition
to himself. Outside this category were only two: Soofi Abdul Hamid Khan, a
refugee, and Chaudhury Muhammad Husain Chatha. The story of the ministry must be curtailed here. It fell in 1953 largely as a result of the anti-Ahmadi
riots which rent the city of Lahore and other areas and resulted in a short
period of martial law (Munir 1954: *passim*).

Daultana was replaced by Malik Sir Firoz Khan Noon who achieved the
position he felt he had been denied in 1947. Noon again drew on members of
the elite for his cabinet retaining Dasti and Leghari and adding, among others,
the controversial Nawab Muzaffar Ali Khan Qizilbash. The Daultana faction
of the League had not forgiven Qizilbash his association with the unpopular
Khizr ministry in 1946. Noon remained Chief Minister until shortly before the
institution of one-unit in West Pakistan. He then yielded to Dasti who made
few changes other than dropping Qizilbash.

Under the one-unit plan the Punjab agreed to accept a severe reduction in
its membership in the Provincial Assembly. It would have only 40 percent of
the members rather than the nearly 60 percent to which it was entitled on a
population basis. This led to a complicated electoral process. The relative
population had changed since the influx of refugees and the beginnings of urban
development. Thus the number of seats from the Punjab was reduced from
197 to 124 but the reduction was unevenly spread. As an interim measure the
incumbent M.L.A.'s were to choose, from among themselves or from outside
the group, district by district, the members of the new unified Assembly, with
some districts choosing more and some fewer than the present membership.
Most of those who belonged to the rural elite were returned, some from districts other than their home. It was clear, however, that in most districts
Daultana and his associates were able to control the vote.

The first Chief Minister, Dr. Khan Sahib, was from the Frontier and not a
member of the Muslim League. In a broad based and short lived cabinet he
included members from all factions, including both Daultana and Mamdot.
Daultana and others pressed for the formation of a Muslim League party in the
Assembly with the clear implication that only the leader of that party could be
Chief Minister. Khan Sahib stoutly refused to join the League. Matters were
brought to a head with a threat of a no confidence motion being carried
against Khan Sahib. Karachi did not wish to upset a carefully constructed
arrangement under which the Frontier would retain the West Pakistan chief
ministership, Karachi in this case meaning especially President Iskander Mirza.
Aisle crossing became a regular part of the legislative proceedings in Lahore
until overnight a new party was created, the Republican Party, pledged to
support Khan Sahib. Care was taken by the Republicans to avoid frequent

votes of confidence and by this means and the probability that at many times they could actually command a majority permitted Khan Sahib and his Republican successors, Sardar Abdur Rashid and Nawab Qizilbash to retain office until October, 1958, when martial law was imposed (Ahmad 1967: 444–451). A 1958 compilation of Republicans and Muslim Leaguers in the West Pakistan Assembly showed that among the rural elite there was about an even split between the two parties, roughly a dozen each. After the departure of Daultana and his associates from the Khan Sahib cabinet the leading family membership in the ministry was (subject to frequent changes of membership) on the order of three of six Punjabis in the Khan Sahib ministry, five of six in Rashid's, and five of seven in Qizilbash's.

On October 7, 1958, President Mirza proclaimed martial law, abrogated the constitution, abolished legislative bodies and appointed General Muhammad Ayub Khan to be chief martial law administrator. Three weeks later Ayub abolished Mirza and assumed the presidency himself. For our purposes here two events are of special importance. One was the Elective Bodies Disqualification Order under which Ayub moved to bar from politics those political figures who, in his view, were responsible for the situation in Pakistan which led to martial law. Twenty leading Punjabi politicians were "EBDOed" of which twelve, including Mamdot, were from among the leading families and most of the others were close political associates of them. Among those barred from political activity (party as well as electoral) were Daultana, Noon, Qizilbash, Iftikharuddin, Dasti and a member each of the Shah Jiwana, Gilani, Gardezi, Sargodha Qureshi, Leghari and Gurmani families. The ban lasted until January 1, 1967.

The second step was the introduction of basic democracies both for local government functions and as an electoral college to select the president and members of the national and provincial assemblies (Ziring 1971: 15–16). The first exercise of the electoral function came in 1962 when those basic democrats elected in 1959 were called upon to choose members of the legislatures. Ayub's was to be a partyless government so all candidates ran as independents and with little interference from above. Not surprisingly a large number of persons who had been elected earlier to legislative bodies, or relatives of them, were chosen to sit in both Rawalpindi and Lahore. At least eighteen, nine to Rawalpindi and nine to Lahore, were elected from among the leading families.

The lack of political organization prior to the election did not preclude the formation of parties inside the assemblies after the election. In the National Assembly an almost equal balance between supporters and opponents of the President resulted. Ayub recognized the need for a party committed to the support of his program. In 1962, after the Assembly opened, a convention of the Muslim League was called. Ayub consented to become president of the Pakistan Muslim League (Convention). Those Leaguers who opposed the President formed the Council Muslim League, claiming direct inheritance from pre-independence days. The elite split again. Daultana, Shaukat and their associates supported, indeed ran from behind the scenes, the Council League. Noon,

Qizilbash, Nawab Malik Amir Muhammad Khan of Kalabagh (d. 1967), by this time Governor of West Pakistan, and others of the elite supported and campaigned for the Convention League. The 1965 elections for both assemblies saw a tightening of political control from above on the basic democrats and the returning to Rawalpindi and Lahore of an overwhelming majority of Convention Leaguers. Noon's son, Qizilbash's brother, Kalabagh's son and others of the old chief families were among those returned, while those who belonged to the Council League were, with very few exceptions defeated. Ayub found that in the Punjab he needed to rely on those whose past was Republican, Muslim League and Unionist in reverse chronological order.

The events of 1969, 1970 and 1971 have been related in many places and need not be repeated here. With Ayub out of office in March, 1969, and Yahya Khan installed as president and chief martial law administrator a new epoch began in Pakistan. Yahya Khan promised that elections would be held and they were in December, 1970.

The Elections of 1970

The ground rules of the election, the conduct of the campaigning, the nature of the participating parties and the results have been discussed elsewhere (Baxter 1971: 197–218). Here we will look specifically at the interaction between the traditional rural elite families and clans and the PPP. The discussion is handicapped to a degree in that no official return of the elections to the National and Provincial Assembly has been published by the Government of Pakistan. Hence, reliance on press reports of results is necessary and these are in some cases incomplete and, even in cases where figures are given for all contestants, may be inaccurate. Nonetheless figures of reasonable acceptability for purposes here can be obtained and used; that is, even with final corrections the magnitude of the PPP vote is not likely to be altered significantly. A further handicap is that there has so far been no definitive "who's who" of new legislators prepared, and identification of all successful contestants is not possible from published sources, especially for the provincial seats.

The results of the two elections are given in Table I, which lists, by district, the percentage of eligible voters who participated, the percentage of seats and votes received by the PPP and the percentage of votes received by the three Muslim Leagues. In the latter the votes of the Pakistan Muslim League (Conventionist), Pakistan Muslim League (Qayyum) and Council Muslim League are accumulated. This papers over differences in program details among the three parties, but it is useful as many of the rural elite ran on one of the three tickets and it is a rough measure of the strenth of this group. It is only rough as some of the elite ran as independents and, as we shall see, some ran on the PPP ticket. Another column gives the percentage of votes polled by a group here labelled "Islamic". Indeed it also papers over differences as it accumulates the votes of the Jama'at-i-Islami, Jamiat-ul-Ulema-i-Islam (both Hazarvi and

Thanvi groups), Markazi Jamiat-ul-Ulema-Pakistan and Jamiat-i-Ahl-i-Hadith. Programmatic differences among these parties are great but each has underlying an appeal based on Islamic principles, albeit differently stated and interpreted (Baxter 1971: 204–206). It is useful especially in those districts near the Indus where the appeal of Islamic sentiments was greater than in other areas of the province. As mentioned earlier, the 1946 Unionist and Muslim League votes are also listed, although these are for rural seats only.

The order in which the districts are listed is according to an index of modernization developed by Shahid Javid Burki (1972: 204–205). While the details can be obtained from the reference just cited, Burki summarizes as follows: "This index was based on a weighting in equal proportions of three characteristics: urbanization, industrialization and education. Urbanization was defined in terms of the proportions of each district in the total urban population, similarly for industrial output and literate population for the entire region." He classified districts as advanced, intermediate and backward, all of the districts in the Punjab falling into one or the other of the first two categories.

The polling for the National Assembly was held on December 7, 1970. The result in the Punjab was a startling victory for the PPP which won 62 of the 82 seats alloted to the province. The Council Muslim League won seven; the Markazi Jamiat, four; the Convention League, two; the Qayyum League, one; the Jama'at-i-Islami, one and independents, five. On December 20, the voters again went to the polls to select members of the provincial assemblies. Of the 180 seats in the Punjab, the PPP won 113. The Council Muslim League with 15 was the only other party to win more than ten seats.

At least 23 candidates from the rural elite can be identified in National Assembly contests. The Council League accounted for eight of these and four won seats (Daultana, Shaukat, the Pir of Makhad and Zakir Qureshi of Sargodha). Each of the three accepting the PPP label were winners (Anwar Ali Noon, Sadiq Husain Qureshi of Multan, and Abbas Husain Gardezi, also of Multan). The other two winners were independents: Malik Muzaffar Khan of Kalabagh and Sardar Sher Baz Khan Mazari of Dera Ghazi Khan. Noted among those who lost were Nur Hayat Khan Noon (Qayyum League), Anwar Tiwana (Convention League), Zulfiqar Qizilbash (Independent), Alamdar Husain Gilani (Qayyum League), Arif Iftikhar (Bhashani group of the National Awami Party) and Sardar Mahmud Khan Leghari (Independent). Winning only nine of the 82 seats (11 percent) the elite slumped to the lowest level ever. In the indirect election for women's seats, the PPP named a member of the Baghbanpura family to one of the seats.

Identification is particularly difficult with candidates for the Provincial Assembly. Among winners ten can be identified as belong to the families listed at the beginning of this article. Five of them were independents (two Legharis and a Mazari from Dera Ghazi Khan being the most prominent), two were from the Council Muslim League and one each from the Pakistan Democratic Party (a Dasti), the Qayyum League (a Gilani) and the PPP (a Gardezi). The Gardezis of Multan who were shut out of pre-independence seats seem to

Table I

The Punjab : Election Data for 1946 and 1970*

	1946 Vote			1970 National Assembly					1970 Provincial Assembly				
District	NUP	ML		Part.	PPP Seats	PPP Vote	MLs Vote	Islam Vote	Part.	Seats	PPP Vote	MLs Vote	Islam Vote
Advanced Districts													
1. Lahore	29.5	67.6		68.6	100	51.9	14.0	20.6	59.3	82	55.5	7.0	8.5
2. Lyallpur	35.4	62.4		60.0	100	56.4	12.1	20.8	60.6	84	51.6	10.0	10.4
3. Multan	28.2	67.4		69.0	78	47.4	25.5	17.4	63.2	79	48.6	24.7	12.0
4. Rawalpindi	11.1	74.7		57.9	100	48.9	19.9	16.9	46.7	88	45.3	35.8	4.2
5. Sahiwal	22.8	77.2		63.7	100	54.9	29.8	10.0	62.1	93	50.8	27.7	3.2
6. Gujranwala	41.7	58.3		72.6	60	49.7	30.4	10.0	69.9	78	42.4	29.3	4.1
7. Sargodha	52.5	47.4		67.5	100	38.6	35.4	9.7	58.0	60	41.1	23.1	16.7
8. Sialkot	19.1	65.8		70.2	75	57.0	12.8	17.2	64.9	100	49.4	20.7	3.2
9. Gujrat	40.0	60.0		63.0	100	30.2	46.0	12.3	62.0	50	27.9	35.8	7.6
10. Jhelum	22.6	77.3		77.0	100	40.9	30.3	11.2	71.9	60	35.2	27.3	3.7
11. Sheikhupura	30.3	69.7		68.9	100	55.0	31.3	4.7	63.6	75	45.4	17.9	8.7
Intermediate Districts													
12. Rahim Yar Khan	—	—		66.8	33	20.7	31.8	32.1	65.4	14	17.7	40.9	16.2
13. Mianwali	43.9	56.1		63.1	0	5.8	32.9	43.3	64.4	0	9.6	48.6	20.9
14. Jhang	19.9	80.0		68.0	0	17.0	—	46.4	63.6	13	14.0	—	17.8
15. Campbellpur	56.7	42.8		60.7	0	23.7	67.5	8.7	53.8	40	35.4	35.8	3.4
16. Bahawalpur	—	—		67.8	—	8.6	30.7	16.7	62.8	20	21.4	6.6	9.4
17. Bahawalnagar	—	—		47.6	67	35.7	22.8	14.0	49.7	67	31.2	42.5	5.4
18. Dera Ghazi Khan	22.8	38.7		52.0	0	12.0	—	38.1	52.5	0	15.5	—	18.4
19. Muzaffargarh	33.9	55.2		64.8	67	27.0	9.3	46.1	62.3	0	14.7	29.9	23.8
Total	33.6	62.6		65.1	76	41.7	24.0	22.8	61.1	63	39.3	22.5	9.9

Sources: For 1946, COI, 1948. For 1970, press reports. Figure for participation in Bahawalnagar presumably is in error.

* Election results by district; the percentage of eligible voters who participated; the percentage of seats and votes received by the PPP, and the percentage of votes received by the three Muslim Leagues. For fuller explanation see text. NUP—National Unionist Party. Sahiwal formerly Montgomery; Sargodha formerly Shahpur; Campbellpur formerly Attock. For 1946, only rural seats are included. Participation is based on valid votes, not on total votes cast including invalid votes.

have been more ready to associate with the PPP although both Gilanis and Qureshis have also joined the party. In the polling for women's seats, the PPP elected Begum Abida Fakr Imam, a member of the Shah Jiwana family of Jhang.

To return to the Burki index and the material in Table I, some general conclusions can be drawn. The PPP performed better in the advanced districts than it did in the intermediate both for the National and the Provincial Assembly. The party won 92 percent of the National Assembly seats in the advanced districts and only 25 percent in the intermediate. For the Provincial Assembly the figures were 79 percent and 18 percent. In vote data as opposed to seat data it can be noted that for National Assembly contests only one district in the advanced group gave fewer votes to the PPP than the highest PPP district among the intermediate group. For provincial contests the picture is less clear but generally the advanced districts gave more support to the PPP than the intermediate. Sargodha appears to be a problem in correlation and this is perhaps explained by the division within the district in which the more highly developed eastern *tehsils* supported the PPP more than the less developed western *tehsils*. The votes for the Islamic group of parties appears very much to follow the course of the Indus River: Mianwali, Jhang, Muzaffargarh and Dera Ghazi Khan, the four highest districts all lie in the western reaches of the province. Campbellpur is an exception, but the leading religio-political figure in the district, the Pir of Makhad, ran on the Council Muslim League ticket. The vote for the three Muslim Leagues tended to be higher in the intermediate districts, especially for the provincial seats where the constituencies are smaller and more susceptible to traditional leadership than to broad appeals.

The appeal of the PPP was not rooted in traditional leadership in the Punjab, with a few exceptions. It was rooted in an economic and social appeal for better housing, more food, improved education and increased health facilities. Although the "confrontation" with India theme was part of the manifesto, reports seem to indicate that as the campaign progressed it receded to the background and the economic and social issues were stressed. The PPP mobilized the youth, Bhutto projected a charismatic personality to this group, and as college students who had learned the PPP program in the cities and towns returned to rural areas (colleges were closed during the final part of the campaign) they acted as missionaries for the PPP. This may indicate a major change in rural politics if the college youth can replace the traditional landed aristocracy and the religious *mullahs* as guides to voting behavior. The Islamic parties often ran on – to use the words of a keen Pakistani observer to the writer – a straight "heaven or hell" platform and only those near the Indus seemed to be greatly concerned. In Jhang, especially, the Markazi Jamiat exploited the Shi'a – Sunni split. The expected strength of the Jama'at-i-Islami in urban areas did not materialize despite that party's reputation for a strong organization. The failure of the Muslim Leagues to unite – although numerous abortive talks were held – no doubt affected those parties' ability to win seats at a rate approaching the rate at which they won votes, but this can be exaggerated. A close look at the seats shows that even if they had united on a single candidate and that candidate were able to poll the combined votes the result would seldom have been changed. In short, a few more seats but probably not to the extent of denying the PPP a majority in both Islamabad and Lahore. The Leagues ran on outdated program of "Islam in danger," a package which does not sell in the more highly developed areas where the issues have become economic rather than religious. One defeated Conventionist told the writer that he lost because he ran on the 1937 and 1946 platform rather than the 1970 issues.

Conclusion

No member of the rural elite can find much pleasure in the results of the 1970 elections. Perhaps individuals, Daultana, Shaukat, those who jumped to the PPP, might find their own picture not clouded but as a group the rural elite was badly beaten and this by a group largely comprising unknowns.

Two points might be made. First, the rural elite needs an "enforcer" of unity. Sir Fazli Husain and after him Sir Sikandar Hayat Khan performed this role. Their successors, Khizr, Mamdot, Daultana, Noon, Qizilbash, Kalabagh, have not been able to suppress personal differences to an extent that unity can be achieved. Programatic differences also entered as Daultana's views on socio-economic issues differ greatly from, say, Qizilbash. Secondly, the rural elite, obviously, does better in limited or controlled elections, as in those prior to independence or those during the Ayub period.

But the changes in the Punjab since the thirties have been great. Agricultural income is higher, education is more widely spread, urbanization and industrialization have increased – perhaps not in each case to the extent desired by Pakistani leaders but the change has nonetheless been vast based on the pre-independence or even 1951 data. The ballot is now available to all and, in 1970, less susceptible to control. One might conclude that the day of the rural elite control of government in the Punjab has ended, but one caution must be noted. The PPP has promised in its manifesto many changes and in another election it may be judged on its performance. Possibly, should the judgment be adverse to the PPP, the electorate might turn again to those groups which have governed in the past. Only another election held on the terms of those in 1970 can determine the future of the landed aristocracy – and whether the PPP has redeemed its pledge to end "feudal" power in politics.

BIBLIOGRAPHY

Ahmad, Nur, Syed
   1936   Mian Fazl-i-Husain, a Review of His Life and Work, Lahore, Punjab Education Press.
   1967   Martial Law-se Martial Law-tak, Lahore.

Azad, Abul Kalam, Maulana
    1959   India Wins Freedom, Bombay, Orient Longmans.
Batalvi, Ashiq Husain
    1967   "Iqbal and the Pakistan Movement", addresses in Lahore, April, 1967, in Urdu.
Baxter, Craig
    1971   "Pakistan Votes—1970", Asian Survey XI: 3 (March): 197–218.
Burki, S. J.
    1972   "Ayub's Fall, a Socio-Economic Explanation". Asian Survey XII: 3 (March):
           201–212.
Coupland, Reginald
    1943   Indian Politics, 1936–1942. London, Oxford.
Darling, Malcolm
    1947   The Punjab Peasant in Prosperity and Debt. Oxford, Oxford. Fourth edition.
Government of India
    1948   Return Showing the Results of Elections to the Central Legislative Assembly and
           the Provincial Legislatures in 1945–46. New Delhi, Manager of Publications.
Great Britain
    1930   Indian Statutory Commission. Volume X. Memorandum Submitted by the
           Government of the Punjab. London, HMSO.
Griffin, Lepel H.
    1940   Chiefs and Families of Note in the Punjab. Revised by G. L. Chopra. Lahore,
           Superintendent of Government Printing.
Husain, Azim
    1946   Fazl-i-Husain, a Political Biography. Bombay, Longmans.
Iqbal, Muhammad, Dr. Sir
    1942   Letters of Iqbal to Jinnah. Lahore, Ashraf.
Jafri, Rais Ahmad, Syed
    1967   Rare Documents. Lahore, Mohammad Ali Academy.
Malik, Hafeez, editor
    1971   Iqbal: Poet-Philosopher of Pakistan. New York, Columbia.
Moon, Penderel
    1961   Divide and Quit. London, Chatto and Windus.
Munir, Muhammad
    1954   Report of the Court of Inquiry ... to Enquire into the Punjab Disturbances of
           1953. Presided over by Justice M. Munir. Lahore, Superintendent, Government
           Printing.
Pakistan People's Party
    1970   Election Manifesto, Karachi, n. pub.
Sayeed, Khalid B.
    1968   Pakistan: The Formative Years. London, Oxford. Second edition.
Tiwana, Khizr Hayat Khan, Malik Sir
    1944   Statement on the Sikandar-Jinnah Pact. Manuscript.
Ziring, Lawrence
    1971   The Ayub Khan Era. Syracuse, Syracuse University Press.

Islam and the New Constitution of Pakistan[1]

FAZLUR RAHMAN

University of Chicago, Chicago, U.S.A.

THE NEW CONSTITUTION of Pakistan, adopted by the National (also Constituent) Assembly on the 10th of April, 1973, and enforced on the 14th of August, is the third constitution in Pakistan's brief history. The first constitution (1956), of a parliamentary type, was enacted by a Constituent Assembly about nine years after its election and was abrogated in October 1958 by a military coup. The second, a presidential-type constitution, was promulgated by a military ruler, Mohammad Ayub Khan, in 1962, and was abrogated in March 1969 by General Yahya Khān, to whom Ayub Khan entrusted power on his own resignation. The new constitution, enacted after the dismemberment of Pakistan in December, 1971, is once again of the parliamentary type, is the first bicameral constitution, and, since it is the result of a freshly elected Assembly, may be said to represent more genuinely the will of the people. Since Mr. Bhutto, in the present delicate situation of Pakistan – both internal and external – wanted the constitution to be based on a consensus of the Assembly, the constitution reflects some heavy compromises with the religious right, a fact which cannot have pleased many extreme leftists in the People's Party of which Mr. Bhutto is not only the unquestioned leader but finally, the sole decision-maker.

But it is not only the compromises on Islam that are in sight in the constitution; what is also concretely present there is a new socio-economic orientation of economic justice and social progressivism. If the constitution can state and reiterate in various contexts woman's essential role in the future development of Pakistan, perhaps it can afford to repeat, along with the previous constitutions, the confused and confusing statement, at the opening of the Preamble, about the Sovereignty of Allah in the Universe, and linking it directly with the delegated sovereignty of the people of Pakistan in Pakistan; or, if it can declare that parliament may enact laws fixing a ceiling on private property or nationalizing industry or other sources of production, it can also afford to drop the word "socialism" or "Islamic socialism" to appease the opposition. We shall examine these issues in somewhat closer detail below; procedurally, it seems convenient to divide the field of Islam under three titles: economics, society, and Islamic propositions including law-making.

---

[1] It would be useful if an earlier article of mine titled "Islam and the Constitutional Problem of Pakistan" is read along with the present one (*Studia Islamica*, XXXII, 4 (December 1970), pp. 275–87.

A. Economics – Islamic Socialism

In the summer of 1966, an intense debate erupted in West Pakistan over the question of the compatibility of socialism with Islam and whether the term "Islamic Socialism" was a meaningful expression or an absurd juxtaposition of contradictories, and has continued ever since. Earlier, this subject had attracted a number of writers in the Middle East and a Syrian scholar and member of the Muslim Brotherhood, Dr. Muṣṭafā al-Sibāʿī, had written a fairly comprehensive work in Arabic in 1959 entitled "The socialism of Islam,"[1] which became widely influential in the Middle East and pioneered a spate of other works, particularly after Nasser's promulgation of "Arab Socialism" in 1962. Judging from their writings, the "Islamic Socialists" of Pakistan were apparently quite unaware of this rich literature and did not exploit it.[2] Much earlier, in the subcontinent, Iqbāl had vigorously denounced Western capitalism, had praised Lenin in a famous poem, "Lenin's Petition to God," had even advocated the abrogation of all traditional religion, if it did not give the peasant and the worker his full due, in a poem "God's Command to Angels," and had roundly proclaimed in a poem "It Is God's Earth" that the earth and its resources cannot become the property of a few. But Iqbāl was equally critical of the materialistic philosophy of Communism and in one of his last poems, "Satan's Advisory Council," decisively repudiated it: He thought that Communism had planted an excellent egalitarian economic system (which is identical with or close to Islam) in the barren soil of materialism. In a letter to Sir Francis Younghusband in 1930 Iqbāl wrote, "If Bolshevism can accept God, it will come very close to Islam. I will not, therefore, be surprised if at some future time Islam overwhelms Russia or Russia overwhelms Islam."[3] Such themes are also given full vent in his letters to Jinnah, where the "atheistic socialism of Jawaharlal [Nehru]" is rejected but the Muslim League's attitude of indifference to the improvement of the lot of the Muslim masses is strongly repudiated as un-Islamic.[4]

In the Pakistani debate of 1966 and since, Iqbal has been heavily invoked by both sides, the socialists appealing to his numerous positive statements in favor of an Islam-based socialism, and anti-socialists to his repudiation of atheistic socialism and communism. Jinnah and Liaqat Ali Khan had both explicitly used the term "Islamic Socialism" (which had actually been used by the pioneer of Muslim Modernism, Jamāl al-Dīn al-Afghānī in Istanbūl in the

---

1 *Ishtirākīyat'l-Islām* (Damascus, 1959).

2 For a short survey of the development of Islamic Socialism in the Middle East, cf. my article "Sources and Meaning of Islamic Socialism," in Donald Smith, ed., *Religion and Political Modernization* (to be published by Yale University Press, Spring, 1974); for some literature in English translation, Hanna, Sāmī and Gardner, G.: *Arab Socialism* (Leiden, 1969).

3 Quoted by Safdar Mīr in the Urdu monthly *Nusrat* (ed. Haneef Ramay), September-October 1966, p. 90.

4 Aziz Ahmad and G. E. Von Grunebaum, *Muslim Self-Statement in India and Pakistan* (1970), pp. 151–52.

1890's). Ayub Khan had proclaimed "Islamic Socialism" to be the goal of state policies in his Introduction to the Guidelines of the Third Five-Year Plan. But the subject had become so controversial and so much pressure was exerted by big business (whose prominent spokesman in the debate was A. K. Sumar, himself a businessman), which found ready allies in the representatives of traditionalism in the Jamā'at-i-Islami and the majority of the 'Ulama (whose very religion Iqbal wanted to be abrogated!) that when the Third Five Year Plan was actually published, the term "Islamic Socialism" was not there. This is not the place to give the details of this debate, of which the most important single epitome is the Urdu monthly "Nusrat" of Lahore, in its September-October issue of 1966. Some highly interesting material was yielded by the debate, and some ingenious interpretations of the Quar'an. On the anti-socialist side, while much of what the religious right said was little more than obscurantism, nevertheless some genuine points were made (just as they had been made earlier in the Middle East) – that is, they express the worry that the term "Islamic Socialism" had been cleverly popularized by the surreptitious voice of the Communists, that should things not work out successfully for, say, a period of two decades or if there are setbacks, this voice will then say, "You see, the adjunct 'Islamic' is responsible for your failures; why can't you just be 'socialist' and forget about Islam."[1] This is exactly what this Voice said to Nasser after the Arab-Israeli war of June, 1967. But this is, after all, a relatively minor point and no socialist ideology consciously based in Islam need worry about it unduly.

When Mr. Bhutto launched his socialist campaign in 1966 after his ouster from the Ayub Government, he seems gradually to have realized that, to get popular support, he must include Islam as an integral part of socialism, even though Mr. J. A. Rahim, a Communist and his chief party ideologue, did not like this, and when he appointed Mawlana Kawsar Niazi, who had risen from the rightist ranks, as the Propaganda Secretary of the Party, Mr. Rahim strongly protested. Nevertheless, in its election manifesto, the People's Party stood squarely on the platform of Islamic Socialism and the very next day after elections in December, 1970, which gave his party an overwhelming majority in the center, Mr. Bhutto hailed the election result as a "great victory for Islam."[2] The fact is that, in any developing country, promises to the masses of an approaching millennium through a liquidation of the exploitative upper classes and vested interests bring favorable results, and, in a country like Pakistan, when this is coupled with an appeal to Islam, the results are assured. It is, indeed, a comment on the stupidity of the right which, in *this* climate, did not show enough perception and continued to harp on the unique Islamicity of private property and the traditional concepts of the relationship between employers and employees.

---

1 Sumār, A. K., in *Nusrat*, op. cit., p. 54, lines 18–21.
2 My paper "The Islamic Experience of Pakistan," in *Islam and the Modern Age* (New Delhi), II, No. 4, p. 1 ff.

But it is relatively easy to be swept atop by a flood of aroused hopes, it is a different story when one assumes reins of affairs of the state. Indeed, at election time the People's Party was not a party but a movement of vast dimensions, a veritable ground-swell, and so there gathered together in its fold elements of all sorts – from Communists through socialists and Islamic Socialists to people of vested interests, even landlords. Whereas this highly mixed character yields a certain flexibility, it obviously makes it difficult to find a firm basis for clear-cut directives. Secondly, and importantly, with the departure of East Pakistan, although Pakistan may have lost some political strength in international affairs, economically this has resulted in sheer gain. For Pakistan, as it stands now, is economically the best part of the subcontinent and has a bright future for development, provided its big neighbor would allow it (and itself) to develop in peace; the direst need of the subcontinent is to re-orient itself from a politico-militaristic stance to a socio-economic development posture. Granted this, Pakistan does not *need* any drastic form of socialism (as, for example, Bangladesh does), but certain necessary adjustments. Thirdly, as we said earlier, since Mr. Bhutto took over power under conditions of severe disadvantage, he felt the need for national consensus and has, therefore, heavily compromised. Finally, an Islamic Socialist state obviously requires a systematic and well-worked-out ideology, and that on an Islamic basis, and also an ideologically-geared governmental structure to implement it. Neither of these is available to Mr. Bhutto.

Despite all this, however, the total omission of "Islamic Socialism" from the Constitution remains a mystery, since the battle-cry of the People's Party for election was precisely this; and, after all, there was nothing wrong with the term; on the contrary, it was pregnant with new possibilities of working the state policies progressively towards a goal where Islamic egalitarianism in a modern setting could be effectively realized. What went wrong? I can only surmise that the two other socialistically oriented parties, the National Awami Party of Wali Khan and the Jam'iyat ul-'Ulama of Hazārvī have become so uncompromisingly entrenched in opposition to Mr. Bhutto that he felt it easier to compromise with his ideological opponents – the moribund rightists. And so, while the Constitution has received heavy doses of *formal* Islam – much heavier than either of the two previous constitutions – as we shall see in the third section of this paper, the essence of Islam was incredibly diluted. Indeed, with the exception of three or four provisions, this Constitution differs little from its predecessors.

These provisions, though they are also general and indirect, are nonetheless important and, when viewed in the light of Mr. Bhutto's initial policies, lend support to genuine optimism. The first is a hint in the penultimate clause of the Preamble that the people of Pakistan have resolved "to protect our national and political unity and solidarity by creating an egalitarian society *through a new order*." Here was a proper place to add the phrase "based on Islamic Socialism," and the omission hits the eye. Nevertheless, the phrase "new order" does clearly imply that the existing order (i.e., the traditional order) is undesirable.

Further, this statement means that only a new, progressive, and just order is the final guarantee for the survival and solidarity of Pakistan, not primarily the defense in mere military terms or the outworn cliches about "Islam in danger."

The second major economic provision is enunciated in Article 3, which says, "The State shall ensure the elimination of all forms of exploitation and the gradual fulfilment of the fundamental principle, from each according to his ability, to each according to his work." The elimination of exploitation was also contained in the two previous constitutions, but the latter half of the article is entirely new. It is obviously a modification of the principle of classical Communism, "From each according to his capacity, to each according to his *need*." But the Communist formula means that those persons who can work more or perform duties meriting higher reward would be denied part of that reward in order to meet the needs of the less fortunate members of society. This idealistic principle was given up in Russia, which, in 1956, expressly admitted "the profit motive." But, apparently, the Pakistani formula cannot mean this, although it has a conscious verbal affinity with it, since, if "ability" meant the ability to work, the formula would become nonsensical and would be translated "those who can work more or perform duties meriting higher rewards will be denied part of that reward in order to pay those who work"! What it presumably does mean is that if, for example, an industrialist increases his capital through the surplus value created by the workers' labor, he will not be allowed to keep all that increase in capital but must share it with workers who will be rewarded according to their work. The phrasing of the formula, therefore, seems to be misleading and it would have been much better to put the matter in simple and direct terms. What the principle does state is, however, a great step in the direction of Islamic Socialism and a clear-cut advance over the two previous Constitutions.

Further, according to Article 38(a), the State shall raise the standard of living of all the people by preventing the *concentration of wealth and means of production and distribution* in the hands of a few... "and by ensuring equitable adjustment of rights between employers and employees, and landlords and tenants." This may be regarded as a commentary on the principle cited in the preceding paragraph, if our interpretation of that principle is correct. The previous constitutions spoke not of "concentration of wealth" but "*undue* concentration of wealth," for one thing. The words "means of production and distribution" are entirely new. This means, first, that means of production and distribution, i.e., the economic base, will be made as broad as possible, but it also means, secondly, that, whenever public interest so demands, any industry, service, or source of production or distribution may be nationalized. Immediately after taking over power, Mr. Bhutto *did* nationalize, i.e., put the management under government control, several basic utilities like gas and insurance. This is, indeed, a basic feature of the constitution in the economic field. Article 18(c) states that nothing shall prevent "the carrying on, by the Federal Government or a Provincial Government, or by a corporation controlled by any such government, of any trade, business, industry or service, to the exclusion, complete or partial, of other persons." In Article 253 (b), it is said that Parliament may make laws to authorize such nationalization.

But the upshot of all this is in Article 253 (a), according to which "Parliament may by law prescribe the maximum limits as to property or any class thereof which may be owned, held, possessed, or controlled by any person." Mr. Bhutto had already, through what the Constitution calls "Economic Reforms," promulgated by ordinances, put a ceiling of 150 acres on irrigated agricultural land. But attempts to lay his hands on the industrialists were unsuccessful. They withheld their investments, locked up their factories, and some of them are even said to have stealthily taken their installations out of Pakistan. The government had ultimately to give in and the then Minister of Industries had to resign. This capital provision rejects the extremist opinions of both the right and the left, yet accepts the basic principle of social justice, i.e., the interference by the State in private wealth, should it become detrimental to the interests of the society as a whole, which is undoubtedly a great achievement.

But two quite basic and closely allied criticisms are to be made of these economic propositions. First, they do not appear as a compact whole but are of a desultory and rambling nature. They appear from the Preamble, through the Principles of Policy, to the "Miscellaneous" provisions. Indeed, so isolated is their character that fundamental questions like the organization of *Zakāt* and the elimination of *Ribā* appear in the Principles of Policy in Articles 2(c) and 38(f) respectively, as though they had little to do with the positive economic policy. The reason is obviously that these two are regarded as "uniquely Islamic" phenomena since they appear in the Qur'ān and are seen as apparently fundamentally different from other economic propositions. Also, their interpretation has become controversial in modern times. As for *Zakāt*, this was the only permanent tax levied by the Qur'ān and the Prophet. The Qur'ān envisages it as a comprehensive tax for all the needs of the society as well as social welfare.[1] But during later Muslim history other taxes appeared without being integrated into *Zakāt* and under colonial domination *Zakāt* disappeared altogether and became a mere private and voluntary charity. It would appear that *Zakāt* has now to be interpreted as a principle of interference in private wealth to satisfy public needs, but this is precisely what the religious right as a whole resists strenuously, clinging to the economic values of the Prophet's time! *Zakāt* in fact is nothing but a blueprint for policies of social justice, and yet the present Constitution – just like its predecessors – puts it in an isolated corner as though it had little to do with the rest of economic life. This leaves the positive economic enunciations of the Constitution as purely secular; they obey an established tradition rather than Islam. And a still greater irony is that these very rightists are always hankering after the restoration of *Zakāt* to its proper position! As for *Ribā*, it was a system of usurious exploitation in the Prophet's Arabia; the Qur'ān, after a series of warnings, banned it altogether. Medieval Muslim lawyers, generally speaking, took this to mean that all

---

1   Qur'ān, IX, 60.

increments on loans are banned, although it continued in practice, thanks to various "legal fictions." Muslim Modernists have contended that *Ribā* meant usury, not interest in the modern banking system, which is development-oriented, but the traditionalists have stuck to their guns, and, ironically, have unwittingly sought to reinforce their position by Marxism! It is to the credit of Ayūb Khan's Constitution that it interpreted *Ribā* as usury (1964 edition, Article 18). But the framers of the present Constitution were apparently afraid and were content with the ambiguous statement that they will "eliminate *ribā* as early as possible."

In the light of the foregoing, it cannot be said that the economic principles of the Constitution are Islamic. The hope undoubtedly is that this procedure will be shielded by the "Repugnancy Clause" (Article 227), which has been enshrined in all Constitutions since 1956, and which states that no law shall be enacted which is repugnant to Islam or injunctions of Islam. But that clause is productive of secular law, *not* of Islamic Law, since in order for a law to be Islamic it is obviously not sufficient that it not be "repugnant to Islam" but that it be derived from Islamic principles. The Repugnancy Clause is inherently incapable of producing a legal system like that of classical Fiqh law (which is genuinely Islamic Law), but a legal system promulgated by the various Sultans in the later medieval period, particularly the Qānūn-law of the Ottomans, which is a secular body of law. It is this fundamental fact which makes all social and economic enunciations of these three constitutions both desultory and non-Islamic. The right procedure would have been to set out all political, economic, and social policies as compact sections and linked organically with the general principles of Islam. This is why in a previous paper I had characterized both the 1956 and 1964 Constitutions as an "Islamic Fetish,"[1] and I am afraid the present Constitution has exactly the same format.

B. Social Provisions

In the social sphere, a major feature of the Constitution is the encouragement it gives to women to enter public life and take on professional careers. The locus classicus (besides equality clauses, inherited from the previous constitutions, in all manner of conduct of life "irrespective of race, color, creed and sex") for this is Article 34: "Steps shall be taken to ensure full participation of women in all spheres of national life," which is an entirely new and highly welcome principle. Some steps the Constitution itself has taken. Ten seats, *in addition to* the two hundred seats for members of the National Assembly (the Constitution is silent on this point concerning the Senate) are reserved for women, while women are also eligible to run for other seats as well (Article 51[4]). In the previous Constitution the number was six, but these six seats were part of the normal number of seats in the legislature, although women could run for

---

1   Fazlur Rahman, *op. cit.* in note 1, p. 285.

other seats as well. But a bold step on this subject is taken in Article 221 (2) where it is laid down that *at least one woman* shall be a member of the Islamic Council, whose minimal strength shall be eight.

The major, indeed, pioneering thrust in this direction, however, was made by Ayūb Khan's Muslim Family Laws Ordinance of January, 1961. That Law not only gave a regular share of inheritance to the orphaned grandchildren against the traditional Muslim practice, but put restrictions on polygyny and regulated the procedure of divorce, abolishing the notorious traditional repudiation of a wife by her husband by the simple utterance of a formula. But Ayūb Khan was, at that time, a military ruler, and it is more than doubtful if a democratically elected ruler in Pakistan can repeat that masterly stroke in the foreseeable future. Indeed, it will be to the credit of the present government if it can protect that Law. For while Ayūb Khan's 1964 Constitution had given absolute protection, the present one apparently does not. It does give initial protection (Article 8[3][b]) to a number of laws included in the First Schedule (pp. 143–47), including the Muslim Family Laws Ordinance of 1961, but says ([4]), "Within a period of two years from the commencement day, the appropriate legislature shall bring the laws specified in the First Schedule – not being a law which relates to or is connected with economic reforms – into conformity with the rights conferred by this chapter." Mr. Bhutto himself and many of his party men are undoubtedly progressive; yet a very large number of Pakistanis not only consider the Muslim Family Laws repugnant to Islam, but look upon them as abridging the rights of Muslim males (although the new census of Pakistan has revealed a preponderance of males over females!) and may well institute proceedings in the National Assembly for the repeal of these Laws.

Of equal importance is the stress on education. In the previous constitution, achievement of universal literacy and of universal, free, and compulsory primary education were envisaged "as soon as is practicable" (1966 Constitution, No. 7 of the Principles of Policy). The present Constitution is much more emphatic and advanced to secondary education, since the State shall "remove illiteracy and provide free and compulsory secondary education within the minimum possible period" (Article 37[b]). It is well-known, however, that in Ayūb Khan's Second Five Year Plan, enforced in 1965, funds provided for education were drastically reduced in favor of economic development. So far as the present government is concerned, not only has it given high priority to education in its actual policies but has laid down a plan in stages, according to its policy statement on education,[1] for completing universal primary education and for the take-over by the government of all private and foreign educational institutions. The government will not only endeavor to make Islamic Studies compulsory – this was also present in the previous Constitution – but will facilitate the learning of the Arabic language (Article 31[2]). This meets a very fundamental desideratum since an adequate knowledge of Arabic is a *sine*

---

1   Government of Pakistan, Ministry of Education, Islamabad *The Educational Policy, 1972– 1980.*

qua non of understanding Islam from its primary sources – the Qur'ān and the Prophetic Sunna. Indeed, the main malady of those who, in Pakistan, have tried to learn Islam has been that most of them do not know Arabic and have been "free-landing" with Islam. But, of course, Arabic is necessary, but not enough: what is equally important is to cultivate a sense of history of the development of Islam over the past fourteen centuries and to compare this development with what the Qur'ān and the Prophet said, and the entire sociologico-historical background which renders the Qur'ān and the Prophet *intelligible*.

The most basic trouble with education in Pakistan and some other Muslim countries, however, is its dichotomy: two systems of education are running side by side, one modern and the other the traditional *madrasas*, untouched by any modern outlook. The former is government-funded, while the latter is privately financed. They are producing men of quite different and incongruous outlooks on life, and incompatible world-views. It would be no exaggeration to say that *two nations* are being produced. No government with the nation's interests at heart can simply go on looking at this fundamentally injurious state of affairs. In Turkey, the impatient Ataturk abolished the old *madrasa* system with one stroke. In Egypt, the famous al-Azhar University experienced a series of reforms in the present century, which widened its curriculum and changed its outmoded methods of instruction. Under Nasser, al-Azhar has been given even a medical and an agricultural college. In Tunisia, President Bourguiba simply lifted the age-old Zaitūna Seminary from the Zaitūna Mosque and replanted it in the University of Tunisia. The Indonesian Government is currently making strenuous efforts to streamline the *madrasas* and in some meaningful way integrate the two educational systems. It is very much to be hoped that the Islamic Republic of Pakistan will, in due course, take steps to improve this grave situation, even though it has found it necessary to state in its educational policy statement referred to above – no doubt with a political end in view – that "status quo shall be maintained" with regard to the *madrasas*. It is also not clear why, in view of the nationalization of education, the Constitution tells so much in the Principles of Policy. None of these institutions, to my knowledge, teaches even Islamic history, let alone general history, philosophy, any modern Western language, economics, or political science.

C. Islamic Propositions and Law-Making

So far as Islam is concerned, the most formidable difficulty faced by the Constitution-makers of Pakistan at the very outset was the location of sovereignty in the new State and whether democracy was Islamic or not. Already before the creation of Pakistan, the leader of the Jamā'at-i-Islamī, Alu'l-A'la Mawdūdī had forcefully contended that Islam could not accept modern democracy since in a democracy people are law-makers, whereas in

---

1   *Ibid.*, p. 37, clause 14.5.

Islam God is the law-giver.[1] Twisting the purely religious sense in which the Qur'ān speaks of God as "sovereign in heaven and earth,"[2] into a modern political sense, Mawdūdī and, following him, the traditionalist ʿulamā, insisted that the Constitution must recognize the sovereignty of Allāh. The idea behind this was, of course, to accept the sovereignty of the Sharī'a Law. The Modernist should have stood firm on the principle of the political sovereignty of the people, because otherwise one would have to admit the ludicrous conclusion that in officially atheistic countries God had set up governments-in-exile! The Modernist, instead, compromised. Hence the opening clause of the Preamble: "Whereas sovereignty over the entire Universe belongs to Almighty Allah alone and the authority to be exercised by the people of Pakistan, within the limits prescribed by Him, is a sacred trust." One would like to know how and through which instrument God had delegated this trust to the people of Pakistan. However, by this compromise, the Modernist managed to avoid a headlong conflict with the traditionalist, and to his own satisfaction, obtained a sanction for *working* democracy. The traditionalist, for his part, thought that *he* had gained what he wanted, viz., a restriction on the will of the people through God's sovereignty. That is where the crux lies in all the three Constitutions.

The Preamble then goes on to say that the State shall establish an order – "wherein the principles of democracy, freedom, equality, tolerance, and social justice, *as enunciated by Islam*, shall be fully observed." In the light of what has been said, the italicized words mean for the Modernist one thing, for the Traditionalist quite another. For the Modernist, democracy, etc., are understood in their modern meaning, for the Conservative, these words serve as a limitation on freedom. For otherwise, these words have no function, since, if the Modernist view is correct (and all Muslim Modernists since the latter half of the last century have been arguing this case with a great deal of plausibility), then Islam apparently enjoined democracy, social justice, etc., not *Islamic* democracy, social justice, etc. These words are, therefore, again a concession to the traditionalists. This is why, in the eyes of the present writer, the form in which Islam has been treated in all these Constitutions is unfortunate. They give the decisive impression of Islam being an artificial adjunct attached to some propositions, while most of the rest of substantive propositions are without any mention of Islam at all. The proper way to produce an authentic Islamic Constitution would have been to write a brief but comprehensive Introduction (or Preamble) where the relevance of Islam to political democracy, social philosophy, economic policies of social justice, treatment of minorities, and international behavior of the State would be set out. Then, one by one, each of these fields would have been treated in a compact and logical manner. Instead, all these fields have been treated in a diffuse and fragmentary manner.

On the subject of Islamization of the society, the Constitution (Preamble, paragraph 5) reaffirms the dicta of the previous constitution that the Muslims

---

1   Mawhūdī, *The Political Theory of Islam*, translated into English by M. Siddiqui (Lahore, n.d.).
2   For example, Qurᶜān, III, 26; LVII, 2; III, 14; XXIII, 88, etc.

of Pakistan will be enabled to order their lives in the individual and collective spheres in accordance with the teachings and requirements of Islam "as set out in Holy Quran and Sunnah." In Ayūb Khan's original constitution of 1962, the term "Sunnah" had been dropped but was restored under public pressure through the First Amendment Act of 1964. The "Sunnah of the Prophet" means the example of the Prophet handed down through Ḥadīth-reports or traditions collected in the third century of Islam by the Sunnis and in the fourth century by the Shī'a. This Ḥadīth literature is quite amorphous and often self-contradictory and modern scholarship has shown that, by and large, it represents, not the Prophet's sayings but the opinions of the very early generations of Islam. Moreover, Shī'a Ḥadīth collections are different from the Sunnī ones. However, it would be unwise to repudiate the Sunnah, for without it the meaning of the Qur'ān itself would often become difficult to settle. What is really required is a historical criticism of the Ḥadīth which would be of enormous help to clarify the situation. We shall presently return to the question of the Islamization of the society.

One highly welcome change in the Constitution is that it has dropped a paragraph contained in the two earlier Constitutions (1964 *Principles of Policy* 1, *Explanation*): "In the application of this principle [i.e., that no law shall be enacted which is repugnant to the Qur'ān and the Sunnah] to the personal law of any Muslim sect, the expression 'Qur'ān and Sunnah' shall mean the Quran and Sunnah as interpreted by that sect." This principle was obviously in contradiction with that Constitution's expressly limiting the authoritative sources of Islam to the Quran and Sunnah only and would perpetuate the authority of different schools of law of classical Islam. It would thus prevent an achievement of uniformity of the law (and morality) of Islam in Pakistan. This writer had pointed out this ugly contradiction to President Ayūb Khan in a letter in 1964.

In Chapter 2, on the Principles of Policy, Articles 29(1) and 30(1) the present Constitution reaffirms what was said in the earlier Constitution, viz., that it will be the responsibility of each organ or authority of the State to act in accordance with these principles in so far as they relate to that organ or authority or a person officially acting on behalf of such organ or authority, and the reponsibility of deciding whether an act of an organ or authority is or is not in accordance with these principles also resides in such organ or authority or a person acting on behalf of them. This means that in this respect each organ or authority of the State is completely autonomous and will not be open to question. The new Constitution, however, probably somewhat inconsistently with the foregoing but certainly representing an overall improvement, lays down in Article 29(3) that annual Federal and Provincial reports shall be prepared and each laid before the relevant Assembly "on the observance and implementation of the Principles of Policy, and provision shall be made... for discussion on such report." If a discussion of such report is to be held, it obviously means that some evaluation of the action of each organ or authority will be made and they cannot, therefore, be all that autonomous. As we shall see below, the Islamic

(Advisory) Council is required by the Constitution (as it was by the second Constitution which, for the first time, provided for it) to prepare an annual report for discussion by the National Assembly.

On continuance of the Preamble, the Principles of Policy (Article 31) also state – like the earlier constitutions – that "steps shall be taken to enable the Muslims of Pakistan, individually and collectively, to order their lives in accordance with *the fundamental principles and basic concepts of Islam* and to provide facilities whereby they may be enabled to understand the meaning of life according to the Holy Quran and Sunnah." Finally, this task is entrusted in Part IX (Articles 227–32) to the Islamic (Advisory) Council. Here, the present Constitution differs in certain important respects from the previous constitutions. The 1956 Constitution had envisaged a Law Commission to prepare a report on the Islamization of existing laws and on such principles and concepts of Islam which can be embodied in legal form and a Research Institute which was to undertake research on Islam and diffuse knowledge on Islam generally. According to the second constitution, an Advisory Islamic Council was provided for, charged both with giving advice on the legal side of Islam and with the task of making recommendations to the Central and the Provincial Governments as to how the Muslims of Pakistan may be enabled to order their lives in accordance with the teachings of Islam. Secondly, it also provided for an Islamic Research Institute which both provided necessary research materials to the Islamic Advisory Council and carried on its own research and dissemination of Islamic ideas. However, during this writer's tenure as Director of the Institute (1962–1968) and membership of the Council (1964–1969), in the Institute and Council there was a continuous tension and frequent conflict between the two: While the Institute espoused a definitely Modernist stance, the general climate within the Council was Conservative and often even reactionary. The Institute was also involved in certain public controversies with the very conservative right. Because of this history, the Institute has been dropped entirely from the new Constitution. But the question is: How will this Council discharge itself of these heavy duties of Islamization, particularly when the members of the Council will all be part-timers and will meet only occasionally, since the Constitution does not speak of the Council as though it were an organization requiring full-time work; indeed, it says that its Chairman, who must be a judge, could be a sitting judge of a High Court or of the Supreme Court (Article 228[4]).

Pakistan, indeed, presents a curious case. It is an ideological state, but it has no known ideology. In the case of Communist or Socialist countries, which are the only other ideological states in the world, their ideological blueprints and even their major policies precede the actual establishment of their states, but in the case of Pakistan, which declares itself to be an "Islamic State," Islam is not yet even known and its "fundamental principles and basic concepts" have yet to be formulated. The trouble is that Pakistani masses are emotionally strongly attached to Islam (as are masses so attached to Islam elsewhere), but the developments or distortions through which Islam has passed during the past fourteen centuries are so diverse and are of such sectarian character that the masses blindly follow these forms. The task obviously is to analyze the history of Islamic development, and to come to some point where a genuine enough perception of what the Qur'ān and the Prophet's struggle were all about may be born. But here even the 'Ulamā and the intellectuals in general do not have any adequate idea of what the Qur'ān was saying, why it was saying it, and what it became through the centuries. This whole question once again leads us to a proper organization of Islamic education and, in particular, to its dichotomy. This being the case, one may genuinely ask: How is Pakistan an ideological state?

According to Article 228 (3) (a), the President shall ensure that "So far as practicable various schools of thought are represented on the Council." This is undoubtedly an excellent principle, since the more broad-based the Council will be, the more points of view will be represented, although, of course, this will require some pateince, since it will not be easy to hammer out the differences. It is not clear, however, what is meant by "schools of thought." In the first place, this term must mean the major traditional sects – i.e., the Sunnis and the Shī'a. But will this include the Ahmadīs? Thorny questions like this are bound to arise. It is to be hoped that the movement of Islamic Modernism, now over a century old, a movement which produced such men as (Sir) Sayyid Ahmad Khan, Sayyid Amīr 'Alī, Shibli, and Iqbal (the intellectual parent of Pakistan) will find adequate representation. Most probably, not all members will be appointed to begin with; the Council can start with any number from the minimum eight upward and the remaining (the maximum seats are fifteen) can be appointed later.

The final report of the Council is made due within seven years. Although the Council's role is "advisory," the present Constitution gives it more authority than did the second Constitution. While according to that Constitution, if reference to the Council by the President or a governor or an assembly is likely to cause delay in handling an urgent matter, laws pertaining to that matter may be made, the present Constitution adds, "Provided that, where a law is referred for advice to the Islamic Council and the Council advises that the law [enacted pertaining to an urgent matter] is repugnant to the Injunctions of Islam, the House, ... the President or the Governor shall reconsider the law so made" (Article 230[3]). But on this point there is some disturbing news and Mr. Bhutto seems (characteristically?) to have gone too far. In Article 230 (4), it is laid down that when the Council presents its report – whether interim (i.e., annual) or final – it will be laid before both Houses of the Parliament and all Provincial Assemblies within six months of its receipt, and Parliament and [each] Assembly, after considering the report, shall enact laws *in respect thereof* (note: *not necessarily in conformity therewith*) within a period of two years of the final report.

The language of the article by itself is not necessarily a cause for alarm, since it does not make it mandatory for the Parliament or an Assembly to *accept* in toto what the report has recommended. But the opposition was apparently refusing to sign the Constitutional document unless at least some of their demands were met, one being that the Islamic Council be given veto power over the Houses of Public Representatives. A front-page article in the weekly "Muslim World" of Karachi (a periodical which essentially gives reliable information about the current political, religious, social, and economic issues in various Muslim countries) in its issue of April 21, 1973 has the following: "President [now Prime Minister since the 14th of August, 1973] Bhutto, in his Aide-Memoire to the Opposition leaders, on the eve of the passing of the Constitution, brought to their notice that Article 230 (4) [partly referred to and partly quoted in the preceding paragraph] *obviously* means that the Islamic Council shall exercise a veto on the powers of the National Parliament. The Opposition demand was accepted by the ruling party in the cause of passing the Constitution by consensus of all parties." The Constitution *was* passed by a consensus of the members of the House present: no vote was cast against it, although there were some abstentions. But this has apparently cost the ideological stance of Mr. Bhutto and his party a good deal.

A new Article (No. 2) has been added in the Constitution declaring Islam to be the State Religion of Pakistan. Article 40 stresses the preservation and strengthening of fraternal relations among Muslim countries based on Islamic Unity and goes on to promise support for developing countries and to foster friendly relations with all countries to try to secure settlement of all issues through peaceful means. Here the support for developing countries (of Asia, Africa, and Latin America) is new, while the rest is more or less a carryover from the earlier Constitutions. Among the Fundamental Rights granted to all citizens, the right of freedom of speech, expression, and the freedom of the press is subject to the overall considerations of the "glory of Islam" and the security of the State. The two earlier Constitutions were content to mention the security of the State only, presumably because a threat to Islam would be considered as a threat to the State since Islam is the declared basis of the State. But Mr. Bhutto, with his eyes ever fixed on the emotions of the masses, considered an explicit mention of the "glory of Islam" apparently necessary.

Finally, a novel feature of the present Constitution is the oaths to be administered to the President and the Prime Minister and, to some extent, oaths to be made by other dignitaries as well – the Speaker, the governors, ministers, members of the Assemblies, etc. (Schedule III). The second Constitution (as well as the first) had laid down that the President shall be a Muslim, but the oaths to be administered to all the dignitaries were about the performance of their duties honestly and in accordance with the Constitution and "in the interest of the integrity, solidarity, and well-being and prosperity of Pakistan." Nothing was said explicitly about Islam. In the present Constitution, in view of the great anxiety constantly expressed by the ʿUlamā in general and the Jamāʿat-i-Islāmī in particular lest an Aḥmadi rise to such high office (in fact, demands have been put forward from time to time to declare Aḥmadis a non-Muslim minority!) – an anxiety which has recently been greatly increased by the fact that many Aḥmadis now occupy key posts in the Armed Forces – the

Constitution provides oaths for the offices of the President and the Prime Minister which lay out the entire traditional credo of Islam: belief in God, in the Holy Books, of which the last is the Qur'ān (for some reason belief in Angels has been left out), in the Prophets, of whom the final is Muḥammad, and in the Last Day. Other oaths also, while they do not speak of the traditional *credo* of Islam explicitly, certainly ask the entrants upon high office "to strive to preserve the Islamic Ideology which is the basis for the creation of Pakistan." The trouble, of course, is that Aḥmadis do not deny the position of the Qur'ān as the last revelation of God to mankind, nor do they believe that there will be another Prophet after Muḥammad with a new law – in fact,the Aḥmadis are so highly conservative and traditional that they follow the Ḥanafī School of Islamic Law – and, to that extent, they do uphold the finality of Prophethood with Muḥammad. It is doubtful whether an Aḥmadī will have any great qualms in making such an oath. Indeed, if there are groups who are much further removed from the core of Islam, these are certain Shi'ite groups whose content and style of worship and prayer has *nothing* to do with those of Muslims and whom the Shi'ites themselves call "extremists." These are, e.g., Druzes and the Isma'īlī followers of the Āghā Khān, although it must be admitted that the present Āghā Khān and his grandfather have done much to bridge the gap between their followers and the Muslim community.

Winding up this analysis, we may again point out that this Constitution is progressive in its social and economic parts, although its progressiveness has been much, very much diluted by the anxiety of Mr. Bhutto to get the maximum support – indeed, consensus – of the National (Constituent) Assembly. The Constitution nevertheless has an unsatisfactorily diffuse and desultory character. All through the Constitution, its maker has had his gaze fixed on the emotional attachment of the masses to Islam and has tried to satisfy and exploit it to the full by going out of the way to inject it with heavy doses of emotional Islam.

REFERENCES

Ahmad, Aziz, and G. E. von Grunebaum,
    1970   Muslim Self Statement in India and Pakistan
al-Sibācī, Mustafa,
    1959   Ishtirākīyat'l-Islām, Damascus
Mawhūdī,
    n.d.   The Political Theory of Islam, trans., by M. Siddiqui, Lahore
Pakiston,
    1973   The Constitution of the Islamic Republic of Pakistan, Islamabad
    1972   The Educational Policy, 1972–1980, Islamabad
Rahman, Fazlur,
    1971   The Islamic Experience of Pakistan, Islam and the Modern Age, New Delhi, II, 4.
    1974   Sources and Meaning of Islamic Socialism, in Donald Smith, ed., Religion and
           Political Modernization, New Haven.
Sumār, A. K.,
    1966   Nusrat, Lahore.

Journal of Asian and African Studies VIII, 3–4

The Emergence of the Federal Pattern in Pakistan

HAFEEZ MALIK

Villanova University, Villanova, U.S.A.

SINCE DECEMBER, 1971 Pakistan's political scene has been dominated by the struggle for power between President Bhutto and the National Awami Party's Chairman, Abdul Wali Khan. This struggle, to an extent, explained the political crisis in Pakistan which followed the seizure of (what the Pakistan Government called), "a veritable arsenal" from the Iraqi Embassy in Islamabad on February 10, 1973, and the dismissal of the NWFP and Baluchistan governors, who belonged to the NAP. Once again a question is being asked: are Baluchistan and the NWFP on the verge of secession in order to create Pakhtunistan? Pakhtunistan could emerge as a separate state if the people in the two provinces are alienated by the Federal Government of Pakistan. However, the odds are that the political elite in the two provinces would not seek confrontation, but exercise all conceivable pressure to gain maximum provincial autonomy in the new Constitution. Behind the facade of the political crisis was a developing constitutional consensus, to which Bhutto and the NAP leaders, including Wali Khan, and his Baluch colleague, Mir Gaus Bakhsh Bizenjo, have made substantial contributions.

The emerging pattern of federalism in Pakistan was reflected in President Bhutto's accord of March 5, 1972 with the National Awami Party (NAP) and Jamiat ulama-i Islam (JUI), and all parties constitutional accord of October, 1972.

Accord of March, 1972

It should, however, be kept in mind that President Bhutto's accord with the NAP and JUI, announced on March 6, 1972 was arrived at after an intense period of crisis which had developed as the result of a contest for power between the PPP and the NAP. This struggle for power was unnecessary, especially at this crucial moment, and it could have been avoided if President Bhutto had not allowed his political lieutenants in the Frontier Province to rupture the PPP-JUI-NAP alliance, which had been brought about since December, 1971.

Why was this alliance ruptured? Basically three issues were responsible for the break down of this alliance:

1) The appointment of governors to the provinces of Baluchistan and the NWFP.

2) The election of female candidates to the provincial legislative assemblies.
3) The introduction of land reforms.

Maintaining their majorities in the NWFP and Baluchistan, the NAP-JUI asserted that the provincial governors should be appointed with their advice and consent. On the other hand, President Bhutto disregarded this demand and appointed members of the PPP as governors. When NAP agitated against governor Raisani in Baluchistan during January, 1971 the agitators were forcefully put down.

In order to undercut the influence and popularity of the NAP in the Frontier Province, the NAP leaders charged that the PPP had organized the Kissan Mazdur Party which was mobilizing the landless tenants against the land owning Khans of the Frontier. Many of these Khans were supporters of the NAP and they felt deeply threatened in their home base, and they blamed the PPP for their rising troubles with the tenants.

The election of female candidates to the provincial legislative assemblies brought the relationship between the two parties to the breaking point. In the Punjab the PPP elected six women to the Legislative Assembly, containing 186 seats; while in Sindh it elected two female members to the Legislative Assembly of 62 members. Simultaneously, however, the PPP nominated female candidates in the Frontier and Baluchistan, and tried to persuade the NAP and JUI members to violate their party discipline and vote for the PPP's nominees. Naturally, these developments created fears in the mind of the NAP leader, Wali Khan, that the PPP was endeavoring to create a dictatorship of Sindh and the Punjab. When Baluchistan and the NWFP legislatures elected the NAP-JUI female candidates, Wali Khan charged that the people have lost confifidence in the PPP leadership.

In view of these developments, Wali Khan and his colleagues in Baluchistan, notably Mir Ghaus Bakhsh Bizenjo, developed a program of resistance to President Bhutto's government, in which regionalism was certainly a point of appeal for the Pathans and the Baluchis. They demanded that President Bhutto should lift Martial Law, call the National and Provincial Assemblies in order to restore democratic institutions in Pakistan. Regarding the land reforms, Wali Khan took the position that only the provincial assemblies were competent to adopt them, and if they failed to introduce these reforms then it was none of President Bhutto's business. Despite his lip-service to Socialism, Wali Khan was not anxious to see his supporters' economic base destroyed by the sledge-hammer of Martial Law.

To strengthen their position, the NAP leaders obtained support from the three factions of the Muslim League, retired Air Marshall Asghar Khan's party, and Jamiat-i-Islami. They started agitation in the Frontier, where appeal was also made in the name of Pakhtunistan. Some of the hotheads openly asked for a confrontation with the national government, if President Bhutto failed to accept the NAP's demands. Consequently, during the months of January and February, a heightened sense of crisis developed in Pakistan, leading foreign observers to report that Pakistan was on the verge of break-up.

Had President Bhutto taken the opposition into his confidence regarding the withdrawal of Martial Law this ugly situation might not have developed. On February 18 he gave an interview to London's BBC correspondent, Ian McIntire, suggesting that he would withdraw Martial Law after introducing agrarian reforms in Pakistan, and after the completion of negotiations with Shaikh Mujeeb and Mrs. Indira Gandhi. The vagueness of his commitment on the withdrawal of Martial Law only heightened suspicions regarding his intentions. Although he announced that the elections to the local bodies scheduled to be held on March 15 would be postponed, and that they would be organized by the provincial governments, the NAP leaders' fears were not allayed. While they welcomed the president's decision, they continued to agitate for the withdrawal of Martial Law and for the withdrawal of provincial governors from Baluchistan and NWFP. These governors were accused of having lobbied for the election of the PPP-sponsored female candidates to the legislatures.

NAP's Political Ideology

The NAP leaders, particularly Wali Khan, have a political ideology which is a hodge-podge of regionalism, secularism, socialism and all-Pakistan nationalism. Wali Khan believes that after the establishment of Bangladesh, Pakistan, as it was originally conceived, has ceased to exist. In his eyes, Pakistan as it stands today is a coalition of four nationalities. He perceives nationalities in terms of their mother tongues and asserts that the new Constitution must be the product of a compromise between these four nationalities.[1] In political terms, this strategy amounts to claiming for the NAP a position of parity with the PPP, the former being the majority party in Baluchistan and NWFP and the latter being the dominant representative organization of the Punjab and Sindh. To Wali Khan the new Constitution would be acceptable if it reflects the true distribution of power between these two political parties in Pakistan.

While this is a regional strategy, Wali Khan has recently endeavored to change his image to an all-Pakistan leader by extending the influence of the NAP to the Punjab and Sindh. If, however, the NAP becomes an All-Pakistan party, it may eventually preempt the JUI, the Muslim League and the Jam'at-i-Islami. This probable development could lead to the emergence of a two party system in Pakistan.

To Wali Khan's debit it may be pointed out that the concept of four nationalities negates the concept of a Pakistani nation, and leaves little ideological room for the Muslim Muhajirs (immigrants) who have settled in Pakistan since 1947. After offering many sacrifices for the creation of Pakistan, Muslim Muhajirs came to the promised land to be Pakistanis and not to become Pun-

---

1   For Wali Khan's ideology see two good studies by Anwar Muzdakiy, Wali Khan Key Siyasat (Lahore: Tariq Publishers, 1972); pp. 141–4; *Bacha Khan Awr Pakhtunistan* (Lahore: Tariq Publishers, 1972).

jabis, Sindhis, Baluchis or Pathans. Not having any commitment to provincial ethos, they are all-Pakistani nationalists *par excellence*. Wali Khan's ethnic ideology creates a crisis of identity, and is a serious obstacle in the development of a homogeneous Pakistani nationalism. However, his attitude is bound to change if the NAP becomes a truly all-Pakistan party, and thus emancipates itself from the narrow confines of ethnic regionalism.

The Averting of the Crisis

Recognizing the explosive potentiality of the NAP'S agitation, President Bhutto invited Wali Khan and Bizenjo to Islamabad for a round of parleys to resolve their differences. Simultaneously, however, Presidential Advisor for Public Affairs, Mr. Mairaj Muhammad Khan gave a statement in which a crucial concession was made to the NAP leaders. He said on March 4, 1972: "His party had no objection to renaming of the Frontier Province as Pakhtunistan or any other name that is adopted by the [Frontier] provincial assembly, but it must be clear that the province would be within the concept and framework of one Pakistan." Negotiations between President Bhutto, the NAP and JUI leaders lasted for three days (March 2, 3, and 4, 1972) and they laid down the principles of compromise to resolve the crisis as well as some principles to frame the future Constitution of Pakistan. The accord, which was finally declared on March 5, turned out to be a point by point compromise between the three parties. The salient features of the accord are:[1]

The Distribution of Power

The NAP-JUI coalition was recognized as the majority party in the NWFP, while in Baluchistan NAP alone would be the majority party. Consequently in both provinces the NAP-JUI alliance established the provincial governments.

The Withdrawal of Martial Law

The PPP proposed that the National Assembly should convene on April 21, 1972 and after passing a vote of confidence in the Bhutto government should approve and confirm the continuation of Martial Law until August 14, 1972. The NAP-JUI wanted Martial Law to be withdrawn on June 7.

It was agreed that Martial Law would continue until August 14, 1972 and the National Assembly would pass a vote of confidence in the Bhutto government.

The PPP proposed that the National Assembly should appoint a committee

---

1   Dawn (March 5, 1972).

of the House to draft a constitution which would be presented on August 1, 1972. The NAP-JUI suggested that the draft constitution should be presented by July 1, 1972 and the National Assembly should be convened on July, 1972. But the parties agreed that the reports of the committee on the constitution should be submitted by August 1, 1972 and that the National Assembly should reconvene on August 14, 1972.

The PPP proposed that when the National Assembly is reconvened on August 14, 1972, it should act only as a constitution making body to guarantee early drafting of the Constitution. The NAP-JUI proposed that the National Assembly should also act as a representative legislative organ. The compromise stated that the National Assembly would make the Constitution as well as ordinary laws for the country until the final draft of the Constitution was produced.

The Interim Constitution

The PPP proposed that the first session of the National Assembly should start on April 21, 1972 for three days. The NAP-JUI proposed that the National Assembly should meet on March 23. The parties agreed that the National Assembly members would be invited on March 23 for participation, and the National Assembly would actually meet on April 14 for three days. During this brief period, specified topics will be discussed, and the debate would be restricted.

The PPP proposed that the National Assembly should meet in order to endorse an interim constitution on the basis of the Government of India Act of 1935, read together with the Independence Act of 1947, along with subsequent amendmets, or on the basis of 1962 Constitution with subsequent amendments. The NAP-JUI leaders insisted that the interim constitution should be the Government of India Act of 1935 and the Independence Act of 1947 with subsequent amendments, and that the Constitution of 1962 should be kept out of the political picture.

President Bhutto conceded the demand of the NAP and JUI leaders on this point, after obtaining their agreement that the debate in the National Assembly would not exceed three days.

The Provincial Legislative Assemblies

The PPP preferred that the provincial assemblies should meet after the interim constitution was adopted, that is on May 1, 1972. On the other hand the NAP-JUI proposed that the provincial legislative assemblies should be convened on April 10. However, it was agreed that the provincial legislatures will be convened on April 21.

Regarding the provincial governors, after a great deal of discussion, it was agreed that until the permanent constitution was adopted the federal government would continue to have the right to appoint the governors in the provinces. As a token of compromise the federal government stated that even during the interim period, governors would be appointed after consulting the majority parties in the provinces.

Future Developments

The PPP-JUI agreement resolved the political and constitutional deadlock in Pakistan, but it also paved the way for the emergence of Pakhtunistan. The attempt to change the name from NWFP to Pakhtunistan need not be considered a secessionist development. Presently all indications are that Pakhtunistan would not move in the direction of Mujeebism. On the federal nature of Pakistan's constitution, the NAP's position moved closer to that of the PPP and other political parties in the country. For example, the NAP leaders indicated that they would like to transfer matters of defense, foreign affairs, foreign trade, currency, including central taxation to the central government of Pakistan. They also indicated their agreement to leave communications, including railroad, civil aviation, telegraph and telephones under the care of the federal government.

Much like President Bhutto, the NAP-JUI leaders recognized that for the industrial and economic development of Pakistan, private business has a great contribution to make. Consequently, the NAP leaders invited Pakistan's financiers and industrialists to invest their capital in the NWFP and Baluchistan, while assuring them that their investments would be safeguarded, and guaranteed by the NAP-JUI governments in these two provinces.

Highlighting the role of private enterprise in the NWFP, the NAP-Minister of Finance, Mr. Ghulam Faruq stated in the Budget (1972–73) speech:

> And so of necessity for the major portion of the Province's development programme, specially the industrial sector, we must look for a more effective and reliable source from a different direction and so out of dire necessity and under compulsion, we have to fall back on private enterprise, already dubbed according to common concept, a sinner. The House, I hope, will appreciate that in the past it was the ineffectiveness of Government operations that paved the way for private enterprise going out of control.
>
> But the private enterprise wedded to the philosophy of profit will ask for its price in the shape of tax holidays, other concessions and a reliable supply of electrical energy and gas.[1]

In the composition of provincial ministries in the NWFP and Baluchistan, the NAP-JUI leaders also reflected a national trend in their agreement on March 11, 1972. In the Frontier, the chief minister came from the JUI, while in Baluchistan the chief minister was provided by the NAP. Wali Khan declared that he would resign his position from the Frontier provincial assembly and

1   Ghulam Faruq, *Finance Minister's Speech: Budget, 1972-73*, Peshawar, Government of NWFP, 1972, p. 5.

retain his membership in the National Assembly. The NAP constitution committee included prominent lawyers including former Justice Sheikh Abdul Hameed, Aziz Allah A. Shaikh and S. M. Zafar, the former Law Minister of Ayub's regime. Wali Khan, Bizenjo, and Arbab Sikandar Khan directed the committee on political matters. These trends indicated that the NAP was endeavoring to become a national political organization.

As a regional alliance, however, the NAP-JUI demanded non-interference in their administrations in the Frontier province and Baluchistan. Hardly had this settlement been implemented when the conflicting strategies began to plague the relations between these two provinces and the federal government. Surprisingly the NAP strategy included: 1) "falling back on private enterprise"; 2) scuttling the land reforms to retain the big Khans' political support, and 3) currying favor with the conservative elements by allowing the JUI ministers to make the study of Arabic in the elementary schools compulsory. (This policy also provided jobs to a large number of half-educated *ulama*.) Simultaneously, however, Wali Khan subjected President Bhutto to his unrelenting criticism to erode his popularity in Sindh and particularly the Punjab, the home-base of Bhutto's power. In July, 1972 the language riots in Sindh lowered Bhutto's popularity, and Wali Khan's image appeared as a probable national alternative in the next general elections.

President Bhutto's counter-strategy operated at two levels. In order to create a sense of distributive justice in these two provinces, he increased their developmental allocations – 100% for Baluchistan, and 119% for the NWFP. To undermine the NAP-JUI alliance the Kissan-Mazdur party was encouraged to pit the tenants against the Khans. From Baluchistan, where Baluchi society is largely tribal and divided between Pakistan, Iran and Afghanistan, Governor Bizenjo was sent to Iran to observe the socio-economic power of Iran and Baluchis' situation. However, the Muslim League (Qayyum group) and the PPP concentrated their attacks on the Ata Allah Mengal government. Retaliating, the Mengal tribesmen attacked some Punjabi settlers in the Pat Feeder area, and the Mengal government also decided to return to the federal government all non-Baluchi employees. To subordinate some rival tribes to the Mengals, the Baluchistan government harassed the Bugtis and the Jamote tribes in Lasbela. Consequently the Jam Sahib of Lasbela, and Mir Nabi Bux Zehri (Vice-President of the Muslim League in Baluchistan) were forced to flee the province, and their extradition was denied by the Sindh government. To escape arrest in the Frontier, the Kissan-Mazdur leaders moved out to the Punjab, where their extradition was also refused. Nevertheless, the relations between the federal and provincial governments remained workable.

In September, 1972 occurred the episode of the London Plot, when the government-controlled newspapers, attacked Yusuf Haroon, Mahmud Haroon (both benefactors of Shaikh Mujeeb and the NAP), Ata Allah Mengal and Wali Khan, who were in London for various reasons. The fact that they had visited convalescing Shaikh Mujeeb could not be denied; what made their reunion "conspiratorial" was the newspapers' assertion that they had advised

Shaikh Mujeeb to persuade Mrs. Gandhi to delay the Indian troops' withdrawal from Pakistani occupied areas. Derisively President Bhutto called them "winter Pakistanis" – who spend summer months in Europe – and denied any knowledge of the London Plot. Some of the federal ministers, however, continued their bitter personal attacks against the NAP Chief, Wali Khan. Against this background was the October, 1972 constitutional accord negotiated between all the political parties of Pakistan.

Accord of October, 1972

President Bhutto took the initiative, while Wali Khan was still in London, to have a broad agreement on federal principles for the new Constitution. By entering into these constitutional parleys the NAP leaders very substantially neutralized their own leader, while the "London Plot" had already cast a shadow over his relatively limited popularity in Pakistan. Unquestionably President Bhutto made substantial concessions to the oppositions leaders, who wanted a parliamentary federal system, while he preferred American federalism. On October 20 the accord was signed by Governors Bizenjo of Baluchistan, and Arbab Sikander Khan of the NWFP (representing the NAP) and Chief Minister Mufti Mahmud (representing the JUI). Out of the murky skies of politics emerged a federal parliamentary system with a Prime Minister as the chief executive responsible only to the National Assembly. A bicameral legislature (the National Assembly and the Senate) was provided, which was empowered to elect the titular president. For 15 years (or three general elections) the vote of no-confidence could be passed by a two-thirds majority of the National Assembly, while simultaneously indicating a successor's name. The power between the Federal Government and the provinces was distributed according to the interim constitution, with residual powers vested in the provinces. However, the interim constitution was weighted heavily in the center's favor.

The 179-page draft of the new Constitution was presented to the National Assembly on December 31, when Wali Khan had returned to Pakistan. Determined to reassert his leadership over the NAP, Wali Khan virtually repudiated the October Accord saying that Bizenjo and Arbab Sikander signed it as individuals and that it needed to be ratified by the NAP General Council. Wali Khan asked to whittle down the Prime Minister's powers, and to have the Senate share with the National Assembly control over the budget. Again, this position reflected Wali Khan's regional strategy. The Punjab, he rightly asserted, having more population (62%) than the other three provinces combined would have untrammeled control over the national resources, if the Senate was denied an allocative role. Bhutto compromised once again and invited the political parties to another round of constitutional parleys to iron out the differences. Responding enthusiastically on January 20, 1973 Wali Khan accepted the offer and it seemed that after all the Constitution would reflect a national consensus. In this hopeful atmosphere exploded the Iraqi Embassy's scandal of February 10, which led to the dismissal of the NAP governors, and chief ministers in Baluchistan and the NWFP.

Emergence of the 1973 Constitution

However, the Government of Pakistan moved rather quickly to normalize relations with Iraq. Iraqi Minister of Education, Dr. Ahmad Abdul Sattar Al-Jawari, visited Pakistan from April 19 to 23, 1973 and had several rounds of discussions with Mr. Bhutto and Minister of State for Defense and Foreign Affairs, Mr. Aziz Ahmad. Both parties frankly discussed Iraqi Embassy's involvement in smuggling of guns to Pakistan. Very shrewdly Iraqis let it be known that the guns were not intended for any political party or a faction in Pakistan, but were meant to be shipped to Baluchis living in Iran.

While this explanation was effectively utilized by the NAP, the Pakistan Government was not pleased with this "diplomatic finesse" of the Iraqis. Finally Pakistan and Iraq resolved to reappoint their Ambassadors, and Iraq reiterated its respect for the sovereignty and territorial integrity of Pakistan. A communique containing this happy understanding was published on April 26, and this unhappy chapter of relations between the two countries was closed.[1]

The NAP-JUI coalition demanded that if the misunderstandings between Iraq and Pakistan had been removed and President Bhutto had accepted Iraq's explanation, there was no reason why their governments could not be reinstated in the NWFP and Baluchistan. Also, the NAP-JUI suggested that if the federal government still suspected their involvement with the Iraqi Embassy, then a high powered judicial inquiry should be held to determine their culpability. Most observers in Pakistan began to suspect that President Bhutto had acted hastily in blaming the NAP and JUI. Practically all the opposition parties came to accept the NAP-JUI's "innocence." Consequently, the opposition political parties coalesced into a United Democratic Front to oppose the PPP's federal government.

President Bhutto now faced the unpalatible choice of either reinstating the NAP-JUI governments in the two provinces, or dissolve the provincial legislatures for fresh elections, or somehow manage to create new coalitions in the two provinces which would form the new governments. President Bhutto adopted the last option, and after considerable juggling created new governments in the NWFP and Baluchistan. Simultaneously, however, he opened negotiations with the opposition parties to achieve a constitutional consensus.

During the first week of April, 1973 the issue of provincial autonomy was resolved and by the time the Constitution was adopted, one could hear no more the outcry of the federal government's dictatorship over the provinces. Some differences remained between the opposition and the PPP in the Nation-

---

1   *The Pakistan Times*, (April 26, 1972).

al Assembly so that the opposition walked out and did not return to the National Assembly until April 11, 1973 when the Constitution was finally adopted.

On April 11 President Bhutto was to wind up the constitutional debate at 11:00 AM in the National Assembly but he did not enter the House until about 1:45 PM. Meanwhile, the Speaker of the House generously invited all back-benchers to make their speeches in order to kill the time. At 12:45 PM an aged leader of the opposition, Mr. Qazi Adil Abbasi, walked into the National Assembly signalling the achievement of a last minute compromise between the opposition and the PPP. Hardly had Qazi Adil Abbasi sat down when the Minister of Law and Parliamentary Affairs, Mr. Hafeez Peerzada, presented a few constitutional amendments for the adoption of the House. A few minutes later some more leaders of the opposition walked into the National Assembly amid loud cheers. Mr. Peerzada introduced some more amendments to the Constitution. Finally at 1:27 PM Mr. Wali Khan and Mr. Bizenjo entered the National Assembly, and were greeted with a thunderous applause. Mr. Peerzada once again introduced some more amendments. When the final vote was counted only three negative votes were cast by one Sindhi and two Punjabi legislators including President Bhutto's former Minister of Law, Mahmud Ali Qasuri.[1] With these three exceptions all members of the National Assembly signed the new Constitution and pledged allegiance to it.

All the amendments were procedural and they hardly touched the distribution of power between the provinces and the federal government, indicating that the issue of autonomy had been settled several weeks ago amicably between the opposition and the PPP. A few minutes before 2:00 PM, President Bhutto entered the National Assembly and made his concluding remarks about the Constitution, reiterating that from now on no polemic would be raised in Pakistan about the federal government's domination over the provinces.

Unlike the Constitutions of 1950 and 1962, the Constitution of 1973 faced the question of provincial autonomy squarely. The NAP and JUI, representing mostly the NWFP and Baluchistan, had expressed their apprehension of the Punjab's and Sindh's economic domination of the two smaller provinces. To allay their fears, a Council of Common Interest (Article 153) was created, consisting of the chief ministers of the four provinces and an equal number of members nominated by the federal government. This Council of Common Interest is to remove economic differences between the federating units and is responsible to the Parliament.

Distribution of water supplies, electricity and natural gas was also constitutionally settled. Any dispute involving these natural resources is subject to the Council of Common Interest's review (Article 155–158). Moreover, the Federal Government assumed the obligation not to deny any provincial government the right to construct and use broadcasting transmitters in the provinces. In any dispute involving this right the issue is to be determined by an arbitrator

---

1   Interestingly enough, as of April 1973, the three dissident legislators were members of the PPP.

appointed by the Chief Justice of Pakistan (Article 159). Parenthetically it may be added that most of these articles had been incorporated in the interim constitution of May, 1972.

The provincial autonomy guaranteed in the Constitution is one thing and autonomy practiced in political terms is entirely different. Maintaining decisive representational majorities in the National Assembly and in the legislatures of the Punjab and Sindh, the PPP can resolve political as well as economic tensions developing in the Punjab and Sindh. However, in the NWFP and Baluchistan, where the NAP-JUI still seem to retain a representational edge in the provincial legislatures over the ruling coalitions, the issue of autonomy assumes not a constitutional aspect, but a practical problem of relationship between the ruling political party and the opposition. To date the PPP and the JUI-NAP have not evolved any workable formula in the exercise of power. Until they do, the debate over autonomy would continue to be a divisive issue in Pakistan.

Bhutto's Foreign Policy, 1972-73

LAWRENCE ZIRING

Western Michigan University, Kalamazoo, U.S.A.

ZULFIKAR ALI BHUTTO's primary interest before becoming President of Pakistan on December 20, 1971 lay in the realm of foreign affairs. Nothing has happened since that dramatic date to indicate he is now less concerned with his country's external relations. While clearly preoccupied with domestic problems, President Bhutto continues to demonstrate an unusual appreciation for the international linkages that influence his programs and generally shape his national objectives. This brief essay aims at examining the key features of President Bhutto's current foreign policy, particularly those which suggest a style or nuance different from that displayed by his predecessors. After mentioning the latter, however, it is important to cite two facts. First, during his tenure as Pakistan's foreign minister in the Ayub Khan administration, Bhutto enjoyed wide latitude in establishing the framework for Pakistan's contemporary foreign policy. And second, Pakistan's foreign policy reflects a continuity with the past that is almost remarkable for its consistency. Hence it is to nuance that we look for a hint of change. It is this and the style of the principal decision-maker that may make Pakistan's foreign policy different from that of his predecessors, a change noticeable more in form than substance. Even a cursory reading of the main parameters of Pakistan's foreign policy assists in illuminating us on this point.

From that day in August, 1947, which marked Pakistan's emergence as a sovereign, independent state, to the time of this writing, Pakistani officialdom has been especially aware of the posturing, declarations, policies and actions of the Indian leaders. The contention always has been strongly held that India seeks to undermine, weaken and eventually destroy the Muslim state (Choudhury 1968; and Burke 1973). It is this conviction that has often kept opposed political groups from intensifying their disputes, and indeed, which provides post-1971 Pakistan with a tenuous equilibrium. Despite bitter political factionalism, strong efforts are underway to prevent a recurrence of the Bangladesh tragedy. As Anwar Syed (1972:27) has written: India "can subvert Pakistan only if Pakistanis, in large enough numbers, are dissatisfied with the prevailing political order. The East Pakistani secession has shown that Pakistan cannot be defended unless the people of her various regions are determined to remain together as one independent nation." While it cannot be ascertained whether provincial loyalties can be transcended, let alone how long inter-province rivalries can be contained, it is clear that Zulfikar Ali Bhutto's performance is predicated on maximizing fear of India in order to keep his detractors from further fractioning the state. At the same time, it is obvious that Bhutto cannot begin to control Pakistani regionalism if he is not prepared to yield to those pressures that it invariably produces (Malik, 1972; 1973).

Zulfikar Ali Bhutto: A Policy Overview

Of Bhutto's several publications, most important is his *The Myth of Independence* (1969). In it he traces Pakistan's external relations, particularly those relating to the major powers, and, with exceptional interest, relations with the United States. This treatise is the clearest delineation of Bhutto's philosophy, perceptions and attitude toward international affairs. Early in his career as a public official, Bhutto voiced disenchantment with Pakistan's almost total reliance on the United States. He was the first member of his generation to rise to a station of political significance, and it was from the platform made possible by these public offices that he publicized a view which veered away from the orthodoxy of the middle and late 1950's. That orthodoxy characterized Pakistan as the *sole* Asian country which the United States could truly depend upon, given the latter's interest in the containment of international communism.

From 1954 until the Sino-India border conflict in 1962, Pakistan's foreign policy began and terminated with the United States, and this proved to be more and more unpalatable to the seemingly more radical, younger generation. Thus as early as the Ayub coup in October 1958, this generation adopted Bhutto as their spokesman and go-between with higher authority. Bhutto's sudden rise to national notoriety was in part a consequence of the several ministerial portfolios he held in the Ayub administration. But a major factor in his skyrocketing popularity was his repeated attacks on the country's "unbalanced" foreign policy. Pakistan, he would argue, should cease posing threats to China and the Soviet Union. By supporting American fears of international communism Pakistan was adding to its list of immediate enemies without strengthening its defenses against India. Moreover, so long as Pakistan was wedded to the United States, it was handicapped in its relations with other Muslim states. Because of these widely broadcast beliefs, Bhutto assembled a large following. He attracted the educated young people, members of the professional intelligentsia, conservative and orthodox Muslims, and politicos with leftist tendencies. Furthermore, when the United States rushed military aid to India after its border skirmish with China in 1962, Bhutto's criticism of the United States was transformed into holy writ. And in the following year when Bhutto succeeded to the Foreign Minister's post, he insisted that the country must modify its long-standing foreign policy if it was to maintain its self respect while protecting itself from the machinations of Indian leaders, who, he declared, were emboldened by the receipt of military hardware from the United States.

Bhutto is credited with Pakistan's warm embrace of China although it is obvious that others before him had laid the foundation for the amicable relations that were to follow. Pakistan recognized the People's Republic in 1950, and Prime Minister H. S. Suhrawardy visited China after a similar visit to Pakistan by Chou En-lai in 1956–57. Foreign Ministers Manzoor Qadir and Mohammad Ali Bogra worked arduously with Bhutto to open commercial and cultural programs with China as well as the Soviet Union in 1960, and discussions on legalizing the border between Pakistan and China were initiated by these same individuals between 1961–62. Still, it was Zulfikar Ali Bhutto who received national acclaim for establishing Pakistan's independent foreign policy.

Bhutto was more vocal on the subject, he also had the foreign minister's portfolio passed to him at a fortuitous moment. Mohammad Ali Bogra's sudden death vaulted Bhutto into the Foreign Office somewhat prematurely. The transfer of American arms to India occurred over the opposition of the Ayub administration, and within months of Mahammad Ali's death. Pakistani anti-Americanism therefore was on the ascendant and Ayub Khan found it necessary to placate public opinion without rupturing Pakistan's relations with the United States. Bhutto was in the best position to satisfy popular sentiment, and in so doing, to help stabilize Ayub's administration.

Given these circumstances, it comes as no surprise that the Ayub-Bhutto relationship should shatter on the issue of foreign policy. Bhutto accompanied Ayub to Tashkent following the 1965 Indo-Pakistan War but the foreign minister disagreed with the terms of the declaration signed in that Soviet city. Although he told Ayub he wanted to leave the government, his resignation was held up for several months thereafter. Nonetheless, once free of governmental responsibilities, he joined other members of the opposition who were seeking to use the Tashkent issue, not only to discredit, but ultimately to bring Ayub Khan down. The failure of the United States to assist Pakistan in its trial with India in 1965 was grist for the mill of the opposition, and Bhutto's ambition was clearly expanded in the heat of the anti-Ayub campaign that followed. The fact that Zulfikar Ali Bhutto set about to organize his own Pakistan People's Party (PPP) rather than join a standing opposition party also illustrates his desire to draw his following into a political arrangement unencumbered by traditional, older political personalities. Over the years all other movements, parties and politicians had been stigmatized in one way or another, and Bhutto sensed that this was his opportunity to begin afresh and from the top.

Even Bhutto, however, could not have anticipated in the winter of 1969 when Ayub Khan's system crumbled, the circumstances whereby he would eventually succeed his erstwhile leader. The Yahya Khan interregnum, the election results of December 1970, and the tragedy of East Pakistan followed by the crucial encounter with India in December 1971, occured with such velocity that it is doubtful anyone on the scene at the time fully grasped the consequences of each daily event. Nevertheless, Bhutto's success at the polls in the December 1970 general election made him the dominant figure in what was then West Pakistan. Hence, when Yahya Khan accepted the India surrender terms, the only civilian with a "national" reputation as well as with the proper leadership credentials was Zulfikar Ali Bhutto. Moreover, the army had had its fill of frontline political leadership. Badly humiliated by Indian arms, it now sought to retire from the scene where it could lick its wounds and attempt the restoration of its once vaunted image. As President Bhutto now had the opportunity to shape Pakistan's foreign policy in his own likeness, this among other pressing affairs of state received his immediate attention.

Bhutto is a firm believer in the theory of interdependence. "World developments have now become so complex and interconnected that no important decision tolls the bell for one people alone." Pakistan, argues Bhutto, is caught up in a web of global proportions and its problems cannot be isolated from those of other nations, nor can these nations ignore what transpires within and against Pakistan. It is Bhutto's opinion that Pakistan's foreign relations can be divided into two segments; the pragmatic where the country is compelled to react to changing world currents, and the sentimental which ties it to a peculiar value system and hence fixed perceptions and preferences. These two segments interact with each other. One may dominate the other at any particular time, but nothing permanent should be concluded from this process. Thus Pakistan must practice, as Bhutto insists today, a "bilateral foreign policy" (Bhutto 1973a). Such an approach permits the country to relate equally to the United States, the Soviet Union, and the People's Republic of China. Bhutto prides himself on having promoted this policy before it was considered fashionable or feasible, and there is no gainsaying the fact that he feels vindicated given the intimate relations developed between the United States, the Soviet Union and China in the last eighteen months. Perhaps secretly, Bhutto senses that Henry Kissinger has stolen a page from his book. In an article in *Foreign Affairs* Bhutto writes:

> By maintaining friendly relations with all the great powers on the basis of principles and not expediency, Pakistan hopes to avoid involvement in disputes and struggles between them. It is part of our new policy that one should refrain from participating in multilateral pacts directed by one bloc of powers against another. Thus we have recently withdrawn from SEATO, in which Pakistan had in any case little part over the past few years. Bilateralism with the greater flexibility it implies will characterize our relations in the future (1973b: 552).

Bhutto cannot fail to recognize the role played by the Nixon administration during the 1971 hostilities with India. Nor can he fail to take advantage of the material assistance the United States is likely to make available to Pakistan in return for its friendship. Hence Bhutto's change of pace and termination of criticism toward the United States. Moreover, the United States is no longer judged an impediment to Pakistan's relations with the communist countries.

President Bhutto also stresses Pakistan's new geopolitical orientation at every opportunity. His country is clearly more intimately linked with Southwestern Asia. By contrast, Southeast Asia is only remotely identified with Pakistan's destiny. It is this Southwest Asian orientation that gives Pakistan a semblance of balance vis-a-vis the dominance of India in the subcontinent. Therefore, Pakistan looks even more fervently than before to Iran, Turkey and other Muslim states. Bhutto has declared that Pakistan is strategically situated at the head of the Arabian Sea and flanks the entrance to the oil-rich Persian Gulf. This means that Pakistan is important to Iran's security and possibly the security of the sheikhdoms along the Persian Gulf. Hence Iran can incrementally add to Pakistani strength vis-a-vis India, while a reasonably sound Pakistan is a significant asset to Iran. The reported plan of the Shah of Iran to purchase approximately two billion dollars in the latest military equipment from the United States, i.e., helicopter gunships, F-5E supersonic interceptors and F-4 fighter bombers, – and, possibly later, F-15 interceptors, would permit the Shah to transfer older weapons, including aircraft to Pakistan. There is also no reason to believe that the United States government would not encourage such a program given the Nixon Doctrine's emphasis of regional self-defense.

As much as Bhutto may wish to publicize the independence of Pakistan's foreign policy, therefore, sincerity notwithstanding, no degree of rhetoric can disentangle the country from a web of global plays and counterplays. South Asia, like other regions of the world, has been made the interest of the major powers and neither Pakistan nor its large and menacing neighbor can ignore or avoid this reality. The Indo-Pakistan War of 1971 clearly placed the United States and the Soviet Union on opposite sides and neither the subsequent visitations by President Nixon and Secretary Brezhnev or the large emphasis placed upon *detente* between their two countries will alter the pattern of rivalry and confrontation in the vicinity of the Indian Ocean and the Persian Gulf. The Soviet Union has historic interests in the area, and it can only pursue them at the present time by undermining the United States twenty-five year association with India. This is not to suggest that the United States has not supplied the Soviet Union with an opportunity to maximize its friendship with India. The United States decision to support Pakistan at the expense of India in the Bangladesh affair was made demonstrably clear when the aircraft carrier U.S.S. Enterprise sailed into the Bay of Bengal. Moreover, the secret documents passed and later published by the columnist Jack Anderson only tended to dramatize in a personal way what was already clear in general terms.

Before the winter of 1971 the United States had managed a delicate equilibrium between the principal antagonists in the region, allying with one side while simultaneously assisting the other. The tragedy that erupted in Bengal shattered this gymnastic diplomatic act, however, and the consequences were not only detrimental to the United States promoted status quo, they also had direct bearing on the degree of latitude open to the indigenous policy-makers. In Pakistan's case, Zulfikar Ali Bhutto may be more, not less, susceptible to major power maneuver; even though he might prove to be less constrained by formal international arrangements.

On January 28, 1972, approximately five weeks after assuming office,

Bhutto addressed his nation on the occasion of the Muslim festival day of Id-ul-Azha. The President was determined not to share in the traditional happiness that marked the day. His words were solemn and remindful of what had befallen the country in the previous month. "We have lost our honor and we have suffered national humiliation," was his theme (Bhutto 1972). Bhutto had just returned from a whirlwind tour to eight Middle East and North African countries. His itinerary included Iran, Turkey, Morocco, Algeria, Tunisia, Libya, Egypt and Syria.[1] On the one hand, such visits aimed at reassuring Pakistan's close and marginal friends that the country was repairing the damage done by the war, and under new leadership was dedicated to playing a significant role in world politics. On the other hand, the country needed a boost in its confidence and the new government sensed that such travels would assist in this effort. On January 30 President Bhutto carried this latter point a step further. Dramatizing his administration's "new" foreign policy, Bhutto revealed he was taking Pakistan out of the Commonwealth. The President's action was prompted by the decision of Great Britain, Australia and New Zealand to recognize the Bangladesh government. In fact, Bhutto called his action "an appropriate countermeasure" (*New York Times*, January 13, 1972). At the same time he revealed that normal bilateral relations would continue between Pakistan and the countries involved. After adding that relations with Britain remained cordial, Bhutto commented that "national honor is more important than pounds, shillings and pence" (*Ibid*). Thus, struggling to restore a sense of well-being to a demoralized population, Bhutto, through his actions and foreign tours, linked Pakistanis with their Muslim brethren in other lands. By breaking with the Commonwealth, he seemed to be cutting Pakistan free of its colonial past. In the latter, Pakistan was thought to be giving up little material advantage. Britain's entry into the Common Market transformed the Commonwealth into little more than an historic relic and the economic value of the organization was judged to be minimal. Taken together, the Middle East tour and the severance of Commonwealth ties aimed at giving the Pakistani people pride in themselves and their new government.

Bhutto's next foreign journey was arranged to reinforce this initial effort. Bhutto visited the People's Republic of China on February 1 and 2, 1972, and on the former date he had a publicized audience with Chairman Mao Tse-tung. Bhutto's visit to China had more than ceremonial significance, however. The President was seeking military stores needed to replenish the Pakistan armed forces, and Premier Chou En-lai's statement that the Chinese were not "ammunition merchants" but would meet Pakistan's defense needs on a gratis basis was considered a very friendly gesture. More important at the moment

---

1 In May, Bhutto would make an even more extensive journey visiting fourteen countries in the Middle East and Africa. They were: Kuwait, The Union of Arab Emirates, Iraq, Lebanon, Jordan, Saudi Arabia, Somalia, Ethiopia, Sudan, Nigeria, Guinea, Mauritania, Turkey and Iran. Bhutto did not visit Afghanistan, Pakistan's northwestern Muslim neighbor, in either journey. A discussion of Pakistan-Afghanistan relations will be found below.

though was China's decision to cancel a $ 110,000,000 debt growing out of the 1965 Indo-Pakistan War while deferring for twenty years the repayment of a $ 200,000,000 loan made in 1970. China also put India on notice that there would be no peace in the subcontinent until all Pakistani territories were evacuated. Nonetheless, there was only the hint that China was going to forward new military supplies to Pakistan, but an understanding to this effect is found in the communique following the visit. Moreover, the Chinese were less fulsome in their condemnation of India as well as their warnings to that country. It need only be recalled that Chi Peng-fei, the Chinese Foreign Minister assured the Pakistani nation in November, 1971, only weeks before the Indian attack, that his government would "resolutely support them in their just struggle to defend their State sovereignty and national independence" (*Pakistan News Digest*, November 15, 1971). Chinese declarations, however, are not always measured by subsequent actions.

President Bhutto's visit to the Soviet Union followed in mid-March, 1972, despite the role played by that communist state in the events of 1971. Bhutto made the trip in order to demonstrate his neutrality vis-a-vis the great powers. Although little of substance emanated from his talks with Soviet leadership, it was agreed in principle to restore economic relations damaged by the war. Another aspect of the visit, however, was Bhutto's projected summit meeting with the Indian Prime Minister, Madame Gandhi. Bhutto wanted to lay Pakistan's case before the Soviet leaders prior to meeting with Madame Gandhi. By so doing it was hoped the Soviet Union would use its influence to resolve some of the larger issues, such as the return of the 93,000 prisoners captured in East Pakistan by the Indian army.

Although Bhutto did not visit the United States during his first year in office, relations with the United States were warm and constructive. On March 30, 1972 an agreement was signed in Islamabad which pledged the United States to continue funding the development of the Indus Basin Hydro-Electric Project. The project underway since 1961 at a cost of two and a half billion dollars is scheduled for completion in 1976, with the United States providing approximately 40 percent of the total financing. The American Charge d'Affaires noted the project helped strengthen the bonds existing between the two countries.[1]

While Pakistan's external fences were being mended and reinforced, the domestic scene was also receiving considerable attention. Of crucial importance in this period was the presidential order lifting martial law and the call to the National Assembly to adopt an Interim Constitution. Both were accomplished between April 17 and 21. The National Assembly also proceeded with the establishment of a committee to draft the new permanent constitution and the date of August 14, 1973 was targeted for its promulgation. President Bhutto also used the occasion to sum up his administration's work in both the domestic

---

1   The United States did not appoint an ambassador to Pakistan until December 1973.

and foreign fields. After noting that the country was stable and beginning to raise itself out of the rubble of the 1971 war, he turned to the subject of foreign policy.

In this section of his speech President Bhutto alluded to his upcoming talks with Madame Gandhi and reiterated a stand he had taken long before his assumption of the President's office. He cited many outstanding differences with India and that Pakistan sought the return of its territory as well as those captured in the war. But he insisted there would be no yielding to a "dictated, imposed peace." He also singled out the Muslim bloc of nations, China and the United States as having demonstrated the greatest friendship toward Pakistan. And so as to give more meaning to this remark, President Bhutto placed Pakistan's policy in its new geopolitical setting:

> The severance of our eastern limb by force has significantly altered our geographic focus. This will naturally affect our geopolitical perspective. The geographical distance between us and the nations of South East Asia has grown. This does not mean that we have lost interest in the welfare of these peoples. Nevertheless, at the moment, as we stand, it is within the ambit of South and Western Asia. It is here that our primary concern must henceforth lie.

> There is the whole uninterrupted belt of Muslim nations ... Clearly we have to make a major effort in building upon the fraternal ties that already bind us to the Muslim world (*Pakistan Affairs*, May 16, 1972).

Pakistan has always looked to the Muslim states for support and encouragement but it is only with Iran and Turkey that it has managed to develop full-blown relationships. First, through the Central Treaty Organization, and, since 1964, with the help of the Regional Cooperation for Development (RCD) – Turkey, Iran and Pakistan, it has engaged in a variety of economic, cultural and military ventures. There is no avoiding the importance of Pakistan to Iran and vice versa and the turbulence on their shared border in Baluchistan is of great concern to both countries. There is also no ignoring the Shah of Iran's alleged fears that the next breakaway nationalist movement may be found in Baluchistan. Despite an outward appearance of friendship toward the Soviet Union, there is the strong belief that the Soviet Union seeks the "liberation" of Baluchistan from both Pakistani and Iranian rule. The Shah is reported in the *Christian Science Monitor* of February 2, 1973, as having "told visitors that Iran would react energetically if Pakistan were threatened with internal breakdown," particularly in proximity to its own frontiers. The seriousness with which the two leaders view the situation can be gauged by the numerous visits that they make between each other's capitals.[1] The joint communique issued on May 14, 1973, for instance, declares that both President Bhutto and the Shah of

---

1 According to the *Christian Science Monitor* "Members of the Shah's government... use the Baluchi argument as one justification for the huge buildup of Iranian military and naval forces in the Persian Gulf and the establishment of two naval bases at Chah Bahar and Jask, on the Indian Ocean." February 2, 1973.

Iran would resolutely stand by each other in all matters bearing on their national independence and territorial integrity."

The troubles in Baluchistan and on Pakistan's frontiers in general were heightened when the Bhutto government revealed that Soviet arms had been smuggled into the country and secreted in the Iraqi Embassy at Islamabad. It was further reported that security agents had discovered copies of a map showing a liberated Baluchi state that stretched from the Soviet border in Iran's northeast province of Khorassan to the Persian Gulf. India has also been implicated in this plot but has denied such allegations (*India News*, July 6, 1973 and July 13, 1973). Baluchi nationalism has its roots in the 1950's but remained inchoate until 1971. The use of Pakistani troops against tribal factions in this vast, desert-like region also has a long history, but the fact that the Army is being utilized at this time must be considered significant. A World Baluchi Organization organized by Mahmoud Hisham Sindjari, and the Baluch Warna, a more radical group under the leadership of Akbar Khan Bugti, were both formed in 1972. Each organization insists on creating a unified, independent and sovereign Baluchi nation, and both appear to have ties to the Baluchistan Liberation Front which operates clandestinely in Iran.

As noted in the beginning of this essay, Pakistan's future may well rest on its ability to cope with dissident provincialists. Military force is not the sole answer, both Iran and Pakistan understand this simple fact. Joint economic projects in the vicinity of the Pakistan-Iranian frontier can be anticipated in a concerted effort to come to grips with the problem. Still, it is not extraordinary that the Pakistan government should announce a large defense budget for the fiscal year 1972–73. The report stressed that approximately 60 percent of all government revenues would be used for refurbishing the armed forces. Of a total budget of 7.43 billion rupees, military spending was anticipated to be in excess of 4.46 billion (*New York Times*, June 18, 1972). With such an outlay for defense it was more than obvious that Pakistan would have to look to its more affluent friends and allies in order to fund its development programs. In this context the United Sates, China, and Iran were envisaged as playing important roles.[1]

The Afghanistan Dilemma

Pakistan and Afghanistan have never been especially friendly. The history of their antagonism is traced from the independence of Pakistan in 1947. Afghanistan did not accept the Durand Line (1893) which established the frontier between the two states and has promoted the creation of a separate

---

1   The Pakistan government labeled all reports that their defense budget was the largest
    ever as "tendentious." It went on to cite the following: "During the last fiscal year
    Pakistan earmarked $ 714 million for defense at the devaluation rate as compared to a
    defense provision in the new budget of $ 402 million. As for allocations in the develop-
    mental sector, the budget makes plain that the exceptional circumstances of the past

Pathan state in the region of Pakistan's North West Frontier Province since that date. The would-be state that the Afghans call "Pakhtunistan," and the movement organized in its behalf has caused the two countries to clash militarily. Border skirmishes have been numerous, with the last serious altercations occurring in the early 1960's. Unlike India and Pakistan, however, Pakistan and Afghanistan have avoided major engagements. Relations between the two countries, therefore, have run between poor and lukewarm. And the neighboring states continue to eye one another suspiciously.

It must be emphasized that Pakistan, more so than Afghanistan, has sought to improve relations. Afghanistan has ignored all Pakistani overtures, turning them aside on the theory that Pakistan is not a free agent and seeks to embroil the land-locked state in a struggle with tne great powers. It is for this reason that Afghanistan not only refused to join the Baghdad Pact (CENTO) in 1955, but was among the first to condemn it. Even the Regional Cooperation for Development (RCD) was judged an instrument of the United States, and Afghanistan has never shown the slightest inclination in joining that organization. It may also be recalled that Afghanistan cast the only vote against Pakistan's admission to the United Nations in 1950. It is against this background that Pakistani-Afghan relations must be evaluated, and the recent developments in Afghanistan which witnessed the overthrow of King Zahir Shah and the return to power of his cousin, Sardar Daoud, point to intensified and not diminishing tension.

If the difficulties in Pakistan's Baluchistan province and Iranian Baluchistan are in any way related to the policy of the Soviet Union, then the re-establishment of Sardar Daoud's power in Afghanistan must be considered ominous. Daoud was the power behind the throne between 1953 and 1963 and perhaps the most vocal proponent of "Pakhtunistan." In 1954, through Daoud's efforts, Afghanistan became the first Muslim country to receive Soviet military

year notwithstanding, Pakistan is determined to press ahead with its program of economic development."

Revenue Expenditure

	1971–72 Budget	1971–72 Budget Revised	1972–73 Rs. in crores Budget
Rev. Collecting Depts.	7.72	5.77	5.30
Debt Service	128.96	156.78	193.56
Civil Admin.	80.56	78.29	90.35
Defense	340.00	426.00	423.00
Grants to Provinces	18.48	25.20	3.98
Others	29.96	25.86	28.85
Total	605.23	717.90	743.44

Source: *Interim Report Series* Pakistan's Fourth Five Year Plan, 1970–75, Vo., 14, No. 9, July-August 1972.

assistance. (Egypt was to receive its first arms shipments in 1955). In 1955 the Soviet leaders visited Kabul and extended long-range economic aid and renewed a treaty of nonaggression. Afghanistan also received military and economic development aid from the United States, and the latter is still continued. In 1956 Daoud signed still another agreement which brought Afghanistan jet aircraft as well as heavy armor and artillery. As a result, both United States and Turkish military assistance was phased out. Soviet advisors replaced both and the Afghan army almost doubled its size, approaching approximately 100,000. Senior Army officers and rank-and-file elements were recruited from the tribal population, namely the Hazaras, Pathans, Uzbeks and Tajiks. Daoud's influence among the undisciplined tribal people was unquestioned. And as he modernized the Afghan army with Soviet assistance, these same tribes became less troublesome for the ruling elite in Kabul. Relative peace among the tribes provided the more sophisticated urban population with new political opportunities.

Although small in size, Afghanistan's intelligentsia in the capital began to assert itself in the early 1960s and their insistence on political reform apparently convinced King Zahir Shah that the medieval political family system was no longer fashionable. The same reform gave the King a chance to rid himself of Daoud's shadow. Hence, Daoud was dismissed from his post and a commoner made Prime Minister. A new constitution was put into force in 1964–65, and Article 24 clearly specified that no member of the royal family could participate in political parties, hold ministerial offices or obtain seats in the parliament or supreme court (Weinbaum, 1972). Daoud did not fight the King's action and accepted the new constitutional order despite his continuing control over the tribal people and Army.

Daoud looked on as Afghanistan fumbled with its new parliamentary experiment. The King still refused to yield his personal power and governments rose and fell with frequent abandon. Riots involving the intelligentsia, particularly the student population of Kabul, were common and by 1969 conservative elements gained control of the parliament. Governmental corruption and inefficiency became especially pronounced when the country was seized by drought and famine conditions took a heavy toll of life. Moreover, the King had promised to establish a political party system but kept postponing the implementation of the proposal. Thus when Zahir Shah departed the country for medical treatment, public discontent was rampant and the scene was set for a dramatic change.

On July 17, 1973, King Zahir Shah was deposed, the monarchy was abolished and Prince Daoud proclaimed the country a republic.[1] It is note-

---

1 ["The King of Afghanistan, Mohammad Zahir Shah, announced his abdication in a statement issued by the Afghan Embassy in Rome. The King was deposed last month while he was visiting Italy.

"In the statement, the 59-year-old former monarch said he would 'abide by the wishes of the people' of his country who had 'welcomed the establishment of a republican regime as their future form of government.' In addition, he said he was placing himself 'as an Afghan citizen under the banner of Afghanistan.' " He did not indicate whether he would live in exile or go home (*New York Times*, August 25, 1973). Ed.]

Table 1

Horizontal Social Groups in Afghanistan

Horizontal Group	Number	Identity	Vertical Element Included in Horizontal Group
1. Elite	2–3 thousand	Royal family Top government officials Wealthy merchants Large landowners Tribal chiefs	Pathans-Sunnis
2. Intelligentsia	8–10 thousand	High government employees Professional men Teachers, students Literati Top religious leaders Army officers	Pathans, Tajik-Sunni but, some Shia Qizilbash
3. Urban Middle Class	800,000 to 1,000,000	Lower civil servants Shopkeepers Scribes Accountants Artisans Literate religious leaders, etc.	Tajiks, Uzbeks, Pathans, some Turkomen and Hazaras
4. Lower Classes a. Urban	8 million		
1. Proletariat	20,000	Factory and semi-skilled workers	Tajiks, Hazaras, Pathans
2. Military, Police, etc.	40,000	Enlisted men in Armed Forces, Police, gendarmerie	Tajiks, Hazaras, Uzbeks, Turkomen
b. Rural			
1. Cultivators	7 million	Small landowners, peasants and semi-nomads	Pathans, Tajiks, Uzbeks, Hazaras
2. Nomads	200,000	Pure nomads, nonculti-vators	Pathans, Turkomen

Note: Population figures are estimates.
Source: "Afghanistan" *An Asia Society Paper*, January, 1963, P. 5.

worthy that Daoud put aside his royal title and assumed the leadership of the country as a Lieutenant General in the Afghan army. Daoud felt compelled to issue a statement on July 25 that the Soviet Union had nothing to do with the coup d'etat. Rumors were already circulating that the Soviet Union had engineered the plot against the King and that Daoud would not hesitate to heat up the "Pakhtunistan" issue with Pakistan. In this context, it is interesting to note that the Soviet Union and India recognized the new Republic on July 19th. Pakistan followed on July 22nd.

Pakistan's early recognition of the Daoud government did not transform Afghanistan into an instant friend. Pakistan's immediate domestic political problems lay along her western frontier. President Bhutto has virtually no power in this heavily tribal belt and he defers to local leadership that does not reflect his Pakistan People's Party interest. Thus when General Daoud announced on July 29th that Afghanistan's "political dispute" with Pakistan is "unresolved," Bhutto could not remain silent or pretend friendship. He is quoted as saying: "The claim for a new state is not new. We have lived with it in the past. But if, God forbid, certain developments should put a strain on our relations, we are quite capable of looking after our national interests" (*New York Times*, August 2, 1973).

Barring Soviet intervention Pakistan should be able to cope with a possible threat from Afghanistan. But the picture is made complicated by the role that India might choose to play, and above all, by the uncertain loyalties of the tribal population, and especially its leadership in the North West Frontier Province. Should the latter decide to join Daoud in a joint endeavor against Bhutto, and should the Baluchistan situation worsen at the same time, Pakistan's future, to say nothing about Bhutto's would be in grave jeopardy. Iran, as already noted, could play a role in such a scenario. A conflict would also indirectly involve the United States. The situation at this writing therefore must be considered fluid. If Daoud is bent on pressing his claim to "Pakhtunistan" Bhutto's new Pakistan could face its most severe test.

India and the Simla Conference

The summit meeting between President Bhutto and Prime Minister Gandhi was slated for June 28, 1972. It was the first face-to-face meeting between the leaders of India and Pakistan since the Tashkent Conference and which Bhutto had attended in his capacity as foreign minister in the Ayub Khan government. Tashkent became a symbol of Ayub's weakness and was ironically exploited by Bhutto in his rise to political power. Now, however, it was Bhutto's turn to meet with Indian leadership, and he was careful to protect himself from his indigenous adversaries who might seek to use the earlier precedent for their own advantage. Granted, Bhutto's situation was not the same as Ayub Khan's when he had met with Indian Prime Minister, Lal Bahadur Shastri. Ayub had led Pakistan into the war with India and it was also he who had decided to lead the country out of it. Bhutto, on the other hand, came to power after a decisive military defeat, and he was not associated with that decision-making process. Bhutto, therefore, could negotiate from a base of political support which Auyb did not enjoy. All the same, Bhutto did not take any chances. Addressing the nation on the eve of his departure, he reiterated the need and his desire for peace but he steadfastly adhered to specific principles. Pakistan, he declared, wants the prisoners returned, its territory restored in the Sind and Punjab, and a solution to the Kashmir problem.

Before this speech the prisoner issue had been among the less prominent concerns expressed by the Pakistan government. But as the months dragged on and the Indians refused to release the POW's, and indeed when it appeared that a number of them would be placed on trial for war crimes in Bangladesh, the Pakistan government could no longer pretend that they were a lesser matter. Time apparently was not on Pakistan's side in this dispute. And despite the material cost, not to ignore the cost in prestige, the Indians were determined to use the prisoners as a major chip in their negotiations. Nevertheless, it seems reasonable to assume that Bhutto felt this was an issue that could be resolved at the summit.

At Simla, President Bhutto was disturbed to find the Indians determined to secure a "No-War" pledge and a formal treaty of "non-aggression" before agreeing to any Pakistani demands. He was sensitive to the interpretation that his opposition could give to such a pact, but perhaps more important, he could not afford to antagonize the armed forces against whom such a treaty would be directed. A treaty of nonaggression might well include articles calling for a mutual reduction in forces which the Pakistan military would not accept. In the opinion of high army officials such an agreement would also mean Pakistan must disengage itself from Kashmir, an unthinkable thought even in the country's current state. Hence Bhutto was compelled to reject even a simple declaration to the affect that Pakistan would resolve never to go to war with India again. It might be noted that the last "No-War" pact between the two countries was signed in 1950. It has been alleged that as a consequence of that act the then Prime Minister, Liaquat Ali Khan, faced a challenge from his military hierarchy, the affair being known as the Rawalpindi Conspiracy. Bhutto had no intention of testing his popularity by accepting such terms from Indira Gandhi.

The Simla talks lasted five days and an accord was signed and publicized, but neither side viewed it with much enthusiasm. In the concrete areas of the accord the following are noted:

Steps shall be taken to resume communications, postal, telegraphic, sea, land, including border posts, and air links, including overflights.

Appropriate steps shall be taken to promote travel facilities for the nationals of the other country.

Trade and cooperation in economic and other agreed fields will be resumed as far as possible.

Exchange in the fields of science and culture will be promoted. In this connection delegations from the two countries will meet from time to time to work out the necessary details.

Indian and Pakistani forces shall be withdrawn to their side of the international border.

In Jammu and Kashmir, the line of control resulting from the cease-fire of December 17

1971, shall be respected by both sides without prejudice to the recognized position of either side. Neither side shall seek to alter it unilaterally, irrespective of mutual differences and legal interpretations. Both sides further undertake to refrain from the threat or the use of force in violation of this line (*New York Times*, July 3, 1972).

The withdrawal of forces noted in the accords was to take place within thirty days following ratification by the appropriate national organs. The question of ratification pointed to President Bhutto's pledge upon entering the talks that he would not impose a settlement on his country. Hence the Pakistan National Assembly met on July 15, ratified the agreement, and legitimated the actions of their President.

The Simla accord did not satisfy India's desire for a "No-War" agreement. Nor did Bhutto agree to recognize Bangladesh. On the Indian side, there was no urgency to release the Pakistani prisoners or to prevent the Bangladesh government from putting a significant number on trial. Moreover, the Kashmir clause did not satisfy Bhutto's continued call that "self-determination" be granted the people of the mountain state.[1] But even the one significant agreement, namely, the withdrawal of forces could not be satisfied according to the agreed schedule. It was not until December that this latter issue was finally resolved. The inordinate delay created new tensions between the two antagonists and whatever goodwill may have been created by the Simla talks was quickly dissipated. Thus the second summit which would have brought Madame Gandhi to Pakistan was put off indefinitely, and the prisoner issue was permitted to fester.

Bilateral and Multilateral Relations

As noted above Bhutto has had to work with a legacy that is not easily transformed. Among other things, he inherited a variety of associations and alliances which in his judgment required a more systematic appraisal of their value and continuing utility. If Bhutto was going to assure China and the Soviet Union that Pakistan did not represent a threat to them while at the same time remaining in the good graces of the United States, it was certainly necessary to steer a middle course between them. Hence the only alliance which Pakistan publicizes is the one which does not involve any of the great powers. This grouping, known as the Regional Cooperation for Development (RCD), was formed in the summer of 1964 between Pakistan, Iran and Turkey. Zulfikar Ali Bhutto was foreign minister at the time and in a speech at the Fifteenth Ministerial Council Meeting of RCD in Izmir, Turkey, on April 7,

---

1 The settlement finally thrashed out on December 7, 1972, made the existent "line of control" in Kashmir a firm boundary for the indefinite future. It is ironic that the very arrangement which Ayub Khan agreed to at Tashkent in January, 1966, and which Bhutto disputed so vehemently, was now an accepted fact. See the author's *The Ayub Khan Era: Politics in Pakistan, 1958–1969*, Syracuse: Syracuse University Press, 1971, pp. 50–113.

1972, Mahmud Ali Kasuri, the then Pakistan Law Minister, identified the President as one of the principal architects of the alliance.

RCD does not address itself to political union. Nor is military affairs a focal point of RCD's deliberations. Rather, RCD continues to represent a group of nation-states having geographical contiguity, harmonious political relations and the mutual desire to improve their economic performance. RCD is an alliance without anger; it is directed at no particular state or states and is relatively free of military encumbrances. RCD focuses specific and exclusive attention upon the positive goals of furthering understanding and generating material progress within the region. Its existence helps to stabilize and ensure the friendly relations now obtaining between the three countries. It is also a further reminder that economic development can be accelerated if nations can find a way to cooperate rather than antagonize one another.

RCD can best be described as an Asian mini-Common Market (Bhutto, 1973). The organization has a complex structure and various components meet on a continuing basis for economic, cultural and informational purposes. It was only in September, 1972, however, that the three countries seriously considered an agreement aiming at the liberalization of trade through the removal of all national barriers.

Bilateral economic and cultural activities with other countries have reinforced this RCD initiative. On October 18, 1972, Pakistan and the United States entered into an agreement extending the work of the United States Education Foundation in Pakistan (USEF/P). A similar cultural and scientific pact was signed with Rumania. In the economic area agreements were completed with Japan, Yugoslavia, Great Britain, France, Italy, the Netherlands, Norway and the Federal Republic of Germany. All were concerned with the rescheduling of debts, or the acquisition of new loans to ease Pakistan over 1972–73.

On November 8, 1972, the Bhutto government took a more celebrated step when it formally announced its decision to withdraw from the South East Asia Treaty Organization (SEATO). The very next day the Pakistan foreign office declared it would recognize the Democratic Republic of Vietnam, and, two days later, the Democratic People's Republic of Korea. Later in the year, East Germany was also recognized. These announcements, taken together, were described by the Pakistan government as a watershed in the country's foreign relations. Although nothing sinister lay behind the decisions, they are of special importance and deserve limited analysis.

President Bhutto was on record since 1962 as having less than genuine interest in Pakistan's western alliances (Bhutto, 1964; 1966; 1969). CENTO in addition to SEATO has been linked with the foreign policy position of the United States, and member states such as Iran and Turkey were pressured by President Johnson to refrain from aiding Pakistan in its war with India in 1965. On numerous occasions, and prior to his becoming President, Bhutto called upon the Pakistan government to withdraw from the alliances. That SEATO, therefore, was considered ripe for cutting is not surprising in the circumstances.

President Bhutto is said to have informed the United States that his country would leave SEATO at an appropriate moment. When that moment did come Pakistan acted within the limits specified under Article 10 of the Treaty and hence did not move rashly. It was also obvious that SEATO ceased to encompass Pakistan after the severing of its eastern wing, and the emergence of the new state of Bangladesh. Pakistan was now geographically removed from Southeast Asia and Bhutto earlier in the year had taken pains to explain that Pakistan's concern would be with South and South West Asia. Moreover, SEATO was organized in 1954 at the urging of the Eisenhower-Dulles administration following the Geneva Accords which ended the French struggle in Indochina. It was intended to put the Chinese on notice that their attempts at penetration of Southeast Asia would be met by the combined forces of the nations of the area, but essentially by the United States.

The alliance, however, was a constant embarrassment to Pakistani leadership which sought to normalize relations with China. Nevertheless, all thought about taking Pakistan out of the alliance had to be weighed against the cost in relations with the United States. Neither Ayub Khan nor Yahya Khan felt they had the clear opportunity to make such a break and yet Zulfikar Ali Bhutto could proceed without fear of serious repercussions. With the United States involvement in Indochina winding down, with Washington-Peking relations established and being nourished, and with Pakistan no longer identified with Southeast Asia, such a decision proved not only painless but perfectly reasonable. Thus when the United States, the Philippines and Thailand all recognized Bangladesh there was no longer a need to sustain the relationship. Furthermore, SEATO countries failed to aid Pakistan either in the 1965 or the more recent 1971 war with India. The utility of the organization to Pakistan had proven to be non-existent.

With this action Pakistan also put all the major powers on notice that it would no longer consider new military alliances as relevant for its requirements. Hence the Soviet Union's pressing of an Asian security pact was taken note of but was to be carefully avoided by the Pakistan government. Pakistan's ties to CENTO are still heavily military but the country is linked with that organization because its principal neighbors, Iran and Turkey, have shown no indication of quitting. The three countries, and particularly Iran and Pakistan as we have seen, are dependent on one another for defensive purposes and in the present unpredictable situation neither country is prepared to take unilateral action simply out of principle. In other works, judged on the basis of cost-benefit analysis, Pakistan needs CENTO and Bhutto is not about to follow the SEATO decision with a like determination. The Middle East, and, in particular, the Persian Gulf, is the most strategic region in terms of great power rivalry in the world today. Moreover, United States national security policy stresses open sea lanes and resource access, and Pakistan is viewed as playing an essential role in this regard. If Pakistan can expect to receive military assistance from the United States it will be with this understanding. At the same time, Pakistan insists on maintaining friendly relations with the Soviet Union. The latter,

however, will also be on notice that its intimacy with India is a prime consideration in their future relationships.

On balance, then, Pakistan's foreign relations will be pursued on a country-
by-country basis with the possible exception of the RCD arrangement. The
United States and China will be treated somewhat equally and efforts will be
made to satisfy the Soviet Union that Pakistan poses no threat to it. But the
relationship with the Soviet Union must be on a different level from that of the
other major powers given that state's support of India. This also means that
Pakistan's principal source of aid in both military and economic spheres will
have to come from the United States, with China supplementing what it can.
Unfortunately, however, Bhutto's reasonably good relations with the Nixon
administration may not be sufficient to satisfy his government's requirements
for assistance, given the low esteem in which Pakistan is held in the United
States Congress. Cuts in Nixon's foreign aid program for 1973–74 do not augur
well for Pakistan. Sufficient residual ill-will exists in the Congress toward
Pakistan to make the likelihood of large-scale assistance most unpromising.

Nor can Bhutto threaten to move closer to China, or indeed to become
more familiar with the Soviet Union. It is difficult to envisage Pakistan being
any closer to China than it is at present. China is not about to take up the
Pakistan cause with India in any fashion different from that followed in the
last eight years. And relations with the Soviet Union are regulated by perceptions of India. Certainly the Soviet Union has more to gain by maximizing its
advantages in India than in Pakistan. And again, Pakistan is linked ever more
closely with Iran and that middle eastern country is not about to alter its
relations with the United States so long as the Shah remains the master of the
political situation.[1]

Pakistan and Bangladesh

Pakistan's relations with Bangladesh remain strained and somewhat
obscure. President Bhutto's release of and assistance in returning Sheikh Muji-
bur Rahman to Dacca has not been reciprocated by the Bangladeshi authorities.
On the contrary, Bhutto has been charged with sheltering ulterior motives. It is
alleged that he seeks a working confederation with Bangladesh, prior to re-
absorbing the east wing into the Pakistan union. The Bangladeshis have therefore turned aside all such suggestions as unrealistic and tantamount to sub-

---

1 Hartirath Singh, editor of the Foreign Trade Review, an Indian publication, is quoted
   as having said: "The meteoric increase in the Iranian armaments has caused tremors of
   anxiety in India. The hazy picture that seems to be emerging—perhaps in the not-too-
   distant future—is one of China-United States-Pakistan-Iran axis." Such rumors as well
   as one in Pakistan insists the Indians and Iraqis are conspiring against both Pakistan
   and Iran by provoking the Baluchi independence movement (*The New York Times,* July 5,
   1973).

verting the nation's independence. It is also important to note that Pakistan continues to direct broadcasts to Bangladesh as well as report the plight of that society since the Indian invasion. Moreover, Pakistan has issued no definitive statement sanctioning or recognizing the separation of a sovereign, independent Bangladesh. Pakistan, with China's help, has also blocked Bangladesh's admission into the United Nations.

The justification for preventing the Bangladesh government from taking its seat in the United Nations remains the prisoner of war issue and the threats to their well-being. So long as Bangladesh insists on retaining and putting on trial some POW's as war criminals, the Bhutto administration refuses to accept the existence of Bangladesh, let alone permit it a seat in the UN. To illustrate this problem there is the statement by Bhutto during a press conference on December 20, 1972. The President explained that many Pakistanis oppose recognition and given the alleged severe treatment of the POW's they were calling upon him "to beat the life out of the Bengalis" living in Pakistan. "Yet they [the Pakistanis] say they can't abandon their brothers. If they're your brothers why the hell are you badgering me to knock the hell out of them here?" When a query followed about the 300,000 Bengalis living in Pakistan being returned to Bangladesh, Bhutto is reported to have replied: "The point is, I don't want to use them as a lever, but if they [Bangladesh] are going to keep our people – 90,000 – and give all sorts of unreasonable and unethical arguments for it, I can't just keep on unilaterally making one gesture after another" (*Pakistan Affairs*, January 1, 1973). In a later interview Bhutto voiced the fear that if trials of Pakistanis are held in Bangladesh, his army would demand that trials be held in Pakistan of Bengalis who are accused of conspiring against the government and nation.

The difficulties in overcoming this impasse are obvious. Neither the Bangladesh or Pakistan governments are strong enough to act independently of their constituents. Mujib was released as Bhutto himself has remarked, while his country was in a "stupor." Had he delayed taking this action it would have been impossible in the circumstances that followed – or so it would seem. Bhutto has since offered to send more than 300,000 tons of rice to the food-short state but Bangladesh has refused to accept this largesse. Suggestions that the Bengali population in Pakistan be exchanged for the POW's have likewise been rejected. In fact, Bangladesh, according to Pakistani authorities, has not indicated they are prepared to negotiate with Pakistan on any terms suggesting mutual compromise. Hence, if a breakthrough is to be achieved, it is India that will have to lead the way. Thus far, however, India is reluctant to force Mujib's hand, possibly fearing that by so doing the Bangladesh leader would lose the much needed support of his followers. The consequences of Mujib's fall could force the Indians either to take more forceful action in Bangladesh or allow for the emergence of a government which might not be in India's best interest. It is not to be concluded that a new Bangladesh government would be any more friendly toward Bhutto's Pakistan. Rather, such a chain of developments could lead to the further radicalization of Bangladesh. Such a development might have direct bearing on the Congress Party's control over the Indian Union and it is bound to have repercussions in Pakistan as well.

Arms and Pakistan's National Security

Pakistan's dependence on outside sources for military hardware is critical. Pakistan has never been able to develop even a minimum defense industry, and its leaders are in a constant quandry on how to obtain the necessary arms to maintain a modern military establishment. Up to the 1965 Indo-Pakistan War the United States was Pakistan's chief supplier, providing an estimated $ 800 million of military goods (Barnds, 1972: 323). Since 1965, however, the United States has kept arms shipments comparatively small. The Johnson administration never could resume the flow in the aftermath of the Indo-Pakistan War and the simultaneous escalation of the American effort in Indo-china. Moreover, the Nixon administration was too consumed with the Vietnamization program, and Pakistan had become too much of a critic of United States policies for it to receive large shipments of armaments. Changes apparently were in the offing, given Yahya Khan's assistance in laying the groundwork for Henry Kissinger's and later the President's visit to Peking. But before the Pakistan government could capitalize on these developments, the tragedy in East Pakistan nullified whatever efforts were underway.

The Nixon administration sought to bolster Pakistan vis-a-vis the threat from India. Relatively small transfers of military equipment were made possible through Jordan, Turkey and Iran but by and large any significant supply of American arms was out of the question. The U.S. Congress was determined to prevent Pakistan from receiving new, large stores of weapons, and the revelations concerning the administrations's "tilt" in favor of Pakistan and away from India only reinforced this determination. It was not until March 14, 1973, that the United States government decided to resume some military shipments.

Up to this date the total embargo on military weapons to Pakistan had been very effective. The Nixon administration, however, decided that some 300 armored personnel carriers, other spare parts and "non-lethal" military equipment could now be passed to Pakistani authorities. The United States government justified its action by noting that: a) Pakistan is in a defensive position since its military defeat in December, 1971; b) in no way can these shipments alter the balance of power which is so preponderantly in favor of India; c) that for political and psychological reasons the shipment is absolutely essential not only to United States-Pakistan relations but also for stabilizing the Bhutto government domestically, and d) it was the United States government's hope that such shipments would make it more possible for Pakistan to reach a political settlement with India.

With the United States announcement, Pakistan was in a position to receive $ 1.2 million in spare parts, parachutes, and reconditioned aircraft engines ordered before the embargo was imposed in December, 1971. The 300 personnel carriers were valued at $ 13 million and this was supposedly contracted for in 1970 and a downpayment made sometime thereafter. An American State Department official noted that this would "wipe the slate clean." Although this may be the case, it was only a token of what Pakistan was seeking and there is the suggestion that more will be forthcoming if the Congress grants the Nixon administration its foreign aid requests. In the meantime the United States signaled its desire to step up assistance to Pakistan when the Agency for International Development made public two loans of $ 60 million to permit the importation of iron, steel, non-ferrous metals, fertilizer and tallow. This followed several other loans dealing with foodstuffs, general commodities, and the continued financing of the Tarbela Hydroelectric Project. The sum total of this economic assistance from March 1972 to March 1973 totaled approximately $ 280 million. In sum: the Bhutto government was no less dependent on the United States than its predecessors.

The Most Recent Phase

Pakistan's foreign policy for the remainder of 1973, and possibly beyond, appeared to focus on President Bhutto's six-day state visit to the United States in July. The sudden illness of President Nixon, however, forced cancellation of the tour but it was rescheduled for September. The consequences at this writing are far from clear. Events move with such rapidity that it is virtually impossible to predict even the most immediate developments with any accuracy. There are, nonetheless, patterns, and these can be traced and evaluated – and from this analysis conclusions can be drawn.

Bhutto is far from secure in his own homeland. The opposition is both vocal and powerful and all Bhutto's gifts of persuasion are required to maintain even a surface equilibrium. The POW and recognition of Bangladesh issues have overshadowed the production of a new constitution and the reinstatement of the parliamentary system. Moreover, solid gains in the economic sector have been generally disregarded, as have a whole series of agrarian, education and social reforms. As in the past, the key issues consuming the highest levels of government are in the sentimental and emotional realms.

It is fair to assert that Bhutto wished to clear away the debris left by the 1971 war with India before the new constitution went into force on August 14, 1973. This meant obtaining the release of the POW's and the simultaneous recognition of Bangladesh. The Joint Statement from India and Bangladesh of April 17, 1973, declared the former's willingness to continue negotiations with Pakistan if the Bhutto government recognized Bangladesh, permitted the 260,000 Biharis living in Bangladesh to leave for Pakistan, and accepted the fact that 195 POW's would be retained for trials as war criminals. The Bhutto government was incensed by the "take-it-or-leave-it" nature of the offer, but agreed to study its contents. Several weeks later it was judged to be entirely unacceptable and Pakistan announced that it was requesting the International Court of Justice to consider the problem under the 1948 Convention of the Prevention and Punishment of the Crime of Genocide. Pakistan argued that under the 1948 Convention only it had the right to exercise jurisdiction over the accused. India, it noted, had no legal justification for transfering the accused POW's to Bangladesh. Pakistan also insisted that the remaining POW's could not be detained while the question of the 195 alleged war criminals was being deliberated. In the case of the 93,000 POW's the Geneva Convention of 1949 concerning the treatment of prisoners of war, of which India is a signatory, was considered binding. According to Pakistan, the Joint Statement of April 17 was in complete contravention of this Convention, and the prisoners should have been returned following the formal surrender.

Despite the bitterness expressed between India and Pakistan, efforts at bringing the antagonists together were made at various levels. The new United States Ambassador to India, Daniel Moynihan, pressed the matter with the Indian authorities while the Nixon administration sought to move President Bhutto closer to a compromise situation. Of special importance was President Bhutto's scheduled trip to the United States. It is not surprising therefore that Bhutto should press his National Assembly for a vote on the issue of Bangladesh. On July 9, 1973, the Pakistan National Assembly in fact did authorize the President to recognize Bangladesh, but it was not a unanimous response. The opposition members in the Assembly walked out of the session and Bhutto accused them of aiding India, who he said no longer wanted Pakistan to recognize Bangladesh. "If we are foolish we will make Moslem Bengal into Hindu Bengal and that is why I want to recognize Moslem Bengal (*New York Times*, July 10, 1973).

Bhutto's continuance in office is seemingly dependent on how he weathers these next several months. The opposition in the Assembly was only symbolic of the real opposition that is to be found among members of the armed forces, the student community and conservative Muslim leaders – all of whom see Bhutto as selling out to the Hindus on the one hand, and possibly the United States on the other. Shades of Ayub Khan! This is why the talks with President Nixon were so vital. The United States had been increasing its economic and technical aid, but what Bhutto was desperately in need of was heightened military assistance. Only such shipments could temper the sentiment in the military and provide Bhutto with the leverage required to resolve, even minimally, the Indian and Bangladesh dilemmas.

It was anticipated that talks with India would commence immediately following the President's return from the United States.[1] Such talks are still

---

1 The new Pakistan-India talks were scheduled for July 24, 1973, and it was anticipated that a second summit would emerge from these meetings. In an obvious gesture of some goodwill India returned 438 sick and wounded POWs on July 11. This brought the total released to 2,264 which includes all the troops taken on the western front in the 1971 war. The Pakistanis months earlier returned all the Indian POWs in their possession (*The New York Times*, July 12, 1973).

planned for a date in August but can the Pakistan leader afford to meet with Indira Gandhi before he has certain assurances from the United States? At the present writing, President Bhutto will not meet with President Nixon before September and much history can be written between now and then.

Postscript

On August 29, 1973, P. N. Haksar, Mrs. Gandhi's special representative and Aziz Ahmed, Pakistan's Minister of State for Defense and Foreign Affairs signed an agreement in New Delhi which held out the possibility of repatriating the prisoners of war and exchanging those populations which found their lot in Bangladesh and Pakistan intolerable. The agreement read as follows:

1. The immediate implementation of the solution of those humanitarian problems is without prejudice to the respective positions of the parties concerned relating to the case of 195 prisoners of war referred to in clauses 6 and 7 of this paragraph;
2. Subject to clause (1), repatriation of all Pakistani prisoners of war and civilian internees will commence with utmost dispatch as soon as logistic arrangements are completed and from a date to be settled by mutual agreement;
3. Simultaneously repatriation of all Bengalees in Pakistan, and all Pakistanis in Bangladesh referred to in clause (5) below, to their respective countries will commence.
4. In the matter of repatriation of all categories of persons *the principle of simultaneity* will be observed throughout as far as possible.
5. Without prejudice to the respective positions of Bangladesh and Pakistan on the question of non-Bengalees who are stated to have "opted for repatriation in Pakistan," the Government of Pakistan, guided by considerations of humanity, agrees, initially, to receive a substantial number of such non-Bengalees from Bangladesh. It is further agreed that the Prime Ministers of Bangladesh and Pakistan or their designated representatives will thereafter meet to decide what additional number of persons who may wish to migrate to Pakistan may be permitted to do so. Bangladesh has made it clear that it will participate in such a meeting only *on the basis of sovereign equality.*
6. Bangladesh agreed that no trials of 195 prisoners of war shall take place during the entire period of repatriation and that pending a settlement envisaged in clause (7) below, *these prisoners of war shall remain in India.*
7. On completion of repatriation of Pakistani prisoners of war and civilian internees in India, Bengalees in Pakistan and Pakistanis in Bangladesh referred to in clause (5) above, or earlier if they so agree, Bangladesh, India and Pakistan will discuss and settle the question of 195 prisoners of war. Bangladesh has made it clear that it can participate in such a meeting *only on the basis of sovereign equality.*
   The special representatives are confident that the completion of repatriation provided for in this agreement would make a signal contribution to the promotion of reconciliation in the sub-continent and create an atmosphere favourable to a constructive outcome of the meeting of the three countries.
8. The time schedule for completion of repatriation of Pakistani prisoners of war and civilian internees from India, Bengalees from Pakistan, and Pakistanis referred to in clause (5) above from Bangladesh, will be worked out by India in consultation with Bangladesh and Pakistan, as the case may be. The Government of India will make logistic arrangements for Pakistani prisoners of war and civilian internees who are to be repatriated to Pakistan. The Government of Pakistan will make

logistic arrangements within its territory up to the agreed points of exit for repatriation of Bangladesh nationals to Bangladesh. The Government of Bangladesh will make necessary arrangements for transport of these persons from such agreed points of exit to Bangladesh. The Government of Bangladesh will make logistic arrangements within its territory up to the agreed points of exit for the movement of Pakistanis referred to in clause (5) above who will go to Pakistan. The Government of Pakistan will make necessary arrangements for transport of these persons from such agreed points of exit to Pakistan. In making logistic arrangements the Governments concerned may seek the assistance of international humanitarian organizations and others.

9. For the repatriation provided for in this agreement, representatives of the Swiss Federal Government and any international humanitarian organization entrusted with this task shall have unrestricted access at all time to Bengalees in Pakistan and to Pakistanis in Bangladesh referred to in clause (5) above. The Government of Bangladesh and the Government of Pakistan will provide all assistance and facilities to such representatives in this regard including facilities for adequate publicity for the benefit of persons entitled to repatriation under this agreement.

10. All persons to be repatriated in accordance with this agreement will be treated with humanity and consideration. The Government of India and the Government of Pakistan have concurred in this agreement. The special representative of the Prime Minister of India, having consulted the Government of Bangladesh, has also conveyed the concurrence of the Bangladesh Government in this agreement.[1]

The above mentioned agreement is a step in the direction of resolving the human dilemma but is does not answer the vital questions concerning the trial of alleged war criminals or the recognition of Bangladesh by Pakistan. It is this observer's opinion that much hard bargaining still lies ahead, and, given the emphasis on the principle of *simultaneity* it could be many months and possibly years before this particular chapter is closed.

BIBLIOGRAPHY

Barnds, William J.
    1972   India, Pakistan, and the Great Powers, New York: Praeger.
Bhutto, Zulfikar Ali
    1964   Foreign Policy of Pakistan, A Compendium of Speeches Made in the National Assembly of Pakistan, Karachi, Pakistan Institute of International Affairs.
    1966   The Quest For Peace, Karachi, Pakistan Institute of International Affairs.
    1969   The Myth of Independence, London: Oxford University Press.
    1972   Radio Address to the Nation, January 28, Islamabad.
    1973a   Address to the Sixteenth Ministerial Council Meeting of the Regional Cooperation for Development, January 11, Islamabad.
    1973b   Address before the National Assembly of Pakistan, April 14, Islamabad.
    1973c   "Pakistan Builds Anew," Foreign Affairs, 51:3, April.
Burke, S. M.
    1973   Pakistan's Foreign Policy: An Historical Analysis, London: Oxford University Press.
Choudhury, G. W.
    1968   Pakistan's Relations with India, 1947–1966, New York: Praeger.
India News, New Delhi.

---

1   The text of this accord will be found in *India News*, September, 7, 1973. Italics have been added.

Jahan, Rounaq
    1972   Pakistan: Failure in National Integration, New York: Columbia University Press.
Malik, Hafeez
    1972   "Problems of Regionalism in Pakistan," presented at the American History Asso-
           ciation, New Orleans, December.
    1974   "Emergence of the Federal Pattern in Pakistan: PPP-NAP Settlement," In,
           J. Henry Korson, ed., Contemporary Pakistan—Problems and Prospects, Leiden:
           E. J. Brill Co.
The New York Times, New York.
Pakistan Affairs, Washington, D.C.
Pakistan News Digest, Islamabad
Syed, Anwar
    1973   "Pakistan's Security Problem: A Bill of Constraints," Orbis, 16, 4, Winter.
United States
    1973a U.S. Foreign Policy, 1972: A Report of the Secretary of State Washington, D.C.
    1973b Foreign Policy for the 1970's: A Report to the Congress by Richard M. Nixon,
           President of the United States, May 3, 1973, Washington, D.C.
Weinbaum, Marvin G.
    1972   "Afghanistan: Non-Party Parliamentary Democracy," The Journal of Developing
           Areas, 7, October, 57–74.
Ziring, Lawrence
    1971   The Ayub Khan Era: Politics in Pakistan, 1958–69, Syracuse, Syracuse University
           Press.

Economic Reforms under the Bhutto Regime*

W. ERIC GUSTAFSON

University of California, Davis, U.S.A.

THERE IS AN Urdu couplet which, in free translation, runs, "The elephant has two sets of teeth, one for eating and one for show." Ripping this couplet rudely out of context – if it had one – I would like to pose the question of the extent to which the economic reforms of the Bhutto regime are for show, and the extent to which they get down to real business. It seems to me that there are some of each, but there is also the melancholy prospect that none of them will work, and we will be left only with the show. Cynicism about Pakistan has become one of Pakistan's most prominent exports, and I hope that I will not add unduly to the supply.

I

In the first burst of reform moves, clearly the "show" motivation was dominant. After an election campaign which made much of the evildoing of Pakistan's twenty-two families, it was only natural that on his second day in office, Bhutto should attack. He seized the passports belonging to the twenty-two richest families and their relatives and dependents, and sealed the borders of the country to all but religious pilgrims to prevent the flight of capital from Pakistan. This act was showing the tusks; it seems hard to imagine that the Government thought it could in fact accomplish much in the way of stemming the flight of capital by prohibiting exit. But the move did provide action, and action which was easy to take.[1]

In January the tempo accelerated. On the second of January it was announced that Ahmad Dawood and Fakhruddin Valika, two prominent industrialists, were under house arrest in Karachi (*Pakistan Times*, 1/2/72, 1:2), and this news was followed in the papers the next day by the announcement of the nationalization under the Economic Reforms Order (1972) of twenty firms, most of which were owned by members of the twenty-two families, with the

*   This paper covers the reform efforts through early September 1973. I am grateful to a number of Pakistani friends for comment. They prefer to remain nameless.
1   New York *Times*, 22 December 1971, 1:6. The passports were later returned at a meeting in Karachi at which Bhutto adopted a somewhat conciliatory tone towards the businessmen. *Pakistan Times* (Lahore), 3/6/72. The President told them that "all restrictions on their travel abroad had been withdrawn to enable them to increase exports."

headline STATE CONTROL OVER TEN INDUSTRIES, and a subsidiary headline FOREIGN INVESTMENT NOT AFFECTED. These twenty firms were supposed to be in ten industries which sounded like what Nehru used to call the "commanding heights" of the economy: iron and steel, basic metal industries, heavy engineering, heavy electrical machinery, assembly and manufacture of motor vehicles, tractor plants, heavy and basic chemicals, petro-chemical industries, cement, and public utilities. The experienced observer of Pakistan's economy would be less bowled over by the list than the innocent reader of the *New York Times*, since he would recognize that Pakistan's capacity in almost all of these areas was slim indeed, and not very much at all was being nationalized (*PT*, 1/3/72, 7:8). Further, Bhutto promised, "It is not the intention of the Government to extend control over other categories of industry" (7:8). No compensation was to be paid to dismissed directors or managing agents, although they – along with other shareholders – were permitted to retain their shares (1:4). The Government was to appoint new managing directors.[1]

The next salvo was fired on 16 January. Under the "Managing Agency and Election of Directors Order, 1972," Dr. Mubashir Hasan, the Finance Minister, announced the abolition of the managing agency system, terminating the agents' agreements and contracts without compensation. (The order simultaneously abolished sole selling agencies.) Control of companies previously wielded by the managing agencies was transferred to the directors of the companies.[2] In strong language Hasan said, according to the *Pakistan Times*,

---

1   Allegations have flown about that the choice of industries to nationalize depended on whether they were run by Bhutto's enemies or not. The San Francisco *Examiner and Chronicle* reported on 16 January 1972, under a picture of Yusef Haroon in a Fifth Avenue apartment decorated with fresh flowers, that he said he "qualifies as a refugee 'because the government has nationalized all my properties, my industries,'" an action he claims was taken 'because of my political differences' with Bhutto" (2A:1). As an aside, the same article gives a clue as to the level of foreign reporting about Pakistan; the article asserts that the 22 families "have surnames like Saigol, Valika, Fancy, Ghandara [*sic*] and Habib." Gandhara Industries (one of those nationalized) was of course named after the ancient Gandhara culture of the North-West Frontier Province, and was the creation of Captain Gohar Ayub Khan, the son of the deposed President, and of his father-in-law, General Habibullah. Political motivation might be looked for here as well, but Gohar Ayub had apparently managed to sell all his shares in Gandhara Industries to the National Investment Trust and the Investment Corporation of Pakistan in August 1969, after his father's fall, curiously enough (Feldman 1972: Appendix B). In any case, a move which appeared to strike at Gohar Ayub's interests would have evoked intense pleasure in many people, even if by that time the gesture might have been a bit too late to have real meaning. Local observers say that the real exercise of political vengeance came with the cancellation (in the closing days of martial law) of the Government's sale of the Bannu Sugar Mills and the Sutlej Textile Mills to General Habibullah. I have been unable to find the text of the Economic Reforms Order. It is doubtless in the *Gazette of Pakistan*, to which I have no access.

2   *PT*, 1/17/72, 1:1. Another eleven industrial units were also taken over the same day, falling in the ten industrial categories previously announced. "According to APP, the Minister said that the Government had taken over all the units it wanted under the

that "managing agencies were one of the worst institutions of loot and plunder through which the 'cream of profit was skimmed by a handful of people who were able to control capital worth about Rs. 50 to 60 crores with an investment of Rs. 50,000 or so.' They had a complete stranglehold over the industry" (*PT*, 1/17/72, 1:2).

The managing agency system was born in India in the nineteenth century. It exists mainly in India and Pakistan, and has long been a focus of criticism. Under this sytem, the management of a company is given over by its directors to a managing agent, a separate corporate entity, which then has a relatively free hand in running things. The opportunities for siphoning off profits and putting them where the shareholders of the actual operating company have no control over them are obviously considerable. Sole selling agents have the same convenient property; goods produced can be sold to the sole selling agent at artificially low prices, thus allowing the profit to appear on the books of the selling agent and under its control rather than under that of the operating company. Under Ayub, the Company Law Commission of 1961 had recommended the "progressive elimination of the managing agency system." The report, although printed in 1963 in an edition of 3,000 copies, was not released to the public. It apparently has been made public under the Bhutto regime,[1] perhaps to place a prop of legitimacy under the actions of 16 January – if they needed one; my impression is that hostility to the managing agency system was widespread. The *Pakistan Times* headed its 18 January editorial "Good Riddance" (4:1). The editorial gives a few snatches of the history of trying to control the managing agency system: the Company Law Commission recommendation; the attempt in 1963 to increase the tax liability of private limited companies; an ordinance of 1968 "empowering the Government to inquire into the affairs of a public limited company and to remove its managing agent if necessary and appoint an administrator. Nor has one heard of any action under that ordinance." Within a few days, the *Times* published "random data collected by some economists since the information gathered by the Central Cartel Law Group set up in 1966 was kept secret," indicating that at least 78 managing agencies, controlling 106 companies, had been abolished (*PT*, 1/20/72, 1:1).

All-in-all, the actions taken represented a mild spurt of nationalization, not affecting foreign enterprises at all (there are few in Pakistan, compared with

---

categories announced earlier. The rest could now start their work in right earnest" (1:3). The *Pakistan Times* on 11 January (3:1), had pointed out that "the 20 units taken over do not include all the major establishments falling in the ten categories selected for immediate state control by the President." See Patel and Memon (1972) for the orders on managing agencies and election of directors.

1 The quotation in the text is from (Pakistan 1963: 126). Security was obviously lacking; I got a copy under the counter from a bookdealer in 1964. Its current public distribution I deduce from its appearance in *Accessions List—Pakistan* 11: 56 (July 1972), published by the Library of Congress PL 480 Project for acquisition of Pakistani books. The chairman of the Commission was Syed Sharifuddin Pirzada, later Attorney General under Ayub. Perhaps significantly, the majority of the Commission were Bengali.

many underdeveloped countries), leaving the financial interest of shareholders intact, and nationalizing industries which, whatever their ultimate importance might be, could hardly be characterized as the industrial powerhouse of Pakistan's economic growth.

The whole nationalization episode appears to have been marked by a good deal of caution. This impression is confirmed by discussions with highly-placed Pakistanis, who claim that the Bhutto regime was unsure of the ability (or the goodwill) of the bureaucracy in running the nationalized industries. According to some, this lack of confidence accounts for the absence of compensation to directors and managing agents. Bhutto is reported to have said, "If we can't make the nationalization work, we'll just hand it back to them." The administration's caution seems entirely well-placed, given the record of the bureaucracy in efficient management (both in Pakistan and in India), but some powerful officials in the administration wanted to go much farther on the route to nationalization.

The President continued to assure the country that "the Government has no intention to take over any more industries" (*PT*, 4/2/73, 3:3), and attached no conditions, at least in the instance just quoted (an address to the Lahore Chamber of Commerce and Industry). The *Pakistan Times* account of the address reported Bhutto as saying that the Government had no intention of taking over any more industries "till new elections were held" (1:1), although the printed text of his speech did not include the remark. In June 1973 the Government took over purchase from the growers of the cotton crop and also the rice export trade, "to ensure the best possible return to the growers," the Finance Minister said (*PT*, 6/21/73, 1:5). Perhaps these forms of economic activity did not count as "industries," but early in September the Government nationalized the 26 mills in the *vanaspati ghee* (cooking oil) industry. *Ghee* is an important consumption item, and nationalization came "because of persistent refusal of industrialists to increase production in spite of their solemn promises to the country and in spite of the incentive of a raised price," as Bhutto put it in an address to a group of industrialists (*PT*, 9/10/73, 1:1). Pervez Tahir's account in the *Pakistan Times* (9/8/73, 4:4–5) gives a list of the malpractices of the *ghee* manufacturers which, if true, goes a considerable distance towards justifying the naionalization (though not of course towards making it work).

Bhutto continued to promise that the Government would nationalize no more units, but added that this was so only if industrialists co-operated by increasing production and "directing their efforts in the best interest of the country," as the *Times* reported the speech. It is not surprising that the nervousness of the private sector continues, despite Bhutto's assurances that "we believe in the concept of a mixed economy in which both private and public sectors play their due share... We, however, do not believe in absolute state power manifesting itself in a totally nationalised, centralised and directed economy" (*PT*, 4/2/73, 1:4). The question is whether the discouraging effect on private investment of the continuing nationalization will be outweighed by its effect in discouraging monopolistic and exploitative practices on the part of the private sector. There is certainly plenty of room for hope.

The final step in nationalization at this writing is the Government's move to purchase the proprietary interest in companies whose management it took over in January 1972. Under the Economic Reforms (Amendment) Ordinance of 1973, the Government suspended trading in the stocks of 18 of the firms, and may purchase the whole or a portion of the shares (or of the proprietary interest) of any of the firms taken over. Compensation may be paid in cash or in bonds redeemable at the option of the Federal Government and bearing interest of one per cent above the bank rate. The Ordinance states the terms for compensation in technical accountant's jargon, but to the bystander innocent of accounting it sounds as though the expropriators will be expropriated in grand style. Compensation will depend on stock market valuations, and according to Pervez Tahir,

> These owners so manipulated the stock exchange quotations that the enhanced operational efficiency of the taken-over units never got reflected correctly. However, the market would certainly have been up if the Government had not suspended dealings. In this way the capitalists have fallen in the trap laid by themselves (Tahir 1973: 4).

A clause enables the Government to exempt shareholdings up to a declared maximum, to protect the small shareholder. The *Pakistan Times* (9/2/73, 7: 1–7) gives the complete text of the Ordinance, which also empowers the Government to reorganize any firm taken over.

II

Next followed a group of labor reforms, within seven weeks of Bhutto's assumption of office, as he pointed out. The full meaning and effect of a number of these would not be clear except to the specialist, which excludes the present writer. Some which look minor may be of major import. I shall nevertheless attempt comment. A number could be lumped under the general heading of fairness to the workers: "a new labour policy which will guarantee to workers their fundamental rights consistent with the requirements of industrial development of the State." A compulsory system of shop stewards was set up, with a grievance procedure to go along with it, with appeal to a Labour Court. Workers will have the option to refer disputes to the Works Council, composed jointly of management and workers. Workers will further have the right to take matters to the Labour Court on their own initiative; this move had previously required the consent of management. "Thus, the workers, while retaining their right to strike, will have the option to get immediate adjudication by the Court." Reasons for firing would now have to be given in writing. The application of the Payment of Wages Act (1936) and the Industrial Employment (Standing Orders) Ordinance (1968) were extended to labor contractors; obviously employers had evaded these enactments by dealing with contractors rather than directly with labor.

A second set of provisions sweetened the pot for labor a bit: payment of

bonus was made compulsory; profit-sharing was upped from two to four percent; the payment by the worker of two percent of wages for medical facilities
was abolished; provision for old-age pensions was announced; and employers
were required to provide education up to matric for one child of each worker.
But Bhutto – most wisely, in my view – stopped short of a minimum wage:
"an increase in money wages will further aggravate the inflationary situation."
Bhutto declared the intention of linking wages to the price level "as is the practice in Scandinavian and some other advanced countries," after inflation had
been brought under control.

But then in the last five paragraphs of his speech, after presenting these
concessions, Bhutto demanded his *quid pro quo*:

> Since the 20th of December, Martial Law notwithstanding, "gheraos and jalaos" seems
> to have become the order of the day. This unruly and rowdy practice, negative in its pur-
> pose, anarchist in its approach, nihilistic in its results has been endured regrettably by
> the Government and the people for over seven weeks ... It is a self-destructive procedure.
> The majority of the people have shown their disgust over these demonstrations of hooliga-
> nism... National leaders have spoken against it... Taking all these factors into account
> now I want to make it clear that the strength of the street will be met with the strength of
> the State.. [This] intolerable form of threat and thunder ... must stop.[1]

Bhutto's problem here was that he clearly had a tiger by the tail. Much of
his urban support came from labor, and the stance of the Pakistan People's
Party on labor issues – and against the 22 families – had emboldened labor
considerably from its old passive attitude. Faiz Ahmed Faiz had predicted at
least thirty years earlier that this would happen, in his poem "Dogs," about the
oppressed of the subcontinent:

> Ye chahen to dunya ko apna bana-len,
> Ye aqa'on ki haddiyan tak chaba-len—
> Koi inko ihsas-e-zillat dila-de,
> Koi inki soi hui dum hila-de.
>
> Once roused, they'll make the earth their own,
> And gnaw their betters to the bone—
> If someone made their misery itch,
> Just gave their sluggish tails a twitch.
> (Faiz 1971: 85)

Labor's new hyperactivity had reached the point where the regime could no
longer control it. Bhutto's response was to make substantial improvements in
procedural matters, increase the real income of workers by a conceivably large
amount, but to brandish the Big Stick – a policy whose success was not noticeable in the next few months.

---

1   All quotations in the above paragraphs are from President Bhutto's address to the nation
    over Radio Pakistan, reported *verbatim* in the *Pakistan Times* (2/11/72, 7:1–3). Complete
    texts of the relevant ordinances are found in Chaudhary (1972a and 1972b). Also worthy
    of note is Haidari (1972).

III

The next major area for reform was land. March 3 was declared a national holiday to celebrate the land reforms, accomplished by a Martial Law Regulation. Briefly, the land reforms cut the limit on holdings per individual (*not* per family) from 500 to 150 irrigated acres and from 1,000 to 300 unirrigated acres. Lands above the ceiling were taken without compensation, and it was announced that they would be given free to the peasants. Installments due from farmers on account of the 1959 reforms were cancelled, and arbitrary ejection of tenants from the land was no longer permitted; they could be ejected only for non-payment of *batai* (the landlord's share of the crop). A number of special features attracted attention, given the background of cynicism about the land reforms carried out under Ayub. (1) No concession or exemption granted under the 1959 reforms was to be retained. Apparently in some cases these were quite substantial. Feldman (1972: 6) reports (with documentation) that the Nawab of Kalabagh and his sons were allowed to retain 18,619 acres on lease. The Nawab was the Governor of West Pakistan under Ayub. (2) Transactions in land in excess of the new ceilings after 20 December 1971 (the date of Bhutto's take-over) were void; apparently there had been many fictitious transfers on the land books in anticipation of reforms, since the new administration had started announcing its intentions in January, and of course the People's Party election manifesto had promised them as well. Also invalidated were land transfers which brought land back into the family through a third party; a clever touch. (3) Civilian officials were required to surrender all lands in excess of 100 acres acquired during their tenure of service or in course of retirement. This provision was of course a response to the widespread view among the public that there had been considerable hanky-panky in land sales to favored officials. President Bhutto noted that "vast barrage lands acquired by the official class both in Punjab and in Sind through disgraceful abuse of power, formed the most sordid and shameful chapter in the story of land-grabbing in Pakistan" (*PT*, 3/2/72, 1:3), (4) Land on the Pat Feeder Canal in Baluchistan, the source of much bloodshed because of its apparent distribution to Government favourites, involving inter-tribal struggles, was to be resumed in its entirety without compensation and distributed to poor farmers.[1]

The tribal areas were exempted from the order – I suppose because of inability to make it stick there, and perhaps because it was unnecessary as well.[2] One concession was worthy of note: if a farmer had installed a tubewell or bought a tractor on or before 20 December 1971, the limit was raised for him by twenty per cent. This gesture to the *kulak* class seems a bit peculiar, but perhaps helpful in somewhat reducing the sting of the reforms to a rather

---

1 Feldman (1972: 202–208) gives some background on the Pat Feeder incidents. Documentation is sparse, and I do not pretend to understand the situation fully.

2 A friend from the tribal areas tells me that only the first reason given in the text holds. He continues, "My grandfather owns miles and miles of land [in the tribal areas] and I am quite sure that he could do with a lot less."

numerous class, without conceding anything of substance to the really big
landlords.[1]

The absence of compensation clearly raised some eyebrows. Rightist
parties in Pakistan had been forced into a position of advocating some land
redistribution, and as Mohammad Jafar (1972) commented, "though the
Rightists never said this in so many words, yet it was common knowledge that
their insistence that the 1956 Constitution be re-enforced was motivated only by
the circumstance that that Constitution had effectively protected the capitalis-
tic interests both of the feudal landlords and the industrialists," and in particular provided for compensation, which a court judgment had interpreted to
mean compensation at market value. According to Jafar, the theoretical bases
for the lack of compensation were two: (1) "...the better and preponderant
view is that private ownership of land, in its absolute concept, is not permitted
in Muslim Law." (2) "...contrary to general thinking on this subject, even
under the British rule in the subcontinent, the State did not recognize an
absolute private right of ownership of land."[2]

Pakistani government publicity pulled out all the stops on the land reforms. A pamphlet of the Department of Films and Publications pointed out
that the limits set were a quarter of what was allowed in Iraq and less than a
sixth of what was allowed in Iran, but there has been no mention that I can
detect in the Pakistani press that the Congress Party in India has introduced
guidelines for ceilings much lower, 18 acres of irrigated double-cropped land or
54 acres of dry land.[3]

Government land in the future is to be disposed of to the landless, not at
auction (which allegedly benefit absentee landlords); the significant exception
here is that Government land will continue to be available to the defense
services, an exception which may have been politically necessary, but as the
Pakistan Times commented the next day, "while nobody will grudge the defense
personnel some reward for their services and sacrifices, grant of this reward in
the form of land is not easily justifiable" (3/3/72, 6:1).

---

1   The announcement of the reforms is in *PT*, 3/2/72. The Land Reforms Regulation, 1972
    (Martial Law Regulation No. 115) was published complete in *PT*, 3/12/73, 1:4 ff. It is
    also available in Sarwar (1972). Some changes were made later: the ceilings were re-
    duced by 20 percent (*PT*, 4/24/72, 1:7; editorial, 4/25/72, 3:1). The limitations were
    from the beginning stated in terms of produce-index units if computations on that basis
    yielded a larger holding. I have ignored these complications, but one effect is that larger
    holdings are permitted in Sind than in Punjab, because of poorer soil fertility.
2   Why general thinking should have been misled is unclear: the British were always
    explicit that the State was the ultimate landlord. See also Rafi Ullah (1972) and Zeno
    (1973), which concerns Guraya (1971), a book advocating limitations on the right to
    property. It was banned under the Yahya regime, on which see Khalid (1972). On
    right-wing theorizing on the land question, the views of Maudoodi (1950), the head of
    the Jamaat-i-Islami, might be interesting, but I have been unable to locate a copy.
3   (Pakistan 1972: 12). In India, actual implementation depends on the States, of course,
    and is apparently moving at a glacial pace. See Ladejinsky (1972) for a most interesting
    analysis—skeptical of the virtue of ceilings taken by themselves—by one of the oldest
    hands in the land reform field.

The amount of land involved appeared considerable: in initial euphoria, the *Pakistan Times* reported an area of three million acres (3/3/72, 1:1). It later reported four million acres (12/18/72, 8:6), and said that three-quarters of that had already been distributed (1/7/73, 6: 1–2). The Government's most recent claim is only that 724,000 acres have been resumed (Pakistan 1973: 11). Large or small, the area will make only a minor dent in rural poverty, given that nearly two million peasants were reported to have no land at all.

IV

On 11 May came what may be the biggest reform of all – although to a large extent it was only the culmination of a gradual process of piecemeal reform. In what was described as a long-awaited move, Bhutto announced the devaluation of the rupee from its old (and largely fictitious) parity of Rs 4.76 to the dollar to a new official rate of Rs 11 to the dollar. The Finance Minister gave a bit of the history of the move towards devaluation in his announcement speech, which took up nearly an entire page of the *Pakistan Times* (5/13/72, 5: 1–7):

> The proposal for exchange reform is not new. It was first mooted as far back as 1963. No positive decision was taken at that time. It was taken up again in 1966. The decision was again postponed. At the end of 1967, the question was raised once again but the decision was postponed once again. Finally, in June 1970, the decision was taken by Yahya Khan in principle and it was decided to [devalue] the currency in October of that year. In February 1971, a written commitment was made by Yahya Khan in a letter to the International Monetary Fund notwithstanding [which] his request for standby credit was turned down. Yahya Khan tried once again to obtain a standby credit and simultaneously gave an undertaking to devalue Pakistan rupee to a dual exchange; one fixed at a rate of Rs 9.50 and the other Rs 11 (excluding one rupee tax) as a floating rate. By then Pakistan's internal situation had become so alarming that the world of finance decided to keep all financial decisions in abeyance until the situation crystalized one way or the other (5:4–5).

The Finance Minister's speech was extraordinarily frank: he refers to "the conspiracy to maintain the existing rate of exchange" (5:2).[1]

The move was much less radical than it sounded in one sense, since in point of fact the bulk of imports had been entering at rates a good bit higher than Rs 4.76, and exports as well were subject to higher rates. Indeed, Pakistan had

---

1 Proposals for exchange reform go back a good bit further than the Finance Minister indicated. See Emile Despres' memorandum to the Planning Board of 1956, proposing an import surcharge for many of the same reasons the Finance Minister mentioned as motivating the devaluation (Despres 1973). The whole area of foreign exchange is absolutely essential to an understanding of the Pakistan economy over the last twenty years, and is much too technical to enter into here in detail, except to state my assessment of the results of the devaluation. Those in need of more technical exposition would do well to turn to a pair of articles by two of my colleagues: Glassburner (1968) and Child (1968).

been running a multiple-exchange-rate system with seven rates, but, as the Finance Minister noted in his speech to the nation, "The most favourable ones are meant for those who are the most favourably placed. The most unfavourable ones are for the least fortunate ones" (*PT*, 5/13/72, 5:2). The picture he painted is a bit overdrawn, but as a two-sentence description, it would be hard to improve.

The major reason for the maintenance of the artifical Rs 4.76 to the dollar, in my interpretation, was the existence of East Pakistan. The East Wing's major export was jute, whose supply and (especially) demand were both thought inelastic. If that were the case, then an across-the-board devaluation would have led to *decreased* export earnings from jute, the country's major foreign exchange earner. A reinforcing factor was that the Central Government controlled the foreign exchange earned by jute; the East Wing got the Rs 4.76, and the Central Government got the foreign exchange, worth far more. Devaluation coupled with an export tax to avoid a decrease in earnings from jute would have been a possibility, but then the taxation of the East Wing would have been rather more explicit than anyone (in power) wanted it to be.

Second, the East Wing offered a protected market for much of West Pakistan's industry. This market had now vanished, and aggressive competitiveness in world markets was called for – and the excess capacity was now there to back it up. The bonus-voucher system had, to be sure, already devalued the rupee for exporters by differing amounts. The effective exchange rates were Rs 5.60 for primary products, Rs 7.81 for semi-manufactures, and Rs 8.61 for manufactures. The difference in rates itself was not readily defensible, and now, with devaluation to Rs 11, all Pakistan exports were at one stroke made more competitive in world markets, although export duties cancelled out a portion of this advantage for primary products thought to be in inelastic demand.[1]

Export figures now argue for considerable success, both in diverting products formerly sent to East Pakistan and in taking advantage of the devaluation. Pakistan is at the crest of an export boom as I write in August 1973, partly the result of high world demand and prices for Pakistani primary products, but significant contributions have been made by cotton piece goods, and lesser contributions by products of small industry: sporting goods, carpets, leather and leather goods. These latter are encouraging portents for the future.

---

1   The export rate calculations are taken from *Outlook* (1972a). The calculations are based on the then prevailing bonus premium of 180 percent. Note the date of the article: discussion of the need for devaluation had been taking place in public. (The reappearance of *Outlook*, banned in effect by the Ayub administration in 1964, is one of the cheering results of the new dispensation of press freedom.) The article cited is quite explicit about the role of the loss of East Pakistan: "As in other aspects of our national life, East-West rivalry had distorted our vision in respect of exchange parity as well" (10). Another article in *Outlook* (1972b) makes much the same points under the title "Three Cheers for Devaluation." (The article is apparently by a different hand.) An added note on the bureaucracy's view of devaluation: the Finance Ministry was apparently leary of the increased budgetary cost (in rupees) of debt service. It was ultimately convinced that increased revenue from export duties would make up for this paper loss.

I take the rapid expansion in these sectors to be largely the result of devaluation, and to presage further improvement. The boom is due for interruption, of course, because of the disastrous floods of summer 1973. (See Pakistan 1973: Ch. VIII and Appendix Table 37, as well as the writings of Burki cited at the end of this article.)

So on the export side there was apparently a considerable boost to the competitiveness of Pakistani exports. On the import side, foreign products have of course become more expensive for many categories of purchasers – and uniformly expensive for all. Several effects seem important here:

(1) The price of industrial imports (both capital and raw materials) will now (hopefully) fully reflect their scarcity value to the economy. Previously the Government had handed imports of industrial goods a gift of the difference between the value of inputs valued at the official rate and the scarcity value in the local economy of these imported goods, realizable either directly (although illegally) or through their embodiment in products to be sold at protected prices on the local market. As the Finance Minister put it, "under the present system of exchange rates [the capitalist] already doubles the value of his money the moment he gets a permit to establish a plant and the loan is approved with nothing whatsoever on the ground" (5:2). East Pakistan enters here in another way. Latterly East Pakistani economists had advanced the argument in high circles in the early 1970's that a devaluation would inhibit the development of East Bengali entrepreneurship, just as it appeared ready to start rolling. These spokesmen wanted Bengali entrepreneurs to enjoy the same advantages which their West Pakistani counterparts had had: possession of an import license at the artificially low official rate was an automatic guarantee of bank credit: banks knew a good thing when they saw one. The argument seems a bit perverse, since in general the old exchange rate system subsidized industry at the expense of agriculture, and East Pakistan was the most heavily agricultural wing. (For a clever argument to this effect see Soligo (1971), who does not draw the moral that since the East Wing was agricultural and the West Wing industrial, interprovincial transfers were involved.)

(2) Luxury consumer goods had previously been imported at the bonus voucher rate (the highest, roughly Rs 13 or 14 to $ 1). This arrangement had what would appear to be the desirable effect of making these luxuries expensive; but these high import prices gave a much higher degree of protection from the world market than was given to capital goods or raw materials, and thus incentive for local production, to a group of goods which had been placed "on bonus because of the lowest priority having been assigned to them in the national objectives," as a Karachi commentator pointed out (*Outlook:* 1972a). Making all imports available at the same high rate will have the effect of raising the incentives for local manufacture of capital and intermediate goods relative to luxury consumer goods.

(3) Since under the new import policy licenses are to be freely available, and all commodity imports – except those completely banned – will be "freely importable," much of the cumbersome machinery for the administration of the

baroque import-control apparatus may no longer be necessary, a considerable saving in national time, energy, and tempers. One might also note that the possibilities for official corruption will be much reduced (as indeed will those of the private sector, since over- and under-invoicing will now be markedly less attractive).

(4) The effect on small-scale industry is worthy of separate note. In all the Byzantine intrigue of the license system, it was the small entrepreneur who found his way most effectively blocked. The Finance Minister was quite explicit here as well:

> At last the small manufacturer will be able to compete with the big producer and will no longer depend on buying raw materials from him in the black market. The big producer will have to work hard to compete with the small man to sell his goods (5:6).

Already the free availability of art silk yarn has led to the mushrooming of small establishments with only a few looms each.

Under the new import policy, industrial plants costing less than Rs 200,000 will be freely importable against cash. This step, if effectively carried out, will mean a tremendous relative boost for the small-scale sector, which has suffered from twenty-five years of neglect. A later announcement made it seem as though hurdles were once more being put in the way of the small manufacturer. The Ministry of Commerce announced that "persons intending to import industrial plants costing Rs 2 lakh against cash and up to Rs 5 lakh against barter/credit, should obtain sanctions of the respective Provincial Governments for the setting up of the new units or expansion of the existing units before applying for the import licenses" (*PT*, 6/7/72, 1:7). A sophisticated local observer points out to me, however, that because provincial governments are unabashedly promotional, and now in competition with other provinces, they will be – *Inshallah* – considerably less likely to place roadblocks in the way of small industry (or large, for that matter) than the "mandarins" (his word) of the central government.[1]

V

The final set of reforms involved the financial sector. The life insurance companies (largely in the hands of the 22 families) had already been nationalized on 19 March – a tempting target. The Government set up a State Life Insurance Corporation of Pakistan on 1 November, with three competing divisions into which the 43 old companies were merged. The action put their Rs 130 crore of assets in the hands of the Government. The assets of the firms were not apparently the prime factor, however. In fact, some of the life insurance sector was near bankruptcy. Eastern Federal, the largest insurer, report-

---

1   When the dollar was devalued in terms of gold by ten percent in February, 1973, Pakistan maintained its gold parity, thus reducing the official rate to Rs 9.90. This enhancement in terms of the dollar was partly cancelled out on the import side by the imposition of additional import duties on consumer goods in the June 1973 budget (*PT*, 6/10/73).

edly had the majority of its liabilities in West Pakistan, but the majority of its assets in East Pakistan, largely in real estate. A dramatic failure in the life insurance sector would clearly have been most unsettling at an inopportune time.

This left banking as the remaining target, also largely in the control of the 22 families. On 19 May the Finance Minister announced a set of procedural reforms, to be embodied in legislation. The banks had long been criticized because they were the private preserve of a small number of the ruling families. The complete text of Dr. Mubashir Hasan's address (*PT*, 5/21/72, 5:3–6) provides a fairly complete catalogue of the alleged misdeeds of the banking sector – some of them of considerable interest, displays of indigenous ingenuity. The reforms sought to curtail the banks' power sharply, but stopped well short of outright nationalization – a step which India had taken in 1969. The reforms in many cases are technical, and I will not describe them in detail, but the basic drift was to introduce a much greater measure of supervision of the operation of private banks by the State Bank of Pakistan, which was now empowered, for instance, to appoint a director of its own for each bank, the director to have no connection with banking. (The motivation of this provision is clear, but it would also seem to limit the potential effectiveness of the State director.) Unsecured loans to directors and their families, firms, and companies, were outlawed, nor could banks any longer make loans to directors and their families against the security of shares. Banks were now constrained in their choice of auditors. A number of similar procedural reforms in sum seemed to promise much less of the sort of overly cozy arrangements under which the banks had been run.

The regime aimed additional reforms at the mal-distribution of credit. Commercial banks will be forced into more participation in agricultural credit, but also in credit to other neglected sectors, in particular local production of machinery, the small-scale sector, and refinancing for non-traditional exports. A National Credit Consultative Council will supervise this end of things. One clever twist is that the Government is to amend the Public Demand Recovery Act to allow banks the power to have their agricultural loans recovered as arrears of land revenue. Although this sounds like grinding the faces of the poor, in fact it is likely to lead to a greater amount of rural credit by providing effective security for loans, which banks now lack (*PT*, 5/21/72, 5:6).

Bhutto clearly put the banking system on notice; to prevent their missing the point, the *Pakistan Times* commented:

> The reform is realistic and well intended, but if it does not work as well as it is hoped, then the Government may have no choice but to nationalise the banks (*PT*, 5/21/72, 6:2).

Bankers would remember that land had been nationalized without compensation.

VI

Where are we left, then? What in these reforms is showing the tusks, and what use of the teeth for constructive reform?

The nationalization seems to be tusk-showing; I expect no great results from it, and the portion of Pakistani industry involved is not large.[1] Performance under nationalization, however, has apparently been surprisingly good; a report to the National Assembly in June, 1973 was most encouraging. (See *PT*, 6/20/73, 6: 1–2, "A Myth Exploded.") Watchful waiting is of course still called for. The abolition of the managing agency system is probably all to the good; it will promote a tendency for greater accountability in corporate affairs, and a better break for the stockholders of the corporations, through easing to some extent the stranglehold of the twenty-two families on industrial affairs. (Representation of minority shareholders has, in particular, been assured through cumulative voting and proportionate representation.)

The procedural labor reforms deserve applause to the extent that they make labourers better able to secure just treatment – even at some cost. But the economic reforms apparently will make employing labor in the large-scale sector considerably more expensive. There is question as to whether this is really a good idea. It is of course soul-satisfying to most of us to see the rich get soaked; but if the soaking largely tends to produce a more pampered class of urban labor at the expense of the rest of the country, and in particular at the expense of those priced out of the employment market by the rise in the costs of employing workers, it is not clear that society at large will have a gain to record. Some action was certainly necessary, and the Bhutto administration seems to have been careful to avoid wild gestures in this area, perhaps to its own initial detriment, since peace on the labor scene was a long time coming, if indeed it has arrived, which seems possible. The *Economic Survey* (Pakistan 1973: 13) reports man-days lost due to strikes, lockouts, and plant closures down in February 1973 to about one-eighth of the half-million lost in July 1972 in the disturbances which continued after the labor reforms. And as far as the effects of the rise in the cost of labor are concerned, the system is apparently proving elastic. It seems likely that capital will be driven to some extent out of the large-scale sector, where labor is organized, and into the small-scale sector, by definition difficult either for labor to organize or the Government to police. Observers tell me that the better-than-doubling of carpet exports in a single year (Pakistan 1973: Appendix Table 37) represents the effects of large-scale capital pumped through a modern putting-out system into the small-scale sector, where wages are much lower.

The land reforms are both tusk and teeth: tusk in that they deliver less than they sound as though they do. The property limitations after all are not on a

---

1 Salamat Ali (1972) says that 82 percent of industry remains privately owned. The figure actually is larger, since small-scale industry is not included in his calculations (or those of anyone else), because there are no decent figures covering the sector.

family basis, but on an individual basis, so that holdings of very considerable size (on a Pakistani scale) are still possible. One is eager for more detail about the actual land distribution; my earlier comments indicate that the amount of land involved has apparently been less than hoped early on. If the provisions on ejection of tenants – or rather on the non-ejection of tenants – can be made to stick, this also can be counted as a substantial achievement: teeth, not tusk. Informed Pakistani friends suggest that they may be *made* to stick in parts of Sind and the N.W.F.P. where the landlords are especially non-supportive of the Pakistan People's Party.

Banking reform sounds like it means business, but *quis custodiet custodes ipsos?* The experience with regulated industries elsewhere in the world suggests that the regulated end up regulating the regulators; one would scarcely be willing to wager large amounts of money that this process would not happen in Pakistan. Reports indicate that life insurance was nationalized (rather than propped up financially and regulated) for exactly this reason: the Controller of Life Insurance was a relatively low-ranking official, and much more subject to manipulation than the Governor of the State Bank of Pakistan, who regulated the banks and was normally an ex-Finance Minister and consequently of considerably higher rank in the Government. The mere existence of the laws (and of the focus of public attention on the banking sector) may make it much more difficult for the industrial families to play footsie with their captive banks and may open up sources of capital to more people in the society. The nationalization of life insurance may have the same effect, if the assets of the new life insurance corporation are not just poured down Governmental ratholes. Tusk certainly; teeth maybe.

The centerpiece of the reforms seems to me to be the devaluation. It is hard to convey to anyone who has not worked through the economics of an overvalued currency rationed by licensing how pervasive and pernicious its effects were, reaching into every corner of the economic life of the country, corrupting everyone it touched, either in the narrow sense of the word "corrupting," or "corrupting" in the sense that it presented a perverse set of economic incentives: encouraging imports, discouraging exports; encouraging foreign-made capital goods, discouraging domestic; encouraging luxury-goods production, discouraging capital-goods production; encouraging the flight of capital, restricting personal freedom. The devaluation can hardly fail to do something simultaneously about all those evils. An important clue to the way the administration regards the matter seems to me is found in the forceful language and great length of Dr. Mubashir Hasan's speech – which he wrote himself – announcing the devaluation. He condemned nearly every evil in the Pakistani economy in the most vivid language and laid the evils at the door of the exchange rate. The tone of the announcement is in great contrast to that accompanying the other reforms: passionate, moving, and intense. And at least eighty percent of what Mubashir Hasan had to say is quite correct, in spite of his vigorous hyperbole: the overvalued currency had encouraged a bizarre variety of cancers in the Pakistani economy and polity, to the point where a Pakistani economist once said to me, "Ah, the glory that was Greece, the grandeur that was Rome, and the racket that is Pakistan!" In the long pull, I think it is the devaluation which will be regarded as Bhutto's greatest single contribution on the economic side of the ledger.

Postscript

After this article had been completed, Bhutto, acting as Prime Minister (having assumed that office on the 14th August) announced a new reform which may ultimately have significant economic impact in a number of ways. On 21 August he announced the abolition of all special services (cadres) in government employment, including of course the elite Civil Service of Pakistan, the focus of much resentment in Pakistan (*PT*, 8/21/73,1; text of statement on 4).

Bhutto had stated earlier that

> in a democratic state where the government is popularly elected, with its main aim the improvement of the condition of the common man, the question of exploitation by the State does not arise (*PT*, 4/2/73, 3:3).

But clearly it does arise, as the Prime Minister noted in his announcement speech:

> It is often averred that the bureaucratic apparatus is a neutral instrument which can be bent to any kind of policy. But this neutrality is mythical. The bureaucracy itself is a powerful vested interest, concerned more with its own good than with the good of the public (*PT*, 8/21/73, 4:4).

Civil service reform had clearly been on Bhutto's agenda; the manifesto of the Pakistan People's Party had noted that a "Socialist regime will need a different structure of administration." The Prime Minister presented the main thrust of his remarks forcefully:

> No institution in the country has so lowered the quality of our national life as what is called "Naukarshahi." It has done so by imposing a caste system on our society. It has created a class of Brahmins or mandarins, unrivalled in its snobbery and arrogance, insulated from the life of the people and incapable of identifying itself with them (4:3).

Although Bhutto did not mention the C.S.P. anywhere in his statement, no one familiar with Pakistan would need special instruction to know what this paragraph was about.

The new system, resulting from the deliberations of the Administrative Reforms Commission, abolishes all the special services and of course the reservation of high policy-making posts for members of these elite services. "Classes" of government servants (I to IV) will no longer exist, and the Prime Minister explicitly stated that, "The road to the top will be opened to all on merit" (4:6).

Bhutto's statement emphasized the role of specialists:

Above all [my italics], the new service structure will enable the Government to gain the full contribution [of] scientists, engineers, doctors, economists, accountants, statisticians and other professionals and specialists, in policy-making, management and administration (4:5).

A "people's government," said Bhutto, "cannot condone a system which elevates the generalist above the scientist, the technician, the professional expert, the artist or the teacher" (4:3–4).

As I noted above in the body of the paper, one of the Bhutto Government's anxieties about its program of nationalization was the fear that the bureaucracy was not up to the task of managing industrial enterprises. Bhutto noted that:

New demands have been placed on the administrative machinery by the various reforms introduced by the Government. Competent persons with experience of running industries are required to take charge of various industries and institutions, financial and otherwise, brought under public control (4:6).

He made special mention that there would be encouragement to lateral entry into the Government service for talented individuals from banking, insurance, industry, and trade.

These reforms promise much new blood and new spirit to make the reforms of the regime work for the good of the people.

REFERENCES

Ali, Salamat
    1972   "The Crisis Continues," Far Eastern Economic Review, 2 December, p. 45.
Burki, Shahid Javed
    1972a "Our Economic Future," Pakistan Times, 13 May, p. 4.
    1972b "Export Oriented Growth," Pakistan Times, 28 May, p. 4.
    1972c "Pakistan's Export Boom," Pakistan Times, 4 and 11 December.
Chaudhary, Muhammad Anwar
    1972a Latest and Most Uptodate Commentary on the Industrial Relations Ordinance, 1969. Lahore: Lahore Law Times Publications.
    1972b New Labour Laws and Policy, 1972. Lahore: Lahore Law Times Publications.
Child, Frank C.
    1968   "Reform of a Trade and Payments System: the Case of Pakistan," Economic Development and Cultural Change 16 (July): 539–558.
Despres, Emile
    1973   "Price Distortions and Development Planning: Pakistan," pp. 133–145 in International Economic Reform: Collected Papers of Emile Despres. New York: Oxford University Press.
Faiz, Faiz Ahmed
    1971   Poems by Faiz, trans. V. G. Kiernan. London: George Allen & Unwin.
Feldman, Herbert
    1972   From Crisis to Crisis: Pakistan 1962–1969. London: Oxford. Appendix B: "Wealth Acquired by Captain Gohar Ayub Khan."
Glassburner, Bruce
    1968   "Aspects of the Problem of Pricing Foreign Exchange in Pakistan," Economic Development and Cultural Change 16 (July): 517–538.

Guraya, Muhammad Yusuf
    1972   Nizam-i-Zakat aur Jadid Ma'ashi Masa'il. Islamabad: Idara-i-Tahqiqat-i-Islami.
Haidari, Iqbal
    1972   The New Labour Policy: Impact and Implications. Karachi: Economic & Industrial Publications.
Jafar, Malik Mohammad
    1972   "Resumption of Land and Compensation," Pakistan Times, 14 March, p. 3.
Khalid, Detlev H.
    1972   "A Book that was Banned," Outlook n.s. 1 (12 August): 12–14.
Ladejinsky, Wolf
    1972   "Land Ceilings and Land Reform," Economic and Political Weekly (Bombay) 7 (Annual Number, February): 401–408.
Maudoodi, Syed Abul 'Ala
    1950   Mas'alat-i-Milkiyat-i-Zamin. Lahore.
Outlook (Karachi)
    1972a   "High Time for Devaluation," Outlook n.s. 1 (22 April): 11.
    1972b   "Three Cheers for Devaluation," Outlook n.s. 1. (20 May): 9.
Pakistan
    1963   Company Law Commission of Pakistan. Report, 1961. Karachi: Manager of Publications.
    1972   Department of Films and Publications. A New Beginning: Reforms Introduced by the People's Government in Pakistan, December 20, 1971–April 20, 1972. Islamabad.
    1973   Office of the Economic Adviser. Pakistan Economic Survey, 1972–73. Islamabad. (Ch. II, "Socio-Economic Reforms.")
Patel, M. Adam, and A. Ghafoor Memon
    1972   The Law of Managing Agency and Election of Directors. Karachi: August Publications.
Rafi Ullah, M.
    1972   "No Compensation in Islamic Law for Land," Pakistan Times, 23 April, p. 7.
Sarwar, Malik Ghulam
    1972   The Land Reforms Regulation, 1972 (M.L.R. 115), with Land Reforms Address. Lahore: Lahore Law Times Publications.
Soligo, Ronald
    1971   "Real and Illusory Aspects of an Overvalued Exchange Rate: the Pakistan Case," Oxford Economic Papers n.s. 23 (March): 90–109.
Tahir, Pervez
    1973   "Changing Mix in Mixed Economy," Pakistan Times, 8 September, p. 4.
Zeno
    1973   "Cultural Notes: Islam and the Right to Property," Pakistan Times, 3 January, p. 4.

Pakistan's Population in the 1970's: Problems and Prospects

LEE L. BEAN
University of Utah, Salt Lake City, U.S.A.

A. D. BHATTI
Population Council, New York, U.S.A.

For advocates of family planning and fertility control, Pakistan, circa 1968, was a nation of hope and promise. Social and cultural conditions in Pakistan were assumed to run counter to those typically associated with rapid fertility declines (see Section II). One could thus argue that if family planning were to be a success in Pakistan, family planning as a voluntaristic approach to fertility limitation had a good chance of success in many of the developing countries where demographic problems seemed most severe.

There were many positive features of the Pakistan family planning program in 1968. Pakistan had adopted a population policy based upon ambitious demographic targets calling for a reduction in estimated birth rates of 20 percent in five years. Starting in selected districts in 1965, by 1968 a nation-wide program was in operation. Available statistics suggested that Pakistan had stimulated a remarkable degree of successful adoption of family planning, often using a wide range of innovative activities.

By 1970 a degree of disenchantment had arisen with respect to Pakistan's family planning program. Leadership of the program had changed with the removal of President Ayub Khan and the dismissal of large numbers of senior civil servants including the head of the family planning program. Statistics related to the family planning program from 1965 through 1968 were viewed with increasing skepticism and entirely new organizational forms were introduced to "make up for the false starts" introduced earlier (see Section III).

The events of 1970 *et passim* have overshadowed the normal operation of social service programs such as family planning in Pakistan and have introduced new demographic dimensions into the development and administration of population policies in the country. Without representative elections, the relative voting strength of distinctive "ethnic" or linguistic groups was unimportant. The 1970 election and the "block" support provided to Sheikh Mujibar Rahman in East Pakistan introduced a new element in the consideration of population policies in Pakistan, even after the break-up of the country into Pakistan and Bangladesh.

While this paper is concerned only with the country of Pakistan as constituted in 1973, the issue of relative population size among various ethnic or linguistic groups cannot be ignored. That issue now focuses on the strength of the four major provinces in Pakistan – Punjab, Sind, Northwest Frontier, and Baluchistan – and the relative strength of the four dominant ethnic groups – Punjabis, Sindis, Baluchis, and Pathans. To what extent these differences will influence the operation of population programs will be explored in Section IV. In Section II, however, we will note that issues of relative population strength have already influenced the collection of population statistics in Pakistan.

Although a new population policy issue has emerged in Pakistan, the social and economic problems underlying the earlier adoption of a strong population policy in Pakistan remain. In this paper, we shall argue that it is the social and economic factors associated with population change which will be most important in the management of population programs in Pakistan, or even in the four autonomous provinces, during the 1970s.

The Population of Pakistan

The Difficulty of Knowing. For the scholar interested in the population of Pakistan, it is important to recognize the degree to which analytical work is restricted by the availability of population statistics and by the quality of those statistics which are available. To utilize a now hackneyed expression, population statistics in Pakistan must be treated with *caution*. Problems associated with population statistics in Pakistan arise from a number of sources: organizational problems, lack of continuity in statistical systems, and the inherent difficulty of collecting demographic data in a country such as Pakistan.

In spite of the existence of the Central Statistical Office, the collection of and analysis of population statistics has been widely diffused in Pakistan since independence. Each of the three censuses carried out since independence has been the responsibility of a special, temporary census office set up within the Ministry of Home and Kashmir Affairs.

The Ministry of Health has been responsible for the collation and analysis of vital events, but this system which eventually depends upon reports by the village chowkidar (village watchman) has never produced adequate reports. To provide current estimates of fertility and mortality, the Central Statistical Office in 1962–65 in conjunction with the Pakistan Institute of Development Economics undertook the Population Growth Estimation (PGE) Survey (Farooqui and Farooq, 1971). In 1968 the PGE was replaced by a different form of survey, the Population Growth Survey-I (PGS-I). Where the PGE study utilized two independent data collection systems to provide pooled estimates of fertility and mortality (continuous registration and quarterly retrospective surveys), the PGS-I utilized monthly retrospective surveys. The monthly system proved unworkable, and in 1969 it was replaced with PGS-II which employed quarterly retrospective surveys. Data from PGS-II have yet to be analyzed and, since the two surveys depend upon quite different method-ologies, the PGS will not provide an accurate time series in conjunction with the PGE surveys.

The discontinuity in statistical series is also seen in the three censuses of Pakistan. The 1951 and 1961 censuses included a "complete" enumeration of the population including questions on social and economic characteristics of the population. The 1971 census as planned was to be undertaken in three phases. First, there was to be a total count (the "Big Count") of the population with few items of information being collected: head of the household, relation-ship to the head of the household, age, sex, and marital status of the members of the household. A second phase was to provide a postenumeration check to validate the accuracy of the "Big Count." From the census lists developed in these first two phases, a sample was to be selected randomly, and details on the socio-economic characteristics of the population collected in what was entitled the HED – Housing, Economic, Demographic Survey. Because of the war, the 1971 "Big Count" was postponed until September 1972, thus coinciding with the language riots in the Sind. This, along with vying for political representa-tion among the four provinces, appears to have resulted in erroneous recording of the population (see below) and delayed further work. The post-enumeration check had not been completed by the spring of 1973, and the HED Survey was postponed until fall 1973.

Aside from the censuses and vital statistics surveys, there are a few other important sources of population statistics. Many of these are associated with the operation of the family planning program. In 1968 a national sample survey of fertility and attitudes toward the practice of family planning was developed under the general auspices of the Family Planning Division. This project, entitled the IMPACT Survey, was under the combined supervision of person-nel, national and expatriate, from several agencies: WEPREC (West Pakistan Research and Evaluation Center), the West Pakistan Family Planning Evalua-tion Center, and NRIFP (National Research Institute for Family Planning), now NRIFC (National Research Institute for Fertility Control).[1] While the field work for that study was completed in 1969, the director of the Family Planning Program in Pakistan refused permission to release the preliminary report. Data from the IMPACT Survey are now being analyzed at Johns Hopkins University and a major publication from that study is anticipated late in 1973 or early in 1974.

Thus at the time of the writing of this paper, the major sources of demo-graphic data for Pakistan remain the 1951 and 1961 censuses. Only the pre-liminary total counts from the 1972 census were available in mid–1973 (Pa-

---

1   We have cited only those agencies in then West Pakistan involved in this major survey.
    Representatives from various agencies in then East Pakistan participated in the planning
    and design of the survey, and assumed major responsibility for the execution of the survey
    in East Pakistan. The study was designed to provide independent estimates for each
    Wing separately.

kistan 1973). Estimates of fertility and mortality can be taken only from the 1962–65 PGE Survey.

Population Impediments to Social and Economic Development: Economic-demo-graphic studies carried out in the late 1950's and early 1970's have often been cited as evidence that the developing countries of Asia, Africa, and Latin America cannot expect to achieve high levels of economic growth without the control of population growth. Perhaps the most important of these studies is Coale and Hoover's *Population Growth and Economic Development in Low-Income Countries* (1958) which focused primarily on India as a case study. Thus the conclusions which indicated the importance of controlling population growth in the context of an economic development plan were easily transferable to and acceptable in Pakistan.

Increasingly over the past five years, such economic–demographic studies have been criticized as oversimplified on the one hand and as political "tracts" representing capitalistic-imperialistic studies of a Malthusian nature on the other hand (Amin 1972). Rejection of such studies on the grounds of unwarranted determinism or on the basis of a particular political ideology is illusory. Whether economic growth can take place in a planned economy in the face of rapid population growth is not the issue. The basic issue is the degree to which population growth slows or impedes social and economic development through the increasing demand for goods and services due to population growth alone, thereby restricting the flexibility of a government in the allocation of funds and resources to economic development and social welfare programs.

This portion of the paper deals with some of the problems being generated in Pakistan by high rates of population growth, following a brief description of the estimates of levels of population growth. While raw numbers reflecting popu-lation growth are intuitively uninteresting, it is worth noting that in Pakistan population growth rates have, in some cases, been deliberately falsified and passionately defended as accurate even in the face of overwhelming evidence of inaccuracies. For example, the Third Five Year Plan accepted a population growth rate of 2.7 percent as a basis for planning while studies available to the Planning Commission at that time indicated a population growth rate in excess of 3.0. The then chairman of the Planning Commission, Mr. Said Hasan, has publicly acknowledged that this lower figure was accepted to avoid pessimism[1]. In addition, officers associated with the 1961 census have consistently argued that the figures collected in the 1961 census were accurate while much evi-dence exists to indicate an undercount of approximately 9 percent.[2] Thus one must recognize that any figure cited below for population represents only one estimate.

---

1   The statement by Mr. Hasan was made at the Seminar on Population Problems in the Economic Development of Pakistan where he chaired the opening session of June 2, 1967 (Pakistan, 1967).

2   Among the numerous population projections prepared for Pakistan, those produced by the Census Organization of the Ministry of Home and Kashmir Affairs utilize the 1961 census figures as a base population without adjustment (Government of Pakistan, Mini-stry of Home and Kashmir Affairs, Census Bulletin 7, May 1968).

Population growth in Pakistan has experienced a rapid acceleration in the past quarter of a century. Between 1901 and 1951, the population approximately doubled, increasing from 17.82 million to 33.82 million.[1] Growth during this period was much influenced by epidemics, particularly the influenza pandemic which, along with other disease entities, resulted in a growth rate of .08 percent between 1911 and 1921, whereas the growth rate was 1.31 percent in the preceding decade and 1.03 percent in the succeeding decade.

It required slightly more than half a century for the population of Pakistan to double after the turn of the century, but the doubling time for the population was reduced to less than a quarter of a century after 1951. If the population figures for 1972 are accepted as accurate, the population of Pakistan increased by 92 percent in a period of 21 years.

It is the opinion of the authors, however, that the population figures provided for Pakistan based upon the 1972 census represent over-counts of the population in contrast to under-counts in the 1961 census. The evidence, however, is sketchy because at the time of this writing only a brief report on the census has been released. Consider, however, the figures by provinces for the period 1951–72.

Table 1
Pakistan Population By Province 1951, 1961, 1972

Area	Millions			Rate of Growth	
	1951	*1961*[1]	*1972*[2]	*1951–1961*	*1961–1972*
Pakistan	33.74	42.88	64.89	2.40	3.45
North West Frontier	4.55	5.73	8.40	2.30	3.19
Centrally Administered T.A.	1.33	1.85	2.51	3.30	2.54
Federal Capital Territory Islamabad	n.a.	0.09	0.24	—	8.17
Panjab	20.64	25.49	37.37	2.11	3.19
Sind	6.13	8.37	13.97	3.11	4.27
Baluchistan	1.09	1.35	2.41	2.14	4.83

1 Pakistan, Ministry of Home and Kashmir Affairs, *Census of Pakistan, Population, West Pakistan Tables* and *Report*, Vol. 3, Table 1, (Karachi: Manager of Publications) 11–58 to 11–77.

2 Pakistan, Census Organization, Interior Division, Islamabad Population Census of Pakistan 1972, *Census Bulletin* 1, *Provisional Tables*, Tables 1 and 2: 1–3.

Note: 1951 population figures are adjusted for the new administrative units of the former West Pakistan.

---

1 The figures cited here are based upon the study by the staff of the Demographic Unit of the Pakistan Institute of Development Economics, *District Boundary Changes and Population Growth for Pakistan, 1881–1961* (East Pakistan Geographical Society, Table XVII, p. 65). The adjusted figures for each census between 1901 and 1961 are as follows: 17.82, 20.31, 31.92, 24.30, 28.69, 33.82, and 42.98 million.

Based upon the reported population figures for 1972 (64.89 million), the reported inter-censal growth rate of 3.45 percent, and the political conditions under which the census was taken, it may be argued that the 1972 census represented an overcount. The census count took place in September 1972, coinciding with the language riots in Karachi and elsewhere in the Sind. At that time, Baluchistan and the Northwest Frontier areas were under the control of the Pakistan People's Party which was vying for political power based upon population representation in the promised new elections.

Differences in growth rates between the two census intervals and among the four major provinces theoretically may be due to variations in migration – interwing migration over the census periods and inter-province migration with respect to province differences in growth – or due to variations in fertility and mortality. None of these factors would seem to account for the high growth figures between 1961 and 1972 or for the intra-province variations in growth.

While there was some net migration from East Pakistan to West Pakistan during the period 1961–1972, the total is probably negligible. However, since details on whether Bengalis were counted in 1972 were not available at the time this paper was prepared, it is not possible to determind whether this figure entered into the 1972 count or not. Assuming that inter-wing migration in no way accounted for the higher rate of population growth between 1961 and 1972, what about the influence of fertility and mortality?

Population projections prepared by Bean, Khan, and Razzaque in 1968 (1968:88) provided a high population estimate for West Pakistan, now Pakistan, for 1970 (July 1, 1970) of 61,579,000 if there was no drop in fertility and a moderate decline in mortality. Using the same projection estimate and linearly projecting the 1970 figure to the period of the 1972 census, one would estimate the population at 64,490,000, or 400,000 less than was reported in the 1972 census.

Consider the underlying assumptions of what appears to be an amazingly accurate population projection. The high population projection developed by Bean, et al. assumes no change in fertility between 1960 and 1970, thus suggesting that the family planning program had no influence on fertility levels. It was further assumed that the crude death rate fell from 17.8 per thousand in 1960 to 12.3 per thousand in 1970.[1] Given the dislocations associated with political disturbances, two wars over the period, and the failure of each development plan to meet health targets, such a reduction in mortality in retrospect appears to be unreasonable. Assuming that death rates declined, however, to about 15 per thousand, this would imply a comparable increase in the crude birth rate of 3 per thousand, suggesting a negative influence of the family planning program. Given the implausibility of these various assumptions, we are led to reject the idea that the reported population figures for Pakistan in 1972 are accurate and that the reported growth rate of 3.45 is without error.

---

1 PGS 1968 published the crude birth rate of 36 per thousand and the crude death rate of 12 per thousand.

Our conclusion is further supported by examining the relative growth by province. (See Table 1.) Over the reported period, two provinces could have been expected to grow disproportionately because of in-migration due to relatively higher employment opportunities associated with differential investments in industry and agriculture – the Punjab and the Sind. Yet the Northwest Frontier province is reported to have grown as rapidly as the Punjab, and Baluchistan is reported to have grown more rapidly than the Sind.

The population of the Sind is dominated by Karachi, and Karachi has clearly continued to grow rapidly over the last decade. However, the growth of Karachi is questionably high, 81.3 percent (increasing from 1.9 million to 3.5 million) during the last census period, and Karachi's growth accounts for only one quarter of the growth of the population of the Sind. Thus it would appear that it is implausible to assume that differences in internal migration can fully account for the variations in provincial growth rates. And at this time, there is no evidence to suggest differential patterns of fertility and mortality of such magnitude as to account for the variations in provincial growth.

Although more direct evaluation of the 1972 census must await the release of more detailed data, the evidence is strongly suggestive that the 1972 census is defective, representing an over-count of the population in contrast to the experience of under-counting the population in the previous census. The only conclusion that one might reach at this time, then, is that the population of Pakistan is growing rapidly, probably in excess of 3 percent per year and current growth rates may be as high as 3.5 percent per year.[1]

The consequences of these high growth rates for social and economic development in Pakistan may be seen in the context of selected population related problems: employment generation, education of the population, and food supplies.

Employment Generation: In "Demographic Aspects of Potential Labor Force Growth in Pakistan," Bean introduced his 1967 study as follows:

> Within the framework of Pakistan's current 20 year Perspective Plan, the Planning Commission has set five explicit development goals; of these, the target of full employment ranks as a monumental task. Its achievement will be strongly influenced by the rate of growth of the population and effective manpower planning. Not only must work be provided for those entering the labor force between 1965 and 1985, but additional employment opportunities must be provided if the level of unemployment and underemployment is to be reduced. This is a major task in its own right since the Planning Commission, combining the concepts of "under-employment" and "unemployment" under the single term "unemployment" estimates its level at 20 percent of the labor force in 1965." (1967:87)

---

1   It is not inconsistent to argue that growth rates may be as high as 3.5 percent a year while arguing that the intercensal growth rate reported at 3.45 percent is too high, since the former refers to current levels while the latter refers to an average figure over twelve years which would perforce require a much higher growth rate currently.

As noted above, the Third Five Year Plan was based upon assumptions of population growth which were not consistent with available data, and failed to take into account under-enumeration in the 1961 census and age reporting errors. Applying constant 1961 labor force participation rates and utilizing the population projections prepared by the Pakistan Institute of Development Economics, Bean concluded that through 1985, the end of the prospective plan period, the Planning Commission had underestimated the labor force by 8 to 12 million persons or 13 to 19 percent, under varying conditions of population growth.

The task of providing full, productive employment for the labor force of Pakistan is unquestionably an important yet sensitive issue.[1] Certainly the measurement of the labor force in Pakistan is difficult (see for example Islam 1964). Unemployment is clearly underestimated, with a reported level of unemployment which is much lower than one would expect due to frictional unemployment in a free market system.

There are several reasons why the issue of full employment for the labor force in Pakistan is sensitive. First, full employment in Pakistan is endangered by the same forces which will lead to successful growth in the agricultural sector. For example, the quantum increase in wheat production in Pakistan during the 1960s occurred with the introduction of the high yield wheat varieties (Mexi-Pak). Between 1966–67 and 1967–68, the index of wheat production (Base: 1959–60 = 100) increased from 112 to 164 and continued to increase through 1970–71 (Pakistan 1972b:85). This type of seed requires relatively high inputs of fertilizer and water, factors consistent with more mechanized forms of agriculture. Unless cooperative farming arrangements are organized with the financial inputs necessary to supply such resources, mechanization of large-scale landholding offers the most productive possibilities. Consequently, small landowners and tenant farmers may be replaced by mechanical equipment. The development of a more extensive system of agriculture thus may restrict employment opportunities in the agricultural sector, even though in Pakistan the net sown area of agricultural land has increased (see below).

Secondly, it has been assumed that surplus labor is generally to be found in agricultural areas, even though urban unemployment is undoubtedly relatively high. Under this assumption, absorption of increasing supplies of labor is

---

1   The sensitivity of the employment issue is reflected in the manner in which population employment statistics are published by the Government of Pakistan. For example, in *25 Years of Pakistan in Statistics, 1947–1972*, none of the 1961 census data on the labor force is published in numerical terms. In the section on "Population," 1951 census data only for the labor force are presented while the 1961 and 1951 census data on literacy, marital status, age and sex distribution, and urban populations are republished. Only urban labor force data for both 1951 and 1961 are presented. In the "Labour" section of the volume, 1961 census data are utilized as a base line for subsequent survey data, but only in percentage terms. One is therefore forced to refer to original sources to determine 1961 census labor force information and to find the basic numerical data from which the percentage distributions are derived for various labor surveys, and the Pakistan Economic Survey of 1971–72 provides no information on the labor force (Pakistan, 1972a).

largely dependent upon industrial growth. Selected industries, such as cotton manufacturing, were heavily dependent upon the East Pakistan market. While much of the export trade has been reoriented – with some positive economic benefits – since the breakup of Pakistan, industrial growth in recent years has been hampered. Because of the political and social problems associated with the changes in government, the war, and civil/labor unrest, the gross domestic product from manufacturing decreased by 3.8 percent between 1970–71 and 1971–2 (Pakistan 1972a:3). Thus to date, the growth of the non-agricultural sector has not, in general, been able to provide employment markets for surplus labor.

Thirdly, female employment in Pakistan is low (Bean 1968) and because of the religious barriers surrounding the appearance and work of women outside of the immediate household, opportunities for female employment may be expected to remain low. At the same time, the greater educational opportunities for females will create a demand for employment which will be difficult to restrict. Thus any form of social change which leads to improved status of women will increase the pressures on the labor market.

Fourthly, Pakistan is systematically pursuing a policy which leads to an unbalanced growth of the labor force. Because of the foreign exchange earnings which accrue through the migration of middle and high level occupational groups, such migration is encouraged. Indeed, during the first part of 1973, contracts were arranged for 300 physicians in Iran while Pakistan is suffering from a lack of physicians, particularly physicians in the public/rural sector.[1] Such a policy which is dependent only upon the short term gains of foreign exchange, can only lead to a labor force stripped of skills, entrepreneurship, and professional abilities.

Thus, while continuing high rates of population growth are creating increasing demands for employment, the policies of Pakistan are more likely to led to unfulfilled expectations for full employment.

Education for All: A policy designed to provide full and universal education for the population has been an essential part of the planned program of social development in Pakistan for years, and with the emphasis on social welfare espoused by President Zulfikar Ali Bhutto, this policy has been reaffirmed. The current education policy of Pakistan announced on March 8, 1972 contained the following elements (Pakistan 1972a: 17):

(a) education to be made universal and free up to class ten throughout the country in two phases, i.e., up to class 8 by October, 1972 and matriculation by 1974;
(b) privately-managed schools and colleges to be nationalized without compensation;
(c) salaries and service conditions for teachers in all privately-managed schools to be brought to par with those of Government schools;
(d) five new Boards of Intermediate and Secondary Education to be set up at Saidu Sharif, Rawalpindi, Gujranwala, Bahawalpur, and Khaipur;
(e) three new Universities to be opened at Saidu Sharif, Multan and Sukkur;

---

1 Contained in an internal office report of the Population Council Iran office (March–May, 1973, p. 1).

(f) the number of universities to be doubled by 1980;
(g) the N.E.D. Engineering College, Karachi and the Sind University Engineering College, Jamshoro to be raised to university status;
(h) a national foundation for book production to be set up.

Certain aspects of this policy such as nationalization, salaries, and boards (b, c, d) are dependent upon administrative/political actions only. Expansion of the university programs and raising of colleges to university status are dependent upon the availability of professional manpower to staff these programs, and retaining highly qualified university personnel is becoming increasingly difficult in Pakistan. The even more difficult part of the policy to implement effectively is the primary target of universal education, and the difficulty to a large degree stems from the demographic conditions extant in Pakistan.

On the one hand, the continuing high rates of population growth mean increasingly larger cohorts of young children requiring education. Consider the number of children between the ages of 5–9 in Pakistan. Bean, et al. estimated that the number of children (male and female) in West Pakistan in this age group was 6.6 million. Under the high population projection, which is roughly consistent with the 1972 census count, there were approximately 9.7 million children in 1970 and there would be 10.9 million in 1975. Thus merely to maintain adequate education facilities in the primary schools, physical facilities and teachers would be required for an additional 1.2 million children between 1970 and 1972 – or essentially creating an education system capable of handling the total primary enrollments of the New York City area. While creating additional facilities is difficult, catching up on educational facilities for the vast number of children currently not receiving education is a monumental task in itself.

In a study entitled "A Demographic Approach to Educational Planning in Pakistan" (1967: 199), Khan noted that early in the last decade, West Pakistan enrollment ratios (the proportion of children in school of a given age cohort) were among the lowest in Asia. Based upon educational statistics for 1962, approximately 44 percent of males between the ages of 5–9 were in school and only 27 percent of males between the ages of 10–14. The picture was even worse for females, 13 percent and 6 percent respectively.

In the light of these low enrollment levels and the increasingly large number of children entering the school ages, Khan concluded: "The educational objectives of the Pakistan long-term perspective plan (then universal education by 1985) are thus not only highly optimistic, they are rather unrealistic, and especially so under sustained high fertility..." (1967: 198). Given the unrealistic nature of the educational target espoused in 1965 – universal education by 1985 – the educational target announced in 1972 must be regarded as statement of political promise rather than a statement of planning commitment. With the existing low levels of education in Pakistan, and the continuing high rates of population growth, universal education cannot be achieved in the forseeable future.

Feeding the Multides. During the 1960s the improvements in agricultural production in Pakistan appeared to assure that Pakistan would soon be self-sufficient in food production. Agricultural outputs increased due to a series of factors. Expansion of irrigation programs, desalinization projects, and land reclamation programs resulted in increased land available for agriculture. In 1960–61, 32,110,000 acres of land were sown, and by 1967–68, this had increased to 35,779,000 (Pakistan 1972b: 82). In addition, Pakistan shared heavily with other countries in the "Green Revolution." With the adoption of the new seed varieties, which for Pakistan with its heavy wheat consumption the Mexi-Pak wheat was most important, production increased dramatically. Between 1955–56 and 1958–59, the average annual wheat production was 3,562,000 tons, and the yield per acre averaged 691 pounds. By 1970–71, the average annual yield was 6,596,000 tons with a yield of 971 pounds per acre, or a yield per acre increase of 40 percent. Thus in terms of cereal grains, Pakistan was not only able to provide for its growing population but was also able to provide for increased consumption. For example, the *Pakistan Economic Survey* for 1971–72 notes that "The consumption of food grains has shown a rising tendency in recent years. After fluctuating in the range of 270–285 lbs. per year per capita, there was a distinct rise to 318 lbs. in 1968–69 and to 350 lbs. in 1970–71" (Pakistan 1972a:21).

Because of recent drought conditions, however, and in part because of dislocations associated with the war, production decreased in 1970–71 and 1971–72. Thus Pakistan which had become a net exporter in the last years of the 1960s became again a net importer. "In 1971–72, however, it became necessary to arrange for imports of food-grains of 7.5 lakh tons in order to control price levels and to maintain daily per capita consumption at 9.6 oz. per day (as compared with 11.05 oz. in 1970–71)" (Pakistan 1972a: 21).

The agricultural achievements in Pakistan during the last decade were indeed remarkable, and were in no small measure due to the "Green Revolution." Certainly there remains capacity to extend the type of agriculture associated with the "Green Revolution" to additional areas in Pakistan through the distribution of the new seed varieties, making available more fertilizers and pesticides. There is a limit, however, to the amount of land which can be included under such agricultural practices, and there are the imponderables – the availability of water. Continued success in agricultural production however is needed, because one certainty Pakistan faces is continued population growth and growing numbers of citizens to be fed: somewhere between 11.7 million and 8.2 million more individuals to be fed between 1970 and 1975.[1]

Conditions Supporting Continued High Population Growth. Pakistan's social and economic development plans for this decade must consider not only the elimination of social inequality, but must also consider taking care of, or providing

---

1   Under the lowest population growth estimate, to maintain the per capita availability of food grains achieved in 1968–69 of 318 pounds, the high output of wheat in 1970–71 of 6,596 thousand tons (or 350 pounds per capita) would have to be increased by 20 percent, assuming all additional food grains derive from wheat.

for a growing population. Employment opportunities are required for an increasing potential labor force, and the new entrants to the labor force for this decade are here now, having been born roughly 10–15 years ago. Educational opportunities must be provided at the primary school level for children born between 1965–70 in the first half of this decade, and for children born in the first half of this decade, facilities must be provided in the last half of the decade· To achieve self-sufficiency in food supplies and to increase nutritional levels, increasing agricultural production is required for the *increasing numbers* of children being born. (Because of the increasing numbers of couples entering the childbearing years of life, even with a rapidly declining fertility rate – see Bean et al. (1968: 91), fertility assumption III – there will be approximately 500,000 more children in the age groups 0–4 in 1975 than in 1970.)

A rapid fertility decline appears less and less likely to take place in Pakistan in the short run. It is important to note that the social and cultural factors in Pakistan do and will continue to support high fertility values. First, women enter marital unions at an early age and marriage is nearly universal. For example, using the Hajnal method which enables one to estimate mean age at marriage from census distributions of the proportion married at given ages, Sadiq reported the mean age of Pakistan women in 1961 at 17.6 (Sadiq 1965: 242). By the end of the childbearing years of life, age 50–54, according to the 1961 census, only 8,894 women in Pakistan had never married. Although widowhood is quite high in Pakistan, it generally does not become significant until after the peak childbearing years. Thus for the group between the ages of 20 and 29, the percentage of currently married women in 1961 was 89.2 percent.

Secondly, within marriages, the social-cultural structure of Pakistan tends to support moderately high fertility values. Many of the variables associated with declining marital fertility simply are not present in Pakistan. Coale, for example, in 1965 summarized the factors associated with the decline in marital fertility (1965: 208):

(1) The decline in mortality. With more children surviving, fewer births are needed to achieve a given family size.
(2) The rising cost and diminished economic advantages of children in urbanized industrial societies. In a rural family children assist in production at an early age and are a source of support for parents in their old age...
(3) Higher status of women. The extension of education to women, women's suffrage, and the employment of women in occupations formerly reserved for males are objective indications of wider opportunity and higher status for women... these changes in opportunity and status promote the spread of birth control.
(4) Religious changes and differences.
(5) The development of a secular, rational attitude.

While Coale notes that there are counter examples to each of these variables, the evidence would seem to suggest that none of these changes which may be associated with declining marital fertility exist in Pakistan at the beginning of this decade.

Infant mortality during the first half of the last decade remained high. A minimum estimate for the period 1963–65 in Pakistan indicated that at least one of each eight children born alive would die before reaching the age of one. Approximately one of each six live births could be expected to die before the age of 14. The uncertainty of knowing that children born would reach adulthood – and therefore would be available to support the parents in their old age – tends to reinforce high fertility.

The status of women remains low in Pakistan. Few are educated (see above) and few are employed – only 6.14 percent of the women age 10 and over in 1961 (Pakistan 1964a).

The population is largely rural and illiterate. In 1961 only 22.5 percent of the population lived in urban areas and only 16.3 percent of the population above the age of 5 was reported as literate (Pakistan 1964b). The Muslim religion tends to reinforce high levels of fertility according to studies by Kirk (1966), and this certainly tends to be borne out in Pakistan.

In summary, all of the factors which would tend to support high fertility levels appear to be present in Pakistan. Furthermore, it is unlikely that one can predict any significant changes taking place in this decade that would substantially influence fertility levels based solely on social and economic changes.

Given these conditions, what might the Government do? The rate of growth of per capita income slowed from the beginning of the last decade to the end of the decade and with the war, per capita income actually decreased by 5.1 percent in 1970–71. Agricultural productivity has slowed in part because of the negative climatic conditions of the past three years. Industrialization has been retarded by labor problems and nationalization programs, and so on. In the face of these negative conditions, therefore, what can one expect from a government policy and program to limit fertility?

Population Policy Implementation in Pakistan

The Government of Pakistan has supported population programs since approximately 1952 and the nature of the policies and programs through 1968 have been summarized in a variety of publications. Because of the complexity of these changes and programs, it is difficult to encapsulate them in a paper of this scope. For a more detailed history of population program activities to 1968, see Bean and Bhatti (1969).

In 1968, Pakistan was operating under a population policy which broadly supported specific demographic goals for fertility reduction to be achieved through a national family planning program. Organizationally, the program operated as a sub-division or division of the Ministry of Health, Labor, and Social Welfare. Between 1968 and 1972 there have been several changes in leadership and levels of governmental authority, but the mandate of the program remained relatively constant. Following a full-scale government review of the program in 1972, it was recommended that family planning be given a broader responsibility and be renamed and upgraded to the Division of Population Planning within the Ministry of Health, Social Welfare, and Population Planning (labor having been taken out of the Ministry). Nevertheless, at the time of this writing, the only significant operational change introduced by these administrative shifts occurred in 1968 with the appointment of a new joint secretary for family planning.

Operationally, family planning in Pakistan from 1965 onward has been a separate group, operating independently of the health program with which it has been allied ministerially. The program stressed the utilization of intrauterine devices and the distribution of conventional contraceptives – condoms and foams, primarily. Sterilizations – primarily vasectomies – were reported to be widely popular in East Pakistan, and some administrative pressures were exerted to increase the rate of vasectomies in West Pakistan without a great deal of success.

Heavy utilization of incentive payments to family planning acceptors was made with respect to IUDs and sterilizations, and incentive fees were also made to "finders" (largely village *dais*) and to the medical personnel responsible for the insertion of IUDs and the performance of sterilizing operations. Conventional contraceptives were sold under a government subsidy.

Stress was placed on having family planning personnel achieve specific targets for IUD insertions, conventional contraceptives distributed, and sterilizations performed. These program statistics were converted into estimates of periods of protection against the risk of pregnancy under a set of simple and questionable statistical assumptions and the protection period (couple years protection) converted by a simple ratio estimate into births averted. Working from the opposite direction, given the demographic target of reducing the estimated crude birth rate from 50 to 40 between 1965 and 1970, the births which must be averted to achieve this goal could in turn be translated into couple years of protection to be achieved, and thence into family planning targets such as IUDs inserted, etc. (Bean, Seltzer 1968).

The combination of large sums of money available for incentive payments and the stress on achieving performance targets clearly established a framework within which misreporting and corruption could take place. Yet the accuracy of the figures and the success of the program were never questioned until late in 1968.

Dissatisfaction with the family planning program in 1968 appeared to derive from two factors. First, the field organization was largely based on the utilization of part time village *dais* (illiterate midwives) to recruit clients for family planning programs. Even if the reported numbers of family planning acceptors were accurate, the productivity of these women in 1968 was very low since on the average a *dai* was recruiting only 1.3 IUD acceptors per month. Secondly, emphasis had been placed on acceptors of family planning methods with little emphasis on developing continuous users of contraceptives (Ahmad 1971).

Thus in 1970 the family planning program introduced a new organizational structure in the Sialkot Division, a structure which, because of its initial testing point, has become known as the Sialkot Project or Program. Under this new program, full-time male and female workers – motivators – were to be utilized to maintain records on a fixed population in order to identify couples in the childbearing years of life, i.e., target couples. The motivator couple concept was based upon the assumption that the success of the family planning program in Pakistan depended on activities which would reach the dominant figures, the males, in the households. Through personal contacts with target couples supported with mass education programs, the motivators were expected to recruit acceptors for the family planning program and to maintain contact over time with the couples. Incentive payments were to be made under this program to the motivators not at the time of acceptance, but at the end of a twelve month period with the payment calculated on the basis of the number of couples recruited and continuing to use contraceptives so that the wife remained non-pregnant for a continuous twelve month period. Longer periods in a non-pregnant state resulted in higher incentive payments. Although there have been no detailed evaluations of this new program, it has been adopted as the model to be expanded throughout Pakistan, and by 1973, it had been introduced into nine districts.

The Record to Date. The performance of the Pakistan family planning program during the period 1965–68 has been summarized in Bean and Bhatti (1968). The performance since mid–1968 may be summarized very briefly (see Table 2). In the first six months of fiscal 1969, family planning outputs continued to rise over all previous periods with outputs by reported IUDs inserted conventional contraceptives distributed, and vasectomies or tubaligations performed. Since that period, family planning performance statistics have continued to decline. Although the records from July 1970 onward are discontinuous, clearly the record for the last six months in 1972 is dismal. Extrapolated to a twelve month period, the data would suggest that the recent performance is worse than the performance during the first year of the developing program introduced with the third Five Year Plan (1965–66).

Table 2
Pakistan Family Planning Performance Statistics 1965–72

Year	IUDs Insertions	Conventional Contraceptives Sold(000)	Sterilizations Vasectomies/ Tubligations
July 1965–June 1966	155,829	23,819	1,365
1966–67	337,880	62,903	1,826
1967–68	425,955	97,167	14,558
1968–69	438,348	102,431	58,435
1969–70	342,952	102,715	10,297
July 1970–Oct. 1970	100,739	31,239	2,187
Jan. 1971–April 1971	72,525	19,352	1,382
July 1972–Dec. 1972	51,595	1,175	1,582

Source: Pakistan Family Planning Council Monthly Reports 1965–72.

The low level of performance of the family planning program late in 1972 as reflected in the available statistics may be due to three factors, singly or collectively. First, the reported statistics may reflect more valid reports of actual performance. Second, certainly the problems associated with the recent war and breakup of the country have made it difficult to maintain and operate social welfare programs such as family planning. Third, the political disputes among the now four provinces in Pakistan have had deleterious organizational consequences and probably operational consequences. For example, under the East-West Pakistan arrangements, family planning was a provincial activity, conjoint with the central government. With the dominance of the Punjabis and refugees in then West Pakistan, a disproportionate number of the senior trained personnel were Punjabi. With the development of the four provinces in Pakistan today, family planning became a provincial activity, conjoint with the new central government. Thus in the Northwest, Baluchistan, and the Sind, many of the Punjabis were replaced with local people, often lacking in both training and experience. Further, provincial governments have not been able to maintain the provincial financial contribution under the economic crisis which has affected the entire country, in spite of the fact that central government funding appears to be ample, largely because of foreign aid provided for family planning from the United Nations Fund for Population Activities and the United States Agency for International Development. Thus, as we shall note in the concluding section of this paper, the politics of population in a fragile state may become more significant in the balance of this decade than ever before in the history of Pakistan.

Population Prospects to 1980

From the point of view of the authors of this paper, there will be several significant population issues in Pakistan at least through 1980. The relative importance of these issues varies, as we shall note below, and all of the issues may become trivial in the face of continuing and mounting political instability now furthered with the change in government in Afganistan and the re-emergence of the Pukhtoonistan issue.

Population Statistics: Continuing Uncertainty. As noted above, recent demographic statistics, particularly the 1972 census, are of questionable validity and no sound basis currently exists for anticipating improved estimates of vital rates or estimates of family planning program activities. However, some recent governmental changes have been made which would appear to strengthen the capacity to generate effective population statistics.

The Census Office has been made a permanent organization, thus establishing the potential for effective long-term planning for the next census. The Census Office has been officially removed from the Ministry of Home and Kashmir Affairs, and is to be combined with the Central Statistical Office in a new Division of Statistics within the Ministry of Planning and Statistics. The integration of census and statistics has not yet been accomplished, and as of mid–1973, the CSO remained in Karachi and the Census Office in Islamabad. Offsetting the benefits which might be derived from an organizationally coherent statistics structure, new duties and responsibilities have been assigned to the Division of Statistics. The President of Pakistan mandated the registration of all adults for the purpose of establishing valid voter registration rolls. Faced with the completion of the census post-enumeration check, the HED Survey and the analysis and publication of the census data, the enormity of the registration program may eliminate any effective planning and development of an improved statistical system for some years to come.

Therefore, given the current state of statistical programs in Pakistan, it is unlikely that adequate population statistics will become available before 1980.

Family Planning in Pakistan. The prospects for a nationally supported family planning program in Pakistan during the balance of this decade hinge upon three questions. Is family planning socially and culturally feasible in Pakistan at the present time? Is the Pakistan government really serious about supporting an effective family planning program? Finally, can fertility control succeed in the face of ethnic and provincial competition for political – representational power?

Is a government-sponsored fertility control program feasible? In Section II of this paper, we outlined a series of conditions which have traditionally been associated with spontaneous declines in fertility in a variety of countries. That is, fertility has declined without the intervention of a government to foster fertility limitation.

There is strong evidence to suggest that some governmentally sponsored fertility limitation programs have influenced the birth rate, and most of the examples are located in Asia; Taiwan, Korea, Hong Kong, and Singapore are good examples. But each of these good examples represents a society culturally and economically distinct from Pakistan: more urbanized, higher levels of education, more industrialization, higher status of women, and so on.

There does not appear to be a country with a level of social and economic development as in Pakistan that has clearly demonstrated that a governmentally sponsored family planning program can induce a *long-term secular decline* in fertility, and there is now little reason to expect that Pakistan will be the first example.

One would expect that family planning would have some effect on fertility, since it would appear that there is some demand for family planning in Pakistan, but there is at the same time no evidence to indicate that the Pakistan family planning program has substantially increased the demand for family planning services.

The demand for family planning services appears to be somewhat limited in Pakistan, and one must question the efficacy of a national family planning program alone to stimulate demand in Pakistan. Nevertheless one must recognize that other government investments in industrialization, educational programs, and other social welfare programs may encourage the adoption and spread of a small family set of norms. But these changes will occur slowly and gradually in the face of a rapidly growing population.

Is Pakistan really serious about limiting the rate of population growth? On the surface, Pakistan had mounted one of the most serious efforts in the world to limit fertility through a family planning program. In the face of left wing opposition to family planning, a high-level government commission reviewed the issues in 1972 and supported continued government activities in population. From this commission arose the recomendation to upgrade and expand the family planning program through the creation of the Population Planning Division.

Nevertheless the Government of Pakistan undermines its family planning efforts through several direct and indirect actions. Family planning remains a conjoint activity of the central government and the four provinces. While under the concept of conjoint activities as defined by the Central Law Minister the central government could assume larger responsibility for family planning, the provinces have been allowed to founder because of inadequate provincial budgets and the assignment of locally acceptable but poorly trained personnel to the family planning program.

In addition, within the central family planning organization, support has not been provided for sufficiently high salaries and for job security to insure stability of the family planning personnel. Related to that issue is the fact that the government is apparently now pursuing a policy indirectly related to the family planning program which limits the possibility of securing the type of high level personnel essential to operate a family planning program. That policy seems to encourage the emigration of skilled manpower as a means of securing foreign exchange. For example, Pakistani physicians, statisticians, and demographers are employed widely in the Gulf States, and the majority of all Pakistani social scientists with Ph.D. degrees with training in population are employed outside Pakistan. Thus it would appear that while Pakistan has mounted a major family planning effort, the government has maintained policies which impede the development of an effective organizational machinery.

Can fertility control programs succeed in the face of ethnic and provincial competition for political representation? The lesson learned through the block voting of an absolute majority of the population of Pakistan which led to the emergence of Bangladesh is not likely to be soon forgotten. Yet in a political/ demographic sense, the idea that fertility control programs can mitigate the development of a more evenly balanced population distribution by province or ethnic group is patently nonsense. The overwhelming numerical superiority of the Punjabis in Pakistan is so great that it cannot be redressed for decades through even the most severe differential fertility control programs.

There is, however, the fact that family planning remains a conjoint activity, and the governments of the Northwest and Baluchistan cannot but be influenced by the thinking of leaders of the socialist countries of the developing world that family planning is neo-colonial and anti-socialist (Amin, 1972). In addition, while population issues – the consequence of population growth on economic and social development – become important in the framework of a centrally planned economy, such issues loom less large at the provincial level. It would appear that population issues are largely viewed, and legitimately so, as important only at the level where economic planning takes place. An important question, therefore, is at what level family planning or population planning programs are controlled in Pakistan.

By maintaining family planning as a conjoint activity between the central government and the provincial governments, the political issues associated with conflicts among the provinces regarding population balance may be short-circuited. But since none of the provinces will have the responsibility for dealing with the issues of population pressure on social and economic development programs nor for dealing with the social and cultural conditions which support continuing high fertility levels, necessary support for population programs at the provincial levels may be difficult to organize.

REFERENCES

Ahmad, Wajihuddin
    1971   "Field Structures in Family Planning." Studies in Family planning 2 (January): 6–13.
Amin, Samir
    1972   "L'Afrique sous-peuplé." Development and Civilization 47–48 (March–June): 59–67.
Bean, Lee L.
    1967   "Demographic Aspects of Potential Labour Force Growth in Pakistan." International Union for the Scientific Study of Population, Sydney Conference, Contributed Papers (August): 87–97.
    1968   "Utilization of Human Resources: The Case of Women in Pakistan." International Labour Review 4 (April): 391–410.
——, and William Seltzer
    1968   "Couple Years of Protection and Births Prevented: A Methodological Examination." Demography, 2: 947–959.
——, et al.
    1968   Population Projections for Pakistan. Karachi: Pakistan Institute of Development Economics Monograph 17 (January).
——, and A. D. Bhatti
    1969   "Three Years of Pakistan's New National Family-Planning Programme." Pakistan Development Review 1 (Spring): 35–57.
Coale, A. J. and E. M. Hoover
    1958   Population and Economic Development in Low-Income Countries. New Jersey: Princeton University Press.
Coale, A. J.
    1965   "Factors Associated with Development of Low Fertility." United Nations: World Population Conference 2: 208.
Farooqui, M. N. I. and G. M. Farooq, eds.,
    1971   Final Report of the Population Growth Estimation Experiment. Dacca: Pakistan Institute of Development Economics (July).
Islam, Nurul
    1964   "Concepts and Measurement of Unemployment in Developing Economies." International Labour Review 3 (March): 240–256.

Khan, M. R.
    1967   "A Demographic Approach to Educational Planning in Pakistan." International
           Union for the Scientific Study of Population. Sydney Conference Contributed
           Papers (August): 192–200.
Kirk, Dudley
    1966   "Factors Affecting Moslem Natality." pp. 561–579 in Bernard Berelson (ed.)
           Family Planning and Population Program; A Review of World Developments.
           Chicago: University of Chicago Press.
Pakistan, (Ministry of Home and Kashmir Affairs) Census Commissioner.
    1964a Census of Pakistan Population 1961. Pakistan-1, Karachi: Manager of Publication
           (June): 5–9.
Pakistan, (Ministry of Home and Kashmir Affairs) Census Commissioner,
    1964b Census of Pakistan, Population: West Pakistan-3, Karachi: Manager of Publi-
           cations (June) 2–78 to 2–93.
Pakistan, Institute of Development Economics
    1967   A Report on the Seminar on the Population Problems in the Economic Develop-
           ment of Pakistan. Karachi (September).
Pakistan, Government Finance Division Economic Advisors' Wing.
    1972a Pakistan Economic Survey 1971–72. Islamabad (June).
Pakistan, Central Statistical Office
    1972b 25 Years of Pakistan in Statistics 1947–72. Karachi: Manager of Publications
           (July).
Pakistan, Census Organization, Interior Division
    1973   Population Census of Pakistan, Census Bulletin-1, Provisional Tables (January):
           1–4.
Sadiq, M. Nasim
    1965   "Estimation of Nuptiality and its Analysis from the Census Data." Pakistan
           Development Review 2 (Summer): 242.

Journal of Asian and African Studies VIII, 3–4

Bhutto's Educational Reform

J. HENRY KORSON

University of Massachusetts, Amherst, U.S.A.

Every new aspirant for political office in an election contest is expected to point out the failures of his predecessors in office, the inadequacy of his opponent(s), and to present to the electorate a more or less clearly defined program intended to cure the ills of his constituency. Such a program must be concerned with the basic needs of the electorate, and must demonstrate a realistic assessment of the feasibility of such a program. A candidate for office expects to appeal to the wishes, desires and ambitions of all the electorate, although he knows that not all will necessarily support him.

In an underdeveloped nation, aside from the political and economic issues which almost always hold center stage in a political campaign, perhaps no other item has as much appeal to the masses as that of universal and free education. Pakistan was left with few resources, economic or educational, at the time of independence in 1947, so that the building process for a complete and modern system of education necessarily had to be a slow one.[1]

Pakistan was founded as a new nation committed to a separate state based on Islamic ideology, but whose system of higher education was largely a replica of the British system, with its concern not with a religious philosophy, but with the arts, letters and sciences of western Europe. Many of the nation's leaders were products of either such institutions in British India or England. (Mr. Bhutto won his B.A. degree at the University of California and took his law training at Oxford. Two of his children are students at Harvard-Radcliffe, while two others are enrolled in the American School in Islamabad.) The ultimate purpose and goal of the educational system established by the British colonial government on the subcontinent was to train a cadre of junior administrators, most of whom could not hope to rise above the level of clerks.

---

1   When President Ayub Khan came to power in 1958, he proceeded to establish a number of Commissions to study diverse national problems. Among them was the National Commission on Education. In 1968, the Embassy of Pakistan in Washington, D.C., issued a pamphlet titled "Pakistan's Development Decade, 1958–68, Educational Reform," which proclaimed the educational advances that had been made during Ayub Khan's regime. "Of all the reforms introduced in Pakistan, I feel personally proud of our educational reforms." It boasted of the achievements of his regime, of which there were some, but played down the failure to achieve the goals set out in the Third Five Year Plan. There were many reasons for the latter, among them the rapid and unabated population increase.

And this sytem of education prevailed until 1947, when India and Pakistan won their independence.

Since Pakistan was founded on the basis of a religious ideology, but whose system of higher education depends so heavily on western educational experience and outlook, it would almost appear to some observers that in matters of education the nation has developed a schizoid personality. On the one hand the political leaders since independence have felt that they have had to maintain the confidence of the *mullahs*, yet on the other hand these leaders have also felt the heavy responsibility of leading the nation into the modern world with all its demands of contemporary technology equipped with an inadequate system of education for its people – not the least of which has been one of the highest rates of illiteracy in the world.

The results of the national election in December, 1970, saw not only the emergence of the Pakistan People's Party as the majority political party in West Pakistan, but Mr. Bhutto as the spokesman for the party and its program of reform in the political, economic and social spheres. Following the end of hostilities between Pakistan and India in December, 1971, the PPP was left as the majority party in the west, with the task of rebuilding a nation not only defeated in war, but with considerable self-doubt as to its future. Mr. Bhutto and his newly-named cabinet quickly rallied to the challenge, and within three months of assuming the office of president announced through his Minister of Education, Mr. Abdul Hafeez Pirzada, a short-range and long-range education plan for the nation for the period 1972–1980. This was termed *The Education Policy, 1972–1980*, and was accompanied by an appendix, *Martial Law Regulations, No. 118*, signed by Mr. Bhutto in his role as Chief Martial Law Administrator on March 29, 1972 (*Policy* 1972).

The permanent constitution was passed by the National Assembly on April 10th, 1973 and authenticated by President Bhutto two days later. Parts of two articles (37 and 38), clearly refer to the government's intentions in the field of education.

"Article 37.   The State shall—
    (a) promote, with special care, the educational and economic interests of backward classes or areas;
    (b) remove illiteracy and provide free and compulsory secondary education within the minimum possible period;
    (c) make technical and professional education generally available and higher education equally accessible to all on the basis of merit;
    (f) enable people of different areas, through education, training, agricultural and industrial development and other methods, to participate fully in all forms of national activities, including employment in the service of Pakistan...
"Article 38.   The State shall—
    (d) provide basic necessities of life, such as food, clothing, housing, education and medical relief for all such citizens, irrespective of sex, caste, creed or race, as are permanently or temporarily unable to earn their livelihood on account of infirmity, sickness or unemployment..."
(*Constitution*, 1973: 17–18).

The Central government has also established the National Education Council with the Central Minister of Education as Chairman. The Council's purpose is to initiate and support research and disseminate its findings and mobilize the latest educational techniques and resources for the improvement of education. It will also maintain and develop cooperation with UNESCO. Ten basic committees will be established to conduct basic surveys and studies and to serve as a resource group to evaluate various programs (*Dawn* 12-3-72).

Reinforcement of the new education policy for the nation by a martial law edict was considered necessary because an important part of the plan called for the nationalization without compensation of all the privately owned and operated colleges beginning September 1, 1972, and all the privately owned and operated schools beginning October 1, 1972, but phased over a two-year period. Only those institutions that the government is fully satisfied are operated on a "genuinely benevolent, philanthropic and non-commercial basis" could be exempted from the application of nationalization.

Perhaps one of the most impressive aspects of the whole enterprise is the fact that the new policy was formulated and announced in a period of less than three months after Mr. Bhutto took office on December 20, 1971. Almost immediately after he assumed office, Mr. Bhutto met with the vice-chancellors of all the universities and requested suggestions for changes, while Mr. Pirzada on January 6th, 1972 met with teachers and students in Islamabad, followed by meetings with provincial officials and others who were invited to contribute their suggestions. Although President Bhutto's new education policy has not only been well received but highly praised in the press, no mention is made and insufficient credit is given to ex-President Yahya Khan in the field of education. Yahya Khan had asked Nurul Khan to develop a new education plan, which was done, but, unfortunately, it was never implemented. Bhutto's policy reflects much of the work that had already gone into Nurul Khan's plan. A sense of urgency pervades the whole policy and one cannot escape the feeling that the government is determined to implement its new program of education for the nation in the shortest possible time.

The new policy, or plan, itself is far-reaching and all-inclusive. It not only calls for the restructuring of the educational system from the primary through the graduate and professional school programs, but special emphasis is placed on the expansion and strengthening of technical training in a wide variety of fields. Although space does not permit a complete review of all the proposals in the plan, the major ones will be pointed up and explored.

Major Proposals

Free and Universal Education

The plan calls for a two-phase program to make education free and universal for all children up to Class X. Because of limited resources, the first phase, which began October 1, 1972, education up to Class VIII was made free for both boys and girls. With the second phase, beginning October 1, 1974, free education will be extended to Classes IX and X in all schools. Depending on response, the government anticipates that primary education will become *universal* up to Class V for boys by 1979 and for girls by 1984, and up to Class VIII in 1982 for boys and for girls in 1987. Some women's groups have already raised questions about the obvious discrimination against girls, but the protests have not been answered directly beyond the expected statements that limited resources would necessarily limit the desired ideal arrangements for the development of universal and free education. The question of making education compulsory has been stated to be the responsibility of the "parents to send their children to school on pain of punishment" (*Policy* 1972: 3). The government recognized the far-reaching implications, and has referred this problem to the provincial assemblies.

Ideological Goals

One of the basic objectives of the new plan will be the "Promotion of understanding and appreciation of the fundamentals of Islam and the basic ideology of Pakistan and their reflection in the code of personal and social life..." (*Weekly Commentary* June 1, 1973), and to achieve this goal the study of Islam will be required through Class X.

Throughout the text of the *Education Policy*, as well as from the periodic pronouncements by political leaders, the concept of useful service to the community and the nation is very apparent. The socialization of the young during the elementary school years is to be conducted by their teachers so that they will be motivated to perform productive service for the welfare of the community. Students will be organized into squads for a variety of tasks, and the dignity of labor will be emphasized. At the middle school level, students will be taught a variety of skills useful to their needs as future members of their communities. Furthermore, "...the People's Government was committed to restore the dignity of teachers so that they could act as guides, preachers and mentors for the moral training of the younger generation" (*Pakistan Times* May 24, 1973).

On May 4, 1973, the Punjab Minister of Education, Dr. Abdul Khaliq was reported in the *Pakistan Times* to have announced that beginning with the 1973–74 academic year, emphasis would be on agro-technical education subjects "to make education more purposeful and useful." He claimed that "there was no room for liberal education, and the major need was for ends-oriented programs and institutions to engage people in productive pursuits." A week later, in the same paper, Dr. Khaliq was quoted as stating that compulsory agricultural and technical education from the sixth class will be introduced in the boys' schools in the Punjab [beginning Sept., 1973], and home economics would be a compulsory subject for girls. This "move toward purposeful education has been taken in the light of the experience of countries like China, the Soviet Union, Cuba and Jugoslavia, in keeping with Pakistan's own conditions." Later in the same month, degrees other than technical and scientific were being referred to in the press as "worthless" (*Pakistan Times* May 12, 1973).

A massive attack will be made on illiteracy among the young through the universalization of elementary education and an equally massive attack will be made on adult illiteracy. For example, beginning September 1, 1973 the provincial government of Sind will launch a literacy program which is planned to reach 400,000 adults at a cost of Rs 8,000,000 (*Pakistan Affairs* August 14, 1973). Egalitarianism will be the keystone in educational opportunity, not only for women but for all underprivileged groups. Academic freedom for teachers and autonomony for institutions within the framework of the needs of the nation will be assured. It is hoped that students and parents, along with teachers and other members of the community will participate in educational affairs. And, finally, a nationwide motivational campaign will be instituted to help persuade parents not only to send their children to school, but to encourage them to participate in the community programs.

Elementary Education (Classes I-VIII)

Beginning October 1, 1972, elementary education was made free in all schools, both government-supported and privately managed. It is estimated that 70 percent of the boys and 25 percent of the girls in the primary school age cohort attend school while 30 percent of the boys and only 11 percent of the girls in the middle school cohort attend school. By 1980 these percentages are expected to increase to 100 percent of the boys and 70 percent of the girls at the primary level and 70 percent of the boys and 40 percent of the girls in the middle school level. These projections also call for the addition of 61,000 classrooms for these school levels, while priority will be given to rural areas and to the education of girls. Where feasible, other facilities will be put into use.

Secondary and Intermediate Education (Classes IX-XII)

Although only 8 percent of the secondary and intermediate school age cohort currently attend school, it is estimated that by 1980 the increase should see 15 percent of the youth in attendance. More important, perhaps, is the planned shift in emphasis of the kind of training offered. About two-thirds of all students are studying liberal arts subjects. The government plan calls for a "...massive shift in enrollment from the arts towards enrollment in science and technical subjects; from an aimless general education to a more purposeful agro-technical education" (*Policy* 1972: 10). This goal is to be achieved by 1980 by maintaining the number of student places in the arts at the present level while increasing the number of places in the science and technical/occupational fields. But since the arts fields largely attract students from the middle class while upward-mobile students from the lower class usually opt for technical training in greater numbers than they do the arts, this plan should not be a goal too difficult to meet. This writer predicts, however, that difficulties might well arise when the growing number of middle and upper-middle class students seek college and university training in the humanities and social science fields which they have traditionally elected in greatest numbers, only to be confronted by a "ceiling" on the numbers to be admitted. Since students from lower income families traditionally seek out the technical fields as the quickest path to occupational placement and upward mobility, it is possible that opportunities in higher education might become more readily available to the latter group than the former. Whether the government will find it necessary to revise the plan at some future date remains to be seen.

Higher Education

Although the announced goals of universal literacy and free education at the elementary levels can be expected to have very broad appeal to the masses, it is from the colleges and universities that a nation must expect to draw its trained staffs of educated men and women for administration, business and industry, and the professions. At the time of independence, there were only two universities in Pakistan, the University of the Punjab in Lahore, founded in 1882, and the University of Dacca in Dacca, founded in 1921. Following independence, the University of Sind in Hyderabad, was founded in 1947; Peshawar in 1950, and Karachi in 1951. Furthermore, before independence there was only one medical college and one engineering college, both located in Lahore. In the same light, only the Punjab and Dacca had law colleges. Since then, several more universities, medical, engineering and law colleges have been opened, all patterned after the British model. As might have been expected, the demand for seats has always been greater than the number available so that expansion of the university system has been quite steady, even though financial support by the central and provincial governments has not always been adequate for the development of the strongest programs. In addition, many students have sought graduate and professional training in established universities abroad, primarily in England, the United States, and Canada.

At present less than 2 percent of the relevant age cohort are enrolled in colleges and universities in Pakistan. Several of the institutions currently in existence are being expanded to full university status. A new University of Baluchistan is being established in Quetta, which includes a new medical school, while N.E.D. Engineering College in Karachi, and the Engineering and Agricultural Colleges in Peshawar, among others, will be raised to the status of universities. Even Azad Kashmir will shortly have its own university, as well as a Board of Secondary Education. A University Grants Commission will be organized to serve as a coordinating agency in order to avoid unnecessary duplication and waste, and, further, to serve as a buffer between the government and the university administrations. The Inter-University Board will serve as the nucleus of the University Grants Commission. Another new university is planned for D. I. Khan and by 1980 the number of universities will have doubled. It is also planned to add six new medical colleges, and to expand some of the existing ones.[1]

The University Ordinance

Long a bone of contention since the days of the Ayub regime, the PPP promised to revise the University Ordinance and rid it of those aspects most obnoxious to the academic community. For this reason it came as something of a shock that, instead of offering greater academic freedom, the control of the universities (in the eyes of the academic community) was to be politicized more than ever before.

Under the new ordinance, the provincial governor will again be the chancellor, while a new office of pro-chancellor has been created which will be filled by the provincial Minister of Education. It is considered by many that this will have an adverse effect on the autonomy of the university, and adds another step in the bureaucratic chain of command. Furthermore, since the provincial Minister of Education is a political appointee, and would serve as the pro-chancellor, he would serve in both the Syndicate and the Senate so that the "university could neither be autonomous nor democratic... he [would be] bound to interfere in the working of the university which would impair its autonomy. Being a politician himself he was sure to inject politics into the university which would vitiate its academic atmosphere" (Editorial, *Pakistan Times* April 24, 1973). The proponents of this measure feel that since the university is the creature of each provincial assembly, the latter is responsible for all agencies under its jurisdiction. Other proponents feel that it is well to have a high-level provincial administrator who is close to the university and participates in its deliberations, understands its problems and needs in such a post – someone who can, indeed, serve as a "friend in court" *vis-a-vis* the Assembly.

The vice-chancellor will be appointed by the chancellor and will serve at

---

1 M. L. Qureshi, Director of the Pakistan Institute of Development Economics, writing in the Pakistan Times (July 23, 1973), claims that the decision to open six new medical colleges cannot be defended. He claims there is no shortage of doctors in the nation, but, rather, a poor distribution of personnel [a common observation even in "modern" nations]. He claims that doctors are induced to leave the country because of higher salaries elsewhere. [Pakistan is a favorite nation for the recruitment of doctors by Arab nations.] In view of the great cost of building new medical facilities, as well as the number of years required to train doctors, Qureshi insists it would make for better government planning to change the system of health care delivery so that doctors would be available in rural areas, and otherwise to make it attractive for doctors to remain in Pakistan.

his pleasure, as will the acting vice-chancellor, who will serve in the absence of the vice-chancellor. In this ordinance, the Syndicate becomes more powerful than the Senate. A number of government servants, including five Members of the Provincial Assembly will be appointed by the government, as will the majority of the members of the Senate (*Dawn* November 24, 1972).

One of the reforms the new University Ordinance calls for is the rotation of department heads on a two-year basis among the three most senior members of each department. The stated purpose of this change is to avoid the solidification of too much power in the hands of one faculty member for long periods of time, and is considered to be an effort to establish a more egalitarian system of departmental governance. This has not been well received by the affected department heads at one university. At the University of Karachi it has been reported that a large number of full professors have applied for "study leave" abroad. "Among them are most of the recently dislodged heads of departments" (*Dawn* November 22, 1972). The vice-chancellor's response to this demonstrated unhappiness on the part of the senior professors was that they can now use their increased free time for research and scholarship! Since all the universities in Pakistan are government supported, they not only depend on the central and provincial governments for their budgets, but also for their administrative control.

At the college and university level, the student community has always been something less than peaceful, and all too frequently tumultuous, if not mercurial, depending on the political issue of the moment. Student groups have been used from time to time by political elements for their own purposes, and, apparently, this activity still continues on the campuses. But aside from this point, the students have always expected and demanded a degree of participatory democracy in the decision-making process of their institutions, and this opportunity has not been available to them in some years. The old university ordinance denied the students any degree of participation and little to the faculty. Under Ayub Khan, the University Senates were done away with. Students could be rusticated; student unions were abolished; graduates could lose their degrees, and faculty fired without due process for a variety of reasons. The new university ordinance does restore the Senate, the majority of which will be made up of elected faculty members as well as ex-officio members, students, and some legislators. The university Syndicate will be made up of elected faculty members, student union officers, government officials and other laymen, although this arrangement has not met universal support of the campuses. Student unions are once again functioning on the campuses. Since the students have always been an important constituency for every government leader, they will serve no less a role for Mr. Bhutto, and it is apparent that he has attempted to cultivate their support, and to use it.[1]

---

1   During the first year of the new University Ordinance (1972–73), it appears that neither the faculty nor the students are happy with it. The students want more representation in the Senate, while both the faculty and the students want more academic freedom and autonomy. There also appears to have been a shift of support by students and faculty

The new university ordinances appear to have been outlined or suggested in Islamabad, but the details were developed and finally approved by each Provincial Assembly for each of the universities. All of the ordinances were approved by their respective assemblies on September 30, 1972. Those of the University of Sind and the University of Karachi are precisely the same, while that of the University of the Punjab differs only in minor respects and is spelled out in greater detail. There are no significant differences. For example, in the composition of the Senate, the University of the Punjab calls for 15 elected faculty members, while the Universities of Sind and Karachi call for 12. It can be safely assumed that the ordinances of the other universities are similar in content.

Centers of Excellence

Another planned change at the university level is the development of Centers of Excellence. These centers will be developed by the University Grants Commission as the need is made apparent, and, from the earliest information available, the fields chosen will largely be in the scientific and technical fields. It is hoped that this development will reduce the nation's dependence on foreign training for its scientists and technicians. The centers will be financed by the central government and will be open to gifted students. The government has appropriated Rs 7,000,000 for this program for the current fiscal year. The University of the Punjab will have such a center in solid state physics; Karachi, marine biology; Sind, analytical chemistry; Peshawar, geology; and Baluchistan, mineralogy.[1]

---

from the PPP in 1970 to the Jamiat-e-Tulaba in 1972. At the first student elections at the University of the Punjab in the latter year, there were serious disruptions on campus when it appeared that the JeT would win handily. The JeT won a substantial victory when the second election was held. It has been reported that the elected president of the student union spends little time on campus, but travels about the province giving anti-government speeches. Since his political position is very anti-administration, he has been arrested twice and released. It should be noted that students and faculty members have always been politically active on the sub-continent.

[1] That Bhutto is serious about the scientific and technological development of the nation can be seen from his State of the Republic Address of August 3, 1973. He announced the establishment of the Pakistan Science Foundation, whose major goals are to be:
   1) To make Pakistani society science and technology conscious
   2) To support scientific and technological research in the universities and other institutions which is relevant to the socio-economic needs of the nation
   3) To promote the utilization of such research, and
   4) To arrest the drain of talent from the country.
In order to implement the above program, the Pakistan Science Foundation Act of 1973 was passed and a budget of Rs 5,000,000 for the first year of operation was provided. Although the National Science Council was formed in 1961, it remained inactive and dormant because of the limitations of its charter and the lack of a full-time chairman. Bhutto has promised to meet with the Council periodically to check on its progress.

The government's emphasis on the shift toward science and technology in the colleges and universities becomes apparent when it is seen that 60 percent of all students enrolled in the nation's colleges and institutions of higher learning are enrolled in the arts programs. The shift in emphasis will be accomplished by holding the number of student places in the arts at the current level while increasing the number of places in science and technology so that the ratio by 1980 will be 30, 30 and 40 percent in the arts, sciences and the fields of technology respectively.

This plan is being supported by the government in spite of the fact that "about 5,000 diploma-holding engineers in the country are faced with starvation" because of a lack of employment, and another "600 have had their employment terminated in the last six months" (*Dawn* November 27, 1972). Yet *The Planning Commission Report* for 1970 claimed there was a need for 12,000 diploma-holding engineers. This kind of miscalculation is an additional aspect of the whole problem of the "educated unemployed" found in many underdeveloped nations, viz., a lack of accurate information on the country's labor force.

The Educated Unemployed

It is a commonly held view that modernizing nations suffer from a lack of scientists and technicians. More frequently found, however, is the paradox of considerable unemployment and underemployment among science and technology graduates. The "educated unemployed" appear to present a problem for many developing nations. One of the major aspects of the problem is the lack of accurate information concerning the numbers of unemployed or underemployed. The number of educated unemployed in Pakistan is estimated by some to be as high as 400,000, largely generalist degree/diploma holders. Recently, however, there has been a great increase in the unemployment of scientifically and technically qualified persons. The unemployment rate is claimed to be 52 percent for applied science M.Sc. degree holders, 44 percent for polytechnic graduates, and 31 percent for M.Sc. degree holders in Economics and Commerce. "The educated unemployed are the nerve-center and the most volatile section of our society. The feeling of being unwanted causes frustration.." (Pervez Tahir, *Pakistan Times* April 24, 1973). Even with the Literacy Corps and the export of trained manpower, Tahir sees no solution to the problem of producing degrees "which can't be marketed," and calls for a rethinking of the educational system and manpower planning. On the other hand, a rough estimate made by the government of Pakistan indicates that there are approximately 20,000 unemployed science graduates, plus an additional 5,000 graduates of the polytechnic institutions. One of the reasons put forth by the government is that private industry prefers to employ uneducated skilled labor at low wages and train them up to the level desired. Another reason offered is the lack of communication between the "industrial sector" and the institutions producing the science-polytechnic graduates.

Some quite consistent sources of employment for some groups of engineers, doctors and other trained specialists in the last decade have been some of the oil-producing Arab nations (as well as other countries). The Pakistan government has usually not discouraged the "export" of trained professionals, because, among other reasons, these people send considerable remittances to their families, and the government is happy to have this additional source of foreign exchange. It has been estimated in some quarters that about one-third of the nation's foreign exchange earnings came from this source in 1972. In fact, a front page item in the *Pakistan Times* (June 1, 1973) highlights the government's efforts to help place engineers as well as other educated unemployed "both inside and outside the country" by having the Manpower Division compile lists of available candidates.

In an additional effort to help alleviate the problem of the educated unemployed the central government has established the National Development Volunteer Program which will be limited to males between the ages of 25 and 40. Qualifications of the applicants will be matched with job opportunities, apprenticeship, or on-the-job training. The volunteers will be enrolled for a period of one year and be entitled to maintenance stipends (*Weekly Commentary* II, 18, pp. 4–5). On May 1, 1973, the central government announced the launching of the program with 1,000 engineers and other technicians to be appointed to the Volunteer program, which will eventually reach 2,500 in number (*Pakistan Affairs* XXVI, no 13, p. 3). Front page advertisements began to appear in the press urging scientists and engineers to enroll in the program, and inviting potential employers to make use of this new service.

The provincial government of Baluchistan is planning to institute a system of "unemployment allowance" for the educated unemployed who are *bona fide* residents of the province. The scale of allowances planned on a monthly basis is:

> Rs 80/ for a matriculate
> Rs 100/ for an intermediate
> Rs 120/ for a graduate
> Rs 150/ for a post-graduate

Since education up to matriculate will be free, and unemployed graduates will receive an unemployment allowance, it would appear that the provincial government of Baluchistan has embraced the ideology of the welfare state. It is also likely that the plan will call for registration of all those who wish to receive the allowance in the National Service Corps, or the National Development Volunteer Program.

In view of the planned expansion of higher education, and in view of the high level of unemployment among the educated group, serious questions must be raised concerning the long-range effects of the new education policy unless government intervention succeeds with its announced plans. Another aspect of the same problem is that women college and university graduates have even greater problems entering the labor force since they must largely conform to the norms of a traditional Muslim society. These norms severely limit their opportunities, and their relatively minor participation in the labor force of the nation contributes heavily to the high dependency ratio of the country (Korson 1970).

The Privately Managed Schools and Colleges. The development and spread of the private schools and colleges was largely a post-independence phenomenon in the large urban centers. Many were licensed as "charitable" institutions, but were, indeed, operated on a profit-making basis that sometimes reached scandalous proportions. Perhaps no other aspect of the new education policy has brought forth as much controversy as the nationalization of the privately managed colleges beginning September 1, 1972 and the privately managed schools over a period of two years, beginning October 1, 1972. It is interesting to note that no compensation was to be paid to the owners and operators of these schools and colleges, and that no property could be sold or transferred by the owners or managers following President Bhutto's announcement on March 15, 1972. The central government maintained the prerogative of exempting those schools and colleges which were located in the federal capital area, while the four provincial governments had the jurisdiction of those institutions in their respective provinces. However, each governmental unit had to be satisfied that such an exempted institution was being operated "on a genuinely benevolent, philanthropic and non-commercial basis" (*Policy* 1972: 19). For example, those non profit-making schools that have maintained high academic standards and good reputations for the treatment of their staffs have been exempted for expropriation. The American schools in Karachi, Lahore and Islamabad fall into this category. As of August 3, 1973, 3,693 schools and 178 colleges had been nationalized (*Pakistan Times*).

The major reasons offered by the government for the expropriation of the schools and colleges are 1) to do away with the profit-making aspect of an educational enterprise, 2) to make schooling more readily available to those children whose families could not afford private schooling, and 3) to bring the whole educational process of the poorer privately managed schools up to government standard. This includes the raising of teachers' salaries to the level of those in publicly supported schools. Many of the private institutions were notorious for underpaying teachers, withholding salaries, and other abuses. It should also be noted that many such teachers were less qualified, and therefore were open to exploitation by the owners and operators of such institutions.

In the course of the summer of 1972 there were numerous meetings between the bishops of the various Christian denominations and government officials. Before the school year opened it was decided to nationalize the colleges but to delay the nationalization of the mission schools to a later date. One of the problems has been the objections raised by the private Muslim schools, viz., that the government intended to delay the nationalization of the Christian schools, but planned to move against the Muslim institutions, – hardly a politically wise action in these unsettled times. In any case, the government's plans did not call for the *acquisition of the properties* of the churches or mosques, but the administration of the schools and colleges functioning within those institutions would be taken over by the nationalization scheme (*Pakistan Times* August 26, 1972; Sardar 1972: 6).

Many of the privately managed colleges and schools in Pakistan have performed a valuable service to the community and nation since they opened their doors, notably those operated by the several Christian missions. The latter, expecially, have established and maintained high academic standards and reputations. Since these institutions have offered essentially western-oriented curricula, they have provided the opportunity for many Pakistani students to pursue advanced degrees at both Pakistani and foreign universities. Since the missionary schools and colleges are English-medium institutions, their graduates have had distinct advantages in pursuing higher degrees whether in Pakistan or abroad. (Almost all teaching in Pakistani universities is done in English.) The administration and faculty of these institutions also have a commitment to provide higher education to their students at cost with no sense of personal gain but rather the satisfaction of serving the students and the community. (The "Government" colleges, as the name suggests, are supported by the provincial governments, and are usually considered the most prestigious among all the colleges.)

Some of the privately managed colleges and schools, however, were operated by their owners for the sole purpose of private gain. Their frequently low level of academic performance was often matched by a relatively weak financial situation which resulted in lower-than-average faculty salaries, and not infrequent payless pay days. The nationalization of the colleges without compensation, then, was designed as a corrective move by the central government. The provincial governments have appointed administrators who send periodic reports to the provincial ministries of education. It was planned to bring teachers' salaries into line with those of government college teachers, but many who had not been paid their salaries since March 15, 1972, were still waiting for redress in this matter in the spring of 1973. As government employees, they are now eligible for fringe benefits previously denied them, although there have been frequent complaints from some of the teachers that some of their basic needs were being overlooked, and that they were, indeed, being treated as second-class citizens.

As of May, 1973, some teachers of the nationalized schools had still not been paid their salaries, some even as far back as March 15, 1972. Another serious complaint was that some government officials considered that the eligibility for pension rights of these teachers from the nationalized schools and colleges began September 1, 1972. the date of nationalization – not the date of their original appointment.

After the announcement of nationalization on March 15, 1972 Prof. Shah F. Haque, Principal of Liaqat College, and a leader of the opposition in the Sind Assembly, claimed it would not be nationalization, but regimentation to place the private institutions under government bureaucracy (*Pakistan Times* August 23, 1972). On the other hand, some of the proponents of nationalization claimed that those elements of the Christian community that opposed nationalization were participating in a "foul conspiracy," and were being exploited by "mischief-mongers" determined to create problems for the government (*Ibid.*). It appears that some operators of private colleges did create problems. When the *Policy* announcing the nationalization of schools and colleges was made public on March 15, 1972, some owners stopped paying teachers' and other staff members' salaries, as well as other financial obligations.

As for the nationalization of the colleges, there is no private college in Baluchistan, while in N.W.F.P. only Edwards College has been temporarily exempted by the provincial government. But of the 135 private colleges in the Punjab and the Sind, all have been nationalized, including the eight colleges operated by various Christian missions, in spite of the fact that they could prove that they were "genuinely benevolent, philanthropic and non-commercial" institutions.

Although the government has not taken over the *properties* of the colleges, they have taken over their administration so that most of the college principals have been retained, but find themselves government employees, and all budget, personnel, administrative and academic matters are under the control of the government. Since the mandatory retirement age for teachers is 58, many teachers over that age have been forced into retirement without the government's willingness to support their pension claims. Many faculty openings have not been filled, while some of the openings at the English-medium Christian colleges have been filled by recent graduates of Urdu-medium institutions and are, therefore, unable to function properly. The missionary colleges have always used English as a medium of instruction, and these two factors have caused considerable unrest among college students.

Since many of the missionary colleges have maintained the highest academic standards, it is felt in many quarters that because of the lack of budgetary support from the government that the level of academic quality will be difficult to maintain. On the other hand, many of the private colleges with the poorest reputations are bound to be improved over the years (provided the government offers sufficient financial as well as other support), so that, in the long run there might well be a "leveling" of academic quality among the nation's colleges.

Schools

The first of the schools to be nationalized were those that catered to the low income groups so that immediate relief could be offered to such families, and also to "improve the lot of the teachers" working in those schools. As of May, 1973, 221 high-fee schools had been exempted, at least temporarily, on the condition that they reserve 20 percent of the seats in each class for outstanding students from low income families (*Pakistan Times* May 27, 1973).

Since the plan called for the nationalization of private schools over a two-year period beginning October 1, 1972, as of this writing many of the mission schools have been spared during the first round of nationalization. However, the threat of ultimate nationalization remains, and there is great anxiety among teachers, students, and their parents. Many of the non-missionary private schools have been nationalized, but it is felt that it is only a question of time (October 1, 1974) before the remaining private institutions will be nationalized. Since many of the missionary schools have always been considered centers of excellence, there is considerable apprehension among their staffs, students and their parents, because without proper financial support it is feared that academic standards will fall.

Many of the same problems faced by the former private colleges now confront the nationalized private schools. Teachers over age 58 have been retired, some with their pensions endangered, and since some of the poorer private schools employed teachers without proper credentials, these, too, have been forced out. Although the poorest schools, should they survive, are bound to gain and improve their performance, once again it is felt that the best of the private institutions will suffer since a "leveling" process will inevitably set in. The major problem, it appears, is that even though the new education plan has considerable support and great public appeal, too much has been attempted too soon, i.e., with insufficient planning and insufficient budget support. For example, many of the nationalized private schools have received little or no money for day-to-day supplies, and must manage with left-over stocks, or do without.

Schools for the Gifted and Talented

Some of the institutions to be taken over by the government will be developed as special schools for gifted students, regardless of their economic background. An example of such institutions is Aitchison College, in Lahore, where in the past only sons of the wealthiest families could hope to attend. In addition schools for the talented students in each district will be established, at first in newly expropriated institutions. Also, separate schools for talented girls will also be established. Each school will have residential facilities and will draw students from each area or district in which it is located.

Illiteracy

Aside from the expropriation of private schools and colleges perhaps no other aspect of the new education policy has received as much publicity as the announced plans for the eradication of illiteracy. This is a problem that many underdeveloped nations have been struggling with, and the results vary widely among these nations. Depending on the "baseline" or starting point, frequently beginning with political independence, and the kind and amount of resources available, some nations have had considerable success, while others have had relatively little. Unfortunately, Pakistan falls into the latter group.

The last census for which results are available in Pakistan (1961), the literacy rate was estimated to be about 20 percent, although the rates varied widely among sex and regional and rural-urban cohorts. The best estimates at the present time show a slight decline to approximately 18 percent, largely because of the continued high fertility rate and the lack of expansion of the educational facilities that had been planned by previous administrations. *Dawn* (December 7, 1972) reports a drop from 18 percent to 15 percent, although it mentioned no time span, or offered a source for this estimate. It is also estimated that there is an annual increase of about one million illiterates per year.

The Education Minister of Sind Province, Mr. Dur Mohammad Usto, has announced an appropriation of Rs 5,000,000 for its adult literacy program. A National Literacy Day was declared for October 1, 1972, and the opening of Education Week. It was celebrated by public appearances and speeches by Bhutto and Pirzada in Rawalpindi. They announced that the central government had budgeted Rs 903,000,000 for education for the current fiscal year, compared to Rs 630,000,000 for the previous year. They pleaded for peace in educational institutions and the avoidance of controversy so that the major goals could be achieved within the time limits set by the government. In Karachi, at least, Literacy Day received a "half-hearted" observance (*Dawn* October 1, 1972).

Although the present goal is to achieve universal primary education for boys by 1979 and for girls by 1984, the problem of adult illiteracy is also an important part of this announced program. It is planned that literacy centers will be established in all villages and towns, in "schools, factories, farms, union council halls, and community centers" (*Policy* 1972: 21). For literacy training alone, the plan calls for 276,000 centers by 1980, for an estimated 11 million illiterates. Short, intensive training courses for teachers are planned, to be supplemented by members of the National Literacy Corps, and other suitable persons. Although a National Literacy Corps was announced during Ayub Khan's regime, patterned after the corps in Iran, the plan was never implemented. Iran's success has been largely due to the use of army personnel in isolated rural and tribal areas, and with the help of college and university graduates who volunteer for a year of national service. Whether Pakistan's leaders would go so far as making a year of national service a requirement for all college and university graduates remains to be seen.

From the pronouncements in the press, as well as editorials in the major newspapers, it appears that the national and provincial leaders of the government are concerned with the problem of illiteracy. The President's wife, Begum Nusrat Bhutto, has been very active in this campaign by frequently appearing before women's groups urging "each one to teach one." How successful the government will be in meeting its targets in the projected time remains to be seen.

Teacher Training and Supply

It is planned that the training of teachers will be reorganized so that larger numbers will become available in a shorter period of time. The plan calls for the introduction of "innovative techniques," which are otherwise not defined.

In March, 1972, the estimated number of elementary and secondary teachers in the country was about 160,000. The estimated *additional* number needed to fulfill the program by 1980 is 235,000, not counting about 300,000 adult and continuing education teachers, both male and female. The 67 teacher training institutions now in operation can produce only 104,000 teachers in the next eight years at the different levels, so that Education as a subject will be introduced at the secondary level, as well as into all the general colleges in order that more teachers will become available in the national pool (*Policy* 1972: 23).

The proportion of women teachers at the primary level is only 30 percent (as against 75 percent in the United States). It is hoped to increase the number and proportion of women teachers in the primary levels so that parents will be encouraged to send their daughters to school. As a traditional Muslim society, this has been one of the major hurdles in any effort to increase the number and percentage of girls in school. It is also expected that with an increased number of women teachers coeducation can be introduced at the primary level. Segregation in schools is rarely ever equal, whether the variable is race or sex, and it is almost always more expensive.

The pay scales of teachers in expropriated schools will be brought up to par with those in the publicly-supported schools, and for those desiring further training, "sabbatical leave with full pay will be granted liberally to them" (*Policy* 1972: 24). One of the long-standing complaints of teachers has been the lack of low cost housing. The new policy calls for the construction of rent-free housing in the future, although no target date is set. One year after the announced education reforms, it was obvious that the planned reforms were not completely effective because college teachers in Lahore had drawn up a list of demands stating that teachers' salaries were being withheld, and that superannuation pensions were not being paid. They blamed "bureaucratic bottlenecks" (*Pakistan Times* March 22, 1973).

Student Welfare

In 1971–72, Rs 20,000,000 was available for scholarships to college and university students. This sum will be increased to Rs 80,000,000 by 1980. In addition, Rs 60,000,000 for interest-free loans will be available, although priority will be given to students in professional schools. In May, 1973, the central government announced that an additional Rs 2,500,000 was being made available for scholarship loans for poor students, the total sum to be divided among the seven universities (*Pakistan Affairs* XXVI, 12, p. 1). Loans will be repaid after students have become earning members in their occupations and professions. In addition, a comprehensive program for the construction of hostels to provide for 8,000 more school and college students at a cost of Rs 40,000,000 was approved by the central government. "Northern and federally-administered tribal areas would receive first priority," while other hostel facilities would be expanded (*Pakistan Times* July 3, 1973). Because of the high cost of books, book banks will be established in colleges and universities and will be available on loan. In addition, low-cost transportation is promised for all students who need such, as well as free medical check-ups. In an effort to reduce the social and economic disparity among students up to grade VIII, uniforms of modest cut and inexpensive materials will be designed. This program will be introduced gradually in various areas so that local sensibilities will not be offended.[1]

National Curriculum Bureau

The new *Policy* calls for the reorganization and strengthening of the National Curriculum Bureau, with Curriculum Centers for each province. It is expected that a wide variety of changes will be forthcoming in the training of teachers, the development of curricula, the development of new textbooks and resource materials. Radio and television will be introduced into the learning process wherever possible, and, by 1980, about 150,000 radio and 100,000 television sets will be distributed to schools and adult education centers, wherever the latter are organized. The use of these sets will be a boon to a wide variety of extension programs in "agriculture, health, education, family planning, and social reconstruction" (*Policy* 1972: 29).

Physical Education and Sports

It is planned that physical education will have parity with other fields of study in schools and colleges and that teachers in this field will have parity with other teachers. Physical education will become an integral part of primary school curricula, and that the field will be up-graded in the colleges. Special

---

1 The Government of Sind has already prescribed the uniforms for all students of the province from Classes I through VIII to become effective in the academic year 1973–74. Girls' frocks will be light blue, white shalwar or pyjama, and white dupatta. Boys will wear camel colored kurta with side pocket and tight collars, and camel colored shalwar or pyjama (*Dawn*, December 23, 1972). The motive for instituting uniform dress for students can be interpreted in various ways. The writer prefers, however, to believe that its major purpose is an effort on the part of the administration to further develop a sense of egalitarianism among students so that manifest differential expenditures for children's clothing are reduced to a minimum. Minister of Education Pirzada has also announced that free books as well as uniforms will be provided for poor students after October 1, 1974.

sports and recreation centers will be established for women, and, in an effort to develop the whole field of physical education, games and sports, a National Sports Trust will be established.

National Foundation for Book Production

For anyone who has taught in Pakistan, the shortage of text and reference books for students is a painful fact of life. It has not been unusual for syllabi distributed to univeristy students to include books that are not only many years out of date, are not even available in any bookstores in the country, and are frequently missing from library shelves. This shortage of text and resource materials has bordered on a national scandal, and, with the relatively limited number of highly qualified faculty members the total result has been seriously reflected in the quality of education that has been available to college and university students.

The new regime has evidently been very conscious of these glaring faults, and, even though the quality of the faculty has been improving over the years as more and more men and women trained abroad return to join the university faculties,[1] the problem of textbook and library resources has continued to plague the educational effort at all levels.[2]

In an effort to mount a frontal attack on the latter problem, the government plans to establish a National Foundation for Book Production to facilitate the production of books and other reading materials needed at all levels of this long-range effort. With the universalization of elementary education, reading materials will be produced locally at low cost by the Foundation which will write, edit, compile, translate, print and publish texts for all the schools, colleges and universities, as well as for the general public. The Ministry of Education's Pakistan Printing Corporation will become the nucleus of the Foundation. It has been announced that the government will no longer observe international copyright laws, and will be free to translate and print "expensive" foreign books. This measure will save much foreign exchange, and reduce the cost of books to the students.[3]

The new ordinance violates both the 1886 Berne (copyright) Convention

---

1 As of October 31, 1973, 3,669 Pakistani students were studying in various foreign countries. (*Pakistan Affairs*, XXVI, 5, February 16, 1973.

2 Even though primary education was to be free, some schools have not been able to furnish books for their students, and many indigent parents do not send their children to school for lack of proper clothing. For this reason, demands are being made that school attendance should be made compulsory by statutory law.

3 According to *Weekly Commentary and Pakistan News Digest*, (II, 2, January 12, 1973) the domestic production of foreign textbooks has already begun, with the expected annual saving of Rs 5,000,000 to Rs 8,000,000 in foreign exchange. The new Textbook Ordinance states, "copyright shall not exist in respect to printing, translation, adaptation or publication ... of any book to be used as a textbook for teaching, study and research purposes in educational institutions" (*Weekly Commentary*, I, 29, December 8, 1972).

and UNESCO's more liberal Universal copyright convention of 1952. No official announcement of such action has appeared in government Gazette notifications. Moreover, under Article 35 of the Stockholm Copyright Act and Protocol, to which the government of Pakistan acceded on November 26, 1969, *one year* must elapse before withdrawal from the convention. A similar clause is found in the UNESCO convention. This appears to be an oversight on the part of the Pakistan government because Section 1(2) of the 1972 Amendment Ordinance states that it shall become effective "at once" (*Dawn* November 20, 1972).

Examinations

Perhaps no other aspect of the educational system in Pakistan has been as sensitive an issue to students at all levels as that of examinations. Mass student failure has been endemic on the subcontinent for years, so that almost any means to pass an examination (or do well) is considered justifiable in some quarters. In some areas of India, for example, students have demanded the right to copy from neighbors during examinations, while in Pakistan the problem of mass failure has been studied by faculty members in an effort to understand and get to the root of the problem (Mangalam 1960).[1]

The Education Policy states that "the existing system of examinations is one of the root causes of the general malaise in our educational system" (1972: 31). The current system offers annual internal examinations from Class I to IX on the basis of which students pass or fail. Mass failure causes many students to drop out and therefore creates an economic loss to the nation. The new plan calls for no annual examinations up to Class VIII. Instead, students will progress through the grades automatically, under a system of continuous evaluation by their teachers. From Class IX there will be a "combination of periodic-cum-annual examinations and a continuous, scientifically graded assessment of the student's achievement, general behavior and aptitude. Eventually, there will be no failures and no repetition of classes up to Class IX" (*Ibid*). In Classes X–XII the system of terminal examinations by the Boards of Intermediate and Secondary Education will be continued for the time being,

---

1 The problem of postponing final examinations upon the request of students so that more time can be allowed for preparation has been a continuing problem for university administrators. The latter wish to avoid any confrontation on what would appear to be purely an administrative matter, but when there is any degree of political unrest, a small group of students are inclined to seize upon this as an opportunity to request a delay for more preparation time. The result has been that the examinations scheduled for 1972, have now been postponed by nine months, which will cause a serious backlog. Students are not awarded their degrees until they have passed their final exams—not after they have completed their course work. According to the *Pakistan Times*, (March 12, 1973) final examinations were to be held April 10, 1973 for students who had completed their work in June, 1972.

although an effort will be made to eliminate long-standing malpractices. The number of Boards will be increased to handle the increased number of students so that there will be one Board for every 25,000 students.

The National Service Corps and Military Training

Next to the campaign to achieve universal literacy, and the nationalization of private schools and colleges, perhaps the most dramatic plan to be proposed by the national government is the creation of a National Service Corps as well as the progressive introduction of compulsory military training for all medically fit males between the ages of 13 to 17 years (Classes IX–XII).[1]

All those passing the Intermediate examination "will be encouraged" to serve one year in the Service Corps, either in one stretch, or consecutively in short intervals during summer vacations. In order to attract young men to serve in the Corps, the following incentives will be provided: a) a monthly stipend, b) uniform allowance, c) preference for selection into institutions of higher learning and/or employment in the private or public sector, and d) the time spent in the Corps will not be counted for purposes of age limit of entry in the services, etc. Although the sex of the volunteers is not mentioned, it is assumed that women will also be expected to volunteer (*Ibid.*).

The major purpose of organizing the Corps appears to be to lend support to the government's attack on illiteracy at all levels; the Ministry of Education will have over-all responsibility for the program, while the provincial governments' education administrations will implement the scheme and arrange for the necessary training. The combination of the two programs, National Service Corps and Military Training is expected to have a major impact on the morale and character of the nation's youth, and help meet the basic needs of achieving universal literacy at all levels as well as meeting military needs. No mention is made of those youths not in school, or who drop out of school before Class IX. It is recognized that a major motivational campaign will be needed to implement both programs.[2]

---

1 Students doing National Service in the Sind are demanding five points concession in their divisional standing for admission to college which the government has promised them. The drive against illiteracy was started in the Sind in December, 1972, with the aid of volunteers from the National Service Corps, and with the announced goal of producing 400,000 adult literates annually. Fifty "leader trainers" have been undergoing special training at the University of the Sind under the supervision of UNESCO specialists in adult education. It is planned to have 1,000 training centers where two leaders will train 200 adults over a two-month period. Special books and other equipment are being prepared for the program (*Dawn*, December 5, 1972).

2 The Vice-Chancellor of the University of the Punjab announced that he hopes to institute a "motivational plan" so that students will take their studies seriously, that would reduce their great interest in "instant gratification," and that teachers would "arouse young people from their sloth and indolence." To achieve this goal, he planned to establish a Counselling and Guidance Committee to determine students' aptitudes and suggest

Religious Education

For a nation that was founded on a religious ideology, it is not surprising that the Policy would call for the compulsory study of Islamiyat up to Class X; that such study will be carefully reviewed from time to time to assure that it will have its proper place in the curriculum and textbooks; that it will not become an isolated item, and that "the values and the spirit of Islam are woven into the warp and woof of our educational fabric" (*Policy* 1972: 37). Radio and television channels will devote substantial time to the recitation of the Quran and its translation.

Administrative Reorganization

Almost everyone who has had any experience with the educational process in Pakistan would agree that the administrative organization (as in so many nations) is cumbersome and unnecessarily complicated. In an effort to reorganize the bureaucratic machinery and, hopefully, to streamline the educational administration of the country and to make it more responsive to the needs of the people, it is planned that a series of Educational Councils will be set up at the national, provincial, district and institutional levels. Membership in the councils will be drawn from all walks of life, and will include representatives of teachers, students and relevant government departments and other agencies. The councils will have the following functions:

"1. to formulate and recommend changes and developments in educational policy
 2. to oversee the implementation of the policies adopted from time to time
 3. to assess and evaluate over-all educational progress in their respective spheres
 4. to initiate and support educational research and disseminate the findings
 5. to harness and mobilize the latest educational techniques and resources for the improvement of education" (*Plan* 1972: 39).

The councils will have 15 standing committees at the national level, 14 at the provincial level, 5 at the district/corporation/municipality/town level and two at the school and college level. Whether this planned major reorganization will prove successful remains to be seen.

Program Financing

From the time the new *Policy* was announced in mid-March, 1972, the first

courses of study for them. Students would also be urged to participate in the Peoples Works Program via manual labor on building roads and buildings on campus, as well as participating in the literacy program for adults (*Pakistan Times*, April 26, 1973).

question universally raised was "How will the program be financed"? And, as might be expected, many were skeptical that the program was nothing more than a propaganda ploy and would never be implemented.

The annual expenditure in 1971–72 in the public sector of education was about Rs 700,000,000 which represents less than 2 percent of the gross national product (*Policy* 1972: 41), one of the lowest in the world, even though UNESCO recommends that developing nations should spend at least a minimum of 4 percent of their GNP on publicly-supported education.[1] The proposed *Policy* calls for a 70 percent increase for the year 1972–73 over 1971–72. Thereafter it is expected that the annual rate of increase will be on the order of 15 percent, so that by 1980 the total expenditure on education will approximate the 4 percent level recommended by UNESCO. The *Policy* calls for the "mobilization of all resources" to meet this goal. To help finance the cost of universal education, the government has levied a tax of Rs 100 per year per worker on all employers who have 20 or more workers (*Pakistan Times*, July 6, 1973).

It is obvious that the heavy emphasis the current administration places on supporting the growth of elementary education is in direct contrast to that of earlier administrations. For example, the allocation for colleges and universities in the First Five Year Plan was more than 50 percent higher than for primary education. Furthermore, the question of allocation becomes somewhat academic when it is learned that of the Rs 580,700,000 appropriated, only 55 percent was actually spent on education (Curle 1966: 53).

Over the years the pattern has not improved noticeably; furthermore, the allocation of the education budget was felt to be disproportionately high for government-supported colleges and universities. For example, for the First Five Year Plan, 29.4 percent of the education allocation was devoted to government-supported colleges and universities, but only 18.0 percent and 26.7 percent for primary and secondary education respectively (*Ibid.*). (The writer is well aware that education costs rise sharply from the primary level upward.)

Another problem that confronts all governments of modernizing nations is the extraordinarily high drop-out rate, and Pakistan is no exception. For every 100 children in the entering Class I age cohort, only 44.6 percent actually enroll, and by Class V only 9 percent are still in attendance. These data are an average of the seven year period 1955–62 (Curle 1969: 52), although the situation has undoubtedly improved since that time. The sharpest drop in attendance occurs during and at the end of the first year. There are many reasons for the high drop-out rate, not the least of which is the poverty of the children's families. Nonetheless, the educational wastage is a challenge to any well intentioned government.

---

1 It had been the practice of previous administrations to allocate higher percentages of the national budget to education than were actually spent. For example, the Third Five Year Plan called for an expenditure of 5 percent for education, yet only about 1.5 percent of the budget was spent on education—one of the lowest in the world (Pakistan: *Basic Facts*, 1966: 115). In 1964, approximately 1.75 percent of Pakistan's Gross National Product was spent on education (Edding and Berstecher, 1969: 56).

Major Project Planning

Of the major projects planned, 14 will be financed exlusively by the central government. Among these are the National Education Council, Centers of Excellence, Centers of Area Studies, The National Book Foundation Scheme, The Peoples' Open University, The National College of Arts, The University Grants Commission, the granting of interest-free student loans, graded basic vocabularies and people libraries, Book Banks in the colleges and universities, including the import of textbooks, and the Councils of Professional Education.

Conclusion

The fact that President Bhutto and Minister of Education Pirzada were able to produce such a wide-ranging plan for educational reform in less than three months after taking office would seem to indicate that such an extensive reform had been uppermost in the president's mind even before he took office. Previous administrations had announced and promised a wide variety of educational reforms, and each five-year plan included projections for expanded educational services. But these goals were rarely ever fulfilled. It has been claimed in some quarters that President Yahya Khan had received an educational reform plan that bore some similarity to the current *Educational Policy, 1972-1980*, but it was never implemented.[1] The expansion of the universities, frequently undermanned and inadequately supported, matched by an actual decline in the literacy rate of the masses, struck many observers as an elitist approach to educational development in a modernizing nation.[2] This is not to say that the spread of primary and secondary schools was ignored. Rather, that a disproportionate amount of the education budget appeared to be spent on higher education.

The continued demand for more college and university places, of course, came from the middle class – undoubtedly more vocal than one would expect the illiterate masses to be. Over the years political agitation and student strikes have caused many colleges and universities to close from time to time, while little has been heard from the illiterate village peasants or the urban workers. The demand for more educational facilities at the primary, secondary and college levels, and the failure of preceding administrations to meet the demand led to the growth of the private schools and colleges. This unfilled need was

---

1   For example, a group of 14 university faculty members, with Dr. Mahmud Hussain, of the University of Karachi as chairman, was appointed in 1969 by the government of West Pakistan to examine the problems and status of the universities. This group issued its report on May 1, 1969, but its recommendations were never implemented *(Report of the Study Group on University Education, 1969)*.

2   In April, 1973, the central government announced that new universities would be opened in Dera-Ismal-Khan, and at Saidu Sharif.

frequently met by entrepreneurs whose major goal frequently was a quick profit on little investment, and at the expense of both teachers and students.

There is little doubt that the new education policy has been widely acclaimed by all segments of the population. In terms of publicity, it has received a very good press, because hardly a day passes without news items reporting day-to-day developments, and almost all laudatory. The missionaries have probably received something less than a satisfactory compromise, but at least the government did not submit to the demands of the extremists who have long proclaimed that such institutions were used to "infect Muslim youth with foreign ideologies," and should be closed down. And few people will lament the losses of those entrepreneurs who operated sub-standard institutions. Such action was long overdue.

Compared to Bhutto's efforts in areas of political and economic reform, one must concede that there has been very little resistance to the new plan. After all, in a nation with such a weak educational base, there are no major organized power centers to oppose the kinds of reforms instituted by the government. Where opposition developed, e.g., from the missionary schools, the central and provincial governments have been sufficiently flexible to reach an accommodation and it is safe to predict that many more accommodations can be expected before 1980, in an effort to achieve the major goals Mr. Bhutto has set out in his new policy. The owners of the private institutions were neither well organized, nor did they enjoy much public support. The "foreign" schools, i.e., American and British, among others, were outside the purview of the new policy.

Not only is great emphasis being placed on achieving universal literacy in the shortest possible time, but universal and free education up to Class VIII beginning September, 1972, and up to Class X two years later is being promised to the people. The nationalization of the private schools may help reach this goal a little sooner than might have otherwise developed, but it is a safe assumption that the masses of the poor and illiterate will not be in a position to readily benefit from these measures overnight. After all, this is a long-term program, the goals of which are to be achieved over an eight-year period.

One can only speculate on the role of the new education policy in President Bhutto's over-all plan. There appears to be a radical reorientation of the educational enterprise, perhaps to facilitate his long-term goal of a more egalitarian society. At one level there appears to be a determined effort to respond to the perceived deprivation of the masses, and on another level a determination to hasten the process of modernization by increased emphasis on training in the technical and scientific fields. The administration probably hopes to see them work in tandem. Furthermore, government officials continue to convey the impression that since it will be funding education at all levels, that those who benefit from it should think in terms of repaying their debt to the nation by serving the people.

A major dilemma that has developed in recent years and undoubtedly continues to haunt the government is that of the educated unemployed. Other developing nations have also been confronted with this problem, and there does not appear to be a ready solution. On the one hand, higher education is the quickest means of gaining occupational placement in the white collar, business and professional occupations of a nation's labor force, and with it the achievement of higher social status. The demand for more seats in the nation's universities is being met by a rapid expansion of educational facilities, yet it appears that the economic organization of the nation cannot fully absorb, in either the private or the public sector, the increasing number of college and university graduates. Perhaps the introduction and expansion of the National Development Volunteer Program as well as the National Service Corps will have the necessary effect in providing the trained manpower needed to implement the government's plans for a more egalitarian society. The achievement of universal literacy in an underdeveloped nation is not only a popular political goal, but the economic value of education has been well established by scholars in the field.

There is no question but that the educational landscape of the nation has changed in the short time that the educational reform has been in force. And this reform might well become the key to the oft-proclaimed "Islamic Socialism" so often bandied about by various political figures in the last quarter century. Education, especially higher education will no longer be a monopoly of the middle and upper classes, because President Bhutto appears to have set the course of the educational enterprise in the direction of egalitarianism.[1]

The administration has made what appears to be remarkable progress in the first year the Policy has been in effect. But two major issues strike the writer as crucial in any effort to predict the success or failure of this new policy by the end of the decade. The first must obviously be financial support. Although it is still too early to make a final judgment on this point, it does appear that the government is making a determined effort in this regard. The allocation for education was increased by 50 percent in the first year, and the plan calls for a 15 percent annual increase.

The second will be far more difficult to assess, namely, fertility control. The first announcement of the census taken in September, 1972, claimed a population of 74,892,000 for what was formerly West Pakistan and is now known as Pakistan – an increase of 51.3 percent over the census count of 1961 (*Census*, 1972). This would indicate an average annual net increase of approximately 3.8 percent, which, if maintained, would indicate a doubling of the nations's population in less than 20 years from the census of 1961. If the first results of this census count are correct, it would undoubtedly have a disastrous effect on government plans for economic development.

For the last several years, family planning officials were claiming that the

---

1 "There are a number of issues being talked about now-a-days. But we are convinced that for us there is only one issue, namely, Islamic Socialism, which, in a nutshell, means that every person in this land has equal rights to be provided with food, shelter, clothing education and medical facilities." Liaqat Ali Khan, August, 1949. Quoted in *President Bhutto's Address to the National Assembly*, April, 1972, p. 42.

net reproduction rate had been reduced to 2.5 percent, an obviously gross miscalculation. The press has reacted to the dangers of the population "explosion," and called for government action to this threat to the nation's well-being. In March, 1972, the *Pakistan Times* carried a full-page advertisement proclaiming the advantages of family planning and stressing that a "small family is a happy family." Since then advertisements have daily carried the same and similar messages, such as "Use oral pills to ensure good health for mother and child," "Wise mothers space births of their children," on the front page of the same paper. In addition, smaller advertisements on inside pages have pointed up the ceiling prices that a consumer should expect to pay for a variety of contraceptives. It is obvious from the retail prices listed that these are highly subsidized by the government. The writer should like to point out that these are startling developments, because such advertisements have never appeared in the press before.[1] Although it has been the official policy of the government since the late 1950's to support fertility control programs, they were not as successful as the officials of the programs claimed.

Unless the government makes a far greater effort in this regard, and unless fertility control measures are more readily adopted than they have been in the past, there is a serious question whether the total effort in the field of education in the next decade will be more than an exercise in futility.

N.B. With the inauguration of the new Constitution on August 14, 1973, President Bhutto assumed the new office of Prime Minister.

REFERENCES

Curle, Adam
    1966   Planning for Education in Pakistan. Cambridge: Harvard Press.
    1969   Educational Problems of Developing Societies. New York: Praeger.
Dawn, Karachi, Pakistan
Edding, Friedrich and Dieter Berstecher
    1969   International Developments of Educational Expenditure, 1950–1965. Paris, U.N.E.S.C.O.
Embassy of Pakistan
    1968   "Pakistan's Development Decade, 1958–68, Educational Reform," Washington, D.C.
Government of Pakistan
    1957   Planning Board, The First Five Year Plan (1955–1960), Karachi.
    1966   Pakistan: Basic Facts, Department of Films and Publications, Fourth edition, Karachi.
    1970   Planning Commission Report, Karachi.
    1972   Education for the Masses, The New Policy, Department of Films and Publications, Karachi.

---

1   After about one month the advertisements disappeared from the *Pakistan Times* as suddenly as they had appeared. One can only speculate on the reasons for the abrupt change.

1972   President Bhutto's Address to the National Assembly, April, Islamabad.
1972   The Education Policy, 1972–1980, Ministry of Education, Islamabad.
1972   The Interim Constitution of the Islamic Republic of Pakistan (As Amended by Post Constitution P.O. No. 1 of 1972), Karachi.
1973   The Constitution of the Islamic Republic of Pakistan, Karachi.
1973   Population Census of Pakistan, 1972, Census Bulletin no. 1, P. no. 27. Islamabad, Census Organization, Interior Division.
Huq, Muhammad Shamsul
1965   Education and Development Strategy in South and Southeast Asia, Honolulu.
Korson, J. Henry
1970   "Career Constraints Among Women Graduate Students in a Developing Society," Journal of Comparative Family Studies, 1, 1, (Autumn): 82–100.
Mangalam, Joseph J.
1960   Study of Student Mass Failure, Study No. 2, Time Perspective and Academic Performance of Students. Lahore: Department of Sociology, University of the Punjab.
Pakistan Affairs, Washington, D. C.
Pakistan Times, Lahore
The New York Times, New York.
Report of the Study Group on University Education. Lahore (mimeo).
1969
Sarwar, Malik G.
1972   The Educational Institutions Take-over Regulations, 1972, (Martial Law Regulation No. 118), Lahore: Lahore Law Times Publications.
Weekly Commentary and Pakistan News Digest, Islamabad, Pakistan.

BOOK REVIEWS

C. M. Turnbull, *The Straits Settlements 1826–67: Indian Presidency to Crown Colony.*
London, Athlone Press, 1967, pp. vi, 428, maps £ 5.50.

In 1826 the newly formed Straits Settlements were the East India Company's remotest possessions, full of dreams and promises but void of certainties.
This work presents in rich detail the mosaic of the next forty years, including an
endless succession of schemes – official and private – which failed to fulfill their
backer's anticipations in Penang, Malacca, and even Singapore. Under the rule
of the Calcutta government, the Straits Settlements were constantly ignored
and development of essential services retarded. Even piracy was slow to be
suppressed in the immediate vacinity of Southeast Asia's busiest commercial
crossroads. Nevertheless by 1867, when the transformation to Crown Colony
occurred, the stability of the Straits Settlements as a unit and the success of
Singapore as one of the world's great shipping and commercial centres was no
longer in doubt. The survival and growing prosperity of the Straits Settlements
in that period clearly was not due to its military role or its prominence in the
Indian imperial system. Miss Turnbull attributes it convincingly to the Strait's
function as a gateway to opportunity and potential wealth for thousands of
immigrant Chinese and Indians and a few hundred Europeans.
   The author skillfully explores the many facets of the Straits Settlements'
development in its first half-century, emphasizing in particular the anomalous
position of the Straits government under British Indian control, the emergence
of an incredibly heterogeneous society in the three settlements, and the growing
involvement of the Straits Settlements in the affairs of the Malayan peninsula.
Moreover, as this work makes abundantly clear, the constant interaction of these
three factors provided the crucial dynamic in the growth of this Indian dependency. Calcutta demanded economy in administration, non-intervention in the
Malay states, and absolute freedom of commerce. This left the Straits government with little money and less authority. "The government had no powers
to exert control over trade and immigration, it had no physical means to put
down piracy, and no legislative powers to deal with Chinese secret societies."
[p. 82]. This very inability of the Singapore to control the activities of Straits
residents led ultimately to intervention in Malayan affairs and to the movement
to transfer responsibility to the Colonial Office.
   It is in her discussion of the movement of Chinese, Indians, Malays and
Europeans into the British territories and the consequent evolution of Straits
society that Miss Turnbull is most fascinating. She never loses sight of either the
differences within each ethnic group or of the conflicts between groups, while
presenting a meaningful general picture of changing patterns of population and
community. The reader must regret with the author [p. v) the paucity of non-
European sources for this history, but within those limits her search has been
exceptionally diligent in a wide variety of official records and other materials,
all brought together in her extensive bibliography [392–409]. The result of

Miss Turnbull's fifteen years of research is an absorbing account of a mostintriguing period in the evolution of modern Malaysia and Singapore.

Sir George Williams University   JOHN L. HILL
Montreal, Canada

Eric A. Walker, *W. P. Schreiner, a South African.* London, Oxford University
    Press, 1971, (first published in 1937), pp. 386, $ 14.50.

This is a standard biography, published in 1937, out of print since 1952
and now reprinted. The reprinting was long overdue.

W. P. Schreiner was "a South African" in a profound sense – representative
of the best kind of humanity that grows in that harsh climate, sadly unrepresentative in a quantitative sense. Of mixed German and English parentage, he
was neither Afrikaner nor quite English, yet could easily be given either of
those labels by political opponents of the opposite group. The first South
African–born Prime Minister of the Cale Colony, he held that thankless office
at the outbreak of the Anglo-Boer War, presiding over a governing party of
which he was not a member, and in the end was opposed by friend as well as
foe.

Like other liberals (and Liberals) of the time he opposed the Milner-Chamberlain imperialism which brought on the war, and he did his best to mitigate
the effects of the conflict on the divided population of the Colony. His personal
reasons for this stance – for instance, his brother-in-law F. W. Reitz was State
Secretary of the South African Republic – made him, again, representative of an
important group.

The most significant aspect of his life, however, was the development of his
mind and heart in relation to the fundamental South African question, race.
Beginning with the ordinary prejudices of his kind, he was still a man for "keeping the Kaffir in his place" when he became Prime Minister. Almost at once
a tour of the Transkei revolutionized his thinking; he called that journey his
"road to Damascus". By 1909, when the draft South Africa Act was before the
Cape House of Assembly, he and old Sir Gordon Sprigg (also a former Kaffir-in-his-place man) stood alone in voting against it. Schreiner voted against it
because of its racially illiberal features, especially the clause requiring "European descent" for members of Parliament. He went to England to lobby against
the Bill, but in vain.

In this liberalism, though not in all other matters, he agreed with his
brilliant sister Olive, the novelist, and others of his often divided and wrangling
clan. The agreements and the disputes, the struggle along the road after
"Damascus", Schreiner's prolix and often boring advocacy, his heart of gold,
indeed "W.P." as a person as well as a statesman, are all well described by
Professor Walker, who resisted the temptation to write more of the Times than
of the Life. It would have been a strong temptation, because Schreiner was
only briefly at the centre of South African affairs, yet all his life on what might
be called the inner periphery.

For those who know Walker only by his History of Southern Africa, notable
for the maximum quantity of information packed into the minimum space, it is

important to say that his other works, including this one, are of a much better literary order and easily digestible. This is a classic biography of a man who was more significant than this role in public life would suggest.

Queen's University   A. M. KEPPEL-JONES
Kingston, Canada

P. B. Harris, *Studies in African Politics.* London, Hutchinson University Library, 1970, pp. 181, $ 4.50.

The publication of separate essays in a single book, only loosely connected and lacking a central theme, usually calls for some special explanation. If the purpose, for instance, is to show, by bringing together the fruits of intellectual labour scattered throughout the years, how the author's ideas on a particular subject have crystallized or matured over a certain period, much of the inevitable overlap and repetition involved in such an exercise may be excused, provided of course that the author and his ideas command wide-spread attention. Unfortunately no such rationale is readily available for the book under review. It has a chapter each on the topics of decolonization and democracy in Africa, the foreign policy of independent African countries, integration in East and Central Africa and one on South Africa and Rhodesia and a conclusion entitled "pointers to the future". The hope that through a number of such diverse topics some new light will be shed on African political life remains unfulfilled, and necessarily so. These issues are too broad and there has been too much proliferation, both in the events in Africa and in the scholarly commentary on them, to permit for this kind of generalized treatment. As a genre the book is at least ten years too late. It belongs to an earlier era in academic writings on Africa when it was, perhaps, still possible to aim at the sweeping phrase and the comprehensive account, without the danger of seeming superficial or haughtily slipshod.

But not only does the book fail to provide any new synthesis or insight, its objective of explaining "African's problems in African terms without reference to norms and concepts derived from other sources" also falls by the wayside. We are told that "African politics is party politics," that is "it is oligarchical," that "Today, much of the old rehtoric and grand ideas of democracy wait outside the conference chambers of the party caucus," that "Post-independence Africa does not lend credence" to the view "that democracy is indigenous to the African" and that "if, therefore, modern Africa throws out the baby of democratic principles with the bathwater of democratic institutions, no one should be surprised. What is important, however, that this has happened and to call things by their proper names." Such conclusions plus the analytical categories used, the single-party state, the role of the electoral system in promoting "democracy," the fate of the Westminster model in Africa, the difference between the "institutions" and the "principles" of democracy (hardly a novel idea), the notion that the institutionalization of democracy in Africa is thwarted by "tribalism" and poverty, the belief that "if civil rule cannot preserve democratic ideals, a resort to the clinical incorrupt standards of the army may well be called for," the assertion that by 1964–5 "Tanzania was associated with radical solutions bordering on Communism," and several similar conclusions and statements not only sound like echoes from the stone-age of political science but betray a robust Euro-centric attitude and ideological bias.

This bias and the inadequacy of the analytical tools used are probably nowhere more evident than in the sections dealing with Rhodesia and South Africa. Rhodesia is presented as just another African country and Rhodesian nationalism as "yet another variant of black nationalism (white African nationalism) and consequently Mr. Ian Smith... as an African nationalist." And on South Africa: thanks to the operation of economic forces "all the minor loyalties in some remarkable way cohere to produce a major loyalty. Rhetorically, this has been described as a 'broad South Africanism'... Hence what emerges is an interplay of ideas and interests." These truly remarkable conclusions of the "political process" emerge after a sketchy historical review occasionally couched in some of the popularized catch-phrases of the contemporary literature on socialization, political culture and behaviourism. Neither in these sections nor in the rest of the book, including the bibliography, is there any evidence of the author's awareness of much of the specialized literature that has been coming out on Africa in recent years. In lieu, there are curious one-liners interspersed containing such elementary truisms as e.g. "the key motive in establishing federations lies in the particular patterns of force peculiar to that society" or "the essential fact to remember about Rhodesia is that it is in Africa." Mr. Harris must have a very low opinion of his readers. After reading his book this feeling, alas, is almost certain to be reciprocated.

McGill University   F. A. KUNZ
Montreal, Canada

C. S. Nicholls, *The Swahili Coast*, New York, Africana Publishing Corporation, 1972, pp. 419, Maps.

More than the edge of the African continent the Swahili Coast has been throughout history the western rim of the South Asian world. Arabs, Indians, and ephemerally, the Chinese have followed its coastline in search of exotic products and all have left their mark. The most evident and singular development from the long contact of Africa and Asia along the narrow littoral has been the rise of a unique Swahili culture and the development of the Swahili language.

To the imperialist nations of the Atlantic the Swahili Coast has seldom been more than a series of minor ports on the route to India and the Far East. By the early nineteenth century the Portuguese had come and gone and the British and French had yet to become interested in its trading prospects. It was the rivalry of these two nations for control of the Persian Gulf, vital to the rich Indian trade, that led them into relations with Muscat and ultimately to the British support of the Muscat colony of Zanzibar. The web of negotiations spun by the ruler of Zanzibar, Sayyid Said, in his attempt to capitalize on the Anglo-French rivalry while maintaining his own independence is the main theme in Dr. Nicoll's study of the coast in the first half of the nineteenth century.

In undertaking the writing of this comprehensive political, diplomatic and commerical history Dr. Nicolls appears to have left few conventional stones unturned. Her present study will therefore remain as the standard description of these aspects of coastal history for some time to come. But the virtues of academic thoroughness are more than a little offset by a historical perspective that is narrow and unimaginative. For the historian not familiar with the Swahili Coast the missing chapter on Swahili society is mourned. Even upon a complete reading of this book one has no clear idea of the human dimensions of the trading towns under consideration. It may be that diplomatic and economic histories of unfamiliar societies inevitably fall flat when they fail to consider the people with whose fate they are ostensibly concerned.

A further general failing of this work would appear to be the author's disinclination to consider events in the Indian Ocean in a wider perspective. The reader searches in vain for comments, however brief, relating the British position in India to their reluctance to take on responsibilities on the East African littoral and to their attempts to abolish the slave trade. As British imperialism was and is a global affair, local policies cannot be comprehended in isolation. So while the present work is commendable for its meticulousness a real appreciation of the Swahili Coast in the nineteenth century awaits the author with a wider view of British imperialism in that era.

Loyola College   MICHAEL MASON
Montreal, Canada

J. F. Ajayi and Michael Crowder. (eds.), *History of West Africa,* Vol. 1. Longmans, London, 1971, Pp. xii, 568, $ 6.00.

In different ways this undertaking by Longmans both compliments and challenges the regional surveys of African history which have hitherto been the preserve of Oxford University Press. One assumes that O.U.P. has not capitulated to the invader and that a kind of bibliographic "Scramble" may be soon witnessed. In any event, Longmans must be praised for being first off the mark in the field of West Africa with a work which is bound to be of enduring value. Professors Ajayi and Crowder owe their greatest success to having secured contributions from a number of scholars who individually have won themselves reputations of the most impressive emminence. A majority of these are from Nigerian universities; Mabogunje, Shaw, Alagoa, Adeleye and Ajayi himself from Ibadan, Crowder and Smith from Ahmadu Bello and Akinjogbin and Horton from Ife. While Hunwick is now at Legon his longest association has also been with Ibadan.

Given the preponderance of scholars from Nigeria it is not surprising that there is a bias of interest in the Central Sudan and the Bights hinterland. There is a further bias against the forest areas especially those in Francophone areas. While Suret-Canal discusses the whole of Senegal-Guinea states, occupying a much smaller area are surveyed in great depth and with great thoroughness by E. J. Elagoa. As a result of this distortion one might come away from a reading of this volume with the feeling that the hinterland areas of modern-day Liberia and Ivory Coast were deserted between the Neolithic and Colonial periods.

While the bulk of the contributions are original a few are certainly *deja vu.*

Curtin's comments on the Atlantic Slave Trade, Alagoa's on the Delta States and Akinjogbin's on Oyo and Dahomey are all encapsulations of larger works. But these aside, it is the originality of the work, rare for such surveys, that is its most striking value. For a start, Thurstan Shaw presents a comprehensive discussion of West African prehistory while Robin Horton discusses stateless societies and the problems which they create for historians. It should be noted here that apart from Horton's references there is nothing on the Igbo peoples of Nigeria, not even a summary of what has thus far been speculated on their history, even though they are one of the most numerous and fascinating groups in the whole of West Africa.

It is the Sudanic areas which receive the most thorough treatment. Smith's article on the early states of the savanna will have no doubt the same repercussions on future considerations of this area as his seminal paper on Islamic revolutions of a decade ago did on discussions on the nineteenth century history of the Sudan. It must be seen as unfortunate that Smith was not encouraged to take his study right up to the nineteenth century for there is no other writer on the broad trends of Northern Nigerian history who can martial such a breadth of learning and who, as well, has the capacity to write the history of society that is at once bold and convincing. John Hunwick, one of the masters of the early medieval period in the Sudan puts that area into the wider context of the Islamic world while John Willis, in a rare appearance as a scholar rather than an academic enterpreneur, does a convincing job in laying to rest the fiction that the fall of Songhai had the same effect on civilization in the Western Sudan as the fall of Rome did on Western Europe.

To the social historian this book, in common with most works on African history, may come as a disappointment. A majority of the contributors seem obsessively concerned with the minutae of dates, events and even numbers. There is, as might be expected from Arabic scholars, a loving observation of the niceties of Arabic orthography as well as a compulsive concern with the development of Islamic institutions. To the non-Arabist this may seem as an unsatisfactory substitute for more general investigation and speculation on the subject of social developments which were either non-Islamic or had a small Islamic content. Hunwick, for example, refers to slaves being used as the labour force upon which the prosperity of Kano was built (p. 216). He seems entirely indifferent to the social concomitants of the introduction of slave labour in the city. It is in the same vein that the advent in Kano of various bodies of foreign Muslims is noted; there is for the most part little analysis of the change in social and economic relations which their coming would have signified.

A critical blindness in the use of conventional sources mars the work of several contributors. Adeleye, for instance, puts enormous strain on the value of the "Kano Chronicle" as a source without indicating that he has given any second thoughts to its reliability. When he writes that Amina of Zaria "emerges as a historical personage" (p. 490) he does so without suggesting that he has given any heed to the vast literature on mythical stereotypes in the histories of pre-literate societies. Yet as far as can be seen there is nothing but the most equivocal evidence to justify discussing Amina as a historical figure. In many ways African history has not liberated itself from its own past; the ghosts and mythical giants of the first histories still wander in and out of ostensibly serious modern histories.

But in the last analysis Professors Ajayi and Crowder have performed a lasting service to African history. In a single volume, modestly priced, elegantly packaged and thoroughly mapped and indexed they have given to us a work which at one supercedes all other texts on West African history and opens to us a trove of new research. One hopes that the second volume in this series will combine originality and readability in the same proportions.

Loyola College   MICHAEL MASON
Montreal, Canada

Alan Peshkin, *Kanuri School Children: Education and Social Mobilization in Nigeria.* New York, Holt, Rinehart and Winston, 1972, pp. 156.

Bruce Grindal, *Growing Up in Two Worlds: Education and transition among the Sisala of Northern Ghana.* New York, Holt, Reinehart and Winston, 1972, pp. 114.

These two additions to the paperback monograph series, "Case Studies in Education and Culture," provide useful comparative data on the dynamics of culture change and the impact of the introduction of "Western" schooling among two peripheral ethnic groups in African nations. As well, the two monographs provide interesting methodological comparisons for the gathering and treatment of such data.

Neither culture group has been salient in the modernization of their respective nation states. The Kanuri are an Islamic society enclave in northeastern Nigeria while the Sisala have been historically even more remote an enclave in the Voltaic region of what is now northern Ghana. Both groups experienced only minimal contacts with European colonials. Significant components of the current processes are more directly related to the political and economic realities of nation-building since the Second World War, although they clearly have their antecedents in the colonial models of assumptions and impositions. In both societies the content and processes of schooling are directly and instrumentally associated with "success" in the modern society despite the fact that the actual experiences of school for individuals are more absurd than otherwise (a condition of *school* not exclusive to African schools or teachers) and the essential outcomes of schooling have been more disintegrative of social and psychological structures than otherwise. Both cultural groups are in a process of rapid transition which, from afar, appears to be highly similar but, from the internal perspectives provided by Peshkin and Grindal, has some fascinating variables for contrast between the two societies.

Grindal uses a fairly standard ethnographic approach in his presentation of the Sisala case. From his lengthy participant observation experience and his personal knowledge of the language, he develops a life-cycle overview of the traditional Sisala society, culture and personality. He draws heavily upon the theoretical models of John Whiting, et al, to convey the sense of integrated wholeness which sustained Sisala culture over generations even though they were a subordinated, peripheral group even among the indigenous societies. This requires well over half the monograph. He then describes the socio-political consequences of British insistence upon establishing a system of "chieftianship" and the socio-economic as well as psychological consequences of the modernization changes for the present older adults. This provides a logical framework for his concluding portion dealing with patterns among modern Sisala youth. Literacy and spatial mobility have been the significant factors of change for Sisala. The empirical socio-economic consequences and assumed psychological consequences are neatly linked by Grindal. He helpfully provides a glossary of important Sisala terms to help convey to the reader the lack of congruence between that language and English – such distinctions, for example, as "fear" in an absolute connotation of visceral panic as opposed to "fear" as an essential component of traditional *respect* and "respect" as a reciprocal attitude "accruing from goodness and generosity".

Peshkin lived and worked in a formal "foreign expert" role and derived his data basically by the use of native student research assistants whom he trained and supervised personally in a rigorous, intensive set of observations over a relatively short time. Essence of his monograph is the presentation of four family case studies derived from these observations. This is made possible at least partly because Peshkin is able to draw heavily upon Cohen's 1967 ethnography of the same people. He combines his data to present "a day in the life" of each instance. Within this framework he identifies significant others and some of their salient life experiences as well as their own roles and attitudes in the day being described. This kind of literary license does not permit Peshkin to deal in depth nor to make the neatly integrated whole and the carefully linked change illustrations that Grindal has provided. However, it does make for a more vital, readable sense of the quality of life among the people described. Peshkin's cases – two male and two female children; two of them rural and two of them urban – are real; they are congruent with Cohen's basic ethnographic description of the Bornu; they are consistent with Islamic patterns observable elsewhere conveying an insight into the pan-Islamic reality as well as into the Kanuri life style. The monograph is a neat literary accomplishment as well as an illustration of a practical ethnographic technique for utilization where traditional participant observation is inhibited. (It should be noted: Peshkin is meticulous in specifying his methodology and its limitations.)

One may have minor arguments with some of the theoretical formulations in both books. Personally, I find Grindal's use of "acculturated" inacceptable as a social category discriminant (the "acculturated literate," the "acculturated illiterate," the "unacculturated") and I find Peshkin's "social mobilization" formulation (derived from K. W. Deutsch) intrusive for my conceptualization of the dynamics of change. These kinds of criticisms are picayunish at most and the points – as well as others of a similar nature – useful challenges to the reader to the extent that he is required to reformulate either his own theories or the data presented in order to fit his own theories.

The two monographs are valuable additions to the sparse case literature on the role of school in the dynamics of culture change. They will be useful to anyone studying about or working in Africa, in Islamic societies, in any developing nation. In fact, my own bias is that such literature should be more frequently required reading among the educators of Western nations who have fostered and imposed the incongruous structures of formal education upon the rest of the world.

University of Victoria   A. RICHARD KING
Victoria, Canada

M. S. M. Semakula Kiwanuka, *A History of Buganda. From the Foundation of the Kingdom to 1900.* New York, African Publishing House, 1972, pp. xv, 322, maps, plans, appendices, genealogies.

This book is presumably intended to serve as the culmination of more than half a century's research into pre-colonial Buganda history. Certainly it super-cedes most of the standard texts that we have thus far seen. Volume One of the *History of East Africa* after a decade of preemminence can no longer be con-sidered as a valuable source for Ugandan history. The myths of Luo domination as espoused by Crazzolara and Oliver as well as the Hamitic hypothesis seem even less tenable than ever. One hopes that the end of what are essentially racialist theories of state building and political domination are near. The prin-cipal instrument for the destruction of these hoary psuedo-historical edifices has been the author's exemplary use of oral tradition; tradition which he has not only collected himself but older accounts which he has assessed with a vision not distorted by the tempting parallels of either Anglo-Saxon or Almoravid invasions. But while Dr. Kiwanuka effectively purges Ugandan history of many of the more insalubrious assumptions of the colonial Africanists his emitic is never violent: his attacks are against ideas not persons.

The strength of Dr. Kiwanuka's careful pragmatic scholarship is at the same time his weakness. While he masses the details of Buganda history he neglects any real interpretation of them. His Chapter Four which deals with Buganda's expansion is a close and tedious study of battles, annexations, victo-ries and plunders which altogether lacks consideration of demography, econo-my, or sociology. It reads like the work of some ancient, diligent chronicler recalling a past lurid in glory but deficient in meaning. From the particular the competent historian generalizes and theorizes, not by forcing alien models upon his material but by seeking explanations in other areas and other disci-plines. Kiwanuka's failure to see beyond the *minutae* of happenings leaves the riches of Christopher Wrigley's compressed economic history of Uganda un-tapped, and Kiwanuka's own work impoverished. It is true that he does make a brief foray into "society and economics" but four pages is no more than a perfunctory gesture. There is more than oversight in the author's failure to take his study beyond the narrowly political – there is a blindness as well. Only marginally more palatable than the Hamitic hypothesis which he assaults is the assumption that political institutions are in continual evolution from the less centralized to the most centralized. This application of the nineteenth century social Darwinism leads him to the conclusion that the Baganda were more "evolved" when they had kings than previously. Such views are perilously close to those which suggest, regardless of the processes or the consequences, that economic "development" in Africa, as presently conceived of by the capitalist West, is progress. Even more obviously startling than his acceptance of the political evolution theory is the author's odd insistence of referring to the past itself with such culture – bound epithets as "gross and cruel" (pp. 129–30).

To the reader patient enough to plod through the dull tunnel which com-prises the central portion of the book the enlightenment at the end comes as a pleasant surprise. The final chapters dealing with the Era of Violence are richly interesting, especially the latter of them. Here the author seems to have found history which is especially meaningful to him. Mutesa, as the king increasingly unable to deal with the complex forces beyond his knowledge, becomes a reality. As the tempo of change accelerates Buganda politics become more frenetic until finally the old forms are devoured in the holocast of advancing imperialism. It is a pity that a few parallels are not made with other areas in Africa for at roughly the same moment things were falling apart all over Africa. Nonetheless we are treated to a lively and persuasive critique not only of imperialism in general but of the activities of Captain Lugard and the writings of Miss Perham in particular. Lugard's murderous proclivity towards seeking immediate solutions in arms rather than in negotiations, his indifference to justice and his callous and frequent perversions of the truth in the interests of his own career are raised and can be seen as complementary to the recent study of his career in Nigeria by Nicholson. The wars in which Lugard participated are seen not as religious struggles but as colonial wars of conquest which turned the Protestant minority in Buganda into a local collaborating ruling class. And what the Protestants were for Buganda, Buganda was for Uganda as a whole.

In all one hopes that Dr. Kiwanuka follows up this work with a volume on the subject of Uganda under colonial rule. One hopes as well that if he chooses the same publishers that they find the means of employing proof readers. There can be little justification for producing a book with as many obvious gaffes in spelling, punctuation and syntax as this one.

Loyola College   MICHAEL MASON
Montreal, Canada

D. A. Low, *Buganda in Modern History*. London, Weidenfeld and Nicholson, 1971, pp. xii, 4 plates, no maps, $ 2.50.
D. A. Low, *The Mind of Buganda*. Berkeley, University of California Press, 1971, pp. xxvii, 4 plates, no maps, $ 8.50.

Professor Low's latest contributions to the literature on Buganda consolidate his position as that of the ex-kingdom's most diffuse and prolific commentator: consolidate rather than extend because very little of what appears in his *Buganda in Modern History* has not been seen before either in journals of elsewhere. The first of his present works under review, then, is a largely unrevised collection of Low's essays, the earliest of them dating from the 1950's. If we are to be grateful to their author it will be for undertaking to bring them together for us, assuming that some of them may be inaccessible.

The range in time of Professor Low's interest spans the whole of a century. His first essay "Conversion, Revolution and the New Regime in Buganda" concerns the period from 1860 to 1900 and his last and only previously unpublished one "Buganda and Uganda: the Parameters of a Relationship" takes us up to the 1960's. The underlying assumption of the author would seem to be that he is addressing the expert rather than the novice for the work includes neither a general introductory sketch of Ganda society nor a map of the kingdom. But this assumption seems to be contradicted by the bits of ethnographic and historical data which are scattered throughout the book and which must be sought out in a piecemeal fashion. Perhaps, besides a little judicious scissors and paste work, Professor Low ought to have considered the dividends to the reader of his providing a general introduction to his subject.

It is evident from his style as well as his sympathies that Low is a subscriber to the colonial school of African history. This school is defined by its interests and its selection of historical evidence. It has a prediliction towards discussing the impact of Europe upon Africa: the Slave Trade, the advent of Christianity, the development of Western institutions, constitutional "advance" and generally the peaceful "development" of British colonies under colonial rule. Its heroes are missionaries sometimes, colonial officials often, commercial adventurers occasionally and Africans almost never. Accordingly the brunt of Professor Low's interest is with the British *and* the Baganda. His point of view is British. His heroes are Sir Andrew Cohen the Colonial Governor (to whom he dedicated an earlier book) not the *Kabaka*, Mutesa, who opposed him, and the constitutional expert (and latterly Low's benefactor) Sir Keith Hancock. Evidence is on paper, in archives and in private hands, and not in the opinions of the illiterate black actors who are regarded, it seems, as a mere supporting cast. As far as can be seen, not a single African was interviewed in the process of Low's researches. An equally telling characteristic of the colonial school is the belief that under British stewardship African peoples "advanced". "Advancement" and "progress" are assumptions which remain undefined. Their anthesis seems to be "atavism", a characteristic of the "King's Friends" (p. 184). Buganda goes forward with Sir Andrew Cohen "a firm believer in African advancement" (p. 106) and backward with the King's Friends. It all seems so simple.

It would do Professor Low less than justice to dismiss him simply as a naive historian of the colonial school. His essay on "The Advent of Populism in Buganda" is original and convincing. As Fallers has said in a comment on the original in *Comparative Studies in Society and History* (p. 445, v.6, 1963) "twentieth century Bugandans are shown to act in ways, and out of sentiments that are understandably related both to contemporary circumstances and to the Ganda past". The author's otherwise original article on the religious revolutions in Buganda was equally valuable in its time although by now somewhat diminished in its importance by the more thorough researches of John Rowe and to a lesser extent, Michael Twaddle. His neat little *vignette* entitled "British Public Opinion and the Uganda Question" is an absorbing study of the role of English and Scottish religious associations in promoting philanthropic imperialism.

The Mind of Buganda subtitled *Documents of the Modern History of an African Kingdom* is apparently aimed at the African history library rather than the African historian. It is a part of that relentless tide of Africana which seems nowadays so indispensable to African studies. The best of such works, such as Thomas Hodgkin's *Nigerian Perspectives* use documents to complement and enliven text and as a result impart to each era a unique flavour. The others, those without an explanatory framework, tend to be unreadable save to those whose literary tastes run to archives. Professor Low's book may be found wanting by comparison to Hodgkin's although, an improvement over some, it does have fourteen pages of introduction for 228 pages of documents.

Loyola College   M. MASON
Montreal Canada

Journal of Asian and African Studies, VIII, 3–4

G. L. Caplan, *The Elites of Barotseland 1878-1969; A Political History of Zambia's Western Province.* Berkeley, University of California Press, 1970, pp. xi, 270, 7 plates, 2 maps, $ 8.50.

Dr. Caplan has undertaken a study that is rare in being both contemporary and coherent: contemporary as it takes us to the near present, coherent insofar as he discusses the present without the obfuscating jargon and theoretical devices which make so much of political science incomprehensible. It is lamentable that there is so little in the field of African history with which to compare his work.

The main burden of Dr. Caplan's study is an examination of an elite which became increasingly reactionary as its authority was diminished first by the agents of the South Africa Company and then by the representatives of the Colonial Office. So while Barotseland stagnated under British over-rule its client ruling class carried on a relentless struggle to maintain its own interests. This they were able to do with only in different success until the post-war period when the Colonial Office came to rely increasingly on them to promote its own neo-colonial projects, such as the Central African Federation, and to serve as a bulwark against the more progressive forces of nationalism. This was the undoing of the king and his fellow rulers. In the end they were abandoned by the British and politically emasculated by their enemies in the government of the new state of Zambia. Caplan's description of the subjection and fall of this class of rulers is commendably correct. Even the most venial of the royal self-servers are spared more than the denunciation of their own deeds. Thus in the case of Sir Mwanawina Lewanika III K. B. E., Central Africa's most gilded marionette, he manages to see virtue in implacability.

The British, as puppeteers, are plainly seen looming over the Barotse stage. One of the most instructive sub-themes here is that of their intentional non-development of Barotseland. Between Lewanika's attempt at developing a modern nation and Kaunda's edict prohibiting labour emigration we see the consistent British attempt to keep Barotseland an impoverished source of labour for white enterprise south of the Zambesi.

Even with independence and the destruction of the privileges of the Lozi elite the story does not end. The continuing problem of Barotseland's poverty combined with the exploitation of the Lozi sense of nationalism and the opportunism of the old Lozi elite remains as one of Zambia's most serious problems. Dr. Caplan's attempt to put this problem in its historical perspective can be considered a vital work in removing African history from the irrelevance in which it has too long bathed.

Loyola College   M. MASON
Montreal Canada

H. E. Guenther, *The Life and the Teaching of Naropa.* Oxford, Oxford University Press, 1963, pp. viii, 109, paper, $ 2.75.

This is an important work for Tibetan specialists as well as all those interested in the development of Tantric Buddhism. First published by Oxford University Press in 1963, it has now been re-issued as a paperback.

Naropa's position and influence in the development of Tantric Buddhism is a crucial one. He came at a point when the long development of Tantric Buddhism had reached a water shed, and his work marks the beginning of a new and rich era of development.

Naropa was born in 1016 in Bengal and came from a middle-class background. At the age of 11, in 1016 A.D. he went to Kashmir then the main seat of Buddishm in India. He was later to return to Bengal, to marry, and then after a period as abbott of Nalanda Monastery, he set out in search of his Guru, Tilopa. Eventually finding him, he was to spend some 12 years studying under him until Tilopa's death in 1069. Naropa himself died in 1100.

The text is a condensation of Naropa's life and teaching taken from a late 12th century manuscript of lHa'i btsun-pa Rin-chen rnamrgyal of Brag-dkar. It appears to be the first authoritative Tibetan account of Naropa's life to be written, and the editor, Guenther, who studied the manuscript over a period at Lahoul, found it, apart from some minor block deficiencis, to be quite clear.

Guenther, who is chairman of the Department of Far Eastern Studies, at the University of Saskatchewan, has divided the volume into two parts. In the first part he gives us the English translation of the text followed, in the second part, by a full and lucid commentary on the philosophical tradition into which Naropa's teaching fitted. Finally, he gives us the complete Tibetan text of the manuscript he uses, a bibliography and a very useful index of Tibetan and Sanscrit technical terms.

The only slight criticism one has of an excellent book lies perhaps in the bibliography. This regrettably is confined only to books mentioned in the commentary and one feels a little regret that the editor did not use the opportunity to round out what is an excellent book by giving us a complete and full bibliography of books in this general area. This is not often done, and it would have been of decided interest and value to any student using the book.

Apart from this small caveat, one has any praise for an excellent and enjoyable piece of scholarship. This book will undoubtedly prove of immense value both to the scholar and to the growing number of students who are rapidly becoming aware of the value and richness of the Tantric Buddhist tradition.

York University   B. C. MacAndrews
Toronto, Canada

FURTHER PUBLICATIONS FROM E. J. BRILL

Contributions to Asian Studies

Sponsored by THE CANADIAN ASSOCIATION FOR SOUTH ASIAN STUDIES, TORONTO Canada.

General Editor: K. ISHWARAN, York University, DOWNSVIEW, ONTARIO, Canada

A series containing scholarly papers. Each volume will cover special areas, of Asian countries, and may be of value for specialists, but also to students and teachers of sociology, anthropology and related social science.

Volume 1: 1971. viii, 204 pages, 8 tables   Gld. 46.—

Contents: INDIA: FAMILY AND MODERNIZATION. D. A. CHEKKI, Kalyan and Gokul: Kinship and modernization in Northern Mysore; K. ISHWARAN, The interdependence of elementary and extended family. – CHINA AND INDIA: MAOISM IN CHINA AND INDIA. HYOBOM PAK, Chinese Communists in the Eastern Three Provinces, 1918–35; J. M. VAN DER KROEF, India's Maoists: Organizational patterns and tactics. – PAKISTAN AND INDIA: POLITICS AND LANGUAGE. W. M. DOBELL, Ayub Khan, a de Gaulle in Asia?; L. HARRIS, The frontier route from Peshawar to Chitral: Political and strategic aspects of the "Forward Policy", 1889–1896; L. ZIRING, Politics and language in Pakistan: Prolegomena 1947–1952. – HONG KONG: VOLUNTARY ASSOCIATION. G. E. JOHNSON, From rural committee to spirit medium cult: Voluntary association in the development of a Chinese town; H. J. LETHBRIDGE, A Chinese association in Hong Kong: The Tung Wah. – MALAYSIA: LAW. INNOVATION AND CHANGE. M. B. HOOKER, Hindu law and English law in Malaysia and Singapore: A study in the interaction and integration of two legal systems; M. C. HODGKIN, Overseas graduates as "Innovators" in two developing countries: Malaysia and Singapore; M. RUDNER, Malayan quandary: rural development policy under the First and Second Five Year Plans.

Volume 2: RELIGION AND SOCIETY IN PAKISTAN. Edited by AZIZ AHMAD. 1971. viii, 105 pages   Gld. 40.—

Contents: F. ABBOTT, The historical background of Islamic India and Pakistan; A. AHMAD, Islam and democracy in Pakistan; S. M. M. QURESHI, Religion and party politics in Pakistan; H. MALIK, The spirit of capitalism and Pakistani Islam; S. MCDONOUGH, The social import of Parwez's religious thought; S. AHMAD, Islam and Pakistani peasants.

Volume 3: 1973. viii, 166 pages, some tables and figures   Gld. 64.—

Contents: CEYLON: REINCARNATION AND BUDDHISM. B. L. SMITH, Sinhalese Buddhism and the Dilemmas of Reinterpretation; I. STEVENSON, Characteristics of Cases of the Reincarnation Type in Ceylon. – INDIA: ECONOMY, POLITICS AND SOCIAL CHANGE. J. L. MURRAY, Peasant Motivation, Ecology, and Economy in Panjab; Y. K. MA-LIK, Conflict over Chandigarh: A Case Study of an Interstate Dispute in India; J. S. UPPAL, Economic Development of Indian States: A Study in Development Contrast; K. G. SAINI, Economic Performance and Institutional Change: the Experience of India. – INDIA: RELIGION. M. MAHAPATRA, The Badu: A Service-caste at the Lingaraj Temple at Bhubaneswar; C. R. PANGBORN, Analysis of a Cliché: Eastern Spirituality and Western Materialism. – INDIA: INTELLECTUALS AND CHANGE. P. C. DEB and L. A. WENZEL, A Dimension of Change in India: Prestige of occupations Among University Students; H. S. SANDHU, The Intellectuals and Social Change in India. – INDIA AND PAKISTAN: FAMILY. J. H. KORSON, Some Aspects of Social Change in the Muslim Family in West Pakistan; I. VERGHESE, Is the Kota Society Polyandrous?

Volume 4: TRADITION AND CHANGE IN THERAVADA BUDDHISM: ESSAYS ON CEYLON AND THAILAND IN THE 19TH AND 20TH CENTURIES. Edited by BARDWELL L. SMITH. 1973. viii, 105 pages.   Gld. 42.—

Contents: B. L. SMITH, Introduction; H. BECHERT, Contradictions in Sinhalese Buddhism; T. FERNANDO, The Western Educated Elite and Buddhism in British Ceylon: A Neglected Aspect of the Nationalist Movement; B. G. GOKHALE, Anagarick Dhammapala: Toward Modernity through Tradition in Ceylon; F. E. REYNOLDS, Sacral Kingship and National Development: the Case of Thailand; S. PIKER, Buddhism and Modernization in Contemporary Thailand; F. B. MORGAN, Vocation of Monk and Layman: Signs of Change in Thai Buddhist Ethics; D. K. SWEARER, Thai Buddhism: Two Responses to Modernity; F. E. REYNOLDS, Tradition and Change in Theravada Buddhism: A Bibliographical Essay Focused on the Modern Period.

JOURNAL OF
ASIAN AND AFRICAN STUDIES

JOURNAL OF
ASIAN AND AFRICAN STUDIES

EDITOR: K. ISHWARAN

DEPARTMENT OF SOCIOLOGY AND ANTHROPOLOGY, YORK UNIVERSITY,
TORONTO 12, CANADA

VOLUME IX

LEIDEN
E. J. BRILL
1974

CONTENTS

CONTENTS

Journal of Asian and African Studies

and

African Studies

EDITOR: K. ISHWARAN

DEPARTMENT OF SOCIOLOGY AND ANTHROPOLOGY
YORK UNIVERSITY
TORONTO, CANADA

Volume IX — Numbers 1-2
January and April 1974

E. J. BRILL — PUBLISHERS — LEIDEN

Journal of Asian

and

African Studies

Volume IX JANUARY and APRIL 1974 **Numbers 1-2**

CONTENTS

W. Wilson, Learning to Be Chinese: The Political Socialization of Children in Taiwan (Cho-Yee To). Hung-Mao Tien, Government and Politics in Kuomintang China, 1927–1937 (Samuel C. Chu). Eduardo Lachica, The Huks: Philippine Agrarian Society in Revolt (Maximo P. Fabella). Visakha Kumari Jayawardena, The Rise of the Labor Movement in Ceylon (Tissa Fernando). Joseph J. Spengler, Indian Economic Thought: A Preface to Its History (Marcus F. Franda). James R. Brandon (ed.), On Thrones of Gold: Three Javanese Shadow Plays (Peter R. Goethals). Michael P. Onorato, A Brief Review of American Interest in Philippine Development and Other Essays (Frank L. Jenista). John Dewey, Lectures in China 1919–1920 (Victor N. Kobayashi). Marcus F. Franda, Radical Politics in West Bengal (Alexander Lipski). Erika Kaneko and Herbert Melichar, Pura Mutuzuma: Archaeological Work on Miyako Island, Ryukyus (Clement W. Meighan). Carlos Quirino, Quezon: Paladin of Philippine Freedom (Michael Paul Onorato). William E. Steslicke, Doctors in Politics: The Political Life of the Japanese Medical Association (David W. Plath). Judith M. Brown, Gandhi's Rise to Power: Indian Politics 1915–1922 (Howard Spodek). Donald H. Shively (ed.), Tradition and Modernization in Japanese Culture (Patricia G. Steinhoff). Wayne S. Vucinich (ed.), Russia and Asia: Essays on the Influence of Russia on the Asian Peoples (John J. Stephan). Leo A. Orleans, Every Fifth Child: The Population of China (Irene B. Taeuber). Rene Lemarchand, Ruanda and Burundi (Yaw Saffu). Ruth Finnegan, Oral Literature in Africa (J. R. Rayfield). G. Wesley Johnson Jr., The Emergence of Black Politics in Senegal. The Struggle for Power in the Four Communes 1900–1920 (Donald Cruise O'Brien). R. T. Parsons, Windows on Africa: A symposium (John M. Janzen). Leslie Bethell, The Abolition of the Brazilian Slave Trade: Britain, Brazil and the Slave Trade Question, 1807–1869 (Myron J. Echenberg). Johnson U. J. Asiegbu, Slavery and the Politics of Liberation, 1787–1861: A Study of Liberated African Emigration and British Anti-Slavery Policy (Myron J. Echenberg). A. E. Afigbo, The Warrant Chiefs. Indirect Rule in Southeastern Nigeria 1891–1929 (Patrick Manning). Yohanan Friedmann, Shaykh Ahmad Sirhindi (Aziz Ahmad). B. I. Obichere, West African States and European Expansion: The Dahomey-Niger Hinterland, 1885–1898 (Martin A. Klein). Clifford Geertz, Islam Observed (Aziz Ahmad). C. P. Ridley, Paul H. B. Godwin, Dennis J. Doolin, The Making of a Model Citizen in Communist China (Samuel J. Noumoff). Romain Yakemtchouck, L'Afrique en Droit international (Yassin El-Ayouty). Nigel Heseltine, Madagascar (Aidan Southall).

JOURNAL OF ASIAN AND AFRICAN STUDIES

The *Journal of Asian and African Studies*, published by E. J. Brill, Leiden, Holland, is a quarterly publication issued in January, April, July, and October. Each number is about eighty pages in length.

The Journal, edited by a board of scholars from all over the world who are specialists in Asian and African studies, presents a scholarly account of studies of man and society in the developing nations of Asia and Africa. It endeavours to fulfill a need in the field in that it unites contributions from anthropology, sociology, history, and related social sciences into a concerted emphasis upon building up systematic knowledge and using the knowledge derived from pure research for the reconstruction of societies entering a phase of advanced technology.

ALL EDITORIAL CORRESPONDENCE, including papers, notes and news covering research projects, associations and institutions, conferences and seminars, foundations and publications, and other activities relevant to Asia and Africa, should be addressed to: K. Ishwaran, Editor, J.A.A.S., Department of Sociology, York University, Downsview, Ontario M3J 1P3, Canada.

BOOKS FOR REVIEW (AFRICA) should be sent to: John M. Janzen, Department of Anthropology, University of Kansas, Lawrence, Kansas, 66044, U.S.A., and (ASIA) to Edward R. Beauchamp, College of Education, University of Hawaii, Wist Annex 2-222, 1776 University Avenue, Honolulu, Hawaii 96822.

BUSINESS CORRESPONDENCE, including subscriptions, change of address, orders for additional offprints, etc., should be addressed to:

E. J. BRILL — LEIDEN, THE NETHERLANDS

Subscription price of Volume IX (1974): Gld. 56.— *plus postage and packing.*

Please do not send money with your order. The publisher will invoice you and will then be pleased to receive your remittance.

MANUSCRIPT STYLE GUIDE

Manuscripts of articles should be not more than 7000 words. Unsolicited papers will not be returned unless postage paid. Submit two copies of the article and retain a copy for your own files. Prepare copy as follows:

1. Type double-spaced on white 8-1/2″ × 11″ standard paper, with a 2″ margin at the left hand side and a 3″ space above the titles of both articles and reviews.
2.* Tables should be typed on separate pages, numbered consecutively and given headings. Footnotes for tables appear at the bottom of the tables. Insert a location note at the appropriate place in text, e.g., "Table 1 about here".
3.* Figures, maps and other line drawings are to be submitted in black Indian ink about twice the intended final size on good quality tracing paper. Insert a location note at the appropriate place in text.
4. Articles and reviews are to be submitted in their *final form* so that they require no further alterations. It is the obligation of authors to carefully proof read their material before submission to the journal. Owing to increasing costs, the publisher is compelled to charge authors for corrections other than printer's errors.

*Tables, graphs, figures, etc., should be used sparingly.

• Bibliographical references should be cited in the text by the author's last name, date of publication and page, e.g., (Anderson 1972: 105) or, if the author's name is mentioned in the text, by the date and page reference only, e.g., (1972: 105). • Footnotes are to appear as notes at the end of articles and are to be used only for substantive observations and not for purpose of citation. • With dual authorship, give both last names; for more than two use "et al" (see 3 below). • If there is more than one reference to the same author and year, distinguish them by using letters (a, b) attached to year of publication in the text and reference appendix (see 2 below). • For institutional authorship supply minimum identification, e.g., (U.N.E.S.C.O. 1971: 67).

Entries in the references should be in alphabetical order of authors and should include: name and initials of author(s), date, title, name of periodical, volume number (arabic numerals to be used throughout), pagination (for periodicals), place of publication and publisher. e.g.,

1. FROLIC, B. Michael
      1971   "Soviet urban sociology". International Journal of Comparative Sociology XII (December): 234–251.
2. GREENBERG, Joseph H.
      1965a   "Linguistics" pp. 416–41 in Robert A. Lystad (ed.), The African World: a survey of social research. New York: Frederick A. Praeger.
      1965b   "Urbanism, migration and language" pp. 50-59, 189 in K. Huyper (ed.), Urbanization and Migration in West Africa. Berkeley and Los Angeles: University of California Press. (Reprinted in Man in Adaptation, the Biosocial Background, ed. by Y. A. Cohen, 259–67. Chicago: Aldine Publishing Co., 1968.)
3. KASER, D., et al
      1969   Library Development in Eight Asian Countries. New Jersey: Scarcecrow Press.
4. SOUTHALL, Aidan W.
      1970   "The illusion of tribe" pp. 28–50 in P. C. W. Gutkind (ed.), The Passing of Tribal Man in Africa. Leiden: E. J. Brill.

Book reviews should not exceed 800 words and should not contain footnotes; references to other works should be incorporated in the text; page references should be given when quotations from the book are included.

Galley proofs of articles will be sent to authors (from the publisher), who should use the standard method of proof correction. Corrected proofs should be returned to the Editor as soon as possible; where proofs are not returned in time, the Editor reserves the right to send the printers his own corrected proof of contributors article which will be the basis of the final article. Proofs are intended for checking, NOT RE-WRITING and authors are most strongly reminded that material should be submitted ready for the printer.

Authors receive 25 free offprints of their article (8 free offprints for book reviews). Additional offprints of articles can be supplied at cost price and must be ordered and paid for when the corrected proofs are returned to the printer.

PUBLISHER: E. J. Brill, Leiden, The Netherlands

Journal of Asian and African Studies IX, 1–2

Technological and Social Changes in a Japanese Fishing Village

TEIGO YOSHIDA

University of Tokyo, Tokyo, Japan

KOICHI MARUYAMA

Hiroshima University, Hiroshima, Japan

EMIKO NAMIHIRA

Kyushu University, Fukuoka, Japan

THIS PAPER documents some relatively rapid socio-economic changes in a Japanese fishing village called Katsumoto-ura. The implications these changes had for village social organization and ritual activities are then discussed. In order to trace changes in the village over time we have done an historical account that covers at least fifty years. The historical data show that the patterns of change in social organization are complex and somewhat cyclical given such a time scale. Furthermore, many modern trends associated with cities such as over-population, social structure influenced by technological change, the rise of producer's interest groups, new employer-employee relations and ecological decline, can be seen in this village, due largely to its economic success.[1]

---

1 The field work on which this paper is based was conducted in the summer and fall of 1964, the fall of 1965, the summer and fall of 1969, the summer of 1971, and in the spring of 1973. The field research was mainly supported by a grant from the Wenner-Gren Foundation for Anthropological Research (#1653), and partly by Special Research Funds of the Research Institute of Comparative Education and Culture, Faculty of Education, Kyushu University. Grateful acknowledgement is made to these institutions. The authors are indebted to Histoshi Ueda, Fujiko Ueda, Kazuto Matsunaga, and Kenne H–K. Chang, with whom the field work was jointly undertaken, for collecting information and analyzing data. While this research was carried out under the leadership of the senior author (Teigo Yoshida), this was a joint research in terms of both field work and analysis. We also wish to thank John L. Fischer, Thomas P. Rohlen, and Jane Bachnik for revising the English style and supplying valuable comments. Part of the results of this research has been published in a paper by Kenne H-K. Chang (1971).

Socio-ecological Setting of Katsumoto-ura

Depopulation, due to the draw of urban employment, is a fundamental fact of life for most Japanese rural communities, however, the village in question, Katsumoto-ura, located on the northern coast of the Iki Island off north Kyushu, has not only succeeded in maintaining its population, but has seen an increase in recent years. In 1963 Katsumoto-ura consisted of 790 households with a population of about 3,500; in 1970 the total number of households had increased to 851 and the population to 3,611 (1,736 males, 1,875 females). Approximately 60 per cent of the total households are now engaged in fishing, and most of the remaining households are connected in some way with the fishing economy of the village as shop-keepers, boat-builders and the like. After graduating from junior high school on the island, most young men carry on their father's occupation as fishermen. Compared to other fishing villages in Japan, Katsumoto-ura has been very prosperous, and this has been achieved primarily as a result of technological development.

Iki Island, on which this village is situated, is located in the Straits of Tsushima between the Korean Peninsula and Kyushu. Iki Island, about 138 square kilometers, is divided into four administrative districts including Katsu-moto-chō (town) on the northwestern part of the island, and the four districts constitute Iki-*gun* (county) in Nagasaki *Ken* (Prefecture). Katsumoto-*chō* consists of two parts, namely, the inland agricultural villages generally called *zai*, and two fishing villages called *ura*: Yunomoto-ura and Katsumoto-ura. All the inhabitants of Katsumoto-ura and the adjacent agricultural villages are devotees of the Shōmo Shrine, to which their tutelary deity is dedicated. The shrine is located on the western seacoast of Katsumoto-ura, and the Shinto priest of the shrine performs communal rituals.

Katsumoto-ura, which lies in an arc around Katsumoto Bay, presently consists of three parts called "ku" (ward): Motoura in the east, Kurose in the middle, and Shōmura in the west. It was formerly divided into two wards, Eastern (Motoura) and Western (Shōmura), and this underlying division still functions in communal and ritual activities. The Eastern ward has been split into two wards, Motoura and Kurose, the latter being newly organized as a commercial area, while the Western ward has retained its identity as Shōmura. Most of the Motoura and Shōmura residents are full-time fishermen. Each of these three wards has several sub-units called *machi* (neighborhoods), which function as the minimal units of township administration as well as of the Katsu-moto Town Fishing Cooperative (Diagram 1).

The Tsushima Straits provide the Katsumoto-ura fishermen with excellent fishing grounds, especially for *buri* (yellowtail), *ika* (squid), and *tai* (sea bream). While some of the Motoura Ward fishermen depend on net fishing, most fishermen of Katsumoto-ura exclusively use hook and line techniques. The squid are caught extensively in the adjacent seas all the year round, though the species vary in accordance with the seasons. The yellowtail are fished only at certain spots in the Tsushima Straits called *sone* (shoal), mainly in the winter

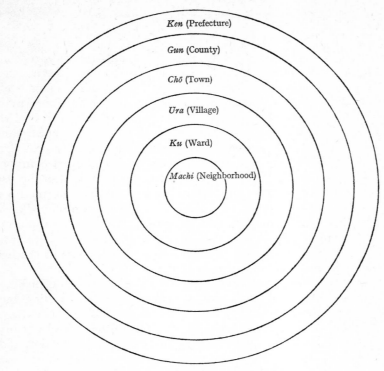

Diagram 1. The size and relationship of the local terms.

season. One of the best *sone* named "Shichiriga-sone" has been practically monopolyzed by the Katsumoto-ura fishermen. Net fishing is prohibited by law around the *sone* for the protection of the resources.

All the marine products are shipped to the main ports of Kyushu and Honshu, namely, Fukuoka, Karatsu, Nagasaki, and Shimonoseki, through the Katsumoto Town Fishing Cooperative which charges a few per cent commission. Fukuoka is about 76 kilometers from Katsumoto-ura. The village is in daily contact with this city in north Kyushu by a regular cargo and passenger ship line, since Fukuoka is socio-economically as well as geographically closer to Katsumoto-ura than Nagasaki, the capital of Nagasaki Prefecture to which Katsumoto-ura administratively belongs. There is even a daily air service between Fukuoka and Ishida-*chō* (town) on Iki Island next to Katsumoto Town. TV and radio broadcasts are received at Katsumoto-ura, and almost all households in the village are equipped with TV sets. Thus, through the development of the transportation facilities and mass media, Katsumoto-ura is no longer an isolated fishing village on a remote island, but has come to be under the direct influence of the modern urban subculture. Yet, much of the traditional village culture has been maintained relatively unchanged until recently.

Former Social Organization and the Development of the Fishermen's Association

According to certain historical records, for about one hundred and fifty years in the 18th and 19th centuries the Katsumoto-ura fishermen enjoyed good whaling in the adjacent seas (Yamaguchi 1939). This fact was orally transmitted to the present inhabitants. According to some aged informants, the fishermen were hired by a few entrepreneurs and were organized into working groups. Fishing techniques were simple and consisted of using spears and nets. This was known as the first period of prosperity at Katsumoto-ura. However, the whale fishery closed in the 1870's because whales stopped coming to the area. Since then squid fishing began to predominate, but most of the people of Katsumoto-ura barely eked out a livelihood as most of the fishermen possessed no fishing boats and were employed by few who did. The employed crew were called "wakkashi" (young men), and this term is still used for the crew. The boat-owner fishermen were under the control of wholesalers (*toiya*) to whom all the fish caught had to be sold. There were 13 wholesalers at the height of their prosperity in the late 19th century.

The relationship between the wholesaler and the owners of fishing boats was based on a contractual arrangement between the two parties, but these contracts lasted for many years and were often succeeded to in the next generation. Since the owner of a fishing boat was committed to selling his catch solely through one wholesaler, he was at the mercy of the wholesaler, and when the market price of fish declined, the wholesaler forced the owner to sell at a lower price. In addition to the contractual arrangement between wholesalers and boat owners, the lack of organizing power among the boat owners to oppose the wholesalers was aggravated by three factors; first, the group of the wholesalers had agreed among themselves not to buy fish from those fishermen in a relationship with other wholesalers, and the wholesalers set the price of fish every ten days at a common meeting; second, the fishermen had no boats large enough to transport the catch themselves to any of the fish markets on the mainland; third, most of the boat-owners had borrowed money from the wholesalers in order to buy their boat and fishing equipment, and their feeling of debts and obligation bound them irrevocably to the wholesalers. The dominance-submission relationship between the wholesaler and boat-owner fishermen is an example of the traditional patron-client (*oyakata-kokata*) relationship in Japan (Bennett and Ishino 1963: Yoshida 1964; Yoshida, Ueda, Maruyama, and Ueda 1969).

The relationship between a boat-owner and his fishermen-crew was also based on a contractual arrangement which was renewed every year on October 10, the time of the annual festival of Konpira Shrine where the fishermen's guardian deity was enshrined. Actually this relationship also lasted longer and was often succeeded to generationally. A crew member tended to feel indebted to his employer, especially when his father or former household head had been employed by the same boat owner. Crew members often were forced to borrow money from their boat-owner, and then had to work for the same boat-owner until they had repaid the loan. Although the relationship between the boat-owner and his crew fishermen was often softened by the sentiments of kinship because the boat-owner frequently hired his crew from his kinsmen, this relationship usually showed the same patterns as those between wholesalers and boat-owners. Thus, the village of Katsumoto-ura was distinctly organized in a linked series of vertical patron-client relationships until the early 1920's. Three strata were clearly distinguished, and there was a hierarchy consisting of the respective links between the wholesalers and boat-owners and between the boat-owners and crew members. While the wholesalers held meetings regularly at each other's houses, the boat-owners had their own gatherings where they made decisions on matters of fishing and elected their representatives for the purpose of negotiation with the wholesalers. Although both the boat-owners and the crew fishermen had been affiliated with the Fishermen's Union since 1908, the Union was practically inactive, and the membership was only nominal.

In the 1920's the increasing poverty of fishermen led them to disputes with the wholesalers, and social conflicts between them gradually became aggravated. Upon the petitions made by fishermen, the local government tried to help them in order to increase marine production. Without the government's intervention the fishermen would have been oppressively dominated by the wholesalers for a longer period. Thus, the fishermen gradually succeeded in selling their catch to other than the originally contracted-to wholesalers, and the wholesalers lost much of their social power by the time the "Katsumoto Yellowtail Feeding Union" (*Katsumoto Buri Kaitsuke Kumiai*)[2] was organized by fishermen in 1930. This union, through the mediation of the Fisheries Section of the Prefectural Office, acquired for the use of its members several fishing grounds which had formerly been under the exclusive control of the wholesalers. Apparently, the activities of the Union served to break down the traditional patron-client hierarchy as the boat-owner fishermen succeeded in terminating their economic dependence upon the wholesalers. While some fishermen repaid their debts to the wholesalers entirely or partly, others did not. But the wholesalers were largely powerless to insist on this. The Union was operated by the leadership of older, experienced fishermen, and was successful. It lasted until the war. During this time the members enjoyed abundant catches of fish, and this can be regarded as the second period of prosperity in Katsumoto-ura. During the war the fishermen suffered from both lack of manpower and fishing equipment.

In 1949 the "Katsumoto Town Fishing Cooperative" (*Katsumoto-chō Gyogyō Kyōdō Kumiai*), including all fishermen of Katsumoto Town, was founded on the initiative of the national government. All fishermen including boat-owners and crew fishermen were included in the Cooperative. Since the establishment of a Youth Division within the Cooperative in 1953 the Cooperative has become

---

2　This Union used a particular technique of fishing, where one throws out bait to lure the fish and then when the fish are feeding one follows up with baited hooks.

very active. Young fishermen (from 15 to 35 years of age) of the Division have promoted the fishing industry through the improvement of fishing technique and the exchange of fishing information between members. The Division of Trust and Savings of the Cooperative encouraged the members to deposit a part of their income. The Women's Division, which was founded in the Cooperative in 1952, helped to increase fishing income through the innovation of a technique for processing dried squid, which is relished by the Japanese. Since the women of the village were not involved in fishing, they were able to spend most of their time in this work and thereby expanded the household economy of the village. Women were tabooed from fishing itself because it was traditionally believed that if a women got in a fishing boat, the fishermen's *funadama* (guardian spirit of the boat) became angry. While the taboo for women in fishing boats is not always strictly observed in recent years, the *funadama* is still respected. The *funadama*, which is said to be a female deity, is enshrined in a small wooden box, and this is placed at the foot of the main mast or in the central part of each fishing boat. The fishermen always pray to the *funadama* before sailing off for fishing and offer some fish and rice to it after fishing. They also perform ceremonies for the *funadama* when launching a boat and during New Year's.

In 1958 the Katsumoto Town Fishing Cooperative began to finance the purchase of new fishing boats equipped with modern marine engines. This loan has been financed by the national government in order to improve the fishing and agricultural economy of the country. Since the interest rate was relatively low (3.5% per annum), many fishermen used the loan system through the arrangement of the Cooperative. The National Association of Fishing Cooperatives (*Zenkoku Gyogyō Kyōdō Kumiai Rengōkai*) also started to finance individual members. Though the interest on the latter's loans was as high as 9% per annum, many of the fishermen applied for them, since some obtained a government grant for paying part of the high rate of interest. It is noteworthy that most of the loans, both government and private, were lent to individual members only through the arrangement of the Katsumoto Town Cooperative, the directors of which stood surety for the financing. In other words, only those fishermen who were judged as promising by the board of directors of the Cooperative were financed. Thus, members of the board of directors of the Cooperative had considerable prestige in Katsumoto-ura. By means of this financing those who had small fishing boats sold them and bought larger ones, and those who did not have any boats and worked as crew members bought new or used boats. Those who had large boats bought even larger ones. Thus the financing policy of the government greatly augmented the number and size of fishing boats. And the immense increase of powerful engine boats distinctly promoted economic development. The present period seems to be the third period of prosperity following the second period of prosperity during the 1930's when the "Katsumoto Yellowtail Feeding Union" (*Katsumoto Buri Kaitsuke Kumiai*) flourished. The government and non-governmental loans were offered to the Katsumoto Town Fishing Cooperative mainly because their fishing industry had been deemed promising.

Technological Development

It was in 1920 that the marine engine was first introduced to Katsumoto-ura. Until then all fishing boats were powered only by oars and sails. In 1922 there were only 6 fishing boats equipped with marine engines while the rest (334) boats were all traditional sailing boats. Since then, however, the number of power-driven vessels increased rapidly to 52 in 1927, 91 in 1932, and 97 in 1936. The number of boats without engines decreased accordingly from 286 in 1927 to 158 in 1936 (Yamaguchi 1939: 525). The rapid adoption of the marine engines by the fishermen allowed them more extensive access to the yellowtail fishing grounds. These included Shichiriga-sone. The abundance of yellowtail at this place had been well-known to fishermen but they could not go there safely without powered engine-boats. Until this fishing ground became easily accessible, the Katsumoto-ura fishermen had relied for fishing grounds upon squid fisheries in the home waters.

The increase of power-driven boats was accelerated by financial aid from the national and local governments as well as by private loans in the post-war period. Table 1 indicates the general tendency of increase in the number of

Table 1

Increase in Number of Powered Fishing Boats

Year	1955	1960	1965	1969	1972
Number	172	245	405	508	549

power-driven fishing boats. In the prewar days all the engines were hot-rod engines of semi-diesel type driven by means of light oil. Since this type of engine was prone to breakdown, a more reliable diesel engine was introduced which has taken the place of the former hot-rod engine. The fishing boat driven by a diesel motor, though more expensive, needs less hands, and is far faster and safer. Thus a three ton boat could be handled by one person. By eliminating other crew men with whom a haul must be shared a boat-owner fisherman could monopolize all the catch. However, this was not always the case. In order to make the best use of an expensive diesel-powered marine boat, the fishermen have found that the size of the boat should be large. Table 2 shows the tendency in size of fishing vessels.

Table 2

Increase in Size of Powered Fishing Boats

	End of 1963	Beginning of 1971	September, 1972
less than 3 tons	243	302	253
less than 5 tons	84	104	96
less than 10 tons	22	72	116
less than 15 tons	2	39	39
less than 20 tons	0	0	42
20 tons or more	0	0	3
Total	351	517	549

This growth in size is still going on; when we visited the village in March, 1973, vessels of the 15 to 20 ton class numbered 63. About 40 boats have been added annually in the last several years, and about 60% of them are over 10 tons. A staff member of the Cooperative told us that the number of boats exceeding 15 tons would soon number 100. But 15 to 20 tons seem to be the limit of the increase, partly because a vessel of more than 20 tons needs much more manpower and this is increasingly harder to obtain, and partly because the tax rate is extremely high for a vessel of 20 tons or more. Moreover, it is not necessary with the hook and line method to employ a vessel larger than 20 tons.

In accordance with the increase in number and size of fishing boats, internal equipment has also been mechanized. Many large boats are equipped with fish radar and even a set of loran. The transceivers have been replaced by better ones. Formerly the Katsumoto-ura fishermen used to all share only a single short wave, but as more fishermen came to use this single band, this type of transceiver was found less effective. At present several radio wave lengths are in use. The use of radio has maintained the safety of the fishermen's lives on the sea, and has facilitated communication with fellow fishermen and fish markets.

Short-wave radio transceivers were first introduced to Katsumoto-ura around 1962 for the purpose of preventing shipwrecks. But they turned out to be more frequently used for exchanging information on fishing at sea than for cases of emergency. It was extremely advantageous for boats to be equipped with transceivers, for they could then follow a school of squid or other fish on the basis of information provided. In fact, boats with transceivers usually enjoy larger catches so that within a year or two almost all of the boat-owners had installed transceivers. While fishing in distant areas, fishermen began to inquire by radio about the catch at each other's fishing grounds. Generally, a fisherman had to be honest over the radio even if he was having a good catch because if he gave misinformation that he was getting only a little in order to monopolize his good catch, he would soon be found out to be a liar when he returned to port. Therefore, in order to maintain his reputation he had to tell the truth. In consequence the transceiver made it technically possible to exchange information at sea, and at the same time, made it impossible socially to keep individual secrecy concerning fishing conditions. Thus the spread of transceivers among fishermen tended to level off the catch, and most importantly, promoted the exchange of information between fishermen. As a result of this spread, it seems, the members of the Youth Division of the Fishing Cooperative succeeded in persuading experienced fishermen to disclose their fishing techniques. Although individual fishermen formerly tried to keep their knowledge of fishing grounds, fishing methods, and fishing equipment secret except from their sons, at the request of the members of the Youth Division the older fishermen gradually gave the young men the knowledge they had acquired through years of experience in fishing. It was often emphasized by the villagers that the fishermen became more open-minded than before.

The improvement of the boat engines, the rapid increase of power-driven fishing boats, the introduction of transceiver and fish radar, and other technological innovations seem to have increased both the total catch of fish and per capita income. While the total catch of all kinds of fish was 907 tons (95 million *yen*) in 1954, it rose to 1,467 tons (218 million *yen*) in 1963, and 1,671 tons (752 million *yen*) in 1971. The total cash deposits of individual members at the Fishing Cooperative in these years were 7 million *yen*, 111 million *yen* and 1,092 million *yen* respectively. It is amazing that during the 17 years from 1954 to 1971 the deposits by members increased 158 times and the gross income increased 8.9 times. In view of the fact that the weight of the catch increased only 1.8 times, we must acknowledge that the rapid rise of fish prices tremendously accelerated the increase of income.[3]

Located so near the coast, Katsumoto-ura is deficient in its supply of underground water. Only several wells in the Shōmura and Kurose wards were in common use until 1961. Women were traditionally responsible for carrying home water in buckets. As a matter of fact, the heaviest and most time consuming work for women was carrying water from nearby wells for domestic uses such as drinking, cooking, and washing. When a nearby well was exhausted as was often the case in summers without rains, they had to carry water from deeper wells more distantly located. The entire village suffered from the shortage of water until 1961, when a waterwork system was completed in Katsumoto Town. This water supply not only improved the sanitary conditions but also enabled women to engage in processing squid in the time formerly taken up by carrying water. Thus the traditional division of labor was considerably affected.

Social Change, Rituals, and New Trends

Let us recapitulate the major social changes of the village of Katsumoto-ura. First, the relationships between the wholesalers and boatowners broke down, bringing about a decline in the socio-economic status of the wholesalers, and accordingly the boat-owner fishermen became economically more independent. These changes appear to be related to the activities of the "Katsumoto Yellowtail Feeding Union" in the 1930's and the increase in the unified collection and selling of fish by the Katsumoto Town Fishing Cooperative since the time of its establishment in 1949. In Katsumoto-ura there are now five households which were previously engaged in wholesaling. Two of these former patrons (*oyakata*) are now acting as local agents for large marine products companies on the mainland; two others are engaged in the processing of dried squid while one of them is engaged in marine transport. None of them possesses the social power he used to have in the 1920's.

Second, the relationships between the boat-owners and crew fishermen broke down due to the tremendous increase of power-driven fishing boats, as

---

3 All the statistical data are based on the official reports of the Katsumoto Town Fishing Cooperative.

a result of which former crew with no boats have become independent boat-owners. Third, the women's contribution to the income of the house-hold through processing squid seems responsible for the rise of their status in family life.

Thus the village of Katsumoto-ura which consisted of several hierarchically organized groups changed into a society of a more egalitarian nature, and the former traditional patron-client relationship has been replaced by a new em-ployer-employee relationship. Leadership in the village has gradually been assumed by the leading officials of the Fishing Cooperative.

Before the establishment of the Katsumoto Town Fishing Cooperative in 1949 the three wards (*ku*) of the village used to maintain more distinctive iden-tities than they do now. For example, Motoura Ward was traditionally known for its net fishing for sea bream; Shōmura Ward for its hook and line method of yellowtail and squid fishing. The ward group sentiments were also reflected in the annual festivals of the Shōmo shrine. In 1930, as members of the "Katsu-moto Yellowtail Feeding Union", the Motoura Ward fishermen began to use the hook and line method as well. Most of the former functions of the ward (*ku*) unit are now assumed by the neighborhood (*machi*), which is the minimum unit of the Cooperative as well as of the Katsumoto Town administration, with the result that the ward unit has largely lost its intermediary position between the village and neighborhoods. This can be related to the process of social integration of the village of Katsumoto-ura.

The "Katsumoto Yellowtail Feeding Union", organized in 1930, consisting of all the fishermen of the Shōmura and Motoura wards, provided the Katsu-moto-ura fishermen with the first opportunity to work jointly using the same fishing technique. As a consequence, the activities of the Union, which con-tinued from 1930 to 1940, contributed to the solidarity of the Katsumoto-ura community as a whole. While some of the farmers of agricultural villages were engaged in coastal fishing, in 1932 the Fishermen's Union at Katsumoto-ura eliminated them from its membership. By this action Katsumoto-ura seems to have strengthened its social solidarity as a fishing village. By the 1950's the hook and line method spread to the entire village. The spread of transceivers also significantly promoted communication between fishermen at fishing grounds. In 1963 in every neighborhood, except in Kurose Ward, largely con-sisting of shopkeepers, a boat-owners' association was organized, which met once a month for the purpose of studying fishing techniques. These organiza-tions did not develop independently, but as sub-units of the Fishing Coopera-tive. The youth group, a traditional association organized at each neighborhood (*machi*), has been re-organized as a sub-unit of the Fishing Cooperative. More-over, such associations as the "Yellowtail Fishing Union" (*Buri Tsuri Kumiai*), the "Sea Bream Fishing Union" (*Tai Tsuri Kumiai*), the "Squid Transport Union" (*Ika Unpansen Kumiai*), etc., were newly organized as sub-units of the Fishing Cooperative, cross-cutting different neighborhoods. Each of these Unions had a local unit in each neighborhood, and many persons belonged to more than two Unions.

Also, one aspect of social control in the village was intensified. In 1905 many Katsumoto-ura fishermen encountered a storm at sea, and 42 of them died; since then the village of Katsumoto-ura has been regulating fishing in stormy weather. This regulation was strengthened in 1949 through the adoption of strict codes by the Fishing Cooperative for the purpose of prohibiting boats from sailing in bad weather. For this purpose red and white flags were raised at the mole of the bay as signals. All the fishing boats of the village have had to follow this regulation strictly without exception until recently, as discussed below. Those violating the regulation have been severely fined by the Cooperative. It seems that these processes, together with the weakening of the social division between the Shōmura and Motoura wards, clearly show the strengthening of the integration of Katsumoto-ura village as a whole, and indicate that the development of the Fishing Cooperative has accelerated the tendency of village cohesiveness.

Various changes observed in the annual festivals of shrines in the village can be understood only in reference to the economic and social changes previously described. The annual festivals of the Shōmo shrine, to which the tutelary deity of Katsumoto Town is dedicated, take place from the 9th to the 15th of October and are most important to the villagers. In these festivals Shinto music and dancing called "*kagura*" are performed by the Shinto priest of the shrine, other Shinto priests and farmers. During the festivals classic plays are staged in the evenings. The most spectacular events of the festivals consist of a boat race and a parade of all the fishing boats with colorful flags in the bay. The race takes place on the last day of the festivals. This boat race was originally a competition between the Katsumoto-ura village and agricultural villages in Katsumoto Town. The competition was between two boats with ten crew members for each: one called "*aka*" (red), which represented the fishing village, and the other called "*shiro*" (white), which represented the agricultural villages. It was formerly believed that the fishing village (Katsumoto-ura) would enjoy a large catch if the "red" boat won and the agricultural villages could expect an abundant crop if the "white" one won. This race thus had an aspect of divination. Later, this boat race was performed not between the fishing village and the agricultural villages but between the two wards: Motoura and Shōmura. This elimination of farmers from the boat race preceded their being eliminated from the Fishing Cooperative, but the direction of the changes in both cases was the same: strengthening of the solidarity of the village of Katsumoto-ura by eliminating the agriculturalists.

After the boat race, whichever won, quarrels were likely to break out between young men of these two ward divisions. Thus this race, reflecting the pre-existing tensions between the two wards, was, in fact, considered by the villagers to intensify the social opposition between them. They explained that for the sake of social unity of the village they abolished the race between these two wards in 1957, and made the neighborhoods, sub-units of the ward, arrange crews every year at the time of the festivals. Thus, since then, the two neighborhoods which present crews for the boat race, have been rotated in the village, regardless of ward affiliation. We observed the boat race in 1964. The spectators were greatly excited, shouting encouragement.

In the festivals of the Shōmo shrine the role of the Fishing Cooperative is extremely important. The membership of the executive committee of the festivals is identical with that of the Fishing Cooperative. The Cooperative organizes and financially supports the festival and other rituals and festivals as well. Thus the Cooperative plays a dominant role in the performances of various festivals in the village.

The disappearance of the ward (*ku*) divisions as ritual units can also be observed in other cases in which social units for worship at the shrines have been either enlarged to the village level or diminished to the neighborhood level. For example, the inhabitants of Motoura Ward formerly worshipped their tutelary deity enshrined in the Innyaku shrine; however, one after another, three of the four neighborhoods of Motoura Ward gradually stopped contributing their financial share covering the cost of festivals and shrine maintenance. The Innyaku shrine is now worshipped by one neighborhood alone. The fact that the shrine lost the nature of tutelary deity for the ward can be attributed to the weakening of the social identity of the ward. The Nyaku shrine, which was originally worshipped exclusively by the descendants of a few pioneering fishermen of Katsumoto-ura, is now worshipped by the entire village. The Konpira shrine, in which the tutelary deity of fishermen is enshrined, was formerly worshipped by the inhabitants of one particular neighborhood called Kotohira but is now worshipped on the village level. The Gion shrine, formerly worshipped by two neighborhoods, has been similarly worshipped at the village level since 1962. Such acts of worship include participation in the festival and financial contribution to the cost of festivals and maintaining shrines.

These changes in the social units which support the shrines can be attributed to the other social and cultural changes previously discussed. More specifically, the two wards of Motoura and Shōmura tended to lose their identity as ritual units in accordance with the development of the solidarity of the entire village of Katsumoto-ura and this process paralleled the increasing importance of neighborhoods as sub-units of the village and the increasing importance of the Fishing Cooperative in village wide affairs. The question then arises as to why some of the ritual units were enlarged to the village level, while some others were diminished to the neighborhood level. One answer to that might be that the worshippers of the tutelary deity of Motoura Ward were diminished to a neighborhood level according to the weakening of the identity of the ward, while the Nyaku and Konpira shrines have become widely worshipped by the entire village because the guardian deities of fishermen were enshrined there. Among the three wards of Katsumoto-ura it is only Kurose Ward that has maintained itself as a ritual unit for performing the festivals of the shrine to which the tutelary deity of the ward is dedicated. This fact seems to imply that the social distinction of the inhabitants of Kurose Ward by their occupation (shop-keeping) has persisted through the years despite the strong tendency to the integration of the village of Katsumoto-ura.

In comparison with the inland farming villages of Katsumoto Town the village of Katsumoto-ura is very prosperous. The people of Katsumoto-ura are proud of attaining economic prosperity, social integrity and superiority over the farmers. Yet, some new trends of differentiation can be observed in the village.

As indicated above, the Motoura Ward fishermen also began to engage in yellowtail and squid fishing by hook and line methods in the winter time, but they never gave up sea bream fishing.

As a result of the increase in the number and size of the fishing boats, the limited areas of good fishing grounds for yellowtail are badly congested with boats during the short fishing season, and communication on a single short wave band became difficult because over 500 vessels became involved. Thus, in 1966 all the boat-owner members of the "Yellowtail Fishing Union" (*Buri Tsuri Kumiai*) organized themselves into twelve groups on a neighborhood basis. These groups all use separate radio bands so that members of the same group at sea can communicate with each other about the location of fish without interference by others. The leaders of all the groups use the common radio band to be used in case of emergency (engine trouble, accident, rescue, etc.). When these fishermen cannot go out fishing in bad weather, members of each group get together at a member's house in order to "study" about fishing by exchanging ideas and information.

Those who own fishing boats of over 5 tons formed a "Squid Transport Union" (*Ika Unpansen Kumiai*) in around 1960. They not only fish squid themselves but transport the catch for others to markets on the mainland for a few percent of commission. The Union consists of four sub-groups, each of which goes out fishing together, forming a fleet of vessels, and each has its own gathering on land in stormy weather. Each sub-group of the Union has its own radio band to communicate within its own group, whereas the leaders of the group have another radio band to communicate with the headquarters of the Fishing Cooperative as well as with each other.

Another union called the "*Makiotoshi* Union" (*Makiotoshi Kumiai*) was organized in the mid 1960's. The fishing technique called *makiotoshi* is a mechanized hook and line method used by larger boats. The members numbered 30 in 1969. Their fishing boats were well equipped with a fish radar and often with a loran. The members of this Union try to find sunken vessels, which generally makes a very good fishing ground for black sea bream. It is said that one sunken vessel will provide a fishing ground that can be worked constantly for a year or more. Since sunken ships are hard to find, these fishermen keep their information to themselves as much as possible. As a consequence, this fishing method tends to enhance group cohesiveness among co-workers, while generating secretiveness and mistrust between groups.

Thus, based on such recent differentiations in fishing activities, different groups and sub-groups have formed, and this trend has begun to weaken the integrity of the village of Katsumoto-ura. This is manifested in, for example, the recent relaxation and final abolition of the communal control of sailing in stormy weather. As indicated before, the Fishing Cooperative stiffened the pre-existing regulations of sailing in 1949. However, since 1969, large fishing boats called "special boats" of over 15 tons have been allowed to go out to sea even when sailing was prohibited because of stormy weather. This was done because the larger boats are well enough equipped to navigate safely even when the sea is too rough for smaller boats. Moreover, the use of red and white flags to regulate the sailing of boats was finally abolished at the annual meeting of the Fishing Cooperative in May, 1972. The reasons for the abolition were: owing to the mechanization of fishing boats, fishing is now safer, and so no serious accidents have recently occurred; and it has become difficult to select persons to judge the weather at 3 to 6 a.m. in winter although this was once an honorable duty. Today only the "Squid Carrying Union" has regulations for its members for fishing in stormy weather. These are put in effect from September to April by hoisting blue, red and white flags.

Although the social integrity of the village of Katsumoto-ura was strengthened by the development of the Fishing Cooperative, the era of economic development seems to have already attained a peak in terms of the availability of fish resources. The decrease of fish is particularly mourned by the old fishermen. They feel that the number of fish now is only about 1/100 of that of the pre-war period, and complain that the poaching boats which have come to Shichiriga-sone from elsewhere have done so much net fishing that they will eventually exhaust the supply of yellowtail even though the Fishing Cooperative is now dispatching a guard boat regularly to protect these resources and the villagers' right to fish yellowtail by hook and line.

The decrease in the quantity of fish is also attributed to the fact that too many boats are now engaged in yellowtail fishing at the fishing grounds even with hook and line techniques. Some of the fishermen blame themselves, saying that there are now too many hands taking out rice from a single rice tub. Apparently technological development has greatly accelerated the decrease in natural resources.

As the quantity of yellowtail decreases, more fishing boats are shifting their emphasis from yellowtail to squid; the former are fished only in winter, while the latter can be taken in all seasons. Thus "special boats" of over 15 tons have begun offshore fishing for squid in the Japan Sea, competing with boats from other places. The squid caught are often sold at ports in northern Japan where the Katsumoto-ura fishermen buy ice and fuel, with the result that they are now away from home for periods of a month or more. This is new for the fishermen, as their fishing grounds used to be limited to the adjacent seas and they brought their catch home daily. As this new deep-sea fishing advances, the fishermen of Katsumoto-ura will be increasingly more involved in social interaction with the larger society as well as in the national economy.

Another outcome of the increase in the number of boats has been a severe shortage of crew men. Many of the boat-owners of the village have been forced to hire from among inexperienced farmers in the neighboring agricultural villages. The boat-owner fishermen have had to train these men before they can efficiently be employed. It was the former's complaint that these inexperienced crew members become seasick easily. The shortage of labor has thus brought about a new employer-employee relationship with inland farming communities, outside of the village.

Along with the tremendous increase of fishing boats, moorings have also become difficult. When there were few power boats, the harbor was spacious enough, but as many of the former crew members have now become boat-owners, they have had to moor their boats far away from their houses. Mooring rental has been practiced. At the most convenient pier in the western part of the bay large boats are moored in two or even three layers. In stormy weather fishermen are afraid that rough waves may make their boats collide and sink. It is practically impossible to further increase the number of boats in Katsumoto-ura because of the mooring situation.

Unlike inland agricultural villages and most rural villages in Japan, most of the fishermen's sons in Katsumoto-ura tend to remain in the village instead of leaving to get city jobs. There are even some cases in which second or third sons, who once left the village to work in cities, have returned to the village to work as fishermen. Due to the system of loans and to the fairly abundant supply of fish in the past it has been relatively easy for young fishermen to obtain power boats and to net higher incomes than salaried men of the same age and educational background. This situation, however, has not only resulted in too many fishermen, but brought about overpopulation in the village. In the limited residence area along the coast there are already too many houses. While two apartment houses were recently built for young fishermen, no more space for houses is available at the present time. This housing problem is another barrier to the further growth of fishing itself as well as to population growth. Some of the Katsumoto-ura fishermen have now been forced to move out of the village to the Yunomoto area. This is not only inconvenient for individual fishermen, but is obviously dysfunctional to the social unity of the village as a highly localized community.

By way of conclusion we should like to emphasize five socio-cultural changes in Katsumoto-ura; first, the leveling out of the class structure accompanying the breakdown of the former patron-client relationships gave rise to the phenomenon of a fantastic rise in the socio-economic status of boat-owner fishermen in the 1930's; second, changes in the power structure were further accelerated in the post-war period by the breakdown of the relationships between boat-owners and crew fishermen as crew men have gradually become independent boat-owners; third, along with the technological and economic development, the village of Katsumoto-ura attained a higher social integration; fourth, there occurred conspicuous changes in the social units responsible for performing festivals and worshipping local deities, and these changes can be largely attributed to the strengthened integration of the village level organization accompanied by the relative weakening of the ward level organizations; fifth, as the economic development attained and passed its peak due to the decrease in natural resources, the fishing techniques have become differentiated, and accordingly, different groups and sub-groups have been formed, with the result that the integration of the village is weakening. As these processes advance, the ways in which festivals and rituals are currently performed will probably be again affected by such changes.

REFERENCES

BENNETT, John W. and Iwao ISHINO
    1963   *Paternalism in the Japanese Economy: Anthropological Studies of Oyabun-Kobun Pattern.*
        Minneapolis: University of Minnesota Press.
CHANG, Kenne H–K.
    1971   "Institutional Changes and Development of the Fishing Industry in a Japanese
        Island Community." *Human Organization* 30: 158–69.
YAMAGUCHI, Asataro
    1939   "Iki Katsumoto-ura no Gyoson Seikatsu (Fishing Village Life at Katsumoto-ura
        in Iki Island)." *Shakai Keizai Shigaku* (Social and Economic History) 9: 387–413;
        515–549.
YOSHIDA, Teigo
    1964   "Social Conflict and Cohesion in a Japanese Rural Community." *Ethnology* 3:
        219–231.
YOSHIDA, Teigo, Hitoshi UEDA, Koichi MARUYAMA, and Fujiko UEDA
    1969   "San'in Nōson no Shinzoku Soshiki (The Kinship System of a Village in the San'in
        Region in Japan)." *Minzokugaku Kenkyu* (The Japanese Journal of Ethnology) 34
        (1): 1–21.

Journal of Asian and African Studies IX, 1–2

The Promotion of Indigenous Private Enterprise in Ghana*

LESLIE E. GRAYSON

University of Virginia, Charlottesville, U.S.A.

AFTER THE OUSTER of the late President Dr. Nkrumah by the National Liberation Council (NLC) in February 1966, the promotion of indigenous private enterprise became one of the objectives of both the NLC and also that of the government of Dr. Busia who took office in September 1969.[1] The Government announced in August 1967 that it will "positively promote and give substantial encouragement to Ghanaian enterprise. Credit facilities and technical assistance to Ghanaian entrepreneurs will be substantially increased."[2] In mid-1968, the NLC issued both a policy paper[3] and a decree[4] on the Ghanaization of business.

By early 1970 pressure mounted to accelerate the pace of Ghanaization.[5] On June 23, 1970 parliament approved the Ghanaian Business (Promotion) Bill[6] which became the Ghanaian Business (Promotion) Act, 1970.[7]

A comparison of the Decree and the Act reveals that overseas business representation and taxi service were Ghanaianized as originally scheduled in 1968, while the Ghanaization of small retail trade was speeded up by three years and certain other businesses (road transport, etc.) by two years. There was considerable debate, both in 1968 and 1970, as to which fields should be restricted to Ghanaians. The principles that influenced the selection of the restricted areas were:[8]

---

* Fifteenth Annual Meeting, African Studies Association, Philadelphia, November, 1972.

1 See also my "The Role of Suppliers' Credits in the Industrialization of Ghana," *Economic Development and Cultural Change* (April 1973), "A Conglomerate in Africa; Public Sector Manufacturing Enterprises in Ghana, 1962–1971," *African Studies Review*, December 1973, "Ghanaian Industrial Strategy: Some Problems for the 1970's," *Economic Bulletin of Ghana*, 1971, No. 3, pp. 3–23 and "A Note on Ghana's Overseas Debt Policy," *Ibid.*, pp. 60–62.
2 *Outline of Government Economic Policy*, Accra, Government Printing Corporation (GPC), no date on publication.
3 *Government Policy on the Promotion of Ghanaian Business Enterprise*, Accra, GPC. 1968.
4 *Ghanaian Enterprises Decree*, 1968, N.L.C.D. 323, Accra, GPC, Effective date of decree was July 1, 1968.
5 Actually it was said in September 1969 that "recommendations aimed at improving certain sections of the decree have been accepted—" *Business Weekly*, Accra, September 22, 1969, p. 5.
6 *Parliamentary Debates*, June 23, 1970, Accra, pp. 1066–1083.
7 *Act*, 334, Accra, GPC, July 3, 1970.
8 *One-year Development Plan*, Accra, GPC, September, 1970, p. 152.

(i) that their operations should fall within the technical competence of the Ghanaian labor force;

(ii) that the size of investment and labor requirement fall within the competence of Ghanaian managerial talents;

(iii) that there is an adequate supply of Ghanaian businessmen with the know-how and experience to enter the selected fields;

(iv) that the take-over of these fields by Ghanaians will create no major gaps nor cause major disruptions in the economy.

The policy of Ghanaization encountered, as expected, some administrative pitfalls. The Government tried to avoid one pitfall with the announcement that "Ghanaians who will allow themselves to be used as 'frontsmen' by foreign business interests in an effort to defeat the objectives of the new policy will face prosecution."[9] Another problem involved the unauthorized amalgamation of "reserved enterprises," i.e., two retail establishments merged, or one acquired the other, so that the annual turnover rose above N500,000 and, therefore, into the non-restricted category. While altering books retroactively (the base was 1967-68) could not have been done without special effort, the relevant agencies of the Ghana Government had neither the staff nor the expertise to check on countervention, if there were any, of the Act. The difficulties caused by these problems were relatively minor, however, and, in fact, one cannot help but be impressed with the smoothness with which the provisions of the Act were put into practice – at least from an administrative point of view.

The only real administrative problem came with the 17 medium-size commercial transport firms which were "taken over" by the Government on June 30, 1971.[10] These companies balked at cooperating with the Government before they were taken over. Approximately one-quarter of the fuel and cargo road transport was owned by non-Ghanaians and the government had to make contingency plans to assure that the flow of supplies would not be disrupted by the Act. In spite of the initial governmental take over, the firms were eventually sold to private businesses, with the original owners receiving compensation for their properties.

Two points should be made at this juncture. One is that the transactions between the Lebanese and Indians on one hand, and the Ghanaians on the other, were commercial transactions, i.e., the price was arrived at after considerable negotiations, except in the case of the taxis, where two governmental appraisers valued the vehicles for the purposes of the take-over. The second point is that all the large and medium size firms, whether European (C.F.A.O., Paterson Simons, Paterson Zochonis, Lennards, S.C.O.A., U.T.C., U.A.C., etc.), Lebanese (El Nasr, M. Captan, S.D. Karam, Assad Fakhry, Fattal Bros., Nassar, etc.) or Indian (K. Chellaram, T. Chandiram, Glamour, etc.) were not affected by either the Decree or the Act.[11]

9   *The Ghanaian Times*, Accra, July 15, 1968, p. 1.

10 *Ghana Gazette*, 1971, No. 46 and West Africa, Week ending July 2, 1971, p. 763.

11 Africanization is, of course, not restricted to Ghana. The Ugandan experience is given in "African Racism—Expelling the Asians," *Wall Street Journal*, November 8, 1972; for

Ghanaian Entrepreneurs – Cocoa Farmers

It is a truism to state that the economy of Ghana is based on cocoa. What needs to be emphasized is that cocoa has always been entirely in African hands and that the farming and selling of cocoa involved and involves considerable entrepreneurship. (Prior to World War II most of the wholesale marketing was in the hands of foreign firms). The growing (and selling) of cocoa goes as far back as 1890. A crucial factor in making Ghana the world's largest producer of cocoa by 1920 was "the specific characteristics of the local population and chiefly their entrepreneurial qualities – the willingness to invest, to grasp the future, to bear risk, to introduce a new commodity and a new technology of production."[12] The cocoa farmer, in Ghana, is not a simple peasant, but a trader and a broker as well as being the cocoa producer. "The Gold Coast has long had an unusually large and active class of comparatively well-to-do middle class merchants with a tradition of enterprise and some proved capacity for it, besides even some small reserve of accumulated capital."[13] A detailed study in the late 50's and early 60's showed that the "migrant farmers of southern Ghana should be regarded as capitalists engaged in the business of cocoa faring."[14] Miss Hill observed that the farmers used land as though it were a savings bank, performed various managerial functions, e.g., employing a labor force and arranging road transport for their and others' crops, and were sizeable creditors. She also points out that they have been functioning in the market economy for over 80 years and that, quoting an 1881 English-Twi dictionary, the Twi language includes such terms as money, interest, capital, invest, save and loan. The Ghanaian cocoa farmer seems to have been an entrepreneur for many decades.

Ghanaian Entrepreneurs – Non-Cocoa Farmers

Miss Hill studied other entrepreneurs in Ghana,[15] namely the Ewe seine fishermen, the cattle owners and traders, both on the Accra Plains and in Northern Ghana; many of the traders in Northern Ghana were Upper Volta nationals. Mrs. Lawson made extensive studies of the entrepreneurship shown by the fishing industry[16] as well as the sophistication of the (fish) traders, all of

Nigeria see "Nigeria Moves Boldly to Gain Control of the Economy," *New York Times*, September 2, 1972, and G. V. Rimlinger, "Indigenisation of Industry," Houston, Rice University Program of Development Studies, Fall, 1972.

12 R. Szereszewski, *Structural Changes in the Economy of Ghana 1891–1911*, London, Weidenfeld & Nicolson, 1965, p. 106. See also R. H. Green & S. H. Hymer, "Cocoa in the Gold Coast," *Journal of Economic History*, September 1966, Number 3, pp. 2994.

13 C. K. Meek, W. M. MacMillan, E. R. J. Hussey, *Europe and West Africa*, London, Oxford University Press, 1940, pp. 81–82.

14 Polly Hill, *The Migrant Cocoa-Farmers of Southern Ghana; A Study in Rural Capitalism*, Cambridge, The University Press, 1963, p. 214.

15 Polly Hill, *Studies in Rural Capitalism in West Africa*, Cambridge, The University Press, 1970.

16 Rowena M. Lawson, "The Growth of the Fishing Industry in Ghana," *Economic Bulletin*

whom were women. Traders exercised control over fishing both as creditors to a highly seasonal industry (in return for an exclusive marketing arrangement; a virtual monopsony, frequently coupled with usurious rates of interest) and by financing seasonal migrations via food and shelter in the host communities. Many of the fish traders were illiterate, as were indeed many other traders in West Africa, yet their market intelligence was, and is, superb. Mrs. Lawson also shows how the traders managed to overcome technological disruption of their marketing-creditor arrangements. When motor boats were introduced into fishing in the early 50's both the financing and the marketing jumped to a size beyond the means of the traders. Enlisting the support of the traditional (and exploited) canoe fishermen, the traders forced the motor boat owners, through a combination of boycott and strike, to market their catch at the traders' terms, and thus re-established the cartelized arrangement.

Trading is very efficient in Ghana. At the retail level it is very competitive,[17] with a correspondingly low profit margin, but this is not the case at the wholesale level. "Mammy traders", controlling such staples as yams, cassava, plantain, and corn, are frequently illiterate but handle huge transactions rapidly, apparently almost always very profitably. Men control the cattle market; my understanding is that in the late 60's the Niger-Mali-Upper Volta-to-Ghana cattle trade was controlled by a cartel of eight men.

There are at least two other areas of entrepreneurship where Ghanaians have played important roles for many years, namely road transport and timber. In the 20's, for instance, the Fori Brothers built a truck transport "empire." Finally, some Ghanaians have assumed increasing entrepreneurial roles both in importing and in manufacturing. J. A. Addison, C. C. K. Baah, Mankoadze, and B. A. Mensah are a few of the Ghanaians in importing. For instance, in 1970 there were ten Ghanaian importers, each with volumes over N1,250,000, and about fifty manufacturing firms have 100% private Ghanaian ownership, employing more than 50 persons.

The Makings of an Entrepreneur in the Ghanaian Setting

When talking about entrepreneurs in West Africa we do not mean a Schumpeterian "innovator," but rather an "imitator" of business practices imported and adopted from industrialized countries who will become active in the small and medium-size industrial and commercial enterprises. Though there are strong entrepreneurial elements in Ghana, there is still a serious shortage of indigenous traders, particularly at the intermediate and large scale

---

of Ghana, 1967, No. 4, pp. 3–24; "Marketing Constraints in Traditional Economies", British Journal of Marketing, Winter 1969, pp. 1–8 and The Changing Economy of the Lower Volta, 1954–1967, London, Oxford University Press, 1972.

17 Peter C. Garlick, African Traders and Economic Development in Ghana, London, Clarendon Press, 1971.

level, and more particularly, industrialists. "Big businesses," of course, were, and are, controlled by Europeans but small and medium-size firms have never had much European involvement, at least not in the former British colonies. Much has been written on this subject, and most of the literature is quite good;[18] it would be redundant to repeat all the hypotheses here. Factors such as foreign domination of big business, lack of African leadership ability or willingness, lack of willingness to commit assets in a fixed form, lack of business education and capital shortage have been extensively analyzed.

A detailed study of Nigerian entrepreneurs has shown[19] inter-regional mobility to be practically nil; only a handful of entrepreneurs were engaged in businesses outside their region of birth. The same study also shows that there has been some movement of clerks and teachers into business even though all "white collar" occupations have high social status in West African societies. Nigerian entrepreneurs did not lack economic motivation, but were in fact driven by a quest for profits and wealth. Yet even though pecuniary drive was paramount, Harris found that[20] firms did not operate at optimum sizes, capacity utilization was very low (while it was claimed that the entrepreneurs faced capital shortage) and efficiency was also very low. The most serious impediment to improved productivity probably was the widespread dispersment of effort and capabilities over several businesses, a phenomenon which is typical not only in Nigeria and Ghana but in most LDCs as well.

Entrepreneurship and Education

One theory frequently advanced is that lack of adequate formal education serves as an impediment to the development of entrepreneurship.[21] There

---

18 B. F. Hoselitz, "Non-Economic Factors in Economic Development," *American Economic Review Proceedings*, May 1957; "The Entrepreneurial Element in Economic Development," in *The Challenge of Development* (ed. by R. J. Ward), Chicago, Aldine Publishing Co., 1967, pp. 122–126; "Social Implications of Economic Growth" in *Readings in Economic Development* (ed. by Johnson and Kamerschen), Cincinnnati, Southwestern Publishing Co., 1972; pp. 53–85, and articles by J. R. Harris, S. P. Schatz, E. W. Nafziger, P. C. Garlick and M. P. Miracle in *South of the Sahara; Development in African Economies* (ed. by S. P. Schatz, Philadelphia, Temple University Press, 1972).

19 John R. Harris, "Nigerian Entrepreneurship in Industry," in *Growth and Development of the Nigerian Economy*, (ed. by Eicher and Liedholm), East Lansing, Michigan State University Press, 1970 and E. W. Nafziger, "Inter-regional Economic Relations in the Nigerian Footwear Industry," *Journal of Modern African Studies*, 6, 1968, pp. 531–542. Nafziger also examines the extended family system in "The Effect of the Nigerian Extended Family on Entrepreneurial Activity," *Economic Development and Cultural Change*, October 1969, pp. 25–33.

20 Harris, pp. 317–18. See also Peter Kilby, *African Enterprise: The Nigerian Bread Industry*, Stanford University, The Hoover Institution, 1965. Kilby also edited a collection of 17 articles, *Entrepreneurship and Economic Development*, London, Collier-Macmillan, 1971.

21 For instance, T. Geiger and W. Armstrong, *The Development of African Private Enterprise*, Washington, National Planning Association, March 1964, pp. 38–44.

seems to be insufficient empirical evidence to prove or disprove this hypothesis. As indicated earlier, many of the cocoa-farmers and traders are illiterates but are doing remarkably well. In Nigeria "the relationship between formal education and entrepreneurial performance is much weaker than had been expected."[22] Another study shows that "the average education of entrepreneurs is probably no higher than that of the population in general."[23] An alternative hypothesis is that the type of education, i.e., educating masses of clerks, is wrong and that what is needed are more technical and management/business schools. A number of proposals have been made to reorient the educational systems[24] but such a drastic change has not yet taken place;[25] therefore, the hypothesis is untested and unproven.

Entrepreneurship and the Lack of Capital

Another theory frequently advanced is that lack of capital is one of the main impediments to the development of entrepreneurship in LDCs. In analyzing this, a useful distinction may be drawn between traditional and "modern" entrepreneurs. Traditional entrepreneurs, say, cocoa farmers, don't seem to lack capital. Miss Hill points out the obvious, that if one behaves like a capitalist, and she makes a good case that the farmers do,[26] then one of their accomplishments is that they get command over capital. In fact, the cocoa farmer – or the Ewe seine fishermen or the traders – manage to obtain capital in spite of a dearth of institutions into which savings can be channeled, and governmental policies that, in Ghana at least, frequently proved to be counter-productive to private entrepreneurship in the last decade. Only the "educated" know how to go about getting loans; these could be Ghanaians as well as aliens.

Turning to the "modern" sector of the economy, in most West African countries it was as much the imperfection of the market as the lack of capital which accounted for the slow emergence of indigenous entrepreneurs. West African economies are small, with the possible exception of Nigeria; they can support only a few highly successful firms in a particular trade or industry, and manage to create, in virtually all cases, an oligopolistic structure. Members of the oligopolistic trade or industry experience no shortage of capital; they can reinvest their profits and can obtain credit. Potential entries do, of course, face a capital shortage, a function more of the oligopolistic market structure than

22   Harris, *op. cit.*, p. 310.

23   E. W. Nafziger, "The Relationship Between Education and Entrepreneurship in Nigeria," *The Journal of Developing Areas*, April 1970, p. 358.

24   Among the many, D. C. Hague, "Education for Industry and Commerce in a Developing Economy," *Economic Bulletin of Ghana*, 1967, No. 4, pp. 27–33.

25   P. C. Garlick, "A Note on Commercial Education in Ghana," *Economic Bulletin of Ghana*, 1960, No. 10, pp. 16–19; G. E. Hurd in *A Study of Contemporary Ghana*, (ed. by Birmingham, Neustadt and Omaboe), London, George Allen and Unwin Ltd., 1967, pp. 224–25.

26   See S. Hymer, "Foreword," In Polly Hill, *Studies in Rural Capitalism*, loc. cit., pp. xvii-xiii.

lack of credit.[27] The last decade witnessed some weakening of the oligopolistic structure of the trading community mostly because of improved infrastructure which made road transport, telephones and telegrams more efficient and relatively inexpensive; improved communications opened up new areas which brought in new traders and they somewhat diluted the cartels. In industry, entry and profitability was and is a function of governmental regulations; whoever receives the import license and a variety of available concessions is viable; whoever does not, is not. The experience of the Federal Loans Board (FLB) in Nigeria from 1956–1962 allowed an empirical testing of whether or not a shortage of capital was an important impediment to the development of an entrepreneur class. After examining the evidence, Schatz concluded that "the belief that a capital shortage is the effective or operating impediment to indigenous private investment is mistaken, that it is an illusion created by a large false demand for capital, and that what really exists is not an immediate shortage of capital at all, but a shortage of viable projects..."[28]

Schatz argues that the "false demand" created consists of both those loan applications that the FLB rejected as not viable and also that smaller category where there was a feasible project but the minimum guarantee required by the FLB before the loan is approved could not be raised. It should not, of course, be concluded from the above that under no circumstances is there a capital shortage but rather it is suggested that lack of financial resources have been greatly over-emphasized as deterrents to the emergence of an African entrepreneurial class.

Entrepreneurship and the "Environment"

There have to be some constraints on the development of entrepreneurs in the LDCs, however, or there would be many more than there are. The most convincing research points to the economic, political, and social "environment" as the main barrier. In a study conducted in the late 60's[29] the following were found to be "environmental" constraints: the (low) level of market demand; lack of foreign exchange; inability to obtain credit, skilled labor or technical assistance; dependence on government officials for licenses and a host of other permits with the dangers (or advantages) of corruption, delay and interference. The technical assistance available, or unavailable, to indigenous entrepreneurs is meant here in the broadest possible sense; other terms used

---

27 M. P. Miracle, "Capitalism, Capital Markets and Competition in West African Trade" in *The Development of Indigenous Trade and Markets in West Africa*, (ed. by C. Meillassoux), London, Oxford University Press, pp. 401–410.

28 Sayre P. Schatz, "The Capital Shortage Illusion: Government Spending in Nigeria," *Oxford Economic Papers*, July 1965, p. 310.

29 P. Kennedy, "Entrepreneurship in the Private and Public Sector in Ghana," *Bulletin*, Institute of Development Studies, Sussex, June 1971, pp. 52–53.

might be "contacts," "business horizon," or "access to information" in the managerial and marketing as well as in the technical sense.[30]

The difficulties inherent in the economic, political, and social environment in West Africa are such that an indigenous businessman, even if he has adequate capital and right amount and kind of education, "will nonetheless have a considerably more difficult time succeeding in business than his equally well-financed and talented counterpart in a more developed economy."[31] Many of the difficulties hinder the foreign and African entrepreneur alike; some hurt the indigenous businessmen more primarily because the foreign enterprises' stronger financial structure helps them weather better the inhospitable environment.

After looking at much of the evidence, one cannot help but conclude that the greatest impediment to the development of entrepreneurship is the business environment itself.

Tentative Evaluation of the Ghanaization Policies

If it is indeed the economic, political, and social environment that is the barrier to the development of indigenous entrepreneurs, the Ghanaization efforts of the NLC and the Busia governments could hardly have had a more inauspicious launching. Since 1968, when the first decree was introduced, the economy has been characterized both by stagnation and an elaborate set of controls. (Actually per capita income has been stagnating, or slightly decreasing, since 1962.) It is ironic to note that at the time of independence (in 1957) or even in 1960-61, the environment for the promotion of indigenous private businessmen was much more favorable. But Dr. Nkrumah distrusted private entrepreneurs[32] and decided to industrialize Ghana via public sector enterprises, starting in 1961; this led to the eventual bankruptcy of the economy and to his ouster. During 1961–1966 public sector activities were promoted at the expense of private businesses; indigenous businesses were at a disadvantage vis-a-vis foreign private businesses simply because the former were weaker and less well established.

In pursuing Ghanaization policies, both the NLC and the Busia governments were motivated by a) wanting to increase indigenous control of the

30   P. Marris, "The Social Barriers to African Entrepreneurship," *ibid.*, "African Businessmen in a Dual Economy," *Journal of Industrial Economics*, July 1971, pp. 231–45 and, with A. Somersset, *African Businessmen: A Study of Entrepreneurship and Development in Kenya*, London, Routledge and Kegan Paul, 1971.

31   Sayre P. Schatz, "Economic Environment and Private Enterprise in West Africa," *Economic Bulleting of Ghana*, 1963, No. 4, pp. 42–56 and Schatz and S. I. Edokpayi, "Economic Attitudes of Nigerian Businessmen," *Nigerian Journal of Economic and Social Studies*, Nov. 1962, pp. 262–63.

32   Ayeh-Kumi, Dr. Nkrumah's economic advisor, said that "Nkrumah did not welcome the growth of a class of Ghanaian entrepreneurs because he regarded them as a group which might challenge the supremacy of the ruling party," "State Enterprise vs. Ghanaian Enterprise," *West Africa*, July 2, 1966.

economy, and b) gaining political support from the existing and potential business community.[33] Regarding (b), all the political parties in the 1969 election were for some kind of a Ghanaization program; businessmen and traders played a significant role in the victory of Busia's Progress Party. They also played a part in the promulgation of the Aliens Compliance Order of 1970 under which tens of thousands of non-Ghanaian Africans who did not hold valid residence permits were deported. The Ghanaization Decree and Act further affected many of the non-Ghanaian Africans legally still living in the country. While the Aliens Compliance Order was not unconnected to the Ghanaian Business Promotions Act, we shall not discuss the former here because it is a subject by itself. Traders and businessmen also played a role under the NLC in the formulation of the Ghanaization decree of 1968. In the Fall of 1967 an Accra businessman, M. K. Batze, submitted a memorandum to the NLC discussing means of curbing the economic activities of Lebanese and Indians.[34] His views were supported by many in the business community; a couple of months later two prominent businessmen, Patrick Quaidoo and W. A. Wiafe, added their voices to the general statement that the economic activities of aliens should be restricted[35]. There is no question but that businessmen became much more a part of the political process than they ever had been during the Nkrumah era.

From an administrative point of view, the major point to be stressed is the fact that the (Ghanaization) Act has been complied with – especially in taxi services and trading. The largest taxi fleet, over 100 vehicles controlled by Fattal Bros., was bought by the Ghana National Trading Corporation. GNTC, in turn, sold the taxis to individual drivers. Ghanaians responded energetically to the opportunities provided by the Act and there appeared to be little economic dislocation in the process. The changeover period passed in an orderly manner. There was neither increased unemployment nor a rise in the rate of inflation because trades and services had to be handed over to Ghanaians. The Ghanaian experience parallels that of Northern Nigeria after the expulsion of the Ibos in 1966. By 1968, "the long awaited Northernization of the urban economy was largely accomplished",[36] and recovery had been achieved.

There were, of course, some difficulties. A few Lebanese and Indians moved to Togo and continued to transact their Ghanaian businesses from there. The most serious problem arose with the enforcement of the Ghanaization of "sole overseas business representation", since the Act inadequately defines the meaning of "sole representation". (Overseas business representation is a highly

---

33   John D. Esseks, "Economic Dependence and Political Development in New States," Annual Meeting of the American Political Science Association, Los Angeles, September 1970 and "Government and Indigenous Private Enterprise in Ghana," *Journal of Modern African Studies*, Spring 1971.
34   *Daily Graphic*, Accra; September 18, 1967.
35   *Ibid.*, November 6, 1967.
36   M. E. Zukerman, "Nigerian Crisis; Economic Impact on the North," *Journal of Modern African Studies*, 1970, No. 8, p. 51.

skilled operation, with the representative having to provide continual and satis-factory service.) Overseas agents claim that they are not "sole representatives" and the onus is on the government to establish that they are. The Government has not pressed its case vigorously thus far, and major European dealers such as Africa Motors, R. T. Briscoe, John Holt, and UTC Motors continue their operations as before. These dealers control imports of spare parts and manage to exercise oligopolistic power over the fairly large car repair market, most of which is in Ghanaian hands. (There would, of course, be no difference if the four importing firms were in Ghanaian hands.)

As indicated earlier, the previous owners of enterprises in the restricted areas received compensation for their businesses. It was the impression of this observer, at least, that by and large compensation was adequate and occasional-ly more than satisfactory to the previous owner. Compensation was worked out privately between the Ghanaian entrepreneur and the previous owner. Ghanaians were anxious to buy, and competed for, the shops and taxies; demand for them outran the supply. They were in a hurry and did not take time, or did not have the acumen, to properly evaluate inventory. Many of the inventories, understandably, were heavily drawn down.

In order to aid indigenous businessmen under both the 1968 decree and the 1970 act, the Government set up a small business loan scheme and an advisory consulting and training service sponsored by the Management Development and Productivity Institute. While it is difficult to gauge the impact of these positive governmental measures, one cannot help but have the impression that they have had only marginal impacts. For one, Ghanaians did not take as much advantage of these schemes as they were expected to and, for another, the Gov-ernment did not provide these services very efficiently. The Government made N1.9 million available for small business credits to be lent at commercial rates of interest but with the Government taking the risk; subsequent allocations raised these credits to N8.2 million. But the Productivity Institute had very few clients. The Productivity Institute could have been put to better use, particularly since in the last ten years controls created a seller's market, which is the worst possible environment in which management principles are either never learned or are forgotten.

To help overcome the credit problem which arose in connection with the takeover of the enterprises, commercial banks were authorized to call on a government guarantee of up to N75,000 per approved client.[37] It was anti-cipated that this would eventually allow a host of indigenous entrepreneurs to apply for loans from the banking system. The private banking system on its own also proved to be helpful as it moved to replace their "lost" customers with new ones. As of mid-1972, the banking system made relatively few loans to new entrepreneurs.

Ghanaization policies were not without critics. It was argued that, at best, it was "much ado about nothing". Ghanaization (of trade in particular) was

---

37   *West Africa*, July 9, 1971 and Standard Bank *Review*, February 1971, p. 11.

insignificant. Critics pointed out that about 80% of the large European trading houses' textile trade had been handled by "market mammies" for decades. It has also been pointed out that all that has really happened is that some businesses have been transferred to Ghanaians, but such a transfer does not make the buyer an entrepreneur. At worst, it was said, Ghanaization policies increased the power of the European trading companies by reducing competition from Lebanese, Indians, Nigerians, and Togolese. There is, of course, no denying that there is some truth in this argument; how much depends on the perform-ance of the Ghanaian traders who replaced the "alien" traders. More serious is the apprehension that Ghanaization will increase the Lebanese and Indian participation in manufacturing, a non-restricted field. The Government stated repeatedly that it encourages both Ghanaian and foreign investors to help develop the country.[38] Since Lebanese and Indians are to be phased out from the protected fields it would be natural for them to move into medium and possibly large scale manufacturing. There is reason to believe that this has already gotten underway. The Chamber of Commerce, the Ghana Manu-facturing Association, and the Association of Ghanaian Businessmen argue that the Government should extend the areas presently restricted (and eventually totally exclude aliens from the economy, except for the large firms in European hands). The Government is reluctant to do this, fearing that Ghanaian entre-preneurs will not be forthcoming fast enough, and that there would be disloca-tion, increased unemployment, and inflation.

The most serious criticism leveled against Ghanaization is the whole idea itself. It has been remarked that such policies would not have been necessary if the Ghanaians had had the capacity previously to compete with the aliens in the trades and services. The Ghanaization Act provided economic opportunities to Ghanaians. Even if some Ghanaians fail in their new ventures, as undoubted-ly they will, others, also Ghanaians, will survive; it will also be Ghanaians who will buy up the failing shops. Moreover, it is to be expected that some of the indigenous businessmen who "make it" in the restricted fields will not only have passed the test of entrepreneurship but will also develop managerial attributes which, in turn, will be transferable to other sectors or to larger enterprises in trade or services.

In conclusion, the Ghanaization policies were distinguished by two charac-teristics: a) to indigenize gradually and b) to do so from the bottom up. Both were geared to the ability and willingness of Ghanaians to increasingly parti-cipate in the economy and to keep the potential economic dislocations to a minimum. Of course, the Ghana Governments did not have to pass the Decree or the Act. However, without them "the economy will continue to rely on foreigners for the simplist type of economic activities and this will certainly raise complex political, social and economic problems for future generations".[39]

---

38 E. N. Omaboe, "Press Release," Accra, July 5, 1968, p. 1.
39 E. N. Omaboe, op. cit., p. 4.

The author was with the Harvard Advisory Group, Ministry of Economic Affairs (Ghana) 1967–1969 and returned to Ghana for the Summer of 1971. This research was supported by the Graduate School of Business Administration, University of Virginia. I wish to thank, for their advice and suggestions, L. T. Wells, Jr. of Harvard University Graduate School of Business Administration, E. Wayne Nafziger of East-West Center, University of Hawaii, an executive of a West African trading company and an officer of the Planning Secretariat, both of whom wish to stay anonymous.

Attitudes of Sierra Leonean Youth Toward Modernization

ROBERT E. CLUTE

University of Georgia, Athens, U.S.A.

Background

SIERRA LEONE is a member of the West African Commonwealth which received its independence from Great Britain in 1961. The British incursion began in Freetown, the primate city and present capital, in 1787 with the return of freed slaves from America, the West Indies and Great Britain. This movement continued and, after the Act of 1807 forbade British subjects to engage in slave trading, the Royal Navy began to capture illegal slave ships and to return the slaves to Freetown regardless of their African origin. Freetown thus became the melting pot of West Africa. The descendants of these people are known as Creoles or Krio. Freetown became a Crown Colony in 1807.[1] The Western influence in education, commerce, religion, political institutions, etc., thus began at an early date and spread from Freetown to the rest of the country. British penetration of the remainder of the country occured relatively late. A Protectorate was established in 1896 and was ruled separately from the Crown Colony until the adoption of the Constitution of 1958.[2]

The predominant party after independence was the Sierra Leone People's Party which held a majority in Parliament and the office of Prime Minister until the elections of 1967. The S.L.P.P. was dominated by the Mende, the most numerous tribe in Sierra Leone. The Prime Minister, Sir Albert Margai, alienated the Temne of the Northern Province, the second largest tribe, by underrepresenting them in the Cabinet and by diverting a disproportionate share of government finances to the Southern Province where his tribe predominated. By the 1967 general elections the standard of living had declined, there were numerous charges of corruption in the government and inflation was increasing at an alarming rate.

In the 1967 elections the opposition Allied People's Congress, which was founded in 1960, defeated the S.L.P.P. and proceeded to form a new government. Siaka Stevens (a member of the Limba tribe of the North which is the third largest tribe in the country) as leader of the A.P.C. became the new Prime Minister. After Prime Minister Stevens received the oath of office, a coup

---

1 J. F. A. Ajayi and Ian Espie, eds., *A Thousand Year of African History* (1965), pp. 328–329, 360.
2 W. E. F. Ward, *Government in West Africa* (1966), pp. 171–172.

was staged by Brigadier David Lansana who was army commander and of the same tribe as Sir Albert Margai. Both the Governor General and Prime Minister Stevens were placed under house arrest and martial law was proclaimed. Three days later a counter coup was staged by the younger officers. Sir Albert Margai and Brigadier Lansana were arrested. The officers claimed that the tribes were polarized and the country was threatened by civil war. A National Reformation Council was established which at the time of this survey was headed by Lt. Col. Juxton-Smith. Prime Minister Stevens fled the country, constitutional government was suspended and parties were outlawed. At the time of this survey, the Spring of 1968, the N.R.C. had failed to raise the standard of living. Although the N.R.C. had initially cleaned up corruption, the sudden affluence of the officer corps gave rise to charges that they were beginning to engage in corruption.[3]

This study is based on a survey of fifth form students and students of Fourah Bay College at the University of Sierra Leone in Freetown. Normally the fifth form is the last grade of secondary school in Sierra Leone. Although a few schools offer a sixth form, the results of this survey would have been too narrow. had it been administered to that form. The age of the respondents varied from 15 to 31 and over with only nine students falling into the 31 or over age category.

Paper and pencil questionnaires were administered by the Political Science students of Fourah Bay College in 29 of the 44 secondary schools in Sierra Leone which covered fifth form work. The survey covers one third of the fifth form students in each province of Sierra Leone. The questionnaires at Fourah Bay College were administered through classes by the writer and likewise cover one third of the student body. The sample has an N of 571 which includes 401 fifth form students and 170 college students.

The survey covered a wide range of questions. Many of the items were taken from a questionnaire administered in Korea by my colleague, Professor Young Ho Lee, of Seoule, and some are also drawn from *The Civic Culture*.[4] This was done in the hopes of making later cross-polity comparisons. Such questions were sometimes altered to meet peculiarly African exigencies. A few items from the larger survey have been selected for this study. These items have been cross tabulated with variables which would normally be expected to have a high correlation with attitudes toward modernization. Sierra Leone is still in the stage of primitive unification and nation building. It is faced with the problem of creating a national economy and a national political system from diverse economic and political subsystems. Therefore, the variables of tribe, province of birth, and province in which the student grew up have been utilized as

---

3   See, for a detailed account of pre-1966 politics in Sierra Leone, Martin Kilson, *Political Change in a West African State* (1966), *passim*. For accounts of the N.R.C. period see Allen Christopher, "Sierre Leone Since Independence," *African Affairs*, Vol. 67 (1968), pp. 302–325; John Cartwright, "Shifting Forces in Sierra Leone," *Africa Report*, Vol. 13 (1968), pp. 26–30, *African Recorder* (May 21-June 3, 1967), pp. 1650–1653.

4   Gabriel Almond and Sidney Verba, *The Civic Culture* (1963) *passim*.

indicators of sub-systems.[5] Religion has likewise been considered by many writers to be highly correlated with attitudes toward modernization.[6] The literature likwise associates income and education with higher rates of social mobilization. Therefore the education of the student, income of the father, education of the mother and education of the father were utilized for cross tabulation.[7] The latter were also considered as indicators of the influence of the father and mother in the process of socialization. The relation of urbanization to modernization is likewise widely recognized by writers on social change and political development.[8] Since this variable is so highly associated with the modernization process both size of birth place and size of the village in which the student grew up were utilized. They were used in order to examine both the effect of urbanization and to determine whether urbanization would be more highly correlated with variables connected with origin of the respondent or whether they would correlate more highly with the area in which the student had received the greatest exposure to social change and development. Age was utilized to provide an examination of exposure to modernization over time in addition to years of the student's education, because the age of students varies much more in African schools that would be the case in most developed systems. Lastly, sex was chosen because of the different social status usually accorded to a woman in traditional and transitional societies.[9]

The dependent variables selected from the survey for analysis were chosen to indicate the attitudes of Sierra Leonean youth toward economic and political development but treatment of the latter is much more extensive. The economic variable merely indicates satisfaction or dissatisfaction with the progress of economic development. The political items were chosen to indicate desired change, disagreement with leaders, commitment to the constitutional institu-

5   See J. J. Spengler, "Economic Development: Political Preconditions and Political Consequences," in J. L. Finkle and R. W. Gable, Eds., *Political Development and Social Change* (1966), p. 257; Gabriel Almond and G. B. Powell, *Comparative Politics: A Developmental Approach* (1966), p. 306 ff.; Richard R. Fagen, *Politics and Communication* (1966), p. 101 ff.; Claude Ake, *A Theory of Political Integration* (1967), pp. 12–13.

6   See Wildred Malenbaum and Wolfgang Stolper, "Political Ideology and Economic Progress: The Basic Question," in Finkle and Gable, *op. cit.*, pp. 190–193; William John Hanna, *Independent Black Africa: The Politics of Freedom* (1964), pp. 4–5, 217, 222–223. Harry J. Benda, "Non-Western Intelligentsias as Political Elite," in John H. Kautsky, *Political Change in Underdeveloped* (1964), pp. 238–251; Everett E. Hagan, *On The Theory of Social Change* (1962), pp. 16–17, 257–258.

7   Karl Deutsch used literacy, income and urbanization as indicators of social mobilization and development, see Karl Deutsch, "Social Mobilization and Political Development," in Finkle and Gable, *op. cit.*, pp. 205–226. For the role of education in development see James O'Connell and David G. Scanlon, eds, *Education and Nation Building in Africa* (1965), *passim*, and George Kimble, "Educational Problems in Sub-Saharan Africa," in P. J. M. McEwan and R. B. Sutcliffe, eds., *Modern Africa* (1965), pp. 354–381.

8   See Gerald Breese, ed., *The City in Newly Developing Countries* (1969), passim.; P. L. Van Den Berghe, *Africa: Social Problems of Change and Conflict* (1965), Part V.

9   See Guy Hunter, "From the Old Culture to the New," and H. J. Symons, "The Status of African Women," in McEwan and Sutcliffe, *op. cit.*, pp. 320–321 and 326–331, respectively.

tions, predisposition to freedom versus authority, and methods by which students would attempt to participate in the process of political decision making.

The questionnaire under study includes both ordinal and nominal data. In the case of ordinal data, gamma[10] will be used without supporting tables for the sake of brevity and in the case of nominal data the percentage and frequencies derived from cross tabulation tables will be utilized. In the latter case tables have often been limited to responses with the highest frequency in cases where the variable includes a large number of categories such as tribe.

Attitudes Toward Economic Development

The survey included a number of items relating to economic development but the scope of this work necessitates that analysis be limited to an examination of the response to one question, namely, "How well is economic development progressing?" Of the 521 respondents, 3.6% answered that development was progressing very well, 35.9% fairly well, 40.0% rather poorly, and 21.5% very poorly.[11] Dissatisfaction has a mild positive correlation with the age of the respondent ($p < .001$, gamma .20), with the years of education of the father ($p < .05$, gamma .21) and a mild negative correlation with year of schooling ($p < .001$, gamma $-.24$). The latter finding would on the surface appear to be a contradiction with the literature contending that high rates of education greatly increase dissatisfaction with economic development as the student's expectancy has been greatly raised without commensurate skills to realize such expectancies.[12] However, the students being examined are not typical in that they do not cover youth who have left school at an early age. Attainment of the fifth form or of college has already placed the student in a relatively advantageous position vis-a-vis the general level of education in Sierra Leone.

As can be seen in Table 1, religion proves to be highly correlated with attitudes toward the progress of economic development. Christians seem to be about equal on this score but Moslems are considerably more dissatisfied. This may be due in part to the fact that Moslems who make up roughly 11% of the population vis-a-vis Christians who make up 8%[13] of the population, have been hampered in the modernization process due to the monopoly of Christianity on health and education through missionary endeavours The poor position of nativists is illustrated by the fact that only 4 students responded that they were

10 On the use of gamma see William Buchanan, *Understand Political Variables*, New York: Charles Scribner and Sons (1969), pp. 225–226, 229.
11 Total percentages do not equal 100 due to rounding.
12 See for example, Frances X. Sutton, "Education in Changing Africa," in O'Connell and Scanlon, *op. cit.*, pp. 192–199; Edward Shils, "The Intellectuals in the Political Development of New States," In Kautsky, *op. cit.*, pp. 204–205, Samuel P. Huntington, "Political Development and Political Decay," in Claude E. Welch, Jr. *Political Modernization* (1967), p. 223.
13 For comparative statistics on African religion and the effects of Christianity on the attainment of status in Africa see Gabriel Almond, *The Politics of Developing Areas* (1961), p. 27.

Table 1
Attitudes Toward Progress in Economic Development
N of Sample = 571

	N*	Very Well %	Fairly Well %	Rather Poorly %	Very Poorly %	X² and Table Probability
Religion	507					19.798, <.02
Protestant	252	2.4	37.7	42.5	17.5	
Catholic	115	0.9	33.0	47.0	19.1	
Islam	136	5.1	22.1	44.9	27.9	
Nativist	4	0.0	75.0	25.0	0.0	
Tribe	500					42.683, <.01
Creole	136	2.2	27.2	52.9	17.6	
Mende	131	3.1	38.2	32.1	26.7	
Temne	76	2.6	27.6	44.7	25.0	
Foolah	18	5.6	22.2	55.6	16.7	
Sherbro	15	0.0	60.0	13.3	26.7	
Kono	24	0.0	37.5	25.0	37.5	
Limba	17	0.0	35.3	64.7	0.0	
Other	83	33.3	34.9	45.8	13.3	
Province of Birth	390					17.896, <.05
West	172	3.5	29.1	47.1	20.3	
North	59	1.7	27.1	55.9	15.3	
South	74	2.7	35.1	39.2	23.0	
East	85	2.4	31.8	44.7	21.2	

N* of Table

nativist in religion. Christian missionary activity began in the Western Area where it is still strongest and where the first modern black African college was founded in 1827. Christianity spread southward to the Southern and Eastern Provinces. The Northern Province, which is predominately Moslem has had relatively little missionary activity.[14] Most schools in Sierra Leone are operated by churches and education is directly related to Christian incursion. There are no free public schools in Sierra Leone. The results of the system are indicated by the fact that 70.4% of the respondents are Christians. The Western and Southern Provinces where Christianity is highest have 18 and 14 schools, respectively, offering education through the fifth form, whereas the less Christian Northern and Eastern Provinces have 5 and 8, respectively, despite the fact that the Northern Province is the largest province in land area and population.

14   See Gerald Windham, "Occupational Aspirations of Secondary School Children in Sierra Leone," *Rural Sociology* (1969), Vol. 35, pp. 40–41, 44.

Only 5 Moslem schools in the country offered education through the fifth form.[15]

Somewhat allied with religion is the relationship of the province of birth to the student's satisfaction with economic development. Again students born in the predominately Moslem North were slightly more dissatisfied with 71.2% feeling that development had progressed rather poorly or very poorly whereas the Southern, Eastern, and Western Provinces scored 62.2%, 66.9%, and 67.4%, respectively. This may be partly explained by the fact that the Northern Province is the least developed part of Sierra Leone.[16]

Tribal origin is also highly related to degree of satisfaction and like province is somewhat allied with the problem of varying stages of development within the economic subsystem discussed above. Although Sierra Leone has 18 tribes, the output of some of the smaller tribes was not reported for the sake of brevity and because of the low cell frequencies created by their small numbers. The seven tribes reported account for 82.3% of the total population and 83.4% of the respondents of this item. The bulk of the respondents are from three tribes, the Mende, Temne and Creole which make up 30.9%, 29.8% and 1.9% of the population of Sierra Leone, respectively.[17]

The Creoles are descendants of the freed slaves. They are not really a tribe, but are statistically treated as such in Sierra Leone. Because of early modernization they have played a dominant role in social, economic and political development. Their atypical situation is reflected by the fact that although they comprise only 1.9% of the country's population they make up 27.2% of the respondents on this item. The Creole confirm the theory of Hoselitz, Rostow and others that marginal people play a high role in economic development.[18] The minority Creole are high achievers who feel threatened since independence as they have lost much political and economic power to the larger, less modernized tribes which have been amalgamated into the country. They are, therefore, among the least satisfied of the tribes. With the exception of the Sherbro, the most satisfied group are the Mende who, because of their size, early introduction to education through Christianity, and their control of the political system until 1967, have been able to make rapid economic advances since independence. The Temne who predominate in the least developed Northern Province are only slightly more satisfied than the Creole. This is probably a dynamic rather than a static response for although the Creole of the Western Area are more highly developed they have fallen in stature since independence, whereas

15   Department of Education, Fourah Bay College, *Training Colleges, Secondary Schools and Technical Institutions, 1967–1968*, no pagination. Two schools were added to the latter data as a result of information collected during this survey. For an account of education in Freetown see Gladys Harding, "Education in Freetown," in *Freetown: A Symposium* (1968), pp. 143–153.

16   C. J. Clarke, *Sierra Leone in Maps* (1966), p. 66 ff.

17   *Ibid.*, pp. 36–37.

18   See W. W. Rostow, "The Take-Off into Sustained Growth," and B. F. Hoselitz, "Economic Growth and Development: Non-Economic Factors in Economic Development," in Finkle and Gable, *op. cit.*, pp. 248 and 282, respectively.

the Temne have improved their economic lot considerably since that time. The Creole have even ceased to dominate in their own, small Western Area as the Temne have migrated in large numbers so that they now make up 27.4% of the households in the area vis-a-vis the Creole who make up 21.7%.[19]

The high satisfaction of the Sherbro with economic development is difficult to explain as they are from one of the poorer areas of the country. The lowest rate of satisfaction of any tribe is that of the Foulah which may be explained in part by the fact that a very high proportion of the Foulah are traders. The devaluation of the British pound on which the Sierra Leone currency is based and extremely high tariffs on imports probably added greatly to their dissatisfaction.

Since a large number of writers insist that economic development is highly correlated with political development,[20] attitudes toward economic development should have considerable carry-over into attitudes toward political development. The prominence of tribe, province of birth and religion (which is closely related to Province) are indicators that sub-systems which have not yet been fully integrated into the national system account for a great deal of the variation in response to satisfaction with economic development. It is worthy of note that these same factors play a rather large role in attitudes toward political development as will be discussed below.

Attitudes Toward Political Development

The fact that Sierra Leone was under military rule and that political leaders were outlawed at the time of the survey precluded the utilization of a number of questions on the political system. However, open-ended questions were answered with candidness and shed considerable light on students' attitudes toward the political system.

Desired Change

For instance, students were asked to list the changes they would like to see in Sierra Leone. Their first responses were coded into 14 categories of which only the three with the highest frequencies are reported here. Of the 438 students responding on this item 34.3% wanted a return to constitutional government, 19.5% wanted to improve education, 10.2% desired a change in leaders and 35.9% fell into other categories. The intensity of the opposition to military rule was obvious from the way the replies were worded and is rather astounding considering that the country was under the rule of the N.R.C. The latter is especially true when one considers that many respondents who were

---

19 Sierra Leone, Central Statistics Office, *Household Survey of the Western Province*, November *1966-January 1967*, p. 12.
20 See for example, R. T. Holt and J. E. Turner, *The Political Basis of Economic Development* (1966), *passim*, and Spengler, *loc. cit.*, pp. 253–268.

timid may have chosen a change in political leaders as a more discrete way of expressing opposition to military rule.

The only variable which was significant and correlated with this item was religion. As may be seen on Table 2, members of all religions gave about equal

Table 2
Desired Changes in Sierra Leone
N of Sample = 571

	N*	Return to Const. Govt.	Improve Education	Change Leaders	X² and Table Probability
Religion	438	%	%	%	66.243, <.005
Protestant	209	34.9	22.0	8.1	
Catholic	103	33.0	22.3	12.6	
Islam	122	35.2	18.0	10.7	
Nativist	4				

N* of Table

priority to a return to constitutional government. Moslems put slightly less stress on education than did Christians, which is interesting in view of the low development of education in Moslems areas. Catholics also expressed considerable concern over a change of leaders. Moslems also evidenced principal concern over two other responses not reported on Table 2, namely, improved agricultural methods and increased transportation and communications.

Should Change be Constitutional?

On this item the questionnaire asked whether the desired changes discussed above should be achieved by constitutional or non-constitutional means. The response was overwhelmingly in favor of constitutional change with 60% of the 466 students who answered the question indicating a preference for constitutional change. Sex proved to be highly correlated (p. <.01, gamma .30) with males showing a greater preference for constitutional change. The education of the respondent's mother likewise proved to be highly correlated (p<.20, gamma —.31)[21] with the desire for constitutional change increasing with a rise in the level of the education of the mother. Students of the Northern and Southern Provinces were most favorable to constitutional change with respondents of both provinces scoring 83.3%, the Western Province had the lowest score, 62.5%, followed by those born in the East, 68.4%.[22] Religion was mildly correlated with the highest response in Catholics and Moslems (83.2% and 83.7%, respectively) and the lowest response in Protestants, 73.8%.[23]

---

21   Note that despite the high gamma significance is very low on this correlation.
22   N = 513, X² 36.834, p. < .05.
23   N = 436, X² 7.056, p. < .05.

Disagreement Between Youth and Leaders

Respondents were asked, "Is there a basic disagreement between youth and the leaders of the Sierra Leone Government?" This item was answered by 435 students who responded with an overwhelming 80.7%, yes. There was a high correlation between age ($p < .001$, gamma $-.31$), student's year of schooling, ($p < .01$, gamma $.32$), and the size of the town in which the students grew up ($p < .001$, gamma $-.36$). Thus disagreement rose with age, declined as the student received more education and rose as the size of the town in which he grew up declined. As indicated in Table 3, religion and province in which the

Table 3
Disagreement Between Youth and Leaders
N of Sample = 571

	$N*$	Yes %	No %	X^2 and Table Probability
Religion	422			5.173, <.02
Protestant	206	78.6	21.4	
Catholic	92	88.0	12.0	
Moslem	121	85.1	14.9	
Nativist	3			
Province				
Grown Up In	397			16.880, <.001
West	171	76.6	23.4	
North	73	95.9	4.1	
South	92	85.9	14.1	
East	61	90.2	9.8	

N* of Table

student grew up were also rather highly correlated with intensity of disagreement. Disagreement is considerably higher in Catholics and Moslems which may be explained by the fact that they tend to come from less urban areas. People who have grown up in the more developed Western Area tend to be a bit less in disagreement with their leaders, but greater discontent is to be found in the three less developed provinces. Although tribe did not prove to be significant and is not reported, it may offer an explanation of the high discontent in the Eastern Province, as all 21 members of the Kono tribe of the Eastern Province said that they were in a disagreement with the leaders of the government. The data offer an interesting contrast to America where disagreement seems to be higher in young people who grew up in more urban areas. It also is in contradiction with the hypothesis of a number of writers that urbanization tends to stimulate social mobilization which in turn creates social stresses which result in strain on the institutions.[24] This may be explained in part by the fact

---

24 See for example, Shanti Tangri, "Urbanization, Political Stability, and Economic Growth," in Finkle and Gable, *op. cit.*, pp. 305–349.

that people from the rural areas are footing the bill for modernization but are not receiving the benefits. In the history of development in the United States this same sort of situation gave rise to the Grange Movement.

Individual Freedom versus Government Control and Authority

The predisposition of students to freedom versus authority in the developmental process was tested by asking whether it would be better to have a political system which would use strong authority and control and get things done or whether it would be better to have a political system which respected political freedom even if it might be more difficult to get things done. Of the 499 students who responded, 60% favored freedom and 40% favored government control and authority. Sex was a significant variable with females being more disposed to authority ($p < .001$, gamma $-.34$). As the fathers' income rose students were more disposed to freedom ($p < .20$, gamma $.30$). Age was mildly significant ($p < .001$, gamma $.27$) with increasing age resulting in greater freedom. Children reared in the South, as shown in Table 4, are con-

Table 4
Control and Authority versus Freedom
N = 571

	N*	Control and Authority %	Freedom %	X² and Table Probability
Grew Up in Province	449			15.679, <.001
West	186	38.2	61.8	
North	88	28.4	71.6	
South	111	48.6	51.4	
East	64	21.9	78.1	

N* of Table

siderably more disposed to authority than children reared in other parts of the country. This may be accounted for by the fact that the Mende, the predominate tribe of the South, are noted for their extreme discipline in rearing children which might tend to produce a more authoritarian personality. Easterners may resent control and authority because that area supplies diamonds which are Sierra Leone's major export but little of the money has been utilized in the development of the Eastern Province. Religion did not prove to be significant, which is interesting in view of the fact that Moslem children would have been more apt to be reared in polygamous marriages.[25] However, the polygamous

---

25   See Windham, *loc. cit.*, p. 45, on the effects of polygamous family backgrounds of Sierra Leone students in regard to occupational aspirations.

family environment evidently does not produce any significantly different results than the children of monogamous marriages.

The Most Effective Way To Influence A Government Decision

Finally respondents were asked, "Suppose several men were trying to influence a government decision, what would be the most effective method? a) working through personal or family connections, b) writing to government officials, c) getting people interested in forming a group, d) working through a political party, e) working through a tribal leader, f) organizing a protest demonstration." In view of the strong commitment of the respondents to constitutional forms as indicated in replies to other items, the results of this question are rather startling. Support of parliamentary form does not seem to be accompanied by commensurate support of the party system. Of the informants, 30.8% preferred a group, 25.5% a party, 16.7% writing to government officials, 14.7% protest demonstrations, 8.3% personal or family contacts, and 4.2% tribal leaders.

As may be seen from Table 5, Mende and Temne people have a greater interest in group action than Krio people. Catholics and Moslems are slightly more inclined to support group action than Protestants. The bulk of the students supporting group action are under 21 years of age. The relationship between group and father's education is curvilinear and peaks on students whose fathers have completed or have had some secondary education. Group support is highest in students who have grown up in the Southern and Northern provinces.

Support of party is higher in Moslems and Catholics. Respondents who have grown up in the Western or Northern Provinces make up 57.7% of those supporting this method. Party interest seems to decline between ages of 16 and 20, but increases rapidly after students reach the voting age of 21. Interest in party increases sharply with the education of the mother.

Support of letter writing is found to be stronger among the literate areas of the nation, as would be expected. The only apparent discrepancy would be the negative correlation that is found between letters and father's education. As father's education increased the support for letter writing decreases. It would be reasonable to assume that as father's education increased there would be additional, often personal avenues of influence open to the respondent which would supersede letter writing. This does not in fact detract from the belief that degree of literacy of a group would tend to influence the trend to support letter writing as a means of influence.

Support for protest demonstrations decreases after the age of 21, more or less in conjunction with the increased interest in party participation. The Krio, who are the smallest of the major tribes tend to favor protest demonstrations (25.0%) more than do the Mende (9.9%) or the Temne (12.3%). Both Catholics and Protestants tend to support demonstrations more than the Moslem element of the population. Those respondents from the more urbanized Western Province, which also contains a high percentage of Krios tend to

Table 5
The Most Effective Way to Influence Government Decisions
N of Sample = 571

	N*	Family %	Letters %	Groups %	Parties %	Tribal Leaders %	Protest %	X² and Table Probability
Sex	511							18.597, <.01
Male	359	10.3	11.4	28.7	27.6	6.4	15.0	
Female	152	3.3	19.1	31.6	26.3	1.3	18.4	
Age	501							70.3, <.05
16	21	4.8	14.3	33.3	28.6	0.0	19.0	
17	74	5.4	18.9	25.7	25.7	1.4	23.0	
18	95	9.5	16.8	32.6	25.3	7.4	8.4	
19	111	4.5	18.0	31.5	18.9	6.3	19.8	
20	60	3.3	11.7	41.7	18.3	8.3	16.7	
21	24	12.5	12.5	16.7	20.8	8.3	29.2	
22–30	104	13.5	5.8	23.1	42.3	2.9	12.5	
31 & over	12	16.7	8.3	16.7	58.3	0.0	0.0	
Tribe	503							37.487, <.01
Creole	132	9.1	14.4	18.9	30.3	2.3	25.0	
Mende	121	5.0	17.4	36.4	24.8	6.6	9.9	
Temne	73	4.1	9.6	37.0	27.4	9.6	12.3	
Other	177	11.3	11.9	30.5	26.6	3.4	15.3	
Religion	490							34.228, <.05
Protestant	243	10.7	15.2	23.9	26.3	2.1	21.4	
Catholic	113	6.2	9.7	34.5	29.2	7.1	13.3	
Islam	130	6.2	14.6	33.1	27.7	8.5	9.2	
Nativist	4							
Province Grown up in	447							46.067, <.001
West	193	10.4	12.4	24.4	28.5	2.1	22.3	
North	84	2.4	7.1	35.7	33.3	10.7	10.7	
South	103	3.9	18.4	35.0	23.3	3.9	14.6	
East	67	16.4	16.4	25.4	20.9	9.0	10.4	
Ed. Mother	474							57.213, <.005
None	274	7.7	12.4	33.2	25.5	8.4	12.0	
Less than 5 years	10	0.0	20.0	70.0	0.0	0.0	10.0	
5 Years	17	0.0	23.5	29.4	23.5	0.0	23.5	
Some Secondary	107	6.5	15.0	22.4	30.8	1.9	23.4	
Secondary	44	9.1	15.9	25.0	34.1	0.0	15.9	
Some College	11	9.0	0.0	18.2	45.5	0.0	27.3	
College Grad	11	36.4	9.1	18.2	9.1	0.0	27.3	
Ed. Father	459							39.994, <.05
None	176	8.0	10.2	35.8	26.1	8.0	10.8	
Less than 5 years	15	0.0	20.0	20.0	33.3	6.7	20.0	
5 Years	23	8.7	26.1	13.0	26.1	0.0	26.1	
Some Secondary	116	8.6	15.5	31.9	23.3	1.7	19.0	
Secondary	63	6.3	12.7	30.2	31.7	1.6	17.5	
Some College	33	9.1	12.1	24.2	33.3	6.1	15.2	
College Grad	33	18.2	6.1	15.2	30.3	9.1	21.2	

N* of Table

support protests much more strongly (22.3%) than do the Northern (19.7%), Southern (14.6%), and Eastern (10.4%) Provinces.

The family is seen as a more effective means to influence decisions by the Krio (9.1%) than by the Mende (5.0%) or the Temne (4.1%). Although the Krio do represent a minority of the population they tend to be more favorably represented in government posts and the professions. The same is true for the Protestant element of the population, of whom 10.7% feel that the family is an effective way to make themselves heard, as opposed to 6.2% for both Catholics and Moslems. Those who live in the Western and Eastern Provinces tend to feel that family is much more important than did those from the North or South. This is especially true of those from the Eastern Provinces. Of these, 16.4% believed in the family as opposed to 10.4% in the West, 2.4% in the North and 3.9% in the South. As might be expected, with an increase in the father's and mother's education, the family comes to be viewed as a much more effective device to gain influence into the decision-making process.

Tribal leaders are seen as the least important means to influence decision-making. They are most favored in the Northern and Eastern Provinces, both of which still retain a strong traditional orientation toward family and tribe. The same is true of the Temne tribe, which shows the most support for this form of input into the system. Moslems and Catholics also tend to favor tribal leaders more than do the Protestants.

Conclusions

The independent variables which correlated with attitudes toward modernization confirm the contention of writers that the persistence of autonomous sub-systems is one of the principal problems of modernization in newly independent, transitional societies. Province, tribe and the closely correlated religious factors appear as consistant forces in the molding of student attitudes. Sex also accounts for considerable variance in attitudes. The education of the mother, in the case of constitutional change, is highly correlated but the background of the father is not. Because of the pattern of incursion which Christianity took in Sierra Leone it is difficult to determine what portion of the religious variable is accreditable to differences in the development of the provinces due to that pattern and what portion might be accredited to the effect of the religion itself on personal values and attitudes. The latter question can perhaps be answered by an analysis of other items included in the survey which have not been covered by this study.

The size of the student's birthplace or the town in which he grew up does not account for a great deal of variance in attitudes. However, in the case of Sierra Leone the cities of Freetown and Bo make an atypical urban situation. Freetown, the primate city has such an impact on the small Western Area and makes up such a sizeable portion of the population of that area that the boundary between the urbanization variable and the province variable is not sharply defined if indeed it exists at all. Bo, the second largest city, likewise presents a problem because it was the primate city of the protectorate before independence and tends to be a Mende seat. Thus the boundary between tribe and the urbanization variables tends to become blurred. Consequently the results of the urbanization variables are probably not very valid.

The year of schooling likewise does not appear to be highly correlated with most factors. Had the data been manipulated to cross tabulate college respondents as a whole with fifth form respondents rather than using the year of education, results would probably have been more highly correlated. However, the yearly increment of change in attitudes after the fifth form is relatively small. This would indicate that a large part of the socialization process has already occured prior to the fifth form which is consistent with the literature on political socialization.[26] As a matter of fact the types of variables found to be highly correlated with student attitudes in the study are the type which would effect such attitudes at a fairly young age. Sierra Leone also suffers from a problem experienced by most West African Commonwealth countries in their curriculum, namely that the curriculum is more appropriate to Britain than to Africa and indeed textbooks are most often British. The latter may account in part for the rather high commitment to constitutionalism and political freedom in the student responses.

The data evidence a high rate of dissatisfaction with economic development. In this they probably do not differ significantly from their elders or peers in other parts of Sub-Saharan Africa.[27] This probably has had considerable carry over to attitudes toward political development in the form of desired changes and disagreement with the country's leaders. The demand for a return to constitutional government, a preference for constitutional change, and choice of political freedom over governmental controls or authority in the political process would indicate a rather high commitment to democracy and existent democratic institutions. However the low commitment to party as a method of influencing government decision making would indicate that the political infrastructure needs to be more fully developed before party attains the level necessary for a sound parliamentary system. This seeming contradiction between ideal attitudes toward constitutional democracy and methods selected for influencing government policy may be the outgrowth of a dual political socialization process. The education institutions highly influenced by the British system create an ideal commitment to democracy while the harsh realities of domestic political life encourage the student to resort to political methods which are not always compatible with parliamentary democracy.

---

26 See for example, R. E. Dawson and Kenneth Prewitt, *Political Socizlization* (1969), pp. 41–52.
27 See Tom Mboya, "An Escape from Stagnation," *Africa Report* (March, 1967), pp. 14–20, 37–39.

Professionalization of Nursing in India: Deterring and Facilitating Aspects of the Culture*

PROSHANTA K. NANDI

Sangamon State University, Springfield, U.S.A.

and

CHARLES P. LOOMIS

University of Houston, Houston, U.S.A.

"A LACK OF PROFESSIONAL STATUS."[1] This statement of the Bhore Report heads a list of conditions characterizing nursing in India in 1946. The report states that in British India there were 43,000 persons for each nurse as compared with 300 persons in the United Kingdom. Twenty seven years since the Bhore Report, the 1972–73 report of the Health Ministry of the Government of India shows the number of nurses to be 83,330 which means that at present there is one nurse per 6500 persons approximately. Although the nation is pressing toward the goal set for nurses trained, the various forces mitigating against the attainment of fully professionalized nursing in India and which, of course, also are the reasons for the low starting point, lie in the culture and society of India. It is the purpose of this paper to present an historical overview of this profession and review some of the components of the society and culture which make for these conditions.

Definition of Concepts

Given the lack of professional status characterizing Indian nursing as was observed in the Bhore Report in 1946, it is necessary that we make our concepts clear before any further discussion of the subject matter. Following Vollmer and Mills (1966: vii-viii), the concept of "profession" will refer only to an abstract model of occupational organization, and the concept of "professionalization" will be used to refer to the dynamic process whereby many occupations can be observed to change certain crucial characteristics in the direction of a "profession". "Professionalism" will refer to an ideology and associated activities that can be found in many and diverse occupational groups where

---

* The authors would like to thank Wayne W. Snyder and Regan G. Smith for their comments on an earlier draft.
1 Report of the Health Survey and Development Committee (1946, Vol. 2: 355) (Sir Joseph Bhore, Chairman). Hereafter this report is called the "Bhore Report" (1946).

members aspire to professional status. In recent works (Wilenski 1964: 137–158; Caplow 1954: 139–140; Kornhauser 1963: 1), the professional model has been conceptualized as being constituted of two sets of specifiable attributes; namely, structural and attitudinal.[2] The structural attributes refer to formalized role-relationships in work including training and socialization. Briefly, they refer to the occupation's becoming a full time vocation, establishing training schools, forming professional associations, and developing a code of ethics. The attitudinal attributes refer to attitudes of practitioners in regard to their work, and consist of: belief in self-regulation, a sense of calling to the field, use of professional organizations as a reference group, belief in service to the public, and a feeling of autonomy (cf. Kornhauser 1963; Goode 1957: 194–200; Gross 1958: 77–82; and Greenwood 1957: 44–55).

An Historical Overview of Nursing as a Profession

In its movement in the occupation-profession continuum, professionalization of nursing in India can be traced historically: nursing in ancient India; toward modern nursing; and nursing in modern India.

The earliest reference to diseases and medicine is found in the Vedas and Samhitas (codes) dating at least 1500 B.C. Wilkinson (1958: 3–4) traces the history of medicine and nursing in ancient India and comments that Ayurveda covers the whole field of medical science, including nursing. It lays down definite rules in regard to the construction and equipping of a hospital. Susrata, the Indian surgeon practicing about 700 B.C., defines the ideal relations of doctor, patient, nurse and medicine as the four feet upon which a cure must rest. Susrata also left behind what is known as Susrata Samhita, his voluminous notes on medicine and treatment. Charak, another physician who practiced about 500 B.C. and was the author of Charak Samhita, described the four qualifications of a nurse viz., knowledge of the manner in which drugs should be prepared or compounded for administration, cleverness, devotedness to the patient cared for, and purity (both of mind and body).

The rise and development of Buddhism about the Sixth century B.C. saw great heights in the practice of medicine. Ahimsa (nonviolence) and compassion for all became part of the Buddhist order. Nursing the sick and alleviating the pain of others became highly valued. However, during this period the practice of surgery declined because experimentation on animals through dissection was against the philosophy of Buddhism.

According to Wilkinson (1958: 5), the most advanced period of medicine in ancient India was from 250 B.C. to A.D. 750. Following this period, a deterioration set in, mainly because of the decline of Buddhism, reestablishment of Hinduistic influence and the resultant rigidification of Hindu social order, and

2   For a summary of structural and attitudinal attributes see Hall (1968: 92–104), especially 92–94.

the Moslem invasion. The period around A.D. 1000 saw hospitals disintegrate not to reemerge until after the arrival of the British colonizers. As we can see, there was no professionalism involved in either the practice of medicine or nursing so far.

British colonization marked the beginning of an era in nursing in India, the accounts of which are well documented (see Sundaram 1970: 353–4, 381–2). With the beginning of the process of colonization by the East India Company, a chartered British trading company, a large number of English soldiers came to India. Although there were doctors in the services of the Company, there were few hospitals or nurses. The only hospital in those early days of the 18th century was one at Fort William, Calcutta, having been started in 1707. When in 1764 a large number of British soldiers fell sick in Madras, a building was rented temporarily to house the sick men. There being no nurses, fellow soldiers did the work of nursing. In 1768, a hospital was started in Madras for which money was raised through public contribution. Three hospitals started operating in 1784 in Bombay but only for the treatment of the Europeans. It was not until 1809 that a hospital for Indians was started in that city. The first training school in Madras for midwives was sanctioned by the government in 1797, but the training was quite poor. Thereafter, hospitals started being built in a slow but steady process. Much of the success in starting new hospitals and nursing facilities is due to the efforts of Christian Missions in India.

The first training schools for nurses were started in 1871 in Madras (general nursing), in 1872 in Delhi (two year certificate course), and in 1882 in Calcutta (for nursing and midwifery). Delhi's Lady Hardinge Medical College Hospital which was started as the first medical school for women in India in 1911 opened a school for training nurses four years later.

It did not take long for the health authorities to realize that the diverse and unstandardized training programs of nurses throughout India needed to be standardized and coordinated. Initial efforts to do so were regional in nature. Following a conference of nurses and medical superintendents of military hospitals in northern India, the North India United Board of Examiners for Missions Hospitals was founded in 1909 to regularize and standardize nurses' training. The idea of standardization of nurses' training soon caught on and several government hospitals joined the Board. The South India and Mid-India Board of Nurse Examiners was founded soon after.

Military nursing originated in India during the First World War. Since 1927 this service came to be known as the Indian Military Nursing Service or IMNS. During World War II, the IMNS increased its scope and quality of services and earned great laurels for itself.

The Indian nurses then did not yet have a professional association or a national body that would create and supervise uniform standards for training and examination of the nurses and midwives. The need for such an organization was obvious. By way of background, it may be noted that in 1905 the Association of Nursing Superintendents of India was formed. A second organization was started in 1909 to offer training for nurses in general. Between these times,

1905 and 1909, other regional associations were formed. An important break-through for the profession came in 1909 when the Nursing Journal of India, a monthly Journal, was founded which serves as the most important vehicle for dissemination of information and professional communication for nurses in India. Finally, in 1922, the Association of Nursing Superintendents and the Trained Nurses Association merged together with the new name and title of the Trained Nurses Association of India (hereafter referred to as TNAI) which soon became the spokesman for the profession. It addressed itself immediately to the problems of the profession and to setting up of standards to upgrade the nurses' training. This body has been influential in instituting important changes – from government legislation to public opinion.

At the prodding of the TNAI, a school offering graduate diploma courses in hospital administration was started in 1943 in Delhi. In Delhi and elsewhere, Sister Tutor Courses were offered. In 1946, two colleges of nursing at Delhi and Vellore simultaneously started bachelor's programs in nursing and their first group of students were graduated in 1950. This was the beginning of collegiate education in nursing in India. In the meanwhile, TNAI, which had been urging and campaigning for some time about the necessity of having a uniform standard of training, finally saw its efforts bear fruit on the heels of India's independence. The year 1947 may be earmarked as the year of the beginning of modern nursing in India. In December 1947, the Indian Nursing Council was constituted by an act of legislature to oversee the curriculum and the program of training of nurses. The Council consisted of eighteen nurses, three midwives, health visitors and one representative from the TNAI indicat-ing the influence of professionalism. Since their inception, the Council and the TNAI have been instrumental in agitating politically for upgrading the standard of nurses' education and service, status and emoluments, and for the general advancement of the profession. Such political agitation has been considered by some (cf. Caplow 1954: 139–140) to be one of the structural steps towards professionalization. From 1951 onward, post-graduate programs in nursing (following a bachelor's degree) became available in India. The College of Nursing at Delhi was first to offer such a one year course on Public Health Nursing. At that time, more and more universities began offering nursing programs for the bachelor's degree. Finally, in 1959, the Master's program in nursing was instituted at the College of Nursing in Delhi. At the time of writing, there are two such graduate schools, but this number falls short of the number needed to prepare in sufficient numbers clinical specialists, researchers, teachers and administrators.

The Indigenous Practitioners

India, like most of the developing countries, is faced with the problems of professionalizing all the roles of the health services. Not only are doctors and nurses with modern professionalized training in short supply, but something like 75 percent of the modernly trained professionals are in cities. Of great importance in the lives of rural villagers, who constitute about 80 percent of India's population, are the indigenous practitioners.

Among the non-professionalized practitioners are some 200,000 vaids who practice Ayurvedic medicine as recorded in Sanskrit in ancient original texts of Hindu literature (cf. Lewis 1958: 265, Swasth Hind 1960: 138). These doctors are like the hakims who practice a similar form of medicine which came in with the Moslems and the Persian script, and are often landowners, wealthy priests and merchants who, in some areas at least, carry on medical practice as a kind of *noblesse oblige* and as side lines (Marriott 1955: 258). Even more common are the magical medicine men who sell various charms to ward off disease, use secret verbal formula and other techniques, and the sacerdotal medicine men such as the priests of the Brahmin caste who practice medicine as a part of the profession of priesthood, but usually limit their medical prescriptions to a number of ritual activities such as making pilgrimages, bathing in the Gangas, the holy river, praying, conducting sacrifices, etc. Also to be mentioned is the snake-bite curer who may come from the lower castes and the religious exorcist who in some ways resembles the faith healer in the West.

The Untrained Midwife or Dai as an Example of an Unprofessionalized Role

The paucity of nurses and the birth of about thirteen million babies each year make the position of midwife or dai critical to Indian demography. Every village has one or two indigenous midwives and, as one recent study shows, nearly 100 percent of the deliveries are conducted by them (see Kakar 1972: 14, 26). The indigenous midwife is preferred over the trained midwife from the Government Health Centres because the former provides the prospective mothers with a number of prenatal and post-natal services which the latter does not. The former is fully cognizant of the cultural patterns and is willing to accept varying rewards in cash or kind depending upon the status of the mother. Zachariah (1972: 251–2, 271) found that increase in the education of husbands reverses this pattern of preference for dais. It is pertinent to note that the 1971 Census figure for percentage literacy in India was 29.34.

A brief description of some of the activities of the dai who generally comes from the lowest castes may throw in relief some problems involved in professionalization of medical status-roles in India. As observed in Lewis' (1958: 47–8) description of a birth taking place in a northern Indian village, the non-professional aspects of the behavior may be easily noted.

The dai, or midwife, of the Bhangi, or sweeper caste, is called in when the prospective mother is in labor. With any sharp instrument which happens to be at hand, the midwife cuts the umbilical cord. This later is buried at the foot of the mother's cot in a hole. It is believed that if not buried or left outside, the cord might be eaten by an animal which would result in the child's death.

After the midwife bathes the mother, the remaining magically unclean water produced from the magically unclean condition of the mother is carried far from the house by the midwife. The newborn child and mother are secluded, if possible, in a separate room. Only the midwife may attend the mother for the first ten days, and no one visits the mother who is believed to be in a state of pollution and defilement. In one village, the midwife received an equivalent of about 4 cents to 25 cents for her services. She also received the clothes worn by the mother during her pregnancy since these are polluted and defiling. If the baby is a boy, the mother is usually more generous to the midwife than if it is a girl.

Other Aspects of Professionalization and the Position of Dai and Nurse

The mastery of the subject matter and techniques of the modern professions and the performance is so important that entrance into them must be in large measure through achievement rather than birth. Whereas the dai or midwife is born to her position, the professional nurse must achieve hers.

Professionalization requires that there be specialization in order to make it possible to have services when no one actor can learn all there is to know about all subjects. The nurse is held responsible for only the area in which she is supposed to have specialized competence. Such specialization as exists in the dai's status-role has been developed by tradition and is diffuse whereas that of the nurse is functionally specific. Professionalization requires that decision making and other actions be carried on in a certain objective, disinterested or affectively neutral manner. For the untrained dai "ancestral tradition is [so] heavy on her that" she ordinarily cannot and does not achieve this objectivity (Bhore Report, Vol. 2, 1946: 397).[3] Professionals are usually paid in terms of society's evaluation of the service rendered and also in accordance with standards that make it possible for them to follow the style of life appropriate for their profession as determined by the value of the society. The payment to the Indian dai or midwife is based upon tradition. It is low as is her rank, because of the defiling "dirty" work she does and seems to have little relation to her importance in the total value system. In fact in India nurses are often recruited from strata which are not greatly superior. Both in terms of income and living conditions provided for nurses in hospitals, the requirements for respectable status of the professional person are seldom met.

The hallmark of the professional person as distinguished from other workers is the extent to which he or she has internalized and conforms to the ethical standards of his or her profession. The ethical standards not only protect the practitioner but also other members of the society and the community. The dai has a traditional *dharma*, an untranslatable term which will be further discussed

---

3 In fact, one of the greatest complaints of the Indian peasants, as reported by Marriott (1955: 262 ff.), is that most of the modern doctors they know, different from the indigenous practitioner and the dai, assume a formal detached attitude.

below and which has some aspects of professional ethics. In general it may be said that the dai's *dharma* lacks the universality or societal protective component of Hippocratic ethics of the medical profession.

Notwithstanding the "particularistic" orientation of and toward dai or midwife, we may summarize the characteristic components of the professional status-role of nurse.[4] As trained she will attain her position and rewards in terms of demonstrated competence and achievement. Her actions, especially in the healing aspects of her status-role are, like those of the physician, basically determined by the universal norms and canons of objective science. Insofar as her status-role demands it she is freed from such affectual ties as those of her family and other non-professional bonds. She is held responsible only in the agreed upon area of her speciality for which she is trained. In many cases the responsibility only applies when "on duty", which differentiates her from the mother who is always responsible for her child. In her training and in her professional associations she internalizes a professional code of ethics which protects her own profession and gives it status and likewise protects the community and society. She is rewarded in terms of salary, living arrangements and all other returns on a scale comparable with that of the other professionals of similar importance and similarly trained, dedicated and competent.

Concepts-Status-Role and Culture

The relation of status-role and culture in Indian society is theorized to have a bearing on the profession of nursing in India. For the sake of clarity these concepts may be briefly discussed and related to the field of nursing.

Status-roles may be defined as that which is expected of an individual because he or she is in a given status or position and acting out the role that belongs with this status or position (see Loomis 1960: 19). We may define culture as all influences which enter behavior but which are not inherited through the genes or blood stream (cf. Loomis 1960: 28–9; Parsons 1961: 963–93).

In general everywhere, as Schulman (1958: 528–37) suggests, the status-role of the nurse has two major variable components. These are the "mother surrogate" or mother substitute role and the professional "healer" role. The expectations for the mother surrogate role may be characterized by tenderness, support, integrity, concern for others, kindness and formal affection. The pro-

---

4 The concepts used here are based upon Talcott Parsons' pattern variables. Early in his use of these concepts he observed that the medical doctor and, of course, the professional nurse were characterized as Gesellschaftlike or instrumentally (not expressively) oriented poles of the variables. The roles involved in this activity were affective neutrality, specificity, universalism and achievement (performance). However, different from the business man or most other professionals the medical status-roles were collectivity-oriented, not self-oriented (See Parsons 1951: 435). See also Parsons (1939: 457–67) and Parsons and Shils (1951: 47 ff.).

fessional and healing aspect of the role may range all the way from these "mother surrogate" contributions which after all are also important in the healing arts to quite different sentiments. Coolly calculated and rational decisions which are necessary to bring the patient from his or her early dependence when he or she required the support of the nurse's permissiveness over the later stages of recovery when the nurse along with the physician and other members of the health team may, in the interest of developing independence and recovery, assume what is called the right to deny reciprocity.

Factors which Deter Professionalization

We have so far referred to professionalization of nursing vis-a-vis the Indian society in a generalized manner. Perhaps this is the time and place to begin our explicit discussion of factors which deter professionalization of nursing in India.

Weakness of Selfhood and Independence

In order that an actor in the sociological sense can be a "true" professional and dedicated to those goals and norms set by his profession, he or she must enter training and be socialized to what may be his or her calling, say nursing. Such training and socialization for the skilled professional must be for a more or less autonomous "self" freed from inhibiting dependencies. It is often stated that Indian women do not develop a "self" except and to the extent that they attain prestige as wife and mother (see Cormack 1953: 193 and 196). For an explanation for this devaluation of selfhood and autonomy, we must turn to the social systems which structure the interaction of individuals and out of which values emerge.

For the Indian villager there are as McKim Marriott (1955: 249) notes three social realms: family and kinship (controlled by limitless mutual trust and demand), village and caste (in which much is controlled by particular obligations and formal respect), and the outside world (composed of the government and market place). Of these three, the kinship or family group and the hierarchical links seem to be most important in determining the nature of self concept. In very few societies is the individual so dependent for his security, identity and dignity as is the Indian on the traditional status-roles in his kin and status groupings, his family and his caste (see Loomis and Boettger 1970: 49).

Beyond the family, the next most powerful influence in the determination of selfhood or the lack of it, is the hierarchical linking relationship provided by caste. Castes structure in a specific manner certain responsibilities and require that behavior be reflected in who can eat together, sit together, smoke together, or speak to one another as equals or near equals. Frequently it is said that "the point of the whole system is to make sure that there will always be some one you can depend upon" (Marriott 1955: 247).

It is against this background of the absorption of the individual, especially the child and woman, into the family and hierarchical structure, that the above-mentioned failure of the self on the part of the woman to develop and become autonomous can be understood.

Authority, Male-Female Relations and Professionalization

A Hindu woman is traditionally shy and submissive as compared with her counterpart in the West. Shyness and submissiveness are considered virtuous for a woman and the socialization process of the Hindus lays great stress on these attributes. A bold woman is out of place. Cormack (1953: 199) argues that because of their submissiveness, Hindu women "do not fulfill their potentialities or fully develop their individual personalities .. but .. they are relatively secure psychologically". The necessity of submissiveness on the part of Indian females, the inexorable taboo against ever touching or being touched by a male outside of the immediate family and before marriage is almost absolute (cf. Cormack 1953: 38).[5] The effect of this training on young females acting out the roles of nurses in hospitals who must help males is obvious.

More will be said of the evaluation and position of women, but here the emphasis is upon restraints against women exercising authority and carrying on activities necessary to nursing especially in relation to males. Among Moslems, especially among those who practice strict purdah, the difficulty for female nurses is even greater than in the other religious groups, because of the tendency among Moslems to think of all women who help or come in physical contact with males outside the family as prostitutes. When physicians add their weight to the powerful forces in Indian culture which prevent the development of selfhood, individuality and self-confidence of women in relation to men and in life generally they deter the professionalization and maximization of utility of the status-roles of women in the health field. The true professionalization of women's roles cannot be achieved until they develop sufficient autonomy, independence and social power as incumbents to carry out the objectives set for the status-roles in question. It will be most difficult for a nurse to carry out the difficult objectives which are built into her status-role if her basic orientation is that of "resignation and submission". Almost by definition, the professional has sufficient influence and autonomy to attain goals set. At present in India, except for a few elite women in public life, such autonomy and influence is lacking.

Evaluation of Womanhood

Since most nurses are women, the evaluation of the female as compared

---

5 Less than a decade later, Cormack on the basis of a study of students in Indian colleges and universities observed a change. Now women generally can protect themselves by their own speech and action. "This is a radical departure from tradition, and clearly indicates that the Indian girl is learning to say 'no'" (Cormack 1960: 101).

with the male sex roles is of importance beyond the consideration of autonomy and selfhood as previously discussed. Several facts about Indian society indicate the advantage the male has over the female in terms of cultural evaluation. In general, infant mortality, always a good index of the level of living and evaluation, has been higher for girls than boys. The sons are considered to be assets because they stay in the family and add to its wealth whereas the daughters are liabilities to be married off with proper dowry.

Abolished long since, two other practices among some Hindus viz., female infanticide and the custom of Sati (i.e., widow immolation at the time of her dead husband's cremation) bring to relief further evidence of lower evaluation of women (see Das 1932: 34 and 77).

Another indication of the lower evaluation of females than males is to be found both in the form of marriage and age of girls at marriage. As Cormack (1960: 114) points out, "One of the most sensitive and poignant themes in India is the marriage of young women to old men – usually widowers with many children". Another explanation for child marriage by Max Weber and Bendix leads us to our next topic. This explanation is based in ritualistic terms, the logic of which runs as follows: At each menses, a girl brought pollution and possible sin, upon herself and her parents in the higher castes (see Bendix 1960: 144n). However, male semen, according to one study (see Carstairs 1958: 83–8, 195–6, 240–1), is believed to be nearly sacred and the chief source of physical, spiritual and mental strength. All these cultural indictments against womanhood bear heavily against the nurse who is supposed to be imbued with professional attributes while taking care of her patient.

Magical Defilement and Pollution

Among the numerous elements in the belief-system of the Hindus, pollution and defilement are, perhaps, most intriguing. In earlier times and still among some conservative Brahmin families, the entrance of a Westerner into a home leads to pollution and defilement, requiring that the home be ritually purified. More defiling even than the Westerner, however, are the untouchables who are now called Harijans and approximately constitute one out of every ten Indians (see Taylor et. al. 1965: 1). Although the practice of untouchability is illegal in India today there is hardly any social intercourse between the ex-untouchables and the caste Hindus.

Important for the consideration of professionalization of the medical services in India, is the fact that pollution and defilement are very frequently focused on body functions, for example, menstruation, shaving, sexual relations, body emissions including blood, and so forth (see Bendix 1960: 145n.). As Weber noted, some sciences in India advanced to the 14th century level of sciences in Europe before the coming of the British. However, surgery, animal husbandry, dentistry and various other activities involving blood, faeces and other body emissions were greatly retarded or never developed. One of Cormack's informants, an Indian nurse, speaks out about nursing:

> "Nursing is socially unacceptable and a real hindrance to marriage. I don't think any family will want me as a member...Nurses because of certain aspects of their work such as handling bedpans – are like 'untouchables'. Also, they are 'indecent' because they go out for night work and so on...Doctors are different; they are so highly qualified they are more or less above suspicion" (Cormack 1953: 170).[6]

The same nurse in commenting about pollution also says:

> "Indian girls become acutely aware of their limitations. For instance, that of not touching boys or men, of eating separately when menstruating, not even drinking water from the same place. It gives them a hostile, derogatory feeling. They are, in fact, treated just like untouchables, and there is absolutely no sympathy involved in it. No one is sorry for girls" (Cormack 1953: 80).

Enough has been written here to indicate that the belief in magical defilement and pollution deters the professionalization of nursing in India.

Non-scientific Explanation of Sickness and its Cure

The germ theory of disease is scarcely known to the mass of the Indian population. One study (Gould 1965: 201–8) shows that in Hindustani, germs may only be depicted as tiny insects. For the villager, sickness is as much a moral as a physical crisis. Some physicians trained in modern medicine and studying village life report that sickness is less frequently believed to be due to the presence of germs than it is to moral weakness which may involve a chain of relationships including diet, blood, semen, or violation of the ethical code. Remedies may be pilgrimages and ritual baths to wash away sins – atonement rather than tonics (cf. Carstairs 1958; Marriott 1955: 256).

Nurses everywhere in India have patients who believe that the "evil eye" caused their disease. It, according to the beliefs of the people, causes smallpox, typhoid, diarrhea, dysentry, hysteria and eye inflammation. Almost no Indian village study fails to mention or discuss the anxiety people have for this danger (cf. Minturn and Hitchcock 1963: 203–361; Lewis 1958: 300–1).

Not very different from the "evil eye" are evil spirits. When 800 parents in eight villages of the Lucknow area were asked, "Can evil spirits cause disease?" three out of four answered, "Yes". The same question was asked of 8,000 parents in a national sample of rural India. The percentages answering Yes, and No, were 54 and 43 (Sen and Roy 1966). It is plain to see that nurses in hospitals and in public health services must for some time talk with patients who believe many of their illnesses and other difficulties are due to an evil eye or evil spirits. Not only must nurses deal with the belief of the evil eye and evil spirit, they must likewise deal with various other nonscientific explanations and procedures. One is the use of the horoscope which is frequently used in choosing a

---

6 Concerning "dirty work" etc., see Hughes (1951: 313–23).

bride/bridegroom in arranged weddings, scheduling travels, making investments, and even as one of the present authors learned, on the prescription of
medical treatment. If willingness to accept medical treatment or surgery
becomes contingent upon horoscopic approval, it does illustrate the absolute
necessity and the great difficulty of getting a patient to accept the goal of
recovery before or as he or she receives medical care.

Factors which Facilitate the Professionalization of Nursing

    Dharma, an untranslatable word which we may arbitrarily say means ded-
ication to one's caste norms and values, may have considerable importance for
nurses. Some similar groups through a process called by Srinivas (1952: 30)
Sanskritization, or taking on the ways stemming from India's past rather than
from those coming from the West, have developed *dharmas* as motivating forces.
For most Hindus, dharma is considered the most important of all values and is
sometimes offered as an explanation for the effort Indians put into their work.
Max Weber (1958: 113) observed that "the Hindu artisan is .. famous for his
extreme industry" and even the casual observer who has worked in other developing areas of the world is impressed by it. Without question it is in large
measure due to the dharma which the individual feels for his important
groupings which induces him to work so hard. With the limitations which the
concept dharma, as mentioned above, has because of its lack of universal[7]
application it should, if nurses adopt it, facilitate professionalization.

    Should nurses in India develop a set of norms and ethical standards com-
parable to those of Western medicine which are more universalistic than most
caste dharmas, there would, in the present authors' view, be an advantage. It
appears also to the present authors that a universalistic principle already
available in Indian culture could assist in eliminating the present tendency to
think of the nurse as defiled because she handles blood and other body emissions.
There is a rule from the law book of Baudhayana which specifies that "every

---

7   Max Weber makes much of this distinction, "...*dharma* differed for every status group,
    hence also for the kings...There was no universally valid ethic, but only a strict status
    compartmentalization of private and social ethic, disregarding the few absolute and
    general ritualistic prohibitions (particularly of killing of cows). This was of great moment"
    (1958: 143–4). He continues: "The resulting 'organic' societal doctrine of Hinduism, in
    default of other standards, could elaborate the *dharma* of each profession solely out of the
    peculiarities of its technique. It thus produced only terminologies for special callings and
    spheres of life, from construction technique to logic as the technology of proof and disproof
    to the technology of eroticism" (1958: 147). Later he writes, "There is no universal 'ethic
    but only a status – and professionally differentiated *dharma* according to caste" (1958: 172).
    He then goes on to mention the eight virtues, once ten in number. He mentions virtues
    listed by Manu condensed into five commandments for all castes: "to injure no living
    being, to tell the truth, not to steal, to live purely, to control the passions. Quite similar
    commandments appear as the first step of Yoga" (1958: 172). "If a stand is taken at all it
    is roughly the following: there are simply several paths and also several goals of holy
    seeking. The monk strives for other worldly personal holiness, while the ritually correct
    lay persons, remaining in the world, seeks this – worldly holiness now and rebirth for his
    forebears and descendants" (1958: 174).

workshop is ritually pure – except distilleries" and .. "In his occupation the hand of the craftsman is pure."[8] This should, as it has in factories and other work places in which workers come in contact with lower caste workers who could defile them, exempt the nurse, orderly and others who are supposedly sources of defilement. It should be noted that physicians because of the cost of their training, their generally accepted importance and other reasons, have overcome the magical defilement which once in India more or less prevented their profession from developing. However, as facts of a recent study indicate, for the nurse to rely alone on her training to overcome this disparagement may be unrealistic. Recently in a study (Sen and Roy 1966) in eight villages in the Lucknow area, 800 parents were asked, "Who is superior? A village Brahmin who is illiterate or a low caste person who has a college degree?" Only one out of four indicated the low caste person with a college degree was superior to an illiterate Brahmin.

The Mother Cult

Despite the lower cultural evaluation of females, "motherhood" in India is considered to be the most sacred and prestigeful value. The worship of mother cult has been a phenomenon in India since time immemorial. This "emphasis on motherhood in the ideology, plus the social implications, plus the psychological necessity in the woman's life to have this one creation, this one power, explains the general attitude toward mother – explains the joy women experience in having children – explains why 'pregnant women are auspicious' .. It gives her a sense of power, security, and success" (Cormack 1953: 151–2).[9]

Because of the "mother surrogate" component of the nurse's status-role, the great emphasis on motherhood in India may be in some ways thought of as favorable to development of nursing.

Models in the Culture – the Brahmins

No Indian nurse, physician and other health practitioner in appraising his

---

8 As organizations, all requiring people of different castes, such as factories, commercial concerns and for the purpose of argument, we may say, hospitals are considered, it would be logical to assume as Bendix and Weber note that these would not emerge according to the logic. However, the law book of Baudhayana which specifies that every workshop is ritually pure – excepting distilleries – *should* and does make it possible for the nurse to cooperate with and serve all castes with no degradation or polluting effect going to either served or serving actor. It is also noted that "the same principle of purity applies to all publicly displayed commodities." See Bendix (1960: 196). See also Weber (1958: 111).

9 It should be stated, however, that there is not complete agreement on the theme of love for mother. See Carstairs (1958); Cormack (1960: 24); Minturn and Hitchcock (1963); and Opler (1959: 140–2). For an interchange on the subject by Carstairs and Opler, see American Anthropologist, Vol. 62, 1960: 505–11.

own professional future in India or in understanding the rank of the indigenous and folk practitioners can fail to contemplate the remarkable influence and prestige of the members of the Brahmins through history. In fact, the Brahmin woman and many others like her who serve as nurses, research technicians and other professionals may be pacesetters for Indian womanhood.

Although at present perhaps of less influence than at some other times in Indian history, to this caste must be attributed an achievement unique in human annals. Without great wealth and usually without armed forces they for centuries remained at the pinnacle of prestige often wielding considerable influence. How did the Brahmins become and remain important for so long? What meaning has this for the nursing profession?

After the heroic period of Indian history as reflected, for instance, in the Rig-Veda, the attribute of holiness came to be associated with influence and power achieved in large part through austerity. It is important to note that most of the folk and indigenous practitioners mentioned earlier in this paper including those Brahmins who are folk healers as well as medical practitioners in villages cannot hope to have their influence unchallenged by other holy men from lower castes who may claim power through austerity or other character-istics. Neither the Brahmin of the past nor the modern medical practitioner can, at least in the rural areas of India, fall back on achievement or hierarchical position to meet these challenges. And, as Marriott (1955: 249) notes: "If Western medicine is to be established not merely in, but as a part of, the middle or inner realms of village society, it must be made to fit the organizational forms of that society." All this calls for adaptation. In the past the non-Brahmin mystics could not be questioned by the Brahmins without throwing doubt on the basis of their own rank. To meet all challenges to their influence and prestige as Weber (1958: 163ff.) notes, the Brahmins encouraged asceticism but attempted to make it compatible with the pride of high ranking intelligentsia so that lower ranking exorcists and holy men without access to Brahmin gurus or teachers and intellectual culture could not compete.

Reports of successful modern medical practice in villages make it apparent that those who will be held in high regard must be able to establish close personal relationships with patients but they must also demonstrate the power of their knowledge. Demonstrated knowledge of human anatomy, ability even to predict child birth or the course of a disease has brought physicians and other health practitioners much prestige. It is not enough to diagnose and prescribe medicines effectively. The nurse, physician and other health practitioners must respond knowingly to questions for which patients want and need answers. Thus, some qualities and achievements important to the rank of Brahmins of old are important to the nurse, and they may serve as models.

Concluding Statement

With the establishment of accredited university programs in nursing, however skeletal, and founding of its professional journal and Association nursing has made structural advancements during the last few decades, especially after India's independence in 1947. On the social front, equality of sexes was enshrined in the Constitution adopted in 1950 giving women identical rights with those of men. What is important for our consideration is the extent to which these legislative changes have come to be practised, and here the findings are inconclusive. While Desai (1961: 48) sees these changes filtering into and affecting even the rural social structure in a qualitative way, Kapur (1971: 5) feels that there is equality more in theory and in the eyes of the law and less in daily life, especially for the rural women and women from the lower middle, and lower echelons of the socio-economic class system (cf. Kapur 1970).

Twenty-seven years since the Bhore Report, despite some structural achievements, socio-cultural as well as structural constraints still weigh against the growth of fully professionalized nursing in India. Nurses' salaries are still low and unattractive to educated young women. Working hours are unduly long. The dwellings allotted them are shabby and comparable to those meant for the lowest-paid public employees. Nurses are denied moral and physical support of various persons constituting their role-set (see Haté 1969: 206), while the student-nurses are often subjected to gross exploitation by the hospital administration (see Krishnan 1971: 3). And, nurses have no other legal avenues (e.g., collective bargaining or strike) for the redress of their grievances but to appeal through proper channels which are highly bureaucratized, authoritarian and often insensitive.[10]

It is more than likely that nurses in the 70's will attain relatively greater professionalism than their sisters in the past. But at the same time, it is unlikely that they would have attained a point of culmination in regard to attitudinal attributes especially "belief in the professional organization as a major reference" and "autonomy" in the near future. In order to break through the societal structural and attitudinal barriers, nothing less than a relentless political, social and educational agitation is called for.

REFERENCES

BENDIX, Reinhard
    1960   *Max Weber – An Intellectual Portrait*. Garden City, N.Y.: Doubleday and Co.
Bhore Report (Report of the Health Survey and Development Committee, Chairman: Sir Joseph Bhore).
    1946   Delhi: Government of India Press (Vol. I and II).
CAPLOW, Theodore
    1954   *The Sociology of Work*. Minneapolis: University of Minnesota Press.
CARSTAIRS, G. Morris
    1958   *The Twice Born*. Bloomington: Indiana University Press.

---

10   On April 1, 1970 the Constitution Bench of the Supreme Court of India ruled that hospitals were not industries as defined in the Industrial Disputes Act. "The decision has far-reaching effect on the functioning of hospitals, employer-employee relations and the welfare of the patients" (Veerappa 1970: 149, 169).

CORMACK, Margaret
  1953   *The Hindu Woman.* New York: Bureau of Publications, Teacher's College, Columbia University.
  1960   *She Who Rides a Peacock.* Bombay: Asia Publishing House.
DAS, Frieda M.
  1932   *Purdah, The Status of Hindu Women.* New York: Vanguard Press Inc.
DESAI, A. R.
  1961   *Rural Sociology in India.* Bombay: The Indian Society of Agricultural Economics.
GOODE, William J.
  1957   "Community Within a Community: The Professions." *American Sociological Review* 22 (April): 194–200.
GOULD, Harold A.
  1965   "Modern Medicine and Folk Cognition in Rural India." *Human Organization* 24 (Fall): 201–8.
GREENWOOD, Ernest
  1957   "Attributes of a Profession." *Social Work* 3 (July): 44–55.
GROSS, Edward
  1958   *Work and Society.* New York: Thomas Y. Crowell Co.
HALL, Richard H.
  1968   "Professionalization and Bureaucratization." *American Sociological Review* 33 (February): 92–104.
HATÉ, Chandrakala A.
  1969   *Changing Status of Women in Post Independence India.* Bombay: Allied Publishers.
HUGHES, Everett C.
  1951   "Work and the Self." Pp. 313–23 in John H. Rohrer and Muzafer Sherif (eds.), *Social Psychology at the Crossroads.* New York: Harper.
KAKAR, D. N.
  1972   "Role of Indigenous Midwife in Family Planning Programme." *Nursing Journal of India* 1 (January): 14, 26.
KAPUR, Promilla
  1970   *Marriage and the Working Women in India.* Delhi: Vikas Publications.
  1971   "Roles and Relationships with Special Reference to the Changing Role and Status of Women." Pp. 1–15 in "All-India Seminar on the Indian Family (Nov. 28-Dec. 2, 1971)." New Delhi: Family Life Centre, Indian Social Institute.
KRISHNAN, Sulochana
  1971   "Status of Women in Nursing Profession." Working paper presented to the Comittee on the Status of Women in India (unpublished).
KORNHAUSER, William
  1963   *Scientists in Industry.* Berkeley: University of California Press.
LEWIS, Oscar
  1958   *Village Life in Northern India.* Urbana: University of Illinois Press.
LOOMIS, Charles P.
  1960   *Social Systems – Essays on their Persistence and Change.* Princeton, N.J.: D. Van Nostrand.
LOOMIS, Charles P. and Shirly BOETTGER
  1970   "Social, Psychosocial and Cultural Aspects of the Nurse-Patient Relationship." *Cohesion* 1 (January): 43–69.
MARRIOTT, McKim
  1955   "Western Medicine in a Village of Northern India." Pp. 239–68 in Benjamin D. Paul (ed.). *Health, Culture and Community.* New York: Russell Sage Foundation.
MINTURN, Leigh and John T. HITCHCOCK.
  1963   "The Rajputs of Khalapur, India." Pp. 203–361 in Beatrice B. Whiting (ed.), *Six Cultures-Studies in Child Rearing.* New York: John Wiley and Sons.
OPLER, M. E.
  1959   "Review of the Twice-Born." *American Anthropologist* 61: 140–2.

PARSONS, Talcott
1939 "The Professions and Social Structure." *Social Forces* 17: 457–67.
1951 *The Social System.* Glencoe, Ill.: The Free Press.
1961 "Culture and the Social System." Pp. 963–93 in Parsons et al. (eds.), *Theories of Society.* Glencoe, Ill.: The Free Press.

PARSONS, Talcott and Edward A. SHILS (eds.)
1951 *Toward a General Theory of Action.* Cambridge, Mass.: Harvard University Press.

SCHULMAN, Sam
1958 "Basic Functional Roles in Nursing: Mother Surrogate and Healer." Pp. 528–537 in E. Gartly Jaco (ed.), *Patients, Physicians and Illness – Behavioral Sciences and Medicines.* Glencoe, Ill.: The Free Press.

SEN, Lalit K., and Prodipto ROY
1966 *Awareness of Community Development in Village India.* Hyderabad: National Institute of Community Development.

SRINIVAS, M. N.
1952 *Religion and Society among the Coorgs of South India.* Oxford: Clarendon Press.

SUNDARAM, S.
1970 "Growth of Nursing in India." *The Nursing Journal of India* 11 (November): 353–4, 381–2.

SWASTH HIND
1960 Delhi: Central Health Education Bureau, Government of India 4 (April): 138.

TAYLOR, Carl C., Douglas ENSMINGER, Helen W. JOHNSON, and Jean JOYCE.
1965 *India's Roots of Democracy.* Bombay: Orient Longmans Ltd.

VEERAPPA, M.
1970 "Supreme Court Verdict Adverse to Trade Unions." *Nursing Journal of India* 5 (May): 149, 169.

VOLLMER, Howard M. and Donald MILLS (eds.)
1966 *Professionalization.* New Jersey: Prentice Hall.

WEBER, Max
1958 *The Religion of India* (Translated to English by Hans Gerth and Don Martindale). Glencoe, Ill.: The Free Press.

WILENSKI, Harold L.
1964 "The Professionalization of Everyone?" *American Journal of Sociology* LXX (September): 137–58.

WILKINSON, A.
1958 *A Brief History of Nursing in India and Pakistan.* Madras: The Trained Nurses Association of India.

ZACHARIAH, S.
1971 "Midwifery Service in Rural West Bengal." *Nursing Journal of India* 8 (August): 251–2, 271).

RESEARCH COMMUNICATIONS

Note: *The Journal of Asian and African Studies* invites communications in the form of short articles and reports about ongoing research, not exceeding 5,000 words, both in the empirical and theoretical fields.

EDITOR

1. Strategies of Rulership: A Critique of Pluralism in India

JAYANT K. LELE
Queen's University, Kingston, Canada

A good deal of literature on political development begins with notions of evolutionary change from tradition to modernity. Analyses of India's democratic form of government which point to a growing pluralism in elite-mass relationships also assume such a movement. Tradition is equated with the prevalence of a central world-view based on myth and religion which legitimates political power. Modernity is equated with the impact of science and technology on society and politics. The institutional framework of traditional societies is taken to be grounded in the unquestionable underpinnings of legitimation constituted by mythical, religious and metaphysical interpretations of reality. These, of course, disappear in modern societies, it is assumed. Instead, the rational interests become the legitimizers of the state (Habermas 1970).

Weber's typology of authority often forms a basis for these evolutionary analyses. For Weber, the traditional authority of the rulers rested on an "established belief in the sanctity of immemorial tradition". As the essential aspect of all traditional authority, he emphasized the consensual community (Weber 1968: 226–235, 1011–1022). The idea of the consensual community as the basis of legitimation of rulers in precapitalist societies is also dominant in Marx's writings. He posits a unity between the rulers and the ruled based on communal ownership of land (Marx 1972: 69–70).

The beginning of modernity is associated with the separation between the state and civil society as public and private realms. Democratic theory, of which the North American pluralism is the most recent manifestation, was based on the ideals of rational order, freedom and formal equality. These were the ideals of the bourgeoisie which came to dominance in Europe on the eve of the separation of the two spheres of life. Marx unmasked the ideological nature of the democratic theory when he showed that the bourgeoisie used the same ideals to monopolize the public sphere when challenged by the deprived workers, peasants and the artisans (Habermas 1962). The Pluralist theory of democracy also constitutes an ideology when it is used to justify the monopolization of the public sphere (Baskin 1950).

Pluralist analysis of Indian democracy does not explore its own ideological character and its practical implications. It equates pluralism with modernity and assumes that the imperfections in Indian democracy stem from the vestiges of traditional or charismatic legitimation. A rational order is eventually expected to emerge leading to greater freedom for the individual and increasing equality among the citizens. Tradition is viewed in this model as having no legitimation problems for the "vested interests" since they represent the unity of the community. The basic problem of the political modernizers, who are usually assumed to be urban, educated aliens, is considered to be that of finding new bases of legitimation (Field 1972).

In order to understand the relative stability of democracy in India a new look at both Marx and Weber is necessary. In the following pages we will present a short exploratory analysis of their insights into the problem of legitimation and their salience to the reinterpretation of democracy in India. It should be treated as an agenda for exhaustive research and not as a complete argument. In order to illustrate the utility of this approach we will sketch a model for the study of democratic politics in Maharashtra state in India.

In his discussion of the variations of the state in precapitalist societies Marx starts with their common origin in presettlement, pre-agricultural tribal property. The latter originates in the capacity of human groups to possess land. The relation to land of the members signifies the fullest social identification. This, in other words, is a society from which the state has not emerged as a distinct entity. The emergent complex societies which follow, especially the Asiatic Society under despotism and the Classical Polis retain, according to Marx, the tribal communal property into the agricultural stage. These are not the communistic societies of the tribal variety, however. Stratification has appeared and the economic surplus of direct producers is appropriated by a new entity, the state. It may be the despot (whom Marx describes as the symbol of the total society) or the urban participate of landowners in the Classical Polis. In both cases the basic type of property is identical; it is the communal form of property.

In this conceptualization of state and society is embedded the basic problem of legitimation of political power. This is, in effect, Marx's answer to the questions: why legitimation and how to secure it. The answer, a simplification of Marx, would be that monopolization of surplus production by an individual or a group is antithetical to the very social nature of human organization; consequently legitimation of such an appropriation must appear in the form of a communal identity or communal function. Thus one learns from Marx that the despot, in the Asiatic pattern, appears as the father of the many communities and that the surplus product belongs to him as if he were the symbol of the inherently supreme unity. In classical antiquity the notion of the community of landowners justifies exclusion of the direct producers (i.e. the slaves) and monopolization of political power.

While it is not necessary to deny the possibility of a genuine sharing of a communal identity or a consensus on the appropriation and disposition of communal surplus between the rulers and the ruled it is not a necessary attribute of traditional authority. Marx was keenly aware of the fact that the same economic basis could produce "infinite variations and gradations in appearance" of the "political form of the relations of sovereignty and dependence" (Marx 1970: 92). These variations, among other things, were often caused by an absence of a genuine unity between the rulers and the ruled. The village communities in Maharashtra from their early settlement are open to this interpretation, as we will see later.

Marx's critique of bourgeois ideology has relevance in those traditional societies where rulers had to consciously legitimize their rule. Under capitalism Marx saw that the individualization of man and privatization of property had nearly reached completion. But even under these conditions the bourgeois ideology continued to use the communal basis of legitimation for justifying the state. Although reciprocity among rational men was supposed to lead to just relations of exchange, the bourgeois constitutional state, now only a superstructure, sought legitimation as a representation of all classes and hence as a guarantor of just exchange. In reality, however, it was neither the guardian of the general interest of the society nor were its laws the embodiment of human freedom.

The bourgeois state did not perform according to the ennobled view it had of itself. Private property degraded the state to its own level and against its true meaning, says Marx. The separation of the public domain as independent from all classes and as superior to them thus became a legitimating strategy which kept the actual power relations inaccessible to analysis and public consciousness. In this sense it became an ideology while maintaining the practical illusion of universality. The modern state with its bureaucratic and legislative bodies became an institutional license for sectional interests. The separation of the public sphere of secularized spiritualism from the private sphere of the satisfaction of egotistical needs creates a tension that neither a bureaucrat nor a politician could overcome.

If the bourgeois society witnessed increasing rationality in interaction and a decline in personal authority it was only temporary (Habermas 1962; Cyert and March 1965; Roth 1968). Increasing rationalization of decision-making in the government and industry (use of science and technology, perspective planning, use of systems analyses and cybernetics) has increased the emergence of personal rulerships very substantially. This second stage of rationalization which Weber had seen on the horizon appeared to him to be full of frightening consequences. His solution, as we said earlier, was in personal rulership where a charismatic ruler was to rule in a plebiscitary democracy. That personal rulerships could emerge within the bureaucratic-rational apparatus, Weber failed to see.

We have taken issue with evolutionary interpretations of Marx's and Weber's ideas of legitimation by indicating the lack of consensual community in traditional societies and the prevalence of personal rulerships in modern ones. In fact, Weber himself, in describing the various manifestations of rulerships, such as those in India and China, shows the complex intermixing of various authority types. To him, we suggest, the various types are possible strategies of rulership which may be used singly or in combination, depending on the circumstances (Weber 1968; Mommsen 1965).

We are primarily concerned with the strategic uses of patriarchal, patrimonial, personal and bureaucratic authority. In the pure form of patriarchalism there are no legal limits to domination. The roots are in the authority over the kinship unit. Compliance of those subjected to authority is on the basis of norms derived from tradition. Patriarchalism evolves out of kinship authority and hence the control of the means of production is clearly located in the hands of the patriarch. The important "strategic" feature of patriarchal rule, therefore, is the emphasis placed on custom and tradition. It is coupled with a minimization, in overt interaction and rhetoric, of the coercive possibilities for violations.

In a patrimonial rule the subjects include not only the kinsmen but a number of service groups. The exploitative power of the ruler depends upon his effective control over the means of production. However, emphasis on the consensual community, whose symbols may be found in traditional village assemblies, common grazing lands and ritual participation by the subjects in the major social, religious and economic events in the patron's household, is by far the most important strategic resource for the ruler. Decline in the salience of these symbols reflects the unmasking of the coercive character of the relationship and calls for the creation of new myths and new symbols and perhaps even a new locus for the sentiments of consensual community.

Another form of authority is that of personal rulership. In its pure form the loyalty of the subjects is based neither on the personal qualities, per se, of the ruler, nor on the legitimating traditions. It is inextricably linked to material incentives and rewards. While it does not derive directly from the established rules or enactments it can exist only within the context of some established and accepted norms of reciprocity. Although it implies personal loyalty to the ruler its basis is in material incentives and rewards and not in custom or feudal fealty. A personal ruler in this case transcends the bases of legitimacy which may have become less tenable, uses them wherever necessary or possible but typically combines them with material incentives in his exercise of rulership (Weber 1968: 1114–1115; Roth 1968: 2–5).

The fourth strategy of legitimation with which Weber deals extensively is the legal-rational authority that goes with bureaucratic domination. The key element of this form of legitimation, for Weber, is the impersonal character of the interactions that have to do with the relationships of domination and subordination. It is governed by legal norms and is function-specific. Both the ruler and the ruled are in a legally defined relationship for a rational pursuit of interests (Weber 1968: 986).

The strategic use of personal rulership is of the greatest significance in our analysis of democratic politics in India. We suggest that it provides the rulers with maximum flexibility in the pursuit of monopolization of the public realm. It gives them recourse to other bases of authority. We have already noted the rise in personal rulership in advanced capitalist and state socialist societies. Personal rulerships also constitute the basic strategy of the political actors in contemporary India. In fact there is continuity through history in the strategic uses of the communal basis for legitimation by the rulers.

In Maharashtra, for example, the villages from the time of early settlement appear to have been units of political domination by the privileged over the vanquished, the aliens, and the newcomers. According to one interpretation the castes originated in the process by which the Northern invaders changed 'the free savage into helpless serfs' with minimum violence and maximum authority (Kosambi 1955: 36).

The resting of ownership of all land in the distant ruler, once perhaps a consequence of a genuine bond of loyalty, later became a myth. It facilitated a mutually beneficial relationship between the lords and the vassals. With the

Moslem regimes even the semblance of community between the subjects and the external rulers, previously derived from shared religion, was gone. The privileged early settlers acquired permanent, inalienable rights to their land. Those who controlled the means of production in the form of land became the managers of the consensual community and began to use it to their own best advantage. They maintained kinship bonds that linked several villages. Thus the dominant agriculturist castes did not live in isolation. They formed a self-conscious regional ruling group equivalent to a class. The political domination in the villages was based on the strategic use of tradition by patriarchal (in dealing with the extended kin) and patrimonial (in dealing with the other dependent castes) rulers. In spite of the changes brought about by British rule, the basic framework of domination persists. Wars and feuds between alien rulers had created rivalries and factionalism within the ruling lineages even before the British arrived. The new system of administration simply intensified the struggle (Kumar 1968). Post-independence democratic politics has also caused some modifications in the structure of village domination. It is now integrally linked with the higher levels of polity through a system of factions and alliances.

> *The Faction:* Schematically, a faction consists of:
> i. The faction leader who belongs to the dominant caste (see Mandelbaum 1970: 358–380) and the adults in the immediate extended kinship unit.
> ii. The heads of other real or fictitious kinship units of the dominant caste who are economically independent of the faction leader.
> iii. The heads of extended kinship units of the dominant caste, who are economically dependent on the faction leader.
> iv. The heads of households from the middle castes.
> v. The heads of the service caste households.
> vi. The tenants and the landless labourers.

The dominant caste in Maharashtra is the Maratha caste. In most villages Marathas constitute a very substantial portion of the total population. However, only a few kinship units within this caste have the concentration of wealth, power and prestige. The latter two are usually the derivative of the first but are often closely linked with the hereditary headman function. The faction leaders are usually from this privileged group. Typically, the two or more factions in the villages are led by members of the same kinship unit. These rival factions consciously coalesce in the event of threats to their dominance by other castes. Such events are, however, rare.

While the rivalries between the privileged kinship units provide the core structure and dynamics of village factionalism the factions themselves are never strictly intra-caste units. In dealing with the dominant Maratha caste the distinction between the privileged inner core and the rest is quite important. A great majority of those who call themselves Marathas were once referred to as Kunbis. They are still treated as somewhat inferior by the elite Marathas. The problem of delineation of the boundaries between the elites and the rest on a lineage-basis is very complex and cannot by discussed here (see Carter 1972; Karve 1961; Karve and Damle 1963; Kumar 1968; and Orenstein 1963). One thing is clear. For the non-elite Marathas and for the middle castes who depend on the elite for access to the means of production the Maratha caste complex constitutes a reference group: a status group to which they aspire (see Damle 1963 and Srinivas 1962). This constitutes a major element in the patrimonial strategies of the elite Marathas. Similarly, the members of the service castes, the tenants and the landless are absorbed into a ritually defined Jajmani relationship. While economic dependence provides the primary basis for the loyalty of followers, its minimization as a source is obviously desirable. A leader can rule with greater freedom if he can show that he must rule because of his traditional role as the ruler and not because of his ability to coerce.

This ritualization of loyalty to the faction leader by members is nowhere more obvious than in the act of voting. The faction leader controls blocs of votes of his supporters in the same way that he commands loyalty in other spheres of action. With an effective insulation of the disadvantaged groups from direct interaction with the external world it is not too difficult to see why the act of voting acquires no other significance than that of a ritualized expression of loyalty to the faction leader. The patriarchal-patrimonial strategy is replaced by personal rulership strategies at the levels of politics beyond the village. The operation of this strategy is best seen in the structure of alliances.

The Alliance:

An alliance is an enduring relationship of support and loyalty between several faction leaders and a person who aspires to a political office within the governmental hierarchy. Typically then, such alliances would exist for every one of the political offices which require electoral support in some form. Primarily, these offices are in the local government sector (Panchayat Samitis and Zilla Parishads), the legislative sector (the state legislature and the parliament) and the cooperative sector (credit, marketing, producers cooperatives and banks heavily subsidized from public funds) (Lele 1965). An alliance is a strategy of personal rulership. Like a faction leader an alliance leader must seek personal loyalty. If he is a faction leader himself he may count on the traditional loyalty of the supporters from his own village. He must secure the loyalty of several faction leaders from other villages. Here the extended kinship ties may sometimes be of help but they may also hinder him. Factions tend to originate within the kinship units of rulers and not between them. Hence for every kin group on your side there is often one on the side of your rival. This in effect nullifies the advantage of kinship ties for the intra-elite competition. For the hegemonic consciousness of the Marathas in times of external threats it still provides a base.

At successively higher levels of hierarchy there are alliances between alliance leaders themselves under the aegis of a higher alliance leader. The important aspect of an alliance relationship is that both patrons and clients have reasonably easy access to alternatives and that tradition does not form the basis of legitimation. Whereas a faction leader legitimizes his domination by a strategic use of tradition, an alliance leader finding himself between the rival faction leaders on the one hand and the formal, constitutional bureaucracy on the other takes recourse to a strategy of personal rulership. What binds the faction and alliance leaders together is the hegemonic consciousness of their common rulership status (Hobsbawm 1971) and an interest in maintaining that privileged position.

Reconciliations, realignments, even graceful acceptance of defeat and a pledge of loyalty to the winner by rivals are common features of the alliance system of politics. The leaders must remain vigilant at all times and must keep the fences mended at all levels of their alliances. Loss of support at one crucial level may cause sufficient uncertainty about the ability of an alliance to deliver the rewards and the stable structure may begin to crumble. The stability of the system lies in the shared interest of the ruling class and not in the existence of a congeries of people with uncommon ends.

The Congress Party is a successful party because it has managed to provide the rural middle peasantry the necessary avenues for enhancement through the mechanism of patronage manipulated by alliances of faction leaders. It is done by maintaining the majority of the population in relative isolation from the points of access to resources.

In conclusion, we have tried to suggest in this paper that the strategy of personal rulership constitutes a crucial mechanism for monopolization of the public sphere by the ruling elite. Whether the society is traditional or modern is immaterial. Pluralist politics flourishes in any society in which there exists a class of privileged rulers who seek to control and monopolize access to the public domain. As a corollary, it requires a population in a state of nearly total dependence in terms of access to the means of production.

In North American politics, pluralism becomes a strategic myth for legitimation of politics as an arena for elite bargaining. The individualist premises are shared by both the population and the elites. The consensual community is transformed into "a fundamental agreement about procedural norms and substantive goals which even the non-political may be socialized to share" (Baskin 1950: 81). Order and stability become the primary goals of a society and its elites. Pluralist groups tend to become the local functionaries of a shrinking decision-making apparatus within the public and the corporate sectors. Their mutual interaction is guided merely by goals of satisfaction of ego-focal interest and material benefits (see e.g., Sevrin 1972). Pluralist theory helps the small class of personal rulers to manipulate the myth of an open political system.

In India the theory of pluralist democracy allows the ruling elite to emphasize the goals of order, stability and gradual change. It gives the middle peasantry an exclusive access to the public realm in which the avenues for the enhancement of privilege are concentrated.

REFERENCES

BASKIN, D.
1972   "American Pluralism: Theory, Practice and Ideology." *Journal of Politics* 32 (1): 71–95.
CARTER, A. C.
1972   "Political Stratification and Unstable Alliances in Rural Western Maharashtra." *Modern Asian Studies* 6, part 4: 423–442.
CYERT, R. and J. MARCH
1965   *A Behavioural Theory of the Firm.* Prentice Hall.
DAMLE, Y. B.
1963   "Reference Group Theory with Regard to Mobility Within Caste." *Bulletin of the Deccan College Research Institute* 23: 11–22.
FIELD, J. O.
1972   *Partisanship in India: A Survey Analysis.* MIT. (Unpublished manuscript).

HABERMAS, J.
1962   *Structurewandel der Offentlichkeit*. Neuwied am Rhein. (I am grateful to Paul Lucardie for a brief English summary.)
HABERMAS, J.
1970   *Toward A Rational Society*. Beacon Press.
HOBSBAWM, E. J.
1971   "Class Consciousness in History" in I. Meszaros (ed.), *Aspects of History and Class Consciousness*. Routledge and Kegan Paul.
KARVE, I.
1961   *Hindu Society: An Interpretation*. Deccan College.
KARVE, I. and Y. B. DAMLE
1963   *Group Relations in a Village Community*. Deccan College.
KOSAMBI, D. D.
1955   "The Basis of Ancient Indian History, I." *Journal of the American Oriental Society* LXXIV (4): 330–337.
KUMAR, R.
1968   *Western India in the Nineteenth Century*. University of Toronto.
LELE, J. K.
1965   *Local Government in India*. New York State College, Cornell University.
MANDELBAUM, D. G.
1970   *Society in India*. University of California.
MARX, Karl
1970   *Capital*. Volume 3. International Publishers.
MARX, Karl
1972   *Precapitalist Economic Formations*. International Publishers.
MOMMSEN, W.
1965   "Max Weber's Political Sociology and His Philosophy of World History." *International Social Science Journal* XVII (1): 23–45.
ORENSTEIN, H.
1963   "Caste and the Concept of 'Maratha' in Maharashtra." *The Eastern Anthropologist* 16: 1–9.
ROTH, G.
1968   "Personal Rulership, Patrimonialism and Empire-Building in the New States." *World Politics* 20 (2): 194–206.
SEVRIN, W.
1972   *The Company and the Union*. Alfred Knopf.
SRINIVAS, M. N.
1962   "A Note on Sanskritization and Westernization," in *Caste in Modern India and Other Essays*. Asia Publishing.
WEBER, Max
1968   *Economy and Society*. Bedminister Press.

2. Diffusion of Innovations in West Africa: A New Look at the Western Model

DAVID G. FRANCIS and JESUS RICO VELASCO
The Ohio State University, Colombus, U.S.A.

Several questions have arisen in attempts to employ the theoretical and methodological orientations of western diffusion research to study the adoption of new ideas in developing societies. Contradictory theoretical arguments have developed even within the western nations concerning various aspects of the diffusion process. An example is the viability of the concept of an ordered series of "stages" leading to adoption (North Central Rural Sociology Sub-committee for the Study of Diffusion of Farm Practices, 1955; Lauvidge and Steiner 1956; Wilkening 1961). Similar questions have arisen from research findings in developing nations. The result has been confusion as to which findings can justifiably be compared.

Diffusion research has figured prominently among the efforts of rural sociologists for several years. As interest has spread to the developing nations, however, problems have arisen. Sociologists from developing societies trained in the United States have become discouraged and reinforced in their suspicions that western theoretical assumptions may not be useful in explaining the process of adoption in their home countries. In the western societies, for example, a direct and positive relationship has consistently been found between early adoption and such items as education, socio-economic status, and size of the farm or business operation (see Table 1). Research findings from developing

Table 1
Hypotheses of U.S. Adoption Research and Their Support

Hypothesis	Number of Studies	Support
1. Earlier adopters have more years of education than do later adopters	203	74%
2. Earlier adopters have higher social status than later adopters	275	68%
3. Earlier adopters have larger sized units (farms, etc.) than do later adopters	152	67%
4. Earlier adopters are more likely to have a commercial (rather than a subsistence) orientation than are later adopters	20	71%
5. Earlier adopters have a more favorable attitude toward change than later adopters	43	75%
6. Earlier adopters are more highly integrated with the social system than later adopters	6	100%

Source: Rogers, Everett M. and E. Floyd Shoemaker, *Communication of Innovations*, The Free Press, 1971.

nations, though often corroborating such findings, indicate that these relationships cannot be considered universal. Inayatullah (1962), studying diffusion in Pakistan, found no relationship between education, participation in formal organizations, number of social contacts, or income with adoption rates among Pakistani farmers. Garver (1962) reported that the military government in Korea had gaps in its organizational structure that impeded some programs and destroyed the possibility of farmers having direct contact with change agents. This was in spite of the programs' appearing quite similar to those in western nations which diffuse innovative information. Hägerstrand (1968) has stated that:

> An aggregate of complicated circumstances causes keenness, hesitation, delay, or refusal to adopt innovations suggested by signals through the communication network. Part of

the picture is, of course, the personal characteristics of individuals. Another part is the necessity for various time consuming adjustments and preparations before an adoption can be fitted into pre-existing procedures, habits, and value systems.

Early U.S. diffusion research reported differences in age between early and late adopters of new ideas. As an example of the variation in findings between western nations and nations in earlier stages of social and economic development, this relationship was examined using the summary of diffusion research provided by Rogers and Shoemaker (1971).

Table 2 shows that although most of the research, including both hypo-

Table 2
Age Comparisons of Adopters of New Ideas by Place in Which the Study Was Conducted

Hypothesis	Place of Study		No Data on Place of Study	Total
	U.S. or Other Western Nations	Asia, Africa or Latin America		
	(percents supporting hypotheses)			
Early adopters are younger than later adopters (44 studies)	52	36	12	100
Early adopters are older than later adopters (76 studies)	79	16	5	100

Source: Rogers, Everett M. and E. Floyd Shoemaker, *Communication of Innovations*, The Free Press, 1971.

theses stating that early adopters are younger and conversely that they are older, has been conducted in the West, the first is more often substantiated in the developing nations (ratios of 1 : 1.44 versus 1: 4.94) than is the second. This is to say that studies in developing nations more often found early adopters to be younger. Western studies more often found them to be older.

Problems have also been encountered in attempting to apply western-type indices. One example is found in the research done by Keith (1968) in Eastern Nigeria. After determining that it was unrealistic to measure diffusion culminating in adoption because of the losses in sample size, he decided to test for simple awareness of new ideas. The questionnaire concerning 14 innovations was applied to a sample of 1,347 farmers. Even on an awareness basis, however, he found that 50 percent of the sample knew of five or fewer of the innovations. Significant correlations existed only among three of these.

Western sociologists involved in international research, while maintaining that adoption models have cross-cultural utility, are aware of problems in developing nations such as response variability, adopter categorization, definition and measurement of innovativeness and level of adoption, and general cross-cultural difficulties that would affect the application of the models (Doob 1958; Rogers and Rogers 1961; Rogers 1962; Lansburger and Saavedra 1967). One suggestion for improvement has come from Havens. Writing on diffusion in Colombia, he concluded that "...past studies concerning the use of new agricultural techniques have largely overlooked the structual arrangements within which adoption occurs. Therefore, they have not always proved helpful" (1970:50).

These researchers, however, have failed to consider adoption as an aspect of the broader process of modernization. It is the authors' theoretical argument that "adoption" is a function of both the level and timing of societal development. This is to say that increased modernization has a broadening effect on attitudes and resulting changes in the value system. The length of time that a society has experienced a new level of modernization benefits the integration of the value changes. To support this argument, the authors have focused on 180 farmers in nine villages in Togo, West Africa. These farmers were interviewed to measure their rates of adoption of new ideas and practices and to determine the intervening variables that enter into the explanation of adoption. A path analytic model was used to test the validity of previous theoretical assumptions of diffusion research and to support the argument of the societal development approach.

The Study Situation

The region in which the present study was conducted is "LaKara" (region of the Kara River), located in the Central Region of Togo, West Africa. It is one of the four economic regions into which the country has been divided and supports a comparatively dense population. An area of 20,000 square kilometers it is the home of 390,000 people mostly of the Cabrai, Losso, and Kotocoli tribes. The Kotocolis are (muslim) traders and not primarily interested in farming. The Lossos and Cabrais are quite similar in custom; however, the Cabrais dominate LaKara. They are, in fact, quite influential in the national government as a result of the military coup in 1966. LaKara is located about 250 to 400 kilometers from the coast line. The area includes four large administrative "circumscriptions" (sub-regional governmental units).

The Togolese population of LaKara is over 90 percent subsistence level farmers living in scattered villages throughout the area. Each circumscription has one "capital" town of several thousand people. Lama Kara, capital of the circumscription of Lama Kara, serves as the administrative center of the entire LaKara region.

The region is mostly savannah in physical nature, including both plains and mountainous areas. The Cabrai, as the principal tribe, have historically inhabited the mountains. They practice relatively advanced techniques agriculturally. The rocky hillsides have been terraced to protect the thin layer of topsoil from washing away. Stone-lined compost pits receive all crop and livestock residue. A system of private property has developed – perhaps because of the great energy requirements of hillside farming. While some lands of marginal fertility are periodically cultivated, they are "free" communal lands and not cared for so intensively. The communal land occupies almost half of the total land area of LaKara.

The *National Rural Development Service* was established in Togo in 1963. Presidential proclamation also created a Rural Development Center which soon began training agents to work in the *Service* in villages of the rural cantons. These agents, generally secondary school graduates from farm areas, were trained for two years in the knowledge and use of innovative ideas in agriculture. They also received courses in extension methods to aid in communicating these new ideas to the local population.

In 1969, after the first group of rural development agents had been in *Service* positions for three years, data were collected for the present study.

The five innovations examined in the calculation of adoption scores were among many introduced or encouraged by the rural development agents. They included use of chemical fertilizer, use of insecticide on stored grain, raising rabbits, planting a garden, and construction of a well. Adoption scores were calculated on the basis of the date that each of these ideas or practices was first used by each individual. Dates were plotted for each practice on adoption curves and "sub-scores" from one to five assigned, depending upon where each individual ranked in relation to his peers. The addition of these practice sub-scores constituted the adoption score for each respondent.

Methods

If the nature of the relationship between the rate of adoption and individual and structural variables is a function of the general process of modernization or societal development, it is suggested that the network of the relationships among the variables should be assessed in different settings that correspond to variations in societal development. Path analysis is one of the statistical techniques that offers the opportunity to show this network of relationships among several variables. This study attempts to analyze the direct impact of several individual and structural variables on the rate of adoption.

The data were collected during the spring of 1969. Five indicators were selected to represent individual and social characteristics of the farmers and one variable was introduced to report the structural differentiation among the villages.

These independent variables were chosen on the basis of previous research studies. They included:
1. Age (in years)
2. Education (years of school completed)
3. Cash crops raised (zero-one variable)
4. Ownership (scale score of household and transportation items)
5. Aspirations (scale score of intention to acquire household and transportation items)
6. Structural differentiation (scale score of communities' facilities)

The central, dependent variable in the study is the rate of adoption of several new ideas or farm practices. Measurement was according to traditional adoption scale methods (Rogers 1962) as explained.

On the basis of past studies and the current theoretical arguments in adoption research, a causal ordering of the key independent variables was hypothesized and graphically depicted in a path diagram. Age and differentiation were plotted at the left, indicating that they were not dependent upon other variables in the model nor upon each other. These were followed on the right by education and aspirations. Their placement indicated that they were preceded by and related to both age and differentiation. Aspirations was also plotted as being to the right of (i.e., preceded by) education. Next on the right in the model were plotted cash crops and ownership. Arrows were drawn from all of the preceding variables to these two variables. Finally adoption was placed on the extreme right, indicating that it was influenced by all of the preceding variables. Arrows indicating direct influences were drawn from age, cash crops, ownership and differentiation. The path coefficients called for in the model were calculated and "negligible or insignificant" paths were deleted.

The new path coefficients were then calculated as called for in the revised model. Finally, the adequacy of the model was assessed comparing the differences between the original correlations with the predicted values from the path coefficients. If the predicted correlations approached the original correlations, then the model could be assumed mathematically correct. If the predicted correlations deviated considerably from the original correlations, the model would be subject to question. While many researchers solve for the path coefficients called for in the path diagram, they frequently neglect to evaluate the overall adequacy of the model. Thus, the reader is frequently left with the question as to how good a fit the model is to social reality.

Findings

According to the path diagram tested in this study, age and structural differentiation are declared exogenous in the system. That is to say, no time or causality is assumed to operate between the two indicators. The other variables are declared endogenous to the system. That is to say, they are assumed to be determined or influenced by at least one of the preceding variables.

The path coefficients and the recursive equations for the adoption model applied to Togo were subsequently calculated. According to this model, 14 percent of the variation in the rates of adoption of the Togolese farmers was a function of four variables: age, raising of cash crops (usually grain sorghum) for income, ownership, and structural differentiation. Of the four variables, the strongest effect was that of cash crops (.28). The magnitude of this coefficient is an estimate of the net degree of change in the adoption scores of the farmers that would result from a one standard deviation change in the cash crops variable. Next in importance were ownership (.21), the age of the farmer (.18) and the structural differentiation among the villages (.13). Thus, the greater the age, the higher the amount of cash crops and ownership of capital goods, and the higher the structural differentiation, the higher the rate of adoption.

It should be noted that the importance of these findings obviously does not lie in the 14 percent of the variance explained. Rather, the path model indicates that the variables pointed out as being significantly associated with adoption in western situations were of limited utility in predicting adoption in the study situation. One problem may be that at this beginning stage of the development process a narrow range within the dependent variable made it difficult to discriminate significant differences among farmers.

The path model, however, provided other information not realized from the findings of traditional diffusion research. Of most importance was the finding that raising of cash crops and ownership were the variables most closely associated with adoption. Another example was the lack of direct effect of education on raising of cash crops for income. The ability to trace paths which led to adoption was considered at least as useful as tracing the traditional stages through which individuals pass in the adoption process. Such findings are useful for purposes of policy formulation. In the present study, the farmers who sold part of their crops to have a cash income were a different group from those who were high in ownership (notice the slight negative correlation between the two variables in Table 4). Thus, for a change agent interested in getting new ideas accepted, there were two groups of farmers indicated who would be most likely to be interested.

The relationship between ownership and adoption has been documented in many studies. But other relationships may be exposed by path diagrams that are not present at all levels of development. A possible example was the correlation between education and adoption in the present study. Being found insignificant, the path between these two variables was deleted. This was surprising since, as stated in Table 1, most previous research has found significant correlation between these two variables. In the Togolese situation, however, this lack of association is understandable. Education is generally considered as the first step out of agriculture. While traditional plots are maintained for family needs, those with more education have other sources of income, are less dependent upon agriculture, and can thus afford to be less interested in modern agricultural ideas.

Determination of the strength of association between the raising of cash crops and adoption provoked further examination. It was found that the raising and sale of cash crops was highly associated with knowledge of cash crop prices. Among those who sold part of their crops, all were aware of current prices. Of those who did not sell, however, only 9.4 percent were aware of the prices.

Knowledge of cash crop prices, in turn, was closely associated with the number of languages spoken by the respondents (see Table 3).

Testing the mathematical adequacy of the structural path diagram that was developed was one of the most important aspects in the use of this model. The zero-order correlation (Table 4) between any two variables in a recursive

Table 3
Number of Languages Spoken by Respondents and Knowledge of Cash Crop Prices

Languages Spoken	Percent Who Knew Cash Crop Prices
Local dialect only	3.17
Local dialect plus another language or dialect (usually French)	45.50

system can be expressed as the sum of the direct and indirect effects of the independent variables (j) and the dependent variables (i) which are transmitted via other independent variables (k) included in the system (Land 1969: 26). In a fully recursive model with all possible paths drawn, the value of the estimated correlation is identical to the value of the observed correlation. However, when a path or several paths are deleted, the direct effect is less. If the predicted correlation matrix approaches the value of the original correlation matrix, then the model can be considered mathematically correct. This technique of predicting the correlation matrix based on the path coefficients presented in Figure II was utilized in the present study.

The predicted correlation matrix from the path coefficients is shown in Table 4. If a comparison is made correlation by correlation between the two

Table 4
Predicted Correlation Matrix above diagonal, Original Correlation Matrix below diagonal

		x^1	x^2	x^3	x^4	x^5	x^6	x^7
Age	x_1	1.0	.1046	−.3401	−.2111	−.0910	.0288	.1736
Differentiation	x_2	.1046	1.0	.1189	.0907	−.1920	.2487	.1418
Education	x_3	−.3402	.0820	1.0	.3703	−.0742	.1768	−.0305
Aspirations	x_3	−.2112	.0787	.3681	1.0	−.2589	.5196	.0082
Cash Crops	x_5	−.0910	−.1888	−.0401	−.2571	1.0	−.2567	.1859
Ownership	x_6	.0288	.2425	.1613	.5174	−.2553	1.0	.1709
Adoption	x_7	.1736	.1414	−.1033	−.0198	.1866	.1706	1.0

matrices (the original correlation matrix is below the diagonal), it is possible to conclude that, although the traditional independent variables had little explanatory values, the structural path diagram utilized was theoretically and mathematically sound. The deviations between the two matrices are presented in Table 5.

Table 5
Deviations Between the Two Matrices Presented in Table 4

		x^1	x^2	x^3	x^4	x^5	x^6	x^7
Age	x_1	1.0	.0000	−.0001	−.0001	.0000	.0000	.0000
Differentiation	x_2		1.0	−.0369	−.0120	.0032	.0062	−.0004
Education	x_3			1.0	−.0022	−.0341	.0155	−.0728
Aspirations	x_4				1.0	−.0018	.0022	.0116
Cash Crops	x_5					1.0	−.0014	.0007
Ownership							1.0	.0003
Adoption	x_6							1.0

Source: Table 4

As can be seen in Table 5, there is only one deviation correlation higher than .05. It is the correlation between education and adoption. As explained earlier, the reason for the failure of the calculated path coefficient to reproduce the original correlation was the fact that in Togo education is not highly associated with agriculture. Educational attainment is actually considered as the first step out of the village system. These findings provide sound basis for the conclusions reached throughout the study. The remaining deviations are less than .05 which is considered a "good" maximum limit for deviations.

Summary

At the current level of development in the study area of Togo, several of the variable relationships consistently found in western research did not obtain. Education, for example, led respondents away from agriculture to new areas of interest. It is felt that the path analysis model helped to explain the complex pattern of association and focus upon other variable relationships than those traditionally examined. It was thought that the adoption variable would correlate significantly with structural differentiation supporting the argument that adoption is a function of both the level and timing of societal development. This relationship may have been affected by the limited range in the adoption variable. The relationship was somewhat stronger between ownership and structural differentiation. It is suggested that further research be conducted to investigate the full adoption process and elaborate the present theoretical structure to discriminate among societies at different levels or times of social and economic development.

In summary, it can be said that use of the western diffusion model in the study situation has resulted in unexpected and inconsistent findings. These inconsistencies may have been beneficial, however, in stimulating further development of the model and understanding diffusion as one aspect of the overall modernization process.

REFERENCES

DOOB, Leonard W.
    1958   "The Use of Different Test Items in Nonliterate Societies." *Public Opinion Quarterly* 21 (Winter): 499–504.

GARVER, Richard A.
    1962   "Communication Problems of Underdevelopment: Cheju-do, Korea, 1962." *Public Opinion Quarterly* XXVI (Winter):

HAVENS, A. Eugene and William L. FLINN (eds.)
    1970   *International Colonialism and Structural Change in Colombia.* New York: Praeger Special Studies in International Economics and Development.

INAYATULLAH
    1962   "Diffusion and Adoption of Improved Practices." Peshawar: W. Pakistan Academy for Rural Development.

KEITH, Robert F.
    1968   "An Investigation of Information and Modernization Among Eastern Nigerian Farmers." Technical Report 4, Project on the Diffusion of Innovations in Rural Societies. East Lansing: Michigan State University.

LAND, K. C.
    1969   "Principles of Path Analysis," in Edgar Borgetta (ed.), *Sociological Methodology.* San Francisco: Gossey-Bass.

LANSBERGER, Henry A. and Anotonio SAAVEDRA
    1967   "Response Set in Developing Countries." *Public Opinion Quarterly* 31 (Summer): 214–229.

LAUVIDGE, Robert J. and Gary A. STEINER
    1961   "A Model for Predicting Measurements of Advertising Effectiveness." *Journal of Marketing* 25.

North Central Rural Sociology Sub-committee for the Study of Diffusion of Farm Practices
    1955   "How Farm People Accept New Ideas." Special Report 15, Iowa Agricultural Extension Service.

ROGERS, Everett M.
    1962   *Diffusion of Innovations*. New York: Free Press of Glencoe.
ROGERS, Everett M. and L. Edna Rogers
    1961   "A Methodological Analysis of Adoption Scales." *Rural Sociology* 26 (December):
            325–336.
ROGERS, Everett M. and Floyd Shoemaker
    1971   *Communication of Innovations*. New York: The Free Press.
WILKENING, Eugene A.
    1956   "Roles of Communicating Agents in Technological Change in Agriculture." *Social
            Forces* 34.

3. Attitudes to Family Size Among Unmarried Junior Civil Servants in Acra.*

CHRISTINE OPPONG
University of Ghana, Legon, Ghana

The outstanding factor in the decline of population growth in a number of countries over the past eighty or more years has been what Banks has termed the "retreat from parenthood", the fact that many people no longer wish to have the numbers of children that their grandparents had (1954: 4). The earliest signs of these changes in attitudex and behaviour have been noted to take place among the upper middle classes and professionals, followed by civil servants, clerks, teachers and so on (Banks 1954: 5). This shift in attitudes and behaviour has already begun to be documented in Ghana. As Caldwell's study showed, with material collected, just ten years ago, socio-economic and urban-rural residence fertility differentials, though small, already appeared to have come into existence. Changes in the ways of life were seen to be making large families more burdensome for the urban middle class (Caldwell 1968: 187). In the sample he surveyed at that time the women were noted increasingly to regard *four* children as being the right number and men *six*. Ampofo's recent study of women teachers has confirmed these aspirations (1971: 106). It is this apparent retreat from parenthood, at least in its traditional proportions, which we wish to explore briefly in this report, among a set of people already singled out as being in the forefront of such changes by their type of occupations and place of residence.

The Data and the Design

The data discussed have been taken from a study primarily focused on married junior civil servants. Here we are concerned with the unmarried sec-

*   An earlier expanded version of this report was read at the third interdisciplinary Family
     Research Seminar held at the Institute of African Studies, Legon in March 1973, and will
     be appearing in *Legon Family Research Papers* No. 3. The study from which these data have
     been extracted was financed by a generous research grant from the Ghana National
     Family Planning Programme. Special thanks are due to Mr. S. Kwafo of the G.N.F.P.P.
     for his patient help and advice, during the course of the survey.

tion of the sample who were found to be without spouse or child. Our aim is to examine their attitudes concerning family size and family planning.

In research design this project partly resembles that of Caldwell's study of the urban elite (1968) as we are looking at two parallel samples, one of men and one of women. Though both samples are admittedly small, they are quite independent and so we may be able to use the results of one survey to support those of the other. The samples are analytical in nature, not representative, selected specifically for the exploration of variables correlated with differences in attitudes concerning family size and planning.[1] One sample comprised 78 nurses, the other 80 clerical officers.[2] It was precisely because Civil Servants and clerks have elsewhere been frequently noted to be in the forefront of the family size change process along with professionals, teachers and others that we chose them. In particular we were interested in finding out within this category those who were retreating or intending to retreat most rapidly from parenthood.

The data was collected through self-administered questionnaires. Almost all the men and women in the samples were between twenty and thrity years of age the average age of both samples being twenty five. The majority had attended secondary schools and all had been trained locally for their jobs. In both samples about a third were Ga, a third Akan and one sixth or fewer Ewe. Several came from the Northern and Upper Regions.

Over half of the women had fathers in clerical and professional type meployment compared to two fifths of the men. Thus in both spatial and socio-economic terms a large proportion of these two populations is mobile, the Ga members forming the indigenous population.

Family Size: desired/ideal

We found, as have those before us, that the desired family size for the majority was 4, as was the ideal family size (Caldwell 1968; Ampofo, 1971). The number of children wanted ranged between 2 and 6 among the women, and from 2 to 15 among the men, with a greater proportion of the men wanting five or more children (36% as compared with 17%). Ideas as to how many children would be too many or too few were similar, both samples considering an average of 8 children too many and 2 not enough (1.6. was the mean in the case of the nurses).

Nine out of ten nurses and three out of four clerks said that educated people in Ghana want smaller families now than they did twenty five years ago.

---

1 For a discussion of the value of the analytical sample in small scale research see Oppenheimer (1966: 9).
2 One set of respondents comprised clerical officers in nine ministerial departments in Accra. The overall response rate in this enquiry was 78%. The other set of respondents comprised nurses from eight hospital departments and clinics in Accra. In this survey the response rate was 85%. Many thanks are owed to the kind ministry and hospital staff who so graciously helped in the process of data collection. In this report only those nurses and clerical officers have been included who reported that they had never been married and had no children.

They saw the most important reasons for this as being economic and connected with the education and good care of the children, who were thus viewed by the majority as being increasingly expensive.

Family Planning Knowledge and Attitudes

The attitudes of the two samples to the spacing and planning of births in general and to the activities of the family planning programmes may be described as very positive. Knowledge of contraceptive methods was already widespread and about half intended to get advice on Family Planning in the future. The majority approved of timing and spacing of births. Only about one in three however thought that an educated women should stop child bearing at 35 and fewer than two thirds thought that a man should stop having children at the age of 45. Approval of cessation of child-bearing by the age of 35 for women was associated with smaller desired family size aspirations. Advocates of large and small family size norms both tended to be familiar with and approve of contraception.

In summary, the population under study desires numbers of children well below the traditional number, and they approve of the principles of family planning, birth spacing and the activities of the Family Planning programmes. In addition they already have before marriage a certain amount of technical knowledge, and desire more and are prepared to get advice in future.

Desired Family Size and Mobility

We shall now proceed to examine the proposition that there is likely to be an association between desired family size and mobility. As we stated at the outset we have samples of respondents, homogeneous with respect to educational level, marital status, child-bearing, age and type of occupation and place of residence, but heterogeneous with respect to place of origin and parental background variables, including father's occupation. In other words some of the nurses and clerks are locals others are in-migrants, mainly from the Akan and Volta areas; and while many have parents with lower levels of education and occupation than themselves, some are children of clerical workers and professionals. Thus we have a population which varies according to two important variables – social and spatial mobility – and can be classified accordingly into local non-mobiles (Ga with clerical and professional fathers); local socially mobiles, (Ga with manual and skilled fathers); migrant non-mobiles (Akan, Ewe etc. with clerical and professional fathers) and migrant mobiles (Kan and Ewe etc. with illiterate, manual and skilled fathers).

This classification is needed for our examination of a number of propositions concerning the relationship between mobility and fertility. As has recently been pointed out the relation between spatial mobility and fertility has long been the subject of population studies.[3] For example nearly thirty years ago Alva Myrdal was writing of feelings of insecurity, "a psychological translation of the greater mobility of modern times," as being one of the major active motives for family reduction (1945: 54-5); a theme which has been reexamined

in subsequent studies (eg. Kiser & Whelpton 1958: 1355, 1339). It has been
pointed out that the value of many studies concerning the effects of mobility
has been decreased by the failure to hold constant such important variables as
educational status, age, labour force participation, etc., so that the importance
of mobility itself could be assessed. In two recent articles such an attempt has
been made using Puerto Rican data from the 1960 census (Macisco et al. 1969;
1970). These analyses showed that married migrants had lower fertility rates
than married locals.

A number of studies have not been consistent with the hypothesis and it
has recently been suggested that, "Perhaps only when upward mobility represents a shift from the agricultural, traditional sector of society to the industrial
– rather than more or less "normal" upward movement within the industrial
sector – does it have a significant impact on fertility" (Mason, David et al. 1971:
45).

Table 1 indicates that the hypothesized relationship between family size
and mobility is worth exploring in this population of clerks and nurses. For it
is the non-mobile elements of the local Ga population who desire the largest
numbers of children and the socially and spatially mobile migrants, with non-
clerical or non-professional fathers, who want the smallest numbers of children.
In fact the most mobile sector of the population in both social and spatial terms
wants fewer children than it thinks to be ideal.

Table 1
Mean Number of Children desired and thought ideal by Social and Spatial Mobility and Occupation.

Social Mobility	Spatial Mobility							
	Locals				Immigrants			
	Nurses		Clerks		Nurses		Clerks	
	Desired	Ideal	Desired	Ideal	Desired	Ideal	Desired	Ideal
Non-mobile	4.3	4.2	5.3	5.3	3.9	4.0	4.3	4.3
Mobile	3.9	4.1	4.6	4.7	3.8	4.1	4.1	4.4

Once indicated such a possible correlation needs examining and explaining.
The next task is to "specify the chain of relations" that may produce such a
negative association, not only between migration or social mobility and fertility
but also between desired and ideal family size and mobility (Macisco et al.
1970). There are several hypotheses as to why such a connection should appear
and we shall examine one or two of them here:

a) that migrants are more receptive to modern contraceptive technology
(Macisco et al 1969: 178).

b) that mobile migrants are more achievement oriented than the local
populations (Macisco et al 1969: 178).

c) that economic constraints are the most important (as indeed Ghanaians

3 For a comment of this kind and an indication of the volume of such literature see Macisco
et al (1966).

themselves have pointed out eg. Caldwell 1968a: 95). Connected with this may greater feelings of economic insecurity (eg. Westoff *et al* 1961: 169).

Hypothesis I. Contraceptive Technology

As Table 2 indicates the evidence does not support the hypothesis that it is the most mobile sectors of the population who know the most and approve the most of Family Planning methods. The locals, both nurses and clerks, report that they have a wider knowledge of contraceptive techniques, and it is local nurses with the clerical and professional fathers who show the most approval of Family Planning.

Table 2
Attitude to Family Planning Score and Mean Number of Contraceptive Methods known by Social and Spatial Mobility and Occupation*

Social Mobility	Spatial Mobility							
	Locals				Immigrants			
	Nurses		Clerks		Nurses		Clerks	
	F.P. Score	Methods	F.P. Score	Methods	F.P. Score	Methods	F.P. Score	Methods
Non-mobile	6.4	4.2	5.8	2.9	6.0	3.0	6.3	2.3
Mobile	5.5	4.0	5.8	2.3	6.0	3.0	6.0	2.1

*   The F.P. score ranged from 0–7 and indicated degree of support for and approval of Family Planning. Coded responses to five separate questions were used.

Hypothesis 2. Achievement Orientation

As Table 3 indicates in three out of the four possible groups the more mobile do exhibit higher mean scores on an index measuring their readiness to move to get promotion or do a course of further studies. In the fourth case, that of the clerks with clerical and professional parents there is no difference in the mean scores. However readiness to seek promotion and small family size desires did not appear to be correlated.

Table 3
Mean Score on Aspirations Index by Social and Spatial Mobility and Occupation

Social Mobility	Spatial Mobility			
	Locals		Immigrants	
	Nurses	Clerks	Nurses	Clerks
Non-mobile	2.1	3	2.5	3
Mobile	2.1	2.5	2.6	2.8

Hypothesis 3. Economic Constraints and Insecurity

The remaining hypothesis is that concerning the role of economic constraints and insecurity. On the whole the migrants felt themselves to be in
worse financial predicaments than the locals. Three out of the four groups
classified themselves on average as being in an unfavourable position. The locals
all classified themselves as fair on average. Moreover respondents reporting a
desire for large families of five or more were more likely than the rest to assess
their financial situations as being good.

It is not surprising that greater financial problems should become apparent
among the migrants upon whom falls the burden of finding accommodation and
the means of livelihood in a relatively strange environment. The problems of
migrant Ghanaian workers have already been vividly described by Caldwell
and others (1969: 97–8). One point stressed about the urban migrant is his
frequent financial help to kin, both those back home and those who also come
to find work in the town (Caldwell 1969: 97–8). We may therefore examine
the content of the financial exchanges between the respondents and their kin to
see if there are observable differences between the migrants and the rest.

Table 4

*Mean Scores of Indices of Financial Help to and from Kin by Social and Spatial Mobility and
Occupation**

Social Mobility	Spatial Mobility							
	Locals				Immigrants			
	Nurses help		Clerks help		Nurses help		Clerks help	
	to kin	from kin	to kin	from kin	to kin	from kin	to kin	from kin
Non-mobile	3.5	1.6	3.6	2.5	3.6	2.0	2.9	1.4
Mobile	3.1	1.6	4.0	1.8	4.1	1.2	4.2	1.6

*   These indices were based upon responses to 8 questions.

Table 4 shows us that there are indeed differences and that they are in the
expected direction: that is, those who are mobile in both social and spatial
terms are the ones who are shouldering the greatest burden of help to kin including parents, siblings, nephews and nieces. At the same time these same
people are receiving the least financial help from kin. Possibly this flow of help
to others and very little in return may be an important factor affecting these
individuals' assessments of their financial situations.

It would seem on the basis of these tentative findings that it may be very
instructive to pursue further, both in breadth and in depth, these leads regarding the social factors in the life situations of the socially and spatially mobile
elements of the urban population, which may be motivating them to prefer
family sizes smaller than those desired by their peers, whose life histories are
characterised by greater geographical and social stability. Especially fruitful
areas for exploration would appear to be their feelings of economic insecurity

and strain, and a detailed analysis of the flows of resources to and from kin. By so doing we may continue to piece together more of the links in the chain of evidence connecting together such important social facts as migration and family size, and further illuminate the profound effects that migration has upon family life in Ghana (Caldwell 1969: 213).

REFERENCES

AMPOFO, D. A.
    1971   "The Knowledge, Attitudes and Practice of Family Planning among the Women Teachers in Primary Schools in Accra." *Ghana Medical Journal* 10 (2): 100–108.
BANKS, J. A.
    1954   *Prosperity and Parenthood* – A study of Family Planning among the Victorian Middle Classes. London: Routledge and Kegan Paul.
CALDWELL, J. C.
    1968a   "The Demographic Implications of Education in a Developing Country: Ghana," in Addo, et al (eds.), *Ghana Population Studies No. 2*. Symposium on Population and Social Economic Development in Ghana. Legon: Demographic Unit.
CALDWELL, J. C.
    1968b   *Population Growth and Family Change in Africa: The New Urban Elite in Ghana*. Canberra: Australian National University Press.
CALDWELL, J. C.
    1969   *African Rural Urban Migration. The Movement to Ghana's Towns*. Canberra: Australian National University Press.
KISER, C. V. and P. K. Whelpton
    1958   "Social and Psychological Factors Affecting Fertility." *Milbank Memorial Fund Quarterly* XXXVI (3): 282–329.
MACISCO, J. J., et al
    1969   "Migration Status, Education and Fertility in Puerto Rico: 1960." *Milbank Memorial Fund Quarterly* XLVII (2): 167–187.
MACISCO, J. J., et al
    1970   "The Effect of Labour Force Participation on the Relation between Migration Status and Fertility in San Juan, Puerto Rico." *Milbank Memorial Fund Quarterly*.
MASON, K. O., A. S. David, et al
    1971   *Social and Economic Correlates of Family Fertility: A Survey of the Evidence*. R.T.T. North Carolina.
WESTOFF, C., et al
    1961   *Family Growth in Metropolitan America*. New Jersey: Princeton University Press.
OPPENHEIMER, A. N.
    1966   *Questionnaire Design and Measurement*. Heinemann.

4. The Communal Rituals of Korean Shamanism

JUNG YOUNG LEE

University of North Dakota, Grand Forks, U.S.A.

Since Korean shamanism has been centered around the family life which constitutes the basic unity of the religious community, most of its rituals are carried out in the homes. Thus, today the communal rituals are rather rare and insignificant compared to the family rituals.[1] However, in most cases the communal rituals have the same features as the family rituals because of the tribal unit of community life in rural areas. Most rural villages are made up of families of the same ancestral root. They are often the extensions of family life. Thus the communal rituals are important to preserve the unity of the tribe and the village together. However, through the influence of Western civilization and the growing urbanization the communal rituals seem to vanish from sight. Nevertheless, their essence seems to be expressed in some other forms of their life in the community. Thus it is important to study the communal rituals of Korean shamanism to understand the ethos of Korean society. Before examining the actual process of communal rituals, let us observe the sacred places where the rituals are to be held in the village.

As we have already indicated, Korean villages in early days were primarily based on certain tribes. Even though some villages had many different tribes, it is commonly known that one tribe seemed to dominate the others. Because of tribal orientation, the homes are usually concentrated in a certain location where agriculture seems to dominate other businesses. Each village usually has an entrance and an exit where usually the sacred objects are located to protect the village. The sacred objects which create the sacred places are mainly age-old trees, a pile of stones and long poles to which are attached white papers or fabrics. Besides these, sacred places are created by the erection of carved wooden poles which are known as *Chunha-Dăjangkun*. They look like the totem poles standing at the entrance of the village. Since this is quite peculiar to shamanistic tradition in Korea, let us take some time to examine this sacred object.

It is probable that the so-called *Chunha-Dăjangkun* might be derived from the idea of *Jangsung*, which is known in the literature of old Korea during the three kingdoms and *Koryŏ* period. In the writings the *Jangsung* is known as *Jangsang*, which is expressed in terms of *Jangsang-Piŏ*, *Jangsang-Piŏchu*, *Jangsang-Piŏtop*, and others.[2] Since *Jangsung* is almost identical with *Dăjangkun*, it is possible that the word "*Chunha*", which means under the heaven, was added to it later. Whatever the origin of the word "*Chunha-Dăjangkun*", it is important that it became a symbol for protecting homes and villages from the evil spirits. Therefore, it is often called by many different names such as *Salmegi*, *Sŭsalmegi*, *Sŭgumagi*, *Sŭsaldok*, and *Bucksŭ*. For example, the word "Salmegi" might be derived from the protection of the destructive spirit or *Salbang*. The idea of *Sumalmegi* might come from the notion of protecting people from the destructive water. Thus it has its origin in *Sŭlsalbang*. The word "*Sŭgumagi*" might come from the word "*Sugubang*", which means to protect the water hole. Therefore, if we look at the derivation of these words, it is clear that the people in early days were afraid of the destructive spirits, especially the destructive water and wind. In order to ask for protection from these powerful spirits, they

---

1 At the end of the Koryŭ dynastry and during the Yi dynasty (about 500 years) there were various shamanistic rituals carried out by the government. Moreover, until Kycha came to rule Korea, it is believed that shamanism and the government were united. However, after the fall of the Yi dynasty to Japan, the communal rituals seemed to disappear while the family rituals still persist strongly in rural areas.

2 See *Samkuck-Yŭsa*, Chapter 4.

set the *Chunha-Dǎjangkun*, which is very strong, to protect them from these spirits.

If we believe that the idea of *Chunha-Dǎjangkun* came from the original notion of *Jangsǎng*, then it was related to various wooden and stone towers in early days. In the *Koryō* period the Jangsang was known in wooden poles, stone tablets and stone piles. Also there were many kinds and colors of *Jangsǎng* at that time. The sacred place created by the stone piles, which are still found, might come from the idea of *Jangsǎng*. Moreover, the sacred tree, which is usually the oldest and tallest in the village, might be one of the *Jangsǎng* symbols. Even the erection of pagodas or *Top* was to symbolize the meaning of *Jangsǎng* in early days. Therefore, it is possible that *Jangsǎng* became the primordial symbol of other sacred symbols in Korean shamanism. Thereby the importance of *Chunga-Dǎjangkun*, which is directly related to *Jangsǎng*, cannot be questioned.

Various forms of *Jangsǎng* are even found in our time. In most cases we can see the two typical wooden poles. On the upper part of these poles are human faces and on the bodies words such as *Chunha-Dǎjangkun* and *Chiha-Yiujangkun*, or *Sangwun-Chujangkun* and *Hawun-Dǎngjankun*. They represent both the male and female *Jangsǎng*. Sometimes there is a single wooden pole, which is often called *Dockbucksu*. Occasionally the erect stone or rock becomes the symbol of *Jangsǎng*. These symbols of *Jangsǎng* are located in the entrance of the village, at the entrance of shrines or even roadsides, so that people can spend a moment in their sacred presence. However, it must be pointed out that the symbols of *Jangsǎng* do not uniquely belong to the shamanistic tradition of Korea. They are seen in almost all other shamanistic practices such as Mongolian and Siberian shamanistic communities.

Now let us return to the sacred place where the community rituals are to be performed. As we said, the sacred places are created by erecting symbols of *Jangsǎng*, which literally means "long life". Just as the house has a certain place for rituals, the village has a definite place which is regarded as sacred. However, when there is no altar place, it is always possible to create one by erecting the symbols of *Jangsǎng*. In most cases the village makes use of a market place for the temporary needs of community rituals. Once the place of ritual is decided, the process of making the place sacred begins. When the ceremony is over, the place becomes no longer sacred and returns to its secular place. Perhaps one of the peculiar characteristics of Korean shamanistic rituals is the flexibility of its accommodation.

The ritual for the community is known by many names such as *Dongje, Dongshinje, Daidongsinsa, Daidongchisung, Sanje, Sanchunje, Dangje, Dangsanje, Sunwhangje, Tochije, Garije, Rosinje, Jangsungje Mocksinje, Bukunje, or Chunje.* There are many other different names than we have mentioned. However, *Dongje* or the ritual of the village is most commonly used. It is important to notice that the various names are not empty words. Each possesses its own unique character which cannot be generalized. Each tribal village seems to have its peculiar mores which are not easily dismissed. Since shamanism became the foundation of Korean civilization, it is important to remember that the peculiar forms of mores and customs are closely associated with the shamanistic rituals. Because their rituals are somewhat varied according to different provinces, there is no way to generalize the phenomena of community rituals as a whole. Each village may have different gods and different forms of rituals. Therefore, in most cases professional shamanesses who are invited for the ritual can assist the master of ceremonies who is elected by the village. In the family ritual a woman acts as master of ceremonies. However, in case of the community ritual, a man becomes master of ceremonies. Here the selection of a man as master of ceremonies is due to social responsibility which is usually attributed to the men. When the ritual is held for the community, it is no longer a domestic affair and, therefore, a man is elected for the job.

It is important to distinguish between the ritual which is participated in by professional shamanesses and that in which they do not assist. In both cases, however, the master of ceremonies is a man who is elected by the people. When professional shamanesses are used for the ritual, it is called "*Kut*" rather than *Je*. Both of them make use of the same word, but are pronounced differently to distinguish between the non-professional and professional rituals. For example, in the northern province the non-professional ritual is called *Dangje*, and the professional ritual is called *Dangkut*. Let us look first at the community ritual which does not make use of professional shamanesses.

Since the community ritual cannot be generalized, we must look at a certain case study of one particular situation. This case study was done at Hucksuck Village which is located on the outskirts of Seoul.[3] The entire population of this village when the case study was done was about five hundred people. At the entrance of the village there are two old trees, one being taller than the other. The taller one, which is on the right side, is the symbol of male god, and the short one on the left is the tree of female god. There is also a black rock, from which the name of the village may be taken, which is called *Sinbău* or the sacred rock. Next to this rock is a tree which is called the sacred tree. Part of this sacred tree was used to build a shrine which is called *Hangang-Sinsa*. This shrine is dedicated to the god known as *Sangsandodang-Sinrung*, and this area is called *Sanchi-Sundang*. Funds to pay for the ritual are gathered by the families in the village. The date is based on the lunar calendar. The small ritual is held on July first and the great ritual on October first of every year. Those who participate in the actual ceremony of the ritual are about seven or eight people who are selected from among those people who are regarded as clean. If a man has died or a child been born in that year, the family is regarded as unclean. Also, all the women are regarded unclean for this particular ceremony. Thus all the men who participated are to be selected from a clean house. Among them one man is selected to be the master of ceremonies. In most cases the mayor of the village is asked to be the head of it. However, those who have been selected to perform the ritual are responsible for carrying out not only the preparation of the offerings, but other ritualistic procedures as well. It takes a few days to prepare for the great ritual on October first. They put out the lefthand twisted ropes of straw to signify the sanctity of the altar area and white papers are placed along the ropes to prevent other people from intruding in it. They put the *Jangsăng* at the entrance of the village to signify that the great ritual is to be held. They put a white cloth on the sacred tree to signify the presence of the spirit. Under the sacred tree many offerings are made. Some of them are beef, rice cakes, white cooked rice, grains, persimmons, and other fruits. Incense is

---

3 This case study was made by Akiba and described in Chijo Akamatzu, *Chusen Husok no Kenkyu*, Vol. II, pp. 204ff.

burned and wine is poured in a cup before they bow down twice. Again the wine is poured in a couple of times when they worship the spirits. The master of ceremonies then starts to read the prayer while other participants continue to bow down. When the reading of the prayer is over, there is a service in unison. Next, seven participants give honor to the gods by pouring wine into the cup. Each of them exchanges the wine with the gods and turns the cup about three times upon the fire of the burning incense and then bows down twice after taking the wine. This is, therefore, much like a communion service by those who represent the people of the village. When this communion service is over, they take the white papers, amounting to the number of families of the village, and fold them one by one in the form of a tube and burn them before the people, the master of ceremonies calling the name of the family being represented in the white paper. While the tube of paper is burning with candle fire on the altar, he says, "This is the *Shogi* of so and so. Please bless the family. Let the *Shogi* go up!" If the *Shogi* or burning paper goes upward, it is a sign of good fortune. The higher the ash goes, the greater the fortune of that family will be. When the ash comes down without going up, it is a sign of misfortune. When the burning of papers is over, the foods and wine are shared by the families represented in the ritual. Then they take them to their homes where they enjoy the communion meal together.

As we said, at the entrance of the village *Jangsăng* is erected for the ritual. Actually, the real service begins with the erection of this *Jangsăng* in the early morning. Those who are elected to carry out the ritual go to the *Jangsăng* and place a simple ceremonial sign and bow down before it. This *Jangsăng* which is placed before the village is made of the sacred tree to prevent evil spirits from entering the village during the service. The carving of *Jangsăng* begins the night before the day of the great ritual. It usually takes an entire evening to complete. It must be ready by the early morning of the day of the ritual. Once it is placed, it lasts a year until the next year's ceremony. It stands to protect the village people for an entire year until replaced by the new *Jangsăng*.

As we have seen, the community ritual by non-professional people, which is called *Dongje*, is rather simple. However, the ritual which is assisted by professional shamanesses is much more glamorous than the one we just described. Let us now look at the village *Kut* at Duckmulsan, which is located north of Seoul. Duckmulsan is a small village which is surrounded by rocky mountains. On the slope of the mountains there is a sacred tree which is called *Maul-Sonang*. The area surrounding the sacred tree is known as sacred ground and is protected by the village. Under the tree there are blue dresses for the gods of the village, countless straw shoes and white papers. The small straw shoes are often dedicated to the tree before climbing up the mountain. There are statues of three Buddhas and other divine spirits next to the sacred tree. There is also a divination stone for a safe journey. When the stone is erected, it is understood to be good fortune. However, if it does not stand, it is a warning for the coming journey up the mountain side. Within this area of the sacred tree and stones can be seen the village which consists of about forty houses. There is no special place of interest in the village other than the sacred places. There is a small shrine which is closely protected by the people in the village. It has a tile roof which is colorfully designed and has a small courtyard which is surrounded by a fence. The central figure of the shrine is no doubt *Chaiyung-Janggun* who stands in the center of the sanctuary. A few women's statues are standing along with him. Next to him are his children, one girl and two boys who bow before him. On his left side is a statue of *Byulsung-Janggun*. Besides them there are many other statues such as Three Buddhas, the god of the Seven Stars, the Dragon King, the god of the Mountain, and others. On the sides of the entrance sacred bells are hung from the ceiling. There are also interesting items such as a blue dragon sword, small and large mirrors, lamp stands and other sacred instruments.

Further inside the village there is a place where the wife of *Chaiyung-Janggun* is dedicated. This is called *Buindang*, which is rather insignificant compared to *Janggun's* shrine. Inside of the shrine there is a statue of the woman or *Buin-* Behind it there is a large sacred mirror on the wall. Beside the mirror are statues of Buddha and other divines. There is an area of ground which is called *Bon. hang-To* or *Dodang-To* where many rituals are held. This ground is sacred because of a sacred tree which is know as *Bonhang-Namu* or *Dodang-Namu*. This tree is grown inside the area of the sacred rock and regarded as the most sacred object in the village. Because of this sacred tree, the sacred ground becomes the place where the most important communal ritual, *Dodang-Kut*, is held biannually.

Dogan-Kut then is held once every two years. It is usually held in the third month according to the lunar calendar. In selecting the date of that month, the people in the village are called to the sacred ground, *Dodang-To*, where they are asked to write down numbers instead of names on papers. The papers are wrapped around small beans and thrown into water. Of these, the two beans that float best are selected. Those represented by these two beans become the masters of the ceremony. The date of the ritual is then decided according to their fate numbers or *Unsu*. The day of the ceremony is supposedly decided on the 14th of March. When the date is chosen, it is posted on the *Dodang-Namu* or the sacred tree. From March first to the thirteenth eating of beef is prohibited and wine is brewed for the sacred use. When the thirteenth comes, the professional shamanesses start to make offerings to different gods. Men in the village take baths and go to worship *Chaiyung-Janggun* who is brought to the sacred ground and placed in *Kutgak*. After the worship they pour wines to him. This *Kutgak* is made of timbers which are supplied by each home of the village. A list of every family and its wishes is found on the altar. Since the main purpose of this ritual is to ask the gods for blessings for each home, it is most important to list the names of those who are involved in the ritual.

As we have indicated, the ceremony actually begins a day before the actual day of the ritual. On the afternoon of March 13, a day before the actual date, we can see the people carrying the poles with the colorful paper attached. People fill the streets as well as other sacred shrines and places in the village. In fact, everyone in the village seems to be in the streets. One of the typical affairs on the afternoon of the day before the ritual is a colorful parade of people with the shamanesses. Usually the chief shamaness leads the parade, and other shamanesses follow her. Then the group of young people, who wear long hats called *Sanmo* and put white bands on their foreheads, follow the shamanesses. These young people are called *Kutchungba* and they hold hands with those who call themselves *Sadangba* and march in the street, beating drums to attract the attention of other people in the street. When they come to a certain place, they call everyone and start to sing and dance. When the music and dance are over, the chief shamaness starts to tell the old legend of the gods. People then offer food and money. It ends with the worship of their ancestral gods in unison. When the parade is over the shamanesses visit every house and offer prayers. The people in turn give money or crops to the shamanesses as a means of their support for the shrines and the gods. This visit is often called *Gemung-Dori* or evangelistic mission. Thus the day before the actual ceremony is spent in parade and visitation of homes in the village.

When evening comes the sacred ground is filled with women in white clothes. Around the *Kutgak* where the principal god, *Chaiyung-Janggun*, is temporarily placed, the crowd of women go through the ritual of purification. In the courtyard of the *Janggun* shrine there is a bonfire surrounded by the groups of people from the village. Inside the altar room are burning candles reminding them of the sacred presence of their ancestral spirits. As darkness deepens, people tend more and more to forget themselves and enter into a mood for dancing. Thus the evening ends with the joy of dance and music which is an important part of the community ritual of seasonal offerings to the ancestral gods. However, everything they do is part of the sacred ritual. During this evening at least two *Kuri* or ceremonial steps out of the twelve *Kuri* of *Chungsin-Kut* or the ritual of seasonal offerings are completed.

Early the following morning the main portion of the ritual begins. Since this is the actual day of the ritual selected by the village, it is the most important day for the people. Among other ceremonies, worship of *Bunhang-Sin* or the great god of the village is the most significant event. This worship service is held inside of the *Kutgak* where *Chaiyung-Janggun* is placed for this ritual. People become very serious at this time. Shamanesses wear red hats and red clothes for this service. The people are led by the shamanesses to perform a delicate service of prayer and worship. When it is over, the shamanesses perform divinations to find out the will of *Bunhang-Sin*. The people then dedicate their offerings of money to the altar. On the fifteenth of March there is the so-called *Madang-Kut*, which literally means the ceremony of dedication of the ground. The chief shamaness takes a sword and places it on her shoulder and starts to dance in front of the *Kutgak*. This ceremony is known as *Janggun Kuri* because it is to please *Janggun* or the general. When the dance is complete, there is also a divination using a metal container which is supported by a jar into which people are asked to throw coins. The next is known as *Makdong* or curtain boy, who with *Janggun* shoots arrows in all directions. It signifies the actual destruction of evil spirits in the surrounding area. The final *Kuri* is *Ditchan* which concludes the ritual. At this time two shamanesses take trumpet-shaped carriers on their backs into which are placed the cooked grains and pork. They go out into the street and throw them on both sides of the street to feed the evil spirits.

When the final *Kuri* is over, it is almost evening. The *Kutgak* is torn down and *Chaiyung-Janggun* is carried to the original location in the shrine. People gather together, taking the sacred poles, beating drums, and walk around the sacred ground about three times from the right and then another three times from the left. After this they scatter over the sacred places and enjoy the sunset and beautiful spring weather. While the people enjoy the sunset, the elected officials of the ritual, assisted by the professional shamanesses, prepare for the *Pulsa-Kut* which is a service of dedication to the Buddha. It is prepared in front of the sacred spring after the ground is completely cleansed. The white rice cakes are dedicated on the Buddha rock. Shamanesses wear ritualistic hats and long robes and dance around with the music. While they dance, others set up a great caldron into which is poured the sacred water. The sacrificial cows and pigs are cut in pieces by the elected officials and placed in the caldron where they are boiled. By that time the sun is already set and the area becomes dark. When everything is cooked, it is dedicated to the Buddha and then is shared by the people who participated in the ritual. This is the last but the most meaningful service of communion, not only with the Buddha and the ancestral spirits, but with friends. This last supper is eaten under dim oil lamps in the open air. The fresh mountain air and the beautiful moon rising from the East conspire to fill the hearts of the people with the presence of *Numen*.

As we have observed, it takes a full three days to complete the community ritual of seasonal offerings. The main purpose of this ritual becomes clear when we examine the main figures to whom the offerings and services are rendered. It is no doubt the importance of *Bunhang-Sin* or the god of the village, or the god of the ground, who becomes the center of worship. The temporary sanctuary is created in front of the *Bunhang-Namu* in order to make the god of the village or *Bunhang-Sin* in the center of the worship. Another important figure is *Chaiyung-Janggun* who represents the defender of the village. He actually presides over the ritual since he is moved to the temporary sanctuary on the sacred ground. It is probable that the two gods, the god of the village ground and the god of protection, are united in the ritual because of the importance of protection of the village from disease and other disastrous effects. Thus the protector becomes as important as the owner of the ground. We see that the combination of these two gods is symbolized in the combination of two powers, the power of heaven and of earth. The *Chaiyung-Janggun* represents the heavenly father and *Bunhang-Sin* represents the earth mother who has produced the village ground. Therefore, the former always takes an active and creative position while the latter takes a passive and receptive role.

It is important to notice that the professional shamanesses always take the subsidiary role in the ritual. Just as they assist the house master in the house rituals, they also assist the officials of the ceremony who have been elected by the people in the village. In the process of election the method of divination is used. It is important that the selection of representatives be by the will of god, rather than of people. Therefore, it is believed that god's will is known in a means of chance or the divination which becomes the vehicle of divine expression. In this respect from the beginning to the end man is receptive to the divine will. Therefore, the basic hypothesis is that the spirit is yang and matter is yin, or the divine is yang and people are yin in their roles. This basic hypothesis is clearly expressed in almost all forms of shamanistic ritual, since what is happening in the world of matter presupposes the activity of the spirit. However this idea is not something unique to shamanistic practices. It is a common trait of almost all the primitive religions in the world. We also observe that shamanism is synthesized with Buddhism. As we have seen, *Pulsa-Kut* or the ceremony for the Buddha becomes the cumulative effect in the community ritual of seasonal offerings. Buddha is elevated above other divine spirits and is seemingly independent of the others. The ancestral spirits are intimately related to shamanistic religion because of the national ancestor, *Dangkun*, or the founder of the Korean people, who was a great shaman himself.[4] However, Buddhism, coming from a foreign country, never became a genuine expression of shamanism, even though it was added to existing traditions. In other words, the synthesis between Korean shamanism and Buddhism is not as complete as the synthesis between Korean shamanism and Korean ancestor worship. We have noticed it clearly because in this particular case the service for the Buddha is separately performed from the community *Chungsin-Kut*. It is not always true that the *Pulsa-Kut* is separately performed from the rest of the shamanistic rituals. It is often observed, however, that the foreign root of Buddhism has caused a somewhat superficial homogeneity in the growth of Korean shamanistic tradition.

4   Kim Tuk-hwang, *Hankuck-Chongkyo-Sa*, Seoul, 1963, pp. 17ff.

Review Article*

Cheikh Anta Diop, *The African Origin of Civilization. Myth or Reality.* Edited
and Translated by Mercer Cook. Lawrence Hill and Co., New York, 1974, pp.
xvii, 316, illustrations, bibliography, index.

The beginnings of this book were avowedly political. C. A. Diop, in his
preface, informs us: "I began my research in September 1946; because of our
colonial situation at that time, the political problem dominated all others."
The first published outline of his views on "African anteriority" appeared in an
article, "Toward a Political Ideology in Black Africa" which appeared in 1953
in the organ of the RDA students in Paris, *Voie de l'Afrique Noire (loc. cit.)*.

After that appeared *Nations Nègres et Culture*, Paris, 1955, and *Anteriorité
des civilisations Nègres*, Paris, 1967. The present volume is composed of selections
of chapters from these, plus "Reply to a Critic," and a new preface and conclusion by the author. The translator-editor has added some notes in addition
to those of the author.

The Black African Political Ideology as set forth by Diop involved not only
ideas on "strategy and tactics in the struggle for national independence",
"concepts on the creation of a future federal state, continental or subcontinen-
tal," "thoughts on African social structures", "the past and future of our
languages [and] their utilization in the most advanced scientific fields as in
education generally", but also "all our ideas on African history" *(loc. cit.)*.

The "decolonization of history" has since become a familiar movement and
has helped to alter the kind of history once written by Cultru, Claridge, Burns
and others who had had experience in colonial service, missionary churches, or
other enterprises in Africa. But this has applied mainly to the modern period of
interaction between Africans and Europeans and the immediately previous
period as represented by Europeans to have existed on the eve of their arrival.
Diop goes back far beyond that – to ancient Egypt.

What does Pharonic Egypt have to do with the struggle for independence of
Senegal and the rest of Black Africa? The answer was already given by Africa-
nus Horton in 1868 in his *Vindication of the African Race:* "Why should not the
same race who governed Egypt once more stand on their legs and endeavor to
raise their characters in the scale of the civilized world?"

Few believed that the colonized Black Africans were the same race as that
which had governed ancient Egypt, and despite Horton's exhortation progress
toward independence was slow. Diop set out to convince the world that not
only was Egypt a black civilization, but that it was the first civilization and
that everyone else obtained the beginnings of their civilization from Egyptian
Blacks. Thus white barbarians had once received the gift of enlightenment from
Negroes but were now so ungrateful as to conquer and exploit them. This gave
the struggle against colonialism a poignancy and tended to make any statement
by a white suspect, no matter what the subject.

Independence for the French territories and for much of the rest of Black
Africa came in 1960. There must be more to the argument of Black "anteriority"
than mere political strategem or we would not have had the publication in 1967
of further argumentation nor the publication now of this translation.

Cheikh Anta Diop is virtually alone in attempting to relate in an extensive and systematic way the data concerning ancient Egypt and that of the rest of Africa, a problem that demands attention. One reason why so few others have ventured on this task is that the scope is so enormous and the nature and variety of technical problems is therefore so formidable. The result of neglect of this field is that hardly anyone can claim full competence to assess Diop's formulation (nor do I); most Egyptologists know or care little about the rest of Africa (though this seems, perhaps, to be changing) and most Africanists know little of Egyptology (and there's little indication of change here). Nonetheless, everyone who is interested in the overall history must deal with this challenge.

Were the early Egyptians Negroes? Possibly. Diop is not the first to assert this argument, and some of his predecessors were white. Or was the Nile Valley north of the cataracts an area of mixture of races in predynastic times, as some Egyptologists believe, or was the population white as many have simply assumed?

That some mixture has occurred at some time prior to the present is undeniable, but were the Blacks there first and did whites come in after the pharonic civilization began, or did the whites later bring in mercenaries and laborers from the south, or had the mixture begun before civilization arose?

Since some, but only some, of the skeletons in predynastic graves have been reported to be negroid, it could be argued that Egyptian culture from the beginning was the creation of a racially mixed population.

Another position is that the problem is a false one. Some contemporary physical anthropologists argue that as race is a combination of traits (skin pigmentation, hair, form, skeletal proportions and other anthropometric measurements), there will be centers where the combination appears in most individuals (as on the Guinea Coast, East Asia, and southern Scandinavia) but in many communities in the Old World between these relatively homogeneous areas the tendency is toward heterogeneity as far as any standard racial categorization is concerned. Thus the "gene pool" of the population of Egypt need not be made to conform to a standard of the norms of any of the more or less homogeneous areas, and in any case no "gene pool" is totally isolated from others.

Some readers might want to note the cautions that this anthropological position implies, but it is perhaps irrelevant to Diop's position because while he doesn't make explicit his definition of Negro his usage suggests that it is broad and is probably therefore not dependent on the physical anthropologist's concept of a combination of traits. In any case, the physical anthropologist is not concerned with some of the problems which interest the historian. What was the nature of the affinities of the Egyptians, biologically and culturally? The answer may have to come in percentages, or broken down to deal with designated traits separately, but an answer of some kind is required: historians are not likely to be satisfied with the physical anthropologists defining the problem out of existence.

This reviewer does not know which of the possibilities will turn out to be the truth and he would be just as happy if Diop's claim is correct but is not satisfied that the arguments are conclusive. It would be fatuous to deny that Blacks had a role in Egypt from an early time but that all Egyptians were then Black remains open to question.

The next crucial question for the Diop thesis is: Was Egypt the earliest civilization?

Elliot Smith tried in many books to demonstrate that this was so, and that thence diffused all over the world traits of Egyptian invention, but his views on innumerable particulars (and more seriously his methods) have been refuted by many specialists. His name is today almost a symbol for ridicule for a mono-maniacal dogmatist.

Cheikh Anta Diop's position, of course, does not depend on Elliot Smith's; the lines of reasoning and development of the argument are quite different, but the expectation of success may be somewhat affected by that failure.

For a long time, due to the sequence of recovery of knowledge by Egyptolo-gists and Assyriologists, it seemed that Egypt was the first state to emerge. Problems of correlating the chronologies recorded by the ancients persisted and archeological inference had to be integrated into the textual data. This problem was attacked by several archeologists, each a specialist on a particular area, in *Relative Chronologies in Old World Archeology*, edited by Robert W. Ehrich (Chi-cago, 1954). A chart (Fig. 1, p. 16) shows Mesopotamia in the Protoliterate Period while Egypt is only beginning the predynastic Gerzean Period. The Mesopotamian Protoliterate Period begins considerably later than the Ubaid Period (chart on p. 52). [The Ubaid Period ushered in the Urban Revolution, *i.e.*, the first city-states.]

The limitations of the symposium format render the Ehrich publication far from being wholly satisfactory, but it was published under the auspices of the American Anthropological Association and the Archeological Institute of America and has enjoyed respect from these professions.

Henri Frankfort, five years before the original publication of *Nations Nègres*, had published *The Birth of Civilization in the Near East* in which he pointed out that cylinder seals where found in Egypt in the late predynastic era. Since cylinder seals were made earlier in Mesopotamia and continued long after to be made there but appear in Egypt only on the eve of the Dynastic Period and soon after disappear as a trait of the Pharonic civilization, "it would be perverse to deny that the Egyptians followed the Mesopotamian example" (p. 123). Certain Mesopotamian art motifs also made the transition to the Nile but, like the cylinders, did not persist there. Egypt already had a virile culture, Frank-fort admits, and was "capable of imposing conformity upon all comers" (p. 122). But the organization of the state and the idea of writing are first manifested in Egypt at that time.

By 1956, Samuel Noah Kramer could entitle a book *History Begins at Sumer* without serious challenge. It seems that the professional Egyptologists and Assyriologists are agreed (as much as any learned profession can ever be) that Sumer preceeds Egypt in time.

This, perhaps, requires only a revision of the thesis for Diop sees early Western Asia almost as Black as Africa. [The Blacks of Elam are discussed more cautiously, and thoroughly, by Frank M. Snowden, Jr. in *Blacks in Antiquity*, Harvard University Press, 1970.] To have an Asian Black anteriority, however, would be less elegant for the conformation of the argument and would loose the title, African.

The battle is not lost, for while Diop does not discuss Frankfort's evidence, it is probable that he would put it under the rubric of conspiracy; for on more than one occasion does he charge that white scholars are playing fast and loose with the evidence. Perhaps the most fantastic context in which he asserts the "insincerity of the specialists" is that this is *proved* by the "Nazi theories" of German superiority to the French since "the French are Negroes"! "They show, in fact, that the Black influence on the Mediterranean is no secret for any scholar: they pretend to be unaware of it, yet use it when they feel so inclined" (p. 117–118). If white scholarship is to be equated with the rantings of paranoid fascists, like Rosenberg and Hitler, then there is no point in discussing the matter.

Yet, the possibility of a widespread distortion cannot be lightly dismissed. Religion, class, political and social ideology, and sex as well as the consciousness of race can affect perception. Currently, we are being served with a flood of publications by women that are revealing the sometimes conscious and some-times unconscious prejudiced (and often fallacious) statements men have long been making about women. The possibility that data has been misinterpreted, or underestimated, because of a particular mind-set is certainly not far-fetched; it is in fact to be expected to have occurred, but this type of human weakness can be overcome by the very processes of scholarship.

Kramer, referring to a cunieformist with whom he had studied, wrote that he "exemplified my ideal of a scholar – productive, lucid, aware of the significant, and *ever prepared to admit ignorance rather than over-theorize*" (*op. cit.*, p. x; italics mine). Most scholars would, I think, agree with that ideal. It is impossible for me to conceive of an international conspiracy to subvert the truth about the color of the early Egyptians or their chronology.

Physics and biology are as prone to controversy as Egyptology so that disagreements in the latter field do not necessarily point to conspiracy.

Diop's writings are sure to be controversial because there are so many hypotheses, as I shall call them, though he deems them facts; one might agree with him on some points but not on others. However the Egyptian problem may be resolved, there is no archeological support for his claim that Nubia antedated Egypt as a civilized society. Even he is diffident about his suggestions that the Yellow race is the result of a mixture of Black and White, and that Africans reached America long before Columbus to introduce Mesoamerican civilization.

The editor chose to exclude "most of the more technical discussions especially the linguistic and grammatical passages" (p. ix). Nonetheless, a statement about the use of linguistics is indispensable since a number of instances remain where Egyptian words are juxtaposed with Wolof words with the implication that they are cognates (*i.e.*, related words from the same root). Wolof is a language of the West Atlantic language family of the Niger-Congo language phylum while Egyptian is a member of the Afro-Asiatic phylum (or Hamito-Semitic as it is also known). Half a dozen years before Diop published, J. H. Greenberg demonstrated this classification, and while some points were resisted there is now more or less a consensus on its basic distinctions (cf. his revised edition, *Languages of Africa*, Bloomington, 1966). If the languages are not related, then cognates, if they are really such, must be borrowings. The likelihood of this in the case of Wolof/Egyptian is remote for temporal as well as spatial reasons.

The confidence a reader may have in how Diop treats words may be in-

fluenced by his quotation from Genesis X, 9–11, which we get in this form:
"The beginning of his [Nemrod's] kingdom was Babylon, Arach and Akkad, all
of them in the land of Sennar" (p. 102). The Revised Standard Version in
English (last revised in 1952) gives Shinar. Sennar is in the Nilotic Sudan (but
probably didn't have that name in antiquity) while Shinar is the Semitic term
for Sumaria. (How Babylon was to be accepted as being in Sennar is not
explained.) If the Egyptian and Wolof words have been as loosely dealt with as
Shinar/Sennar, we need not wonder at their number.

We should take note of the subtitle which poses the question, myth or
reality? If the reality of the thesis cannot be affirmed, can its mythic nature? An
affirmative here does not seem out of order for a myth is a sacred story and the
whole treatment of the author has the tone of sacrality.

Robert MacIver, a political scientist, wrote: "By *myths* we mean the value-
impregnated beliefs and notions that men hold, that they live by and for.
Every society is held together by a myth system..." (*The Web of Government*, p.
4–5).

Myth and political ideology are certainly not synonymous but they do often
overlap. Myth is not exclusively of ancient fabrication; but mythopoetic minds
appear in every generation. Diop, it seems to me, created a myth to go into the
myth-system that served the Francophone African anti-colonialist movement.
Negritude was another part of this myth-system.

Finally, I feel constrained to say that the weaver of myth is a little understood type of creative person, likely to be underrated because we underrate
myths. The modern view emphasized that myth is not the same as scientific
truth; the implication is that it is therefore false. That does not necessarily
follow. Myth is its own kind of truth. It is the truth of the spirit, arising from
legitimate human aspiration. That is why Hocart, that insightful British anthropologist, called it "The Life Giving Myth." The poet O'Shaunnessy
described the myth-maker well:

We are the music makers
We are the dreamers of dreams
Wandering by lone sea-breakers
Sitting by lonely streams
World-losers and world-forsakers
Yet, we are the movers and shakers
Of the world forever, it seems.

A world in need of betterment will not despise myth-makers; a perfect
world need not fear them for they are, as the poem goes on to show, only
catalysts for the discontent of the populace so that:

"one man with a new song's measure
can go out and topple them [the old empires] down"

This is significant here because I think this characterization is more in
keeping with Cheikh Anta's temperment and personality than the impression
one is apt to get if confronted with certain passages taken out of his overall
framework. When I first dipped into *Nations Nègres* I supposed that it had been
written by a fiery fanatic. Later it fell to me as privilege and pleasure to become
acquainted with Cheikh Anta Diop and I was surprised to find him such a
gentle person; it is, I believe, his strong conviction which permits him to be
intense but calm. Because he has the sensitivity of the creative artist, it is pain-

ful for this reviewer to set out nakedly my judgement. He has known that I was empathetic but unconvinced, respectful but critical, and it is with a certain sorrow that I accepted the request to undertake the professional task of essaying a public assessment of the major product of Cheikh Anta Diop's life-work.

Now that the colonial period is over, and *Négritude* seems to be declining, there is perhaps little but inertia to keep a myth of African anteriority going; it has been translated into English by a professor-emeritus of Howard University, and thereby perhaps launched on a new political career, for however much political progress Senegal may have made, the struggle for racial equality in the New World has still a good way to go.

If English-speaking Blacks adopt the Diop hypotheses, it is to be hoped that they will follow his eschewal of racial pretentions: the difference between races, physically and tempermentally, derives from climate and not biology (p. 111–112). Diop is not a racist in that his teachings cannot, by themselves, lead to a conception of Black superiority. Diop has not gone as far as Jean Paul Sartre, who suggested that a little reverse racism to counter the established white racism could be a good thing. (How you then get rid of it, he doesn't say.) Sartre would agree, of course, that for one racism to replace another would be no progress for humanity.

Without the atmosphere of racism no one would be very much concerned, except as a point of curiosity, what complexion the Egyptians had or whether they were first or second in the advent to civilization. But we have had this saturation of racist thinking, from which hopefully we are emerging, and we've had Europeans proclaim that Africans were among the "child races of mankind" unable to rise above barbarism without the tutelage of Europeans (Lord Lugard, *The Dual Mandate*), and some have interpreted African history as a series of invasions of white "Hamites" leavening the dark mass of African populations since the mixed groups were "quicker witted" than the unmixed Negroes (C. G. Seligmann, *The Races of Africa*).

The impact of this negative image must have serious consequences for the formation of the personality of black individuals (cf., *e.g.*, *Black Self-Concept*, ed. by J. A. Banks and J. D. Grambs, New York, 1972). Though some may be persuaded that they are actually inferior, others will resist such a designation and fight back with whatever weapons are available, including myth.

It is worth noting that though ethnocentrism is common, racism is not a normal condition. Through the Greco-Roman period, Snowden found, there was a "conviction that race is of no consequence in judging a man's worth" (p. 216).

The attitudes of Europeans toward race in the early modern period was apparently, on the whole, little different: "Soon after 1500 the king of Portugal welcomed an ambassador from the king of Benin, and found him 'a man of good speech and natural wisdom'. A son of the king of Kongo, studying at Rome, was made a bishop in 1518. 'There are two black princes of Anamsbu here,' Horace Walpole was noting in his London dairy for 1749, 'who are in fashion at all assemblies,' being received at Covent Garden with 'a loud clap of applause.' At about the same moment another young man from the Gold Coast, Anthony William Amo, was awarded a doctorate of laws by the University of Wittenberg, appointed counsellor of state by the Court of Berlin."

(Basil Davidson, *The African Genius*, Boston, 1969, p. 289).

Unfortunately, this general acceptance of a normal state of human equivalency regardless of physical characteristics was not to persist. Arguments in defense of the slave trade (in the late 18th century), of slavery (in the nineteenth), and of economic exploitation of formerly enslaved populations, as well as of colonialism (in this century) contributed to the growth of a myth of inferiority of darker skinned peoples. This grotesque idea has caused, and is still causing, incalculable injustice and misery to many peoples in many parts of the world. Not the least harm done by racial prejudice is the effect of suppressing the dignity of a Black individual. But it is not too much to hope that racism will be overcome and a normal intellectual atmosphere will permit a nonpoliticized approach to historical problems.

Boston University DANIEL F. MCCALL
Brookline, Massachusetts

BOOK REVIEWS

John Peter Neelson, *Student Unrest in India: A Typology and a Socio-Structural Analysis.* München, Weltforum Verlag, 1973, pp. 101.

In this short volume, Mr. Neelson attempts to provide both a survey of the now rather substantial literature on student activism in India and an explanation of the causes of student unrest. He succeeds more adequately in the former task than the latter, and his volume is a useful guide to the literature. Several case studies of student unrest are cited in order to give the reader a "feel" for specific incidents. But the bulk of the volume is a discussion of the causes for unrest – such issues as the sociological characteristics of the participants, the role of youth in the Indian social structure, elements of traditional Indian society which impinge on students, and an analysis of the socio-structure aspects of what the author calls "non-realistic" conflict.

The author's basic hypothesis seems to be that student unrest is caused mainly by the fact that the socio-political role of the student in modern India has too many conflicts with the traditional society of India and with the current economic situation. For example, certain expectations are part of the traditional family structure. The student often comes into conflict with these expectations when exposed to modern education and the modern economy. Similarly, the academic system is based on "universalistic" criteria while much of traditional society, including of course the caste system, is based on "ascriptive" elements.

While a thought provoking discussion, this book has many weaknesses. Its main problem is that it is too brief to adequately deal with the many issues it raises. Such a broad overview is a difficult task, and the author is simply unable to bring together the various elements into a coherent whole. Significantly, there is no summary chapter in the book. Further, the academic reality of the Indian student is almost totally ignored. Many of the other commentators on student activism in India have dealt at length with the contribution of the "student condition" (the examination system, collegiate organization, etc.) to student unrest. And there is little consideration of the broader political situation in the country, and particularly the situation in Kerala and West Bengal, which have had active and rather effective leftist political movements on campus. Thus, while this volume raises a number of useful issues concerning Indian student unrest, it provides no explanations for this unrest, and posts no workable theoretical framework.

University of Wisconsin   Philip G. Altbach
Madison, U.S.A.

James C. Ingram, *Economic Change in Thailand, 1850-1970.* Stanford, Stanford University Press, 1971, pp. 352, Charts, Tables, $ 10.00.

When the first edition of Professor Ingram's book appeared in 1955 it fulfilled an urgent need and has become the standard reference work for the economic history of Thailand. Since then substantial additonal work has been done on the Thai economy mostly, but not exclusively, on developments beyond the period covered by that edition (1850–1950).

A few scholars raised questions concerning the validity of the information and analysis of that early period including such matters as the structure of production before and after the advent of specialization in rice exports, the policies which were followed, etc. Professor Ingram could have decided to apply himself to the revision of that historical work. He chose, instead, to concentrate on the addition of two new chapters summarizing more recent history (1950–1970).

This is his privilege. By the same token, the readers who were prone to overlook certain deficiencies in the old edition – in view of the long period covered, the scarcity of data, and the embryonic state of development analysis at the time – are likely to be more demanding of the new chapters. In other words, the somewhat disparate approach which was acceptable in the old edition is no longer entirely satisfactory. One looks in vain in the new chapters for an overall picture of the Thai economy (a model if you like) which would allow the reader to interrelate the information provided in the individual sections.

In some places there are also indications that Professor Ingram is not fully familiar with the available literature. This is particularly evident in sections where he departs from "straight" economic history to engage in problem analysis. For example, he seems oblivious of the existence of several articles by this reviewer, which omission sometimes affects the analysis.

A good case for highlighting the points made so far is his treatment of the important matter of the "rice premiums" (export taxes). Here he summarizes conflicting arguments and information from a number of authors without arriving at a conclusion regarding central issues such as the developmental impact of the premiums or alternative methods of taxation. These, as well as most other aspects of the premiums issue, were systematically analyzed already in a lengthy 1965 article.* Among other things, it was shown there that one can come down in favor of the premiums on the basis of economic analysis, specifically including the incorporation of rational response by farmers. It is surprising therefore to read Professor Ingram's assertion (p. 256) that such arguments can be derived only "by imputation" from statements of government officials. Similarly with regard to the effect of the premiums on other sectors, other segments of the population, the balance of payments, etc.

Despite such deficiencies it is a useful reference work, especially for the earlier period. The author also helps prospective readers by pointing out discontinuities and other deficiencies in the available data.

University of Illinois   ELIEZER B. AYAL
Chicago, U.S.A.

---

* See Eliezer B. Ayal, "The Impact of Export Taxes on the Domestic Economy of Underdeveloped Countries," *Journal of Development Studies* (1), July 1965.

Vincent Brandt, *A Korean Village, Between Farm and Sea.* Cambridge, Massachusetts, Harvard University Press, 1971, pp. 252, $ 8.95.

Anthropologists must have more fun than other social scientists. At least in the cases of sociology (the reviewer's discipline) and psychology, rigid theoretical or methodological models often restrict creativity to a point of absurdity. The present work of Vincent Brandt, an ethnological study of a single Korean village, represents the best of anthropology: a comfortable blend of enthusiastic description combined with an extremely important, but non-scholastic theoretical model. The perspective is social-structural, but is derived mostly from other anthropological sources.

Although Korea is usually described as a homogeneous culture, recent observations by Korean and foreign social scientists have uncovered a host of sharp differentiations within the society. Regionalism, social-class differences and occupational differentiations have all been commented upon in the literature. Differences in rural community structure, usually attributed to kinship orientation, provide the focus for Brandt's study. However, rather than to compare a number of different communities, Brandt chose to study a single village (population approximately 700) on the central west coast of Korea. The village studied is a mixed farming-fishing village, not necessarily "typical" of rural Korea as the author appropriately warns, but certainly of a common type in a society bounded on three sides by the sea. In any case, the village provides an excellent case study for the problem under investigation.

The author's principal theme is that two distinct structural models co-exist in this village. One is hierarchical, authoritarian, lineage-based, and dominated by formal Confucianistic ideology. The other is communal, egalitarian, informal, and more akin to what we might suggest to be a Taoist or shamanistic ideology. The two models are similar to Victor Turner's "structure" and "communitas", or Sorokin's "ideal" and "sensate" cultures, respectively. The two models appear to be related to some extent to function, in the sense that the Confucianistic model seems closely allied to farming, and the community model to fishing occupations, but because most of the inhabitants of the village under study engage in both occupations, Brandt understandably has some difficulty in relating observations to economic functions except in a general way. Nevertheless, his wealth of ethnographic material does sort itself out nicely along these two dimensions.

Brandt's findings, and explicit conclusions, suggest that social solidarity in this village stems from the community ethic, which, though subordinated to the Confucianistic, lineage ethic, nevertheless provides social bonds to ameliorate potential conflict endemic in a society dominated by a multiplicity of hierarchical, rigid kinship structures. This is of course an important theoretical point, and one especially pertinent to the understanding of factionalism in Korean society.

Brandt's understanding and penetration of Korean rural society is impressive. Excellent discussions of social control are documented beautifully with anecdotes which could not have been obtained without real acceptance of the author by the subjects of his study. The book is limited in scope, perhaps, but the author mercifully spares his readers with endless generalizations about Korea as a whole. The theoretical implications are sufficiently important so that the book does relate to more than the village under study. All in all, I would rate *A Korean Village* one of the very best books about Korea in the English language, and certainly an important contribution to the study of social structure.

University of Hawaii   HERBERT R. BARRINGER
Honolulu, Hawaii

Richard W. Wilson, *Learning to Be Chinese: The Political Socialization of Children in Taiwan.* Cambridge, The MIT Press, 1970, pp. 203, $ 10.00.

This book attempts to study how elementary school children in Taiwan become members of a certain group with particular political attitudes and distinctive political behavior patterns. Chapter I describes group tradition, child rearing, group consciousness, and achievement; Chapter II discusses leadership and political style in relation to the family, the schools, and political training; Chapter III concentrates on the problem of hostility; and Chapter IV gives the conclusion. This study purports to test the hypothesis that "learned patterns of response tend to generalize to situations other than those in which they were learned, the extent of generalization being a function of the degree of similarity" (p. 9. Note: This hypothesis is borrowed from Albert Bandura and Richard H. Walters' *Social Learning and Personality Development,* New York, 1963). The author spent about six months in Taipei, Taiwan, studying five elementary schools through observation, interviews and questionnaire surveys.

Unique as one of the few studies on the political role of the elementary school in Taiwan, this research utilizes well-designed instruments that, as in the interviews, sometimes vividly illustrate the attitudes, thoughts and opinions of the young children. It provides some insights into the subject.

This study could have been more interesting and meaningful had the author presented his research findings more completely and analyzed them systematically. But, falling prey to an obvious passion for theory and abstraction, he has fragmentized his findings, putting them into somewhat arbitrary and artificial categories and mingling these findings with various western theories of child psychology, personality development, socialization, communication behavior, and political science. Throughout the book, selected examples from the author's observations of the Taiwan schools are used to support the theories of Erik Erikson, Fred Greenstein, Theodore Newcomb, Marion Levy, John Whiting, Irvin Child, James Coleman, etc. In turn, these theories are used to explain Taiwan's educational and social phenomena as seen by the author. Such a liberal use of western theories to interpret an eastern culture virtually suggests that they are universal, whereas in fact, these theories have not been proved to be non-spatial and non-cultural. While some of them might be sound and valid in interpreting relevant phenomena in a certain western culture, from which these theories were generated, they might not be appropriately used to explain the school and society in Taiwan. Being an imposition of ready-made categories upon certain subject matter, this study may have committed the "fallacy of the Procrustean Bed" (see J. S. Wu, "The Paradoxical Situation of Western Philosophy and the Search for Chinese Wisdom," *Inquiry,* XIV, 1971, 1–18).

Although the author shows an explicit awareness of the shortcomings of stereotyping Oriental cultures by some western observers (p. 1), he himself could not avoid doing the same. He prejudges the Chinese as a "face"-conscious people, and then proceeds to document this assumption. According to the author, "face" is the "driving force in creating and sustaining [the] Chinese political system." While making such a gross and emphatic generalization, the author unfortunately fails to discuss clearly the original Chinese term for "face." He says that "face" for the Chinese has two meanings: "The first, *mient-tzu*, is the prestige and reputation achieved through material or social success, ostentation or generosity. The second, *lien*, is 'the respect of the group for a man with a good moral reputation'" (p. 22). This reviewer would like to clarify briefly these two terms as follows:

1. *Mien-tzu* and *lien* are synonymous in Chinese; both mean "face".
2. *Mien-tzu* and *lien* in themselves are neutral; i.e., they do not imply to have "face" or not to have "face". They simply designate "face".
3. *Yu mien-tzu* (having *mien-tzu*) means to have "face". This could be the result of having achieved success or honor.
4. Idiomatically, there is no such term as *yu lien* (having "lien") in Chinese.
5. *Mei mien-tzu* (no *mien-tzu*), or no "face", implies not having status, credibility, or being a failure.
6. *Tiu lien* (to lose *lien*) means to lose "face". This is a stronger expression than *mei mien-tzu*, but the difference is one of degree, not of kind.

Despite the above shortcomings, this book is a valuable publication on Taiwan today. It would be a useful reference for those who have some knowledge about Chinese history and culture.

University of Michigan   CHO-YEE TO
Ann Arbor, U.S.A.

Hung-Mao Tien, *Government and Politics in Kuomintang China, 1927-1937.* Stanford, Cal., Stanford University Press, 1972, pp. 226, $ 8.95.

Until the recent appearance of *The Strenuous Decade* (Paul Sih, editor), books dealing with China during the period of 1928–1937 have concentrated on China's external relations or on the Nationalist-Communist struggle. As a result, even the latest general works on modern Chinese history tend to view the 1930's as a prelude to World War II and the eventual Communist triumph. Now we have Dr. Tien's finely wrought study. While its scope is quite limited as contrasted with the Sih book, it effectively presents an alternative view to those more favorable to the Nationalists (Kuomintang). It has the added virtue of bringing modern social science techniques to bear on certain data, an example of which is the analysis of the background and turnover-rate of county magistrates (Chapter 8). There is also a good deal of descriptive material, in which a number of secondary figures, notably Yang Yung-t'ai, Ho Chung-han and Hsiung Shih-hui, all important supporters of Chiang Kai-shek, have been rescued from neglect.

An outgrowth of the author's doctoral thesis, the book is organized into two halves, focusing on the central and the provincial governments respectively. Each half takes up the general topics of leadership, personnel and finance, and more specifically, decision-making structure, party membership and recruitment of officials. Recognizing the differences in the available national and provincial data, the author wisely chose to adopt different methods of analysis. For instance, there is an excellent chapter on factionalism in national politics, highlighting the various groups supporting Chiang: the Blue Shirts, the Political Study faction, the Whampoa graduates and the CC (Chen Brothers) clique. In contrast, the data on provincial officials are dealt with quantitatively.

Dr. Tien explicitly cautions us not to draw sweeping conclusions from his study, but the tendency to do so is all but inescapable, a temptation to which the author himself is not always immune. Such overall judgements, however, need to be based on studies of much broader scope. In this book there is little discussion of the economic and educational achievements of the time. Key figures, T. V. Soong and H. H. Kung for example, are mentioned only in passing. Even within the scope the author has set for himself, he has not adequately discussed the supporters of Wang Ching-wei and Hu Han-min, contemporary rivals of Chiang. Consequently some of the book's conclusions are less than totally convincing. For specialists an added blemish is the lack of a glossary with Chinese characters, for which the editor rather than the author should probably bear the blame.

These shortcomings notwithstanding, the book deserves careful reading. It makes a strong case against the thesis of the Kuomintang being a viable party pursuing sound policies until its efforts were shortcircuited by the Japanese invasion. Dr. Tien has persuasively argued to the contrary. The party, in his view, never did achieve stability in recruitment and policy making. He reminds us that China in the 1930's was not even ruled by the Kuomintang party, for the regular party organs and apparatus were effectively superceded by Chiang's military organization and personnel. Sould we then regard these developments as indisputable evidence of the failure of the Kuomintang and of Chiang himself? One need only be reminded that Mao Tse-tung in the Great Proletarian Cultural Revolution has similarly undercut the stability of the Chinese Communist Party to be extremely cautious in making any final judgements of the early Kuomintang record.

Ohio State University   SAMUEL C. CHU
Columbus, U.S.A.

Eduardo Lachica, *The Huks: Philippine Agrarian Society in Revolt.* New York, Praeger Publishers, 1971, pp. 268, Annexes, n.p.

The Huk movement has not lacked narrators and analysts. Eduardo Lachica's book is the latest of the growing literature on the Huks. The author is a hardworking journalist on the staff of the *Philippine Herald*. He was trained both at the Ateneo de Manila and Harvard University. This latest attempt is a well-researched, well-written and well-balanced book.

The first half of the book is devoted to a history of the Huks until mid-1959. This is the part which is well covered in numerous books and articles.

Many knowledgeable persons assumed the movement ended there. This is far from the truth as this work will show.

The interesting part of the book starts with Chapter eight onwards. This chapter narrates the revival in 1964 after being inactive for a while. From that date on the "Huk movement returned to its original goal of peasant advocacy and added a new one of establishing a permanent and legitimate logistical base." It also retreated to its original jurisdiction of Pampanga and concerned itself little else outside this area. Revolution was excluded from the organization's objectives.

The next three chapters deal with the establishment of the Mao-oriented New Peoples Army on December 26, 1968; the break-up between Commander Dante and the Manila ideologues; and a chapter on the University of the Philippines, which has proved the leadership of the leftist movement.

Lachica explains the split between Dante and the "ideologues". "An outsider, no matter how intellectually qualified cannot go up the hills to take over the command of the unlettered peasant guerrillas. The traditional distrust for the stranger is a wall between him and the peasants" (p. 198). A second and third reasons are: "the tendency of Filipinos to identify their problem in terms of economic difficulties experienced individually or as members of family units" and finally, a lack of common aspirations between the ideologues and the peasant guerrillas.

This reviewer accepts the conclusion "The Huks, in sum, are the Pampango version of continuing agrarian demonstrations in various parts of the Philippines" (p. 201).

The main strength of the work is the up-to-date materials never before touched by earlier writers, including the New People's Army. It is not an easy task to summarize the movement in fifteen chapters. Unlike earlier works, this one started as an in-depth investigative report. The earlier works were either written as an academic exercise or written by participants. The academic works do not quite capture the leaders as flesh and blood, and the excitement of events are somehow lost in their desire for objectivity. The participants wrote with a tendency to idealize their role or justify it.

Two minor weaknesses are noted by this reviewer. The first is the absence of a bibliography. The bibliography is helpful in tracking fugitive sources. Its absence gives the reviewer a feeling of a "hurried" work. A second weakness is the reliance on unidentified informants. While acceptable in the journalistic trade, it is fatal in a book as it becomes difficult to check on an unidentified informant. Oral interviews have to be used with caution. The two minor errors in no way detract from the whole work. Lachica needs to be encouraged on his premier work.

Lincoln, Nebraska   MAXIMO P. FABELLA
U.S.A.

Visakha Kumari Jayawardena, *The Rise of the Labor Movement in Ceylon.* Durham, Duke University Press, 1972, pp. 382, $ 10.75.

Politics in British Ceylon was mainly a ball game played by British officials in Ceylon, first with a few affluent high-caste families, and later with an English-educated and westernized elite, the products of Britain's colonial educational policy. Ceylon, in contrast to India, had neither a Tilak nor a Gandhi, and neither violence nor non-violence. The masses never played a central role in the nationalist movement and consequently they have been largely ignored by students of Ceylon's history and politics. The result is that we know very little of the aspirations and activities of the Ceylonese masses in the colonial period. Dr. Jayawardena's book has to some extent filled this gap in our knowledge. Her study of the rise of the labour movement from 1880–1933, is the first comprehensive account of the urban working class in British Ceylon, and illustrates its crucial role in many important political events. She not only gives detailed analyses of specific strikes and labour disputes and shows how urban and plantation workers were organized, mobilized and utilized, but more importantly relates these events systematically to social and political developments of the period. The result is an authoritative study of modern Ceylon, of interest to the specialist and general reader alike.

The reviewer's only disagreement is on a matter of emphasis. Dr. Jayawardena seems to believe that there was a marked shift from conservatism at the turn of the century to radical trade unionism in the 1920s. The fact remains though that despite differences in leadership style, the trade union movement of Ceylon was and has remained to this day an elite affair. With but one or two exceptions, the working class of Ceylon has yet to produce labour leaders of any consequence from its own ranks. The most lasting contribution of A. E. Goonesinha, the radical labour leader of the 1920s, was that he introduced the idiom of socialist rhetoric, which was picked up and developed by Marxist politicians of the 1930s and continues to be used with some effect even today. Goonesinha was no radical in any significant sense of the word, and, in fact, became a prominent right-wing politician in the 1940s. And the most vociferous "radical" of the 1920s, Victor Corea, was as much an admirer of the British *raj* as any conservative member of the National Congress. Corea once told the Governor of Ceylon, "I love my country too much to wish to change the stable and strong Government our fathers wisely chose more than a century ago." (Nathan Papers, Rhodes House, Oxford, Corea to Sir Hugh Clifford, 15 April 1927.)

These minor comments apart, I have only the highest admiration for this excellent study. It is a fine example of sound scholarship, insightful analyses and elegant presentation.

University of British Columbia   TISSA FERNANDO
Vancouver, Canada

Joseph J. Spengler, *Indian Economic Thought: A Preface to Its History.* Durham, Duke University Press, 1971, pp. 161, Bibliography, Index, $ 8.75.

In this volume Professor Spengler indicates his considerable knowledge of Indian economics – past and present – while providing a very readable introductory summary of the development of Indian economic thought. As Professor Spengler is quick to point out, this is not a definitive study – it is based on translations and secondary sources and is entitled "a preface" – but was written to "stimulate intensive, organized inquiry."

The first two-thirds of the book deals primarily with the period prior to the Mughal conquest of India, and especially with arthashastra literature and Manu's dharmashastra. Spengler sets forth a number of "dimensions" of Indian society (such as population size and growth, agricultural production, urbanization, transport, and settlement patterns) which, in his view, "set limits to economic behavior at given times and hence to analysis and prescription based on this behavior" (p. 156). Prior to 1750 A.D., Spengler argues, Indian writings about economics amounted to "no more than protoeconomic discussion and direction," although such writings did compare favorably with those found in other societies at the time and "would have permitted the quite efficient functioning of the Indian economy of the day."

According to Spengler, "Economics really came to India with the British in the wake of the collapse of the Mughals," while "The really great upsurge in the development and diffusion of economics came, in India much as elsewhere, in the present century" (p. 161). In general, Spengler is impressed by both the prestige and quality" and the "practitioners in number" of Indian economists since World War II.

This is a useful book, from a number of different perspectives. First, Spengler summarizes in a short space most of the authoritative data available on the physical dimensions of ancient Indian society (food production, population size, yield per acre, and so forth). Second, he spends considerable time describing the organizational dimensions of ancient India and the distribution of decision-making power, relating these matters to prevailing economic theories. While his conclusions are not surprising (he describes an elitist peasant-based society, inhibited by excessive bureaucracy, caste, and a variety of superstitions and cultural values) his work is to be commended for the balanced perspective he has achieved and for his thoroughness in drawing from a diversity of source materials.

The weakest sections of the book are those dealing with the shastras: these sections are for the most part repetitive, detailed descriptions of what can and cannot be found in various sanskrit texts. The most interesting and important parts of the book are those in which Spengler generalizes from his findings, particularly at the end of Chapter 2 and in Chapters 6 and 7.

In his preface Professor Spengler indicates his hope that funds can be found for a "(say) ten-year organized inquiry into the growth of Indian society and the history of the interaction of thought and economic life in India." Unfortunately, he has not made the case for such an inquiry here, although he has provided a useful book nonetheless. Duke University Press should be commended, not only for its very high-quality presentation, but also for a fine addition to the content of its publications on economics.

Colgate University   MARCUS F. FRANDA
Hamilton, U.S.A.

James R. Brandon (ed.), *On Thrones of Gold: Three Javanese Shadow Plays.*
Cambridge, Harvard University Press, 1970, pp. XVI, Photographs,
Tables, Appendices, Note on sources, Bibliography, Glossary, Index,
$ 15.00.

This beautifully produced book, designed both for the general reader and
theatre artist, presents "English versions of three plays from the standard
Javanese wajang kulit (shadow play) repertory". Comprising just over 75%
of the volume and based upon Javanese language play scripts or synopses
published in Jogjakarta (Java) between 1960 and 1964, the three plays (*The
Reincarnation of Rama, Irawan's Wedding, The Death of Karna*) belong to that most
extensive and popular traditional form of Javanese wajang, the Pandawa
dramatic cycle. Although "abbreviated in detail" and representing "only one
way each play might be done" (p. 80), each of these puppet plays remains
"substantially complete" (p. viii) and further includes considerable dramaturgical data on the requisite, intricately meshed supporting roles of the *dalang*
(puppeteer) and the *gamelan* (orchestra). While stage instructions specify the
major physical movements and fights of the puppet actors, additional performance notations account for the Javanese play divisions, scene nomenclature,
dalang activity (his style of narration; his choice of *suluk*, or mood songs; his
signals for controlling the orchestral accompaniment), and the play's appropriate instrumental melodies (*gending*). The balance (almost 25%) of the book
synopsizes the distribution and "dramatic function" of the *suluk* and *gending*
music throughout the three plays (in appendices A and B), gives a sample
analysis of the movement sequences in the "flower battle" fighting scene (appendix C), comprehensively reviews source data in Indonesian and western
languages (note on sources, bibliography) and, to introduce the plays (pp.
1–80), deftly surveys the nature and development of the wajang dramatic art
form in Java. Of the black and white photographs six (full page) illustrate
single puppet profiles (pp. 42–47) and another 126 (of 1/3 page size) illustrate
the screen images of various encounters within the respective plays. Ten
smaller color plates (pp. 50–51, 336–337) show certain details of puppet orna-
mentation and manoever patterns. The glossary and index jointly provide
comprehensive referencing of the entire volume.
     Although long known to be richly and profoundly expressive of classical
Javanese weltanschauung, *wajang kulit* drama to date has either been only
fragmentarily excerpted or broadly summarized in the English language. By
selecting these whole plays for translation Brandon has not only begun to
rectify this imbalance but, as a dramatist, has also succeeded admirably in his
effort to "illustrate some of the wajang's subject matter, thematic content,
mood, and theatrical techniques" (p. vii). The translations, conscientiously
hammered out with the native Javanese language assistance of Pandam Guritno
Siswoharsojo, are unabashedly sensitive both to linguistic and dramaturgical
values – and the formidable translation problems candidly discussed in the introduction. The astutely placed photographs vividly portray the dramatic
versatility – at the *dalang's* trained fiingertips – of the flat leather puppets in
enacting all major scenes. As an introduction for western readers both to the
wajang's raw dramatic power and its intricate theatrical sophistication this

book is outstanding. In portraying traditional Javanese values "in action" its three plays are fascinating.

East-West Center   PETER R. GOETHALS
Honolulu, U.S.A.

Michael P. Onorato, *A Brief Review of American Interest in Philippine Development and Other Essays.* Revised Edition. Manila, MCS Enterprises, 1972, pp. 106, n.p.

This slender volume is an updated and expanded version of the original which appeared five years ago. The title is somewhat misleading as all but the lead article deals specifically with Fil-American political relations between 1916 and 1927. The title essay restates the thesis which has been a unifying element in most of Dr. Onorato's research. Briefly stated, Onorato's premise is that the social, economic and political shortcomings of America's colonial experience in the Philippines were not solely the fault of the United States. He places much of the blame on the shoulders of Filipino leaders and Manuel Quezon in particular. By 1916 the Filipinos were capable of significantly redirecting the United States' Philippine policy but they short-sightedly placed personal and political interests above national needs and thereby hindered the development of a viable Philippine nation.

Each of the succeeding articles attempts to reinforce specifically the general assertion of the lead essay. This interrelationship succeeds in bringing an admirable unity to a collection of published essays, but overlapping statements tend to create an "I've heard this before" feeling for the reader. Not surprisingly, the most detailed of the essays deal with Governor-General Wood who is presented as an able man facing an impossible and thankless task, a foil for the political machinations of Manuel Quezon. The author's arguments in the major essays are well-researched and in all of the articles he writes lucidly and convincingly. Professor Onorato makes a good attempt to present a balanced analysis but can not quite shake his American perspective.

The major weakness of this volume is its sketchiness. Five of the nine essays have less than ten pages of text. In all fairness, the author does preface the volume by stating that the collected articles are chiefly intended to be stimulants to further scholarship but one wonders if it might not have been better to preserve more substantial studies in a volume of this nature. There are a few other minor errors but they do not detract significantly from the work. However, it is intriguing to read about a March 1969 essay which was subsequently published in July, 1968.

Those who are familiar with Dr. Onorato's previous work will find few surprises in this recent publication. His pioneering reappraisal of Leonard Wood continues with few modifications. The short but pithy essays will fuel late-night discussions among Philippine historians and may stimulate deeper analysis. The book regroups previously scattered research and for this reason should be in the library of Filipinists who do not have ready access to the various Philippine periodicals in which the essays first appeared.

Baguio, Philippines   FRANK L. JENISTA

John Dewey, *Lectures in China 1919-1920.* Translated from the Chinese and
  edited by Robert W. Clopton and Tsuin-chen Ou. Honolulu East-West
  Center Book, University Press of Hawaii, 1973, pp. vi, 337, $ 12.00.

Although John Dewey was a most prolific writer, several important presen-
tations of his ideas never reached print. One was a book, about three-quarters
completed, which purportedly wove together the strands of his entire philosophy. Dewey lost the manuscript while returning from a summer in Nova
Scotia to his New York apartment.

Another was lectures presented in China during Dewey's sojourn there from
1919–1921. Although he had intended to publish them, as he had done for the
Reconstruction in Philosophy talks presented in Japan in 1919, even his notes for
the China lectures have not been recovered. But there were close Chinese
followers who were Dewey's former students at Columbia University, and so the
lectures were translated into Chinese and published almost immediately after
they had been delivered.

The book under review is a retranslation of some of these lectures. Its
editors, laboriously translated over a hundred lectures; thirty-two of them are
included in this volume, while the remainder have been made available in
typescript at the University of Hawaii library. An annotated list of these latter
lectures is included in the appendix.

This unusual project of returning Dewey's words into English is justified
partly on the grounds that since Dewey had a strong influence on Chinese
intellectuals and educationists during the twenties, the lectures may add to the
fund of knowledge needed to understand Chinese intellectual and social currents of that period. Professors Clopton and Ou also consider the retranslations
of use to those studying Dewey's development as a philosopher.

The two series of lectures selected for this volume were delivered at the
Peking National University and are titled, respectively, "Social and Political
Philosophy" and "Philosophy of Education." The selection of these, rather than
the other lectures, for publication is sound for they include Dewey's first
formal statement of his social and political philosophy as derived from his
experimentalist viewpoint to a group of people eager for a new China. The
lectures on political thought include Dewey's attitude towards Marxism,
social reform and alternatives to revolution. They are particularly interesting
when viewed from today's perspective, for they show how American liberals
– and Dewey was indeed a patron saint of liberalism – have progressed in their
appraisal of China under communism. Dewey was certainly a poor prophet
when he spoke in one of his lectures to the Chinese that "...people are tiring of
Marxism..."

The selection of his lectures on education is also fitting because, as the editors indicated in their introduction, Dewey had a profound impact on school
practices. Dewey's viewpoint has been criticized by social reformers for its
tentativeness, a stance not conducive to a strong commitment to a specific
program of social action; but in the area of education, as shown in these lectures,
he proposed specific suggestions on how to reform schooling; one can readily
understand why Dewey had a greater appeal to educationists, rather than to
those who ventured into the arena of government and politics.

A limitation of the book is its introduction, which is worthy, but all too

brief, for here was an opportunity for the editors to include an extended discussion of the impact of Dewey's ideas in Chinese intellectual and political
circles. There is also a lack of critical tone in the assessment of Dewey's ideas
and in the analysis of Dewey's followers in China from a 1970s viewpoint. One
suspects, for example, that the following for Dewey in the twenties, although
well-intentioned, was due more to an interest by Chinese "liberals," in en-
hancing their own status as intellectual elites, rather than in confronting the
immense problems of their huge country.

Nevertheless, these omissions should not detract from the fact that this is a
nice and interesting volume, carefully assembled by two devoted Dewey
scholars, extremely well-written, and perhaps more readable than Dewey himself in the original.

University of Hawaii   VICTOR N. KOBAYASHI
Honolulu, Hawaii

Marcus F. Franda, *Radical Politics in West Bengal.* Cambridge, M.I.T. Press,
1971, pp. 287, $ 12.50.

Marcus Franda, who has been involved in Bengal studies since 1959,
provides us with a careful analysis of the baffling intricacies of Bengal leftist
politics. In particular he addresses himself to two questions: 1) why is West
Bengal one of the two Indian states – the other being Kerala – where the Communists have been able to share in the decision-making power, 2) why have the
Communists failed fully to capitalize upon Bengal's revolutionary potential?
Franda clearly shows how the radicalization of politics was brought about
primarily by the decline of Bengal in the twentieth century. "Once they [the
Bengalis] swayed the destinies of India; now they cannot even determine their
own." Shift of the capital from Calcutta to New Delhi and of political power
to the Hindi-speaking heartland of India diminished the significance of
Bengal. The *bhadroloks,* a western educated high caste elite, responsible for
Bengal's glorious renaissance in the nineteenth century, were frustrated by
their loss of power. Searching for a new regional identity and regional power,
many *bhadraloks* were attracted to Marxism. They also bore a grudge against
the Congress party which was closely associated with the shift of power and
which they blamed for the Bengal Partition of 1947. Until 1966, however, the
relatively cohesive Congress Party was able to control West Bengal. In that
year, as a result of a disagreement over food policy, the Congress Party split,
enabling an anti-Congress alliance of Communists and other largely leftist
parties to form a coalition government. But the Communists were riddled
with factionalism. Eventually three Communist parties came into being: the
Communist Party of India (CPI), the Communist Party of India-Marxist
(CPM), and the Communist Party of India-Marxist-Leninist (CPML). Each
of the three Communist parties in turn suffers from factionalism. External factors, such as Sino-Soviet tensions, and the Chinese attack upon India, contributed greatly to differences over party strategy. More important still for an
understanding of factionalism is a phenomenon inherent in Indian culture as
well as regional peculiarities. "Ethnoconceptualization," i.e. the reproduction

in the political sphere of caste structures, has to be considered. Factionalism is
further strengthened in Bengal by sub-regional loyalties and by an authoritarian
leadership pattern. Franda's study was completed at the height of political
turbulence in Bengal. Understandably he could not foresee events, such as the
Indo-Soviet Friendship Treaty, Indian intervention in Bangladesh, and the
Congress electoral victory in 1972. However, all the factors responsible for
bhadralok discontent still continue to exist. Abject poverty of the masses remains
and with it Bengal's revolutionary potential. Thus Franda's analysis has long
range meaningfulness.

California State University   ALEXANDER LIPSKI
Long Beach, U.S.A.

Erika Kaneko and Herbert Melichar, *Pura Mutuzuma: Archaeological Work
on Miyako Island, Ryukyus.* Asian and Pacific Archaeology Series No. 4.
Honolulu, Social Science Research Institute, University of Hawaii, 1972,
pp. xiii, 163, Plates, Figures, $ 4.50.

The published literature on the archaeology of the Ryukyu Islands is
exceedingly limited and what is available in English is virtually nothing. The
publishing of any excavation data must therefore be welcomed as a significant
and useful contribution of new information, and the value of having some
verifiable facts in this near-vacuum of publication in English more than makes
up for criticisms which may be made of details of the report.

In passing, the older literature offered considerable speculation about the
possibility that Japan was originally inhabited by peoples moving up through
the islands to the south. The archaeology so far done in the Ryukyus certainly
does not yet offer any support for such a theory, since all cultural remains so far
reported are relatively late and clearly marginal to Japanese culture history
(which itself has been shown to have much greater antiquity than was formerly
believed).

The present report is no exception, since the survey of Miyako Island turned
up no ancient sites and the site reported here (Pura Mutuzuma) extended to
historic times, being abandoned in A.D. 1714 according to historical documents.
A considerable amount of trade pottery shows much occupation in the early
Ming dynasty (14th and 15th centuries); the beginning of the occupation is
not clear but there is apparently little beyond a few sherds and marine shells
that could be older than about the second century A.D.

The descriptive reporting is meticulous and highly detailed, including
not only conventional archaeological field data but a variety of technical
information – identifications of bones (mostly cattle), shells, and soil chemistry.
Most valuable is the detailed description of pottery which permits comparison
of the pottery found with sherds from other regions.

Historical data on the site come from a variety of documentary sources and
from the trade materials including porcelains, celadons, and a couple of coins.

Comparative archaeological analysis is limited by the paucity of archaeological excavations done in the Ryukyu Islands. The full value of this report
cannot be realized until there is a corpus of data on Ryukyuan archaeology.

This study goes so far beyond the details previously presented that some of the data presented have no clear relevance to anything else but stand as almost isolated research data. What this report does accomplish is to begin building up the necessary data for archaeological conclusions, and in adhering to most rigorous standards of careful data presentation, the authors have insured that their study will remain a cornerstone for archaeology of the later periods in the Ryukyus.

University of California   CLEMENT W. MEIGHAN
Los Angeles, U.S.A.

Carlos Quirino, *Quezon: Paladin of Philippine Freedom.* Manila, Filipiniana
   Book Guild, 1971, pp. xvi, 419, n.p.

There is no question that Carlos Quirino is the loyal Boswell to Manuel L. Quezon, late president of the Philippine Commonwealth. His first biography of Quezon in 1935 must be viewed as a well-written campaign document. At the time it purported to be an important study of the rise to power of the most important Filipino Leader of the first thirty-five years of the twentieth century. In 1935, Quirino, as a young Filipino journalist, was both bewildered and charmed by the charismatic Quezon. He is still loyal to his chief in this new and supposed definitive biography. This loyalty unfortunately has affected the quality of the work. The author was unable (perhaps due to his intense involvement with his subject) to use recent critical studies of Quezon's role in Filipino politics or Philippine-American relations lest he was forced to admit serious weaknesses in Quezon's character. He seems unwilling to see his chief as anything more than a warm, albeit hard-hitting, human being devoted solely to the nationalist aspirations of his people. He refuses to accept facts concerning Quezon's abilities to manipulate people and events to further his own personal ambitions even if it meant sacrificing or postponing the realization of those aspirations, such as, independence from the United States.

It is both unnecessary and perhaps impossible due to limitations of space to point out small mistakes or even the larger errors in fact. Suffice to say that no serious student of the subject will fail to read the works of three American historians of the period: Gerald E. Wheeler, Theodore Friend, and this reviewer. Their studies were avoided or used selectively. While it is difficult to imagine anyone attempting to understand the complexities of Filipino politics and Quezon's place in Philippine history on the basis of Quirino's book, it is nevertheless regretable that many readers, especially Filipinos, will use the biography to form judgements on the nature of Philippine politics and/or Philippine-American relations without realizing its limitations.

The book is divided into twenty chapters that are arranged chronologically. The weight given by Quirino to the pre-Commonwealth era, *i.e.*, before 1935 (284 pages out of 385 pages of text) indicates that he was unwilling to attempt any meaningful examination of the Commonwealth period or the war-time government-in-exile. Any real assessment of Quezon's presidency would reveal the serious deficiencies of the author's hero. It is easier to look at Quezon as the hard, two-fisted exponent of Philippine nationalism fighting reactionary

American governors general then admit that the man could not lead his
people effectively once he became chief executive of the Philippines.

It is unfortunate that the present work, which is basically an updating and
expansion of *Quezon: Man of Destiny*, is not much more than a collection of
anecdotes strung together in a highly polished narrative purporting to be
scholarly in nature. A serious, critical study of Manuel L. Quezon still needs to
be written.

California State University   MICHAEL PAUL ONORATO
Fullerton, U.S.A.

William E. Steslicke, *Doctors in Politics: The Political Life of the Japanese
Medical Association.* New York, Praeger Special Studies, 1973, pp. 302,
$ 17.50.

The world media these days are fond of depicting Japan Incorporated as a
monolith. But the stereotype makes little sense when set against the amount of
diversity and conflict within the Japanese domestic scene. Political pressure
groups have been a part of that scene throughout the modern century, and
during the last generation they have grown in numbers, in variety, and often
in power. Professor Steslicke has come up with the first book-length study in
English showing us one such influential pressure group in action.

A physician in private practice in Japan earns much of his income by directly dispensing the medicines he prescribes. When legislators sought to end this
practice in the 1950s the Japan Medical Association sprang to new vitality. The
Association won that fight handily, but for most of the time since then it has
been locked in extended wrangles with the state and with other pressure groups
over how best to operate the national health insurance system.

At times the JMA has been flamboyant, as in the summer of 1971 when
50,000 doctors boycotted the insurance system for a month. But most often the
Association has to sustain the kind of political polylog familiar to physicians'
organizations elsewhere – negotiating and dickering concurrently with cabinet
ministers, diet members, political party leaders, welfare ministry officials, and
other health related groups.

Steslicke sketches this wider picture but puts most of his energy into a case
report on JMA struggles for insurance system reform in 1960–61. He is generous
with footnotes and draws inferences with scholarly care. But the price of this is
a sometimes monographic monotone that tends to smother the human comedy
which is politics anywhere. I'm sure it's no easy task to keep the narrative clear
when one has a cast of characters as long and as interlinked as that in the *Tale
of Genji*. Steslicke manages to keep the narrative clear and orderly, and specialists in Japanese politics will relish the detail he packs into his account. Others
may wish for less detail and more pointing up of the import of key events in the
struggle.

Anyway a lot more people need to become a lot more aware of the pluralism of Japanese domestic politics, and I hope that Steslicke's work will
inspire reports on other such organizations. One lasting impression from my
recent stay in Japan is that client and consumer organizations have swiftly been

gaining clout and are taking seats around the domestic policy table. It's a far cry from the participant democracy of new-left vision, but it is no mere aping of Western models. The West is grudgingly admitting that it may have something to learn from Japan in economic matters. Perhaps there are some lessons in politics as well.

University of Illinois   DAVID W. PLATH
Champagne-Urbana, U.S.A.

Judith M. Brown, *Gandhi's Rise to Power: Indian Politics 1915-1922.* Cambridge, At the University Press, 1972, pp. xvi, 384, Glossary, Biographical Notes, Bibliography, Index, $ 19.50.

Dr. Brown, Lecturer in History at the University of Manchester, sidesteps the often-accepted notion of "charisma" as the factor underlying Mahatma Gandhi's spectacular, if brief, success in forging a broad-based Indian nationalist movement. She seeks instead more mundane and more rigorously analyzable explanations. Her carefully constructed, lucidly argued book demonstrates that Gandhi built his movement by attracting to himself a wide, geographically diverse spectrum of local leaders who brought with them already mobilized groups of followers. By recruiting these "subcontractors," Gandhi simultaneously brought their clients under his umbrella.

The alliances which Gandhi forged with these leaders often proved temporary. They were issue-oriented ententes, easily terminated with the passing of the specific issue. The deflation and fragmentation of the nationalist movement following the failure of the non-cooperation campaign of 1920–22 proved that Gandhi's organization was neither monolithic nor pan-Indian, but rather a coalition of lower-level leaders. Secondly, the diversity of groups in pluralistic India always threatened Gandhi's movement with internecine warfare; controversial decisions such as support for the Khilafat movement and rigid adherence to non-violent methods ensured the participation of some of the subcontractors, but pushed others out from under the umbrella. Finally, Brown questions the extent of popular involvement with Gandhi's Congress. Although masses of Indians worshipped Gandhi as (semi)-divine, mass *political* mobilization for the national cause was an illusion. Only "the western educated of the once backward areas and .. some vernacular literates from town and countryside who had acted as subcontractors .. and saw in nationalist politics .. a means of forwarding and protecting their interests" (p. 356) were actually organized.

Brown builds her case carefully, chronologically, beginning with a perceptive view of Gandhi's experience in coalition building among diverse Indian groups in South Africa. She emphasizes the localized nature of his first campaigns in India after his 1915 return home: Champaran, 1917; Kaira, 1918; and the Ahmedabad textile strike, 1918. Gandhi made these first tentative steps in places as yet largely untouched by the nationalist movement and among new men like Rajendra Prasad and Vallabhbhai Patel whom Gandhi saw as potential national leaders under his supervision. Subsequent chapters on the Rowlatt Satyagraha of 1919, the Khilafat movement, and the non-cooperation struggle illustrate on an all-India canvas the strengths and weaknesses of Gandhi's choice of issues, methods, and coalitions.

The data are largely original source materials: records of the Government of India and the collected works of Gandhi. Two elements grate: more rigorous editing would have further transformed the detail-laden, dissertation style and, substantively, somewhat more attention might have been paid to the importance of Gandhi's personality and unorthodox strategy in holding his allies together.

Brown's important contribution helps focus attention on the nuts-and-bolts of interest aggregation in the expanding Indian political nation of the recent past. It raises several significant questions for further research: Did Gandhi, at least occasionally, appeal to the adulatory masses over the heads of the local leaders and thus assert leverage against the subcontractors? What was the significance of primarily non-nationalist issues like *khadi*, anti-untouchability, and village uplift on the anti-imperial campaigns? In his relationships with regional allies, was Gandhi adapting yet another traditional Indian form – the patron-client relationship – or was he formulating a fundamentally new link? Finally, an equally sophisticated analysis of Gandhi's subcontractors might be a useful next step in pushing forward the important direction of inquiry to which Brown has brought us.

Temple University   HOWARD SPODEK
Philadelphia, U.S.A.

Donald H. Shively (ed.), *Tradition and Modernization in Japanese Culture*. Princeton, Princeton University Press, 1971, pp. xvii, 689, $ 14.50.

This volume is the fifth in the series of studies on the modernization of Japan resulting from the Association for Asian Studies' Conference on Modern Japan. It is of the same high calibre as its predecessors. Each chapter represents a serious attempt by a reputable scholar to understand one very specific facet of cultural modernization in Japan.

In the first four chapters, Soveak, Nagai, Shively and Keene provide fascinating, detailed insights into four issues of the Meiji era: the Iwahura Mission experience as recorded in its official report; the development of the Meiji educational system; the middle Meiji reaction of Japanization; and the cultural effects of the Sino-Japanese war of 1894–95.

Parts Two and Three deal more specifically with the individual producers of new cultural forms in the arts, and how they grappled with western techniques and aesthetic values. The topics range from drama to music to oil painting to poetry, and, of course, fiction and literary criticism. Despite the careful attention paid by the authors to aesthetic and technical problems particular to each art, the studies are all both intelligible and illuminating to the non-specialist. Rosenfield's analysis of western-style painters and their critics, Malm's piece on the westernization of music and Ortolani's study of Shingeki are notable for their success in going beyond biography to the analysis of general developments in the respective fields. Within the more limited confines of individual biographical studies, Hibbett's analysis of Natsumé Soseki stands out for its careful and perceptive handling of psychological concepts.

The final three articles deal with aspects of culture in the broader sense.

Viglielmo's paper on the young Nishida succeeds more as interesting biography than as a tracing of the sources of his philosophical ideas, but it does make Nishida seem more accessible. Blacker judiciously applies a general social science proposition about millenarian cults to the new religions of Japan. Miller's study of *keigo* offers the rather startling finding that Japanese use of politeness levels has become more complicated in recent years, rather than being simplified as a result of westernization and modernization.

Taken as a whole, the volume is an important addition to English-language studies of Japan, although many of the individual contributions have been published already in other forms. The papers show evidence of the cross-fertilization provided by the Conference on Modern Japan. The editor's preface and introduction to each section provide excellent continuity for the varied selections.

The book's expense is for once mitigated both by its length and the extremely helpful color plates and musical transcriptions which accompanied the Rosenfield, Haga and Malm articles. My only complaint is that it took five years to get the book into print.

University of Hawaii   PATRICIA G. STEINHOFF
Honolulu, U.S.A.

Wayne S. Vucinich (ed.), *Russia and Asia: Essays on the Influence of Russia on the Asian Peoples*. Stanford, Hoover Institution Press (Hoover Institution Publications 109), 1972, pp. xiv, 521, Notes, Index, $ 15.00.

The phrase "Russia and Asia" evokes such a welter of relationships that prospective readers might question the feasibility of treating so diffuse a subject in a single (albeit hefty) volume. Asia's staggering diversity precludes the term from conveying more than a largely contrived identity. After all, what do Japan and Jordan have in common? Moreover, Russia's association with this massive chimera is complicated by the fact that the tsarist empire and the Soviet Union have been simultaneously a part of as well as distinct from Asia. *Russia and Asia* nevertheless successfully deals with these complexities by a felicitous combination of expertise and editorship.

All ten essays comprising the book derive from a conference on "the Russian Impact on Asia" held at Stanford University in 1967. To introduce the subject, Nicholas V. Riasanovsky skillfully traces the evolution of Russian conceptions of Asia starting with Kievan apprehension and Mongol-inspired trauma and proceeding through the curiously "European" perspectives of self-proclaimed anti-westernizers to the apocalyptic visions of twentieth-century "Eurasianists". Richard N. Frye and Wayne S. Vucinich offer instructive insights and provide practical information on Russian and Soviet oriental studies respectively. Remaining papers explore Russia's impact on European Muslims and the Caucasus (Alexandre Bennigsen), Armenia (Vartan Gregorian), Georgia (David M. Lang), Central Asia (Manuel Sarkisyanz), China (Mark Mancall), Japan (George Alexander Lensen), and Siberia and the Far East (Ethel and Stephen P. Dunn).

The essays draw material mainly from published sources and present a compressed synthesis of rather large topics. Nearly all of the authors adopt a straightforward historical narrative. A few hypothesize fresh interpretive frameworks such as the "paradigmatic perceptual scheme" which Mancall adduces to explain China's divergent responses to Russia and the West. Collectively, the papers summarize how Russia advanced upon, struggled with, and in some cases subjugated and absorbed a wide variety of Asian peoples. Modes of culture transmission expressed through nationality policies are elucidated with particular effectiveness. More systematic attention might have been devoted to comparing the impact of particular institutions (e.g. the Orthodox Church) on various Asian societies. Although bibliographical references are extensive, their usefulness would have been enhanced by systematic updating.

Russia and *Asia's* most valuable contribution is to bring into focus an important but hitherto fragmented subject. It draws together and distills a wide range of scholarship previously scattered throughout journals and monographs. It opens new vistas for western orientalists who want to learn more about their Soviet colleagues. Hopefully, it will foster a wider appreciation of Russia's enduring and multifarious involvement with peoples living between the Golden Horns of Istanbul and Vladivostok.

University of Hawaii   JOHN J. STEPHAN
Honolulu, U.S.A.

Leo A. Orleans, *Every Fifth Child: The Population of China.* Stanford, Stanford University Press, 1972, pp. 191, $ 8.50.

The questions of the population of the People's Republic of China are intricate and controversial. Data are sparse, access limited, and argument rampant. Leo Orleans presents a brief, nontechnical, and imaginative resume of the state of the statistics, the probable course of the changing population, and the relevances to China's future and that of her neighbors. Chapter 1 describes "The population record", Chapter 2, "Vital statistics and population growth". Chapter 3 considers "Urban population", Chapter 4, "Population distribution and migration". Chapter 5, the longest, concerns "National minorities". The sixth and final chapter is entitled "Implications and consequences", including manpower problems, food resources, and power politics.

Mr. Orleans believes that China's population is important to China, to Asia, and to the world, and that those who spend their time studying China from the outside have a responsibility "...to make our evaluations and opinions available, and be prepared to accept the consequences". In his assessment, the political, economic and social developments and transformations resulted in changing rates of population growth and changing patterns of migration that may not insure the future of the People's Republic of China but that avoid Malthusian doom, urban disintegration, and rural collapse. Birth rates declined early along with death rates; China averted the rates of increase of 3.0 percent a year or more than plague so many less developed countries. Controlled migration to cities, stimulated exodus from them, and transfers of youth and educated adults from cities to communes prevented the vast concentrations of marginal people in cities and added contingents of the educated and the skilled to the rural areas.

The basic adjustments in rates of growth and types of migration were conducive to the resolution of the central problems of population. The concentration of manpower in the rural areas and the associated educational and economic policies may yield solutions to the problems of employment that are so intractable elsewhere. Declining rates of population growth and increasing productivity may yield solutions to the population-food difficulties as economic growth proceeds. And, given the internal resources, the massive problems of development, and Chinese pragmatism, external expansion is unlikely.

Princeton University   IRENE B. TAEUBER
Princeton, U.S.A.

Rene Lemarchand, *Ruanda and Burundi*. New York, Praeger, 1970, pp. 562, $ 12.50.

Professor Rene Lemarchand's excellent articles on Rwanda and Burundi which preceded this book always gave promise of a first–rate study of these two little known ex-kingdoms in Central Africa. With the publication of *Rwanda and Burundi* by Praeger/Pall Mall in their useful and successful series on the recent political history of African countries, this promise can now be said to have been fulfilled beyond the wildest expectations of at least one fastidious African Africanist; and it is indeed pleasing that the book won the coveted M. J. Herskovitz Award for 1971 because the book certainly does exhibit various strengths.

First of all, the study is obviously not a rushed one: it has matured in the thick bush of Rwanda and Burundi as well as in the libraries of campuses in America and elsewhere. Rushing to publish has been the ruin of not a few works by other American Africanists one could mention, who have been strong on library materials and concepts but thin on "bush materials" and hard data. Professor Lemarchand clearly knows the countries, the people, and their history. There is rich description of the impressive scenic beauty as well as the desperate poverty that the two countries present to the visitor; there is a careful if somewhat schematic historical survey; and there is analysis of the changing relationships within what are quite clearly caste-ridden, feudalistic societies, the feudal idea being however shorn of its specifically European connotations and attributes. The link of history with the present happenings is constant and most illuminating, again in contrast with some other American Africanists, Professor Bretton, for instance, who seem to deprecate the effort to show how traditional social institutions and history press on present politics. And as the study was not the result of the increasingly normal six month stint in the country to be written about, the author got to know members of the elites well enough to write with a freshness of detail and portraiture which personal knowledge enhances.

The second strength of the book lies in the compulsive theoretical awareness on practically every page. The theoretical significance of political phenomena is arrested to be sharply and lucidly commented upon, in a constant debate with other authors, before the narrative and analysis are taken up again. Social change, particularly the revolutionary brand of it, is made the focus of analysis of the politics of these two newly-proclaimed republics, and so all the concepts and vehicles associated with social change – traditionalism, political mobilization and modernization, rural radicalism, violence, military coups, etc. – naturally make their worthy appearance; and they are all tidily and meticulously indexed. Rwanda and Burundi are pegs on which are hung large theoretical discussions about social change.

Thirdly, there is a comparative perspective induced by the need to explain why it is that two virtually identical societies, with significant similarities in social stratification, historical experiences in their pre-German, German and Belgian phases, comparable in size and resources, nevertheless experience different evolutionary modes and rates at the terminal phase of the colonial period and the immediate post-colonial period. Rwanda experiences a bloody revolution, in the whole of the decolonization process in Africa rivalled only by the Zanzibari revolution of 1964, whereas Burundi does not. Why? This is the basic comparative question the book sets out to answer. And the answer is that while there were identical structures and tendencies in the two societies, the Rwandese examples were always more pronounced and extreme, more inflexible and rigid.

These differences in degree which come to constitute differences in kind, at least in their outcome, in the manner in which fundamental social tensions and stresses are resolved, are repeatedly summarized in several passages. For instance, Burundi's caste system is shown to be more variegated, more flexible, and this is contrasted with the far sharper differentiation in the Rwandese system (pp 23 & 24). The lower degree of centralization of the authority structure of traditional Burundi, added to by the German policy of fragmenting the Mwami's power (p. 62), a policy which the Belgians also pursued (p. 74), is to be contrasted with the far greater degree of centralization in Rwanda, in part the result of exactly reverse policies of the colonial powers. Even the pattern of geographical spread of the ruling Tutsi differed in the two countries and apparently had different and significant implications for the revolutionary potential of the two societies. There is a contrast of Burundi's geographically concentrated Tutsi population, and therefore less visible Tutsi yoke over relatively large areas, with the Rwandese pattern of wider dispersal of the Tutsi overlord. Similarly, the pattern and rate of Tutsi education in the two territories differed: the Tutsi of Rwanda tended to be better educated than their counterparts in Burundi, and this tended to reinforce the sense of collective Tutsi superiority far more in Rwanda than in Burundi (p. 75). Thus, "not only was the premise of inequality less prominent in Burundi than in Rwanda, the lines of demarcation between groups were drawn at different levels in each society. Whereas the main line of cleavage in Rwanda was between Hutu and Tutsi, in Burundi the crucially important distinction was between the princes, on the one hand, and the Hutu and Tutsi on the other. The criteria of ranking, in other words, did not involve ethnic differences as much as differences of lineage and power." Thus, the familiar distinction between consistent and cross-cutting cleavages, or the less familiar one between hegemonic and ruling castes, to be identified with Rwanda and Burundi respectively, is the answer to the basic comparative question the book sets out to answer.

The one solitary criticism I have of *Rwanda and Burundi* is that there is a tendency to be repetitious. The book, I believe, could be slightly shorter and consequently possibly slightly cheaper. But repetitiousness is often the careful teacher's insurance against inattention and perhaps misrepresentation. And, in any case, when comparison involves the juxtaposition of two entire societies, a certain amount of repetition is perhaps inevitable.

St. Anthony's College   YAW SAFFU
Oxford, England

Ruth Finnegan, *Oral Literature in Africa.* Oxford, Clarendon Press, 1970.

Ruth Finnegan has undertaken the enormous task of producing "an introductory survey which could sum up the present knowledge of the field and serve as a guide to further research… useful not only to those intending to do specific research on African oral literature but also to those with a general interest either in Africa or in literature generally." (p. vii). She has, I believe, achieved her purpose.

The book is divided into four sections. The first discusses the nature of oral literature, the ways in which African oral literature has been studied in the last two centuries, and the social and linguistic background of African oral literature. It gives a good survey of modern concepts in all these areas. Chapter 3 is especially useful for readers who are unfamiliar with African languages and is especially stimulating for those interested in the wider implications of relationships between language and literature.

The remaining three sections are devoted respectively to poetry, prose, and "some special forms", i.e., drum language and literature and drama. Poetry is treated under the headings: Poetry and patronage; panegyric; elegiac poetry; religious poetry; special purpose poetry; lyric; topical and political songs; children's songs and rhymes. Prose comprises two chapters on prose narratives, one on problems and theories, the other on content and form, and a chapter each on proverbs, riddles and "oratory, formal speaking, and other stylized forms".

The reader may feel that this is not the best possible arrangement. The categories are based partly on form, e.g., poetry or prose, proverbs or riddles, and partly on function, e.g. religious poetry, topical and political songs. This raises all sorts of problems. Many pieces of oral literature fall into two or more categories, and in some cases the collector of a piece has not given enough information to enable it to be assigned to a functional category. Purely formal categories might be easier to use, for there is considerable cross-cultural agreement about distinctions between poetry and prose, proverbs and riddles. But the same item may be used for different purposes in neighboring cultures: is "John Brown's Body" a religious song, a war song, a political song or a children's song?

But to use purely formal categories would separate items which should go together; as Finnegan explains, a proverb is often an allusion to a story and would be meaningless in a culture which did not also contain the story. To use purely formal categories would be to sacrifice meaningfulness to convenience. There is even more objection to purely functional categories. For versions of the same item may be found in different contexts in neighboring, or even in the same cultures. Is "John Brown's Body" religious poetry, war poetry, a political song or a children's song? Its function cannot be properly understood unless it is considered under all these headings. Yet Finnegan's mixture of formal and functional categories has the disadvantages of both bases of classification in that things that should be together are separated, and disparate items may be included under one heading.

It is not easy to suggest an alternative arrangement. A possible one might be based on culture areas, such as those set out in Jacques Maquet's *Civilizations of Black Africa*, which are based on historical as well as geographical principles, and which included the new cultures of modernized Africa.

However, Finnegan's book is so well indexed, cross-referenced, footnoted and "bibliographed" that her arrangement of the material does not in the least impair the book's usefulness to many types of readers. The folklorist interested in the structure of oral literature will find here a wealth of material. The ethnographer and social anthropologist can add a dimension to their understanding of African cultures and societies. As all available information about the performance and social setting of the items of literature is carefully recorded, the book is an invaluable reference work for anybody working in any aspect of African culture.

It is also an excellent piece of literature in its own right. Besides being a gold mine for scholars, it is a delight for the general reader. Finnegan conveys the richness and joy of the African imagination. The people and animals and spirits of Africa live, laugh, weep and quarrel between the covers of her book.

York University   J. R. RAYFIELD
Toronto, Canada

G. Wesley Johnson Jr., *The Emergence of Black Politics in Senegal. The Struggle for Power in the Four Communes 1900–1920.* Stanford, Stanford University Press, 1971, pp. 219, Notes, Index, $ 8.75.

The scope of this work is greater than the sub-title suggests, including as it does a review of the development of electoral politics in the Senegalese Communes from the introduction of mass elections in 1948. It is projected as the first of two volumes, the second of which will deal with the period from 1920 to 1945. The author's intent is to document the development of African political leadership within the urban enclaves of the Senegalese Communes (Dakar, Rufisque, Gorée, St. Louis), a development which is seen as a fore-runner of later African nationalist politics in Senegal and elsewhere. And the documentation brought to bear on this theme is indeed impressive – including a thorough investigation of the archival materials in Paris and Dakar, as well as a series of interviews with those political elders who survive.

French and other scholarship, inspired by an influential article by Pierre Mille in 1901 (*Journal of the African Society*), has long seen the Four Communes in the pre-1945 period as dominated by rotten borough politics. In this view the historical accident of a mass African electorate merely led to a chaos of manipulation dominated by the money of large French companies and the coercive resources of the colonial administration. The elected urban and territorial representatives, and the single Deputy to the French National Assembly, might indeed be Africans, but they were pawns in a French game. The companies bought the votes of a largely illiterate electorate, and the administration where necessary falsified the election results.

The author of this study sets out to correct this established view, which he regards as the reflection of an anti-African bias in the colonial sources. He shows that the African mass electorate may not have been as readily manipulable as was previously assumed, and that African voters forced the displacement of French representatives first by mulattoes (in the period 1906–1914) and then by those of full African descent. His attention is sharply focussed on the 1914 election for a Deputy to Paris, when the first African Deputy (Blaise Diagne) triumphed in a bitter struggle with French and mulatto opponents. This was the first election in Senegal to be run by secret ballot, although the non-falsification of the results by the administration remains somewhat enigmatic.

Diagne, who retained his position as Deputy to his death in 1934, is the principal subject of the latter part of this study. And his career is indeed of absorbing interest. His early electoral campaigns were apparently tinged by anti-white sentiment (expressed in the vernacular), but his duties in Paris were consistently taken up with the defense of colonial political and commercial interests. During the First World War he was appointed High Commissioner for military recruitment, and his travels in West Africa helped to enlist thousands for service in the slaughterhouses of Flanders. He came to a remunerative agreement with the Bordeaux companies, and later defended the administration in its use of forced labour. In the early nineteen-thirties he twice served as Deputy Minister of Colonies. He served the purposes of colonialism, certainly, as did later Senegalese politicians, but he was also respected and even feared by French colonial officials. One senior administrator referred in an official note to his "haughty and brutal dishonesty". Here is a very good subject for a political biography, and nobody is better equipped then Dr. Johnson to undertake such a task.

School of Oriental and African Studies   DONALD CRUISE O'BRIEN
London, England

R. T. Parsons, *Windows on Africa: A symposium.* Leiden, E. J. Brill (Humanities Press, New York), 1971, pp. x, 202, $ 12.50.

This volume will be of interest to Protestant churchmen who, continuing to hold an optimistic view of their role in African affairs, wish to become involved in concrete programs there. Specific problem-issues are analyzed and offered plausible solutions – insights through particular "windows" – in this symposium written by Protestant missionaries from Europe and North America together with three African church leaders. Thus in the first "window" Kodwo Ankrah examines nepotism, tribalism, and administrative paralysis in Ghana, and the problem of refugees; Haldor Heimer explains the appeal and strength of independent churches in Luluabourg, Zaire; Kikiyu evangelist Moses K.

Waweru gives a personal testimony of his work amongst the pagan Masai; Lawrence Henderson examines the (to him) problematic correlation of ethnic identity to Protestant denominational affiliation in Angola; Enoch Mulira of Uganda proposes ways of overcoming illiteracy of the millions; James R. Stull ponders over the state of medical care in Liberia in the face of continuing traditional healing; editor Robert Parsons proposes a model for a trans-ethnic church in Nairobi; J. H. Hellberg suggests what the role of the church must be in medical work in Africa; and the late Sidney Gilchrist offers an ennobling profile of African churches that have suffered in Angola at the hands of Portuguese colonizers.

Whatever else might be said about this view of Africa as problems-left-to-be-solved, it is first of all a document of how reality is perceived by missionaries and churchmen, not surprisingly, to be fraught with burdens to be overcome. What is surprising, and open to criticism in this reviewer's mind, is the manner in which issues are conceived: not in terms of nation-building, economic development, or the evolution of the arts and professions, but in rather sordid issues such as nepotism, tribalism, refugees, and remaining pagan tribes to evangelize; or ethnic and linguistic particularism and separatist religion. It is a back-handed attempt to deal with the entire continent. Here and there a more positive picture emerges of the obverse to the "problems". Especially in Henderson's and Parsons' writing a view is projected of what the church, and African society perfected, ought to become: a multi-ethnic fellowship unencumbered by contemporary cultural particularities. This is all very well and good, but hardly in accord with surrounding reality, nor with the direction of the church itself. The missions and their daughter churches, by admission of several of the writers, are ethnically particularist. But there is more. In the solutions to the issues a peculiar image of the church emerges in which pagans, Catholics, and independent separatist groups are shunned, and made over into part of the problem.

Despite its worthwhile analyses and recommendations, this book leaves the reader with the somewhat discomforting impression that the contributors wish everyone could be brothers on earth; but in *my* camp, if you please.

University of Kansas   JOHN M. JANZEN
Lawrence, U.S.A.

Leslie Bethell, *The Abolition of the Brazilian Slave Trade: Britain, Brazil and the Slave Trade Question, 1807–1869.* Cambridge, At the University Press, 1970, pp. 425, $ 13.50.
Johnson U. J. Asiegbu, *Slavery and the Politics of Liberation, 1787–1861: A Study of Liberated African Emigration and British Anti-Slavery Policy.* London, Longmans, Green, 1969, pp. 231, $ 11.40.

These two works belong to that already voluminous body of literature devoted to British Anti-Slavery and Abolitionist policy in the nineteenth century. Both studies would probably not have been undertaken or published had earlier writers not been so strongly committed to the romantic humanitarian school founded by Coupland. Though neither writer is consciously revisionist, both move us further away from the Coupland view even as they feel obliged to pay lip-service to the "Saints", Wilburforce, Sharp and their successors. While neither goes so far as to endorse the Eric Williams thesis about the primacy of economic motives, both offer clear evidence that economic considerations motivated British policy towards the Brazilian slave trade, and towards the liberated Africans and the West Indian planters.

Bethell's work shows that British enthusiasm for abolition of the Brazilian traffic was impeded by considerations of *realpolitik*, the need to keep most favoured nation status – and even informal empire – over Portugal and its ex-colony in the New World. On the Brazilian side, the long suspect thesis pioneered by Gilberto Freyre about Luso-Brazilian racial tolerance and the benign nature of slavery also takes a further beating. When Brazilian abolition of the slave trade came in the 1850's, it was the product not of humanitarian impulses in either Brazil or Britain, but the result of Palmerston's high-handed and exasperated gunboat diplomacy. Indeed, we learn from Bethell that during the debates in Brazil over a proposed abolition law in 1931, some of the strongest supporters were racists who opposed the trade because they disliked and feared the racial imbalance that was already resulting from the extensive importation of Black Africans. Brazil did not in fact actually abolish domestic slavery until 1888, half a century after the British and a quarter of a century after the United States.

Bethell successfully integrates the more familiar British official sources with the rarer Brazilian archives, and what emerges is an efficient if somewhat dull book. Mechanically, the work is a model dissertation-turned-book; the prose is clear, the bibliography comprehensive, the footnotes intelligible. But it is written for the specialists in Brazilian and British history who are able to weave their way through the laborious process leading to abolition. Only the most stout of heart Africanists will want to make the effort to follow what is a peripheral theme to African history.

Johnson Asiegbu's subject, though the title could have more clearly indicated this, is British policy towards liberated African slaves who emigrated *to the West Indies* after emancipation in 1834. He is not concerned with, and virtually ignores, those Africans who, after a stay in Freetown, returned to Nigeria, especially, and played the vital role of a pro-British incipient African bourgeoisie. Asiegbu demonstrates clearly that, in the face of pressure from the West Indian planters, the British government shut its eyes to the frightening similarities between the traffic in "voluntary" free labour and the disreputed slave trade, ostensibly over since 1807 as far as British citizens were concerned. The greatest abuses in this new scheme occurred in the period from 1847–49, when cheaper, slave-produced Brazilian and Cuban sugar threatened to drive the British West Indian product off the market. Under this pressure the British stopped insisting on the presence of a supervising British officer aboard private carriers, and mortality rates in this new version of the Middle Passage climbed alarmingly towards a high of one-third of the "voluntary" passengers. (Asiegbu estimates the total "voluntary" emigration between 1840 and 1861 at roughly 100,000 persons.)

Two factors combined to end the policy of liberated African labour emigration in 1861. First came the problem of dwindling supply of "liberable" Africans as the Brazilians, especially, cut down on the trade in the 1850's.

Second, and more important for the history of Africa, the local West African palm oil trade began to suffer from its own shortage of labour, and British West Indian planters turned more and more to Asia for a labour force. Thus economic and not humanitarian pressures forced a change in British policy.

Valuable though these findings are, Mr. Asiegbu's account is marred by sloppy presentation and a general lack of analysis. The book's introduction and conclusion are especially weak and poorly written, and offer virtually no discussion of the author's aims or findings. Instead Asiegbu gives a maudlin and confused interpretation of the debate between the Coupland and Williams schools. The opening chapter on the beginnings of Sierra Leone adds nothing, and in fact suffers from serious neglect of the Africans' own views, especially the strong criticisms men like Ottobah Cugoano and Olaudah Equiano levelled against humanitarian paternalism. Finally, the book is thin for the price involved; of the 230 pages, only 160 are text and the rest Appendices, only a few of which are at all important to the work.

Mr. Asiegbu promises a follow-up study, the impact of liberated Africans on West Africa after 1861. This will be welcomed, and it is to be hoped that there will be greater emphasis on African attitudes and actions and less on British policy. Thirty years ago it could have been said that British policy towards the slave trade and slavery was a major theme in African history. Then, the impact of liberated Africans upon their respective West African societies was hardly appreciated. Today, the major theme is rather the role of these men as members of a new class of proto-bourgeoisie, most of whom enthusiastically transmitted British religious, political, economic and even imperial ideas to large parts of West Africa.

McGill University
Montreal, Canada

MYRON J. ECHENBERG

A. E. Afigbo, *The Warrant Chiefs. Indirect Rule in Southeastern Nigeria 1891–1929.* New York, Humanities Press, 1972, pp. xv, 338.

The subject matter is familiar: systems of administration in colonial Africa. But the approach has changed with the times. In place of the British analyzing and justifying the colonial system they dominated, we now have the Nigerians criticizing the colonial system they lived under. Among the objectives of the exercise, presumably, are to reinterpret the colonial period from a viewpoint more appropriate to Nigerians, and to help establish viable Nigerian political institutions. The long dispute over the nature of direct and indirect continues in these pages. In the process, Lord Lugard comes in for some hard knocks, as do such defenders of Lugard as Margery Perham and Lucy Mair. Other colonial figures, notably Sir Ralph Moor, receive some praise.

The book is a study of the Warrant Chiefs from the nineteenth century until the Women's Riot of 1929 in Owerri and Calabar provinces. Following a rather comprehensive background chapter on "indigenous politics" among the Ibo, Ibibio, Ijo and Ogoja peoples, the narrative follows the growth of the Native Courts under Moor, and the appointment of Warrant Chiefs to sit on the courts. Then from 1914 to 1919, Lord Lugard is seem as attempting to establish uniform local government all over Nigeria, and hence forcing his Northern model on the South. In the meantime, the people came to lose their fear of colonialism, and the chiefs became more agents of the administration than local leaders. The weakness in the local government system began to show the moment Lugard left, and various reforms were attempted. Finally, with the idea that a Native Treasury was necessary to support the Native Courts, the government substituted a direct tax on men for the previously required forced labor. In 1928 the collection of the tax went quietly enough. But in 1929 the women of Owerri province, fearing that they too were to be taxed, led an uprising now known as the Women's Riot. The result was that the British dismantled the local government system, and started over again.

In summary, Afigbo says three traditions came into conflict: the indigenous political tradition, the tradition of Sir Ralph Moor, and the tradition of F. D. Lugard. Conflict over the small differences between the last two, he says, obscured the great difference between the first and the others, at least until the Women's Riot.

The work of reinterpreting the colonial period is now seriously underway, and Afigbo is an able contributor to that tradition. He writes with clarity and wit, so that it is difficult to miss his point. He has relied heavily on local archives and interviews, and the details of his book bring to life the flavor of local politics in Nigeria.

The concentration on the role of Lugard brings both strengths and weaknesses. Lugard and Lugardism are the main subject for almost half the book. Much is to be said for de-mystifying the man, for proving him to be a mere mortal, and for criticizing his autocratic nature and his political mistakes. But to make him a scapegoat, to make him a symbol for all that is wrong in British administration rather than for all that is right, does not seem to lead anywhere. At points, Afigbo seems almost to be suggesting that Lugard was the cause of the Nigerian Civil War. It is fairly important to distinguish between problems brought about by Lugard himself, and those brought about by British rule in general. Indeed, Afigbo argues that under any conditions, the British would have been induced to set up a local government system little different from what they actually set up. On the one hand the system could never have worked, but on the other hand Lugard made it even worse. These two lines of argument tend to conflict.

Perhaps this apparent contradiction could be resolved by taking a broader view of the colonial system than simply administrative policy. What, for example, were the forces which caused Lugard to propose a unified administrative system? What were the conflicts between the aims of British rule and the objectives of Nigerians? The study of politics and administration is the obvious place to start work. But we will surely understand the rise and fall of the Warrant Chief system better, and the place of Lugard in that process, once the social and economic history of colonial Nigeria has been more carefully filled in. It is to be hoped that Nigerian historians will move in greater numbers into these areas in the coming years, rather than concentrate solely on politics.

A note on sources: the book goes into greatest detail among the Ibo, which seems justified. But since an important step in the argument is that the British built up the system of Native Courts and House Rule among the Ijo and then misapplied it to the Ibo and others, it is a significant error not to have cited the important work of E. J. Alagoa on the Ijo.

McGill University   PATRICK MANNING
Montreal, Canada

Yohanan Friedmann, *Shaykh Ahmad Sirhindi*. Montreal, McGill University Press, 1971, pp. xiv, 130, $ 9.50.

The work under review is based on a Ph. D. dissertation submitted by the author to the Institute of Islamic Studies, McGill University. The author has had access to some very rare manuscripts in the Asafiyya Library, Hyderabad, Andhra Pradesh. He has a keen insight combined with a high degree of scholarship, and the work under review is a significant contribution to the study of the thought of the 17th century Indian mystic Shaikh Ahmad Sirhindi, on whom much has been written from varying religious and political angles. Sirhindi was a great leader of the Naqshbandiyya Order of Islamic mysticism, a full scale study of which has been recently undertaken by Professor Hamid Algar of the University of California at Berkley.

While Dr Friedmann studies in some detail the mystical thought of Sirhindi, whose main contribution to Indian Sufism was his re-evaluation, re-definition and re-orientation of the doctrine of phenomenalogical monism, the author's principal concern is the examination and criticism of the more recent historiography about Sirhindi which tends to regard Sirhindi's orthodoxy and propaganda as a reaction to Akbar's policies of secularism in the administration of the empire, and of composite eclecticism in religious outlook. Dr. Friedmann sharply rejects this recent view of Sirhindi, and views him essentially as a mystic. While, no doubt, there is a great deal of validity in Dr. Friedmann's criticism, it is by no means conclusive. Though the politicization of Sirhindi has been carried to extremes, there is no doubting the evidence of Sirhindi's own letters; quite a few of them are concerned with politics or rather with the restoration of orthodoxy in the Mughal empire. But Dr. Friedmann is quite right in assuming that the influence of the Naqshbandiyya on Aurangzeb has been overrated. There is no denying the fact that unlike his brother Dara Shukoh and his sister, Jahan Ara, Aurangzeb had an unmystical mind. At any rate, even in the Naqshbandiyya of the 18th century Sirhindi's political view had almost disappeared and its place had been taken by the eclecticism and tolerance of Mirza Mazhar Jan-i Janan whose influence spread to Syria, Iraq and Turkey.

University of Toronto   AZIZ AHMAD
Toronto, Canada

B. I. Obichere, *West African States and European Expansion: The Dahomey-Niger Hinterland, 1885–1898*. New Haven, Yale University Press, 1971, pp. x, 400, $ 15.00.

Brick by brick, thesis by thesis, the temple of truth is being built. Region by region, graduate students have fanned out over the land shining their light into unknown corners of what was once called the dark continent. This book was one of those efforts, a doctoral thesis submitted to Oxford University in 1967. Judging by the absence of any reference in the text or in the bibliography to the works of Ross, Izard, Argyle and Polanyi, it was not revised between that date and 1971, the date of the preface. In spite of this, the work is competent, represents a thorough and intelligent reading of the archives and fills a significant gap in the historical literature. Obichere's subject is the French push into Dahomey and the hinterland area stretching from Borgu to the Mossi states.

Obichere is writing about an area, most of which was little known in Europe at the time – Dahomey excepted – and had to be explored before the colonial powers could even be sure what they were claiming. The account, like most narratives of the scramble has elements of the absurd. The flag followed not commerce, but the first map-maker into areas whose resources were little known and whose value to the colonial powers was never developed. We might even say that the area was later underdeveloped. Obichere describes the conquest of Dahomey, the scurryings of explorers, and the military expeditions sent forth by eager governors of three nations anxious to make their mark on history. Once mighty Dahomey was beaten, internal divisions elsewhere were exploited, repeating rifles generally prevailed, and the final task was left to diplomats in Europe unwilling to risk war over distant and unfamiliar lands. Surprisingly, and I think correctly, Obichere argues that economic factors were the most important of the many stimuli to this expansion:

> The competition for territory in the hinterland was primarily a result of the desire to ensure the economic viability of the coastal possessions whose commerce and prosperity depended on the uninterrupted flow of trade.

The colonialists often also exaggerated the wealth of areas they sought.

The book has several short-comings. First, it is based completely on sources in European archives. Obichere has consulted neither oral traditions nor African archives, which are often fuller and franker. Second, he has chosen to study a large area over a short period of time. This results in a very shallow picture of the African side of the interaction, of African perceptions and of the meaning of the conquest to the conquered. This is more a work of European history, than a study of Africa. Third, Obichere has paid little attention to economic history or to the various economic interests operating in the area. Lastly, the book reads in places too much like what it is, a thesis. The narrative is detailed, the analysis is brief.

When better books are written on this area, they will go more intensively into processes of change and of interaction within the area. I hope Obichere writes them. This book is a beginning, but there are still too many dark corners.

University of Toronto   Martin A. Klein
Toronto, Canada

Clifford Geertz, *Islam Observed.* New Haven and London, Yale University Press, 1968, pp. 136, $ 5.00.

The short book under review is the reproduction of Dwight Harrington Terry Foundation lectures on religious development in Morocco and Indonesia by Clifford Geertz who is Professor of Anthropology in the University of Chicago.

The very approach of Professor Geertz is fascinating. He has chosen the two countries, Morocco and Indonesia, situated at the geographical – and cultural – extremes of the world of Islam. In both countries he examines their classical styles, their "scriptural interludes", and their struggle for reality. The short book underlines basically the difference in the interpretation of Islam in the two countries studied. In the author's own words: "...they have participated in the history of that (Islamic) civilization in quite different ways, to quite different degrees, and with quite different results. They both incline towards Mecca, but, the antipodes of the Muslim world, they bow in opposite directions."

This would illustrate how entertaining the author's style is. The book, however, suffers from two shortcomings. The author gives the impression that his knowledge of the historical background of Morocco is not profound; and that he does not sufficiently take into account the magnitude of Buddhist and Hindu influence on the Indonesian Islam. The book as a whole, and its general argument, also leaves one with an unsatisfying impression of superficiality. But this would be judging the work as history. As a piece of anthropological investigation it may leave quite different impressions.

University of Toronto   Aziz Ahmad
Toronto, Canada

C. P. Ridley, Paul H. B. Godwin, Dennis J. Doolin, *The Making of a Model Citizen in Communist China.* Stanford, The Hoover Institution Press, 1971, pp. 404, $ 9.95.

The Making of a Model Citizen in Communist China is a volume which deserves a place, for contradictory reasons, in the library of all who are concerned with the political and social processes of the People's Republic of China. The authors have provided us with an excellent collection (146 in number) of translations drawn from a set of elementary school grammar readers (yü-wen) covering the first five years of elementary schooling. These texts were issued between 1957 and 1964 being drawn from the curriculum of Peking and Shanghai. The documents themselves, therefore, provide an excellent source for studying early socialization and to a considerable degree, permit us to understand the horizon of values for the first generation of Chinese to enter the school system after the revolution. On the other hand, this volume is a superb example of what scholarship should not be. The analytic section of the volume covering the first 208 pages is filled with inconsistency, prejudice, distortion and most of all a lack of understanding of both the nature of the Chinese revolution as well as its link to the educational system.

Among the assumptions stated early in the study is that western society is stable, resulting in adults accepting and transmitting accepted values, whereas in China the adult population may not pass on positive attitudes (page 4). Passing over this dubious characterization of western society, how do the authors validate their assumption about China? They tell us that "the Communists leadership is undoubtedly trying to change positive attitudes toward Kuomintang China that may have been created by the family" (page 101); however, most parents recognize the effect positive attitudes toward the KMT would have on their children's future and would therefore refrain from expressing such attitudes (page 102). This tautology is deficient in both substance and logic. This same inadequate presentation is reflected in the analysis of Mao Tse-tung. On the one hand, we are told that Mao is portrayed as a "Sun God" (page 111), while an analysis of the statistics drawn from the authors' methodology displays in their "Central Theme" analysis 48% of the texts are concerned with the values of the new society compared with 16.5% devoted to Mao (page 135), while in their "Main Topics" analysis "recommended behavior" leads the list with 24.75% with Mao fifth in order of frequency of occurrence with 5% (page 182). The authors in addition criticize the Chinese compilers of the readers for including "fictionalized texts" (page 21). One of these stories relates to the struggle between a poor starving child in the U.S. with a wealthy lady's dog outside of a dog restaurant, while another refers to a black African who is attacked and killed by a lion while a film-maker shoots his film. While granted they are symbolic, how fictionalized are they when we find more nutritionists hired by pet food companies in Canada than are employed by manufacturers of human food, and somewhere between 28 and 107 black people in Macon County Ala. dead from untreated syphilis, the result of an experiment begun in 1932 and carried on until the summer of 1972? The central dis-service of the analysis is the unwillingness of the authors to present the Chinese view of how they understand the dialectical development of society. Rather than this, we are presented with a view that China is a society of schizophrenics tormented by the contradictions between ingenuity and obedience, kindness and pro-social aggression, evil of the past and accomplishments of the past, ideals and reality. In their summary, the authors state that achievement should ideally result in competition and personal ambition and they lament for the Chinese who must sacrifice this for society. What is a sacrifice for Ridley, Godwin and Doolin is a virtue for hundreds of millions of Chinese.

McGill University   SAMUEL J. NOUMOFF
Montreal, Canada

Romain Yakemtchouck, *L'Afrique en Droit international*. Paris, R. Pichon et R. Durand-Auzias, 1971.

Professor Yakemtchouk has written a scholarly treatise which explains in its first chapter the African conceptions of international law, and supports his assessments through analysis of indepth cases which cover the rest of his work. The historical, political, developmental and motivational backgrounds that he presents prior to his entry upon the case studies, is an excellent interdisciplinary formulation of the reasons for the variety of stands which Africa takes on issues of contemporary international law. Thus his introductory chapter plays the role of both introduction and summary for the rest of his book which also deals with the following case areas: recognition of state and government (chapter II); succession to treaties (chapter III); the problem of frontiers (chapter IV);

peace and war (Chapter V); the international regime of waterways (Chapter VI); maritime relations (chapter VII); bilateral technical co-operation (chapter VIII); the right to work (chapter IX); equality of economic "treatment" (chapter X); investments (chapter XI); African regionalism (chapter XII); and Africa and the United Nations (chapter XIII). There are also annexes, an index of names, and a wealth of bibliographical and substantive footnotes.

The basic thrust of his book, which is lucidly written and soberly argued, is a dichotomy of Africa's reserve towards rules of international law which were formulated by the very Powers which colonized and fragmented the Continent, and Africa's readiness to adhere to the precepts and provisions of international law which uphold the exclusivity of national sovereignty (except in matters relating to African regional co-operation, integration and unity).

African States, he points out, consider that the development of international law was done without either their knowledge or their consent, and that it was imposed on them instead of being accepted by them. With this in mind, the author focusses on what he calls the elements and characteristics of the young African international law, regardless of its lack of clarity and in spite of its chances of longevity. The international law of the African States bears the imprint of the main problems which, as the author puts it, agitate the political life of the Continent and which preoccupy its leaders, namely, apartheid and decolonization. Active support of the armed struggle against the Powers which still administer dependent territories is considered relevant to ethics and justice. In this connection, the author states: "Mais l'Afrique estime que le droit des peuples a l'autodetermination revêt un caractère obligatoire, et que sa validité a au moins autant de poids que le principe de l'interdiction du recours à la force". This is an important example of what the author considers as a process of African regionalization of international law. However, he draws attention to the important fact that the reconversion and adaptation of international law is a gigantic task, and that the African States, preoccupied with their pressing economic and social tasks have not replaced the rules of law which they have denounced with new rules. Otherwise, the author argues, how could one regulate, on a purely national basis, international navigation, air transport, telecommunications, postal service, copyright...etc? In support of his argument, he cites a relevant conclusion reached by the Congress of African Jurists of 1966 as follows: "Les acquis juridiques du développement historique constituent un fonds commun de savoir, de formules et de solutions qui peuvent et doivent être utilises par les Etats neufs..."

The African emphasis on "the imperative of sovereignty" is given by the author a full treatment throughout his book. Such an emphasis, the author asserts, is due to psychological, historical and sociopolitical reasons, the most important of which is the fact that as a result of the struggle for African independence, sovereignty was made the supreme objective. Consequently, African States insist that their relations with the outside world be based on the principles of equality, non-interference in internal affairs, and respect for national dignity.

The author advocates, as do other writers who support pan-Africanism or inter-African co-operation, that African States should take concrete steps in the direction of limiting the notion of exclusive internal jurisdiction, gradually and progressively, in favour of inter-African co-operation based on inter-dependence. It is in this context that he describes the primacy of international law over

national law, a primacy which is affirmed in the majority of African constitutional documents, especially as they relate to African unity. His reference to
the Constitutions of Ghana and Cameroon, among other Constitutions which
contain provisions dealing with African unity, is illustrative.

The author deals at length with Africa's attitude of reserve toward the
International Court of Justice (ICJ) which has developed as a result of the
Court's judgement in the South West Africa (now called Namibia) cases
delivered on 18 July 1966. Here it will be recalled that in November 1960,
Ethiopia and Liberia which were Members of the League of Nations which
entrusted South Africa with the Mandate for "South West Africa", instituted
contentious proceedings against South Africa which covered the Mandatory's
obligation to furnish annual reports on its administration to the United Nations
General Assembly and its contraventions of the Mandate's provisions. In its
judgement, the ICJ, by the President's casting vote, the votes being equally
divided (7 to 7) found that the Applicant States could not be considered to have
established any legal right or interest in the subject matter of their claims and
accordingly, the Court decided to reject them.

This judgement, as the author aptly points out, affected adversely the
conception of the African States as to the role of the ICJ in the world of today.
The judgement was regarded by Africa as "contraire à la Charte," "d'inspiration politique", and "une échappatoire pour éviter de traiter la question
de fonds". Following that, the United Nations General Assembly, on 27 October 1966, voted to withdraw the Mandate, and on 19 May 1967, it established
an international body to administer "Namibia" pending its independence.
Here it should be pointed out that the visits earlier this year by U.N. Secretary-
General Kurt Waldheim to the Republic of South Africa and Namibia, and the
subsequent visit by Foreign Minister Muller of South Africa to the U.N. for
consultations with the Secretary-General are in direct relation to that 1967
General Assembly resolution and other resolutions.

It could therefore, be said that in undertaking this study, Professor Yakemtchouk brought together, in an effective way, the various postulates which he
had previously advanced, and has updated the early writings on the same
subject by scholars such as Ibrahim Shihata and R. P. Anand in the mid
1960's.

St. John's University   YASSIN EL-AYOUTY
New York, U.S.A.

Nigel Heseltine, *Madagascar*. New York, Washington, London, Prager Publishers, 1971, pp. x, 334, $ 11.00.

This is the best general account of Madagascar to appear in English so far.
It is much more systematic and coherent than the more journalistic publications
which have previously appeared. The author was recently economic adviser
to the President of the Malagasy Republic and travelled to every corner of the
island, as the President of the *Academic Malgache* remarks in his preface.

The book provides a background description of the land, climate, fauna and
flora; a survey of the views most generally held on the origins of the Malagasy
peoples; a sound and quite thorough account of the state and politics from

1800 up till 1970 and concluding chapters on the economy and development prospects. The picturesqueness, the mysterious paradoxes, anomalies and contrasts of the Great Red Island are well conveyed, and a sensitive and profound appreciation of Malagasy culture and its variations is displayed. Reasonable objectivity is achieved in presenting the political and religious clashes of English and French, Protestant and Catholic and the relative development potential of the Malagasy on the one side and the still pervasive French companies on the other.

It is hardly the author's fault that he has reproduced the views of older writers on Malagasy kinship and family structure which recent studies have shown to be incorrect. The Merina were divided into locally endogamous communities which cannot be described as clans or as patrilineal. It is a pity that having correctly remarked that distinct tribes do not really exist, the author calls the named territorial groupings clans although they have none of the characteristics of clans. It is typical of the tribal myth that the proverb *Malagasy daholo, tsy misy avakavaka* (We are all Malagasy, there are no distinctions) should be translated instead "We are all Malagasy, there are no more tribes!" Nor did access to tombs follow patrilineal rules. The Betsileo are rather similar and the whole island is best seen as exhibiting varieties of cognatic kinship (as is true of most of Indonesia), with somewhat stronger emphasis on short patrilines here and there, and ubiquitous tendencies to stratified ranking of endogamous groups. Nor is there any sound evidence of matrilineal survivals. Certainly the rights of maternal uncles are not to be so interpreted.

Some miscellaneous small points require comment. It is perhaps misleading to speak of Tananarive as vividly alive till far into the night, for the fearful retreat into the shuttered house in all the villages of the plateau does affect the capital as well. The rival Catholic and Protestant churches of these villages are surely quite contrasted architecturally, not "often of identical design". The reference to "Swahili *lambas* of East Africa' is wrong, there is no such term in Swahili. It is essentially Malagasy. Protestant and Catholic missions do not both stretch back equally early in the nineteenth century, for the London Missionary Society had a virtual monopoly from the 1820s to the 1860s. It is misleading to speak of smooth transition to independence since the savagely suppressed rebellion of 1947 was an essential part of it, with strong repercussions to-day. The "wild cattle" referred to are usually described as "feral" and there is no evidence of indigenous wild cattle in Madagascar, Luis Mariano's prolonged visits in the early seventeenth century can hardly be called "sporadic landings". There are no "distinct racial types" in Madagascar, but a great though continuous range of variation in physical characteristics not only between coast and plateau but even within small localities. The Makoa are certainly not a distinct tribe in Madagascar but are descendants of Mozambique slaves who came from the Makoa or neighbouring groups in northern Mozambique. It is quite outlandish to imply causal influence by suggesting similarities between Malagasy, Nilotic, Hamitic and Fulani cattle keepers. There is no evidence to prove that the herina were either better organised or more culturally evolved until they came in touch with external influences and began their rapid development at the end of the eighteenth century, however, they certainly occupied the Betsimitatatra long before the nineteenth century. The name of the French envoy Le Nyre de Vilers is consistently mis-spelled as is Wanderobo (p. 54).

The figures for secondary schools run by the religious missionaries seem to be omitted from the table on p. 86. Betsileo hats are not rimless, but those of the coastal, especially south-western peoples. Further fanciful interpretations of "Vazimba" are unfortunately added to the already long speculative list. The disintegrative effects of excessive forced labor on the structure of the herina state in its latter days are underestimated.

The author is very sanguine about development prospects, despite the fact that real income per head in Madagascar fell slightly during the Development Decade. He stresses the dynamism and potential skill of the Malagasy, as comparable to that of the Japanese. The eclipse of the Suez Canal puts Madagascar back on the great ocean routes, well-placed for re-export industries; with enormous hydro-electric potential; a possible meat export of up to 200,000 tons per annum from the huge western herds, rivalling that of Uruquay; production of both temperate and tropical fruits for the air freight market; great tourist potential in the vast sandy beaches of the west coast, and the attractions of a stable political scene (though recent events cast a little more shadow here).

University of Wisconsin   AIDAN SOUTHALL
Madison, U.S.A.

FURTHER PUBLICATIONS FROM E. J. BRILL

Contributions to Asian Studies

Sponsored by THE CANADIAN ASSOCIATION FOR SOUTH ASIAN STUDIES, TORONTO Canada.

General Editor: K. ISHWARAN, York University, Downsview, Ontario, Canada

A series containing scholarly papers. Each volume will cover special areas, of Asian countries, and may be of value for specialists, but also to students and teachers of sociology, anthropology and political science.

Volume 1: 1971. viii, 204 pages, 8 tables   Gld. 46.—

Volume 2: RELIGION AND SOCIETY IN PAKISTAN. Edited by AZIZ AHMAD. 1971. viii, 105 pages   Gld. 40.—

Contents: F. ABBOTT, The historical background of Islamic India and Pakistan; A. AHMAD, Islam and democracy in Pakistan; S. M. M. QURESHI, Religion and party politics in Pakistan; H. MALIK, The spirit of capitalism and Pakistani Islam; S. McDONOUGH, The social import of Parwez's religious thought; S. AHMAD, Islam and Pakistani peasants.

Volume 3: 1973, viii, 166 pages, some tables and figures   Gld. 64.—

Contents: CEYLON: REINCARNATION AND BUDDHISM. B. L. SMITH, Sinhalese Buddhism and the Dilemmas of Reinterpretation; I. STEVENSON, Characteristics of Cases of the Reincarnation Type in Ceylon. – INDIA: ECONOMY, POLITICS AND SOCIAL CHANGE. J. L. MURRAY, Peasant Motivation, Ecology, and Economy in Panjab; Y. K. MA-LIK, Conflict over Chandigarh: A Case Study of an Interstate Dispute in India; J. S. UPPAL, Economic Development of Indian States: A Study in Development Contrast; K. G. SAINI, Economic Performance and Institutional Change: the Experience of India. – INDIA: RELIGION. M. MAHAPATRA, The Badu: A Service-caste at the Lingaraj Temple at Bhubaneswar; C. R. PANGBORN. – INDIA: INTELLECTUALS AND CHANGE. P. C. DEB and L. A. WENZEL, A Dimension of Change in India: Prestige of occupations Among University Students; H. S. SANDHU, The Intellectuals and Social Change in India. – INDIA AND PAKISTAN: FAMILY. J. H. KORSON, Some Aspects of Social Change in the Muslim Family in West Pakistan; I. VERGHESE, Is the Kota Society Polyandrous?

Volume 4: TRADITION AND CHANGE IN THERAVADA BUDDHISM: ESSAYS ON CEYLON AND THAILAND IN THE 19TH AND 20TH CENTURIES. Edited by BARD-WELL L. SMITH. 1974. viii, 105 pages.   Gld. 42.—

Contents: B. L. SMITH, Introduction; H. BECHERT, Contradictions in Sinhalese Buddhism; T. FERNANDO, The Western Educated Elite and Buddhism in British Ceylon: A Neglected Aspect of the Nationalist Movement; B. G. GOKHALE, Anagarick Dhammapala: Toward Modernity through Tradition in Ceylon; F. E. REYNOLDS, Sacral Kingship and National Development: the Case of Thailand; S. PIKER, Buddhism and Modernization in Contemporary Thailand; F. B. MORGAN, Vocation of Monk and Layman: Signs of Change in Thai Buddhist Ethics; D. K. SWEARER, Thai Buddhism: Two Responses to Modernity; F. E. REYNOLDS, Tradition and Change in Theravada Buddhism: A Bibliographical Essay Focused on the Modern Period.

Volume 5: 1974, viii, 102 pages

Contents: A. INDIA AND PHILIPPINES: CULTURE, RELIGION AND REINCARNATION. GEOFFREY BURKHART, Equal in the Eyes of God: A South Indian Devotional Group in its Hierarchical Setting. – DONN V. HART, Culture in Curing in Filipino Peasant Society. – ARVIND SHARMA, The Notion of Cyclical Time in Hinduism. – IAN STEVENSON, JAMUNA PRASAD, L. P. MAHROTA, K. S. RAWAT, The Investigation of Cases of the Reincarnation Type in India. – B. INDIA, INDONESIA AND NEPAL: POLITICS AND EDUCATION. REUVEN KAHANE, Social Conditions leading to Military Dominance: the Case of Indonesia. – HORACE B. REED, Education and Land in Nepal: Complementary Reforms. – GLYNN WOOD, Egalitarian and Technocratic Goals in Educational Growth: The View from Mysore.

Journal of Asian

and

African Studies

Volume IX	JULY and APRIL 1974	Numbers 3-4

CONTENTS

CONTENTS

and B. S. Strong, Circumpolar Peoples: and Anthropological perspective (Richard Slobodin). John A. Harrison (ed.), South and Southeast Asia. Volume 3 of the Association of Asian Studies' Thirtieth Anniversary Commemorative Series (Howard Spodek). Douglas L. Wheeler and René Pélissier, Angola (Immanuel Wallerstein). S. O. Anozie (ed.), Language Systems in Africa. The Conch (Rose-Marie Weber). E. Hermassi, Leadership and National Development in North Africa: A Comparative Study (A. M. Abu-Hakima). Tung Wei (ed.), Communist China: A System-Functional Reader (John F. Copper). W. Norman Brown, The United States and India, Pakistan, Bangladesh (Robert I. Crane). James Ngugi (Ngugi Wa Thiong'O), Homecoming. Essays on African and Caribbean Literature, Culture and Politics (Max Dorsinville). Gerald Moore, Wole Soyinka. Modern African Writers (Max Dorsinville). Jeremy Boissevain and J. Clyde Mitchell (eds.), Network Analysis: Studies Human Interaction (William G. Flanagan). John Gallagher, Gordon Johnson and Anil Se 1 (eds.), Locality, Province, and Nation: Essays on Indian Politics, 1870–1940 (Robert Eric Frykenberg). Trygve Lötveit, Chinese Communism 1931–1934: Experiences in Civil Government (Eugene Lubot). Justus Ml van der Knoef, Indonesia after Sukarno (Roger K. Paget). William E. Henthorn, A History of Korea (Spencer J. Palmer). V. Craijanzano, The Hamadsha. A Study in Moroccan Ethnopsychiatry (Raymond Prince). Alexander Spoehr, Zambozanga and Sulu: An Archeological Approach to Ethnic Diversity (Daniel J. Scheans). Richard N. Henderson, The King in Every Man: Evolutionary Trends in Onitsha Ibo Society and Culture (William B. Schwab). Robert C. Lester, Theravada Buddhism in Southeast Asia (Amnuay Tapingkae). Raghaven N. Iyer, The Moral and Political Thought of Mahatma Gandhi (Robert L. Youngblood).

JOURNAL OF ASIAN AND AFRICAN STUDIES

The *Journal of Asian and African Studies*, published by E. J. Brill, Leiden, Holland, is a quarterly publication issued in January, April, July, and October. Each number is about eighty pages in length.

The Journal, edited by a board of scholars from all over the world who are specialists in Asian and African studies, presents a scholarly account of studies of man and society in the developing nations of Asia and Africa. It endeavours to fulfill a need in the field in that it unites contributions from anthropology, sociology, history, and related social sciences into a concerted emphasis upon building up systematic knowledge and using the knowledge derived from pure research for the reconstruction of societies entering a phase of advanced technology.

ALL EDITORIAL CORRESPONDENCE, including papers, notes and news covering research projects, associations and institutions, conferences and seminars, foundations and publications, and other activities relevant to Asia and Africa, should be addressed to: K. Ishwaran, Editor, J.A.A.S., Department of Sociology, York University, Downsview, Ontario M3J 1P3, Canada.

BOOKS FOR REVIEW (AFRICA) should be sent to: John M. Janzen, Department of Anthropology, University of Kansas, Lawrence, Kansas, 66044, U.S.A., and (ASIA) to Edward R. Beauchamp, College of Education, University of Hawaii, Wist Annex 2-222, 1776 University Avenue, Honolulu, Hawaii 96822.

BUSINESS CORRESPONDENCE, including subscriptions, change of address, orders for additional offprints, etc., should be addressed to:

E. J. BRILL — LEIDEN, THE NETHERLANDS

Subscription price of Volume X (1975): Gld. 64.— *plus postage and packing.*

Please do not send money with your order. The publisher will invoice you and will then be pleased to receive your remittance.

MANUSCRIPT STYLE GUIDE

Manuscripts of articles should be not more than 7000 words. Unsolicited papers will not be returned unless postage paid. Submit two copies of the article and retain a copy for your own files. Prepare copy as follows:

1. Type double-spaced on white 8-1/2″ × 11″ standard paper, with a 2″ margin at the left hand side and a 3″ space above the titles of both articles and reviews.
2.* Tables should be typed on separate pages, numbered consecutively and given headings. Footnotes for tables appear at the bottom of the tables. Insert a location note at the appropriate place in text, e.g., "Table 1 about here".
3.* Figures, maps and other line drawings are to be submitted in black Indian ink about twice the intended final size on good quality tracing paper. Insert a location note at the appropriate place in text.
4. Articles and reviews are to be submitted in their *final form* so that they require no further alterations. It is the obligation of authors to carefully proof read their material before submission to the journal. Owing to increasing costs, the publisher is compelled to charge authors for corrections other than printer's errors.

   *Tables, graphs, figures, etc., should be used sparingly.

- Bibliographical references should be cited in the text by the author's last name, date of publication and page, e.g., (Anderson 1972: 105) or, if the author's name is mentioned in the text, by the date and page reference only, e.g., (1972: 105). ● Footnotes are to appear as notes at the end of articles and are to be used only for substantive observations and not for purpose of citation. ● With dual authorship, give both last names; for more than two use "et al" (see 3 below). ● If there is more than one reference to the same author and year, distinguish them by using letters (a, b) attached to year of publication in the text and reference appendix (see 2 below). ● For institutional authorship supply minimum identification, e.g., (U.N.E.S.C.O. 1971: 67).

Entries in the references should be in alphabetical order of authors and should include: name and initials of author(s), date, title, name of periodical, volume number (arabic numerals to be used throughout), pagination (for periodicals), place of publication and publisher. e.g.,

1. FROLIC, B. Michael
    1971   "Soviet urban sociology". International Journal of Comparative Sociology XII (December): 234–251.
2. GREENBERG, Joseph H.
    1965a   "Linguistics" pp. 416–41 in Robert A. Lystad (ed.), The African World: a survey of social research. New York: Frederick A. Praeger.
    1965b   "Urbanism, migration and language" pp. 50-59, 189 in K. Huyper (ed.), Urbanization and Migration in West Africa. Berkeley and Los Angeles: University of California Press. (Reprinted in Man in Adaptation, the Bio-social Background, ed. by Y. A. Cohen, 259–67. Chicago: Aldine Publishing Co., 1968.)
3. KASER, D., et al
    1969   Library Development in Eight Asian Countries. New Jersey: Scarcecrow Press.
4. SOUTHALL, Aidan W.
    1970   "The illusion of tribe" pp. 28–50 in P. C. W. Gutkind (ed.), The Passing of Tribal Man in Africa. Leiden: E. J. Brill.

Book reviews should not exceed 800 words and should not contain footnotes; references to other works should be incorporated in the text; page references should be given when quotations from the book are included.

Galley proofs of articles will be sent to authors (from the publisher), who should use the standard method of proof correction. Corrected proofs should be returned to the Editor as soon as possible; where proofs are not returned in time, the Editor reserves the right to send the printers his own corrected proof of contributors article which will be the basis of the final article. Proofs are intended for checking, NOT RE-WRITING and authors are most strongly reminded that material should be submitted ready for the printer.

Authors receive 25 free offprints of their article (8 free offprints for book reviews). Additional offprints of articles can be supplied at cost price and must be ordered and paid for when the corrected proofs are returned to the printer.

PUBLISHER: E. J. Brill, Leiden, The Netherlands

Introduction

ROGER D. ABRAHAMS AND JOHN F. SZWED*

THIS GATHERING OF ARTICLES is a harvesting of some of the second fruits of the Black Studies movement. *Discovering Afro-America* is our designation for this scholarly dimension of the growing recognition of the integrity and power of black individuals and communities. These essays, written by young scholars with a variety of backgrounds, demonstrate that one major area of this discovery is in cultural continuities.

Not that this is really a discovery from the historical point of view. It is really a rediscovery of some of the verities which have reemerged every twenty-five or thirty years in the last century. And the most important of these: that Afro-Americans have a unique history and culture not wholly stemming from the desperate experience of enslavement, racism and poverty.

Perhaps the most important aspect of the discovery of Afro-America has been the growing recognition that blacks have been studied before, often by blacks, and often in a very insightful manner. There is some poignancy to the story, however, for it both startles and saddens to read documents of other generations as *they* discover Afro-America and to see that we are still embroiled in the same controversies, dealing with much the same range of data (though certainly somewhat more fully described today) and confronted with the same contradictions and paradoxes. How sad it is, for instance, to read the dialogue between E. Franklin Frazier and Melville Herskovits at an ACLS meeting on Afro-American studies in 1940 to realize that we are still arguing about the same matters. (See especially the Woods, Thompson, and Hannerz essays here.) And how much sadder, even, to realize that most of the very good scholarship involved in this controversy is buried in arcane publications. What we have left of the Herskovits-Frazier confrontation that is readily available, for instance, are their *chefs d'oeuvre, The Negro in America*, and *The Myth of the Negro Past*, but no apparatus to help the student understand the contradiction, and point out the limitations of both men's approaches. This is why argumentative survey of scholarship pieces (such as Hannerz') seem so crucial in the development of Black Studies.

It may be of some value, as we have recently done a bibliographical work concerning Afro-America (Szwed and Abrahams, in press) to give a brief survey of writing in this area.

* The editors gratefully acknowledge the dispatch with which the contributors dealt with us, the help of Frances Terry in typing the manuscripts, and the financial assistance of the National Institutes of Mental Health, MH 17216 and the American Philosophical Society.

If we look at the writings on black culture in all of the Americas some striking similarities appear. Beginning in the mid-1600's and continuing forward there is an abundance of writing in the form of travel accounts and slavers' journals. At first, these early writers dealt with the question of whether or not slaves were humans, and therefore subjects for justifiable slavery. The debate centered on whether what slaves did constituted genuinely human behavior. And throughout there was also the question of whether the slaves were able to become "civilized": that is, capable of changing their behavior to conform to that of the Europeans. But at the same time, questions were raised as to whether or not the Europeans themselves might become savages through their contact with Africans in the already feared tropics and semi-tropics of the New World. Certainly, these writings show an awe of African culture patterns: their particular beliefs in the supernatural, their religious ceremonies often held outdoors at night, their music and dance, their talk. This concern led to the writing of guidebooks for potential planters and European emigrants that were in their own way ethnographic accounts.

A second phase of writing began in the early 1800's when abolitionists and missionaries (often the same people) concerned themselves with what would have to be contended with in converting slaves to Christianity, and whether or not emancipation would work in a multi-racial, multi-cultural setting. Again, there was a concern with "native" ways, their exoticism; only now instead of seeing slaves as savages, they were more often than not seen as children, capable of learning. So, for example, North American abolitionists and apologists for slaves wrote enthusiastically of spirituals and various expressions of other-worldly faith, often completely ignoring all of the other aspects of mundane, day-to-day life.

In a third phase, that which followed the abolition of slavery, there were several divergent types of writing. One, by ex-slaveholders and their children, was an expression of sentiment for the "old types" who were passing, the people who were said to be happier and healthier under slavery. Here, "native ways" were recalled and described as a reminder of why blacks could only survive under the domination of the plantocracy. But in the British West Indies, where ex-slaves were in the vast majority or, in the case of Haiti, which had successfully abolished slavery by revolution, the "native" middle class recognized the same cultural features that the slavers and missionaries noted, but with some argument that these represented creative cultural accomplishments. This latter tradition of writing continues today, usually in the form of locally printed pamphlets, and leading most recently to a call among the local literati for a folk-based literature and national culture: e.g., writings on Haiti by Jean Price-Mars on Haitian folktales and religion, or for the former British West Indies by Olive Lewin, Olive Walke, Louise Bennett, Rex Nettleford and others, in defense of calypso, creole speech, carnival, folktales, and the like.

The situation in the United States was quite different, however. With a great preponderance of whites in economic and social control, and with the imposition of severe Jim Crow laws in the nineteenth century, blacks and black defenders among the whites were inclined, like the abolitionists of an earlier period, to deny the existence of black cultural patterns, to refute their musical and choreographic abilities, their unique religious rituals, and anything which distinguished them culturally from whites.

Starting in the 1930's and reaching a peak in the 1950's, a fourth phase developed following the extension of social science techniques in the forms of criminology, social work, and psychiatry. Now, black cultural patterns were seen as manifestations of pathology, a deviance from North American "mainstream" standards resulting from the various manifestations of injustices and racism. In the British West Indies, this was the position associated with Madeline Kerr and Edith Clarke; in the United States it was the position of Abram Kardiner and Lionel Ovesey, Gunnar Myrdal, E. Franklin Frazier, William H. Grier and Price M. Cobbs, and many, many others.

Three very powerful exceptions must be noted here. In the United States, as noted, Melville J. Herskovits applied the comparative method of anthropology to what appeared to be on the surface a strictly North American phenomenon, and found many overriding similarities of culture shared by the black peoples of West Africa and most of the countries of the New World. In Cuba, Fernando Ortiz, a lawyer and criminologist, had initially been interested in the pathological aspects of black life, but abandoned that position to become Cuba's chief scholar of Afro-Cuban culture. Similarly, in Brazil, Arthur Ramos, a psychiatrist, had initially seen Afro-Brazilian culture as merely manifestations of the primitive mind, but later came to be the chief advocate and scholar of African cultural retentions in that country.

The 1960's seem to have been the occasion for giving ethnographic and novelistic accounts of "ghetto street life" in its narrowest sense – hipsters, hustlers, and mackmen; sweet talk and getting over; drugs, freak's balls and stone violence. A new and gaudy sentimentalism, yes, but also an alternative to the experience of Uncle Toms, OEO, the Moynihan Report and the somnambulistic prose of the social ameliorists. Though these critics may accuse them of dilettantism, cross-cultural coprophilia, or worse, students of the street can observe (as Zola and Flaubert) that such life exists and must be described and understood. Nonetheless, a new perspective of Black American life is indicated, one that balances the exotic and arcane with the everyday and prosaic.

In much the same way, the hard-won argument for Afro-American culture as an historically and culturally distinct entity now needs to be enhanced by studies that interrelate (one almost writes "integrate") the various American ethnic cultures. But where we once saw such studies as inevitably demonstrating white over black, – African ways lost in the sweep of European culture – new facts are now emerging in new scholarship: Leslie Fiedler's shrewd reading of American mythology; Eileen Sothern's finding in black influences on European court and military music; William Stewart and David Dalby and J. L. Dillard's writings on the black forces at work in American and European languages; Karl Riesman and John F. Szwed's work on the African and Afro-

American elements in Joyce's *Finnegan's Wake* and in this volume, Peter Wood's argument concerning blacks teaching whites agricultural technology; these and many more are in the works.

Behind all this, too, are a group of inspired scholars presenting black history in a tough culture-based direction: Eugene Genovese, Engleman and Fogle, Herbert Guttman, John Blassingame, Sterling Stuckey, and, in this volume, William H. Wiggins, Jr.

The tone of the new scholarship is neither apologetic, defensive, nor patronizing. It emerges from an historical situation, a political reality, but it is also firmly fixed on previously untreatable data. Surely, some of the inspiration for this new manner and means of doing Afro-American scholarship arises from those black scholars who are, at the same time, practitioners, activists, and artists. (See for instance, Leonard Goines in this volume.)

What can we expect from Afro-American cultural studies in the next ten years? First of all, the questioning of the social models of analysis used in the past will certainly continue and intensify. Furthermore, numerous cultural continuities between specific 18th and 19th century Old and New World populations will become clearer, both through the use of demographic data, and through in-depth analysis of art – and life – style elements. (See Robert Thompson's article for an example.)

There is every reason to expect that new techniques and methodologies in linguistics, sociolinguistics, kinesics and proxemics, indeed literary analysis will focus interest on different manifestations of Afro-American culture, especially those correlating with aspects of social structure. (See, for instance, Dan Rose's article here.)

Finally, because of the unique configuration of sociocultural elements in Afro-America, new perspectives are arising which will have influence on practitioners of disciplines in dealing with other materials. We already see such a development in language study (especially concerning pidgins and creoles), and treatments of spirit possession and trance behavior in anthropology and psychiatry.

We also have faith that black culture will go on without analysis. Its track record is already pretty well-established.

Journal of Asian and African Studies IX, 3–4

Research in the Black Ghetto: a Review of the Sixties[1]

ULF HANNERZ

University of Stockholm, Stockholm, Sweden

THE IMAGE of the United States which dominated social thought in the fifties was that of the affluent homogeneous mass society. The end of ideology had been proclaimed and social critics seemed mostly concerned with conformism in suburbia. The state of race relations seemed to be a problem largely confined to one section of the country, the South, and it tended to be conceptualized mainly in the legalistic terms of desegregation. Then, in the sixties, came the rediscovery of conflict, poverty and ethnicity. A war on poverty was begun, the civil rights movement became transformed into one of black power, and there were riots in large northern cities where huge areas had become black ghettos. No longer could one use the ideas of the fifties in characterizing American society and identifying its problems.

The thrust of social research is necessarily in some way related to the general intellectual climate in the society where it is conducted. As the United States went from the fifties to the sixties, the social sciences may have had some influence in causing the changes in the perception of society, but even more significantly, these changes called forth a new interest in problems and research orientations which had been absent, dormant, or in other ways neglected in the preceding period. The body of research which I will review here is one which is to a very great extent a product of this new climate. It had no counterpart in the fifties; and if there are indications that it will not have one in the seventies either, this is to suggest once more the discontinuity between the decade which we recently passed through and that in which we are now.

I refer to the studies of black life carried out in northern ghettos, by researchers who might be either anthropologists or sociologists in terms of professional identification but who went about their work in a way which tends to be regarded as typically anthropological: i.e., as participant observers in which researchers get directly involved in ongoing everyday events in the ghetto community and thereby achieve a reasonably well-rounded picture of its way

---

1 This paper was presented at the Nordic Association for American Studies Conference, "The Urbanization Process as Reflected in the Social Sciences and Literature," Kungälv, Sweden, June 20–23, 1973.

of life. It is this style of working, rather than a shared theoretical perspective, which makes me refer to the studies involved as "a body of research."

It may seem curious that the studies to be discussed here, little more than a handful, should be deemed a particularly unusual contribution to knowledge about one sector of American society, since race relations have clearly been a major field of study from the very beginning of American social science. A closer look at that field, however, reveals that a close-up view of black life has not in fact been achieved with any great regularity. Much of what has passed for knowledge about black life has been arrived at by way of studies from a distance, such as analyses of official statistics of welfare agency case materials, or by way of piecemeal investigations of isolated problems, comfortably handled through survey methods not requiring intensive, long-term involvement with the black community. Only in the thirties and early forties, in a period of social ferment which in some ways may have been like the sixties, was there a concentration of studies which gave anything like a picture of black life as a whole, including such works as Johnson's *The Shadow of the Plantation* (1934), Dollard's *Caste and Class in a Southern Town* (1937), Powdermaker's *After Freedom* (1939), Frazier's *The Negro Family in the United States* (1939), *Deep South* by Davis, Gardner and Gardner (1941), and *Black Metropolis* by Drake and Cayton (1945). But as the titles indicate, most of these dealt with the South. Black Americans had not yet become to such a great extent a northern urban people.

Moreover, much of the research on race relations does not focus on the black community at all. The black American has often been the "invisible man" in his country, to use the title of Ralph Ellison's novel, and to a surprising extent this has been true even in a field of research where one would expect him to be conspicuous. [2] One prominent example is that most celebrated of all studies in the field, Myrdal's *An American Dilemma* (1944). The dilemma in question is, after all, a white dilemma; Myrdal gives primary attention to "what goes on in the minds of white Americans." Of more than 1300 pages in this massive compendium, hardly more than 30 are devoted to the black life to which the researchers of the sixties have devoted most of their attention.

To be sure, problems of American race relations cannot be understood without regard to the operation of white mainstream America. It would be a mistake, however, to see black Americans only as a passive party in either maintaining or changing these relations; yet to some extent American social science seems to have succumbed to such a perspective in much of the literature. In 1963, before the pattern of the sixties had crystallized, one leading American sociologist, Everett C. Hughes, asked, in a presidential address to the American Sociological Association, why sociologists had not foreseen "the explosion of collective action of Negro Americans toward immediate full integration into American society" (Hughes 1963: 879). A few years later, he might have asked why they had also failed to foresee the growth of black separatism. Part of the answer

---

2   See for instance recent overviews of the field by Lyman (1972) and Vander Zanden (1973).

to both questions may have been that for some time they had not in fact made the study of the black community a particularly important component of their race relations research.

I should add that as the pendulum swings, we are now again hearing pleas for more research on the role of white America in the current racial situation. The current concept among anthropologists interested in American society is that there is a need to "study up" (Nader 1972), to realize how dependent everyone is on the holders of power, and to analyze the exercise of that power. Certainly there could hardly be any research that is more important. Yet two points should be made in this connection. One is that this is not a return to what we might identify as the major trend in the white-oriented race relations inquiries of the past, which tended to be concerned with racial prejudice and its psychological bases rather than with the working of the power structure. The program of "studying up" would involve above all the study of "institutional" or "structural" racism, succinctly delineated by Friedman (quoted by Vander Zanden 1973: 39–40) as follows:

> ... decisions are made, agendas structured, issues defined, beliefs, values and attitudes promulgated and enshrined, commitments entered into, and/or resources allocated, in such a way that non-whites are systematically deprived or exploited. It should be emphasized that ... intentions of the actors, or the formal statements of the relevant norms, laws, and values, are irrelevant to whether an institution is acting in a structurally racist manner. What counts is whether its actions in fact distribute burdens and rewards in a racially biased fashion or defends or supports other actors who are making biased distributions.[3]

"Studying up" then can be clearly identified with one strand in the social thought of the seventies, following more logically on the concerns of the sixties. Even so, it ought not to be pursued with such intensity that the understanding of continuity and change in the black community suffers. For the latter will still be more than a passive recipient of outside influences, and white Americans are still in need of understanding how their black countrymen live.

Participant observation is one of the simplest ways in which a social scientist can go about gathering his data, yet is a very costly way of doing so. By getting close to everyday life, by being at hand to observe its occurrences, one will also become to some extent a participant. Whoever uses this approach, then, gets an inside view of more or less the entire undivided way of life of the social unit with which he is involved.

We are, in some sense, all participant-observers in our own ways of life. Being a participant-observer professionally comes about by feeding the information one gets into a scholarly analytical framework, and more often than not, with doing so in a social unit which is not one's own. From the point of

---

3   There is a close parallel between this notion and the concept of "structural fascism" introduced by the Norwegian social anthropologist, Ottar Brox (1972).

view of the community under study, the participant is in some ways like a child; he does not yet know enough to participate fully and competently in local life. Curious as he may be about it, he does not always know what about it that he does not know, and so some of his learning will necessarily come about through his mistakes. As he continuously participates as much as he can in what goes on, however, he not only observes others but receives constant feedback on his own behavior. As time goes on, he acquires a relatively complete knowledge of what it is like to be a member of this community. But it is a very personal and sometimes difficult learning experience, and it is bound to take time.

Compared with quick surveys by way of questionnaires, then, the participant-observer makes a considerable investment of time and personal commitment. No doubt one personal reason for a great many going through this, is that it can be a very satisfying kind of experience. There are also important scholarly reasons, however, for this form of data gathering. First of all, anthropologists, who are the leading protagonists of this approach, have tended to practice it in exotic non-western societies in which there has been no other reasonable starting point for acquiring knowledge about how life is lived. One cannot start out in an alien cultural context with a questionnaire developed in one's own society. It is a well known fact that to stupid questions one gets stupid answers, and there are many examples in the lore of anthropologists of how questionnaires may be cross-culturally stupid, by being framed in terms which simply make no sense in another cultural framework.

We are now finding our complex western societies much more heterogeneous than we perhaps used to suspect. Although everybody in a nation might in some way share some common culture, classes, regions, ethnic groups, occupations and other groupings also have cultures of their own. And to learn about these, we may need participant observation as much as in a more conspicuously exotic society. There are in fact a couple of particular reasons for employing it here. The easy assumption of cultural sharing is a treacherous one, only to be revealed as false by someone with the experience of having participated directly in more than one of the cultures concerned. Furthermore, in most western societies, one group, perhaps a numerical majority, views its own way of life as the "normal" one for the entire nation, and regards other ways as deviations, not only in a statistical but also in a moral sense. This group may also have the power to punish, formally or informally, those who behave differently. With the changed perception of American society in the sixties, there has been renewed recognition of the WASPs, the White Anglo-Saxon Protestants, as group performing such a function.[4] But the dominant group not only punishes those who break its rules of conduct. It also holds them up for general inspection, so that members of other groups will become more or less familiar with them. Exposure to mass media and a universal system of education are some of the

---

4 The interplay between factors of behavior and factors of descent in the position of the WASPs is too complex to discuss here, although the latter must obviously also be taken into account.

efficient ways in which all members of a western society will learn of the mainstream culture of the society. One might say, then, that members of a minority group become to some extent bicultural, insofar as they know both the mainstream culture and their own alternative. Those who are themselves of the mainstream, on the other hand, do not have equal access to minority cultures.

The social sciences have often been used to bring knowledge about the minority ways of life to the members of the mainstream of society. To the extent that the members of the minorities regard the social scientists as representatives of the mainstream, however, and to the extent that they perceive the mainstream as hostile to minority life styles, they may try to give the researchers the impression that their conduct is only minimally different from that of the mainstream. Being fairly knowledgeable about what the latter entails, they may well succeed in doing so if the researcher's contact with their community is only fleeting and superficial.

Participant observation is particularly necessary as an approach to research in groups, then, which are in some way in conflict with the dominant group, and which might therefore tend to engage in impression management toward it. This is one reason why this mode of research has had a renaissance in American social science in the sixties, when so much of the rediscovered diversity has also involved conflict, not only in the case of ethnic minorities but also in the case of, for example, sexual minorities or the criminal underworld. [5]

The case for participant observation, however, does not end when the researcher has acquired sufficient cultural competence to formulate intelligent and fairly specific questions about the way of life he is studying; nor does it end when those who engage in it are willing, in principle, to answer any questions that an unfamiliar researcher might want to read off an interview schedule. Also there is no perfect fit between a person's real behavior and his ability to verbalize about it, at a high level of analytical awareness. If, for example, one is studying sex roles; even the most cooperative group of informants are unlikely, to be able to provide all the information one wants through interviews. We cannot assume that they notice, or can readily be made to notice, all the ways in which they are engaged in evolving or maintaining such roles in their spontaneous everyday behavior. Rather, the researcher had better place himself in situations where children learn about masculinity and femininity, where young people or adults of both sexes interact, in and out of the family context, and where people of one sex get together in peer groups to gossip about their encounters with the other sex. Certainly, participant observers do not dispense with interviews. But they tend to be long, intensive, informal, searching and open-ended and thus rather different from the ordinary questionnaire technique. And they must grow out of extensive first-hand observation.

It should be added that participant observation has disadvantages; these are not confined to its being time-consuming and perhaps uncomfortable to

---

5   For some further examples of the uses of participant observation in these fields see Polsky (1967), Humphreys (1970), Douglas (1972) and Newton (1972).

the person involved in it. There is the problem of representativeness. The participant observer, like most people in a community, can interact intensively with relatively few people, but it may be desirable to generalize for many in scholarly reporting. Of course, one should try to specify carefully the social characteristics of the people with whom one has been involved, so as to give some idea of how far a generalization can be carried; and one may be able to cross-check certain kinds of data for a larger population through supplementary methods. But one cannot do this for all one's information, and in a conflict situation such as that of the black ghetto, for an accepted participant observer suddenly to don another kind of researcher's cap may be impossible or even harmful to his future efforts as a participant. The problem of representativity is, then, one which the participant observer must live with. But he is prepared to do so, realizing that his information about the group which he has come to know is likely often to have considerably greater validity than that reached through other methods.

One of the signs of public concern with the situation in the ghetto was that several studies carried out in this manner grew out of two relatively large research projects, both funded by the National Institute of Mental Health, the federal government research agency which is particularly involved in studies of human welfare. One project was carried out in St. Louis, known by the name of the research location, the ill-reputed Pruitt-Igoe public housing project (its official title was "Social and Community Problems in Public Housing Areas"). Out of this research have come three books, *Coming Up Black* by David A. Schulz (1969), *Behind Ghetto Walls* by Lee Rainwater (1970), who led the project, and *Tomorrow's Tomorrow* by Joyce A. Ladner (1971), as well as various shorter publications. The focus in the first of these books is on growing up in the black ghetto, in the second on family life, and in the third on the situation of the black young woman. These topics, however, are obviously not easily distinguishable from one another, so that in reality their contents overlap considerably, and one might equally well describe their common subject as patterns of family and peer group life among the ghetto dwellers. The second larger project was located in Washington, D.C., where the Health and Welfare Council of the National Capitol area had NIMH support for its study of "Child Rearing Practices among Low Income Families in the District of Columbia." Its best-known product is Elliot Liebow's book *Tally's Corner* (1967), but there is also a second book, Camille Jeffers' brief and rather modest *Living Poor* (1967). While Liebow centers his study on a group of black men, mostly marginally employed or unemployed, and the various facets of their lives, Jeffers' book is an account of women's life in a public housing project. In the case of both these larger projects, then, the official titles have not circumscribed the research fields too narrowly; the Pruitt-Igoe study is not totally preoccupied with the peculiar problems of public housing, and the Child Rearing Study in Washington, D.C., also spread itself over a wider field. In Liebow's book, for example, the father role of the men he studied is dealt with specifically in one out of seven chapters. As a further case of a larger project engaged in ghetto-related research, I might mention the Urban Language Study of the Center for Applied Linguistics, likewise in Washington, D.C., which was concerned with black dialect and its social context. This was the project to which my own work was organizationally linked, with an emphasis on sex roles and on wider patterns of neighborhood and community life and resulting in the book *Soulside* (1969).

If public concern for once allowed the organization of somewhat larger research teams to move into this field, however, there was still room for the efforts of individual scholars, as shown by the other studies. One of them, *Deep Down in the Jungle* by Roger D. Abrahams (1964), is not strictly a product of the sixties, as Abrahams began his work in this field slightly earlier, but it and Abrahams' later work relates so clearly to this period that I think it must be discussed in connection with it. *Deep Down in the Jungle* has a topic which may seem rather different from those of the work previously mentioned, as it deals with the folklore, often rather obscene, which Abrahams collected from the men of a black neighborhood in Philadelphia, but it is really to be seen as an expressive aspect of black social organization. In a later more synthesizing work, *Positively Black* (1970), Abrahams also discusses black expressive perform-ances in this light. Another work which treats one of the black folk arts as an expression of themes in black life more generally is Charles Keil's *Urban Blues* (1966), an analysis of the role of the blues singer and his relationship to his ghetto audience, a work which began the debate over the concept of "soul". (The latter, of course, was the symbol of "ultimate blackness" which came to the fore during the sixties.) Keil's work was based in Chicago; so was that for another of the more specialized studies during the period, *The Vice Lords* by R. Lincoln Keiser (1969), an analysis of the organization of one of the larger street gangs of the city.

Yet other facets of black life are illuminated in another Chicago-based study, Gerald D. Suttles' *The Social Order of the Slum* (1968), based on observa-tions in a neighborhood where blacks, Italians, Puerto Ricans and Mexicans live next to each other. With its emphasis on inter-ethnic relations, however, this study falls somewhat outside the scope of our interests here. Another study, finally, which is also somewhat marginal but which can in some ways be said to be a part of the ghetto research is *Black Players* by Christina and Richard Milner (1972), a study from San Francisco of black pimps and their prostitutes (the latter of which are often white). It may be noted here that the pimp, as the term is generally used in the ghetto, is not a procurer but rather the lover, coach, and rather authoritarian boss of one or more prostitutes in his "stable". Although the prostitution involved is not specifically aimed at the ghetto so that this enterprise can be said to exist only at the fringes of the black community, the flamboyant idleness and power over women of the pimp is sometimes provocatively held up as a male ideal by ghetto men who, as we shall see, cannot easily cope with the more conventional American definition of the male role. For that reason, a study of the black pimp has a particular place in ghetto research.

Besides these books, there are numerous articles and unpublished works, such as some dissertations which have not made their way into print; but we can probably get a satisfactorily well-rounded view of recent research in the black ghetto by focusing on the studies mentioned. Together, they can give a more well-rounded picture of the ghetto than a single participant observer, moving within constricted circles, can easily do in a heterogeneous community. Thus Rainwater and Schulz tend to emphasize family life, Liebow and I give greater emphasis to the life of ordinary men than women, Ladner deals with a younger group of women than does Jeffers, and Keiser, Keil and the Milners each deal with more specialized male roles or contexts, in ways which can be more or less easily related to the picture which we have of the ghetto as a whole.

Undoubtedly, the most important theme of these studies has been the impact of poverty on life in black urban communities. The concern here has not been only with sheer material deprivation as such, but with its consequences for the behavior and social relationships of those affected. In response to the perceptions of the majority of Americans that such things as crime, violence, drunkenness and broken families are typical of the black ghetto, a great many of the researchers have seen it as a major task to show that these disreputable characteristics occur less frequently than is commonly thought, and when they do occur they tend to be the results of deprivation. These studies should thus counteract those interpretations in the tradition of vulgar racism which suggest that blacks are inherently inferior; but if this among sophisticates might be considered flogging a dead horse, it should be noted that they also constitute a critique of the prevalent tendency, also in well-disposed and influential circles, to equivocate about the determinants of ghetto "pathology" and think of piecemeal treatments which do not focus on the economic situation. The most important example of the latter is probably the "Moynihan Report," informally named after its main author, Daniel Patrick Moynihan, who suggested in this government document that the instability of the family was at the roots of many ghetto ills, without giving equal emphasis to the role of poverty in disrupting family life. [6]

The major interest of several scholars could thus be phrased, following Lee Rainwater (1970: vii), as the study of "the dynamics of socioeconomic inequality." Although racial discrimination was understood to be what kept many blacks on a low income level and was realized to have certain other effects as well, there was a tendency in these studies not to see anything uniquely black about the ways in which people reacted to the economic situation. Furthermore, there was little in this ghetto life that could not be accounted for in terms of economic and other external pressures. As succinctly stated by Rainwater (1970: 4), the paradigm is that:

---

6   The report itself is included, with a review of the debate over it and reprints of major contributions to the debate, in a volume by Rainwater and Yancey (1967).

> *White cupidity*
>   creates
> *structural conditions highly inimical to basic*
> *social adaptation (low income availability, poor*
> *education, poor services, stigmatization)*
>   to which Negroes adapt by
> *social and personal responses which serve to*
> *sustain the individual in his punishing world*
> *but also generate aggressiveness toward the self*
> *and others*
>   which results in
> *suffering directly inflicted by Negroes on them-*
> *selves and on others.*

This pathological condition is often studied within focus on family organization. There is great diversity in family arrangements in the black ghetto; and survey data show that in terms of composition, at least, the most frequent arrangement in most areas is that of mainstream America – i.e., father, mother and children sharing one household. However, the ghetto has a significantly higher than average number of households where there is no adult male playing the roles of husband and father. Adults who form the core of such households are one or more women; if there are adult men in the household, they may be the brothers or sons of the women, or more loosely attached male partners who do not fully play husband and father roles in the conventional sense. These men or earlier partners may be the fathers of the children of the household. The women are unmarried or separated. This is the household composition which is the basis of one definition of matrifocality, or female-centeredness. One could also construct a definition of matrifocality, however, which is based on household behavior, rather than composition. Even in many households with a conventional composition the husband-father might be a rather marginal figure in household activities. There is no scholarly consensus on definitional problems here, and there is certainly much heterogeneity in the organization of ghetto households. Yet a great many of them share the characteristic that there is considerable strain between men and women, and the outcome is frequently that the male leaves the household.

By now fewer people in western society would be prepared to assert that it is necessarily more wrong for women to have the greater power in the family than it is for men to have it, in line with the traditional family form. As domestic arrangements generally become more flexible in the wider society, one might ponder the possibility that other Americans will take less note of what they have long considered the deviation of black Americans from normal family patterns. Thus far, however, "broken families," the rather dramatic term commonly used for households which are matrifocal in composition, have generally been compared to the conventional model, and the black people who have been involved in them have often been held directly responsible for their aberrations.

The economically inclined analysis of black family forms emphasizes instead that poverty and low status provide the basis for the difference between these forms and that favored by mainstream America. If a certain degree of male dominance has been established as proper according to convention, this is because the husband and father has normally been able to function as major or sole breadwinner, to provide his household with a satisfactory anchoring in the status scale of the society, and to serve as the family specialist on external relations generally. Many low-income black men have not been in this position, however, and thus their status has been threatened not only in the job situation but also at home. Part of the conflict within the household has consequently been directly due to the economic situation, as women have wanted more resourceful husbands and men have wanted more respect. For neither, of course, can easily free themselves from the impact of the mainstream model of what a family should ideally be like, although they may perceive it somewhat selectively.

Further factors in the causation of marital conflict and matrifocality can be indirectly connected to poverty. When ghetto men see themselves as barred from rewards normally available to men in American society, they may seek an alternative male role which promises some satisfactions. Some of the other forms of behavior which mainstream society frowns upon may thus also have an economic derivation. There is certainly in the wider society as well a subterranean convention that toughness, daring, sexual adventurousness, drinking and an assortment of other items also constitute characteristics which are masculine rather than feminine; and many ghetto men elaborate these, perhaps in one combination or other with highly persuasive verbal skills and fashion consciousness, into another general type of masculinity which is well established in the black ghetto. It is obvious that a man who tends toward this side of the male role spectrum may find it even more difficult to play the husband and father roles prescribed in mainstream culture, and so this alternative may lead to even greater estrangement within the household. But working arrangements may be established whereby a man in this kind of role functions, on a short-term basis, as the companion of a woman, with a more marginal commitment to her household. And it is also important to realize that this is a male role which may be validated to a high degree in interactions within the all-male peer groups, in varying states of cohesion, to which several of the ghetto studies have given intensive attention.

By way of this kind of interpretation, then, economic deprivation can be seen at the roots of household instability as well as of interpersonal violence, alcoholism and a variety of other forms of expressive behavior, mostly masculine, which have tended to be offensive to the mainstream mind. It may certainly be recognized that some of these reactions to poverty may be detrimental in a very real sense to the ghetto dwellers themselves, although ultimately they should not be held responsible for them. However, the behavior of the ghetto dwellers may be as good an adaptation to the existing situation as one could find. The openness to interaction which a stranger to the ghetto may find overwhelming and perhaps even slightly immoral may have survival value, particularly when paired with some healthy scepticism toward the other's motives. Thus networks of relationships are established which may come to good use as resources may be channeled through them in situations of need. If some ghetto men end up in alcoholism and self-destructive uncontrolled violence, then a great many others may use similar elements of action more moderately to arrive at as satisfactory a definition of self as may be deemed possible, and some men may even play the alternative role with such finesse and charm as to satisfy even material needs; this is the case of pimps and other small-scale illicit entrepreneurs (but this, of course, may involve an exploitation of other ghetto dwellers). And if a great many matrifocal households have a troubled existence, they might not have been better off had a man been present, forced to enact the conventional provider and authority role in so ambiguous and unsatisfactory a manner as to cause frequent conflict.

In a recent review by the Jamaican social historian, Orlando Patterson (1972), he identifies three main currents in the writing of black history: catastrophism, contributionism, and survivalism. For the catastrophist historians, he suggests,

> black history in the New World is simply one long disaster, a chronicle of horrors in which blacks experienced every conceivable form of exploitation, humiliation, and anguish at the hands of the white oppressors (Patterson 1972: 29).

We might perhaps see catastrophism as the major tendency in the post-war writing of the history of black Americans. It is a tendency which one is tempted to identify with white liberal scholars, although it has certainly had prominent black followers as well. The contributionists, on the other hand, seem more often to be black, and frequently amateur historians. Their objective has been to show notable black achievements; as this line of work has traditionally been practiced, it has tended to be a matter of either retrieving from obscurity black individuals who have played a part in some notable historical, cultural or technical development, or identifying some already well-known historical figure as being of at least partial African ancestry.

Survivalism, finally, involves an emphasis on the ways in which elements of African cultures persisted in the black community through slavery and into the present. The leading scholar of survivalism has been an anthropologist, the late Melville J. Herskovits, whose book *The Myth of the Negro Past* (1941) has probably only recently drawn more interest from the historians of black America. The myth to which Herskovits referred is that which suggests that Africa had no culture worthy of that designation, or that in any case it was lost with slavery and the slave trade so that it was not a factor at all in the life of black America. Herskovits' response was to catalogue a great many cultural phenomena occurring in the New World which were manifestly or probably of African origin, and to detail the ways in which African cultural elements had evidently been reshaped to fit into their new contexts while still retaining signs of their past. From the evidence he presented, however, it was clear that more Africanisms survived in Latin America and the Caribbean than in North America, although they were certainly not absent in the latter area.

If we look now to the relationships between catastrophism, contributionism, and survivalism, we can see that the latter two share an interest in viewing black Americans as an active force, with its own cultural tradition and creativity, while catastrophism has focused on what whites have done to blacks. On the other hand, contributionism has often limited itself to black creativity within the framework of white mainstream culture, i.e., in such approved fields as technical inventions, political patriotism, or the fine arts. Only survivalism has more consistently dwelt on the cultural autonomy of the black community. This has meant that the most clearcut conflict has been between catastrophism and survivalism, as it has been a corollary of the former view that blacks in America lost their African culture as they were inducted into American society. This conflict was most clearly spelled out, some thirty years ago, in exchanges between Herskovits and a leading catastrophist, the black sociologist E. Franklin Frazier. Until recently, the great majority of scholars seem to have judged the catastrophists the winners of this battle. In the last decade, however, it has turned out that they may have claimed the victory too soon.

The socioeconomic interpretation of contemporary ghetto life involves a brand of catastrophism, with varying degrees of clarity and intensity of expression. The emphasis is on the deprivation of the black community and its consequences. Certainly, one cannot look away from this deprivation, or other ways in which ghetto dwellers suffer at the hands of the wider society, as a fundamental condition of ghetto life. To focus on only this, however, would be less satisfactory if one hopes to arrive at a relatively full picture of ghetto life. Although generally undertaken in a reformist – or even revolutionary – spirit, the study of ghetto deprivation may give too little attention to the collective creativity and traditions of the black community which constitute more than a minimal forced response to the conditions imposed on it by the outside world. Polemically, it may even be described as a kind of narcissism on the part of the majority, seeing its own power reflected in the powerlessness of the black community. John F. Szwed (1972: 171), in a recent critique of social science research on black America over a considerably longer period than that under review here, has commented that too many scholars whose position of political partisanship have found approval among their peers have gotten away with shabby research where black people as cultural creators have been sacrificed, turned into mere ciphers. At worst, he suggests, although this may have been accomplished in the name of radicalism, it comes to little more than the racist position which also denies the full humanness of blacks.

The studies considered here, are less vulnerable than most to such accusations – participant observation, after all, must necessarily involve sensitivity to others as human beings. Yet the issue of recognition of black creativity and black traditions is not wholly irrelevant.

The best example is perhaps Elliot Liebow's study *Tally's Corner*. Liebow, certainly, cannot be accused of being a poor observer of human life. Yet he is committed to a socioeconomic interpretation of ghetto life – working, for one thing, under the aegis of a research project based on such assumptions – and the way in which he orders his observations and pursues his argument makes his perhaps the most unequivocally catastrophist of the recent studies. In a vivid formulation on which his critics have tended to fasten, Liebow (1967: 223) suggests that similarities in ghetto ways of life over generations are largely the results of socioeconomic pressures constituting

> a simple piece of social machinery which turns out, in rather mechanical fashion, independently produced look-alikes.

The response to this, by one critic, has been to assert that *Tally's Corner* is "one of the most significant attempts in recent years to discredit the idea of the black culture" (Davidson 1969: 164).

"Culture" is obviously a key concept here. It is central in anthropology – not quite so much so in sociology – but is more often used as a kind of shorthand sensitizing term than as a concept of great analytical rigor. According to the anthropological usage it is a whole interconnected way of life of a group the members of which learn their culture in their interactions with one another, the organization of thinking and acting of a group. To acquire this culture one must participate in group life.

As long as this concept is used in the study of small, stable, homogeneous and relatively independent communities it remains rather uncontroversial. When it comes to understanding the dynamics of group life in a large, complex society, where a group is in constant contact with others, however, analyses in cultural terms must become much more subtle in order not simply to confuse the issues. When Liebow, in the statement quoted above, largely denies the existence of a black ghetto culture, he reacts to one oversimplified use of the culture concept, but in his reaction he unfortunately accepts the oversimplification.

Liebow, with other scholars, protests against the concept of a "culture of poverty" which became popular in the sixties. With several precursors, this particular formulation came from Oscar Lewis' (1959, 1961) studies of lower-class Mexican families. Lewis implied by this term that life in poverty was an interconnected whole, typical of the lowest stratum in modern class societies. Poverty for one part of the population was the product of the structure of the entire society, and as a way of life tended to become stabilized, as the poor learn their culture from one another, particularly between generations.

While Lewis had intended the concept to serve as a tool of social criticism, it soon became evident that it could be perverted. In some circles – journalists, educators, and policymakers more often than social scientists – there was some tendency to focus narrowly on "culture" as this learning process within a relatively autonomous group. The poor thus were themselves to blame for their poverty, by learning from each other and thus perpetuating self-destructive behavior. The term culture of poverty, was an unusually convenient catch phrase for this old idea, one which seemed to lend it some scientific respectability. Consequently, scholars who were convinced that only changes in the economic structure of society could eradicate poverty found it necessary to mobilize forces against this understanding of a culture of poverty, and Liebow was obviously one of them. [7]

In agreeing to a battleground defined by the most corrupt use of a culture of poverty concept, unfortunately, these anthropological and sociological critics tended to ignore basic understandings of contemporary anthropological cultural analysis. Anthropologists do not assume nowadays that a way of life acquires and maintains its form independent of its environment. Rather, cultural ecology, the branch of anthropology which inquires into the interaction of a group with external factors of influence is one of the liveliest areas of the discipline. Following this, the culture of poverty seem more usefully approached as an adaptation to poverty, rather than a cause of it. This is fully in line with a socioeconomic interpretation of ghetto life; it is in no conflict, for example, with Rainwater's paradigm of ghetto social dynamics as quoted earlier in this paper. But in suggesting, by the use of the culture concept, that this adaptation is a collective product, learned to a great extent from other members of the community and maintained in interaction among them, one clearly rejects the more extreme notion that the poor are "independently produced look-alikes". To argue along the latter line would seem to overlook what goes on inside the poverty stricken community itself, in the households and peer groups of the black ghetto. [8]

An emphasis on a cultural interpretation of reactions to poverty is a stance, developing out of one particular dialogue, as are many others in the various branches of studies of black America.

Let us return to Szwed's criticism that many studies of black life have not taken sufficient account of black Americans as cultural creators. Cultural interpretations of adaptations to poverty are perhaps free of this accusation, insofar as they have pointed to ways in which ghetto dwellers have responded to deprivation with inventiveness. The further question arises then, as kind of: what are black Americans apart from being poor? Socioeconomic interpretations lead us to regard blacks as social scientists now tend to look at "deviant" groups generally – i.e., if one changes the conditions which create deviance, everything will return to normal. But what here could be regarded as deviance

---

7 Two recent volumes by Valentine (1968) and Leacock (1971) give a good view of these criticisms of the culture of poverty concept.
8 I have argued the point that there is a cultural process of adaptation more fully elsewhere (Hannerz 1969, 1970a, 1972).

and what would be normal? It is highly questionable whether black Americans have veered away from a mainstream American pattern of life which was once theirs. Their African ancestors clearly had a cultural heritage very different from European immigrants. Catastrophists, of course, imply that this heritage was wiped out with the arrival of the slaves. It is hard to conceive of a people suddenly ceasing to act in accord with their established modes. Rather, black American ways of life it would seem were influenced throughout the American experience by three kinds of forces: the weight of black community tradition, the pressure to conform to mainstream American culture, and the particular structural conditions deriving from being placed quite consistently at the bottom of American society. While the socioeconomic interpretations emphasize the latter of these forces, the scholars who have taken the most pronounced culturalist view have devoted most attention to the first of them, urging that life is something different from and more than what white Americans would have made it. Black Americans in this view have certainly incorporated much of mainstream American culture into their repertoires. But the situation is still best viewed as one of culture contact, involving a process of acculturation in which peoples of different cultures influence one another. Somewhat ironically, such proponents may point to the same structural forces on which socioeconomic interpretations have focused, using them to explain why the acceptance of mainstream culture may have been less than complete. Concentrated in particular positions in the social structure, blacks have also been insulated from much direct mainstream cultural communication. This fact has recently drawn more interest in historical study – where not so long ago Stanley Elkins[9] could depict an almost total dependence of the slave on his master (Elkins 1959), there is now an emphasis on the "under-life" of the plantation, the community life particularly of the field slaves, which had a certain degree of autonomy and was well hidden from the view of owners and overseers (cf. Blassingame 1972). Even today, many ghetto dwellers may have only fleeting contact with white Americans for long stretches of their lives. Since such interaction is usually basic to efficient cultural transmission, these circumstances may have provided the conditions for some black cultural autonomy. For one thing, it may have facilitated to some extent the adaptation to socioeconomic deprivation, in conflict with mainstream norms. As those groups of the wider society which serve as major anchorage points of the latter seem more distant, one may more easily attribute some degree of moral legitimacy to other modes of action which are widespread in one's own community. But also, one may continue to transmit such elements of one's group tradition which remain relatively unaffected by socioeconomic circumstances, without much interference from the outside.

Of the scholars mentioned above, particularly Roger Abrahams and Charles Keil have emphasized the autonomy of the black American cultural tradi-

---

9   A reader including the more important scholarly responses to Elkins' thesis has recently been edited by Lane (1971).

tion, but they represent a larger group of scholars whose work have taken somewhat different forms. Abrahams' field of specialization is the study of verbal performance while Keil is an ethnomusicologist. Both, then, are primarily concerned with communicative forms, an area where the position of black cultural autonomy is not at all difficult to argue. Few would deny that black American music such as blues and jazz draws partially on different traditions than Euro-American music, and although there is controversy concerning the provenience of black folklore, the latter is obviously not the same as that of white Americans. It is easy, also, to understand why communicative forms could be maintained in a way which draws more significantly on an independent tradition, since they are not so immediately susceptible to socioeconomic pressures as are, for example, family forms.[10] Recently there has also been great interest in black American dialect; scholars such as Joe L. Dillard (1970, 1972) and William A. Stewart (1970) have devoted much attention to the origins of this dialect in creole language forms developed on African and European bases before and during slavery. Those who interpret ghetto life in socioeconomic terms and those who emphasize a separate cultural tradition are then often speaking of different things.

Keil is an anthropologist, Abrahams an anthropologist-folklorist. Their culturalist views reflect a degree of difference between anthropology and sociology. Although some anthropologists engaged in ghetto research have emphasized socioeconomic factors, there seems to have been a greater tendency for the sociologists to do so, while anthropologists have played much the more important part in taking note of independent black culture,[11] a replay of the survivalist-catastrophist debate. The reasons are probably not difficult to ascertain. Sociologists tend to work in their own society and to view the culture of the majority as a given. Groups who do not act in line with that culture are likely to be viewed as deviants, explicable in terms of the structure of their own society. Anthropologists, on the other hand, given their relativist and comparatist traditions, expect to find cultural difference and explain it, as such, rather than as deviance. Furthermore, their concerns include the historical cultural links between blacks in the United States and Africa, and between other areas of the New World.[12] These anthropologists have, in fact, posited an Afro-American continuum, including black communities in the Caribbean,

---

10 Yet we should apparently not go so far as to suggest that any kind of society can have any kind of music. Szwed (1970: 220), in an essay on musical change in black America, suggest that "song forms and performances are themselves models of social behavior that reflect strategies of adaptation to human and natural environments"; the blues, for example, as an aggressive, secular, individualist form of music may have eased the transition from agrarian society to mobile, wage-labor urbanism.

11 It may be noted, however, that Abrahams, in the first edition of *Deep Down in the Jungle* (1964), did not take the strong culturalist position he has done more recently, in the second edition of that book, in *Positively Black*, and in various other publications.

12 After their ghetto research, Abrahams has gone on to work in the Caribbean and Keil in West Africa. Although they could not have drawn on these experiences in the works discussed here, this may serve as evidence of their orientation in the study of black Americans.

much of Latin America, and North America as far up as the Canadian seaboard (cf. Whitten and Szwed 1970). While socioeconomic interpretations of some flexibility may be relevant to this whole area, it also provides a map of varying degrees of strength in black cultural traditions which provides interesting possibilities of comparisons for the culturalists in ghetto research. The anthropologists may thus bring a particular sensitivity to cultural differences into this field of study. One might be aware of the risk, on the other hand, that they might occasionally favor such interests and interpretations over others because of a "bias of exoticism" (cf. Naroll and Naroll 1963, Fischer 1969). At best, their orientations and those of sociologists should be complementary.

Abrahams and Keil differ from other ghetto research not in that they are survivalists in the strict sense of the word. They acknowledge the work of Herskovits and others in showing that black Americans should be seen as an ethnic and not merely poverty-stricken group, but they are not particularly concerned with tracing Africanisms as such. They take it as a basic assumption that they *are* dealing with a culturally distinct group with its own heritage. Perhaps this is the major difference: they feel no need to *explain* distinctive black forms of behavior in terms of anything else. Furthermore, they study spheres of life where the elaboration of distinctiveness is particularly notable, such as music and verbal performances, though they do relate these phenomena to areas of everyday culture in ghetto living. Keil's study of the urban blues singer, for example, is not only an inquiry into a particular black occupational category, but also an analysis of the bluesman's importance as a living symbol: of the troubled male-female relationships of the ghetto; and of the alternative male role which we have noted earlier. The bluesman is a community hero who through his performances validates the ghetto experience. Thus, particular individuals may, because of their highly visible and stylized ways of life, stand as points of cultural anchorage for large portions of the ghetto population. Something similar could be said about the dramatic styles of black pimps as studied by the Milners, although these authors do not carry a cultural analysis very far in this direction. As far as Abrahams' work on types of verbal performance is concerned, he also shows how folk poetry serves as a storehouse for a ghetto philosophy, again with some emphasis on the male role. And he has also devoted considerable effort to showing, in several works, how verbal talents are given great weight as a part of this role in many New World black communities.

Culturalist interpretations such as those by Abrahams and Keil have contributed greatly to our understanding of the elaboration and relative autonomy of ghetto ways of life, and of the part which particular institutions and activities may play in providing foci for distinctive orientations. It is a recognition of their achievement that one can think of and hope for similar studies which would map, for example, the current role of black churches and radio stations in communicating black culture. Although there is widespread agreement concerning the central place that the church has long had in the black community, there is a dearth of modern studies utilizing current forms of intensive analysis of, for example, cultural symbolism. Such studies would be particularly important as the diversity of church life in the ghetto is likely to give organized religion a rather different shape than that which it had in the small southern rural community. The radio station, on the other hand, is obviously a much newer black institution, but in those cities where it is found its disc jockeys in particular can take on a similar role in cultural communication to that of bluesmen or ministers of the church. The "soul" concept of the sixties, standing for the essence of the black experience and style, obviously had some of its roots in religion and was popularized efficiently in black radio and music.

With all this work, nevertheless, the limits of cultural autonomy still need study and description. Bennett Berger (1967), in reviewing Keil's *Urban Blues*, noted that much of what Keil describes as characteristic of black culture may be reworded in terms of adaptation to poverty. And when Abrahams, in *Positively Black*, describes in the form of a cultural theme the agonistic style of interpersonal relationships among black Americans, there seems to be little difference between his observations and those which others have used in analyses of the consequences of socioeconomic deprivation – the battle of the sexes and so forth. This is not to say that these culturalist interpretations are failures. Rather, both those who lean toward cultural studies and those who lean toward a socioeconomic framework of analysis tend to ignore each other. Though their respective emphases may be suitable to describe different aspects of ghetto life, interpersonal relationships clearly involve both adaptation to material circumstances and cultural styles of communication. Agonistic style may be both part of a cultural heritage and a likely adaptation to current circumstances. Contemporary structural conditions may serve to maintain an established cultural tradition, not only by keeping ghetto dwellers somewhat isolated but also by providing conditions where the behavior directed by tradition is as adaptive as any other. What one might wish for, then, is a more careful synthesis of culturalist and socioeconomic analytical perspectives, which would give us a more detailed picture of the continuous interplay between black cultural tradition and American social structure. With some historical depth this could also give an understanding of the cumulative nature of the former; for certainly, black American tradition is no longer only a matter of an African heritage but also the shared experience of slavery and southern rural poverty, as well as traditions already evolving in the urban setting.

Perhaps one obstacle to synthesis involves the sociology of researchers. If one mapped the social networks of the scholars concerned, culturalists interact intensively in the main with one another and with, among others, linguists and musicologists sharing similar interests, engaging in a constant exchange of information and ideas, and largely supporting each others' views. Those more directly oriented toward issues of social policy, tend also to be in close touch with each other, working on problems defined as related to poverty. Finally, a number of individual scholars, whose research contributions have sometimes been of a descriptive rather than analytical nature, are not closely linked to either group. Between the two major groups there tends to be little personal contact, nor do they attend closely to the strong points of each others' works. More such attention would obviously be needed to make progress toward a successful synthesis.

However the synthesis must also include a third element besides black cultural tradition and socioeconomic pressures: inputs of mainstream culture. The autonomous black culture is an elusive entity. In one context it may come clearly to the fore; in the next, one wonders if one sees anything that other Americans would not do. In addition, one discovers quickly enough that some ghetto dwellers seem much closer to mainstream culture than others. Such culturally learned modes of thinking and acting which ghetto dwellers do not share with mainstream Americans, then, do not make up a "whole" culture, an entire design for living. Rather, it is "thick" in some areas of life and "thin" or non-existent in others. And even where it is "thick," ghetto dwellers are often aware of the mainstream alternative. The different ways of performing the male role is a major example. Mainstream culture is communicated within the ghetto, and it is continuously flowing into it from the outside, through mass media, schools, and in countless other ways. We must not exaggerate ghetto cultural autonomy. In such a situation, old anthropological notions of culture, developed in much less complex communities, may not be very satisfactory. One needs a conceptual framework where the possibility is recognized that an individual can have more than one culture in his repertoire, that he can switch between these cultures quickly and that he can drift between them over a longer period. I have myself tried to develop a concept of biculturalism as a tool for understanding the ghetto cultural situation, and another anthropologist who has more recently engaged in ghetto research, Charles A. Valentine, has also noted the utility of such a concept (cf. Hannerz 1969, 1970a, 1970b; Valentine 1971).

Ghetto dwellers may vary a great deal in the extent to which they make use of either culture, even when both are included in their repertoires, so that some conform rather closely to mainstream culture while others tend to act more consistently in line with black alternatives and yet others seemed to follow a course somewhere between these. Certainly socioeconomic constraints constitute one factor determining the choice, as those who can better afford it tend to have something more resembling a mainstream way of life. But in order to make the bicultural framework of analysis more fully satisfactory we would also need to have a more detailed picture of relative competence in and orientation toward the two cultures as well as of other factors influencing their actual use.

Furthermore, we should perhaps not yet take for granted that either mainstream or black culture is homogeneous enough to make a model involving only two cultures absolutely adequate. With these qualifications and hints toward further development, however, I believe that a bicultural model is a useful approximation of ghetto reality.

REFERENCES

ABRAHAMS, Roger D.
  1964   *Deep Down in the Jungle*. Hatboro, Pa.: Folklore Associates. (2nd ed. 1970, Chicago: Aldine.)
  1970   *Positively Black*. Englewood Cliffs, N. J.: Prentice-Hall.
BERGER, Bennett M.
  1967   "Soul Searching". *Trans-action* 4(7): 54–57.
BLASSINGAME, John W.
  1972   *The Slave Community*. New York: Oxford University Press.
BROX, Ottar
  1972   *Strukturfascismen och andra essäer*. Stockholm: Prisma.
DAVIS, Allison, Burleigh B. GARDNER and Mary GARDNER
  1941   *Deep South*. Chicago: University of Chicago Press.
DILLARD, Joe L.
  1970   "Non-Standard Negro Dialects: Convergence or Divergence?" in *Afro-American Anthropology*, edited by Norman E. Whitten, Jr., and John F. Szwed. New York: Free Press.
  1972   *Black English*. New York: Random House.
DOLLARD John
  1937   *Caste and Class in a Southern Town*. New Haven, Conn.: Yale University Press.
DOUGLAS, Jack D., (ed.)
  1972   *Research on Deviance*. New York: Random House.
DRAKE, St. Clair and Horace R. CAYTON
  1945   *Black Metropolis*. New York: Harcourt, Brace.
ELKINS, Stanley M.
  1959   *Slavery*. Chicago. University of Chicago Press.
FISCHER, Ann
  1969   "The Personality and Subculture of Anthropologists and their Study of U.S. Negroes". in *Concepts and Assumptions in Contemporary Anthropology* (Southern Anthropological Society Proceedings no. 3.) edited by Stephen A. Tyler. Athens: University of Georgia Press.
FRAZIER, E. Franklin
  1932   *The Negro Family in the United States*. Chicago: University of Chicago Press.
HANNERZ, Ulf
  1969   *Soulside: Inquiries into Ghetto Culture and Community*. New York: Columbia University Press.
  1970a   "What Ghetto Males Are Like: Another Look", in *Afro-American Anthropology* edited by Norman E. Whitten, Jr., and John F. Szwed. New York: Free Press.
  1970b   "The Notion of Ghetto Culture" in *Black American* edited by John F. Szwed. New York: Basic Books.
  1972   "The Study of Afro-American Cultural Dynamics". *Southwestern Journal of Anthropology* 27: 181–200.
HERSKOVITS, Melville J.
  1941   *The Myth of the Negro Past*. New York: Harper.
HUGHES, Everett C.
  1963   "Race Relations and the Sociological Imagination". *American Sociological Review* 28: 879–890.
HUMPHREYS, Laud
  1970   *Tearoom Trade*. Chicago: Aldine.
JEFFERS, Camille
  1967   *Living Poor*. Ann Arbor, Mich.: Ann Arbor Publishers.
JOHNSON, Charles S.
  1934   *Shadow of the Plantation*. Chicago: University of Chicago Press.
KEIL, Charles
  1966   *Urban Blues*. Chicago: University of Chicago Press.

KEISER, R. Lincoln
 1969   *The Vice Lords*. New York: Holt, Rinehart and Winston.
LADNER, Joyce A.
 1971   *Tomorrow's Tomorrow*. Garden City, N.Y.: Doubleday.
LANE, Ann J., (ed.)
 1971   *The Debate Over Slavery*. Urbana, Ill.: University of Illinois Press.
LEACOCK, Eleanor B., (ed.)
 1971   *The Culture of Poverty: A Critique*. New York: Simon and Schuster.
LEWIS, Oscar
 1959   *Five Families*. New York: Basic Books.
 1961   *The Children of Sánchez*. New York: Random House.
LIEBOW, Elliot
 1967   *Tally's Corner*. Boston: Little, Brown.
LYMAN, Stanford M.
 1972   *The Black American in Sociological Thought*. New York: Putnam.
MILNER, Christina and Richard MILNER
 1972   *Black Players*. Boston: Little, Brown.
MYRDAL, Gunnar
 1944   *An American Dilemma*. New York: Harper and Row.
NAROLL, Raoul, and Frada NAROLL
 1963   "On Bias of Exotic Data". *Man* 63: 24–26.
NEWTON, Esther
 1972   *Mother Camp: Female Impersonators in America*. Englewood Cliffs, N. J.: Prentice-Hall.
PATTERSON, Orlando
 1972   "Rethinking Black History". *Africa Report* 17 (9): 29–31.
POLSKY, Ned
 1967   *Hustlers, Beats and Others*. Chicago: Aldine.
POWDERMAKER, Hortense
 1939   *After Freedom*. New York: Viking.
RAINWATER, Lee
 1970   *Behind Ghetto Walls*. Chicago: Aldine.
RAINWATER, Lee, and William L. YANCEY
 1967   *The Moynihan Report and the Politics of Controversy*. Cambridge, Mass.: The M.I.T. Press.
SCHULZ, David A.
 1969   *Coming Up Black*. Englewood Cliffs, N. J.: Prentice-Hall.
STEWART, William A.
 1970   "Understanding Black Language", in *Black America* edited by John F. Szwed. New York: Basic Books.
SUTTLES, Gerald D.
 1968   *The Social Order of the Slum*. Chicago: University of Chicago Press.
SZWED, John F.
 1970   "Afro-American Musical Adaptation", in *Afro-American Anthropology* edited by Norman E. Whitten, Jr., and John F. Szwed. New York: Free Press.
 1972   "An American Anthropological Dilemma: The Politics of Afro-American Culture", in *Reinventing Anthropology*. Dell Hymes, ed. New York: Pantheon.
VALENTINE, Charles A.
 1968   *Culture and Poverty*. Chicago: University of Chicago Press.
 1971   "Deficit, Difference and Bicultural Models of Afro-American Behavior". *Harvard Educational Review* 41: 137–157.
VANDER ZANDEN, James W.
 1973   "Sociological Studies of American Blacks". *Sociological Quarterly* 14: 32–52.
WHITTEN, Norman E., Jr. and John F. SZWED, (eds.)
 1970   *Afro-American Anthropology*. New York: Free Press.

"It was a Negro Taught Them", a New Look at African Labor in Early South Carolina*

PETER H. WOOD

The Rockefeller Foundation, New York, U.S.A.

W HEN COL. JOHN BARNWELL of South Carolina laid siege to the stronghold of the Tuscarora Indians in the spring of 1712, he noticed a special ingenuity in the fortification. "I immediately viewed the Fort with a prospective glass and found it strong," the commander wrote. Not only were there impressive trenches, bastions, and earthworks to ward off attack, but heavy tree limbs had been placed around the fort making any approach difficult and hiding innumerable "large reeds & canes to run into people's legs." What struck Barnwell particularly was the fact that, according to the fort's occupants, "it was a runaway negro taught them to fortify thus." At that early date blacks and whites had lived in the region for scarcely a generation, and it is not likely that this slave, identified only as "Harry," had been born in Carolina. Instead it seems probable that he had grown up in Africa and had lived in South Carolina before he was "sold into Virginia for roguery & ... fled to the Tuscaruros" (*Virginia Magazine*, July 1898, 44–45). If Harry's African know-how caught the South Carolina commander off guard, it may also startle modern historians, for this obscure incident exemplifies an intriguing aspect of Afro-American history which has not yet been adequately explored.

Colonial South Carolina is an excellent place to begin searching the cultural baggage of early black immigrants for what anthropologists have termed "carryovers". More slaves entered North America through Charleston (called Charlestown until 1783) than through any other single port, and no other mainland region had so high a ratio of Africans to Europeans throughout the eighteenth century as did South Carolina. Early migrants from Barbados and other places where black slavery was well-established brought Negro workers with them when they could afford it. In the initial years after 1670, however, most English settlers hoped to meet the colony's intensive labor needs in other ways. Attempts were made to procure a steady supply of European

---

* An earlier version of this paper was read to the Organization of American Historians in 1972. Material appearing here is presented in a fuller context in Peter H. Wood, *Black Majority: Negroes in Colonial South Carolina from 1670 through the Stono Rebellion.* (New York 1974).

workers and to employ neighboring Indians on a regular basis, but neither of these sources could meet the demand. Within half a century Negroes constituted a majority of the settlement's population, and additional black slaves were being imported regularly from Africa.

That such a large percentage of early South Carolinians were Negroes has never been thoroughly explained, though basic contributing factors have long been recognized: European racism, colonial precedent, and the proximity of the African trading routes. No other workers were available for such extended terms, in such large numbers, at so low a rate. Indeed, such slave labor was so has always seemed almost inevitable. And perhaps for this very reason, the question of whether Negroes brought with them any inherited knowledge and practical skills from the African continent has seemed irrelevant to white historians. Though the anthropologist Melville Herskovits challenged "The Myth of the Negro Past" more than thirty years ago, the American historian has tended to uphold the legend that blacks had no prior cultures of any consequence, or that if they did, little could have survived the traumatic Middle Passage (Herskovits 1941). (McPherson (1971:32–39) indicates that a few historians have considered some carryovers, but little attention has been given to the importation of any practical kinds of cultural information.) Africans, according to this approach, were imported *in spite* of being thoroughly unskilled (or perhaps in part *because* of it). And it followed from this that the central chore which faced European masters was one of patient and one-sided education, so that "ignorant" slaves could be taught to manage simple tasks.

Yet in actuality something very different seems to have taken place. In the earliest years of colonization slaves who had passed through the Creole culture of the West Indies demonstrated unsuspected talents. Within several decades the necessity for labor of any sort led to an increase in the size and diversity of the Negro population, and a further variety of African skills emerged which were strikingly appropriate to the lowland frontier. Slaves, therefore, were far from being the passive objects of white instruction. A process of mutual education took place among the slaves themselves, despite initial language problems. And many of these workers, regardless of legal status, occasionally ended up teaching their masters. Africans, as will be made clear, sometimes proved knowledgeable and competent in areas where Europeans remained disdainful or ignorant. Hence the problem faced by white Carolinians during the first and second generations of settlement was less one of imparting knowledge to unskilled workers than of controlling for their own ends black expertise which could, as in Harry's case, be readily turned against them.

Though hitherto unacknowledged, the comparative advantages which Africans possessed over Europeans in this New World setting can be seen in a variety of different ways. South Carolina, first of all, was in a different geographic zone from England and from all the earlier English colonies in mainland North America. This fact was pleasing to white settlers on one level, but disconcerting on another, and they were slow to make the adjustments necessary for life in a somewhat alien semi-tropical region. John Lawson, an amateur naturalist who explored the Carolinas at the start of the eighteenth century, commented that if English colonists "would be so curious as to make nice Observations of the Soil, and other remarkable Accidents, they would soon be acquainted with the Nature of the Earth and Climate, and be better qualified to manage their Agriculture to more Certainty." But he went on to admit, as would Jefferson and others after him, that Europeans seemed to become less careful and observant rather than more so in the unfamiliar environment of the American South (Lawson 1967 [1709]: 80, 81).

West Africans, on the other hand, were not only more accustomed to the flora and fauna of a subtropical climate generally, but they possessed an orientation toward what Lévi-Strauss has called "extreme familiarity with their biological environment, ... passionate attention ... to it and ... precise knowledge of it" (Lévi-Strauss 1966: 5). Even prior to the 1600's black slaves had established a reputation for being able to subsist off the land more readily than Europeans in the Southeast. A century before the founding of Carolina, when Negroes were sent to work on the fortifications at St. Augustine, a Spanish official had written approvingly, "With regard to their food, they will display diligence as they seek it in the country, without any cost to the royal treasure" (*Colonial Records of Spanish Florida*, 1930: 315). In Carolina their ability to cope with this particular natural world was demonstrated, and reinforced, by the reliance Europeans put upon them to fend for themselves and others. Instances of black self-sufficiency (like instances of Indian assistance) made a lasting impression upon less well acclimated whites, and as late as 1775 we find an influential English text repeating the doctrine that in Carolina, "The common idea ... is, that one Indian, or dextrous negroe, will, with his gun and netts, get as much game and fish as five families can eat; and the slaves support themselves in provisions, besides raising ... staples" (Land 1969: 67).

By far the largest number of people entering South Carolina during the colonial period came from West Africa, and, in the course of a century of immigration, items indigenous to parts of that vast region were transported with them. For example, though white colonists would debate at length which European should receive credit for introducing the first bag of rice seed,[1] it is possible that successful rice cultivation, to be discussed separately later, followed the arrival of seeds aboard a ship from Africa.[2] Often the botanical

---

1   Landgrave Thomas Smith, Dr. Henry Woodward, an anonymous sea captain, and a treasurer of the East Indian Company all took or received the credit at some point. A letter of Nov. 4, 1726 (overlooked by historians), from Jean Watt in Neufchatel makes the claim "that it was by a woman that Rice was transplanted into Carolina." Records of the British Public Record Office Relating to South Carolina (hereafter abbreviated as BPRO Trans.), xii, 156–157.

2   At the end of the eighteenth century the Abbé Raynal wrote: "Opinions differ about the manner in which rice hath been naturalized in Carolina. But whether the province may have acquired it by a shipwreck, or whether it may have been carried there with slaves, or whether it be sent from England, it is certain that the soil is favourable for it" (Raynal, London, 1798, VI, 59).
   The first edition of this work, in 1772, offered only the shipwreck theory. The tradition

imprecision of contemporary Englishmen makes it hard to say exactly which plants were introduced and when. Semantic confusion about Guinea corn and Indian corn provides a case in point. Maurice Mathews reported during the initial summer of settlement that along with Indian corn, "Guiney Corne growes very well here, but this being ye first I euer planted ye perfection I will not Aver till ye Winter doth come in" (South Carolina Historical Society, *Collections*, V, 333). This grain or some subsequent variety clearly took hold, for in the next generation Lawson reported Guinea corn to be thriving; he noted it was used mostly for hogs and poultry, while adding that many black slaves ate "nothing but" Indian corn (with salt) (Lawson 1967 [1709]: 81). A definition offered by Mark Catesby in 1743 reveals that Indian and Guiney corn had become interchangeable in English texts, if not in actual fact:

> *Milium Indicum.* Bunched Guinea Corn. But little of this grain is propagated, and that chiefly by negroes, who make bread of it, and boil it in like manner of firmety. Its chief use is for feeding fowls.... It was at first introduced from Africa by the negroes (Catesby 1743, appendix, xviii).

Catesby also recorded "The Leg-worm, or Guinea-worm" among the "insects" he found in Carolina, and Lawson listed among varieties of muskmelon a "guinea melon" which may have come from Africa. Others mentioned the "guinea fowl" or "guinea hen," a domesticated West African bird which was introduced into North America during the eighteenth century. Henry Laurens of Charleston (like George Washington of Mount Vernon) acquired seed for "guinea grass," a tall African grass used for fodder (Lawson 1967 [1709]: 81–83; Mathews, II, 1193).

The West African and Carolinian climates were similar enough so that even where flora and fauna were not literally transplanted, a great deal of knowledge proved transferable. African cultures placed a high priority on their extensive pharmacopoeia, and details known through oral tradition were readily transported to the New World. For example, expertise included familiarity with a variety of herbal antidotes and abortives (Vansina 1971: 443; Curtin 1968: 215). A South Carolina slave received his freedom and one hundred pounds per year for life from the Assembly for revealing his antidote to certain poisons; "Ceasar's Cure" was printed in the *South Carolina Gazette* and appeared occasionally in local almanacs for more than thirty years (*S. C. Gazette*, May 9, 1750; Webber 1914: 78; On Caesar, cf. Duncan 1972: 64–66).

Although certain medicinal knowledge was confined to specially experienced slaves (some of whom were known openly as "doctors"), almost all blacks showed a general familiarity with lowland plants. Negroes regularly gathered berries and wild herbs for their own use and for sale. John Brickell noted of slaves in Carolina, for example, that "on Sundays, they gather Snake-Root, otherwise it would be excessive dear if the Christians were to gather it" (Brickell 1911 [1737]: 275). The economic benefits to be derived from workers with such horticultural skills were not lost upon speculative Europeans. In 1726

---

of a Madagascar origin has been popularized in Heyward 1937. On slaves from that region, see Platt 1969: 548–577.

Richard Ludlam urged the collection and cultivation of special plants upon which the cochineal beetle (an insect used to produce red dye) might feed and grow. According to Ludlam:

> Two or Three Slaves will gather as many Spontaneous Plants in one day, as will in another Day regularly Plant Ten Acres, by the Same hands and for the Quantity of Plants Growing here on the Banks of Rivers & in the multitudes of Islands on the Sea Coasts, I can Safely Assure you... Thousands of Acres might, at a Little Charge, be Stock with them.[3]

Bringing a greater awareness of the environment with them, foreign slaves were better able to profit from contact with native Indians than were their equally foreign masters. A variety of plants and processes were known to both West African and southeastern American cultures, and such knowledge must have been shared and reinforced upon contact. Gourds, for example, served as milk pails along the Gambia River in much the same way calabashes had long provided water buckets beside the Ashley[4] (Grant 1968: 24; Lawson 1967 [1709]: 149). The creation of elaborate baskets, boxes, and mats from various reeds and grasses was familiar to both black and red (Lawson 1967 [1709]: 195–196), and South Carolina's strong basket-weaving tradition, still plainly visible on the roadsides north of Charleston, undoubtedly represents an early fusion of Negro and Indian skills (Smith 1936: 71).

The palmetto, symbol of the novel landscape for arriving Europeans, was well known to Africans and Indians for its useful leaf. They made fans and brooms from these leaves and may well have entered into competition with Bermudians who were already exporting baskets and boxes made of woven palmetto (Lawson 1967 [1709]: 14; Corry 1968 [1807]: 66). An authority on Carolina furniture writes that "The very early inventories frequently mention Palmetto chairs or Palmetto-bottom chairs" (Burton 1955: 36–37). The skill and labor behind these traditional items may well have been primarily African, as suggested by one surviving mortgage. In 1729 Thomas Holton, a producer of chairs and couches, listed as collateral three of his Negro slaves: "by name Sesar, Will, and Jack by trade Chairmakers (Wills, Inventories, and Miscellaneous Records, 1729–1731:27).

Through the first two generations of settlement Indians were common among the Negroes in lowland Carolina, both as fellow slaves and as free neighbors (Cf. Dundes 1965: 207–219; Hudson 1971). But the number of Indians steadily declined, and as their once-formidable know-how dissipated it was the Negroes who assimilated the largest share of their lore and who

---

3   A copy of this letter (Jan. 10, 1726) is in volume II (labelled volume III) of the typescript marked, "Charleston Museum, Miscellaneous Papers, 1726–1730," South Caroliniana Library, Columbia.

4   It is impossible to say whether it was Africans or Indians who showed white planters, around 1700, how to put a gourd on a pole as a birdhouse for martins (that would in turn drive crows from the crops) or who fashioned the first drinking gourd which would become the standard dipper on plantations.

increasingly took over their responsibilities as "pathfinders" in the Southern wilderness. Blacks became responsible for transporting goods to market by land and water and for ferrying passengers and livestock. From the first years of settlement the primary means of direct communication between masters was through letters carried by slaves. Charleston set up a local post office at the beginning of the eighteenth century, and by 1740 there was a weekly mail going south toward the new colony of Georgia and a monthly post overland to the north via Georgetown and Cape Fear, but with the exception of these minimal services the responsibility for delivering letters in the region fell entirely to Negro boatmen and runners throughout the colonial period (Cooper and McCord, II, 188–189; *S. C. Gazette*, September 17, 1737; May 3, 1739; November 20, 1740).

There is no better illustration of white reliance upon black knowledge of the environment than the fact that slaves became quite literally the guides of their masters. Contemporary records give adequate testimony. John Lawson, travelling from the Ashley to the Santee by canoe at the start of the eighteenth century, relates that at one point a local doctor "sent his Negro to guide us over the Head of the Swamp" (Lawson 1967 [1709]: 20–21). A public official such as the Provost Marshal would sometimes be loaned a slave boy "to Show him the way" between plantations (*Journal of the Commons House Of Assembly, 1726–1727*, 119). In October 1745 a white traveller coming from Philadelphia recorded in his Journal: "had a Negro to guide us the Road being Intricate" (Pemberton *Diary*, 1745), and in the same month a minister of the Society for the Propagation of the Gospel wrote that his parishioners had urged him to purchase a family of three Negroes.

> I consented [he wrote] not knowing full well the ways and management of country affair[s] ..., and was obliged also by extream necessity to buy 3 horses with bridles and saddles, one for me, another for my wife, and the other for a Boy servant, for it would be impossible for me to go through the Parish between the woods without a Guide (Boschi 1949 [1745] 185).

In 1770 William De Brahm would observe that slaves, besides being stationed at their masters' gates to offer hospitality to white travellers, were often sent with departing guests "to cut down small trees in the way of carriages, to forward and guide through unfrequented forrests, ... [and] to set them over streams, rivers and creeks" (Weston 1856: 179). It is not an unrelated fact that ever since colonial times Negroes have commonly served as guides to white sportsmen in the Sea Islands and throughout the coastal South (Cf. Crum, Chapter IV).

It is striking to find black familiarity with the land more than matched by familiarity with the coastal sea. Although Europeans were unrivaled as the builders and navigators of oceangoing ships, there was little in the background of most white immigrants to prepare them for negotiating the labyrinth of unchanneled swamps and tidal marshes which interlaced the lowland settlement. Afro-Americans drew on a different heritage. Some slaves had scarcely seen deep water before their forced passage to America, and none had sailed in ocean vessels; yet many had grown up along rivers or beside the ocean and were far more at home in this element than most Europeans, for whom a simple bath was still exceptional (Cf. Turberville 1929: 126, for history of English bathing). Lawson, describing the awesome shark, related how "some Negro's, and others, that can swim and dive well, go naked into the Water, with a Knife in their Hand, and fight the Shark, and very commonly kill him" (Lawson 1967 [1709]: 158). Similarly the alligator, a fresh-water reptile which horrified Europeans (since it was unfamiliar and could not be killed with a gun), was readily handled by Negroes used to protecting their stock from African crocodiles (Grant 1968: 13, 23; see also Schaw 1922: 149–151).

Most importantly, a large number of slaves were more at home than their masters in dugout canoes, and these slender boats were the central means of transportation in South Carolina for several generations while roads and bridges were still too poor and infrequent for easy land travel.[5] Small canoes were hollowed from single cypress logs by Negroes or Indians, or by whites whom they instructed in the craft.[6] To make the larger canoe known as a pettiauger two or three trees were used, giving the boat additional beam for cargo without significantly increasing its draft; fifty to one hundred barrels of tar or rice could be ferried along shallow creeks and across tidal shoals in such vessels.

These boats were frequently equipped with one or even two portable masts for sailing and often ventured onto the open ocean (Lawson 1967 [1709], 103, 104, 107; Clontes 1926: 16–35; Cf. McKusick 1960). Their design may have represented a syncretic blend between European, Caribbean, and Indian styles on the one hand, and on the other hand diverse coastal traditions from West Africa, where cypress wood was used to fashion both round and flat bottomed craft (Batutah 1929 [1325–1354]: 333; Hakluyt 1904: 18; see also Wax 1968: 474, 478). Negro crews, directed by a black "patroon", managed these boats, and many of their earliest rowing songs were apparently remnants recalled from Africa (McCrady 1899: 516; Fisher 1953: 8).

The fact that dexterity in handling cypress canoes was an art brought from Africa is underscored by an advertisement for a runaway in the Virgina colony.

---

5   In 1682 Thomas Newe found that horses brought from New England were still scarce and expensive, "so there is but little use of them, all Plantations being seated on the Rivers, they can go to and fro by Canoo or Boat as well and as soon as they can ride." Newe added that "the horses here like the Indians and many of the English do travail without shoes" (Salley 1911: 184).

6   The English experience in Carolina must have been comparable to that of the French among the Island Caribs of the Antilles at the same time. Breton (1665, reprinted 1892), 331 states:
      The French learned from the Savages to hollow out trees to make canoes; but they did not learn from them to row them, steer them, or jump overboard to right them when they overturned: the Savages are not afraid of overturning, wetting their clothes, losing anything, or drowning, but most French fear all of these things... Every day one sees disastrous accidents.

The notice concerned "a new Negro Fellow of small Stature" from Bonny on the coast of Nigeria; it stated that "he calls himself Bonna, and says he came from a Place of that name in the Ibo Country, in Africa, where he served in the Capacity of a Canoe Man" (*Virginia Gazette*, December 24, 1772). In South Carolina slave men were often advertised in terms of their abilities on the water: "a very good Sailor, and used for 5 years to row in Boats, ... a Lad chiefly used to row in Boats," "a fine strong Negro Man, that has been used to the Sea, which he is very fit for, or to go in a Pettiaugua," "all fine Fellows in Boats or Pettiau's." So many Negroes brought these skills with them, or learned their seamanship in the colony from other slaves, that black familiarity with boating was accepted as axiomatic among whites. In 1741, when Henry Bedon advertised two Negro men "capable to go in a Pettiauger" who had been "going by the Water above 10 Years," he added that the pair "understands their Business as well as most of their Colour" (*S. C. Gazette*, April 6, 1734; April 11, 1739; January 31, 1743; February 18, 1741).

"Their business" often included fishing, and it is not surprising that in the West Indian and southern colonies Africans quickly proved able to supply both themselves and their European owners with fish (Wax 1968: 475–476). In Charleston, an entire class of "fishing Negroes" had emerged early in the eighteenth century, replacing local Indians as masters of the plentiful waters (*S. C. Gazette*, November 5, 1737). (For an excellent discussion of fishing slaves as a privileged subgroup, see Price 1968.) "There is ... good fishing all along this Coast, especially from October till Christmas," wrote James Sutherland who commanded Johnson's Fort overlooking Charleston harbor during the 1730's, adding (perhaps with fisherman's license), "I've known two Negroes take between 14 & 1500 Trouts above 3 feet long, wch make an excellent dry fish" (Coe Papers, undated). A French visitor whose ship anchored not far from Johnson's Fort early in the next century found himself "in the midst of twenty-five dugouts,"

> each containing four Negroes who were having excellent fishing, such as one might well desire on the eve of Good Friday. Ten minutes doesn't go by without there being hauled into the dugout fish weighing from twelve to fifteen pounds. After they are taken on the line, they are pulled up to the level of the sea where one of the black fishermen sticks them with a harpoon (Montlzun 1948: 136; see also Price 1968: 1372).

Skill with hooks and harpoons was complemented by other techniques more common in Africa and the Caribbean than in Europe. The poisoning of streams to catch fish was known in West Africa (Fyfe 1964: 96), and fish drugging was also practised in the West Indies, first by Island Caribs and later by Negro slaves. They dammed up a stream or inlet and added an intoxicating mixture of quicklime and plant juices to the water. They could then gather inebriated but edible fish from the pool almost at will (Price 1968: 1366, 1372; Quigley 1956: 508–525). Inhabitants of South Carolina in the early eighteenth century exploited a similar tactic, for in 1726 the Assembly charged that "many persons in this Province do often use the pernicious practice of poisoning the creeks in order to catch great quantity of fish," and a public whipping was imposed upon any slave convicted of the act (*Statutes*, III, 270; the misdemeanor seems to have continued; cf. *S. C. Gazette*, April 6, 1734).

West African Negroes may also have imported the art of net casting, which became an established tradition in the tidal shallows of Carolina. The doctor aboard an American slaving vessel off the Gold Coast in the mid-eighteenth century recorded in his journal: "It is impossible to imagine how very dextrous the negroes are in catching fish with a net, this morning I watch'd one man throw one of 3 yards deep, and hale it in himself with innumerable fish" (Wax 1968: 474; see also Whitten and Szwed, pictorials, 11th p.). Weighted draw-string nets, like the dugout canoes from which they were cast, may have represented the syncretic blend of several ancient Atlantic fishing traditions (Price 1968: 1374). The men who could handle nets could also mend them; in 1737 a runaway named Moses was reported to be "well known in Charlestown, having been a Fisherman there for some time, & hath been often employed in knitting of Nets" (*S. C. Gazette*, November 5, 1737). The prevalence of Negro commercial fishermen in the Southeast, as in the Caribbean, continued long after the end of slavery, and blacks who man shrimpboats in present-day Carolina earn their living at a calling familiar to many of their West African forebears. [7]

No single industry was more important to the early settlement in South Carolina than the raising of livestock. While the first generation of Englishmen experimented unsuccessfully with such strange crops as grapes, olives, cotton, rice, indigo, and ginger in the hopes of finding an appropriate staple, their livelihood depended in large measure upon the cattle and hogs that could be raised with a minimum of labor. Beef and pork were in great demand in the West Indies, and these at least were items which the English had long produced. But even here there was an unfamiliar element. According to traditional European patterns of animal husbandry, farmers confined their cows in pastures, milked them regularly, and slaughtered them annually. Since winter fodder was limited, Europeans maintained only enough stock through the cold months to replenish their herds in the following spring. This practice made little sense in a region where cattle could "feed themselves perfectly well at no cost whatever" (Thibou 1683) throughout the year. Stock grew lean, but rarely starved in South Carolina's mild winters. Colonists therefore might build up large herds with little effort, a fact which could benefit the settlement but which dismayed the Proprietors in London. It has been "our designe", they stated indignantly, "to have Planters there and not Graziers" (South Carolina Historical Society *Collections*, V, 437–438).

Africans, however, had no such disdain for open grazing, and many of the slaves entering South Carolina after 1670 may have had experience in tending

7   Frederic G. Cassidy (1967) points out that the Doulla-Bakweri language of the Cameroon River area provided the Jamaican Creole word for the crayfish or river prawn. "This part of Africa, indeed, took its name from the plentiful shrimp or prawns in the river: *Cameroon* is from Portuguese *camarao* 'shrimp.' "

large herds. Melville Herskovits, along with others, has pointed out that although domesticated cattle were absent from the Congo region due to the presence of the tse-tse fly, such animals were common along much of the African coast to the north and west. Stock was even traded for export on occasion. In 1651, for example, the English Guinea Company, precursor of the Royal African Company, instructed a captain to barter liquor at the Gambia River for a "Cargo of negers or Cattel" to be carried to Barbados. People of the Gambia region, the area for which South Carolina slave dealers expressed a steady preference, were expert horsemen and herders. English visitors expressed high admiration for their standards of cleanliness with respect to dairy products, and contemporary descriptions of local animal husbandry bear a striking resemblance to what would later appear in Carolina. Herds grazed on the savannahs bordering the river and in the low-lying paddy fields when the rice crop was off; at night stock was tethered within a cattlefold and guarded by several armed men (Herskovits 1930: 67, 72, 73; Donnan 1930–1935, I, 129; Grant 1968: 24–25).

As early as the 1670's there is evidence of absentee investors relying upon Negro slaves to develop herds of cattle in Carolina.[8] Even when the white owner lived within the province, the care of his livestock often fell to a black. The slave would build a small "cowpen" in some remote region, attend the calves and guard the grazing stock at night. When Denys Omahone sold a fifty-acre tract to a new white arrival in the 1680's the property contained, besides the Indians who still inhabited it, four calves, three steers, five sows, one boar and a "Negro man by name Cato" (South Carolina Archives, Miscellaneous Records A, 1682–1690: 318–319).

This pattern continued. In 1690 Seth Sothell gave his father-in-law one of several large landholdings "And thirty head of Cattle belonging to ye Said Plantation and one Neg[ro] Man" (South Carolina Archives, Archdale Papers, item 26, January 25, 1690; cf. Dunbar). Upon the death in 1692 of Bernard Schenckingh, a well-to-do Barbadian migrant with four estates, the appraisers of his James Island holdings reported that "In sight and by account

---

8 In 1673, for example, Edmund Lister of Northumberland County, Virginia, bought one hundred acres of land along the Ashley River on Oyster Point from an illiterate laborer named John Gardner. Lister sent three men south ahead of him to prepare the land (not an unusual practice), but he died the following year before taking up residence. One of those he had sent ahead to South Carolina was an indentured servant named Patrick Steward with only several months left to serve, but the others were apparently black slaves experienced with livestock, for in 1676 Lister's widow stated in a bill of sale that her "Dec[d] Housband, did formerly Transport Severall Negros, out of this Colony of Virginia, into Carolina and did there Settle them upon a Plantacon, together w[td] Some Cattle." The holding may have been considerable, for the widow received 10,000 pounds of good tobacco for the land, Negroes, and stock from a Virginia gentleman who was himself an absentee owner of slave in Carolina (South Carolina Archives, Records of the Secretary of the Province, 1675–1695, 39–41; Salley 1944 (1671–1675): 59, 66–69). It was long ago suggested that the particularly numerous slaves in the Narragansett country of Rhode Island played an important role on the renowned stock farms of that region (Channing 1886: 9–10).

apeareth 134 head of Cattle [and] one negro man" (South Carolina Archives, Records of the Secretary of the Province, 1692–1700: 38). Half a century later the estate of Robert Beath at Ponpon included, "a Stock of Cattle ... said to be from Five Hundred to One Thousand Head ... Also a Man used to a Cow Pen and of a good Character" (*S. C. Gazette*, March 19, 1741).

At first the Carolina settlement occupied a doubly colonial status, struggling to supply provisions to other English colonies. [9] The development of a trade in naval stores soon enabled the settlement to become a staple producer in its own right, but it was the cultivation of rice as an export commodity which came to dominate Carolina life in the course of the eighteenth century. Despite its eventual prominence, the mastery of this grain took more than a generation, for rice was a crop about which Englishmen, even those who had lived in the Caribbean, knew nothing at all. White immigrants from elsewhere in northern Europe were equally ignorant, and local Indians who gathered small quantities of wild rice had little to teach them.

Though England consumed comparatively little rice before the eighteenth century, the cheap white grain was a dietary staple in parts of southern Europe by 1670, and Carolina's Proprietors were anticipating a profit from this crop even before the settlement began (S. C. Historical Society *Collections*, V, 15). When the colonists could show nothing for their efforts after their first seven years, the Londoners wrote impatiently, "wee are Layinge out in Severall places of ye world for plants & Seeds proper for yor Country and for persons that are Skill'd in plantinge & producings ... Rice oyles & Wines" (BPRO Trans., I: 59). But there is no direct evidence that the Proprietors followed through on this promise, or that they responded helpfully to later requests for guidance (*Journal of the Commons House of Assembly*, 1698: 36).

Nevertheless, during the 1680's, perhaps after the arrival of a better strain of rice seed from Madagascar, the colonists renewed their efforts to grow rice, but with only marginal success through the 1690's (Salley 1919; Gray, I: 277 ff.; Clowse 1971: 123–132. See also *South Carolina Historical and Geneological Magazine*, January and April, 1931). An eighteenth-century Englishman recalled:

> the people being unacquainted with the manner of cultivating rice, many difficulties attended the first planting and preparing it, as a vendable commodity, so that little progress was made for the first nine or ten years, when the quantity produced was not sufficient for home consumption (*Gentleman's Magazine*, June, 1776, 278–279).

Similarly, Governor Glen would later claim that even after experimenters had begun to achieve plausible yields from their renewed efforts around 1690,

---

9   A letter from the Reverend John Urmstone in North Carolina, July 11, 1711 (quoted in Land 22–23), typifies conditions which had prevailed in South Carolina slightly earlier. Urmstone stated, "the planter here is but a slave to raise a provision for other colonies," adding:

> Men are generally of all trades, and women the like within their spheres, except some who are the posterity of old planters, and have great number of slaves, who understand most handicraft. ...

they still remained "ignorant for some Years how to clean it" (Glen 1951 [1761]: 94).[10]

In contrast to Europeans, Negroes from the West Coast of Africa were widely familiar with rice planting. Ancient speakers of a Proto-Bantu language in the sub-Sahara region are known to have cultivated the crop (McCall 1964: 69). An indigenous variety (*Oryza glaberrima*) was a staple in the western rain-forest regions long before Portuguese and French navigators introduced Asian and American varieties of *O. sativa* in the 1500's. By the seventeenth and eighteenth centuries, West Africans were selling rice to slave traders to provision their ships. The northernmost English factory on the coast, James Fort in the Gambia River, was in a region where rice was grown in paddies along the riverbanks (Herskovits 1930; Donnan 1930–1935: I; Grant 1968: 24–25). In the Congo-Angola region, which was the southernmost area of call for English slavers, a white explorer once noted rice to be so plentiful there as to bring almost no price (Grant 1968: 24–25; Parrish 1942: 227n.).

The most significant rice region, however, was the "Windward Coast," the area upwind or westward from the major Gold Coast trading station of Elmina. An Englishman who spent time in Sierra Leone on the Windward Coast at the end of the eighteenth century claimed that rice "forms the chief part of the African's sustenance." He went on to observe, "The rice-fields or *lugars* are prepared during the dry season, and the seed sown in the tornado season, requiring about four or five months growth to bring it to perfection" (Corry 1968 [1807]: 37; cf. Fyfe 1964: 20, 29, 77). Throughout the era of slave importation into South Carolina references can be found concerning African familiarity with rice. Ads in the local papers occasionally made note of slaves from rice-growing areas (Donnan, I: 375, 377–380, 413, 428, 438, 442. See also Mannix and Cowley 1962, opp. 146), and a notice from the *Evening Gazette*, July 11, 1785, announced the arrival aboard a Danish ship of "a choice cargo of windward and gold coast negroes, who have been accustomed to the planting of rice."[11]

---

10 Glen added at this later date (p. 95): "The only Commodity of Consequence produced in South Carolina is Rice, and they reckon it as much their staple Commodity, as Sugar is to Barbadoes and Jamaica, or Tobacco to Virginia and Maryland."
    In 1691 a Frenchman named Peter Jacob Guerard received a two-year patent on "a Pendulum Engine, which doth much better, and in lesse time and labour, huske rice; than any other [that] heretofore hath been used within this Province," but there is no indication that the device itself succeeded, or that it helped to spur further invention as hoped (*Statutes*, II, 63). Guerard came to South Carolina in April 1680 aboard the *Richmond* with a group of French Huguenots. He was a goldsmith by trade and served as collector of the port in 1696 (*South Carolina Historical and Genealogical Magazine*, XLIII (Jan., 1942), 9–11). His pendulum device may have been nothing more than a pestle attached to the limb of a tree so that it would swing back up after each stroke into the mortar below.

11 The most dramatic evidence of experience with rice among enslaved Africans comes from the famous rebels aboard the *Amistad* in the nineteenth century. Thirty-six slaves from the Sierra Leone region were shipped illegally from Lomboko to Cuba, and in the wake of their successful shipboard uprising they eventually found themselves imprisoned in New

Those Africans who were accustomed to growing rice on one side of the Atlantic, and who found themselves raising the same crop on the other side, did not markedly alter their annual routine. When New World slaves planted rice in the spring by pressing a hole with the heel and covering the seeds with the foot, the motion used was demonstrably similar to that employed in West Africa (Herskovits 1937: opp. 100; Bascom 1941: 49). In summer, when Carolina blacks moved through the rice fields in a row, hoeing in unison to work songs, the pattern of cultivation was not one imposed by European owners but rather one retained from West African forebears (Bascom 1941: 45; Glassie 1968: 117). And in October, when the threshed grain was "fanned" in the wind, the wide flat winnowing baskets was made by black hands after an African design (Huggins, Kilson, Fox 1971: opp. 128; Herskovits 1958: 147).

Those familiar with growing and harvesting rice must also have known how to process it, so it is interesting to speculate about the origins of the mortar and pestle technique which became the accepted method for removing rice grains from their husks. Efforts by Europeans to develop alternative "engines" proved of no avail, and this process remained the most efficient way to "clean" the rice crop throughout the colonial period. Since some form of the mortar and pestle is familiar to agricultural peoples throughout the world, a variety of possible (and impossible) sources have been suggested for this device (Glassie 1968: 116–117). But the most logical origin for this technique is the coast of Africa, for there was a strikingly close resemblance between the traditional West African means of pounding rice and the process used by slaves in South Carolina. Several Negroes, usually women, cleaned the grain a small amount at a time by putting it in a wooden mortar which was hollowed from the upright trunk of a pine or cypress. It was beaten with long wooden pestles which had a sharp edge at one end for removing the husks and a flat tip at the other for whitening the grains. Even the songs sung by the slaves who threshed and

---

Haven. There they were interrogated separately, and excerpts from the interviews drive home this familiarity with rice in personal terms:

He was a blacksmith in his native village, and made hoes, axes and knives; he also planted rice.

There are high mountains in his country, rice is cultivated, people have guns; has seen elephants.

He was caught in the bush by four men as he was going to plant rice; his left hand was tied to his neck; was ten days going to Lomboko.

He was seized by four men when in a rice field, and was two weeks in traveling to Lomboko

He is a planter of rice.

His parents are dead, and he lived with his brother, a planter of rice.

He was seized by two men as he was going to plant rice.

5 ft. 1 in. high, body tattooed, teeth filed, was born at Fe-baw, in Sando, between Mendi and Konno. His mother's brother sold him for a coat. He was taken in the night, and sold to Garlobá, who had four wives. He staid with this man two years, and was employed in cultivating rice. His master's wives and children were employed in the same manner, and no distinction made in regard to labor (Barber 1969 (1840): 9–15).

pounded the rice may have retained African elements (Herskovits 1958: 147; Parrish 1942: 13, 225–233, plates 7 and 8).

In the establishment of rice cultivation, as in numerous other areas, historians have ignored the possibility that Afro-Americans could have contributed anything more than menial labor to South Carolina's early development. Yet Negro slaves, faced with limited food supplies before 1700 and encouraged to raise their own subsistence, could readily have succeeded in nurturing rice where their masters had failed. It would not have taken many such incidents to demonstrate to the anxious English that rice was a potential staple and that Africans were its most logical cultivators and processors. Some such chain of events may even have provided the background for Edward Randolph's report to the Lords of Trade in 1700 that Englishmen in Carolina had "now found out the true way of raising and husking Rice" (BPRO Trans., IV, 189–190). Needless to say, by no means every slave entering South Carolina had been drawn from an African rice field, and many, perhaps even a great majority, had never seen a rice plant. But it is important to consider the fact that literally hundreds of black immigrants were more familiar with the planting, hoeing, processing, and cooking of rice than were the European settlers who purchased them.

Despite the usefulness of all such African skills to the colony's development, there existed a reverse side to the coin. While it is clear that Negro South Carolinians made early contributions to the regional culture, it is also clear that they received little recompense for their participation and that they were bound to respond to this fact. Slaves quickly proved that the same abilities which benefitted Europeans, such as gathering herbs and guiding canoes, could also be used to oppose and threaten them. The connection between black expertise and black resistance, suggested by the story of Harry's skill in protecting a fort against white soldiers, can be illustrated in a number of areas.

The raising of livestock provides a case in point. As cattle and hog production grew, it provided numerous whites with the substance for increasing their holdings in Negroes (Salley 1911: 172), and European observers marvelled at this growth (Nairne 1710: 13). Slaves, on the other hand, benefitted little from this enterprise in which they were involved. Consequently they began to utilize their skills to the disadvantage of the white society. Negroes often helped themselves to the livestock which they tended, and the regulations for branding stock which were introduced by the government before 1700 did little to deter this practice. Slaves altered brands with such dexterity that in the Negro Act of 1722 their owners denied them the right to keep and breed any horses, cows, or hogs whatsoever (*Statutes* II, 106; VII, 382). Nevertheless, livestock rustling by Negroes continued, and in 1743 the Assembly was obliged to draft "An Act to prevent Stealing of Horses and Neat Cattle," which went so far as to declare, "it shall not be lawfull hereafter for any Slave whatsoever to brand or mark any horses or neat Cattle but in the Presence of some white Person under the penalty of being severely whip[p]ed" (*Statutes* III, 604; cf. IV, 285 (1768).

A law passed the following year required that Negro ferrymen, suspected of transporting fellow slaves, were to be accompanied by a freeman at all times (*Statutes* III, 626; ix, 72, 1731). By then it had been apparent for decades that the skills of black boatmen could be a liability as well as a source of profit to white colonists. As early as 1696 an act had been passed, patterned on laws already in force in the West Indies, which threatened any slave who "shall take away or let loose any boat or canoe" with thirty-nine lashes for the first offense and loss of an ear for repetition (*Statutes* II, 105. See Higham for a similar law on Antigua). Related acts in the eighteenth century prohibited unfree Negroes from owning or using any boat or canoe without authorization (*Statutes* VII, 368 (1714), 382 (1722), 409–410 (1740)). Such repeated legislation underscores the fact that slaves who were involved in building and manning these boats inevitably found occasions to use them for travel or escape.

Among the Negroes whose seamanship was most valuable and also most problematical for whites were those who served aboard Charleston pilot boats or were otherwise knowledgeable in local navigation. The possibility that slaves would make such strategic skills available to an international rival was always a source of concern for English settlers. There was alarm, for example, during hostilities with Spain in 1741 when the Negroes from Thomas Poole's pilot boat were carried to St. Augustine by a Spanish privateer (*Journal of the Commons House of Assembly, 1741–1742*, 272). At that time colonists were well aware that for several decades Bermuda had suffered serious depradations from Spanish vessels piloted by Bermuda Negroes who had defected (Wilkinson 1950: 112; cf. Wood 350). Four years later a slave named Arrah was seized from Hugh Cartwright's schooner and "great encouragement was offered to be given him by the enemy if he would join with them against the English, and assist them as a pilot for ... Carolina." When he stoutly refused and succeeded in making his way back to Charleston after several years, the grateful Assembly granted him his freedom by a special act (*Statutes* VII, 419–420).

Black knowledge of herbs and poisons was the most vivid reminder that Negro expertise could be a two-edged sword. In West Africa, the obeah-men and others with the herbal know-how to combat poisoning could inflict it as well, and this gave slaves a weapon against their new white masters. In Jamaica, poisoning was a commonplace means of black resistance in the eighteenth century, and incidents were also familiar in the mainland colonies (Patterson 1969: 265–266; Mullin 1972). In South Carolina the administering of poison by a slave was made a felony in the stiff Negro Act of 1740 which followed in the wake of the Stono Rebellion (*Statutes* VII, 402). Eleven years later an additional law was written, stating that "the detestable crime of poisoning hath of late been frequently committed by many slaves in this Province, and notwithstanding the execution of several criminals for that offence, yet it has not been sufficient to deter others from being guilty of the same" (*Statutes* VII, 422–423).

The statute of 1751 suggests the seriousness with which white legislators viewed the poisoning threat, for they attempted belatedly to root out longstanding Negro knowledge and administration of medicinal drugs. It was enacted, "That in case any slave shall teach or instruct another slave in the knowledge of any poisonous root, plant, herb, or other poison whatever, he or she, so offending, shall, upon conviction thereof, suffer death as a felon; and the slave or slaves so taught or instructed" were to receive a lesser punishment. "And to prevent, as much as may be, all slaves from attaining the knowledge of any mineral or vegetable poison," the act went on, "it shall not be lawful for any physician, apothecary or druggist, at any time hereafter, to employ any slave or slaves in the shops or places where they keep their medicines or drugs." Finally, the act provided that "no negroes or other slaves (commonly called doctors,) shall hereafter be suffered or permitted to administer any medicine, or pretended medicine, to any other slave; but at the instance or by the direction of some white person." Any Negro disobeying this law was subject to the most severe whipping which the colony's Assembly ever prescribed. Yet even this strict legislation was apparently not enough to suppress such resistance, for in 1761 the *Gazette* reported that "The negroes have again begun the hellish practice of poisoning" (*S. C. Gazette*, January 17, 1761; Aptheker 1969: 143–144; Marburg and Crawford 1802: 430).

The matter of poisoning was discussed at length in a letter which Alexander Garden (the Charleston physician after whom Linnaeus named the gardenia) sent to Charles Alston, his former teacher in Edinburgh, in 1756 (Waring 1964: 225–226). Garden stated his candid belief that while some masters had been "actually poisoned by their slaves," numerous other deaths were listed as poisonings by local doctors as a device to "screen their own ignorance." Nevertheless, actual instances of poisoning intrigued him, and he put forward a scheme "To examine the nature of vegetable poisons in general." Garden took most seriously the implications that black proficiency derived from Africa. He requested from Alston, "assistance in giving me what information you could about the African Poisons, as I greatly and do still suspect that the Negroes bring their knowledge of the poisonous plants, which they use here, with them from their own country." He even went so far as to state explicitly that it was part of his plan, "To investigate the nature of particular poisons (chiefly those indigenous in this province and Africa)." But his scheme was of little avail at a time when European knowledge of African flora was still so limited.

Europeans entering South Carolina did not anticipate black skills or the uses to which they might be put. Indeed, most were ignorant of the environment they entered and of the labor they purchased. But white settlers soon realized that African workers possessed expertise which could be exploited and knowledge which was to be feared. Within several generations, the Europeans had imparted aspects of their culture to the slaves and had themselves acquired practical knowledge in matters such as ricegrowing (Corry 1968 [1807], 65–66). Consequently, Negro skills rapidly lost distinctiveness during the middle decades of the eighteenth century. By that time, however, black South Carolinians had already contributed significantly to the colony's initial growth, and ironically these early contributions, although threatening at times,

served to strengthen rather than to weaken the European rationale for perpetuating an African labor force. A full generation before the American Revolution, race slavery had become a firmly established institution in the region,
and white patterns of exploitation and fear were destined to run their lengthy
course.

REFERENCES

1775   *American Husbandry*. London. (Reprinted in Aubrey C. Land).
APTHEKER, Herbert
    1969   *American Negro Slave Revolts*. 2nd ed. New York.
BAKER, H. G.
    1962   "Comments on the thesis that there was a major centre of plant domestication near
            the headwaters of the River Niger". *Journal of African History* 3: 229–234.
BARBER, John Warner
    1840   *A History of the Amistad Captives*. New Haven. (Reprinted New York, 1969).
BARNWELL, J.
    1898   *Virginia Magazine of History and Biography*, VI (July): 44–45.
BASCOM, William R.
    1941   "Acculturation among the Gullah Negroes". *American Anthropologist* XLIII: 43–50.
BATUTAH, Ibn (Muhammed ibn abd Allah)
    1929   *Travels in Asia and Africa, 1325–1354*. Translated and selected by H.A.R. Gibb.
            London.
BOSCHI, Charles
    1949   To S.P.G. Secretary, Oct. 20, 1745. *South Carolina Historical and Geneological Maga-
            zine* L (October): 185.
BRETON, R. P. Raymond
    1892   *Dictionnaire Caraibe-Francais, 1665*. (Reprinted Leipzig 1892.)
BRICKELL, John
    1737   *The Natural History of North-Carolina*. London. (Reprinted, Raleigh, 1911).
BURTON, E. Milby
    1955   *Charleston Furniture, 1700–1825*. Charleston.
CASSIDY, Frederic G.
    1967   "Some New Light on Old Jamaicanisms". *American Speech* XLII: 191–192.
CATESBY, Mark
    1743   *The Natural History of Carolina, Florida and the Bahama Islands*. London.
CHANNING, Edward
    1886   "The Narragansett Planters". Johns Hopkins University Studies in Historical and
            Political Science, Series 4, No. 3. Baltimore.
CLARK, J. D.
    1962   "The spread of food production in Sub-Saharan Africa". *Journal of African History*
            3: 211–228.
CLONTES, F. W.
    1926   "Travel and Transportation in Colonial North Carolina". *North Carolina Historical
            Review* III (January): 16–35.
CLOWSE, Converse D.
    1971   *Economic Beginnings in Colonial South Carolina, 1670–1730*. Columbia.
CONNER, Jeanette Thurber, trans. and ed.
    1930   *Colonial Records of Spanish Florida* III (June 4, 1580). Deland, Florida.
COOPER, Thomas and David J. McCord, eds.
    1836–1841   *The Statutes at Large of South Carolina*. 10 vols. Columbia.
CORRY, Joseph
    1807   *Observations upon the Windward Coast of Africa*. London. (Reprinted, London, 1968).

CRUM, Mason
1940   *Gullah: Negro Life in the Carolina Sea Islands.* Durham, North Carolina.
CURTIN, Philip D.
1968   "Epidemiology and the slave trade". *Political Science Quarterly* LXXXIII (June): 119–216.
DONNAN, Elizabeth, ed.
1930–1935   *Documents Illustrative of the Slave Trade to America.* Washington.
DUNBAR, Gary S.
1961   "Colonial Carolina Cowpens". *Agricultural History* XXXV: 125–130.
DUNCAN, John D.
1972   "Slave emancipation in colonial South Carolina". *American Chronical, A Magazine of History* I (January): 64–66.
DUNDES, Alan
1965   "African Tales among the North American Indians". *Southern Folklore Quarterly* 29 (September): 207–219.
FISHER, Miles Mark
1953   *Negro slave songs in the United States.* New York.
FYFE, Christopher
1964   *Sierra Leone inheritance.* London.
GLASSIE, Henry
1968   "Patterns in the Material Folk Culture of the Eastern United States". University of Pennsylvania Monographs in Folklore and Folklife, No. 1. Philadelphia.
GLEN, James
1761   *A Description of South Carolina.* London. (Reprinted in Chapman J. Milling, ed., *Colonial South Carolina: Two Contemporary Descriptions.* Columbia, 1951).
GRANT, Douglas
1968   *The Fortunate Slave, An Illustration of African Slavery in the Early Eighteenth Century.* London.
GRAY, Lewis Cecil
1933   *History of Agriculture in the Southern United States to 1860.* Washington.
HAKLUYT, Richard
1904   *The Principal Navigations, Voyages, Traffiques & Discoveries of the English Nation,* X. Glasgow.
HERSKOVITS, Melville J.
1930   "The culture areas of Africa". *Africa* III: 67–73.
1937   *Life in a Haitian Valley.* New York.
1941   *The Myth of the Negro Past.* Boston.
HEYWARD, Duncan Clinch
1937   *Seed from Madagascar.* Chapel Hill.
HIGHAM, C. S. S.
1921   *The Development of the Leeward Islands, 1660–1688.* Cambridge, England.
HUDSON, Charles M., ed.
1971   "Red, White, and Black, Symposium on Indians in the Old South." Southern Anthropological Society, *Proceedings,* No. 5. Athens, Georgia.
HUGGINS, Nathan I., Martin KILSON, Daniel M. Fox, eds.
1971   *Key Issues in the Afro-American Experience.* New York.
Journal of the Commons House of Assembly, 1726–1727.
LAND, Aubrey C.
1969   *Bases of the Plantation Society.* Columbia.
LAWSON, John
1709   *A New Voyage to Carolina.* London. (Republished with introduction and notes by Hugh Talmage Lefler, Chapel Hill, 1967).
LÉVI-STRAUSS, Claude
1966   *The Savage Mind.* London.
McCALL, Daniel F.
1964   *Africa in Time-Perspective.* Boston.

McCRADY, Edward
     1899   *The History of South Carolina Under the Royal Government, 1719–1776.* New York.
McKUSICK, Marshall B.
     1960   "Aboriginal canoes in the West Indies", in Sidney W. Mintz (comp.), *Papers in Caribbean Anthropology.* Yale University Publications in Anthropology, No. 57. New Haven.
McPHERSON, et al., eds.
     1971   "African cultural survivals among Black Americans", in *Blacks in America: Bibliographical Essays.* Garden City.
MANNIX, Daniel P. and Malcolm COWLEY
     1962   *Black Cargoes: A History of the Atlantic Slave Trade, 1518–1865.* New York.
MARBURG, H. and W. H. CRAWFORD
     1802   *Digest of the Laws of Georgia.* Savannah.
MATHEWS, Mitford
     1938–1944   *A Dictionary of American English.* Chicago.
MONTLZUN, Baron de
     1948   "A Frenchman Visits Charleston, 1817." *South Carolina Historical and Genealogical Magazine* XLIX (July): 136.
MORGAN, W. B.
     1962   "The forest and agriculture in West Africa". *Journal of African History* 3: 235–240.
MULLIN, Gerald W.
     1972   *Flight and Rebellion: Slave Resistance in Eighteenth-Century Virginia.* New York.
NAIRE, Thomas
     1710   A Letter from South Carolina. London.
PARRISH, Lydia
     1942   *Slave Songs of the Georgia Sea Islands.* New York.
PATTERSON, Orlando
     1967   *The Sociology of Slavery, An Analysis of the Origins, Development and Structure of Negro Society in Jamaica.* London.
PEMBERTON, James, *Diary of a trip to South Carolina, 1745,* entry for October 17, original in Library of Congress, mfm. in South Caroliniana Library, Columbia.
PLATT, Virginia Bever
     1969   "The East India Company and the Madagascar slave trade". *William and Mary Quarterly*, 3rd ser., XXVI (October): 548–577.
PRICE, Richard
     1968   "Caribbean fishing and fishermen: a historical sketch". *American Anthropologist* LXVIII: 1363–1383.
QUIGLEY, Carroll
     1956   "Aboriginal fish poisons and the diffusion problem". *American Anthropologist* LVIII: 508–525.
RAYNAL, Abbé
     1798   *Philosophical and Political History of the Possessions and Trade of Europeans in the Two Indies.* 2nd ed. London.
Records of the British Public Record Office Relating to South Carolina, 36 vols. (1663–1782). (In the South Carolina Department of Archives and History).
SALLEY, Alexander S., ed.
     1911   *Narratives of Early Carolina, 1650–1708.* New York.
     1919   "The Introduction of Rice Culture into South Carolina" (Bulletins of the Historical Commission of South Carolina, No. 6). Columbia.
     1944   *Records* of the Secretary of the Province and the Register of the Province of South Carolina, 1671–1675. Columbia.
SCHAW, Janet
     1922   *Journal of a Lady of Quality,* edited by Evangeline W. Andrews and Charles M. Andrews. New Haven.

SMITH, Alice R. Huger
1936   *A Carolina Rice Plantation of the Fifties*. New York.
South Carolina Historical Society, Collections, in the South Carolina Department of Archives and History.
SUTHERLAND, James
Undated letter in the Coe Papers (Documents of the Lords Commissioners, 1719–1742). South Carolina Historical Society.
THIBOU, Louis
Letter in French dated September 20, 1683 and typescript translation in the South Caroliniana Library, Columbia.
TURBERVILLE, A. S.
1929   *English Men and Manners in the Eighteenth Century*. 2nd ed. London.
VANSINA, Jan
1971   "Once upon a time: oral traditions as history in Africa". *Daedalus* C (Spring): 442–468.
WARING, Joseph I.
1964   *A History of Medicine in South Carolina, 1670–1825*. Charleston.
WAX, Darold D.
1968   "A Philadelphia surgeon on a slaving voyage to Africa, 1749–1751". *Pennsylvania Magazine of History and Biography* XCII (October): 474–478.
WEBBER, Mabel L., comp.
1914   "South Carolina Almanacs, to 1800". *South Carolina Historical and Genealogical Magazine* XV (April): 78.
WESTON, P. C. J., ed.
1856   Documents Connected with the History of South Carolina. London.
WHITTEN, Norman E., Jr., and John F. SZWED
1970   *Afro-American Anthropology: Contemporary Perspectives*. New York.
WILKINSON, Henry C.
1950   *Bermuda in the Old Empire*. London.
Wills, Inventories and Miscellaneous Records, in the South Carolina Department of Archives and History.
WOOD, Peter H.
1972   "Black majority: Negroes in colonial South Carolina from 1670 through the Stono Rebellion". Ph. D. dissertation, Harvard University.

"Lift Every Voice": a Study of Afro-American Emancipation Celebrations

WILLIAM H. WIGGINS, Jr.

Indiana University, Bloomington, U.S.A.

FREEDOM is the Afro-American's magnificent obsession. Each period of our history, slavery, reconstruction, urban migration, the Harlem Renaissance, the two world wars, civil rights and the current age of Black Power, is another chapter in the story of Afro-Americans struggle to be free. This struggle has been long with many defeats, e.g. the rise of Jim Crow laws after reconstruction and the rash of Afro-American lynchings after World War I, and some periodic victories, e.g. the election of Blacks to local, state and federal offices during reconstruction and the present age of Black Power and the federal civil rights legislation passed during the career of Dr. Martin Luther King, Jr. Throughout this struggle freedom has been the objective, the goal. The tactics have been as divergent as the ballot or the bullet, integration or separation, religion or politics, cultural awareness or economic acumen, emotional rhetoric or written reason, but the single prize sought by all Afro-Americans has been freedom.

The fifty-seven year period from 1808 to 1865 is a watershed in this freedom struggle. In this period of little more than half a century, Afro-Americans took part in and benefited from those movements and events which culminated in their emancipation from slavery. Their primary means of registering this complaint against slavery and the joy of freedom were a series of little-studied emancipation celebrations. The first one was celebrated on January 1, 1808 to commemorate the termination of America's foreign slave trade and the last one began on June 19, 1865 to celebrate the arrival of freedom's sweet sound to east Texas (Quarles 1967: 14–19).

Though they all share the common theme of Afro-American freedom, these celebrations were fashioned by differing historical circumstances. In addition to January 1, 1808 and June 19, 1865, four other celebrations originated with the issuance of some state or federal edicts of freedom. July 4, 1827 signaled slavery's end in the state of New York; August 1, 1834 marked the termination of English slavery in the West Indies; April 16, 1862 was the date that Congress ended slavery in the District of Columbia; and February

1, 1865 was the day that Congress passed the Thirteenth Amendment.

Four of these celebrations began with the issuance of varied proclamations of emancipation. On May 9, 1862 General David Hunter, Commander of the Department of the South issued an order freeing all the slaves in South Carolina, Georgia and Florida; on September 22, 1862 President Abraham Lincoln issued his "preliminary proclamation" which gave the seceding states one hundred days to change their pro-slavery position; on January 1, 1863 Lincoln issued his historic Emancipation Proclamation and set in motion the hallowed "Day of Days" celebrations; and on June 19, 1865 General Gordon Granger landed at Galveston, Texas and read a governmental order freeing all of the slaves in east Texas and thereby initiating the Juneteenth celebrations. One celebration, the Jerry Rescue Day, began on October 1, 1851 in Syracuse, New York when a group of white citizens freed a slave named Jerry and sent him to Canada.

The origins of the remaining seven celebrations are not as easily explained. Just as many of their slave celebrants had no known birthdates, these celebrations have no certain year of birth. And, by the same token, just as the parentage of most slaves is suspect, the historical circumstances which bore these events are not known. They cannot trace their lineage back to a Congressional Act, or an heroic act of abolition, or a presidential proclamation. Their celebrants simply say that on some past May 5th, 8th, 20th, 22nd, 28th, 29th, and August 4th and 8th their ancestors learned that they were free.

Collectively, these celebrations divide into three major catagories: secular, sacred and secular/sacred. August 4th and 8th, May 8th, 20th, 28th and 29th, and June 19th are secular emancipation celebrations which draw heavily from American rituals and culture. The 4th of July celebrations have served as their model. The morning parade was one item borrowed and fashioned to the Afro-American theme of freedom. Their line of march included smart stepping brass bands, pretty "prancing horses," local orders of Masons, Shriners, Knight Templars and other fraternal organizations, resplendent in their parade dress. However, the theme of freedom was ever present. Often the floats depicted the historical fight of Afro-Americans for freedom. And there were symbols and slogans in abundance, too. One placard carried the slogan, "Fourteen slaves brought here in 1619." In some parades axes were carried to symbolize death to the slave owner and torches were carried in others to symbolize their hard-earned freedom. But the most effective symbol was the ex-slaves who were placed at the end of the march. And in Brenham, Texas, the black citizens elected their parade queen, "The Goddess of Liberty."

There were negative white reactions to these parades. Afro-Americans in New York shifted their observance to July 5th with the hope of not angering the whites. But these measure did not always work. For example, during the July 8, 1862 emancipation celebration in Ithaca, New York, two white men appeared in black face and "grotesque" dress and tried to disrupt the parade with their demeaning antics.

These parades ended at the picnic area where marchers and celebrants

enjoyed good food and warm fellowship. A must item on the menu was barbe-
cued meat, expertly prepared the night before, and ice cream made at the park
during the day. At Juneteenth celebrations great quantities of "red soda water"
were guzzled by youngsters. Allensville, Kentucky's August 8th celebration was
a time of fun and fellowship according to Mrs. Bennie Mae Smith. She recalled
that:

> the Methodists had their picnics at their church and the Baptists would have their's at
> their church. I remember at one church the band was standing up playing, 'Will there be
> a star in my crown?' and the band at the other church started playing, 'No not one.'
> (Laughter) Well, anyhow there was always a lot of fun. I mean you could talk about it
> from one year to another.

This "jollyfication" spilled over into the other picnic activities. Numerous
games were played, e.g. egg races, sack races, horseshoes, croquet, checkers and
all sorts of children's games. There were spectator sports like "tie downs,"
boxing matches and bicycle races. However, the biggest spectator sport was
baseball. East Texas hamlets like Paris and Daingerfield often closed their
downtown business sections in order to attend the big "Juneteenth" baseball
game.

Memorals of Juneteenth baseball heroics abound. Judson Henry was an
oldtimer who performed one of these never-to-be-forgotten feats. It was June
19th in Daingerfield and they were playing their arch rival, Jefferson. The
score was tied at 2 and 2 and Mr. Henry recalled that:

> I come up with two outs, two strikes and I hit that ball right across the centerfield fence.
> And man, you talking about... And this was money now. And, and we had such a crowd
> out there in those days till what they'd do, they'd split this money equally among the
> players. And we had... our portion for that day was $ 4.00 a man on our side. And when
> they got through having a time down there they taken me up $ 16.00.

However, Floyd "Skeet" Martin's memories are not as pleasant. His
spectacular last-out catch saved a 3 to 2 victory for the Rockdale Tigers over
Georgetown, Texas. The moment was electric! According to Mr. Martin
"four girls come out of the stands and grabbed him," but the fans did not pass
the hat to show their appreciation for his heroics and sadder still neither of the
four young girls offered their hero "a piece of pussy."

Drum dancing is popular among celebrants of the May cycle of celebrations. This Africanism is practiced in the four state area of Georgia, Florida,
Alabama and Mississippi. Each May 8th blacks on east Mississippi plantations
would celebrate their freedom by beating drums, singing and "dancing all
night." On May 28th Afro-Americans in the neighboring Alabama towns of
Eufaula and Rutherford engaged in similar activities. Mrs. Bass recalled how
the "old people" attired in "long dresses" formed "line walks" and danced to
the beating of the drums during Eufaula's emancipation celebrations. And
Mrs. Johnson told how the celebrants danced "their troubles away" to the
music of "large" and "small" drums carried by young boys and played by old

men. As this drum orchestra moved through the crowd they would stop periodically, the people would form a circle and individuals or groups would "jump in the circle and dance."

Revered Thomas J. Flanagan was so inspired by the poetic movement of the May 28th dancers at Thomaston, Georgia, he wrote this poem:

It was the 28th of May
And merry makers gay
Hurrahed for the Emancipation.
When Lincoln by decree
Made black men free...
When Lincoln by decree
Made all black men free
And gave a new step to the nation.
The day was fair
And the crowd was there
But somehow the spirit didn't come
Till old Uncle Lit
Stepped out...
Till old Uncle Lit
Hit the grit
And began to beat that drum.
The old drums rowded...
Went bow, bow, bow
And roddy, dow, down and bip.
And the mud...
And the dust flew
As Uncle Lit's crew
Danced...
Danced about beating that drum.

Other field workers have observed drum dancing at recent July 4th celebrations in Como, Mississippi. George Mitchell describes the activity in a manner which closely parallels the descriptions of drum dancing still done in Alabama's Chattahoochee River Valley and the central Georgia town of Thomaston on May 28th and 29th emancipation days (1971: 49–57). But Mitchell is at least partially wrong in his contention that: "The fife and drum music of the band, very close to pure West African, is found nowhere else in the United States" (1971: 51–53). Drum dancing was also recorded as being an integral part of Trinidad's August 1st emancipation celebrations (Hill 1972: 24). These fragmentary descriptions of the May and July celebrants drum dancing only vaguely suggest the sophistication of a Trinidadian Calinda. But undeniable is the cultural fact that blacks in these two places used the West African way of expressing their joy of freedom by beating drums and dancing to their rhythms.

These secular celebrations reached their zenith in popularity during the 1920's. However, there was a sharp drop in their cultural acceptance by the 1940's thanks to World War II. Afro-Americans who had fought for the preservation of the "four freedoms" came home determined to be Americans in the fullest sense of the term. For the first time these secular celebrations were shunned by the young and educated blacks. Deep ideological cleavages developed between older and younger Afro-Americans. In Onion Creek, Texas, a creative attempt was made to bridge the gap: the Juneteenth program was observed on July 4th. However, it failed to soothe either party.

And although they are not as strong as they once were, traditional allegiances still exist. Many Afro-Americans in east Texas, western Louisiana, southwestern Arkansas and southern Oklahoma still agree with Holsey Johnson's assertion that: "The biggest day in the United States was the 19th of June." Many blacks brought up observing August 4th and 8th celebrations in Tennessee, Kentucky and portions of northeastern Arkansas, southeastern Missouri and western Virginia prefer these dates over July 4th because "it wasn't our Independence." And many of the Afro-Americans in the Chattahoochee River Valley second these sentiments of Mrs. Hubert: "the 28th of May was far more existing than the 4th of July." Despite these allegiances, the secular cycle of emancipation celebrations is almost extinct, with celebrations being limited primarily to such traditional areas as Allensville, Kentucky for August 8th, Onion Creek, Texas for June 19th and Thomaston, Georgia for May 29th.

January 1st and February 1st are sacred celebrations based upon the rituals and culture of the black church. In contrast to the day-long secular observances, these affairs are programs of several hours duration. In most cases they are held in black churches and sponsored by ministerial alliances or civic organizations like the local Voter's League, the Urban League and the NAACP. The Watch Night service and the Sunday morning service have been adapted to fit the emancipation celebration. The former service of singing, praying and testifying has been used with only limited success.

But strangely enough, the first January 1st celebration followed the Watch Night format. In cities like Boston and New York racially mixed congregations came together early on the last night in 1862 to spend those last few hours singing and praying with the hopes that they would see America repent of her sin of slavery and dedicate itself to freedom for black and white citizens from that moment on. Soon after midnight their prayers were answered when a copy of President Lincoln's Emancipation Proclamation was read to them moments after it arrived by telegraph. After the reading of the freedom statement there was much applause and speech making in praise of President Lincoln for having the courage to issue such a statement, and of the eternal God for giving him the wisdom to see that it must be done.

However, the Sunday morning worship service has been the model most extensively used. The singing of freedom songs and the reading of a freedom document have been added to the sermon-centered eleven o'clock worship service. In both instances there has been much cultural fermentation before the current freedom song and document were selected. In the case of the song, black celebrants had sung such spirituals as "Free at Last," "Go Down Moses" and "Many Thousand Gone," abolitionist tunes like "John Brown" and patriotic songs like "America" and "The Star Spangled Banner" before settling on "Lift Every Voice and Sing," a song that they lovingly renamed "The Negro [and more recently Black] National Anthem," soon after it was written in 1927. By the same token, the Declaration of Independence, the January 1, 1808 federal statue ending America's slave trade, New York's July 4, 1827 freedom proclamation, Great Britain's August 1, 1834 emancipation proclamation, the federal statute of April 16, 1862 ending slavery in Washington, D.C. and Lincoln's two freedom proclamations of September 22, 1862 and January 1, 1863 were some of the freedom edicts read at sacred emancipation celebrations before there was a consensus for the last document.

This stilted document has been filtered through the filter of Afro-American culture and distilled into a powerful statement of freedom. Since its issuance in 1863 the reading of the Emancipation Proclamation has evolved from a straightforward news report to a highly developed genre of oral narration within the Afro-American culture. Tradition has also dictated that the reader of this precious document must be young, preferably in his late teens or early twenties, and a female, though young men have been selected with some success. Reverend William Holmes Borders eloquently discussed the importance of the Proclamation for many Afro-Americans and the criteria used to select the reader of this statement.

> Whenever they found a person or wherever I found a person who could really do it with understanding, it was a great and glorious thing. But it's difficult to so find, for a person to get into it, vicariously, this reading of the Emancipation Proclamation so that it is a burning fire for the audience. It's difficult; it's really difficult, certainly difficult. I'm sure that Lincoln did it well the first time it was verbally done. I'm sure he did his Gettsburg Address with fervor and that fire is still burning in both. But Lincoln passed through the suffering. He made the great decisions. He was President when this country's backbone had been popped and when its skull had been busted. And having passed through those experiences he wrote them. He came to them repeatedly and the fire flamed but the more because he was in it, a part of it. And he, I'm sure did them very much better than, than the persons who followed. But every now and then we pick up a person who was zealous, who knew it, who could share it. And when we did it was a woman most of the time.

This amazing statement reveals much about black attitudes toward the Emancipation Proclamation as a document and the aesthetics of reading it at a January 1st Emancipation Day celebration. First of all, the document's content is now rivaled by its oral form. In less than a century, this historical document has become a piece of classical Afro-American literature. For in just the same tradition with the blues singer's interpretation of his song's lyrics being the ultimate source of its vibrance, so too is it the case with the reader of the Emancipation Proclamation. Like the preacher who will follow her on program, the reader must make the document her own by coming to fully understand it and combine her personal emotional reaction with the historical significance of the document for Afro-Americans. And, secondly, the reader's primary aim to "set an audience afire" with her reading of Lincoln's Proclamation is the same goal of other black oral artists, the most notable being the black preacher who fashions another historical document, *The Bible*, into an emotionally moving oral art form, the sermon, which reflects his personality and sets his congregation on fire.

Mrs. Ethyln Kirby gave a brilliant artistic rendition of the Emancipation Proclamation during the 1972 Columbus, Georgia celebration. After the congregation sang "We Shall Overcome," she slowly rose from her seat, dramatically walked to the lecturn, mesmerized the congregation as she flattened out the text of her presentation and began to speak in an emotional tone and cadence reminiscent of the black preacher:

> I: America, I saw you grow. I saw your rocks and rills, thy woods and temple hills. America, I saw your military forces on land and sea... Alabama... Arkansas... Florida... Georgia... Mississippi, North Carolina, South Carolina, Louisiana, and Virginia... I saw you. I saw you ignore the warning of God and Lincoln's Preliminary Proclamation...
>
> Cong: Yes.

This moving piece of oratory took just under ten minutes to perform. An analysis of this narrative reveals several techniques of narration found in other genres of Afro-American folklore. First of all, the Proclamation is "framed" between opening and closing formulas fashioned from verses of the song, "America." The opening formula sets the historical stage for President Lincoln issuing the Emancipation Proclamation. The listing of the confederate states is similar in technique to Dr. King's calling the roll of freedom's ring in his "I Have a Dream" sermon. These are the southern states which will feel the brunt of the Union Army's fury. Secondly, the ending is traditionally Afro-American in two ways. Firstly, it is an excellent example of the short twist ending, so prominent in the secular toast and the sacred sermon (Abrahams 1970: 97). And, secondly, the rhymed couplet ending is the basic oral block upon which such structured genres as the toast and some contemporary black poetry are based (Wiggins 1971: 56–68). Also worthy of note is the fine sense of rhythm which is built into the reading of the Proclamation itself. Each important idea is punctuated with a loud "amen!" or "yes!" from the congregation. This call-response pattern creates a rhythm which both inspires the reader and gives flowing movement to a document written in an offical non-rhythmical way.

January 1st and February 1st, especially January 1st, are the most viable of the three types of emancipation celebrations. January 1st celebrations have maintained their form and broadened their geographical influence. In addition to being annually observed in the Confederate states of Virginia, the Carolinas, Georgia, Alabama, the border states of Maryland and West Virginia, and all of the New England states, it has moved into other celebration regions. For example, it has replaced the May 28th celebration in Eufaula, Alabama, the September 22nd celebration in Indianapolis, Indiana, the April 16th celebration in Washington, D.C., and co-exists with surrounding August 4th and 8th celebrations in Memphis, Chattanooga and Nashville, Tennessee and June

19th celebrations in New Iberia, Louisiana. This vibrance and longevity can be best explained by the celebration's intimate relationship with the black church, the tap root of the Afro-American experience.

April 16th and September 22nd are sacred/secular emancipation celebrations rooted in both American and Afro-American rituals and culture. In a real sense these celebrations reflect the "double-consciousness" of the Afro-American experience. The July 4th parade and picnic are borrowed from the American experience and the January 1st emancipation day service is taken from the Afro-American struggle. The April 16th celebrations began with a noon parade which was routed by the White House and through downtown Washington, D.C. fraternal drill teams and brass bands from nearby Virginia and Maryland swelled the parade ranks to three divisions. The march ended at one of the local churches where a rousing emancipation speech was given by some noted race leader. These celebrations peaked in the 1880's and were almost extinct by the turn of the century.

The September 22nd celebrations expanded this sacred-secular pattern. It was observed for a longer period of time and by a much larger geographical area. Ohio, Indiana and Illinois were the three states who annually celebrated this "black man's 4th of July." Indiana had the most celebration sites and Terre Haute was the strongest celebration site. Each year Afro-Americans from Vigo County and the surrounding communities would gather for a celebration which began with a mid-morning parade down Wabash Avenue, Terre Haute's main street, and out to the city park. At the picnic grounds celebrants bought tasty barbecue and other picnic food from "stands" run by local civic and religious groups, watched baseball games, bicycle races, boxing matches and heard brass band tunes and political speeches. In 1888 Frederick Douglass spoke at the picnic. When night fell an emancipation celebration service was held at a local church. These celebrations peaked during the 1920's – there were two celebrations, parades and all, held in Terre Haute, September 22, 1927 – and slowly declined afterwards reaching almost total extinction after World War II. The two dominate causes were a rising sense of patriotism and the integration of the public schools.

There have been some efforts made to make various sacred and secular celebrations balanced sacred/secular affairs. However, the celebrations have rejected all efforts to broaden their appeal. For example, only a few January 1st celebrations, like Phenix City, Alabama and Charleston, South Carolina, still have pre-program parades. However, most of the more viable ones like Atlanta, Georgia and Nashville, Tennessee have rejected the parade and emphasized the two-hour-plus noon service. Some efforts have been unsuccessfully attempted to balance June 19th and May 28th celebrations with religious services. An emancipation sermon was added to Rockdale, Texas' 1972 Juneteenth celebration, but it was poorly attended and caused one celebrant to scoff, "I ain't never heard of no damn preaching on the 19th of June!"

Reverend J. C. Cook recalled this humorous memory from an unsuccessful attempt to add an emancipation sermon to an Alabama May 28th celebration.

Although gathered in the church, the celebrants' mood was more one of fun and fellowship. Frustrated by their lack of respect and attention the preacher finally shouted: "'THESE FOLKS GOING TO HELLLLLL!' One man stepped out who'd been drinking, said, 'LET 'EM GOOOOOOOOOOOOOOOOOO REVEREND!' And that's the way they went on." (Laughter)

From 1865 to 1900 emancipation celebrations served as annual days of thanksgiving for freedom. Local efforts were also started to aid the widows and feed the hungry of the race. However, the dominant movement of this period was to have one of these days declared a national holiday. Many of the celebrations already had quasi-holiday status. School children were exempt from classes on April 16th in Washington, D.C. and September 22nd in Terre Haute, Indiana. A similar privilege was accorded Afro-American workers who celebrated these two dates, June 19th, August 8th and the May cycle. Mrs. Bennie Mae Smith summarized the custom well when she said: "They done told the boss man (laughter) that they want off that day. And the white man in that area understand."

There have been varied official recognitions of these days. The Terre Haute mayor issued city proclamations extoling September 22nd, the accomplishments and contributions of the Afro-American community. Similar proclamations have been recently issued honoring June 19th in Oklahoma City, Oklahoma. The 1972 Texas House of Representative passed a resolution recognizing "'Juneteenth' as an annual, though unofficial, holiday of significance to all Texans and, particularly, to the blacks of Texas, for whom his date symbolizes freedom from slavery" (*The Dallas Morning News* 1972: 10A). In 1903 Indiana Afro-Americans began a movement to make Congress declare either January 1st or September 22nd a national Afro-American holiday.

Major R. R. Wright was successful in securing state and federal recognition for February 1st. In the early 1940's he successfully lobbied to get the states of Maine, West Virginia, Ohio and Pennsylvania to pass bills declaring February 1st National Freedom Day in honor of the date in 1865 when Congress passed the Thirteenth Amendment. He was also able to acquire an annual funding budget of $ 5,000.00 from Pennsylvania when Edward Martin was governor. Unfortunately, Major Wright, an ex-slave who lived to be president of a college, founder of a bank and international entrepreneur, died before President Harry S. Truman signed his National Freedom Day Bill into law in 1948. This bill which gave the Afro-American his first national black holiday reads in part:

> Resolved that the President of the United States is authorized to issue a proclamation designating the 1st day of February of each year as National Freedom Day for the purpose of commemorating the signing by President Lincoln, on February 1, 1865 of the joint resolution adopted by the Senate and the House of Representatives of the United States proposing the thirteenth amendment to the Constitution of the United States of America. (*National Freedom Day Program* 1973: 10)

Major Wright's affection for the Thirteenth Amendment is also seen in his successful lobby to get a Thirteenth Amendment Commemorative Stamp issued for the 1940 New York's World Fair.

From 1900 to the present there has been a fragmenting of the celebrations' functions. Most of them have devolved into social affairs. Windsor, Canada's August 1st celebration has become the most commercial, openly billing itself as "the world's greatest freedom show." And what a show it is, annually attracting crowds of 30,000 or more to its parades, carnivals, beauty contests, talent shows, etc. August 4th and 8th, May 29th and June 19th have become "emancipation homecoming celebrations." Sponsors now hold these celebrations on the weekend nearest the original date. This allows former residents now living in the urban west and north to travel home for a joyful weekend of food, fun and fellowship. January 1st and February 1st have remained celebrations dedicated to racial uplift. They are still observed on their original dates and they have consistently stressed such primary issues as voting, racial pride, economic boycotting and full civil rights. In the case of some January 1st celebrations this civic interest has been aided by the fact that during the 1930's their sponsorship was taken over by the Urban League, the NAACP and local Voter Leagues.

The Black Power movement of the 1960's has caused a neo-emancipation day celebration movement in certain August 4th, June 19th and September 22nd celebrations. Black students at Indiana University attended a 1972 September 22nd celebration at Bloomington, Indiana's Second Baptist Church. The sponsor, pastor Ernest Butler, held the celebration because he "saw a need" for more racial awareness among the black students and Bloomington's black community. A similar June 19th revival has taken place in Oklahoma City, Oklahoma. Young black members of BLAC, Inc. (Black Liberated Arts Center, Inc.) rekindle the spirit of Juneteenth by reading original poetry, freedom speeches and entertainment. And Manchester, Tennesee black citizens have revived their August 4th celebration, making it a time when former residents come back home and "rap" about the past, present and future of Afro-Americans in America.

Unfortunately, many cultural nuances have been lost in these renovations. For example, the importance of the freedom document is greatly diminished. In some celebrations it is not read and in others it is read without a hint of the oral artistry historically associated with it. And the sense of a quasi-holiday is lost. Oklahoma City's celebrants purposely chose Sunday to celebrate Juneteenth, completely disregarding the old honored custom of holding this secular celebration on a week day and not dishonor the Sabbath. This is the current state of Afro-American emancipation celebrations as they begin their second century of existence in America.

In conclusion, I must say that this study could not have been done using the traditional elitist approach to Afro-American studies. My point is painfully underscored by the fact that it is only at this late date in our country's history that a thorough study has been made of Afro-American Emancipation celebrations. Before my study their existence was affirmed by only a handful of articles and a few brief tangential references in other studies. It was only by going to the field and collecting oral data from the books with one back, individual members of America's Afro-American community, that I was able to complete my research. Without their unselfish assistance, America would never know why they annually "Lift Every Voice and Sing."

REFERENCES

ABRAHAMS, Roger D.
    1970   *Deep Down in the Jungle: Negro Narrative Folklore from the Streets of Philadelphia.* Chicago: Aldine Publishing Co.
HILL, Errol
    1972   *The Trinidad Carnival: Mandate for a National Theatre.* Austin: University of Texas Press.
MITCHELL, George
    1971   *Blow My Blues Away.* Baton Rouge: Louisiana State University Press.
QUARLES, Benjamin
    1967   "Historic Afro-American Holidays". *Negro Digest* (February): 14–19.
WIGGINS, Jr., William H.
    1971   "'I Am the Greatest': The Folklore of Muhammad Ali". *Black Lines* II (Fall): 56–68.

    ————

    1972   "Austin Wire: Juneteenth Recognized By House". *The Dallas Morning News* (June 20): 10A.

    ————

    1973   "31st Anniversary Celebration". *National Freedom Day Program* (February): 1–16.

INFORMANTS

BASS, Lula L. (Mrs.)
    A public school teacher in Columbus, Georgia. She is about 30 years old and attended May 28th celebrations as a child in southeastern Alabama.
BORDERS, William Holmes (Reverend)
    One of the outstanding preachers in America and pastor of Wheat Street Baptist Church, Atlanta, Georgia. Reverend Borders is about 65 years old and has spoken at various August 1st, May 5th and January 1st celebrations.
COOK, J. C. (Reverend)
    Pastor of the Greater Mount Zion Baptist Church, Phenix City, Alabama. Reverend Cook is past 70 years old and has attended both May 28th and January 1st celebrations during his lifetime in Alabama's Chattahoochee River Valley.
FLANAGAN, Thomas J. (Reverend)
    Presiding Elder in the African Methodist Episcopal Church and author of the column, "Up From Georgia with My Banjo," a series of poems published by The Atlanta Daily World newspaper. Reverend Flanagan is over 70 years old and has attended May 28th and January 1st celebrations during his life-time in Georgia.
HENRY, Judson
    Owner of the Chatterbox Cafe in Hawkins, Texas. Mr. Henry is over 70 years old and played for Daingerfield, Texas' baseball team on past Juneteenths.
HUBERT, Agnes (Mrs.)
    A public school teacher in Columbus, Georgia. She is about 30 years old and attended May 28th celebrations in southeastern Alabama as a child.

JOHNSON, Bennie Mae (Mrs.)

Housewife and aunt of Mrs. Hubert. She is in her mid 50's and returns annually for May 28th celebrations in southeastern Alabama.

JOHNSON, Holsey

Farmer who lives near Brenham, Texas. He is about 60 years old and has attended Juneteenth celebrations all of his life.

KIRBY, Ethlyn (Mrs.)

A resident of Columbus, Georgia. She is about 30 years old and has read the Emancipation Proclamation at other January 1st celebrations.

MARTIN, Floyd "Skeet"

A farmer who lives near Rockdale, Texas. He is in his mid 50's and has played in past Juneteenth baseball games.

SMITH, Bennie Mae (Mrs.)

A housewife who lives in Louisville, Kentucky. Mrs. Smith is 72 years old and has attended each August 8th celebration in Allensville, Kentucky since she married her childhood sweetheart Mr. Claude Smith and moved away.

An Introduction to Transatlantic Black Art History: Remarks in Anticipation of a Coming Golden Age of Afro-Americana

ROBERT FARRIS THOMPSON

Yale University, New Haven, U.S.A.

THERE ARE, it seems to me, at least three parts to any study of Afro-American visual creativity in transatlantic perspective: (1) the identification of strategic West and Central African visual traditions, travelling in the minds of blacks to the Americas during the period of the infamous Atlantic Trade; (2) the citation of persisting strands from these ancestral patterns, now richly inter-woven and recombined by Afro-American artists, and the definition of their vibrant creativity on its own terms – i.e., taking pains to scan the horizon for signs of departure, development, and grand cultural achievement, as well as originating impulse; (3) the definition of a common ground of philosophic assumption, the mediating process of world-view, accounting in part for similarities in form and function characterizing Afro-American creative vision.

African formal influence, in American-born black art history, can be inferred where resemblances are consistent and multifacetted. The criterion of identification therefore is: complexity of relationship. Just as systematic dif-ferences reveal the special bond linking Spanish and Portuguese to common Italic roots, so degree and kind of shared visual themes argue for historical links between African and Afro-American creativity.

The method used to identify such influences is straightforwardly compara-tist. In the sheer act, for example, of juxtaposition of one form of Nigerian wrought-iron staff with a similar Afro-Brazilian iron object from Rio de Janeiro whole histories of formal persistence suddenly leap to life. In Yoruba cities the presence of the herbalist-diviner may be identified by the possession of such staffs, often shaped with a circle of iron birds at the top, disposed under a (usually larger) iron bird which culminates the staff. The same staff occasionally turns up in the Yoruba-influenced sectors of Rio de Janeiro around 1941: same iron medium, same circle of birds under a bird of commanding position at the summit of the staff.

Mechanically, the theme's continuity can be "explained" by a history of slaving, linking portions of the traditional culture of the Yoruba of west Nigeria to the culture of certain ports of Brazil – as well as western Cuba. These slave trade mediated contacts were recent, persisting well into the middle of the last century and in some instances they were massive. Yet the deeper level of intellectual communication, embedded in the function of such staffs, related to healing and collectedness of mind, seems the real key to their amazing motion across time and space. For how to explain, otherwise, the fact that during the period 1945–1974 the use of such staffs has spread from the Yoruba-influenced barrios of western Cuba to Puerto Rico and the Puerto Rican sectors of the United States urban northeast. The secondary migration of the bird-staff, now sometimes merely suggested by new shapes which seem closer in form to the Western weather-vane than to originating Yoruba impulses, can only partially be related to original slaving histories and ethnicity. Clearly larger issues of universal intellectual appeal and the fulfilling of spiritual needs across cultures are involved now. Yet the focus achieved by such forms, however changed, in cultic presentation is still strongly flavored with African influence. Yoruba bird-staffs, wherever they appear in the New World and the Old, honor the god of medicine, Osanyin, guardian of the personal balance, health and mental equilibrium of a human being. They honor the deity with the sign of mind (the commanding bird at summit), the sign of the head or intellect, sometimes complicated by the conquest, also by mind, of all evil, the latter symbolized by the gathering of minor birds. Leaves which assuage fevers and clarify a person's mind are logically associated with such staffs. Significantly, most herbalists in the Yoruba religion, whether in Nigeria or even in Union City, New Jersey own such staffs or know something of their use and meaning.

Confirmation of an artistic influence is always delicate. But I think that in the illustration just given, deliberately chosen for its density of philosophic reference, historical imprint is so clearly rendered that we can concentrate on problems of meaning and iconic communication and take the fact of on-going diffusion for granted.

This point applies to those provinces of western Cuba, namely Matanzas and Havana, where scraps of at least two vernacular languages of eastern Nigeria, namely Efik and Ejagham (Abakpa), in Cuba called Efi and Abakuá, and possibly a third, Efot (Afro-Cuban: Efó), are spoken by a few thousand men belonging to an important all-male society (Ngbe) which came from these parts of the Bight of Biafra during the first half of the 19th century. Unsurprisingly, in a context of linguistic reinstatement, the visual parallels linking Nigerian Abakpa and Afro-Cuban Abakuá are striking. In both West Indian and African manifestations of Ngbe (leopard) society ritual the same masked spirit-messenger, representing a leopard king from another world, come to judge the quick and the dead, dramatically appears and postures with virtually identical sacred gestures. The form and decorative details of the messenger's costume, allowing for minor modification in Cuba, are almost indelibly persistent: checked fabric, raffia ruff at the joints, generous sash about the waist, conical headdress, cloth-covered disk at the back of the head, fronds in one hand, staff of office in the other.

This visual continuity is spectacular. The purity reflects not only late and illegal importation of cultic practices from eastern Nigeria as late as the 1860's, or little more than one hundred years ago, but also the dynamic quality of the originating tradition perpetuated in consciously cultivated ethnicity, given perennial vitality by the intense aesthetic satisfactions provided by a shared cult repertory of gesture, mime, and calligraphy – all marvels of black creative communication. These costumes and associated gestures were sacred and as such dissembled change within a presentation of timeless truths.

Altogether different from Cuba and Brazil is the art history of the maroons (runaway slaves) of the interior of Surinam, a territory north of Brazil and east of Guyana, in northern South America. Here slaves, some from the Gold Coast and Dahomey, many others from Kongo and Angola, escaped coastal plantations and set up independent settlements in the forests of the interior. They waged guerilla warfare against the colonial powers on the coast and ultimately won their independence about the middle of the 18th century.

In the process, Surinam maroons carved out an African-influenced style of life within the tropical rainforests, in terrain not unlike that of their ancestors. They were able to bring to this environment African ideas about the making of secular objects – combs, calabash containers, garments, doors, in direct contrast to the sacred nature of art in the New World from Nigeria and Cameroon among Yoruba and Abakuá cultists. The influence of African civilizations upon the art of Surinam was rendered diffuse by this very secularity, because bans on blatant change, as in the making of sacred images, for the most part did not apply. Trends therefore ran their course to brilliant effect. Nevertheless, there was always, as Richard Price tells us, "a strong feeling for, a love of, things considered 'African' thus an ideology of allegiance to 'Africa' but this was a very generalized Africa – 'things African' as opposed to 'things Western', relating to cultural resistance" (Price 1972). In sum, origins seem obscure, innovations clear.

In the complexity of the Surinam situation African influence seems difficult to trace. I shall suggest, in future works, a provisional point of origin, or points of origin, inferred from the existence of drums, some 18th century carved calabashes, and other early Afro-American art forms in Surinam showing clear relationships to parts of Africa. These works were shaped and shaped anew in the continuing local exploration of new forms. Novel modes of decoration were discovered, thereby, within old outlines. Decorations were combined and re-combined on the surface of the forms until the very profile of an object, as in the curving of a flat-sided comb by an especially innovative artist, might respond to the oscillation of imagination.

Some outlines held firm, however, to disclose, paradoxically, a clearer notion of ultimate sources in change than in continuity. This seems to have happened where creativity emphasized, in rearrangement and placement of accent, an original fund of formal ideas. In following this history we discern many overlaps, where Surinam artists arrived at formal conclusions remarkably similar to those obtaining among the arts of some provinces of West Africa today, notably the kingdoms of the Akan with their northern and eastern neighbors.

Slaves from these territories figure, culturally speaking, prominently (but not exclusively) in the Surinam slave trade. It is useful to compare an early 18th century royal chair (asipim) from northern Ashanti with an early 20th century door, probably from the northern Saramaka village of Gansee in Surinam. So far as I know, the function of these objects was similar. Allegedly, the Akan chair was carved about 1700 by the ruler himself. The present owner, king of the town of Agogo in Ghana, maintains that the motifs selected by the early 18th century ruler in the making of his chair emphasized his knowledge and the embodiment of his power. In Saramaka, according to Richard Price, "more than anything else the door shows the skill of its carver (whose house it graces) and therefore says something personal in a way different from an object made in order for display" (Price 1972). Hence there is a kind of concordance in functions: the chair and door were made by their original owners as testaments of skill and ingenuity.

By the same token, the mode of decoration of the two objects, although evolved within different classes of form, is also broadly similar: even-banded scrollwork, which does not modulate in width, is caused to flow in symmetrical arabesques, fusing curves with straight lines; brass studs follow and emphasize the flow of the lines which are, in turn, outlined with negative space in openwork.

Note that we have compared shared decorative motifs, in the making of furniture and doors, which is something different from matching iron staffs with iron birds made in Nigeria and Brazil. The distinction indicates artistic change in Surinam and the spread of creative patterns through many media. In addition, the comparison, which is arbitrary and in itself assumes a generalization, makes the door "look African" when actually the particular configuration which lends the portal its special elegance was not fully evolved in Surinam until the early 20th century. The Surinam door is also lean and tough in comparison with the courtly opulence of the plated chair from metropolitan Akan, however related the phrasing of line and void.

Yet when we return to the roots of Surinam art, in approximately the early 19th century, the stencil-like outlining of simple forms, playing straight line against curved, seems more and more Akan, as if we were approaching an originating tradition. A minor difficulty emerges at this point: the earliest-known art of the blacks of Surinam seems tentative and crude, perhaps in renewal of ancestral form through simplification. Such tentativeness makes sense in a context of runaways emerging from slavery in a challenging rain-forest.

The fact that we lack for Haitian/Dahomean, United States/Kongo, Mexican/Manding and Angola connections the documentary fullness which characterizes the art of Surinam or the Yoruba-influenced cities of the north-east of Brazil makes of the study of these further historical relationships largely surmise. Yet comparison of sources reveals parallels, probable lines of influence and inspiration, and, sometimes, unquestionable histories of abiding influence.

At the end it becomes clear that we are dealing with a rich and important reality in the history of world art, five currents falling under the rubric of a grand transatlantic tradition:

1. Art for the gods: Yorubaland and Dahomey/Cuba, Brazil, Haiti, Puerto Rican New York.

2. Art for secular display: Akan, Gã, others/Surinam

3. Art as initiation and road to the dead: Cross River/Western Cuba

4. Art as magic: Kongo and Angola/Georgia, South Carolina, Cuba, Brazil

5. Art as shelter, basketeering, masking, and iron: Manding/Mexico, Brazil, USA

Differences of artistic achievement and availability of published materials demand, at present, various strategies of presentation, from a privileged concern with meaning in Yoruba art or formal change in Surinam, to a frank fragmentation of relation, through want of documents, in the telling of artistic influences apparently stemming from Manding and from Kongo. Part of the problem embodies reflections of original differences separating Manding culture from Kongo, and so on, and part stems from different histories of development and change in Afro-American visual art, ultimately resulting in discrete Afro-Cuban, Afro-Brazilian, Gullah, and other developments.

The life of these forms has occurred in relation to seemingly eternal ideals of symbolized generosity and power. I have called this shared philosophy "an aesthetic of the cool," after an ancient African idiom for the fullness of social balance within the deepest capabilities of men and women. "Coolness" in this subsaharan and Afro-American sense does not refer to moderation of coldness, nor to *sang-froid* except as parts of a deeper structure of belief. The idiom certainly does not cite the Western convention for lack of social warmth, as in the phrase, "why was he cool to me today?" for nothing could be farther from the strong connotations of social equanimity and positive sentiment which attach to African-influenced usages of the term. To be cool means to become composed in a sharing sense, to remember the way one ought to be. To be cool means to return, to laughter, people, and responsibility. There is a probative force to the artistic traditions of the cool, to the idealist assertion that powers of balance are inherent in the deepest strengths of men and women. Black cool is an idiom of *social balance* ("cool country") and *internal* or *spiritual balance*, the sign of clear conscience ("cool heart") when one returns to oneself in an ideal sense, achieving or rediscovering character, when what one does and what one ought to be are one.

In the traditional civilizations of West Africa the locus of the cool is held to be the head. This is richly suggested by statuary and by the behavior of living persons: doctrinal firmness of facial expression is considered the proper mask for those who accept responsibility for human continuity; one striking African extension of this universal quality of self-control is to freeze the face of the active dancer, as well as the presiding judge or elder. The former phenomenon, very strange by Western standards which teach the separation of bodily gaiety from sobriety, so that dancers smile and mourners look sad, is very pervasive in the artistic cultures of West Africa. This quality of self presentation in the dance was one of the first "discoveries" by Western observers of the dance in Africa. Two writers independently described faces frozen by a sense of higher authority at opposite ends of the black artistic empire, the Cape of Good Hope in the autumn of 1673 and Louisiana, at a sugar house, before 1863. From the Cape:

> They take the greatest delight in dancing which they perform with astonishing gesticulations. If they have the least feeling for religion, it is in the observation of the dance that they must show it... the males, with their bodies leaning forward, stamp on the ground vigorously with their feet, lustily chanting in unison with rising and falling intensity, and with a fixed expression on their faces (Schapera 1933: 13a).

And from early 19th century Louisiana:

> a double shuffle in a thumping ecstasy, with loose elbows, pendulous paws, angulated knees, heads thrown back, and backs arched inward – a glazed eye, intense solemnity of mien (Russell 1863: 258–259).

Intensity can be matched with ecstasy, fixed expression with solemnity of mien, opposing immobile face with the pulsations of the body. This is important. For some Westerners, as we have seen, utterly take for granted a connection between corporeal gaiety, in the dance, and smiling. In marked contrast, the dancers at the Cape and in Louisiana demonstrated via the dignity of their mien that their muscularity was purposefully asserted, not a spasm.

The date and far-flung quality of these citations suggests a measure of antiquity for the concept of the cool in the dance, an African resolution of the paradox of mind within body: energy illumines the muscular beauty of the body in motion while the head commands the excitement as a silent emblem of composure.

There is another dimension to the cool, showing that African and Afro-American composure is more than display of self-control. Cool is also a sign of positive transition to ideal worlds. The "glazed eye" of 19th century Afro-Louisianians implied that while dancing they had been translated from this existence to another world. The facial seal qualified the nature of this other world, a realm of pure order and controlled pleasure, not dissociation or unconsciousness. This is the manner, in the dance, by which some traditional West Africans and their New World descendants living in traditional culture are led to the state of spirit-possession. Like a vessel from above, they are filled with the power of the ancient gods of Africa, abolishing time and space, revealing the richness of the world into which they disappear: they are *home*. And home was where the kings dwelled, where the ancient cities of the civilizations of the west of Africa were, gathered in spiritual riches and collective moral vigilance. When possessed, these were not dancing slaves nor rustics; these were children of the gods.

The grandeur of the tradition perenially imparted strength. In the midst of the turbulence of the festival was the learning of valor under provocation, balance in competing rhythms, and the sweetness of matched densities of interest and common purpose. These assertions require explanation. The aesthetic of the cool, as a mode of mastering reality, seems to carry through the vast changes that characterize the black experience. Values of cool, generalized dignity contributed to social stability when black men and women were challenged by virtually overwhelming problems of life and death.

Shared heroism is therefore a part of the cool, an African truth which reached the ears of the American black man as early as childhood, when he listened to tales told besides the shacks of the rural south. Consider in this vein a tale from the blacks of Georgia, first published in 1888, and recently reprinted in standard English:

> Brother Lion was hunting and he spotted Brother Goat lying down on a big rock, chewing with his mouth. He crept up to catch him. When he got close to him he looked him over carefully. Brother Goat kept on chewing. Brother Lion tried to find out what Brother Goat was eating. He didn't see anything near him except the bare rock on which he was lying. Brother Lion was surprised. He waited for Brother Goat. Brother Goat kept on chewing and chewing. Brother Lion couldn't understand this, so he came up close and said, 'Hey, Brother Goat, what are you eating?' Brother Goat was startled when Brother Lion rose up in front of him but he kept up his courage and answered, 'I'm chewing on this rock and if you don't leave, then when I'm through with it, I'm going to eat you.' This bluff saved Brother Goat. A brave man will get out of difficulty, where a coward will lose his life. (Stewart 1970: 125)

To keep up courage is a form of cool. A person ideally works out strategy behind a mask of calm. The British are also said to possess this gift, nonchalance under fire (Hemingway's "grace under pressure"), a quality sometimes parodied in films. But the difference is: the black protagonist maintains calm to inherent dramatic point, with an audience close at hand, whereas, say, the solitary mountain-climber, an oddity by African communal standards of heroic action, is almost a paradigm of the individualist nature of much Western heroism. The cool hero shares his heroism by leavening his performance, where possible, with humor and other invitations to audience participation, even in the process of being challenged. He more than keeps his head; he has the presence of mind to direct both audience and enemy in a crisis situation. Of course, not every man can rise to such a destiny. But Malcom X is one who did:

> I was walking down the aisle and a big, beefy red-faced cracker soldier got up in front of me, so drunk he was weaving, and announced loud enough that everybody in the New Haven railroad coach heard him, "I'm going to fight you nigger." I remember the tension. I laughed and told him, "Sure, I'll fight, but you've got too many clothes on." He had on a big Army overcoat... He took that off, *and I kept laughing* [underlining mine] and said he still had on too many. I was able to keep that cracker stripping off clothes until he stood there drunk with nothing on from his pants up, and the whole car was laughing at him and some other soldiers got him out of the way. I went on. I never would forget that — that I couldn't have whipped that white man as badly with a club as I had with my mind. (Malcolm X, 1966: 72)

Malcolm, by cool, extended laughter was able to involve a tense audience in relaxing comedy and to transform, through his powers of concentration, the enemy into a self-destroying buffoon. The passengers in the coach were drawn, in spite of themselves, into supportive roles, orchestrated by the definition his courage gave to the event, by the continuation of his laugh, which finally became *their* laughter. Therein, perhaps a difference between coolness in the black sense, as dramatized sharing of courage, and individualist *sang-froid*.

A world-view in which the essence of morality is conceived to be generosity more than suffices as a model by which ideal societies can be structured. The world of the cool is like Atlantis again immersed in water, for traditional West Africans define water as a mirror of mediation in the very image of its coolness. However, in the African instances, unlike the Atlantis of Mediterranean invention, "cool persons," as members of the Ijaw civilization of the Niger Delta term good-natured men who keep out of litigation and love to dance, are real and never drown.

Not without reason, the prevailing association of water and coolness with purity of existence, in the African imagination, are the black gods of Haiti believed to reside in a fabled "island at the bottom of the sea" (*zilet en bas d'l'eau*) corresponding to, among possible models, the mythic underwater city of Ode Kobaye, a city at the bottom of the river, where one of the twelve major gods of the Yoruba is believed to reign in glory; not without reason are the gods of the Afro-Cuban religion kept as stones immersed in fresh water or liquid within vessels (Bascom 1950), for if water is coolness, an idealized state, and gods are come from a zone where ideals by definition are splendidly realized, then cool water (or equivalents) form a most proper setting of the divine. In fact the relationship likening water to coolness, to reconciliation and regained purity in proximity to the divine, is a pervasive element of many West African traditional religions.

In another study I have shown how dictionaries of West African and Central African languages show that the semantic range of the term, cool, includes associations of bodily beauty, healing, calm, order, and social mediation (Thompson 1974: 43–45; see also Thompson 1969). I am not saying that all African peoples at all times and all places operated in affinity with this principle. Such a sweeping statement would be absurdly easy to disprove. I am saying, however, that the concept lives in the minds of the legitimate heirs of traditional West African life, in zones affected by the Atlantic Trade, as well as in the imagination of their New World blood relatives, and, for the purposes of this survey, that will suffice.

In a strict West African and Afro-American sense, therefore, it is being asserted that mystic coolness is an ancient charter for entire black civilizations passing through fire and passing through heat (African wars, slavery, imperialism, colonialism, racism, hate) to affirmation and self-determination.

Many Westerners, particularly the recent young, have been using the ecstasy and the brilliance of the arts of cool people, even performing these traditions, without considering their philosophic power. The tradition is known, as an idiom of the streets, but rarely comprehended for what in fact it is: *a symbolically generous aesthetic organization of social reality*. This does not mean that cool people are generous at all times; it does mean that art persuades them, reminds them, resituates them within what they ought to be.

Travesties of misunderstanding continue to exist because most denizens of the cities of the West, from minstrels through Picasso to rock, have perceived only through reflection, mimesis of vogue, the traditions of the cool. They have rarely really known the world from which these moral principles came. None other than Hegel himself, after a series of spectacularly false assertions about African character says: "at this point we leave Africa, not to mention it again For it is no historical part of the world; it has no movement or development to exhibit. Historical movements in it – that is in its northern part – belong to the Asiatic or European world .. Africa is the Unhistorical, Undeveloped Spirit" (Hegel 1956: 91–99). Absolutists' assumptions of like spirit, the whole school of those who minister to "underdeveloped" or "developing" nations, continue to block by lack of awareness the appreciation and just estimation of black indigenous philosophy.

This brief essay suggests a trek back to the truth, to a whole world of black performance in vision and symbolized generosity. Cool art from Africa from the beginning of this century has showered the world with assuaging brilliance and sensuous discipline. There is a debt that has to be acknowledged.

A most important aim of a coming golden age of Afro-American studies, therefore, will be the portrayal, through art history, of the transatlantic contribution of the aesthetic of the cool to world philosophic advancement. Cool, like Greek sculpture, is a classical tradition, bound to a rational order of life. Yet within its forms and manifestations change, spontaneity, motion, and initiative, answering to the imperatives of life, are reconciled and given space and body so that the heritage is ever full of pleasure, life, and blood.

Cool is complex balance. Line merges with oscillation, motion flows within arrest, naked flesh encloses purity of mind, to make a single leap of faith. The whole of the being – in overlapping concepts, "whole statement" motion (*mbandu*)[1] in Zaïre, "getting it together" in the Black United States – is cast in art towards targets of social affirmation. The serious student of Afro-Americana will bear witness to different sorts of socially creative balance, accomplished through complex proliferations of aesthetic, sharp contrasts in time and space. For example, Western women, in Nigeria and Surinam, soon learn to abandon their habit of wearing a light green sash in combination with a dark green skirt; the traditional black women of these provinces of the great circumatlantic aesthetic tradition show them another way, the wearing of fiery orange against green, red against blue, deliberate high-affect collisions of color which, in the aggregate, strongly suggest that dress among cool people can be another kind of

---

1   Informant: Piluka Ladi, a Musuku migrant now working in Kinshasa, Zaire. I am grateful to Beatrice Luwefwa Kiyema, herself a Musuku, for checking the translation of the term, *mbandu*, and suggesting the phrase, 'whole statement' which I use here.

bodily incandescence with which to mark, by contrast, for special consciousness, the depth of their facial hauteur in public presentation. It is interesting that recently a writer for the New York *Times* was apparently surprised to learn from the famous Afro-American athlete, Walt Frazier, that his was a *learned* (reporter's italization) cool. "And now, Frazier tells us, it is a *learned* cool — learned from Elgin Baylor of the Los Angeles Lakers in Clyde's rookie year (1967–68). Clyde was more emotional in those days, and one night, while waving his arms and gritting his teeth to pressure Baylor, the all star forward looked at Clyde as if to say, 'Hey, young-blood, what you think you doin?' Then Baylor went into his moves as though the rookie weren't even there. Clyde was so impressed that he has been Mr. Cool ever since" (Lemesrud 1974: 16). The artistic freezing of the human face, possessed of black intelligence, becomes, among the knowing followers of the cool, an object of universal awe. To dance or perform athletic or jurisprudential wonders with a cold face is to enact the force of reason. The human condition is momentarily led to points of calm, there to find sources of renewed illumination. The rhetoric is light years removed from the insistence upon things gutted by circumstance that marks so much of the writing in the past on Africans and Afro-Americans (see Szwed 1974). But until we consider, through artistic mediating forces the dreams and loves of Africans and Afro-Americans, as well as their politics and social structure, we shall never know black people.

REFERENCES

BASCOM, William
    1950   "The focus of Cuban Santería". *Southwestern Journal of Anthropology* (Spring).
HEGEL, G. W. F.
    1956   *Philosophy of History*. New York: Dover Publications.
LEMESRUD, Judy
    1974   Review of "Rockin' Steady: A Guide to Basketball & Cool", New York *Times* Book Review (March 24), 16.
MALCOLM X (with Alex Haley)
    1966   *The Autobiography of Malcolm X*. New York: Grove Press.
PRICE, Richard
    1972   Personal communication, September 18.
RUSSELL, William H.
    1863   *My Diary North and South*. Boston: T. O. H. P. Burnham.
SCHAPERA, I.
    1933   *The Early Cape Hottentots*. Capetown: Van Riebeeck Society.
STEWART, William A.
    1970   "Understanding Black language" in John Szwed (ed.), *Black America*. New York: Basic Books.
SZWED, John
    1974   "An American anthropological dilemma: the politics of Afro-American culture" in: Dell Hymes (ed), *Reinventing Anthropology*. New York: Random House, Vintage Books.
THOMPSON, R. F.
    1969   "Aesthetic of the Cool". *African Arts* VII, 1 (Autumn).
    1974   *African Art in Motion*. Berkeley and Los Angeles: University of California Press.

Journal of Asian and African Studies IX, 3–4

Detachment: Continuities of Sensibility Among Afro-American Populations of the Circum-Atlantic Fringe

DAN ROSE

University of Pennsylvania, Philadelphia, U.S.A.

DURKHEIM AND MAUSS in their monograph, *Primitive Classification* (1963), argue that social arrangements between actual members organize thought into categorical, conceptual schemes. Further, category and hierarchy are felt to correspond homologously to social category and social hierarchy. Among any collection of persons in continued association there is membership differentiation into disjunctive social categories, such as age, sex, clan, neighborhood, ethnicity, and class. Persons also accord one another, even in the most egalitarian social situations, rankings that organize members hierarchically. The organizing features of cognition, hierarchy, and category, then, are precisely those most apparent features of any collection of affiliated persons.

The homology between cognitive arrangement and sociological arrangement may also be perceived between cognitive social processes and the actual process of experiencing. Research emphasis so shifted is directed at discovering how social persons order their immediate, ongoing interactions. The ordering of situated interactions is simultaneously both moral and cognitive; it is only arbitrarily that one separates the moral from the cognitive order. In face-to-face, or even forms of mediated social interaction, members negotiate their social encounters largely through the exchange of talk. Talk is both morally and ideationally ordered so speakers may give and receive messages, exchange stories, exhibit their societal workings through parable, sanction courses of action, mention proverbs, and the like. The closely meshed interactive organization that individuals in contact with one another achieve concertedly may be termed the *subsequential ordering* of their experience.

Further, I will equate the cognitive with the aesthetic. The aesthetic may be considered a dialectic of production and appreciation. In ordinary talk, as in high art, there are performers who do impeccable jobs at producing a saying, story telling, criticizing, or reminding. Proper appreciation is duly rendered during subsequent conversation on the spot or later retrospective replays of the event. The paradigm of exquisite aesthetic talk is clearly composed of the *story form.* Much moral work in conversations, such as subtle reminders, baiting, or blatant sanctions, are performed with the social power a finely told story wields.

The story form displayed during conversation, at once creates and preserves the *subsequential ordering* of elapsed social events. The told story preserves ongoing social encounters for listeners and pictures for them those social arrangements in that event that the talker finds aesthetically impeccable, politically salient, personally satisfying, and socially telling. To give it from the hearer's perspective, a talker employs the story form to presently convince hearers, produce relief from boredom, pass the time, sell himself, make bids for further regard, discredit his hearers, perform for third parties at the expense of his apparent recipient, generate humor, etc. In living out our lives in interaction and in recounting those moments of engagement, we exhibit a subsequential ordering of experience. The story preserves and creates a sense for listeners of originating encounters. In this report, both encounters originating from fieldwork and story-preserved accounts in fiction are exhibited as data for analysis, and as evocative material for reader's understanding of ethnographer's experience.

During fieldwork my godson, a friend, Boycie, and a girlfriend, Katherine, of my wife, said some things that made no sense by themselves. They were just things informants toss off, the stuff that goes on in everyday talk. These comments stayed in mind so naggingly that when I read black Barbadian fiction, what I'd heard during fieldwork came suddenly alive. Then I searched for some way of principalling what I'd read and what I'd heard. After reading further into West African works of fiction it was confirmed: there was something there.

This paper is about detachment as description and as "story" in its broadest sense, aesthetic detachment among Afro-Americans and Africans around the Atlantic fringe. If the claim seems as convincing at the end of the paper as it did to me when I realized what apparently was going on, then our conceptions of cultural continuity among Afro-Americans will be further substantiated. It is an odd kind of urban ethnography when some very ordinary comments dropped in the course of pleasant conversation or to pass the time become informative of a whole population's aesthetic sensibilities. Nevertheless, this paper can be read as an attempt to come to terms with exactly that intuition.

II

The anthropological fieldwork on which this paper is based was undertaken in a black urban locale.[1] This was a space where my wife, Karen Rose, and I lived for two years and began picking up a selection of the experiences that some Afro-Americans in Philadelphia, Pennsylvania have. We lived on 14th Street in Philadelphia, on a trolley line. Our neighbors were black and we

1 Support for this research was made available by the Center for Urban Ethnography, the University of Pennsylvania, under Public Health Service Grant 17216. I appreciate the encouragement in the investigation of Afro-American sensibilities from John Szwed, Roger Abrahams, Karl Reisman and Sally Yerkovich. Comments on an earlier version of this paper were made by Robert Farris Thompson and are much appreciated.

associated entirely with them and not with members of an academic community or a network of Caucasian friends. We did not reveal our academic identities. This meant that the people who knew us and observed us figured we were deviants, either hiding from the police, dodging the draft, or dealing in drugs.

I apprenticed myself as an auto mechanic to Telemachus Combs, who ran his own transmission repair shop. We lived next door to the garage so our lives were circumscribed. What we lacked in range of acquaintance we made up for in depth of relations with neighbors around us. Our next door neighbor was Ivery, who had six children. She was a welfare recipient living above Telemachus' garage. Ivery was terribly ashamed of her alcohol addiction. Due to her shame she refused contact with her consanguineal and affinal kinsmen in the city. What we all had in common was spatial proximity. Although Telemachus lived in West Philadelphia, his daily round was largely a function of his work on 14th Street. He arrived around 8:10 a.m. and left the garage between 6 and 10 p.m. He once mentioned that he did not know what he'd do without South Philly. He had worked off and on in the area for nearly twelve years.

The locale on 14th Street can be thought of as a small social space having a reality of its own – a social unit with some integrity. It tended always toward being an intimate space in which one felt familiar, at home, engaged, and actively prohibited from much that occurred. As such it was a small – if not closed – moral universe in which the individual's existence was very much a function of his local identity and the sanctions brought to bear on his performances. By a person's local identity I refer to the combination of his social and personal identities (Goffman 1963) that have particularly emerged in relation to other persons in that place. Because one's local identity is limited to others in immediate proximity, persons create naturally bounded social spaces in their continuing contacts. It was in this locale that the following remarks were made in their casual way.

1. One afternoon I was walking to the store with my godson, Ivery's boy, Godfrey. He was at that time ten years old. He told me that he had been in a fight at school. The other boy had called him some names. He took umbrage at them and said that he was going to call the other kid some names in return. I asked him what names he was going to call the other boy. He said, "I'll call him whatever comes out my mouth." [2]

2. Karen had a good deal of access to information through knowing the women on our street. One of her friends, Katherine, was sitting in a rocker in our living room, exchanging her dreams with us. Katherine was twenty at the

---

2 Consider the autonomy of the mouth as rendered in the West African novels, Nwapa (1970: 125); Oyono (1970: 50, 71; 1971: 34). Clearly the function of giving the mouth its own autonomy is to provide distance between oneself and one's words. Given the creation of this distance, then, it's more difficult for others to attribute responsibility for utterances to the talker. It is a ritualized attempt to remove oneself from the social dangers inherent in one's own speech productions. Commonly, of course, it is the detached mouth which gives voice to the descended 'spirit' in both African and Afro-American religious practice.

time. She was regularly attending the meetings of a local motorcycle club. In her dream she was being introduced to members of the club. She shook the hand of each member as she was introduced to them. She reported that as she shook the person's hand, her hand came off in the other person's grip, like a glove. She said that it seemed perfectly normal in the dream (as it always does in dreams) to have one's hand detached in that way.

3. I was sitting with Boycie in front of an engine rebuilding firm where he had once been employed. We were waiting for the valves of an automobile engine head to be ground and seated. We were looking over the southern blocks of the city. The high-rise slum clearance project buildings were the tallest profiles on the horizon. They were only a couple of blocks away. Boycie waved his arm, encompassing the area, and asked,

"See all this space?"

I said, "Sure," looking around.

He said, "I'm fucking all this space."

A single person, I thought, profaning by his existence a whole section of the city.

From these brief recountings, two essential distinctions may be made: first, that parts of the body seem to have a life of their own, as a detached hand, and as a mouth which apparently utters words autonomously from the rest of the human being; and second, that a person might be wholly detached from others such that he can see himself as profaning everyone else, as committing a sexual act with a section of the city, as being somehow over against the space in which he existed, or as existing detached from that space in a way that he could, if he chose, enter it as in sexual congress. Parts of the world also have this same effective agency.

Among Afro-Americans there are numerous constructions made with prepositions which phrase relations in social space quite clearly. The momentary relationship between two ends of a social tie becomes evident in prepositional use. Examples include the preposition *behind*, to marry *with*, to get *next to*, to be *in to*, to be *down*, and to fuck *over*.

Body parts, persons in social space, and the contents of the world such as women, buses, sugar, cities, ghosts, or whatever is relevantly identified, can be endowed with a conceptual and active autonomy (Hawkins n.d.). Not only do bodies have a conceptual autonomy but they may be detached in another style by rendering human form into animal form. Animal behavior is then read back onto individual's behavior, in that way generating humor (see Bohannan 1967: 264). Achebe's story, "Sugar Baby", shows how sugar is animated and referred to as if it were a person:

> I caught the fierce expression on his face in the brief impulsive moment of that strange act; and I understood. I don't mean the symbolism such as it was; that, to me, was pretty superficial and obvious. No. It was rather his deadly earnestness.
> It lasted no more than a second or two . Just as long as it took to thrust his hand into his sugar bowl, grasp a handful and fling it out of the window, his squarish jaw set viciously. Then it crumbled again in the gentle solvent of a vague smile.
> "Ah-ah; why?" asked one of the other two present, or perhaps both, taken aback and completely mystified.

"Only to show sugar that today I am greater than he, that the day has arrived when I can afford sugar and, if it pleases me, throw sugar away." (Achebe 1973: 95)

This aesthetic sensibility, of treating pieces of the world and selves as autonomous, will be termed "detachment". In West Africa, especially, the practice of being *cool* is a form of interactive detachment. Thompson (1973: 41) writes: "Manifest within this philosophy of the cool is the belief that the purer, the cooler a person becomes, the more ancestral he becomes. In other words, mastery of self enables a person to transcend time and elude preoccupation" (see also Thompson, 64-65 for further detail on detachment).

III

The justification for collecting black behavior from the United States, the Caribbean, and West Africa, and putting it in a heterogeneous and complex category is not easily made, nor consensually recognized as legitimate. There is one argument worth attending, however, in presenting such a case. Despite critiques and detractors, Herskovits (1958) made a strong brief for the continuity of some of the West African sensibilities in the New World. While doing fieldwork, I was sensitized to the data in two ways. On the one hand, there was the claim that Afro-Americans were deculturated and resembled poor whites of the same class. On the other hand, I was urged to look out for what might prove to be deep features that black Americans had kept alive as practices in their everyday lives. Furthermore, I believe that living locked into a locale with little relief from it required a deep participation in people's mundane lives. Since the interrogative form is not a legitimate device on 14th Street for acquiring information, we were required to participate as best we could to acquire local norms. It was through trial and error that we received tutoring, not in carefully scheduled questions. Our information was rather more participants' awareness than observers' knowledge.

One could look for places in social systems such as the slavery situation where African norms for behavior were indigenously preserved. White educational socialization of the blacks, particularly of the formal variety, was, in North America, especially poor, with recent minor improvement. A second sector of life, cohabitation, and the norms for relating between men and women were not under white scrutiny. The small domestic economies and polities in day-to-day realities could easily be preserved and, as I argue in this report, were, under the plantation system.

To round out the picture on the practice of detachment which runs through black sensibilities and to provide evidence of the way it is produced, I want to turn to accounts taken from Nigeria and Barbados. Both Tutuola's West African experience and Lamming's Barbadian one complement Achebe's little story on sugar and the reported field experience of the writer. The intended reason for including excerpts from fictionalized accounts is to enable the reader to participate in a minor way in the experience that members have of their own social systems. Achebe, Lamming, and Tutuola may be read as sociological sophisticates of their own social and aesthetic forms. Furthermore, passages taken from their writings may evoke the reader's sense of the organization of experience fieldworkers usually try to acquire.

In Tutuola's *Palm Wine Drunkard*, the palm wine drinker, apparently a young man, has lost his palm wine tapster. The tapster fell from the palm tree while attempting to procure the juice and died. The drinker was unable to entertain his friends because he had nothing to offer them in exchange for their company. He then set out to remedy the situation by searching for the tapster in heroic quest beyond the land of the living. Tutuola continues with the first person narrative (abridged):

> I reached another town which was not so big, although there was a large and famous market. At the same time that I entered the town, I went to the house of the head of the town who received me with kindness into his house. I told him that my name was called "Father of gods who could do anything in this world." As he heard this from me, he was soon faint with fear. After that he asked me what I came to him for. I replied that I was looking for my palm-wine tapster who had died in my town some time ago. Then he told me that he knew where the tapster was.
>
> After that he told me that if I could help him to find out his daughter who was captured by a curious creature from the market which was in that town, and bring her to him, then he would tell me whereabouts my tapster was.
>
> Before that time, her father was telling her to marry a man but she did not listen to her father; when her father saw that she did not care to marry anybody, he gave her to a man himself, but this lady refused totally to marry that man who was introduced to her by her father. So that her father left her to herself. So, one day she went to the market on a market-day as she was doing before, or to sell her articles as usual; on that market-day, she saw a curious creature in the market, but she did not know where the man came from and never knew him before.
>
> He was a beautiful "complete" gentleman, he dressed with the finest and most costly clothes, all the parts of his body were completed, he was a tall man but stout. As this gentleman came to the market on that day, if he had been an article or animal for sale, he would be sold at least for... [two thousand pounds].
>
> By and by the market closed for that day then the whole people in the market were returning to their destinations etc., and the complete gentleman was returning to his destination as others did, then she was following him (complete gentleman) to an unknown place.
>
> But when they had travelled about twelve miles away from that market, they left the road on which they were travelling and started to travel inside an endless forest in which only all the terrible creatures were living.
>
> As they were travelling along in this endless forest then the complete gentleman in the market that the lady was following, began to return the hired parts of his body to the owners and he was paying them the rentage money. When he reached where he hired the left foot, he pulled it out, he gave it to the owner and paid him, and they kept going; when they reached the place where he hired the right foot, he pulled it out and gave it to the owner and paid for the rentage. Now both feet had returned to the owners, so he began to crawl along on the ground, by that time, that lady wanted to go back to the town or her father, but the terrible and curious creature or the complete gentleman did not allow her to return or go back to her town or her father again and the complete gentleman said thus: – "I had told you not to follow me before we branched into this endless forest which belongs to only terrible and curious creatures, but when I became a half-bodied incomplete gentleman you wanted to go back, now that cannot be done, you have failed... Even you have never seen anything yet, just follow me."

When they went furthermore, then they reached where he hired the belly, ribs, chest etc., then he pulled them out and gave them to the owner and paid for the rentage.

Now this complete gentleman was reduced to head and when they reached where he hired the skin and flesh which covered the head, he returned them, and paid to the owner, now the complete gentleman in the market reduced to a "SKULL," and this lady remained with only "Skull." He was humming with a terrible voice and also grew very wild and even if there was a person two miles away he would not have to listen before hearing him, so this lady began to run away in that forest for her life, but the Skull chased her and within a few yards, he caught her, because he was very clever and smart as he was only Skull and he could jump a mile to the second before coming down. He caught the lady in this way: so when the lady was running away for her life, he hastily ran to her front and stopped her as a log of wood.

By and by, this lady followed the Skull to his house, and the house was a hole which was under the ground. At the same time that they entered the hole, he tied a single Cowrie on the neck of this lady with a kind of rope, after that, he gave her a large frog on which she sat as a stool, then he gave a whistle to a Skull of his kind to keep watch on this lady whenever she wanted to run away. (Tutuola 1953: 16–22)

The detachment of body parts is thematic in West African mythic consciousness (Herskovits and Herskovits 1958: 243–245; Beier 1966: 48–49; Gbadamosi and Beier 1968: 5–7; Delane 1966: 6, 16, 30, 53, 101; Fagunwa 1968: 28).[3]

What has been exhibited so far, especially in the work of Tutuola, is the detachment of body parts, not the detachment in space that Boycie profanely talked about. Next, the topic of detachment of bodies in space will be drawn from the literature and discussed. I would argue that this second form of detachment *is more primary* than the first one already exemplified. The detachment of parts of a body is really an aesthetic detachment of pieces from a whole – pieces from a whole body that works together, usually, normally, as an ensemble of articulated members. The aesthetic detachment of the bodily parts, with the body being a model of the social universe, is really a *reduction*. The human body is a model of the body politic and a mapped reduction of society's workings – exactly what George Lamming seems to be getting at in describing offspring as *Natives of My Person*, which I'll discuss later.

What I want to suggest next are the methods of interaction between persons in ordinary encounters – detachment during encounters – that underlie the more aesthetic expression of detachment. The experiences in the social encounters of inclusion and exclusion, and the particular ways these are patterned, are considered to be ordinary to, and to underlie aesthetic inclusion and exclusion – or attachment and detachment.

The argument, preceeding the further examples, is this: detachment in social relationships, during encounters, creates the experience in the mind that

---

3 Bodily detachment in space is a feature of all trickster figures, not only in West Africa, but among aboriginal North Americans among others (see Radin 1956). The claim is modest, that African populations experience bodily detachment one way, Amerindian populations, another. The point is a researchable one. How is it that detachment is experienced given the social encounters – exchanges and grievance redresses – patterned among a population? This is *the* research question.

permits persons to create aesthetic productions modelled after features of that social experience. The Caribbean example that Lamming offers is like the example taken from Boycie's profanation of space. Individuals, rather than body parts, have their own (sometimes unfortunate) social autonomy.

In this following abstract from his novel, Lamming animates three young boys who are about ten years old. They are talking about events in Creighton Village. One of them, Trumper, tells the other two about Jon, a young man who was mainly known for his skill at pitching marbles. At the time of the incident that Trumper is telling about, Jon has been living with a young woman named Jen. He has had two children by her. He was also been attending services at a small church, the Free for All Brethren. He and the minister's daughter, Suzie, got along well, and she became pregnant by him. The minister, Brother Bannister, told Jon that he ought to marry his daughter Suzie so as to save Brother Bannister from embarrassment. Jon at this point told the mother of his children, Jen, that Brother Bannister wanted him to marry Suzie and threatened to shoot him if he did not. Jen threatened to poison his guts out if Jon married Suzie instead of marrying her. After all, she argued, she was the mother of his children.

Jon, to discharge his obligations, promised to marry both Suzie and Jen and somehow managed to schedule the ceremonies for the same day. One ceremony was to take place in the large church and the other wedding was to take place in Brother Bannister's church. Jon did not show up to claim either bride. When the respective congregations heard he had showed up for neither they bawled for murder and the two clergymen viciously denounced one another.

Instead of going to either church, Jon ran to the cemetery and climbed a large mahogany tree. From that roost he was able to observe both church doorways. He stayed in the tree, entranced, until nightfall, then he came down and the next morning the people found him sitting among the tombstones devoid of his senses. Lamming continues the story by putting these words in the young boys' mouths.

...Trumper said, "... Jon thought the weddin 'had to be, an' he went there to see who would take his place."
"But nobody could take his place," Boy Blue said...
"It didn't make no difference," Trumper said... "This is what I mean... We all get a feelin' inside that certain things got to be, an' it make no difference what is, or what's not, that particular thing gottabe. For instance the sun. When you see the sun you know there gottabe light. An' don' say something wrong with yuh eyes, 'cause the sun ain't got nothin' to do with that. Is simply and purely a question of if there's sun there gottabe light. An' you don't ask any questions 'cause there ain't no questions to ask. An' with the sea, 'tis the same. When you touch the sea with yuh toe you know there gottabe wet. An' you don't ask questions 'cause there ain't no questions to ask. What maybe or maybe not don't matter, 'cause if there be sea there gottabe wet. In the said, same way, if there's weddin', if priest an' preacher, and church an' bride, if all these things is there, then there gottabe weddin' an' it ain't have nothing to do with what maybe, or maybe not, if there's these things, church, priest, preacher, an' so on, then there gottabe man. If there's weddin' there gottabe man. Deep inside you, you know there's gottabe that, if there's those other

things, an' you don't worry yuh head, 'cause it ain't have nothin' to do with you. There's
no need to worry, so you just sit an' wait to see what'll happen... [Jon] was simply an'
purely sayin' to himself that 'though he be in the tree, if there's weddin' an' all that,
there's gottabe man, an' deep down he expect a man to go in. Is the sea an' the toes all
over again."
"That would make it that there wus two Jons," Boy Blue said, "one in the tree an' one in
the church, whichever church he did choose."
"P'raps three Jons," Trumper said, "'cause there wus as much weddin' preparation in
one church as there wus in the other."
"Three Jons," Boy Blue repeated, "one in the tree, an' one in each church. But it don't
make sense... It ain't what the preacher does call logical."
"P'raps it ain't," Trumper said, "but that don' make it not so. Logical or logistical, or
whatever they call it, is logical or logistical an' so on, an' sense is sense, as we all know,
but all that ain't got nothin' to do with what is..."
"I don't care what you say, Trumper," Boy Blue said. "You can't be in a tree an' two
churches at the said same time." There was an urgency in his voice.
"I don't know," Trumper said. "P'raps you can if you feel you can." (Lamming 1970:
131–142)

It was earlier claimed that the aesthetic experience of detachment could
be rendered as a social experience of detachment. The best place to look for
such experience in ongoing social interactions seems to be economic exchanges
of the most mundane sort between tied persons. A good example of mundane
economic exchanges occurs in the kind of sexual-economic-religious exchanges
that Jon, Jen, and Suzie were into. Since exchanges and arguments about
exchanges are rule-governed obligations, our cut into the data is to search for
the obligations binding parties on a moment-to-moment basis. We want to
know the rules that underlie the conducting or discharging of obligations
between relevant members. Once the rules are shown, they can pretty well
account for the conduct of experience during social encounters. This experience
and the rules that underlie it, are then seen as the cognitive organization that
gives rise to the specific possibilities of aesthetic as well as interactional productions, and potentially in the same event.

There were three Jons. The Jon in the tree, the Jon that was supposed to
marry Suzie, and the Jon that was supposed to marry Jen. The three Jons that
the boy's gossip detected, corresponded homologously to Jon's obligations. He
was obliged to marry two different women. And he was additionally obligated
to himself to remain in the land of the living. It is through the rule-governed
discharging of obligations that, in a moment, I wish to pursue the investigation.

One can focus on the process of corporeal detachment that the young boys
effected in their gossip concerning Jon, Jen and Suzie. The moral process of
detachment can be found to produce the way objects in the world are experienced. As offered before, objects, including parts of the body, have an
autonomy, a quasi-life of their own. The question then is: how is it that experience is so structured among persons that the world seen as made up of
detached parts, bodily and socially, may be rendered so as to produce aesthetic
artifice and enjoyment?

Two notions employed so far can now be put together: the binding obligations members have to one another and may attempt to get out of, and the sub-sequential ordering of experience during interactions. Before defining the way that obligations tie up parties, consider that the way one obligates others and discharges obligations to them is done in lived time, during originating events. If A owes B money, or a favor, then at some subsequent time A must either pay B off or B must request a return. The involvement in obligations to others, and the paying off of others comprises the temporally ordered subsequentiality sustaining social relationships.

What is of interest is a person's management of his and others' entangled obligations to one another. The drama comes in when an individual is obligated to several others at once, as Jon was to Jen and Suzie. That's when the fun starts because onlookers and the knowledgeable get to see the inherent con-flicts built into their human culture played out in familiar, specific, and locally exciting ways.

All human societies must solve a problem of social form, in this case the social form for a given actor being "equally" binding obligations. There are ethnospecific, culturally located means for solving the problem of being bound to two parties simultaneously. Jon attempted to remove himself bodily from the two obligations by taking himself out of the action. A wife with a lover in addition to her husband may feign in a playful "good morning" greeting to her husband that she has no other such involvement (Robbe-Grillet 1965: 121). In either case, the person doubly obligated must manipulate impressions of him-self in culturally recognized forms. In so doing, he and others concert their experience of their subsequentially ordered moral universe.

It is precisely in this way that actors manage to manipulate their position between more or less equal obligations. The sequentially organized experience of self and other is generated and sustained in culturally specific modes. This experience of self and other during immediate social contact is then available as a fundamental structuring of experience in a variety of situations with numerous other actors. It is available in one's head as a cognitive patterning one uses to reflect with, create aesthetic objects with, process stimuli with, or formulate utterances with. The moral and the cognitive are thus bound up in a whole package of organized experiencing that actors use, the better with which to creatively understand their world.

The third incident I want to examine happened in Philadelphia in the garage. It involved Telemachus, Raymond, and Dave and Frank. Raymond was a nineteen-year-old black kid who did unskilled mechanical work, pulling transmissions, doing tune-ups, brake jobs, and the like. Raymond used to work for Telemachus but went to work across the street at Frank's auto garage. Dave, an Italian like Frank, did the mechanical work in that shop. Frank managed the garage, a glass installation shop, a whorehouse, and his apart-ment houses. Although Raymond had worked directly under Dave, he was hired by Frank and had known Frank longer. Both Raymond and Frank had lived and worked in the neighborhood most of their lives.

Telemachus said to me late in the afternoon, "Raymond called me this morning and again this afternoon. This morning he wanted to know if I would buy some automatic transmission clutches. This afternoon he called back to see if I had decided yet."

"How much did he want for them?" I wanted to know.

"He said he wanted seven dollars for the set. He said that he took them from over at Frank's because he wanted to hurt Dave. He didn't have to tell me he stole them. Now I know too and that is the same as if I had done it."

Nothing more came of the incident that day. But the next morning around nine o'clock Frank came into the shop to talk to Telemachus. Frank asked Telemachus to ask Raymond to return the clutches. They had missed them and Raymond was the only person who could have taken them. I could not hear Telemachus' response to Frank's request. Maybe for Frank it was unsatisfactory because a couple of hours later Dave came into the shop. That in itself was very unusual because Dave, who was running Frank's garage at that time, would have nothing to do with Telemachus. He had been inside Telemachus' doorway only once or twice before and then only on business.

Without formality he asked Telemachus, "Did Raymond get in touch with you?"

"Yes, he called on the phone yesterday," Telemachus answered.

"Did he offer to sell you some transmission clutches?"

"Yeah," Telemachus said. He avoided looking at Dave.

"What did he want for them?"

"Seven dollars."

"Give him the seven dollars if he calls again. And if you talk with Ray, tell him that he isn't fucking with boys, he's going to end up in the drink," Dave said.

"I don't want to get involved in this," Telemachus told him.

"Okay, I'll tell him myself," Dave said; and he walked out.

Later in the late afternoon Raymond came and said to Telemachus, "Dave asked for the clutches back. I told him I knew who took them and I could get them back for him. Dave asked me how much and I told him six dollars. Dave said to me, 'Get them and you can have the money.' When I brought them back, Dave took them and told me that if he ever caught me taking anything from there again he would hurt me."

Telemachus was looking at Raymond with his eyes squinted. He said, "M-hmm," accompanying Raymond's story.

Raymond continued, "I respect Dave for acting like a man, and not like Frank. Frank has to ask somebody else to tell me, instead of coming to me himself. I really wanted to hurt Frank. I would like to sugar his car. The trouble is, around here everybody knows me and they would pin it on me if his car got messed up."

After Raymond left, Telemachus said to me, "I think he's trying to make up for the time he hurt me and took all that stuff.[4] He steals from Frank and brings the stuff to me."

_____
4   Raymond once stole three hundred dollars worth of goods from Telemachus' garage to

Raymond, by stealing the clutches from Frank and Dave, could be considered to be what is called in black children's arguments, the *instigator*. That is, Raymond instigated a confrontation between Frank, Dave, and Telemachus. Telemachus was between obligations, but by removing himself from this slot made Raymond the middle person. Raymond attempted to place Telemachus between himself and Dave and Frank. (Dave and Frank may be considered here as holding a single structural position.) Telemachus perceived that he was between obligations and told Raymond that since he knew that the clutches were stolen that he was as culpable as Raymond, he was in effect a thief, if he bought the transmission clutches. He then attempted to remove himself from his structural position between obligations when Dave confronted him in the shop and asked him to tell Raymond that Raymond was not dealing with boys. Telemachus said he did not want to be involved. Nevertheless he was, by having contacted Raymond.

Raymond, too, was between obligations: he stood between Telemachus and Frank and Dave. He had committed a felony against Frank and had furthered his delict by jeopardizing Telemachus' relations with Frank. At that point Frank was angry with him and Telemachus was piqued. On either side he had a litigation going and no solace.

The ordering of experience during Afro-American litigations when they are concerned with persons placed between obligations may be formulated as follows: if a person is placed by another between obligations, rather than siding with either, he attempts to extricate himself equally from both. This is social detachment from obligation. The detachment is furthered because it is usually the case that each member in the round of litigations is a defendant. Also, each can hold an accuser's slot. This double fact means that no coalitions are formed, two against one, with any durability. Each member is legally isolated when he is accused. The isolation is rotated in the round of litigations.

Raymond was in this case the *instigator*. The rule for instigator's action is this: an instigator attempts to provide evidence that will contaminate the relationship between two parties who are tied in some way. Raymond attempted to insert his theft of clutches between Telemachus and Frank. Since Telemachus rented his repair shop from Frank, the strategy on Raymond's part was to jeopardize the amicable landlord-renter relationship Frank and Telemachus had going for them. Raymond, after all, could have sold the clutches any number of places if he had just needed the money. The instigator, then, also contributes to the creation of detachment from obligation by inserting evidence to jeopardize constituted relationships. In so doing he alienates partners from one another and creates social distance between them, particularly if they litigate and hard feelings result.

It should be noted that these instigations receive their power because they are introduced in front of other persons. Such litigious acts receive their power

---

redress a grievance. Stealing here can be seen by all parties as a mechanism for the redress of a grievance.

from the instigator's attempt to discredit or embarrass a person publicly. These incidents are very much the stuff of gossip in Afro-American urban locales, so that everyone involved has his reputation on the line. The way the principals discharge themselves determines their skill at playing this moral game.

There is a rule which apparently holds with little exception: persons who are confronted with their delicts deny or redefine their culpability. When Dave confronted Raymond with the theft of the clutches, Raymond, rather than owning up to having taken the clutches, claimed that he knew who took them and claimed as well that he could obtain them for Dave. In this manner, Raymond detached himself from his part in having taken the clutches, maintained face in the presence of accusation and threat, and wholly redefined his own identity.

By detaching himself from Dave's imputed identity of him as thief, Raymond redefined his identity to being the person who knew who the thief was. In this manner he escaped a given identity and acquired a self-selected one. He generated a divorce or detachment from his own history, his autobiography, and created a retrospective version of himself.

These rules underlie subsequential social ordering of experiencing. The actor, in the preceding examples, attempts to exempt himself from obligations through a detached persona and to insert evidence that will tear at the fabric of social ties other persons have underway. This methodology for interpersonal equality insures that each character be as isolated as all the others, that the tied persons will not be able to over-obligate others such that they'll have too many debts to collect on, and thereby achieve higher status through access to more resources.

In this process of own and other social distancing within already constituted relationships, the ego and person's identity is accorded an autonomy. As Radcliffe-Brown taught us, the socially created social identity of members is then imputed as an ontology for the universe. Things in the world, like their human model, are considered to have certain qualities. Although to members, the world they think they live in is actually what they've made of one another. The active autonomy of a hand, a handful of sugar, a mouth, or oneself in a social space is the effective autonomy of actors' identity created during the experiencing of self and other in subsequent social encounters. The discharge of obliged turn and return, what is owed and how exemptions are worked out, afford a closer look at the way experience itself is constructed. I wanted to show in the story form that the sense of detachment – a human moral and cognitive act, like classifying – occurs in a special way among Africans and Afro-Americans. The conceptual work of the detachment of bodily parts was reduced to the detachment persons *experience* with one another when face-to-face as they actually detach themselves from their obligations to one another.

Not all is detachment and autonomy. It should be stressed that while there is much in the social encounter that produces disaffiliation, there is a dialectic. Disaffiliation, autonomy, and alienation within sequencing are meshed simultaneously with affiliation, interdependency, and involvement. Detachment creates social distance while affiliative moves create social attachment. Lamming, once again, provides the example. After the publication of his recent novel, *Natives of My Person* (1972), he was asked during an interview (Kent 1973: 4) what the title of the book meant. He answered the question this way:

> In 1958, during a visit to Ghana, I was spending some time with an Ashanti family, and the father showed me a post card which presumably was a Christmas card he had made to send out to friends, business associates and so on. On this post card were about 25 or 30 people of different ages who, to my surprise, I learned were his children. But what the post card said was, "These are all natives of my person." Many years later – I think 12 years later – when I was coming to write this novel you are referring to, that phrase leaped out of my consciousness as the title that was exact for what was happening here – that everything going on in the book was in a way a native of my person, that I might in some way contain all of that experience, that anything created from that experience became, in that manuscript, *Natives of My Person.*

Social attachment is created in lived time, and detachment is an alienation within constituted expectations between obligated persons. When looked at more formally these are terms of disjunction and conjunction, continuity and discontinuity. Instead of looking at category and hierarchy, we have looked to inclusion and exclusion as temporally ordered cognitive organizational phenomena. More deeply we can ask what are the organizational principles that underlie the grammar of inclusion and exclusion, what can be gathered, what shall remain separated? Added to the insight of Durkheim and Mauss, we might now ask, what are the rules within any given population for persons' inclusion in a given category, their exclusion from a particular category, who and what may be talked about and where, in the human, storyable scheme of things?

Both in direct social contact and in the story form there is a subsequential ordering of the experience of inclusion and exclusion. This human cognitive-moral activity is specifically patterned by the way persons are obliged to conduct their most mundane, microminiature economic affairs and disagreements over definitions of the situation and outcomes of exchanges. These sensibilities of face-to-face contact become analogized, elaborated, and built into norms in the story forms – say, gossip, about the small dramas occurring between persons in everyday life.

Based on this admittedly anecdotal data, I would posit the hypothesis that continuities of sensibility have remained among populations of African descent and that we can enter this world aesthetically through the ways in which they conceive of the uses of detachment. There is, in other words, a kind of special rhetorical style by which the body or the social group is temporarily dismembered, a dismemberment that maintains the entity in some ultimate sense. These sensibilities have been preserved in the most usual face-to-face interactions. This detachment has the quality of being patterned in intimate social relations and in stories within a specific historically tied population. It is, to be sure, a human attribute, patterned elsewhere among other populations in other ways; but the style of the detachment and the places in which this motive is employed seem significantly related in Africa and Afro-America, probably as some dimension of the sensibility-style Thompson calls "the aesthetic of the cool."

REFERENCES

ACHEBE, C.
1973 *Girls at War and Other Stories*. Garden City: Doubleday.
BEIER, U.
1966 *The Origin of Life and Death*. London: Heinemann.
BOHANNAN, P.
1967 "Drumming the Scandal among the Tiv", in P. Bohannan (ed.), *Law and Warfare*. Garden City: Natural History Press.
DELANE, I. O.
1966 *Owe L'Esin Oro Yoruba Proverbs, Their Meaning and Usage*. Ibadan: Oxford University Press.
DURKHEIM, E. and M. MAUSS
1963 *Primitive Classification*. Chicago: University of Chicago Press.
FAGUNWA, D. O.
1968 *The Forest of a Thousand Daemons*. London: Nelson.
GBADAMOSI, B. and U. BEIER
1968 "Not Even God Is Ripe Enough". *Yoruba Stories*. London: Heinemann.
GOFFMAN, E.
1963 *Stigma*. Englewood Cliffs: Prentice-Hall.
1974 *Frame Analysis: An Essay on the Organization of Experience. New York: Harper and Row.*
HAWKINS, Screamin' Jay
"A Thing Called a Woman". *What That Is!* Philips PHS 600–319.
HERSKOVITS, M.
1958 *The Myth of the Negro Past*. Boston: Beacon Press.
HERSKOVITS, M. and F. HERSKOVITS
1958 *Dahomean Narratives and Cross-Cultural Analysis*. Evanston: Northwestern University Press.
KENT, G. E.
1973 "A Conversation with George Lamming". *Black World*, March.
LAMMING, G.
1970 *In the Castle of My Skin*. New York: Collier.
NWAYA, F.
1970 *Idu*. London: Heinemann.
——
1972 *Natives of My Person*. New York: Holt, Rinehart and Winston.
OYONO, F.
1970 *Boy*! New York: Collier.
1971 *The Old Man and the Medal*. New York: Collier.
RADIN, Paul
1956 *The Trickster*. New York: Philosophical Library.
ROBBE-GRILLET, A.
1965 *Jealousy*. New York: Grove Press.
THOMPSON, R. F.
1966 "An Aesthetic of the Cool". *African Arts*, VII, 1.
TUTUOLA, A.
1953 *The Palm Wine Drunkard*. London: Faber & Faber.

Journal of Asian and African Studies IX, 3–4

Reflections on the State of Black Music and the Black Musician

LEONARD GOINES

City University of New York, Manhattan, U.S.A.

SINCE THE LATE NINETEENTH CENTURY, music education in the United States has been dominated by a cultural bias based on the assumption that Western European music is superior to any other in the world and consequently the only music worthy of serious academic study and scholarship. Resultantly, all forms of black music were systematically excluded from the curriculum and Americans, both black and white, have been taught, either through direct means or omission, that black music of the United States (blues, gospel, rhythm and blues, jazz, etc.) lacks the logic, objectivity, sublimity, morality and craftsmanship of Western Art Music.

Ironically this view is prevalent in predominantly black institutions as well as the white ones. Institutions such as Howard and Fisk Universities which should have been meeting the needs of black musicians for black music have, since their inception in the nineteenth century, fostered a curriculum which, until recently, had been devoted completely to Western European art music. So much so, in fact, that it was possible to get into serious trouble by just getting caught playing jazz in one of the practice rooms. Several black musicians who have become jazz and popular music superstars since their student days have often spoken of the discouraging experiences they encountered while attending these schools because their musical interests were not "classically oriented."

The black educators who established the music departments of these black schools, in most instances, modelled them after their white alma maters. This in itself would not have produced such disastrous results. The vast majority of them, however, also felt that black music was inferior and were ashamed of the elements which made it unique. Consequently black institutions dedicated themselves to the task of producing black performers, composers and music educators thoroughly grounded in the principles and theory of Western art music. Black music was studiously avoided, especially blues, jazz and the hated gospel music. Only elaborately arranged spirituals, which approximated the styles and forms of "classical" music were tolerated.

This is further complicated by the fact that when pressure was placed upon teachers and administrators by black students protesting the absence of black music courses, their reasons were often misinterpreted or conveniently misunderstood. Some even believed that the academic study of black music should be viewed as racism in reverse. This, of course, was a silly outlook and an offensive one. It can no more be viewed as racism for a black student to trace the history and development of black music from its African beginnings than it is for his white counterpart to trace the history and development of white Western music from its European beginnings.

As you can easily surmise, when I entered the Manhattan School of Music during the fifties there was no possibility of studying black music in any shape or form. Trained in the symphonic or operatic tradition, black students were graduated from such institutions with a number of desirable but unusable skills. The curriculum did not provide many of the necessary skills for us to make a living from music. Though we were well prepared as symphonic instrumentalists few of us were being accepted into symphonic or other "legitimate" orchestras.

The fact of the matter is that we went to colleges, conservatories, and universities to prepare ourselves for performing careers and found that, in most instances, there was little correlation between the type of music and performing practices we were taught in school and those we actually needed and used. In our actual work situations we primarily functioned in jazz and popular oriented big bands and small ensembles as found in nightclubs, theatres and recording studios.

The problem is pretty much the same today in respect to both training and employment practices. While qualified and experienced black instrumentalists, singers, conductors, and composers have been rolling out of schools like Julliard, Eastman, Peabody and the Manhattan School of Music in large numbers, there are presently only five black players in the "big five" symphony orchestras of the country while a token number are used in the other performance areas. And though, as a result of student demonstrations a few years back, most institutions offer at least a one semester survey course in black music, and many support a school jazz workshop or laboratory band, few institutions, black or white, offer the comprehensive type of program needed to adequately prepare students focusing on black areas of performance. Notable exceptions are a very few schools that offer a jazz major or its equivalent. Lead by North Texas State University, Southern University, Indiana University, University of Utah, University of Miami and the Berkley College of Music these schools collectively offer programs leading to degrees with a jazz emphasis, a degree with a major in studio work (radio, T.V., and recording studio performance) as well as big and small band performance, arranging and historical studies.

I recently spoke with an extremely well trained and versatile jazz musician who has taught on the college level for over twenty years. Currently working towards his Ph.D. at a northern state university he was extremely upset at the time. Being required to analyze a body of music for a class assignment he had chosen the works of John Coltrane. The project was vetoed. Not only was Coltrane's music unacceptable but the instructors, knowing next to nothing about jazz, were aware that they were unequipped to evaluate it.

Though overt brainwashing and censorship are generally considered to be alien to our American way of life, subtler and less sinister variations are utilized. Many music educators, for example, accomplish similar unfortunate results by demanding that their students espouse their opinions of which forms of music or musicians are the greatest or most vital. The following statement from a very popular textbook exemplifies this practice:

> Traditional music [Western art music] is middle class in orientation and is regarded as "cultural" and edifying while jazz is low class, strictly for fun, and often linked with dancing, courtship and sex. Traditional music is deliberate, a composer's art preserved in a written score; jazz is spontaneous, a performer's art preserved only on records. The danger that traditional music runs is getting rarefied in the ivory tower. The danger that jazz runs is getting dirty in the market place... In harmony, pulse, musical form, and range of expression, most persons with extensive musical experience find jazz comparatively meager, once the initial "kicks" have worn off ... Jazz is a minor art having its own integrity and liveliness, and probably it cannot bend too far without losing many of its characteristic virtues. (Jansen and Kerman 1968: 291)

If black music had been handled in a realistic manner in textbooks written by these authorities rather than either being completely ignored or approached from an ethnocentric point of view, there would be little need for the concentrated efforts which are presently required. Hopefully this need will diminish in the future. I have personally studied courses in twentieth century music, however, where the word jazz, for example, posed influence on composers such as Ravel, Debussy and Stravinsky. Needless to say there was no mention of gospel or rhythm and blues even though most of todays' popular music forms are based on them in one form or the other.

Likewise, my formal training as a historian or ethnomusicologist in the area of black music was equally limited. There were practically no courses available to me dealing specifically with the black musical experience. There was also a lack of suitable literature and materials for use in personal research activities. This was understandable in terms of the low regard in which black music was held. But it was also due, in part, to the tendency of the white scholar to approach the subject from an ethnocentric point of view, evaluating it only by white Western standards. Consequently, much of their materials failed to provide the necessary insight from a psychological, sociological or historical point of view. While research into their own music by black Americans was almost non-existent.

Faced with these problems I had no choice but to think in terms of personal field work. Using a combination of personal funds and research grants I began doing field work in Africa, North America, Latin America, and the Caribbean which has enabled me, over the course of some twenty years, to amass a vast amount of materials and information on black music from these areas.

II

While much attention is being centered upon the development of black music today, very little thought is directed toward the black musician and the circumstances surrounding his struggle for existence. Historically denied access to "white" musical areas and organizations, because of social reasons, and robbed of his success in black American music because of economic ones, he has constantly sought new means of expression.

As might be expected, however, few black musicians have been permitted to share in the gigantic profits gathered from their musical experiences and expressions. Even today, when multibillion dollar industries are involved in the dispensation of black music throughout the world, only a handful of black performers show consistently high earnings while the vast majority are concerned with sustaining themselves on the visceral level.

In addition to out and out economic exploitation, the black musician has had to absorb social indignities during the course of duty that could fill several volumes.

Billie Holiday, Roy Eldridge, Lena Horne and many others who worked with the big white bands of the 1930's such as Artie Shaw, Charlie Barnet and Benny Goodman have all related tales of personal discrimination ranging from being denied accommodations at the hotels where the bands were playing and staying, in addition to being refused meals in the restaurant and sometimes not being permitted to perform.

It is even more poignant to note that such overt discrimination could take place in the 1960's with such an internationally renowned musician as Duke Ellington.

Duke Ellington was the subject of much controversy in 1965 when the Pulitzer Prize Award Committee decided not to give a music prize that year, rather than give the award to him.

In *The Crisis of the Negro Intellectual,* Harold Cruse makes the following statement:

In 1965, Duke Ellington, America's greatest exponent of orchestrated jazz music and composition, was turned down for the Pulitzer Prize citation for "long term achievement" in American music. In the New York Times' story, the Pulitzer Prize advisory board gave no reason for refusing the citation to Ellington. For just about forty years, he has been, by general popular and professional acclaim, the foremost jazz orchestra leader and composer in America. This turn-down indicates that the same old, ethnic-group war for cultural supremacy in American music is still being waged. Ellington was quoted as saying: "Fate's being kind to me. Fate doesn't want me to be too famous too young..." One cannot explain how or why an Ellington does not achieve his due recognition today while the Gershwin-type musicians achieved status and recognition in the 1920's for music alleged by many to have been stolen outright from Harlem nightclubs... the role of the Negro as entertainer is still being used, manipulated, and exploited by whites ... years after the 1920 era, Duke Ellington has outplayed, outcreated, and outlasted all the Benny Goodmans and Paul Whitemans — yet the situation has not changed very much. The question of Ellington and the Pulitzer Prize is a surface issue. The prize itself is not really that important, but what lies behind the denial of the prize is a whole history of organized duplicity and exploitation of the Negro jazz artist – the complicated tie-in between booking agencies, the musician's unions, the recording companies, the music publishers, the managers, the agents, the theatre owners, the nightclub owners, the crooks, shysters, and racketeers. The Negro creative intellectuals have to look into the question of how it is possible for a Negro jazz musician to walk the streets of large cities, jobless and starving, while a record that he cut with a music company is selling well, both in the United States and in Europe. The impact of the cultural tradition of Afro-American folk music demands that the racially corrupt practices of the music-publishing field be investigated. (1967: 107–111)

You might begin to ask at this point – how is it possible for the black artist to be exploited in this manner without having a definite means of recourse?

The answer is pure and simple. Whites are in control of the mass media. By this we mean recording, radio, T.V., film, video tape, live broadcast, and the written word. Though the vast majority of American popular music on radio, T.V., etc. is black or black derived, representative black performing artists in all areas – jazz, R&B, soul, gospel and other religious music are almost non-existent. Jazz musicians in particular are becoming extremely aware and vocal in this regard.

Beginning in the sixties black musicians, especially those involved in the type of music labeled "avant garde" jazz began to form a peculiar group who displayed a particularly high level of social consciousness. While reflecting the Afro-American experience in general they saw themselves at the vanguard of the urban black communities. Articulate musicians such as Archie Shepp have proven to be among the more sensitive and active members of their society in voicing protest against the low status of black people and their art forms. Their unrestrained, aggressive, and often angry music is many times designed to un-shackle itself from European influences that have been superimposed upon it. Being equally interested in socio-political activity as well as aesthetic grati-fication they see their music as being reflective of the black community at large and as becoming instrumental in the salvation of the American population – both black and white alike. Archie Shepp makes the following statement in this regard:

> The Negro musician is a reflection of the Negro people as a social and cultural phenome-non. His purpose ought to be to liberate America aesthetically and socially from its in-humanity. The inhumanity of the white American to the black American as well as the inhumanity of the white American to the white American is not basic to America and can be exorcised, gotten out. I think the Negro people through the force of their struggles are the only hope of saving America, the political or the cultural America. (Jones 1968: 154–155)

Many people do not realize that it is possible for a recording artist to make little or no money in royalties for record sales unless large numbers are sold. This is due to the fact that production costs (which include studio expenses, processing and packaging expenses, fees to other musicians appearing on the album and others) are paid by the record company in advance but are deducted from the royalties of the featured artist.

For years black musicians have attempted to circumvent white economic and artistic control of the black music market by starting their own recording companies. Problems always arose when it came to distribution, however, as these companies were part of the white establishment too. Many musicians have tried a mail order service in addition to having records sold in the black and college communities. In the recent past black musicians have been consolidating their efforts and as a result have brought more far reaching corporations into being.

The most successful of these labels at the moment is Strata-East. Strata-East Records, Inc. which involved only a few musicians when pianist Stanley Cowell and trumpeter Charles Tolliver formed the company in 1971, has grown to include albums by such wellknown artists as: Max Roach, Harold Mabern, Gary Bartz, Lonnie Liston Smith, Pharoah Sanders, Leon Thomas, Don Cherry, Cecil McBee, Richard Davis, Kenny Dorham and Roy Haynes. The biggest problems they faced when they began producing were of course promotion, air play and distribution. The growth of college radio stations has offered a partial air play solution while their impressive list of albums has enabled them to deal directly with commercial distributors. The unique feature of the company is that the artist – company royalty breakdown is basically reversed. The artist who in most cases functions as his own producer, receives about 85% while the company retains 15%.

Further, because many jazz musicians, prior to the fifties, had no knowledge at all of contracts and other legal documents which he encountered, he signed anything placed in front of him; not realizing that a contract is a mutual agreement between parties involved and if it is not satisfactory to one party it could or should be amended or revised accordingly. Donald Byrd, the well known trumpet player and former Chairman of Howard University's Department of Jazz Studies, cites this lack of legal knowledge as one of the main vehicles for the exploitation of black musicians over the years. Consequently his department offered courses in the legal protection of music and musicians. Byrd is indicative of the dedicated musicians who are returning to the classroom in a concerted effort to bring meaningful experiences to those black musicians who have been systematically excluded from the college curriculum for so long. In addition, organizations such as New York's Collective Black Artists and the Chicago-based Association for the Advancement of Creative Musicians are gearing themselves toward the assimilation and dissemination of knowledge and techniques about and for the advancement of black music and musicians.

These organizations stress several long term, vital needs or goals. The need for extensive promotion and distribution of jazz records is top on the list. This is followed closely by the need to develop an educated jazz audience – largely by bringing jazz to the schools. And, equally as important, the necessary cooperation needed from various media such as radio and T.V. as they hopefully present and disseminate live and recorded jazz.

The above mentioned groups, in addition to several others such as Jazz Interactions, Jazzmobile, and the New York Jazz Museum have touring programs which present concerts and workshops in schools and in the community which are designed to educate as well as entertain.

In line with their media needs, a group of demonstrators led by Rahsaan Roland Kirk and the late Lee Morgan disrupted the Merv Griffin and Dick Cavett shows to dramatize their demands for more jazz and black artists on commercial television. During the month of October 1970 the Jazz and People's Movement, as the demonstrating musicians called themselves, set forth a list of aims which were designed to bring about more jazz specials on television which would educate the public to jazz, expose deserving talent, and present the music in its historical context. Operating on the premise that black artists must be aware of and relate to the political, economical, and cultural forces that control their lives, their main thrust was to direct attention to the exclusion of deserving black creative artists by the mass communications media. Needless to say no giant steps were taken to shift this focus.

As we have seen, some strides have been made by black music and black musicians in the recent past. It is very evident, however, that there is still much to be done. Courses in black music must adequately prepare their performers, composers, critics, and most important of all their audience by providing musical training that is both realistic and comprehensive. A student who wishes to become a jazz musician, critic, or work in related fields, for example, will hardly achieve that goal if he or she analyses Bach chorales exclusively, reads only Western European musical history, plays only Beethoven and Mozart sonatas and are faced with professors who feel that blues, jazz and rhythm and blues are not worthy of serious discussion in their classrooms.

REFERENCES

CRUSE, Harold
    1967   *The Crisis of the Negro Intellectual*. New York: William Morrow & Co., Inc.
JANSON, H. W., and Joseph KERMAN
    1968   *A History of Art and Music*. New Jersey: Prentice-Hall, Inc.
JONES, LeRoi
    1968   *Black Music*. New York: William Morrow & Co., Inc.

BOOK REVIEWS

Jerome Cohen (ed.), *Pacific Partnership: United States-Japan Trade: Prospects and Recommendations for the Seventies*. Lexington, Mass., D.C. Heath, 1972, pp. xiv, 270, $ 12.50.

This is a disparate collection of essays on aspects of the Japanese economy and of U.S.-Japanese trade and payments relationships. It was assembled under the auspices of the Japan Society's Committee on Economic Policy Studies; it was edited and summarized by Dean Cohen as Chairman of the committee. The optimistic "partnership" title may be a whistle in the dark. Its apparent purpose was to check the apparent drift toward economic warfare between the two countries, as embodied particularly in the rise of American protectionism (the Burke-Hartke Bill in the U.S. Congress). The Businessmen's Advisory Committee of the Japan Society also supplied a chapter on "Policy Recommendations," less "enlightened" (from a conventional economist's jaundiced viewpoint) than the remainder of the volume, but more enlightened than one would expect from the National Association of Manufacturers or the AFL-CIO.

Characterizing these essays as "disparate" has reference to their levels of technical sophistication and their audience appeals. Dean Henry Rosovsky's "overview" of Japan's economic prospects (Chapter 1) and Dean Cohen's own concluding summary (Chapter 11) will be the most helpful to the general public. This reviewer has only the most minor of quibbling differences with either one. The Rosovsky chapter has already been reprinted separately, and may even be influential in policy formation.

Next in ascending order of difficulty are three surveys of Japanese trade and payments, by Dr. Patricia Kuwayama, Professor Warren Hunsberger, and Dr. Lawrence Krause (Chapters 3, 5, and 6, respectively). These contain only minimal "apparatus," but assume acquaintance with the international economist's technical vocabulary. In addition and perhaps inevitably, these chapters overlap with each other somewhat; Krause's chapter on private investment is the most heavily weighted with novel material.

Of greater technical interest to economists are three chapters (2, 8, and 9) co-authored by Dr. William Rapp. These all cast the principles of "infant-industry protection" and "learning-by-doing" into quantitative form by means of a device which I hereby christen "Rapp's Law," although its coverage is incompletely specified. Quoting Cohen's literary restatement (p. 252) of the moral of Rapp's several logarithmic diagrams: "For Japanese industry total cost per unit in constant yen declines by a characteristic amount (usually 20 or 30 per cent) each time accumulated productive experience (total amount ever produced) doubles." I am myself skeptical of many such empirical generalizations inadequately supported by theoretical rationalization, for reasons Professor Paul Samuelson has assembled better than anyone else:

[T]he fact that counter-trends have about canceled each other out can be regarded as a coincidence, and provides no guarantee of repetition. [We have] learned how treacherous are economic 'laws' in economic life: e.g., Bowley's Law of constant relative wage share; Long's Law of constant participation in the labor force; Pareto's Law of unchangeable inequality of income; Denison's Law of constant private saving ratio; Colin Clark's Law of a 25 per cent ceiling on government expenditure and taxation; Modigliani's Law of constant wealth-income ratio; Marx's Law of the falling rate of real wage and/or the falling rate of profit; Everybody's Law of a constant capital-output ratio. If these be laws, Mother Nature is a criminal by nature. Experience has also taught me not to be necessarily suspicious of coincidence; in many cases, even if they do not explain the facts, they do describe the facts, up until they cease to describe the facts."*

There are, finally, two somewhat bristlingly econometric chapters, a projection of the Japanese foreign trade position to 1980 by Professor Kazuo Sato (Chapter 4) and a study by Professor Gary Saxonhouse of the Japanese-American "textile confrontation" (Chapter 7). Sato piles Assumption Pelion upon Assumption Ossa, and ends with a set of conclusions which do not seem either particularly exciting or much better than crude futurology. Saxonhouse, on the other hand, deduces from his econometric equations that (1) "Import competition" is only a minor element (as compared with technological changes and wage rate increases) in explaining the decrease of total man-hours worked in the American industry, and that (2) Japanese textile exports to the U.S. have not been affected greatly in 1972–73 the 1971 restrictions upon man-made and woolen textile export. So one might well ask, what is the confrontation all about, or, as Saxonhouse puts it, "Why the political flap?" His conclusion is that the "representative organs of labor and capital" on both sides, are not organized "to represent accurately the views of the industry in general" (p. 196). Another possibility is that Saxonhouse's econometrics was not available to these organs in advance, or that they might not believe his results anyway.

So rapidly do times change in Japanese-American trade relations that this book, prepared at a time when the Japanese were running huge export surpluses and the Americans huge import surpluses, appears at the time when the overall trade imbalance problem seems close to solution. (One plausible reason may be an 18-month lag in the effectiveness of the late-1971 currency revaluations, a condition suggested to the reviewer by Dr. Krause as holding quite generally for trade among the more developed countries.) To some extent, therefore, the volume suffers from a kind of anachronism, possibly endemic to the present state of international economics, which we can hope to overcome in the present generation.

Duke University   M. BRONFENBRENNER
Durham, U.S.A.

---

* Paul A Samuelson, "A Brief Post-Keynesian Survey," in Robert Lekachman, (ed.), *Keynes' General Theory: Reports of Three Decades* (New York: St. Martin's Press, 1964), p. 336. (Running quotation).)

Nishida Kitaro, *Art and Morality*. (Translated by David D. Dilworth and
Valdo H. Viglielmo). Honolulu, The University Press of Hawaii, 1973,
pp. 216, $ 8.00.

Ever since Art suffered its massive identity crisis in Europe during the 19th
century its theoreticians have postulated that its shaken integrity must be re-
established or re-defined unless it be regrettably placed on the list of endangered
species. As a result Art has often been considered in terms of distinct quantities,
of self-contained objects which function solely for the evocation of sensory
stimuli without any intentions of conceptual references beyond their physical
parameters. This is clearly evidenced in the omnipresent dictum, "Art for
Art's sake".

Nishida Kitarō (1870–1945), influential founder of the academic Kyoto
School of philosophy, expands such a limited attitude as he assumes the position that the "truth" of an object is not wholly contained within its physicali-
ty, rather it is also contingent upon the "self" and its sensory, intuitive, and
conceptual response to that phenomenon including its "a priori". During the
immediate "aesthetic activity" the subject and object become one in the "actual will", that which allows infinite freedom in creative choices. The knower
and the known lose their dialectic distinctions when there is a heighten awareness that the vital spirit bubbling beneath Nature's physical facade is the same
as the spirit of the "self". Thus the focus and the content of the "aesthetic activity" is Man's 'inner self', Man becomes the "aesthetic object", the primary
object of consideration in a "pure experience".

The knowledge gained from the aesthetic experience, dependent on
Man's ideational and emotional faculties, is a more profound "truth" of the
human condition. It is this which constitutes the necessary content for significant Art. "Truth" is realized when Man is the object hence it is both beautiful
and of a optimum moral level. Art and morality are of a similar nature in that
they depart from the experiential "world of objectivity" armed with "free will"
to search out the problems of "truth". They essentially differ from each other
in that Art continues in the realm of infinite subjectivity and morality is
eventually manifested in the institution of Religion becoming more practical in
function.

Nishida systematically investigates these complex interrelationships, as well
as others, in a manner derived from the systems of logic of such distinguished
"Western" philosophers as Kant, Bergson, and Fichte. It is primarily Kant's
laws of "a priori" and his "Categorical Imperative" which gives philosophical
unity throughout this dense work. Along with these "Western" influences
(predictable ones concerning the "internationalism" of 20th century Japan)
Buddhism's monistic world view is ever paramount. If there is a weakness in
this ambitious work it perhaps is in this regard. Using forms of "Western"
logic to deal with the metaphysics inherent in Buddhism weakens its meta-
phorical references.

California State University   GENE COOPER
Long Beach, U.S.A.

Burton Pasternak, *Kinship and Community in Two Chinese Villages.* Stanford, Stanford University Press, 1972, pp. 174, $ 8.50.

Much of the strictly anthropological literature on Chinese society consists of detailed and comprehensive ethnographic reports dealing with single villages. In this volume Pasternak departs somewhat from this tradition by comparing his findings from separate field studies of two villages, one Hakka and the other Hokkien, in different regions of southern Taiwan. He also limits himself to describing only those factors that bear (or might be supposed to bear) on the differential strength of agnatic kinship organizations and "cross-kin" associations in the two communities. The discussion of the effects of different climatic and agricultural conditions is valuable, particularly with regard to irrigation systems, and cultural ecologists and students of development should be pleased with the clear and cogent historical descriptions of such factors as they pertain to these two villages.

The central problem that the book addresses is an important one: Why were some southeastern Chinese villages dominated by single corporate patrilineages while others were composed of small and weak collections of families with numerous different surnames that might or might not participate in alliances that crossed agnatic categories. In an attempt to account for such differences, Pasternak makes the following inductive generalizations from his two cases:

"Ultimately, in conjunction with other materials from southeastern China, our comparison of [the two villages] suggests two hypotheses. One is that small agnatic groups were most likely to develop into single-lineage communities on open frontiers where competition for strategie resources was minimal, whereas the need for cooperation across agnatic lines for purposes of exploiting the environment or for defense tended to generate or reinforce the development of multi-lineage communities. Another is that higherorder (i.e. nonlocalized) descent groups resulting from an aggregative process seem to be associated with situations were territorially discrete and numerically weak agnatic groups have been confronted by a large and persistent common enemy (pages 18 and 19)."

The scientific validity and value of such generalizations is doubtful, but the philosophy of science cannot be adequately discussed in a book review, and I will therefore limit my critique to an evaluation of Pasternak's material and to the brief mention of factors bearing on his problem that he ignored or played down.

The contrast between the two villages seems forced in some respects, particularly on pp. 116–17, where intervillage conflict in the Hokkien case was cast in the frame of agnatic units, while similar difficulties in the Hakka area were described in community or ethnic terms. Again on pp. 120–21, the small budget of the Hokkien village and the proportionately large amount carried over to the succeeding year were said to signify a lack of public interest in community affairs in contrast to the Hakka village where a wealthy "cross-kin" corporation exists for unique historical reasons. The problem of the representativeness of the two villages for their respective ecological and ethnic regions is never addressed. Having myself worked throughout an area in West Central Taiwan that included nearly 200 settlements, I can attest to marked differences among neighboring villages with regard to the strength of agnatic corporations and the extent that significant relations transcend kinship and community. I know of a number of Hokkien villages in my region which were founded under similar frontier conditions and which have similar agricultural economies, some of which resemble one or the other of Pasternak's two cases. Only historical explanations can account for the forms that their community organizations have taken.

Pasternak provides good and convincing historical explanations for the differences between his two villages, but is apparently not satisfied with them. The generalized hypotheses he proposes are not likely to satisfy others because they ignore some well documented facts that bear on his problem. There is, for instance, the traditional defensive position of the Hakka on the mainland that complicates any comparison of particular Hakka and Hokkien community organizations. There are know cases in which single surname villages have become multisurname, and other cases in which multisurname villages have come to be completely dominated by one agnatic unit, as well as some cases in which one lineage has replaced another in the same village over a century or so. There are other sources of lineage wealth besides agricultural production, such as business or government service. Higher order agnatic organizations are known to have been created by the rural gentry for political purposes unrelated to defense or ethnic opposition.

In his conclusion, Pasternak cites the meager collection of studies of other villages in southeastern China (including Taiwan) which he claims support his hypotheses, although the ethnographic facts could be argued differently. In conclusion, I am of the opinion that convincing evidence supporting Pasternak's hypotheses is lacking, and the value of his book lies in the unique historical and ecological explanations for the ways in which his two villages differ.

University of Illinois   LAWRENCE W. CRISSMAN
Urbana, U.S.A.

Robert S. Ellwood, *The Feast of Kingship: Accession Ceremonies in Ancient Japan.* Tokyo, Sophia University Press, 1973, pp. viii, 175, $ 10.00.

The relation of the imperial institution to Shinto remains a relatively uncharted field in Western scholarship, with few publications. Ellwood's book, with its thorough research of Japanese materials, is the most systematic investigation of the religious dimension of the ancient imperial institution, and for this all Western readers are indebted to him.

Ellwood's book is actually three works in one: 1) a comparative overview of ritual kingship in five cultures (Egyptian, Mesopotamian, Chinese, Polynesian, and Altaic); 2) a survey of the development of early Shinto as the background of the accession ceremonies; 3) an analysis of the ritual of the *Daijō-sai* (accession ceremonies) and its text in the tenth century *Engi-shiki*. Only a few general insights from these three areas may be mentioned in a brief review.

The comparative overview of ritual kingship reveals a general phenomenology: kingship is given by the gods, the death of a king brings chaos to the society, the power of the king is related to that of his ancestors, kingly power is concentrated in regalia, and sacrificial offerings accompany the accession. The

Japanese *Daijō-sai* reflects some of the same features, but also possesses its own distinctive characteristics, such as its special relationship to the traditional Japanese harvest festival.

The survey of the development of Shinto treats the complex origins and diverse character of Shinto. Tracing archaeological evidence and early writings, Ellwood counters the usual interpretation of Shinto as "nature-worship," with the thesis "that the fundamental thrust of Shinto, ancient and modern, is sociological" (p. 43). Also treated are a number of interpretive difficulties within early Shinto: the clan *kami*, the religious significance of ancestors, ancient shrines, mythical traditions, the role of shamanism, the solar goddess Amaterasu, and the harvest festival.

Analysis of the *Daijō-sai* focuses on the preparatory purification and the priestly families in charge of the rituals as well as the sacred fields (for growing the rice to be made into ritual sake), and the erection of ritual buildings, before discussing the ceremonies themselves. The ceremonies draw on the rich repertoire of ancient Shinto, ranging from rites of purification and invocation to symbols of fertility and hints of shamanism. Ellwood concludes that the *Daijō-sai* "is a miniaturization of the genius of the Shinto religion" that exemplifies a Shinto related to both nature and history." His study shows that the (Japanese) "imperial idea...is properly set into a sacramental, agricultural, and archaic setting" (p. 153).

One of the important contributions of this book is the concrete demonstration of the Japanese imperial institution in its initial setting, showing that it was not primarily an office of political power. Some of the interpretive framework for the discussion of these rituals deserves further documentation. For example, much of the argument hinges on the relationship between pre-agricultural and agricultural elements of the ritual. Ellwood sees a "critical transitional period" passing from a mythological to a historical worldview which seems to presuppose three major cultural stages: pre-agricultural, agricultural, and "historical." Because this framework tends to determine the characters of the *Daijō-sai*, should be further documented and discussed.

Western Michigan University   H. Byron Earhart
Kalamazoo, U.S.A.

Rhoda L. Goldstein, *Indian Women in Transition: A Bangalore Case Study.* Metuchen, N.J., The Scarecrow Press, Inc., 1972, pp. 172, $ 5.00.

During recent years, attitudes in many countries toward field research conducted by Americans have become quite negative. This is particularly true in India. Thus, the work conducted by Dr. Rhoda L. Goldstein as a Fulbright Research Scholar at Bangalore University in 1966–1967 takes on additional value precisely because research of this kind would seem to be impossible in the foreseeable future.

The research, conducted under the guidance of the Sociology Department of Bangalore University, utilized a 20% sample of woman graduates of the class of 1965. With 99 in the sample, 97 questionnaires were completed. The questionnaire, which is both complete and well-designed, concentrates on attitudes toward marriage and employment among this group which is pre-dominantly middle class and Hindu. Moslems and Christians provided 9% and 15% respectively. The median age of the respondents was 22.

The interview procedure shows considerable adaptation to the Indian social milieu. It is this attention to the sensitivities of the interviewees which is most worthy of praise and which contributes in large part to the successful aquisition of information. The research assistants included two Brahmin and one Christian who shared both the educational and social background of the young graduates. Interviews in the home were conducted within the family situation, with other members of the family present. For the most part, the team was welcomed as honor guests. Frankness and sincerity seems to have prevailed on the part of both the young graduates and their relatives in an-swering all questions.

One of the major impressions from the survey was of the time-filling nature of advanced education. With marriage taking place at a later age (early twenties) than was formerly true in India, college work is an excellent way of spending the intervening years after graduation from secondary school. Educa-tion is considered an advantage to marital chances (only 8% feel that it is a hindrance). In addition to providing a better selection of potential husbands for the father whose primary duty it is to arrange the marriage contract, educa-tion of the woman is supposed to provide her with better ability to "adjust" to the circumstances of married life and the implications of living in a different joint family. The need to keep busy at something (such as education) lest one get into trouble reflects a continuation of traditional attitudes toward feminine sexuality.

Dr. Goldstein's study demonstrates that the educated woman in Bangalore still thinks and acts within traditionally accepted patterns. The single woman who has accepted employment still lives with the family and, for the most part, contributes her salary to the family for joint administration. While 35 out of the group can accept the idea of a career without marriage as life-fulfilling, this viewpoint is still within the context of chaperonage and protection.

Direct quotations from many of the interviewees add reality to the statisti-cal study. One feels a sense of compassion for some of the respondents in their explanations of attempts to find "suitable" employment.

One could wish that the median age of the sample had been slightly older. It is the feeling of this reviewer that interviewing the class of 1965 which had been graduated for less than two years inevitably meant a kind of immaturity and nostalgia for the college experience on the part of many respondents. The nature of the transition itself is therefore somewhat different from what one might anticipate of those who had been away from college for some years.

While the sample is small, the analysis is very thorough. Because of this, because of the combination of charts, commentary, and quotation, Dr. Gold-stein's study should be read by those interested in learning more of the attitudes of middle class women of India, one of the few countries in the world to promote a woman to the rank of Prime Minister.

University of Hawaii
Honolulu, U.S.A.

Mary F. Gray

N. H. N. Graburn and B. S. Strong, *Circumpolar Peoples: an Anthropological perspective.* Pacific Palisades, Goodyear Publishing, 1973, pp. 236, No price given.

This is a very good textbook on a neglected subject. The format is a selective survey with varying emphases. Nine Arctic and Sub-Arctic societies are concisely examined: the Samek or Lapps, the Yakuts, Evenks (Northern Tungus), Kutchin, Naskapi, Aleuts, and Eskimos. (I have followed the authors in applying the -s plural sign in some cases and not in others.) These chapters do not follow a repetitious outline. Thus, the Samek chapter stresses regional variety and intercultural relations; that on the Yakuts, "political-military organization"; for the Northern Evenks, shamanism and world-view are described; for the Chukchi, bilateral social organization; and so on.

Besides the introduction, there are three generalizing chapters. Throughout, a large amount of heterogeneous information has been skillfully reduced to lucid and reasoned summary.

The work is entitled *Circumpolar Peoples*, not *Circumpolar Culture*. There is little on the region as a culture area – $1\frac{1}{2}$ pages on "common cultural characteristics," although in addition a number of inter-ethnic comparisons are made. There has been a good deal of discussion, especially in the Scandinavian literature, of common or widespread aspects of northern cultures. Some reflection of this discussion would have been relevant.

The annotated bibliographies should be very helpful to undergraduate students. There is little evidence that the authors have consulted non-English sources; the result is, for some areas, a certain thinness; e.g., in dealing with modern Soviet Asia. For example, I do not recall any mention, beyond a single reference, of fictional, poetic, folkloristic, and historical literature by Siberian authors of aboriginal and Russian descent. Though much remains untranslated as yet, its existence is a significant fact.

More serious is the reliance, for classification of languages in northern Soviet Asia, upon "the listings of Levin and Potapov, 1965." Even in 1956, when *Narody Sibiri*, edited by Levin and Potapov, was published in Russian, the validity of a Ural-Altaic language family was questioned. In *YAzyki Narodov SSSR*, volumes II and II (1966), Uralic and Altaic are regarded as quite separate at the family Level; Glyn Lewis's *Multilingualism in the Soviet Union* (1972) summarizes the situation. Graburn and Strong's list of "linguistic families" for the region is misleading in several respects, especially in that the "families" listed are not comparable in time-depth and level of generality.

Outstandingly good, on the other hand, are the succinct discussions of Arctic bilateralism, Eskimo social structure, and recent Samish and Greenlandic social history.

By the way, it seems to this reader that the case for the use of "Inuit" instead of "Eskimo" is identical to that in favour of "Samek" instead of "Lapp". The authors have here missed a change to lead the way in anthropological literature.

A few minor errors are mentioned in hope that they can be corrected in the subsequent editions which the book merits. There are misprints in the names Hallowell (p. 9), Shirokogoroff (p. 56), Strachan Jones (p. 107), and Mailhot (p. 108). June Helm has not published "with June MacNeish" (p. 215), since the two names refer to the same person. I do not believe that the late Duncan Strong did fieldwork in Alaska, as stated in p. 74, footnote.

Physically, this paperback is well produced, with legible type, clear and attractive maps, and sensible charts.

McMaster University   RICHARD SLOBODIN
Hamilton, Canada

John A. Harrison (ed.), *South and Southeast Asia. Volume 3 of the Association of Asian Studies' Thirtieth Anniversary Commemorative Series*. Tucson, The University of Arizona Press, 1972, pp. 246, $ 3.75.

This selection of fifteen "pathbreaker" articles culled from the thirty year record of the *Far Eastern Quarterly* and its successor *Journal of Asian Studies* highlight the growing skills of scholarship in the South and Southeast Asian studies. The editors apparently sought representation by discipline, for the contributions originate in at least ten different fields. All, however, reflect the hallmarks and *raison d'etre* of area studies: at least some degree of multidisciplinary synthesis and considerable linguistic expertise.

Freedman and Toply, anthropologists, compare Chinese religious organization in Singapore with that in the villages of the mainland and find both a (temporary?) disjuncture between religious and political organization and an end to the previous close relationship between local shrine and its surrounding neighborhood. Barrier examines the interaction between the Arya Samaj religious reform organization and the Indian National Congress in the Punjab around 1900. Staal demonstrates the precision of linguistic analysis as a method of studying cultural diffusion between the great and little traditions in India.

A few of the articles are more narrow in disciplinary scope but reflect another of the characteristics of area studies. They require particularly deep immersion in the culture of the region. They include Brohm's dissection of the Buddhist overlay on the animist religions of Burma; Pelzer's illustration of man's despoliation of the southeast Asian countryside; Potter's revision of the standard classification of Hindu philosophical systems; and Dimock's locating Tagore in the tradition of Bengal's Baul poets. The three pieces by Indian scholars, as might be expected, also exhibit intimate familiarity with local culture and, in addition, employ the analytic tools of Western social science to reveal it in a new light: Srinivas depicts Sanskritization and Westernization as alternative processes of upward mobility in the caste system; Kothari and Maru exhibit the mutual modifications in both traditional caste forms and modern political techniques as caste becomes a recruiting ground for political mobilization; and, in the most touching piece in the collection, the late Irwate Karve evokes the shared joys and tribulations which enfold diverse people, at least temporarily, as they make a pilgrimage in Maharashtra.

Despite the marked sophistication and erudition of each of the articles individually, the collection as a whole remains a non-book. Scholars with the specialization and interest to read the articles will probably already have done so in the original journal, especially since it is the organ of the large and prestigious Association of Asian Studies. Those without the requisite training and interest will probably find the book over their heads. As a "review of the best in American scholarship on South and Southeast Asia over the past thirty years" (p. ix), the volume sorely lacks an introduction which would place these articles into the context of the major developments in recent scholarship. The sampling alone, without this context, seems uninstructive. It has none of the thematic cohesion of the better surveys in specific problems such as Crane, ed., *Regions and Regionalism in South Asian Studies*, Frykenberg, ed., *Land Control and Social Structure in Indian History*, and Singer and Cohn, eds., *Structure and Change in Indian Society*. Those topically oriented collections have joined together past questions, current resolutions, contemporary research methods, and lines of inquiry for the future. Since the present volume has no such theme, it has greater need of a comprehensive introduction to their scholarly context. The three page introduction by Geertz barely scratches the surface. It provides only a small fraction of the coverage necessary to transform a collection of major, but rather unrelated articles, into a useful record of the immense progress of American research in the past generation.

Temple University   HOWARD SPODEK
Philadelphia, U.S.A.

Douglas L. Wheeler and René Pélissier, *Angola*. New York, Praeger, 1971, $ 11.00, pp. ix, 296.

This volume on Angola is part of the Praeger series designed to present an overview of individual African countries. As such, one can justly ask how it serves the purposes of two audiences: the student who wishes an introduction to the particular country, and the specialist who seeks a creative synthesis. This particular volume in the series has the additional problem that it is really two books: one on Angola up to 1960 by Douglas Wheeler, and one on Angola since 1960 by René Pélissier.

As an introductory overview of the period up to 1960, the book has no rival in any language. It is competent, clear, informative. As an overview of the period since 1960, it has many rivals, most notably and most recently the book by Basil Davidson. Pélissier's section suffers by comparison. Davidson's book may be said to have the biases of an engaged partisan but it is alive with the flavor of a war of national liberation. Pélissier's account has the sterility of an outsider who seeks to put distance between himself and the situation he describes. Particularly as an introduction, this is unfortunate.

And for the scholars? Here too one must treat Wheeler and Pélissier separately. Pélissier does not add very much to what is already known. To be fair, he does not pretend to do this, Pélissier having envisaged his role as speaking primarily to the first audience. This is not true however of Wheeler. Wheeler happens to have an unpublished doctoral dissertation on Angola in the period between 1836–1891. He therefore took the occasion of this book to give us a short version of this thesis in chapter 3. He thereby has made a very useful contribution to the scholar who might otherwise have never seen this important material.

What story does Wheeler tell in chapter 3? In his words, it is the story of the expansion of a "barren sovereignty". To my mind, it is really the story of the impact of British world hegemony on Portuguese colonial policies. Wheeler sums up the basic dilemma quite well:

> Britain's policy on Portuguese expansion north of Luanda presented a paradox. To Portugal, the ending of the slave trade could not be achieved without extension of sovereignty, but this was anathema to Britain, since Portuguese expansion (and the accompanying customs duties) would inevitably curtail the freedom of trade enjoyed by British merchants. (pp. 52–54)

Britain won out, here as elsewhere, in the beginning, because British opposition plus African resistance was more than a weak European country like Portugal could overcome: "As of 1861, African traders and warriors rather than the Portuguese controlled most of the interior of Angola, and Portugal was as yet impotent to change the situation" (p. 56).

But then came the Scramble, not surely in any way the result of Portugal's increased strength, but a sign of the beginning of Britain's decline. "Portugal attempted to make up for lost centuries" (p. 61). Expansion became possible, in Angola and elsewhere. Even so, "Many Portuguese considered it little less than a modern-day miracle that Portugal retained vast Angola" (p. 62). Not a miracle at all; just a deal. But what a difference it would have made for the MPLA if the western border of Zambia lay at the edge of the more populated and more wooded areas of Angola.

There is much else to be found in this chapter and the subsequent ones of great interest: the decline of Creole culture which accompanied the decline of the African commercial bourgeosie in the late 19th century; the ups and downs of Boer-Portuguese relations; proto-nationalism of the *assimilados* of Luanda in the 19th century; an intelligently acerbic view of Portuguese colonial policy under the republic ("forced labour...was as bad as if not worse than under the ailing Bragança monarchy. [p. 110]"); the misplaced African faith in the European left (prior to Sqlazar). All of this analysis is not focussed as clearly as I would have liked it to be: on the steady process of the incorporation of ever more land, labor, and capital into the capitalist world-market, a process which has been accelerating since the Second World War, again in Angola as elsewhere. But the reader can intrude his theoretical framework to flesh out the data presented, here as elsewhere.

McGill University   Immanuel Wallerstein
Montreal, Canada

S. O. Anozie (ed.), *Language Systems in Africa. The Conch*, Vol. 4, No. 2, Sept. 1972. Published as a special issue, 1973, pp. 114, $ 8.75.

The six papers in *Language Systems in Africa*, as Sunday O. Anozie notes in his introductory remarks, hardly comprise an integrated collection. Yet they represent those two aspects of language investigation that are of constant concern to us: the structure of language as a reflection of the human mind and its place in the workings of society. The emphasis here is clearly on the second:

the social significance of language in written, spoken and – of special importance in Africa – surrogate forms.

Anozie's own spirited paper is a continuation from the previous *Conch* of his thinking on structurology, an approach to African poetics. In this part he examines the contribution that generative transformational linguistic theory might make to its development. The primary difficulty here is that the theory of syntactic structure, exemplified in some detail by the brief examination of a grammar of Igbo, is inherently too limited to provide a framework for poetics. Questions of artistic language creation, literary translation, and the psychology of cognitive systems, simply cannot be met by the theory. It is therefore no surprise that Anozie finds that his attempts to apply it to African literature do not take him far.

J. H. Kwaben Nketia's "Surrogate Languages of Africa" is a valuable overview of the field, well worth reprinting here. He describes the sorts of messages played on the "talking drums", their message forms, their correspondence to the spoken language, and their expressive and referential functions. He draws widely from the literature and from his experience among the Akan to give a picture of the range of phenomena associated with the surrogate systems, rather than a strictly comparative or a comprehensive analysis for one people.

In his chapter, Lloyd W. Brown takes on Marshall McLuhan, that most modern of observers, to drub him for the oldest of Western offenses with respect to Africa – the perpetuation of old untruths and the construction of new ones. Drawing support from Achebe, Fanon, and Senghor, he attacks McLuhan's *Understanding Media* for its breezy assertions about African social organization, the choice of the African as the symbol of sinister Western flaws, and – here is the relevant concern for language – the insistence on literacy as the unique defining characteristic of civilization. Except to lend graceful passion to his position, the support is unnecessary; McLuhan is clearly irresponsible.

The challenge of being responsible in linguistic research is examined by Ben G. Blount in his paper on language study in Africa from an anthropological perspective. In particular, he points out that language use may well influence the methods and outcomes of research. In this respect he is not only self-conscious about techniques, but places them in the context of a principal concern of current language study, that is, language behavior as a shaper and reflection of social relations. B.I.C. Ijomah's paper, in fact, is a valiant but uneven attempt to lay out the theoretical foundations for the study of speaking. The bulk of the paper is given to an analysis of language functions in terms of Parsonian action models. Although enlivened by examples from African experience, the exposition is stunted in the limits of these few pages.

Edgar C. Polomé's contribution exemplifies the sorts of studies now under way to examine the larger socio-political context of the face-to-face behavior that is of interest to Ijomah and Blount. In an admirably thorough manner, he describes the language situations in Zaire and Tanzania, presenting each country's language policy, supporting institutions, and people's receptivity to them, reminding us again of the richness of Africa as a field for the study of language in human affairs.

McGill University   ROSE-MARIE WEBER
Montrial, Canada

E. Hermassi, *Leadership and National Development in North Africa: A Comparative Study.* Berkeley, University of California Press, 1972, pp. 241, plates, $ 8.50.

This book represents a case study of change in, and development of, the three Maghribi states of Morocco, Algeria and Tunisia, which led to their emergence as national states in the second half of the twentieth century.

In his study of this change, Dr. Hermassi, unlike similar studies by Western scholars on the developing countries of the Third World, who try to adjust their case studies to European or Western patterns of "Modernization", Dr. Hermassi develops a process of his own, a process which springs from Maghribi local circumstances. He sees this evolution going through the problematic passages of national integration, institutional competence, economic development and distributive justice. All these pose formidable difficulties for the state elite or leadership which had to shoulder the responsibilities of the expected transformation of their societies into modern national states.

The choice of the Maghrib as a case study by the author is, indeed, very opportune because. "In analyzing a particular society, a social scientist enjoys an advantage if he knows the society intimately from having lived in it, for he can then sense the motives and feelings of the members." Dr. Hermassi is the product of the same Maghribi society which he analyzes in this book. Thus, unlike other sociologists who discard the importance of historical formative factors in the evolution of the modern national states, Dr. Hermassi finds, with good reason, that this is not so with the Maghrib. He believes that, in order to comprehend current social problems, one must study their origins in the society's past history (p. 157). No wonder, therefore, that he devoted the first ninety pages of his study to a discussion of the history and traditions of the Maghribi societies. He called upon Ibn Khaldun, the well known fourteenth century Tunisian sociologist, historian and philosopher for inspiration and guidance in matters relating to the nature of the structure of societies in general and the Maghribi society in particular (pp. 15–21). However, historical background only paves the way for the implementation of the author's ideas on what brought about the effected change in the Maghribi society, and how that society was transformed from medieval tribalism into modern nationhood. This change was the result of the part played by the elite in the developmental processes. This role of the Maghribi elite covers more than a half of the book. Details of political, economic and social evolution are subjected to the author's critical scrutiny.

Though Dr. Hermassi tends to convey to his reader a persuasion of the cohesiveness of the three Maghribi societies by emphasizing certain similarities common to all of them such as the tribal structure and religion, he could not discard other factors of dissimilarity. Hence, with the departure of the French colonial rule from North Africa, as a result of the Maghribi struggle for independence, these latter factors led finally to the establishment of three separate national states in the region instead of one. The reader was led to believe a united Maghribi state would be the natural replacement of the colonial rule, a fact that did not materialize. The author tends to blame the Maghribi leadership, as a whole, for being unable to produce that unity. He apparently seems to have forgotten the vast differences among the elites of the three political systems, in those three parts of North Africa, which managed, independently, to throw off the colonial yoke. For he himself tells us that "There have been three essential, competing definitions of political reality in every Maghribi society". The first orientation he calls scriptualism (Islamic heritage), the second liberal modernization and the third mobilization (pp. 93–99). Thus, the elite in each Maghribi society were of such diverse, if not even antagonistic beliefs, which could hardly help in establishing a united Maghribi state. Morocco, the author goes on to tell us later in the book (p. 143), inherited even a marginal elite, while Algeria a heterogeneous elite, and Tunisia a homogeneous one.

Throughout his analytical discussions of the role played by the Maghribi elite in achieving their objectives of the establishment of the three modern states of Morocco, Algeria and Tunisia, Dr. Hermassi was clearly focussing on the local structure, tribal and urban, of Maghribi society. He did not try to draw any comparisons with other Arab Middle Eastern states. Such comparisons could have helped him appreciate the shortcomings of the Maghribi elite who did not live up to his expectations in building a united Maghrib. For the medieval and colonial heritage, both in North Africa and the other Arab countries, is, more or less, similar. He, perhaps, avoided making these comparisons because of limitations imposed by the nature of his study. Yet by comparing the North African societies in the manner Dr. Hermassi presents in his scholarly work, the reviewer is convinced that "the Maghrib has become more intelligible". The reviewer shares, with the author, the hopes that the near future will see an integrated and united Maghrib. The three Maghribi states certainly complement one another, not only in the geographical lay out, but also in cultural tradition as well. Dr. Hermassi should be congratulated on producing this cohesive and solid piece of academic research.

McGill University   A. M. Abu-Hakima
Montreal, Canada

Tung Wei (ed.), *Communist China: A System-Functional Reader.* Columbus, Ohio, Charles E. Merrill Pub. Co., 1972, pp. 470, $ 5.95.

Despite the recent widespread and intense interest in the Chinese Communist political system there are few books which deal with this subject in a comprehensive manner. Most scholars in the field have more specialized interest or emphasize a methodology which does not lend itself to a general assessment of China's government and politics. In addition, many students of China feel that they lack reliable data to write a broad synthesis of recent Chinese politics.

Wei's objective is to fill this gap. He organizes this book according to the system-functional approach: China's political system is analyzed on the basis of how the system is organized and how it works. This approach is common in analyzing other political systems; but it has seldom been applied to China. It assumes that China can be studied like any other political system and sufficient data are available to do this.

Wei draws on a variety of sources from several disciplines: history, psychology, sociology, economics, as well as political science. This broad analysis gives the reader a clear idea of what politics means in China where almost all behavior has political significance. Yet this approach is not exclusively for the scholar; Wei points out that this book is designed for the intelligent layman.

Wei separates this work into five sections: (1) History, Geography and Political Myth, (2) Social Structure and Political Socialization, (3) Elites, Groups, Political Participation and Communication, (4) Political Integration, Political Structure, and the Allocation Process, and (5) External Environment and the Problems of Capability and Stability. Each plays a special role in providing the system-functional analysis that the editor seeks.

In Section 1 Wei selects writings which provide a brief historical and demographic background; then two Chinese Communist writings are inserted – Mao and Lin Piao – after which two scholars assess the importance of the cult of Mao and the problem of authority in China. This section affords the reader a background to contemporary problems which are in large measure a carry-over from China's historical political system.

Section 2 contains an analysis of China's social structure in terms of problems which the Communists inherited, and their attempts to deal with Chinese society in political terms. This is done under the rubric of political socialization. Interpersonal relations and the family are examined first; then the methods the regime used to enhance political control while centralizing political power are assessed.

Section 3 delineates the structure of elites in China and examines the problems of political participation and communications. Several different kinds of elites are defined; and the "Red versus Expert" problem is a central theme in looking at both the composition of elites and how they function.

In Section 4 a more in-depth look – especially employing interdisciplinary tools – is used to elucidate how the political process actually works. The focus is on four facets of political control: the process of eliminating disruptive elements, political indoctrination, the Chinese Communist political machine, and the reallocation of values.

Section 5 affords an analysis of the Chinese state in its external environment. Here Wei endeavors to combine the cultural model, the national interest model, and the political ideology model to assess China's foreign policy capabilities and goals and problems.

Utilizing the structural-functional approach, Wei analyzes Chinese politics in the broad sense. For example, the reader can view China in the context of the following comparative models of study: traditional-transitional development, open-closed society, orthodox-revisionist ideology. The reader can also draw comparisons with the Republic of China on Taiwan.

Wei has collected a large number of sources. And, since approximately half of the selections were written after 1965, this book presents an up-to-date appraisal of the Chinese political system – including changes during and after the Cultural Revolution. Also the editor supplies an introduction to each section with comments on methodology and theory enabling the reader to connect various aspects of politics broadly defined.

Communist China: A System-Functional Reader would make an excellent textbook for a course on Chinese government. It is also recommended to both the scholar and layman with an interest in the politics of China.

University of Maryland   JOHN F. COPPER
Far-East Division
San Francisco, U.S.A.

W. Norman Brown, *The United States and India, Pakistan, Bangladesh.* Cambridge, Harvard University Press, 1973, pp. 462, $ 16.00.

W. Norman Brown, the leading Indic scholar and authority on South Asia in the United States, has produced a third, revised edition of his well-known *The United States and India and Pakistan.* The present edition is not only brought up to date but also contains considerable material on the crisis that led to the creation of Bangladesh. In the ten years that elapsed between the second and third editions, major changes took place in South Asia and these are fully treated in the present version.

The volume under review is, if anything, more comprehensive, perhaps more exhaustive, than the previous editions. The first five chapters are concerned largely with the sub-continent prior to 1947, while the remaining twelve chapters are primarily devoted to developments in South Asia since 1947. The treatment, as in previous editions, is essentially topical rather than chronological. Thus, there is a chapter on "the Quarrel over Kashmir", on "Social Progress and Problems" and on "Foreign Relations". Each of these provides detailed information on its subject matter for the most recent three decades.

Though the presentation borders, at times, on the encyclopedic, and is frequently descriptive in character, the book is marked by intimate knowledge, sympathetic understanding, and passages of brilliance.

In my judgment Chapter 7 "Hindu-Muslim Communalism", which is excellent, should logically have appeared just before Chapter 6 "The Winning of Independence", because many of the developments Dr. Brown reports in the sixth chapter rest upon or were substantially influenced by communal issues which he has so well covered in his seventh chapter. The rest of the book, however, seems to me to have been placed in the most useful logical sequence.

While granting that the period since Independence is the more important to undergraduate courses in this country, and therefore merits the space accorded to it by the author, I must record my own feeling that Dr. Brown's great abilities as a scholar would have been even more fully deployed if at least half of the volume had focussed upon the epoch prior to 1947. This is not a quantitative argument, but rather an assessment of the even more permanent contribution Dr. Brown would have made had he placed greater emphasis on aspects of and trends in South Asian history, culture and tradition, as background to what has transpired in the last 30 years.

Thus, for example, the exhaustive chapter on "Political Parties" gives the reader a relatively brief but thorough summary of every political party in India, Pakistan and Bangladesh (such as one would find in a political science textbook on comparative political parties) as well as detailed examination of each election which has taken place, but the volume says less than it might have about the origins of the political party system and the ways in which the party system works, with special reference to historical, cultural factors. There is also a detailed account of the Indian constitution and its properties, as well as the vacillation in constitution making in Pakistan, with little evaluation of how the system works in practice. There is, for instance, a discussion of a Martial Law Regulation of 1959 regarding land reform (p. 337) which tells the reader what the Martial Law Regulation said but does not evaluate the ways in which or the extent to which the Regulation was implemented in practice. An account of the factors in Pakistani society which militated against any meaningful implementation of the 1959 Regulation would have given the reader perspective and background in terms of which the efficacy of the Act could have been judged.

Because of the topical organization of the volume it can readily be used in different kinds of undergraduate courses on South Asia. Chapters on various topics can easily be assigned by the instructor in terms of his or her own course syllabus. That imparts to an exhaustive study, such as this, a flexibility for classroom use that is wholly commendable. One would have to make extracts from a dozen different volumes to pull together for a course the same range of materials and data Dr. Brown has so carefully incorporated into his volume.

He has also provided several very useful statistical summaries in an Appendix and a lengthy and valuable bibliographical essay which is organized by subject matter.

We are all deeply in debt to Professor Brown for an authoritative work that will stand us in good stead for another decade.

Syracuse University   ROBERT I. CRANE
Syracuse, U.S.A.

James Ngugi (Ngugi Wa Thiong'O), *Homecoming. Essayson African and Caribbean Literature, Culture and Politics*. New York, Lawrence Hill and Co., 1973, pp. 155.
Gerald Moore, *Wole Soyinka. Modern African Writers*. New York, Africana Publishing Corp., 1972, pp. 114.

Except for Ezekiel Mphahlele (*The African Image* [1962]; *Voices in The Whirlwind* [1973] and Leopold Senghor *Liberté I: Négritude et Humanisme* [1964]), the presence of the African creative writer in the field of literary theory and criticism has not manifested itself in book-length essays, bearing the writer's perspective in comprehensive form. A growing tradition of criticism has been (and is still) produced by academic critics, but the student of African literature interested in hearing the voice of the actual creators reflecting on their craft and attendant concerns has had to rely on the occasional article or lecture published in a learned journal or assembled in some collective form due to the resourcefulness of a Per Wastberg, Christopher Heywood or G. D. Killam. In any case, whether as a sequel of cultural colonialism or as a sign of scholarly activities that should not be restrained by one form of nationalism or another, much of the scholarship and research in African literature has been (and is) carried out by non-Africans. Against this background, Ngugi Wa Thiong'O's *Homecoming* emerges as a meangingful event: it is, hopefully, a signal that a necessary correction is in progress, the African writer is coming home and staking claims for domains he is in a privileged position to articulate.

But Ngugi's book is important also in that his is the first book of essays by an Anglophone African writer that calls for an understanding of the Black experience relating Africa to the West Indies and, implicitly, to the U.S. Central to Ngugi's unitary vision is a call for total decolonization that is to substitute a socialist order responsive to Black people's history and needs for the capitalist framework, the legacy of colonialism that can only maintain Africa and the Third World in a state of subservience belying *de jure* political independence. The imperative of total liberation runs through essays dealing with such Fanonian mainstays as National Culture, Violence and Culture, or analyses of individual African and West Indian qriters such as Soyinka, Achebe, Lamming, Selvon and others who have all dramatized the plight of individuals alienated and fragmented because of an historical condition over which they seem to be powerless. Ngugi's design is undoubtedly reminiscent of the philosophy of Négritude at its best. But since Ngugi belongs to the generation that follows Senghor's, filial aggressiveness translates itself in Soyinka's understanding of Négritude in the image of a tiger who pounces not in some hypothetical Parisian living room but in the back alleys, the avenues and forest paths trod by black feet. One finds echoes of Black American rhetoric as well, the kind which at present calls for a Black Aesthetic linking Black writers of the world, but which in denying the White critic the freedom of speech or thought in the matter dissociates itself from the humanism of Négritude.

Homecoming is a seminal effort, it is a breakthrough in terms of insight and articulation of premises towards the definition of the Black experience in a truly decolonized world. Much of the theoretical orientation is indebted to Frantz Fanon; but coming from an important African writer living and working in Kenya, the book augurs of possibilities whose realization can only be welcome. One could criticize, on the other hand, the randomness of the subject matter (the essays were written and published during the Sixties for various audiences), the unilinear reading of the West Indian material, or one could even be so malicious as to suggest that in not specifying the kind of socialist order anticipated Ngugi functions within a vague Marxist frame of reference which cannot be distinguished from the Capitalist alternative if the purpose is to rid Africa and the Third World of Western imperialist models. However, one cannot ask more of a writer than generosity of vision and eloquence to sustain it. Ngugi has both.

Gerald Moore's *Wole Soyinka* is the first in a series of monographs on modern African writers designed to bring to students and scholars in African literature information, suggested approaches and other helpful material for a proper evaluation of the works of important writers. The series aims at being resource oriented. Judging from Moore's initial efforts, the project, of which Moore is the General Editor, starts on a note of excellence. Soyinka's total output up to 1969 (poetry, drama and fiction) is reviewed in the detailed, though here conventional, form of textual explication (plot, summary, etc) and in juxtaposition with the author's life. The text is well presented, illustrated appropriately with scenes from the plays, and an index is supplied. There is little one can disagree with; the book is not designed to elicit critical debate. One could quibble about a certain slant typical of the tradition of scholarship

Moore is heir to: the insistence placed on Soyinka's training at the Royal Court Theatre, in London; his tutelage under G. Wilson Knight at Leeds University; and a general *je ne sais quoi* that makes at times for the uneasy feeling that one is being taken on a tour by a sleek guide, so disturbingly efficient as to substitute his oracular skills for the landscape. Shades of Prospero and Caliban!

Essentially, though, Moore's book is good, solid spadework which, interestingly enough, strikes a nice balance with Ngugi's *Homecoming*. Perhaps in that balance lies an answer to the debate regarding the proper interpreters of African literature and culture: the vision and its articulation can but be the African writer's, the scholarship concerned with supplying the tools for analyzing the vision is for all to share.

McGill University   MAX DORSINVILLE
Montreal, Canada

Jeremy Boissevain and J. Clyde Mitchell (eds.), *Network Analysis: Studies in Human Interaction*. The Hague, Mouton and Company, 1973, pp. 271, fl 30.25.

Add to the growing bibiliography of social network literature a collection of articles further demonstrating the diversity of research situations in which the method may be applied. Social networks is of course that nearly sociometric methodology pioneered by John A. Barnes' study of Bremnes in the early 1950's ("Class and Committees in a Norwegian Island Parish" *Human Relations*, VII: 39–58) which many thought would deliver social science analysis from the static confines of structural functionalism. But social network is in fact a methodology rather than a theoretical replacement (it took us a while until this was recognized) and a thoroughly demanding methodology (in terms of time and effort) at that. Nevertheless it became a popular field orientation through the 1960's and it seems that everyone nearly everywhere was employing it – or thought or said they were. Social networks, as a body of research, became confused. Like the centipede, the method had grown so many legs in preparing for its leap from structural functionalism that once it became aware of all of them it didn't seem possible that they could all be made to work together. Researchers began to come together to discuss the method and the Boissevain/ Mitchell collection is the product of one of the annually organized symposia of the Africa Studiecentrum at Leiden (1969) which focussed upon the critical topic of the theoretical aspects of the network approach with special reference to research in Africa. It is, however, a book much more concerned with the application of social network methodology, than with the geographical area in which it is applied.

It should be remembered that one of the editors, J. Clyde Mitchell, had presented a somewhat similar collection of network research, published in 1969 (*Social Networks in Urban Situations*: Manchester University Press). A fair question to ask would seem to be to what extent does the present volume represent an advance over the earlier one. (While the Leiden conference was held the same year that the Mitchell book was published, there were four years of development between actual publication dates.) Progress could be measured here as some drawing up of the loose methodological and conceptual strings of social networks. It is somewhat dishearting although not altogether surprising to read in this regard the editors' comments that many of their contributors are still working with "rough and ready methods which may be refined or discarded" (Boissevain, ix), and that "network analysis is still in its infancy" (Mitchell, 34). It is true that a bare twenty years have passed since the inception of the method. It is also true that the method's conceptual requirements are likely to drive a researcher to the brink of his or her capacity for coherent abstraction, and that the tracing out and analysis of interpersonal linkages in amorphous non-corporate social "bodies" in shifting arenas of activity is likely the most ambitious sort of inquiry for a social scientist. Taken together these factors indicate that this is an approach the details of which may take some time to be worked out. Yet one may begin to feel a bit anxious at this juncture about the current stage of development and begin to anticipate growing numbers of inquiries from critics as to the nature of the emperor's clothes. Bruce Kapferer, a contributor to the volume and himself one of the most capable practitioners of the art of network analysis, writes quite frankly that "The high expectations which have been advanced concerning the utility of the concept "social network" have largely not been realized even allowing for the recent introduction of the concept into sociological and anthropolocial usage" (83). But this is not the theme or tone of the book, and rather than a sense of urgency there is still that general sense of housecleaning through operationalization, and experimentation, that characterized the 1969 Mitchell collection. And, perhaps, this is the way for science to proceed in going about its business.

However, as it stands, the Boissevain/Mitchell book is not a replacement for the earlier collection treating the same general topics. Surely, anyone familiar with social networks will recognize the importance of Kepferer's piece where Elizabeth Botts' findings are reconsidered outside the structural functional framework which was implicit in her analysis. Mitchell makes an important clarification by indicating that the conceptual dichotomy between networks and corporate groups is a false one and that we may merely deal at different levels of abstraction by referring to one or the other. There is as always among network writers that self conscious attempt to tighten up the process of analysis and the conceptual definitions in all of the contributions. But the collection is in sum a catalogue of the possibilities and issues of the network approach; this and the earlier Mitchell collection together comprise a bigger, but not complete catalogue; and the big job of social networks remains to be done. The definitive statement remains to be made and any number of collections that leave the reader to his or her own devices as to how to make sense of it all can't do this nor can they really be faulted for failing to do it. At this stage a different format is required.

While the suggestion may seem to blow the approach out of all proportion in terms of its present importance in social science research, I would propose that there is a need for dialogue in the growing sub-field of social networks, and that movement which depends on the dialectics of exchange which in turn depends on the slow process of publication, critique, and reformulation is inadequate to serve the need for coherence in such a rapidly growing area. It seems that little less than a regularized interdisciplinary conference and periodically published forum providing a focus of attention for comparative purposes, such as a newsletter, will provide the integration required to advance what still seems a promising methodology. Certainly the present collection further indicates this promise, as well as the need.

University of Connecticut   WILLIAM G. FLANAGAN
Storrs, U.S.A.

John Gallagher, Gordon Johnson and Anil Seal (eds.), *Locality, Province, and Nation: Essays on Indian Politics, 1870–1940*. Cambridge, Cambridge University Press, 1973, pp. 325, $ 9.95.

This volume consists of a reprint of the entire issue from *Modern Asian Studies*, volume 7, part 3 (July 1973). Each of its seven essays, the writing of which was supported by the Social Science Research Council's Modern Indian History Project, is devoted to detailed examination of a single theme. Taken as a whole, these essays are of such quality as to warrant wide circulation and the critical review which comes with their reprinting. Even when findings are most questionable or most likely to provoke controversy, the combinations of new data and new insights are stimulating enough to provide fuel for much historiographic discussion and revision in the next generation. Even so, treatment of the subject is far from all encompassing. Rather, samples of locality and province and region are taken to throw light upon the imperial structure and the emerging consciousness of nationhood. Perhaps the strongest essay and certainly the one with greatest specificity is the remarkably stimulating examination of the development of political activities within agrarian society of Madras Presidency between 1880 and 1930. According to David Washbrook, ideological considerations played a much less significant role in the integrating of local societies than did their mutual sharing of government positions which provided opportunities for finding, establishing, and extending networks of patronage and influence. This thesis is most attractive; however before it can be accepted and before we can be convinced as to the growth of one (or two) Presidency-wide, broadly encompassing network of patronage, more careful documentation and systematic substantiation must be provided. The ultimate beauty of Washbrook's paradigm is that it seems to work. Next in degress of local specificity are the two essays on Bengal. Gordon Johnson deals with the period from 1904 to 1908 when Bengali political activities lay in the very vortex of the nationalist movement. John Gallagher, on the other hand, covers those years, from 1930 to 1939, when Bengal was in decline and the Bengal Congress could do nothing to restore the past splendor of India's former premier Presidency. Two more essays concern politics in North India, especially in the United Provinces. C. A. Bayly shows the relationships between financial interests, especially various Baniya banking groups in cities of North India, and leaders of various communal, revivalist, and nationalist political groups. His descriptions of *mahajan* families, particularly those of Allahabad, reveal how patronage of religious causes contributed to the developing fusion of political interests of upper India. Francis Robinson, focusing upon Muslim separatists, explains how the Muslim community in the United Provinces could join the Congress in efforts to bring about political changes. Finally, two essays have a more All-

India frame of reference. One of these maintains a much lower profile, sticks more closely to empirical data, and is altogether more tidy. Richard Gordon, tracing the differences which developed in 1919–20 between those who wanted to work within the new legislative councils and those who wished to boycott constitutional collaboration, makes a careful analysis of political tactics. Anil Seal, on the other hand, allows himself to be fettered neither by close attention to evidence nor by careful precision in concept usage. His essay, serving to introduce the whole volume, is disappointing. His arguments that political life in India occurred at many levels and that political leaders played many, often seemingly contradictory roles can hardly be considered fresh or profound. But it is especially in his use of concepts, such as "imperialism" and "nationalism", that his work is flawed.

But let me elaborate:

Concepts are instruments of analysis, tools for understanding. If these are never precisely defined, never given sharp cutting edges, or used with clear consistency, historical materials can be bludgeoned into shapeless incomprehensibility or, in other instances, never dented at all. Concepts are, after all, words – not about mere words nor merely about words. They are abstractions, words made by word-producing beings, not only to describe what such being do but how what they do is shaped by what they think – by ideas. What is done and how it is done is related to how the doers see themselves and their world; and this in turn depends upon the concepts (i.e. expressed in words) through which they look. Thus, telling us what he meant by "imperialism", especially if his usage were abnormal, and how what he meant might be manifested within phenomenological occurrences, so as to be identified, should have been an important part of Seal's work. By refusing to take this trouble, he not only presumes too much but his usages appear to suffer from so much inadvertent "slippage" in focus or inconsistency that his concept has meant different things in different contexts. Moreover, even beyond this, presuming that, as a social theorist, he saw his concepts within a larger structural world of concepts, his words ought to have defined and delimited his world, especially in important things which are human and social. Is his "imperialism" like a butterfly which can be caught in a net and examined as a specimen? If his "imperialism" is observable, should he not have given us some rudimentary presuppositions, some clues of what it *was*, what of its features could be *counted*, and where the phenomenon in question ends and features of another phenomenon begin. For a concept of such profound importance and ubiquity and complexity, surely more could be expected than some sort of vague feeling that what Seal saw was a huge, monolithic being, a breathing monster of organic composition having a single and rational nervous system by which self-serving, if not diabolical, impulses were transmitted. But where was that privately held set of political motivations held by certain groups of overzealous, super-patriotic British "nationalists"? When was imperialism as a personal aspiration transmitted into a systematically organized public ideology and by how many persons was imperialism held to be a "true faith"? When and how and in what form did imperialistic motivations become transmitted into "national" policy on behalf of the British realm? And by how many British and among which British subjects was this ideological virus most rampant? Did imperialist impulses originate in London or did they emanate from Calcutta and New Delhi? Were they greater in volume and potency in one period than in another? Even so, were occurrences of this phenomenon so different in one place from another or in one period from another as to alter the very essence of the phenomenon itself? In short, if many of Seal's statements were turned upon their heads or if what he declares about nationalist politics were also ascribed to imperial politics, most of his assertions would have been just as valid. Yet the undercutting edge of scorn for one and of apologetic concern for the other brings the quality of his entire methodology and scientific detachment into question. He should have stayed closer to shore, in the shallower waters where his feet could touch hard empirical data. Instead he went into waters too deep apparently presumed to theory beyond his depth.

University of Wisconsin   ROBERT ERIC FRYKENBERG
Madison, U.S.A.

Trygve Lötveit, *Chinese Communism 1931–1934: Experiences in Civil Government.* Copenhagen: Scandinavian Institute of Asian Studies, 1973, pp. 290, 30 Sw. Crs.

This book contributes to our understanding of the Chinese Communist Party during its Kiangsi Period. During this time severe political and ideological conflicts eventually led to Mao Tse-tung's removal from power. Victory for the Moscow-trained twenty-eight Bolsheviks resulted in the displacement of Mao's moderate policies by a more leftist line. It also meant the abandonment of Mao's guerrilla tactics against Kuomintang troops. The decision to adopt the more conventional strategy of fighting from fixed positions proved to be ill-conceived, and its failure forced the Communists to embark on the historic Long March. Only then, in the midst of the Long March, did Mao's position as leader become relatively secure.

Trygve Lötveit, research fellow at the Scandinavian Institute of Asian Studies in Copenhagen, sets two goals for his study. One is to describe the complex organizational network which developed in the Kiangsi soviet. The second is to trace the effects of the shift to the left in such areas as the administration of justice, land reform, and finances. Despite its title, Lötveit's book is limited to a study of the Central Soviet Area. This soviet, usually called the Kiangsi Soviet, encompassed territory along the Kiangsi-Fukien border and included some three million persons. Lötveit does not deal with the half dozen or so other Chinese Communist soviets which existed in the 1930's. Moreover, his analysis is largely based on the Ch'en Ch'eng Collection of documents on Chinese communism, gathered by General Ch'en during his military campaigns in the 1930's. (See Tien-wei Wu, "The Kiangsi Soviet Period: A Bibliographical Review on the Ch'en Ch'eng Collection," *The Journal of Asian Studies,* XII, 2 (February, 1970), pp. 385–412.) This is a valuable resource on the Kiangsi Soviet, but it has its limits. Lötveit frequently comes up against these limits, and he must either give speculative answers or no answers at all to some questions. Nonetheless, he does succeed in deepening our understanding of the Kiangsi Soviet.

Lötveit begins with a detailed account of the structure and function of soviets at the hsiang, district, county, and provincial levels. One is immediately struck by the efforts made to politicize a traditionally non-political peasant society. The mass-meetings, local organizations, and complex administrative apparatus could hardly fail to leave their imprint on the peasants of the Kiangsi Soviet. Those who were reluctant to participate were subjected to incessant, though usually polite, persuasion visits by local cadres. What is revealed, then, is the gradual evolution of mass-line politics and the techniques which insured mass involvement. As Lötveit points out, this elaborate mass-line machinery could be used both to listen to the people and to coerce them. However, his discussion of the nature of the central government leaves the impression of policies dictated from the top. The National Soviet Congress, selected on the basis of democractic centralism, rarely played an independent role. It was a rubber stamp for the Central Executive Committee, which in turn was controlled by the presidium. Suggestions from below may occasionally have found their way to the top. But there is little doubt that basic decisions were made by a very small group of leaders, and the elaborarate administrative network functioned mainly to implement these decisions.

As the composition of leaders altered, policy shifts occurred. With the decline of Mao Tse-tung's influence and the rise of the twenty-eight Bolsheviks, a distinctive drift to the left occurred. Lötveit's study sheds some new light on the consequences of this shift in the areas of justice, land policy, and finances. Initially, the judicial system had the dual objective of administering justice and educating the masses in Soviet law and ideology. Consequently, some care was taken to hold formal proceedings, open to the public, and to follow consistent legal principles. With the swing leftward revolutionary motives became more important than legal considerations. Punishing counter-revolutionaries took precedence over protecting the innocent from injustice. In the later period of the Kiangsi Soviet, dating approximately from February, 1934, there develops an atmosphere which Lötveit terms "red terror". It is epitomized by the Commissar of Justice who wrote, on March 1, 1934: "One ought not to hinder the interests of the revolution because of legal procedure." The result was widespread killing of reactionaries, with few legal constraints.

Land reform policies followed a zigzag course, but they too grew more revolutionary toward the end of the Kiangsi Period. Early policies of confiscation and land distribution were often characterized by an excess of zeal. This led to mistakes such as the confiscation of land from middle peasants and excessive harshness toward rich peasants. In an effort to avoid alienating possible allies a new and more cautious policy was enunciated in October, 1933. Under this program efforts were made to rectify previous injustices. However, some counter-revolutionaries took advantage of this new climate to wage a counter-offensive, and a March, 1934 order swung policy once again to the left. Spurred by growing military pressure from the Kuomintang, this policy resulted in greater expropriations of land and materials from reactionary classes and further killing of landlords.

Communist financial policies followed the familiar path from moderate to revolutionary. At first the tax burden on the masses was relatively light. But as economic pressures mounted, particularly due to rising military expenses, the government imposed greater demands on the masses. Initially, the masses were persuaded to make "voluntary" requests for an increase in their tax rate. Then

JOURNAL OF ASIAN AND AFRICAN STUDIES

they "voluntarily" purchased several issues of government bonds, which were never redeemed. Finally, the peasants were encouraged to "loan" rice to the government to feed the army. Lötveit sees these decisions as part of a broad ideological pattern. As the government turned leftward it departed from moderate financial policies in favor of appeals based on revolutionary zeal. Cadres were sent to "struggle" against anyone whose fervor was inadequate.

In finances, land policy, and justice the Kiangsi Soviet moved ever leftward. This change in leadership and philosophy produced the decision to wage a conventional war against the Kuomintang, contrary to Mao's preference for guerrilla tactics. Also, the more extreme, or leftist, political and economic policies alienated potential allies and undermined mass support. Mao's judgment was vindicated by events. Lötveit's study is in accord with the conventional picture of the Kiangsi Soviet. His contribution lies in the details and the new dimensions he adds.

Wheaton College   Eugene Lubot
Norton, U.S.A.

Justus M. van der Kroef, *Indonesia after Sukarno.* Vancouver, University of
    British Columbia, 1971, pp. 261, $ 6.00.

This genre of scholarship is as valuable as it is chronically unappreciated. Unfortunately the reception leads authors, including van der Kroef, to adjust stated purpose to market sensibilities. What the author in the present volume terms "a brief survey", "intended for the general reader," I would call essentially a prose digest of several years' worth of dozens of secondary sources, American intelligence reports, embassy news summaries, newspaper accounts in Indonesian and English. In the absence of other serious digest writers on Indonesia, van der Kroef deserves considerable gratitude for his persevering efforts methodically to set down this material in some orderly form. If he has been unappreciated, it is surely in part due to a certain scholarly snobbery regarding synoptic digests. The present volume is stuffed with fact material, and I found myself repeatedly jotting down information for my own edification, unrelated to the writing of this review. Valuable fact material would of course be even more valuable, and errors correctable, if there were footnotes to assist verification and further research.

Perhaps the basic criticism of this book is that it is neither fish nor fowl. The infusion of ideological point of view and plentiful if sporadic conceptual and theoretical analysis make it inadequate as a digest. The preponderant bulk of nearly raw descriptive material in selective areas of Indonesian events makes it inadequate as a coherent general summary of the post-Sukarno era. In selective areas of van der Kroef's concern, such as Wast Irian, constitutionalism, and foreign policy, the reader is drenched in description, often obscure or recondite to the point where even the specialist flounders in an attempt to find interconnection, thread or relevance. The sporadic, disjunctive nature of theoretical passages, some of which are individually very good, seems to lend further confusion, since there is no attempt to tie chapters together.

If at one point Sukarno's star is pictured as doomed from the moment of the "coup" in September, 1965, the assertion elsewhere that two years later he still had a good chance of saving his political neck, makes no sense. If one reads that Indonesia's basic principles in foreign policy have remained unchanged from the pre-coup period, one is then perplexed to remember an earlier assertion that Indonesia in 1963–1965 had been a diplomatic front man for Communist China in the Third World. If present Government power is documented as unchallengeable and campaigns against a phantom PKI are suspected to be red herring, then it is difficult to square the author's easy acceptance of an ever present communist menace.

Van der Kroef has tempered his tendency to use megalomania, communist conspiracy, totalitarianism and the chicom menace as major analytic tools. They do still appear, but in between there now also appear distinctly un-Dullesian, even neutral, concepts like power, self-interest and authority. One is left with the suspicion that if, in the immense energies and encyclopedic knowledge of this author, digest writing and analysis could be separated, both endeavors would benefit.

University of Colorado   ROGER K. PAGET
Boulder, U.S.A.

William E. Henthorn, *A History of Korea.* New York: The Free Press, 1971,
   pp. 256, $ 9.95.

Professor William Henthorn is widely recognized for his concise scholarship. In Korean studies his probing research into ancient history, language, fine arts and the Mongol invasions of Korea, have prepared the ground for this comprehensive coverage of Korean history. *A History of Korea* is 250 pages of very readable, compact, interpretive essays reaching from pre-historic times to the end of the Yi dynasty. Modern history in the twentieth century is not covered.

Although chronologically organized, the book is characterized by the freshness of its topical analysis. The author draws upon an impressive range of basic Chinese, Japanese, and Korean source materials but happily the finished product is condensed and simplified. Scholarly impedimenta is at a minimum: no footnotes, no prolonged or complicated lists of technical terms or references, the maps are all clearly intelligible, and the charts are well conceived.

The book has five sections: (1) The Land; (2) The Archaeological Record; (3) The Early Tribal Peoples; (4) The Three Kingdoms; (5) Late Silla; (6) Early Koryŏ; (7) Late Koryŏ; (8) Early Chosŏn; and (9) Late Chosŏn. There are four appendixes. Unlike the proforma appendixes of most scholarly books, Henthorn's are a crowning achievement. They comprise insightful essays on Korean language, foundation myths, major themes of Korean history, and an excellent summary bibliography, topically arranged. The discussion of foundation myths – certainly the most complete of any now available in the English language – is worth the price of the book. As I see it, the only thing conspicuously lacking is a good set of photographs. Those fine discussions of the Koguryŏ tombs deserve at least one good picture (preferably in color) to replace the relatively inane drawing on page 27.

Henthorn's history is well suited for an introductory course at the college level, but its insights should find resonance in a much wider world than that.

Brigham-Young University   SPENCER J. PALMER
Provo, U.S.A.

V. Crapanzano, *The Hamadsha. A Study in Moroccan Ethnopsychiatry.* Berkeley, University of California Press, 1973, pp. xiv, 258, $ 12.00.

The Hamadsha are members of a Moroccan religious brotherhood that traces its ancestry to two Muslim saints of the late seventeenth century. Their chief claim to fame is their propensity to head-slashing and other self-mutilation while in a state of trance during their healing ceremonies. In spite of this flamboyance, they have received little attention from Western scholars and Crapanzano's excellent account is therefore a valuable contribution.

The study is divided into three main parts. The first is concerned with historical aspects including both what is actually known about the founding saints and the legends about them. The Hamadsha is linked with the Sufi tradition, but whereas the Sufis are concerned with experiencing direct contact with the divine, the Hamadsha is primarily a healing group which employs the holiness (*baraka*) of the saints as a power to heal and protect against the damaging effects of spirits (*jnun*). Part II deals with the component institutions of the Hamadsha complex and their intricate interrelationships. The Hamadsha is also analyzed as an institution to facilitate the integration of newcomers into the city by providing them with a rich network of social relationships. Part III, which was the most interesting for this reviewer, is devoted to the therapeutic activities of the brotherhood. There is an excellent chapter describing the local theory of disease and therapy and chapters on the importance of pilgrimage to a shrine in healing, on the trance dance (*hadra*), and on the "explanation of therapy".

In its healing function the Hamadsha serves a primarily low-income sector of the population. It is particularly geared to the healing of illnesses attributed to spirits – especially spirits with names and distinctive personalities (as opposed to other, less well developed and more or less "faceless" entities). Spirit-caused illnesses include paralyses, deafness, mutism and other afflictions of sudden onset which are regarded as resulting from being "struck" by a *jinn;* other illnesses are due to *jinn* "possession" and include episodes of unconsciousness, convulsions, tremors, speaking in tongues, or "sudden and abrupt, often meaningless changes in conversation or activity; flights of thought and so forth".

One spirit which is especially closely linked to the Hamadsha is *Aisha Quandisha.* The Hamadsha brotherhood consider themselves to be her special devotees. In *Aisha* we meet that very familiar figure of mythology and folklore, the seductive, destroyer of men. One informant's description will best communicate her flavour:

A man is walking along a road, and suddenly his vision blurs. He thinks there is something wrong with his eyes, but in fact it is Aisha... When he comes to an isolated crossing or path, she takes him by the hand... Suddenly they find themselves in a big garden with a lot of food, near a well-furnished house. Lalla Aisha takes the shape of a woman the man loves and desires. She has the same features as the beauty, but they are slightly exaggerated. Her bust is eighty centimeters. They make love. Afterward she asks him what he wants to do. The man says he is single and wants to marry. Lalla Aisha says she wants to do the same. "We'll make a vow (ahd) to God," she says. She tells him not to tell anyone, not even his mother. If he does, she'll have his throat. She tells him that she will sleep with other men. "I'll help you with money," she says... "If you do not do what I say," she says, "then you'll not have me or any other woman."

The spirits usually inflict disease when they have been offended. They are quite touchy! In dealing with such illnesses, the healer may drive the spirit away (a relatively uncomplicated one-shot affair), or he may attempt to establish a working relationship between the afflicted and the spirit. The unnamed *jnun* are usually handled by exorcism; the more developed spirits, like Aisha are usually drawn into this latter kind of symbiotic alliance.

In curing an illness inflicted by a named jinn, it is first necessary to establish his identity by means of dreams and various kinds of divination. Once the identity has been established, one must discover what the *jinn* wants through consultation with a seer. The patient may be required to make a pilgrimage, carry out a sacrifice, wear certain clothing or finance a possession ceremony (*hadra*). In some cases (presumably in which the patient is suffering a more severe form of pathology), an intimate ongoing relationship with the *jinn* may be necessary with a series of possession dances, pilgrimages and sacrifices.

As has been noted one of the demands of the spirit may be that the patient have a *hadra* performed. This ceremony involves the leader of the local Hamadsha lodge, several types of musicians and a band of male and female devotees. The performance lasts for several hours and follows a prescribed sequence; the women engage in a peculiar jacknife possession dance while some of the men may slash or mutilate their heads which bleed profusely. The men are believed to be influenced or possessed by Aisha and slash themselves because it is her bidding. The patient himself may also be required to dance and may become involved in the self mutilations.

Crapanzano presents us with a cogent interpretation of the dynamics of the healing process at a number of levels: cultural, individual, and physiological. An important aspect has to do with the tensions between the sexes in Moroccan society. Attitudes to women are highly paternalistic and women endure a lowly status; men are called upon to be domineering and authoritarian. Aisha the voluptuous sorceress and destroyer is the collective projection of the bad male conscience, and the *hadra* is a public expiation demonstrating a symbolic castration of the male to redress the balance. Of course the matter is much more complex and Crapanzano leads us into many absorbing side paths. He also promises to deal with individual illustrative case histories in a future volume.

This is a highly readable book. Crapanzano is one of an increasing number of anthropologists and psychiatrists who have taken pains to come to grips with the viewpoints and theories of their opposite numbers. Ethnopsychiatry is coming of age and this book is an important landmark in this fascinating enterprise.

Mental Hygiene Institute   RAYMOND PRINCE
Montreal, Canada

Alexander Spoehr, *Zambozanga and Sulu: An Archeological Approach to Ethnic Diversity.* Ethnology Monographs, No. 1, Pittsburgh, Department of Anthropology, University of Pittsburgh, 1973, pp. 298, Maps, Illustrations, Photographs, Appendices, Bibliography, N.P.

The subtitle of this excellent monograph is modestly misleading. The archeological approach used was not the usual kind of empiricist site excavation, rather it was a finely focused, problem centered, "... experiment in historical archeology" [p. 274]. Indeed, even this is something of an understatement because the author's archeological data was masterfully combined with the materials of ethnohistory and ethnology to produce a time perspective on four ethnic groups, Subanum, Tausug, Samal, and Zamboanguenos, "...which archeology, ethnohistory, and ethnology singly could not provide" [p. 274].

Central to this "experiment" was the author's utilization of evidences of internal and external trade as indicators of ethnic group interaction and intergroup status relations. This interest was not a gratuitous by-product of the materials recovered, but was derived from Spoehr's conviction that trade, by and large, has been neglected by archeologists in spite of the fact that it is an important and recurring theme in the culture history of Southeast Asia. Although he had multiple aims in mind the crux of the author's experiment was the desire to give some time depth to the complex ethnic picture in the Zamboanga-Sula area. As the exigencies of tropical archeology would have it the archeological data pertaining to this problem "...are necessarily limited, a result of both the test excavation procedure employed and the difficulty experienced in finding suitable sites" [p. 274]. In point of fact some of them are simply puzzling. An example of this is the percentages of European tradewares recovered from Fr. Pilar, a Spanish garrison post, and from a number of Tausug *cottas* or forts, on Jolo Island. These wares, according to Spoehr, were not present in quantity in the area until well after the start of the 19th century. Yet remains from that period showed that 7.0% of the Jolo ceramic materials were of European origin while inside of Fr. Pilar they accounted for only .00053 of the recovered sherd materials. Thus, if one didn't know better a not unwarranted conclusion *on the basis of the archeological record* would be that Fr. Pilar was a Muslim stronghold designed to control the European settlements on Jolo Island! Thanks to the historical and ethnological data supplied by Spoehr such a surmise cannot be made. Paradoxically, then, the unevenness of the site materials reported on, and the author's control over them and related materials, help to make the strongest case for the necessity and correctness of his approach.

In addition to this the monograph provides a number of excellent examples of what materials ethnoarcheologists should be interested in and, how they should be reported. Among these are (1) a detailed construction history of Ft. Pilar, (2) a fine study of present day Samal earthenwares and their distribution and (3) a useful and standardized typological approach to *both* the recovered earthenwares and trade potteries, particularly the Chinese. These features alone would make the volume a must for those interested in Philippine and Southeast Asian archeology. But, as noted earlier there is much more to this volume. Indeed, its major contribution lies in its sophisticated treatment of archeological, historical and ethnological materials as means and not as ends

in the search for an understanding of regional culture history. Such a reminder has been badly needed by many of us involved in the study of these and
related matters.

Portland State University   DANIEL J. SCHEANS
Portland, U.S.A.

Richard N. Henderson, *The King In Every Man: Evolutionary Trends in
   Onitsha Ibo Society and Culture*. New Haven and London, Yale University
   Press, 1972, pp. 576, 48 figures, 4 appendices, bibliography, index, $ 25.00.

Richard N. Henderson's analysis of the Ibo world is not only highly informative but also greatly enlarges our knowledge of the Ibo culture. The study
is primarily concerned with the changes that occurred in West African Ibo
society before the end of the nineteenth century. The author reconstructs
traditional Ibo culture from evidence drawn from written sources, oral traditions and recent ethnographic field work carried out in the Ibo city of Onitsha
from September 1960 to July 1962. Since the study provides very little information about field techniques, interviews, representativeness of informants and the
general collection of data, it is difficult to judge the validity and general reliability of the great mass of interesting data presented.

In the preface and introduction the author explains his theoretical orientation and argues that Onitsha should be viewed as an evolving society combining the autonomous, acephalous, village group characteristics of Ibo culture
plus developing institutions of royalty, kingship and related political structuring. In general terms Henderson sees Onitsha as combining characteristics
of tribal social systems with those of an emerging city-state, similar to the city-
states of the ancient Grecian world. Fortunately, most of the book is concerned
with the analysis of Ibo culture and the author's evolutionary theories intrude
only in the first and last chapters.

The study is essentially divided into four parts with Part I being a historical
reconstruction of Ibo culture from 1500 to 1800. A broad overview is presented
describing related people (i.e., Ijaw, Igala, Tiv, Beni and other, closely allied
Ibo city-states) with the author indicating that the Onitsha region may be
affected by at least four different political and cultural spheres of influence.
Most of the historical reconstruction is based on Onitsha oral traditions, royal
geneologies, myths and publicly acknowledged stories associated with specific
lineages, village segments and particular kings. A good case is argued for the
for the authenticity and accurate transmission of the oral data but there is
always some doubt about this kind of soft data unless it is supported by other
hard evidence that is more scientifically and empirically based.

Part 2 analyzes the elementary structures of Onitsha society and the author
outlines the major values and religious doctrines of Onitsha culture. He indicates that the social life of Onitsha was firmly rooted in concepts of filiation
and descent with a marked emphasis on ancestor worship. Men were dominant
with women being seen as weak without the structural reinforcements of the
male roles. A sharp correlation is also drawn between settlement patterns,
property and patrilineage structure. Henderson's analysis clearly indicates that

the web of kinship was a major social force in Ibo culture affecting most of the roles and relationships in the society.

In Part 3, Henderson analyzes the "ozo" title system, the kingship and the institution of chieftaincy. It is in these evolving political relationships that he enlarges our knowledge of Ibo culture possibly opening up new vistas of political analysis. He shows in great detail the various steps and arduous tasks that a man must undertake to become an "ozo" man, a titled man. The evolving kingship structure is also dissected and all its ramifications examined. The kings were seen as closely bound to the patrilineage and as upholders of clan symbols. They were also looked upon as sacred individuals who were seen as servants of the powerful spirits. Most unusual were the "hidden kings" who Henderson argues were kings, "in the full sense of the term". Below the kings were three ranks of chiefs, who like the kings had a close relationship to the lineages and exerted great power over the people.

In the final section, Part 4, social change in pre-colonial Onitsha is ana-lyzed. It is in this section that the author explains his evolutionary theories and indicates the social development of Onitsha. Although this study is a major contribution to the analysis of Ibo culture and packed full of new and inter-esting data about Ibo city-states, his evolutionary thesis appears to be a bit weak. Whether one can establish broad political sequences in highly divergent cultures is quite questionable under any circumstances. The author's argument that Onitsha may have political and social elements that may resemble, in an evolutionary sense, a Greek city-state is not too well substantiated. Some form of kingship and chieftaincy were evolving in Onitsha along with developing commercial activities but with the exception of these very broad similarities the comparison seems to lack verification. Nevertheless, regardless of this criticism, this study is an excellent contribution to our understanding of Ibo culture and may open up new avenues of research in our investigation of Ibo society.

Temple University   WILLIAM B. SCHWAB
Philadelphia, U.S.A.

Robert C. Lester, *Theravada Buddhism in Southeast Asia.* Ann Arbor, The University of Michigan Press, 1973, pp. 201.

Theravada Buddhism in Southeast Asia is intended, in the words of the author, "to communicate the major features of the present-day practice of Theravada Buddhism in Southeast Asia in the perspective of scripture and history." Prof. Robert Lester has achieved this intended purpose. This book is highly recom-mended for laymen as well as for specialists in the field of Buddhist studies. Prof. Lester's method and treatment of the subject are a departure from the view of Theravada Buddhism as primarily monastic and world-denying. The author's suggestion that the Buddhist monk may be of significant influence towards the progressive, social, economic and political change in Theravada Southeast Asia is worth examining. The author must be admired for his at-tempt to get an in depth perspective of the Theravada tradition not only from the historical and doctrinal context but also from the anthropological perspec-tive.

Theravada Buddhism in Southeast Asia consists of two parts. The first part deals with the three main features of Buddhism, namely, The Buddha, The Dhamma, and The Sangha, each of which is treated in the light of the scripture and tradition. Part II deals with the practice of Buddhism: the author describes three main elements, namely, The Way of the Monk, The Monk and Society, and The Way of the Laity.

Prof. Lester's treatment of the chapter, The Monk and Society, is commendable and his interpretation of the role of the Monk in the Theravada Society is quite accurate. The Monk's influence in primary education in these Theravada countries should not be minimized. In view of many "development-minded leaders" the Monk should be restricted to the teaching of ethics and spiritual subjects, and the lay educators should be responsible for the teaching of secular subjects. As Prof. Lester has observed correctly, the Monk in modern times is increasingly well educated both in the spiritual and secular subjects and, therefore, is capable of teaching secular subjects, and in most instances, may be even more effective than the lay teacher.

The most significant chapter in this work is the author's interpretation of the role of Theravada Buddhism in "change". I agree with Prof. Lester that on the surface there have been changes in the Theravada countries with regard to the education of the Monk, and the progressive outlook on the part of Sangha as well as of government leaders. There seem to be many significant innovations with respect to the education of the Monk. There are also many signs that both the Monk and the Laity have become more sophisticated in this modernizing world. However, Prof. Lester's view on Theravada Buddhism and Change might be too optimistic. Superficially, the available data seem to point to a bright future for the Theravada countries. However, one can only wait and see if these new signs of development will really effect substantial change.

Regional Institute of Higher   Amnuay Tapingkae
Education and Development
Singapore

Raghaven N. Iyer, *The Moral and Political Thought of Mahatma Gandhi.* New York, Oxford University Press, 1973, pp. xiii, 449, $ 12.50.

Despite the large body of literature about Mahatma Gandhi's life and work, there is a paucity of scholarly studies concerned primarily with the interrelationship between Gandhi's moral philosophy and his political concepts. The few serious studies of Gandhi's moral and political ideas have generally concentrated on Gandhian "techniques", and in the process have tended to obscure the richness and depth of Gandhi's thought. Professor Iyer, in contrast, has focused on the metaphysical and moral presuppositions of Gandhi's concepts, and has taken care to place them within the context of Gandhi's personal intellectual development and the broader philosophical traditions of India and the West.

The book can be divided roughly into two separate, yet interrelated, parts. The first part is concerned with an examination of Gandhi's criticism of modern civilization and his prescription for its transformation. The discussion includes a review of Gandhi's attitudes toward religion and politics; his emphasis on the need for a moral commitment to absolute values; his faith in the goodness of human nature and human perfectibility; and his belief in the importance of the individual. The second half of the book is devoted to an analysis of the genesis and morphology of Gandhi's concepts of *satya, ahimsa, satyagraha, swaraj*, and *swadeshi*. Emphasis is given to the importance of *satya* and *ahimsa* as the cornerstone of Gandhi's thought and how these two concepts are intimately related to his other ideas.

Basically, Gandhi felt that the hope of modern civilization lay in the moral and spiritual renewal of receptive individuals who, by their example, would stimulate a reform of the existing social order. Such a renewal, however, required a continual quest for the ultimate truth (*satya*) by nonviolent (*ahimsa*) means. But in order to effect change in a revolutionary way, according to the limits of *satya* and *ahimsa* and the prevailing sociopolitical climate, Gandhi developed the concept of *satyagraha* or active resistance to authority as well as the twin notions of selfrule (*swaraj*) and self-reliance (*swadeshi*). Gandhi also stressed the inseparableness of means and ends in his teachings and writings, arguing that just ends ultimately cannot be obtained by unjust means.

This book represents an important contribution to our understanding of Gandhi's philosophical concepts. Professor Iyer has skillfully presented the nuances and interrelationships of Gandhi's ideas without judging them on the basis of their political results, and as a consequence has succeeded in providing a comprehensive picture of Gandhi as a moral and political thinker. Clearly, *The Moral and Political Thought of Mahatma Gandhi* deserves serious consideration not only by students of Gandhi, but also by those concerned with the brutalization of man in modern civilization.

Arizona State University   ROBERT L. YOUNGBLOOD
Tempe, U.S.A.

FURTHER PUBLICATIONS FROM E. J. BRILL

Contributions to Asian Studies

Sponsored by The Canadian Association for South Asian Studies, Toronto
Canada.

Editor: K. Ishwaran, York University, Downsview, Ontario, Canada

A series containing scholarly papers. Each volume will cover special areas, of Asian countries, and may be of value for specialists, but also to students and teachers of sociology, anthropology and political science.

Volume 1: 1971. viii, 204 pages, 8 tables   Gld. 46.—

Volume 2: RELIGION AND SOCIETY IN PAKISTAN. Edited by Aziz Ahmad. 1971.
viii, 105 pages   Gld. 40.—

Contents: F. Abbott, The historical background of Islamic India and Pakistan; A. Ahmad, Islam and democracy in Pakistan; S. M. M. Qureshi, Religion and party politics in Pakistan; H. Malik, The spirit of capitalism and Pakistani Islam; S. McDonough, The social import of Parwez's religious thought; S. Ahmad, Islam and Pakistani peasants.

Volume 3: 1973, viii, 166 pages, some tables and figures   Gld. 64.—

Contents: CEYLON: REINCARNATION AND BUDDHISM. B. L. Smith, Sinhalese Buddhism and the Dilemmas of Reinterpretation; I. Stevenson, Characteristics of Cases of the Reincarnation Type in Ceylon. – INDIA: ECONOMY, POLITICS AND SOCIAL CHANGE. J. L. Murray, Peasant Motivation, Ecology, and Economy in Panjab; Y. K. Malik, Conflict over Chandigarh: A Case Study of an Interstate Dispute in India; J. S. Uppal, Economic Development of Indian States: A Study in Development Contrast; K. G. Saini, Economic Performance and Institutional Change: the Experience of India. – INDIA: RELIGION. M. Mahapatra, The Badu: A Service-caste at the Lingaraj Temple at Bhubaneswar; C. R. Pangborn. – INDIA: INTELLECTUALS AND CHANGE. P. C. Deb and L. A. Wenzel, A Dimension of Change in India: Prestige of occupations Among University Students; H. S. Sandhu, The Intellectuals and Social Change in India. – INDIA AND PAKISTAN: FAMILY. J. H. Korson, Some Aspects of Social Change in the Muslim Family in West Pakistan; I. Verghese, Is the Kota Society Polyandrous?

Volume 4: TRADITION AND CHANGE IN THERAVADA BUDDHISM: ESSAYS ON CEYLON AND THAILAND IN THE 19TH AND 20TH CENTURIES. Edited by Bardwell L. Smith. 1974. viii, 105 pages.   Gld. 42.—

Contents: B. L. Smith, Introduction; H. Bechert, Contradictions in Sinhalese Buddhism; T. Fernando, The Western Educated Elite and Buddhism in British Ceylon: A Neglected Aspect of the Nationalist Movement; B. G. Gokhale, Anagarick Dhammapala: Toward Modernity through Tradition in Ceylon; F. E. Reynolds, Sacral Kingship and National Development: the Case of Thailand; S. Piker, Buddhism and Modernization in Contemporary Thailand; F. B. Morgan, Vocation of Monk and Layman: Signs of Change in Thai Buddhist Ethics; D. K. Swearer, Thai Buddhism: Two Responses to Modernity; F. E. Reynolds, Tradition and Change in Theravada Buddhism: A Bibliographical Essay Focused on the Modern Period.

Volume 5: 1974, viii, 102 pages   Gld. 48.—

Contents: A. INDIA AND PHILIPPINES: CULTURE, RELIGION AND REINCARNATION. Geoffrey Burkhart, Equal in the Eyes of God: A South Indian Devotional Group in its Hierarchical Setting. – Donn V. Hart, Culture in Curing in Filipino Peasant Society. – Arvind Sharma, The Notion of Cyclical Time in Hinduism. – Ian Stevenson, Jamuna Prasad, L. P. Mahrota, K. S. Rawat, The Investigation of Cases of the Reincarnation Type in India. – B. INDIA, INDONESIA AND NEPAL: POLITICS AND EDUCATION. Reuven Kahane, Social Conditions leading to Military Dominance: the Case of Indonesia. – Horace B. Reed, Education and Land in Nepal: Complementary Reforms. – Glynn Wood, Egalitarian and Technocratic Goals in Educational Growth: The View from Mysore.